THE

HISTORY

OF

HARVARD UNIVERSITY.

VOL. I.

G. G. Smith Sc.

HARVARD UNIVERSITY.

with the procession of the Alumni from the Church to the Pavilion, September 8 1836

THE HISTORY OF HARVARD UNIVERSITY.

By JOSIAH QUINCY, LL.D.,

PRESIDENT OF THE UNIVERSITY.

VOLUME I.

BOSTON:
CROSBY, NICHOLS, LEE, & CO.,
117 Washington Street.
1860.

University Press, Cambridge:
Printed by Welch, Bigelow, and Company.

TO

THE ALUMNI OF HARVARD UNIVERSITY

THIS WORK IS RESPECTFULLY DEDICATED

BY

THE AUTHOR.

PREFACE.

THIS History had its origin in the following circumstances. In March, 1836, the Author accepted an invitation from the Corporation of Harvard University, to prepare, as President of the institution, a discourse, to be delivered on the second centennial anniversary of its foundation, in commemoration of that event, and of the founders and patrons of the seminary. From the researches, into which he was led by this undertaking, it became apparent that these topics could not be satisfactorily investigated before the day fixed upon for the celebration. The Author, therefore, decided to prepare such a general sketch of events and characters as might be comprised within the limits of an occasional address, and to announce his intention of attempting to do justice to the subject in a work of a more enlarged form and permanent character.

Various considerations concurred to produce this determination. Many of the circumstances attending the foundation of the College, and much of its subsequent history, the lapse of time had already involved in obscurity. Important public documents were lost. Some of the early records of the institution had been destroyed by fire. Those which remained were contained in two or three decaying volumes, the loss of which would render it impossible to trace consecutively the events of its early history. In 1809, the importance of such a work was perceived, and its immediate preparation was urged on the sons of the College, by Buckminster, as ripe a scholar, and a genius "touched to as fine issues," as any one who was ever graduated at Harvard College; on the ground that, if delayed, "it would soon become impracticable."* For nearly thirty years a vote of the Corporation, requesting the President to prepare a History of the University, had stood upon the records of that board, and the execution of such a work had long been an object of desire among the friends of the institution. The laborious zeal of the late Benjamin Peirce, Librarian of the seminary, had indeed eventuated in a publication of

* See an eloquent appeal to the Alumni of the University, in an address "on the Dangers and Duties of Men of Letters," pronounced before the Phi Beta Kappa Society, by J. S. Buckminster, and published in the "Monthly Anthology" for September, 1809.

great merit and usefulness, possessing the traits of that soundness of judgment and accuracy of investigation so eminently his characteristics. But his History of the University being left incomplete * by his death, the interesting information and valuable materials he had collected with great industry and research, although in many respects thoroughly wrought and fully developed, yet in others were only partially prepared, and in a state to excite rather than to satisfy curiosity.

A knowledge of facts could now be obtained, which might soon be lost, concerning founders, patrons, and officers of the institution, whose wisdom and exertions had contributed to its character, its success, and even to the continuance of its existence. To rescue these facts from oblivion was acknowledged by all to be a solemn duty,—a duty, which the Author, reflecting upon his relation to the seminary, and upon the circumstances which had led him to researches subsidiary to such a design, deemed to be upon him imperative. To render an appropriate and just tribute to the merits, sufferings, and sacrifices of these founders, patrons, and officers, was the conclusive motive to this undertaking; and, since no duty is more incumbent upon seminaries of learning, than the commemoration of the virtues and labors,

* See the Editor's preface to Mr. Peirce's History of the University.

which have contributed to their existence and prosperity, a greater extension has been given to the biographical notices in this work, than is usual in a general history.

Every effort has been made to render the work complete, exact, and worthy of the institution it was designed to illustrate. In addition to the archives of the College, and those of the Colony and State of Massachusetts, the use of the books and manuscripts belonging to the Massachusetts Historical Society and to the American Antiquarian Society has been liberally afforded to the Author. Many ancient papers and manuscripts have been submitted to his inspection by those individuals in whose hands they now rest. The thread of the narrative has, however, been chiefly drawn from the records of the Corporation and Overseers; and no fact deemed generally important and interesting, which they contain, has been intentionally omitted. When views concerning motives, characters, and events, are expressed, differing from those generally entertained, the original documents from which they result are invariably annexed. The desire to place these authorities in the hands of the public, and to preserve from loss original papers, illustrative of the manners and characters of a former age, has led to an enlargement of the Appendix to each volume far beyond the original design.

To render the history more complete and useful, the outline of events has been brought down to the present day; but a particular notice of living characters has been avoided, except in cases where gratitude demanded a tribute to the bounty or extraordinary services of individuals; and in such cases it is confined to the language of records or public documents. A similar course has been pursued in respect to the narrative of contemporaneous events, which has been restricted to facts deemed necessary or important to be known.

A History of Harvard University, written by the President of the institution, and published with the sanction of the Corporation, may be regarded by the public as rendering the College or the Corporation responsible for the views and sentiments it contains. The Author of this work, therefore, deems it his duty explicitly to state, that the narrative of facts and circumstances here given is exclusively the result of his own research and selection, and that, for the views and opinions it expresses, he is alone responsible.

In collecting materials for this work, and particularly those relating to the lives of benefactors and patrons of the institution, the obligations of the Author to individuals have been too numerous to be specially acknowledged. His thanks, however, are particularly due to the following gentlemen, for important documents, or aid: to Benjamin Peirce, Professor of Mathematics and Natural Philosophy in the University, for placing at his disposal a collection of papers made by his late father; to the Rev. Samuel Sewall of Burlington, for permitting the free use of the curious and graphic diaries of his ancestor, the Hon. Chief Justice Sewall; to John Belknap, Esq., for a like permission to use a manuscript collection, made by his father, the late Rev. Jeremy Belknap, D. D. To the Hon. John Davis, James Savage, Nathaniel G. Snelling, the late and lamented John Farmer, and Alden Bradford, Esquires, and to the Rev. Joseph B. Felt, the Author is under obligations for occasional assistance in difficulties, which their intimate acquaintance with the early history of Massachusetts peculiarly qualified them to resolve.

The benefit which all works printed at the University press derive from the taste, judgment, and assiduous fidelity of its superintendent, Charles Folsom, Esq., is too generally known and appreciated to need to be here acknowledged. But that gentleman's long and intimate acquaintance with the concerns of the University, and the deep interest he takes in every thing affecting its character and prosperity, have led him to bestow on the details of this work an earnest attention and solicitude, which have largely contributed to its correctness, and created a sense of obligation, which it is not less the Author's pleasure than his duty to express.

This work, having been prepared without any view to personal emolument, was, when completed, offered to the Corporation, who accepted it, resolved to publish it by subscription, and appropriate the proceeds of the sale to the increase of the beneficiary fund of the College.

When apprized of this intention, the publisher, John Owen, Esq., in a spirit of liberality and zeal for the interests of the institution, voluntarily relinquished all compensation for his services, and thus secured the entire net proceeds of the work to be devoted to assist indigent students in the University.

The sketch of "Gore Hall," which forms the frontispiece to the second volume, was kindly contributed by Mr. Richard Bond, the architect of the building.* And the account of the Centennial Celebration was prepared, and the proceedings and speeches on the occasion were collected, and chiefly arranged, by a Committee appointed by the alumni.

To his eldest daughter (Eliza S. Quincy), the Author is indebted for the design and original sketch of the frontispiece to the first volume, and also for the original sketches of all the vignettes, with the exception of the first

* The engravings on steel in this work were executed by Mr. George C. Smith, of Boston. Those on wood, excepting the Pavilion, by Mr. J. A. Adams, of New York.

three College Halls, (which are reduced copies from an ancient engraving,) the Medical College, and the Pavilion. The labor of preparing the Index was voluntarily assumed by her, and has been executed with fidelity and exactness. Indeed, the work itself, in its progress through the press, owes to her continued vigilance, much of the accuracy, which it is hoped will be found in it, and which, from the multiplicity of its details, and the constant pressure of official duties, it would have been scarcely possible for the Author otherwise to have attained.

November 30th, 1840.

CONTENTS

OF

VOLUME FIRST.

CHAPTER I.

CHAPTER II.

CHAPTER III.

CHAPTER IV.

CHAPTER V.

CHAPTER VI.

CHAPTER VII.

CHAPTER VIII.

CHAPTER IX.

CHAPTER X.

CHAPTER XI.

CHAPTER XII.

CHAPTER XIII.

CHAPTER XIV.

CHAPTER XV.

CHAPTER XVI.

CHAPTER XVII.

CHAPTER XVIII.

CHAPTER XIX.

APPENDIX.

LIST OF THE ENGRAVINGS.

HISTORY

OF

HARVARD UNIVERSITY.

CHAPTER I.

Centennial Celebration in 1836. — Origin and Design of this History. — Vote of the General Court of Massachusetts Bay, in 1636. — Bequest of John Harvard. — His Name conferred on the Seminary. — Early Donations. — Nathaniel Eaton. — Henry Dunster elected first President. — His Administration. — Charters of 1642 and 1650. — Contributions of the Colonies. — Resignation of President Dunster. — His Death. — State of the Finances of the College.

Origin and design of this History.

On the 8th of September, 1636, the legislature of the Colony of Massachusetts Bay passed an act, which resulted in the foundation of Harvard College. Two centuries after that day, on the 8th of September, 1836, the Corporation, the Overseers, the officers of government and instruction, and the sons and friends of the institution, assembled within its walls to commemorate that event.

An extract from the Address, delivered by the President of the University on that occasion, at the request of the Corporation, will explain the origin and design of this History.

CHAPTER I.

Centennial Address in 1836.

"The design of this celebration is neither temporary excitement nor transient effect. We have not assembled, on some popular holyday, to witness the play of dazzling and delusive words. We come, as children, to the beloved home of our literary parent, on her birthday, with greetings and gratulations, — with simple and child-like offerings, to be valued, not for their beauty or material or workmanship, but for their truth and fidelity, as evidences of interest and attachment, as acknowledgments of blessings received, and of hopes fulfilled. We come, in her presence, to express filial and to cultivate fraternal affections; asking for reminiscences of her early years; inquiring if research have rescued aught concerning her from the ruins of time; bringing hearts disposed to magnify the minute, and to at tach importance to what is common; prepared to hear again the thrice-told tale of her infant days, and to listen to the touching memoirs of her poverty and weakness; — to us interesting, not from the greatness of the recapitulated events, but from our gratitude for experienced benefits; bearing in their train joys, which children alone know, and which strangers can scarcely be expected to share, or even to understand

"Harvard University was established under the auspices of the earliest class of emigrants to Massachusetts Bay. It was, from the first, intimately connected with political and religious opinions and events. In every period, its destinies have been materially affected by the successive changes, which time and intellectual advancement have produced in political relations and religious influences. It is impossible rightly to illustrate its early and later history, without referring to these connexions, and tracing to them much of the adverse, as well as prosperous, fortunes of the seminary.

The history divided into four periods.

"The events which have affected the fortunes of Harvard College, during the last two centuries, may be advantageously arranged and considered, in relation to four great periods; each embracing about fifty years. The first period terminates with the College charter, granted in 1692 by the first Provincial legislature, assembled under the charter of King William and Queen Mary. The second extends from this time to the accession of Holyoke to the presidency, in 1736. The third includes the succeeding years to the accession of Willard, in 1780. The fourth embraces the time subsequent.

"During the first period, the College was conducted as a theological institution, in strict coincidence with the nature of the political constitution of the colony; having religion for its basis and chief object. Although the charter of the College gave it no sectarian bias, it was, without question, regarded by both the clergy and the politicians of the period, as an instrument destined to promote and perpetuate the religious opinions predominating at the time. The seminary, during this period, will be seen amidst poverty and suffering; depending for its existence on a precarious, and often penurious, benevolence; soliciting aid, and repulsed; in want, and its own funds withheld; in distress, and relief denied or postponed; sometimes tossed on the waves of political, sometimes on those of religious controversy, and, amidst the conflicts of both, raising as high as the times required, or its resources permitted, the standard of the literature of the country.

CHAPTER I.

"In the second period, bitter controversies will be found springing up between those religious parties, into which the Congregational sect divided immediately after the new principle of political power introduced by the charter of William and Mary had deprived it of that supremacy, which the old charter had secured to the Congregational clergy. Of these the College was often the field and sometimes the object. In consequence, its sky was occasionally obscured, and its progress embarrassed. It regularly, however, advanced under new and not inferior auspices. High Calvinists, indeed, regarded it with diminished favor, and even began to look elsewhere for instruments to propagate their sentiments and extend their power. But new friends to it arose; its usefulness became acknowledged; and its resources increased.

"In the third period, the divisions of the Congregational sect grew wider and more marked. They prosecuted their animosities, notwithstanding, with a subdued temper, partly from experience of the unprofitableness of such controversies, and partly from a fear, entertained in common by all the parties formed out of those divisions, of the increasing power of the Episcopalian sect; which, at this time, began to display its standard with great boldness, supported by the favor and funds of the transatlantic hierarchy. While the leaders of each division were actively engaged in one common cause, they naturally composed, or treated with a politic tenderness, their mutual differences. The political aspect of affairs began also, early in this period, to foretell the coming revolutionary tempest. Amid the preparations for the contest, which led to national independence, religious animosities were suspended; nor was their voice heard during the din and excitement of that struggle. In the mean time the College was permitted to remain in a state of comparative tranquillity; viewed, indeed, by some of the Calvinistic sect with coldness and jealousy, and its officers charged by some with being Arminians, and even suspected of more fearful heresies. Embracing, however, as the College did with equal warmth and openness, the cause of American Independence, it at the same time acquired a well-deserved popularity, and shared, in common with all the other institutions of the country, the pecuniary losses and embarrassment consequent on that contest.

"During the fourth and last period, extending to our own time, the College, now raised to the rank of a University, partook, with the country at large, of the vicissitudes following the war, and subsequently of the prosperity, which ensued upon the adoption of the federal Constitution, and on an orderly arrangement of State and national affairs. From this time the seminary began to regard itself, and to be regarded by others, as an institution devoted exclusively to the advancement of science and general literature; — as a tree, destined to support and develope all the objects of human knowledge and pursuit, in proportion to their respective value and importance; of which Theology should be always a branch, but no longer the stem.

"In each of these periods, the occasion requires, that, as we pursue the order of events, the causes of that prosperity, which the seminary now enjoys, should be traced to the character of its founders and patrons, and to the literary, political, and religious influences of successive times; and, above all, while passing down the series of succeeding years, as through the interior

CHAPTER I.

of some ancient temple, which displays on either hand the statues of distinguished friends and benefactors, that we should stay for a moment in the presence of each, doing justice to the humble, illustrating the obscure, placing in a true light the modest, and noting rapidly the moral and intellectual traits, which time has spared; to the end that ingratitude, the proverbial sin of republics, may not attach to the republic of letters; and that whoever feeds the lamp of science, however obscurely, however scantily, may know, that, sooner or later, his name and virtues shall be made conspicuous by its light, and throughout all time accompany its lustre.

"From this view, it is apparent that the occasion requires, not an oration, but a treatise; not an address, but a History.

"Like the historian, then, of ancient times, when, on Grecian soil and like solemn occasion, were assembled, as now and here, the wise, the learned, the pious, and the great, let us also strive to beguile the passing hour with an appropriate story of former years; and like him too, leave it half told, when hearers give signs of weariness, or when the herald shall proclaim that the time has come for the feast and the games."

Origin of the College.

On recurring to the origin of this seminary, our first feelings impel us to wonder and admire. That intellectual men should early contemplate an institution for the instruction of youth in the higher branches of science might be expected, and is in conformity with the usual practice of mankind. But this has ever happened after time had given validity to their occupation of the soil, and external enemies had been conquered or conciliated; after those roots of discord, which naturally spring up among new combinations of men, had been extirpated or overpowered; after wealth had begun to flow in, and a sense of security, combining with a sense of prosperity, had given power and expansion to the spirit of benevolence. At such a stage of advancement, institutions, having for their object varied, high, and exact scientific education, might be anticipated.

Now, wonderful as is the fact, this institution was projected under circumstances in every particular the reverse of these. It was not among the later, but among the earliest thoughts of our ancestors. They waited not for days of affluence, of peace, or even of domestic concord. The first necessities of civilized man, food, raiment, and shelter, had scarcely been provided; civil government and the worship of God had alone been instituted, when the great interests of education engaged their attention. Their zeal was not repressed by the narrowness of their territorial limits, not yet extending thirty miles on the seacoast, nor twenty into the interior; nor yet by the terror of a savage enemy, threatening the very existence of the settlement; nor by the claims on their scanty resources, which an impending Indian war created; nor by the smallness of their numbers, certainly not then exceeding five thousand families; nor yet by the most unhappy and most ominous to their tranquillity of all, the religious disputes, in which they were ever implicated. It was under a combination of disastrous and oppressive circumstances, any one of which would have deterred men of less moral courage and intellectual vigor from engaging in any such general design, — on the eve of a war with the fiercest and most powerful of all the native tribes, — the Antinomian

CHAPTER I. controversy at its highest and most bitter excitement, — an unexplored wilderness extending over their fragile dwellings its fear-inspiring shades; — in the daytime, the serpent gliding across their domestic hearths, or rattling its terrors in their path; in the night, their slumbers broken by the howl of the wild beast, or by the yell and warwhoop of the savage; — it was amidst a complex variety of dangers, which, at this day, the imagination can neither exaggerate nor conceive, that this poor, this distressed, this discordant band of Pilgrims set about erecting a seminary of learning, and appropriated for its establishment a sum "equal to a year's rate of the whole colony"! For a like spirit, under like circumstances, history will be searched in vain.*

The record is as simple, as its object was noble and
1636. its spirit elevated. Two centuries ago, on the second Thursday and eighth day of September, that General Court first assembled, among whose proceedings is the following record. "The Court agree to give Four Hundred Pounds towards a School or College, whereof Two Hundred Pounds shall be paid the next year, and Two Hundred Pounds when the work is finished, and the next Court to appoint where and what building."

To this date we trace the origin of the seminary. This is

> . . . . "gentis cunabula nostræ,
> . . . . uberrima regna."

* "Within ten years after the little flock landed at Salem, a College was endowed by them and established. It is questionable, whether a more honorable specimen of public spirit can be found in the history of mankind." — DWIGHT'S *Travels in New England*, Vol. I. p. 481.

CHAPTER I. 1637.

The year ensuing (1637), the General Court appointed twelve of the most eminent men of the colony "to take order for a college at Newtown." All of them names dear to New England, on account of their sacrifices, their sufferings, and virtues. Among these, there were, of the clergy, Shepard and Cotton and Wilson; of the laity, Stoughton and Dudley; and, above all, Winthrop, the Governor, the guide and the good genius of the Colony. Soon afterward the General Court changed the name of the town from *Newtown* to *Cambridge;* a grateful tribute to the transatlantic literary parent of many of the first emigrants, and indicative of the high destiny to which they intended the institution they were establishing should aspire.

Notwithstanding the zeal displayed, and the encouragement thus liberally promised, yet, such were the poverty, danger, and disunion of the time, that it would have been altogether impossible for them to carry their design into effect, had not an event, wholly unanticipated, supplied resources applicable immediately to its execution.

John Harvard. 1638.

In the year 1638, while they were only contemplating its commencement, John Harvard, a dissenting clergyman of England, resident at Charlestown, died, and bequeathed one half of his whole property, and his entire library, to the institution. From the amount of his bequest, he must have been among the most wealthy emigrants. It was equal to, if not double, that which the colony had ventured even to promise; and, besides, was capable of being applied at once to the object. An instance of benevolence thus striking and timely, proceeding from one who had been scarcely a year in the country, was accepted by our fathers as

CHAPTER I.

an omen of divine favor. With prayer and thanksgiving they immediately commenced the seminary, and conferred upon it the name of Harvard, thus acknowledging him as its founder.

Of John Harvard history gives little information, and that very imperfect. That he was educated at Emanuel College, Cambridge, emigrated to this country in 1637, and was immediately admitted a freeman of the jurisdiction and a member of the church in Charlestown, is all that is known concerning him with distinctness and certainty. His contemporaries had few opportunities to become acquainted with his character. He had been but a year in the country, and during the whole time probably the destined victim of consumption, which in that short period brought him to his grave. The historians of the time apply to him the epithets of "reverend," "godly," "a lover of learning." How true and efficient a patron of it he was, this seminary is both a witness and a monument, more durable than one of marble or granite.

The catalogue of his library, consisting of two hundred and sixty volumes, still exists among the archives of the seminary, and indicates not only his professional studies, but also his general scholarship. Besides a formidable array of veteran champions of the ancient church militant, such as Ames and Aquinas, Bellarmine, Beza, and Broughton, Chrysostom and Calvin, Duns Scotus and Luther and Pelagius, there are works of more general literature, such as Bacon's and Robinson's Essays, Bacon's Advancement of Learning, Minsheu's Guide to the Tongues, Heylyn's Geography, and Camden's Remains, all works, at that time, of recent publication. The classical department of his library was even more rich and select. In it were Homer,

Isocrates, Lucan, Plutarch, Pliny, Sallust, Terence, Juvenal, and Horace, the last with Stephanus's Notes and a folio Commentary. Such are the only indications, that remain, of the literary and intellectual tastes of our founder.

The scanty records* of the period even leave some doubt as to the amount of his bounty. Let it have been more or less, it is equally entitled to the epithet "*munificent*," so justly conferred on the bequest of John Harvard,† in that eloquent tribute to his memory, occasioned by the erection, some years since, of a monument to him at Charlestown, by the alumni of the College.

Whatever was the amount, it was the half of his whole fortune, and his entire library; and this from a man, who, although he had no children, left a widow and general heirs who were dear to him. It was also the earliest, the noblest, and the purest tribute to religion and science this western world had yet witnessed. It was equally timely and unexampled. Wisely and justly did our ancestors inscribe his name upon the seminary, and acknowledge him as its founder, who had, at a moment so seasonable and critical, afforded that efficient aid, which alone enabled them at once to give it existence.

The example of Harvard was like an electric spark falling upon materials of a sympathetic nature, exciting immediate action and consentaneous energy. The magistrates caught the spirit, and led the way, by a subscription among themselves of two hundred pounds, in books, for the library. The comparatively wealthy

* See Appendix, No. 1.

† See "An Address at the Erection of a Monument to John Harvard, Sept. 28th, 1828, by Edward Everett."

CHAPTER I.

followed with gifts of twenty and thirty pounds. The needy multitude succeeded, like the widow of old, "casting their mites into the treasury."

The early records of the College indicate the universality of the will, at the same time that the nature of the gifts exhibit, in a strong light, the simplicity and the necessities of the period. "When we read," says Peirce,* the learned and laborious historian of the University, "of a number of sheep bequeathed by one man, of a quantity of cotton cloth worth nine shillings presented by another, of a pewter flagon worth ten shillings by a third, of a fruit dish, a sugar-spoon, a silver-tipt jug, one great salt, and one small trencher-salt, by others; and of presents or legacies, amounting severally to five shillings, one pound, two pounds, &c., all faithfully recorded with the names of the donors, we are at first tempted to smile; but a little reflection will soon change this disposition into a feeling of respect and even of admiration."

Early donations.

How just is the remark of this historian! How forcible and full of noble example is the picture exhibited by these records! The poor emigrant, struggling for subsistence, almost houseless, in a manner defenceless, is seen selecting from the few remnants of his former prosperity, plucked by him out of the flames of persecution, and rescued from the perils of the Atlantic, the valued pride of his table, or the precious delight of his domestic hearth;—"his heart stirred and his spirit willing," to give according to his means, towards establishing for learning a resting-place, and for science a fixed habitation, on the borders of the wilder-

* History of Harvard University, p. 17.

ness! The inhabitants of the country contributing from their acres, or their flocks; those of the metropolis from their shops and stores; the clergyman from his library, and the mechanic from his tools of trade! No rank, no order of men, is unrepresented, in this great crusade against ignorance and infidelity. None fails to appear at this glorious clan-gathering in favor of learning and religion.

At this period it would be in vain to attempt to recall from oblivion the names of men, some of whom, it appears by the record, made it the condition of their gifts, that they should be unknown; and none of whom looked, or sought, for other applause than that, which

> "Lives and spreads aloft by those pure eyes
> And perfect witness of the All-judging, ...
> As he pronounces lastly on each deed."

Nathaniel Eaton.

The bequest of Harvard occurred during the time that the infant seminary, with the title only of "school," was under the superintendence of Nathaniel Eaton. Of this man nothing has been transmitted worthy of being repeated. He was "convented before the magistrates," and convicted of being passionate, quarrelsome, negligent, and cruel. On account of the scandal of his conduct to religion, and the apprehensions it might awaken in parents, he was fined and dismissed. His delinquencies are minutely recapitulated in Winthrop's "History of New England," and sufficiently justify this severity.* It appears also, by the remarks of Mr. Savage, the exact and scrutinizing commentator on Winthrop, that, at no subsequent period of the College history, has discontent with commons

* Winthrop's History of New England, with Notes by James Savage, Vol. I. pp. 308-313.

CHAPTER I.

been more just and well-founded, than under the huswifery management of Mrs. Eaton. "It is perhaps owing," he adds, "to the gallantry of our fathers, that she was not conjoined in the perpetual malediction they bestowed on her husband."

By the fiscal accounts of Eaton, it is apparent, that the superintendence of the building then erecting, the receiving of donations and applying them, were all intrusted to his discretion. On his dismissal, these powers were transferred by the General Court to Mr. Samuel Shepard, who performed those duties until the arrival in the country of the Rev.

Henry Dunster. 1640.

Henry Dunster. This occurred in the autumn of 1640; and his qualifications for the office were so conspicuous, that he received, from the magistrates and elders, promises and encouragements* sufficiently alluring to induce him to accept the appointment, with the title of "President."

During the first six and thirty years after the foundation of the seminary, its history offers little to awaken general interest, except events in immediate connexion with the characters and fate of the first two presidents, Dunster and Chauncy. Both of them were able, faithful, and earnest. Both pious, even to the excess of the standard of that quality, which characterized the times. Both were learned beyond the measure of their contemporaries; and probably, in this respect, were surpassed by no one, who has since succeeded to their chair. After years of duty unexceptionably fulfilled, both experienced the common fate of the literary men of this country at that day; — thankless labor, unrequited service, arrearages un-

* See Peirce's History of Harvard University, Appendix, p. 79.

CHAPTER I.

paid, posthumous applause, a doggrel dirge, and a Latin epitaph.

Among the early friends of the College, no one deserves more distinct notice than Henry Dunster. He united in himself the character of both patron and President; for, poor as he was, he contributed, at a time of its utmost need, one hundred acres of land towards its support; besides rendering to it, for a succession of years, a series of official services, well directed, unwearied, and altogether inestimable.

Under his administration, the first code of laws was formed;* rules of admission, and the principles on which degrees should be granted, were established; and scholastic forms, similar to those customary in the English Universities, were adopted; many of which continue, with little variation, to be used at the present time. The charter of 1642 was probably, and that of 1650 was avowedly, obtained on his petition.† By solicitations among his friends, and by personal sacrifices, he built a President's house. He was instant in season and out of season with the General Court, for the relief of the College in its extreme wants. The Commissioners of the United Colonies stood to the people of New England, in that day, somewhat in the relation in which Congress now stands to the people of the United States. They had, however, only the power to recommend measures, not to enforce them. Dunster formed the plan of concentrating upon the College the patronage of all the Colonies. Under his auspices, a memorial was addressed by Mr. Shepard, pastor of the church in Cambridge, to those Commissioners, for a general contribution for the main-

1642.

Commissioners of the United Colonies.

* See Appendix, No. XXVII. and No. LXVII.

† Ibid., No. LXVIII.

CHAPTER I. tenance of poor scholars at the College, to the end, that "the Commonwealth may be furnished with knowing and understanding men, and the churches with an able ministry." The tenor of this memorial strikingly illustrates the simplicity and the poverty of the times. It entreats the Commissioners to recommend "to every family throughout the plantations (which is able and willing to give) to contribute a fourth part of a bushel of corn, or something equivalent thereto," which, it declares, would be "a blessed means of comfortable provision, for the diet of such students, as stand in need of support." The Commissioners approved the plan, and made the recommendation requested.*

The patronage thus extended by these Commissioners to the seminary, gave them some claim to have a voice in its concerns. Accordingly, in 1646, they recommended to the General Court of Massachusetts, to take some course with the parents of the scholars, "that these, when furnished with learning, remove not into other countries, but improve their parts and abilities in the service of the Colonies."† There was some reason for the apprehension this recommendation indicates; for, of the *twenty* scholars, who had been graduated at the College prior to 1646, *twelve* had actually then gone to Europe, all of whom found employment there; and *eleven* of them never returned to this country.

1647. In 1647, Dunster, who never omitted any opportunity to be useful to the College, addressed a letter to the Commissioners, containing various inquiries for their advice and direction; "touching cases," says he,

* Hazard's State Papers, Vol. II. p. 17. † Ibid. p. 74.

CHAPTER I.

"difficult to myself, and which may be dangerous in time ensuing to others, unless regulated by your counsels."

Contributions of the Colonies.

By this memorial it appears, that the contributions from the Colonies had amounted to fifty pounds per annum. But, if the first proposition of one shilling a family had been attended to, it would have amounted to much more; for, although "some families give, some withhold." By the same document it also appears, that a principal part of the President's maintenance arose out of "stipends from the scholars"; that the College building, in roof, walls, and foundation, was out of repair; that the library was defective in all manner of books; especially in law, philosophy, physics, and mathematics, "the furnishing whereof," the memorialist adds, "would be both honorable and profitable to the country in general, and in an especial manner to those scholars, whose various inclinations to all professions might thereby be encouraged."*

Again, in 1651, Dunster urges upon the Commissioners the decaying condition of the College buildings, and the necessity of their repair and enlargement; and, in reply, the Commissioners promise to propound to the several Colonies, to give "some yearly help, by pecks, half-bushels, and bushels of wheat"; 1651.
adding, by way of hint to the "General Court of Massachusetts," (and one not altogether unnecessary,) "that if they would please to give a leading example, the rest may probably more readily follow."†

Dunster's usefulness, however, was deemed to be at an end, and his services no longer desirable, in consequence of his falling, in 1653, as Cotton Mather

* See Hazard's State Papers, Vol. II. p. 84.

† Ibid. p. 197.

CHAPTER I.

expresses it, "into the briers of Antipædobaptism,"* and of his having borne "public testimony, in the church at Cambridge, against the administration of baptism to any infant whatsoever."

It was time, in the opinion of our worthy ancestors, for them to bestir themselves, when the pious Mitchel himself declared, that his own faith in the orthodox doctrine of Pædobaptism had been so shaken, and such "scruples and suggestions," in respect to it, "had been injected into him by Mr. Dunster's discourses," that he did not dare to trust himself within reach of their "venom and poison," it being "not hard to discern that they came from the *Evil One*."†

Indicted by the grand jury for disturbing the ordinance of infant baptism in the Cambridge church, convicted by the court, sentenced to a public admonition on lecture day, and laid under bonds for good behaviour, Dunster's martyrdom was consummated by being compelled, in October, 1654, to resign his office of President, and to throw himself on the tender mercies of the General Court.

President Dunster resigns. 1654.

There is a simple, touching pathos, in the following "Considerations,"‡ he submitted to that body in the ensuing November, showing why he should not be compelled at once, for the convenience of his successor, to quit the President's house.

"1st. The time of the year is unseasonable, being now very near the shortest day, and the depth of winter.

* Magnalia, Book IV. chap. 4, § 10. † Ibid.

‡ These "Considerations" bear date the 10th day of November, 1654; and were probably presented to the General Court (among whose papers they were found) after his formal petition, made in consequence of his resignation, on the 4th of November, 1654.

"2d. The place unto which I go, is unknown to me and my family, and the ways and means of subsistence, to one of my talents and parts, or for the containing or conserving my goods, or disposing of my cattle, accustomed to my place of residence.

"3d. The place from which I go, hath fire, fuel, and all provisions for man and beast, laid in for the winter. To remove some things will be to destroy them; to remove others, as books and household goods, to hazard them greatly. The house I have builded, upon very damageful conditions to myself, out of love for the College, taking country pay in lieu of bills of exchange on England, or the house would not have been built; and a considerable part of it was given me, at my request, out of respect to myself, albeit for the College.

"4th. The persons, all besides myself, are women and children, on whom little help, now their minds lie under the actual stroke of affliction and grief. My wife is sick, and my youngest child extremely so, and hath been for months, so that we dare not carry him out of doors, yet much worse now than before. However, if a place be found, that may be comfortable for them, and reasonably answer the obstacles above mentioned, myself will willingly bow my neck to any yoke of personal denial, for I know for what and for whom, by grace, I suffer."

"The whole transaction of this business is such, which in process of time, when all things come to mature consideration, may very probably create grief on all sides; yours subsequent, as mine antecedent. I am not the man you take me to be. Neither if ye knew what, should, and why, can I persuade myself that you would act, as I am at least tempted to think

CHAPTER I.

you do. But our times are in God's hands, with whom all sides hope, by grace in Christ, to find favor, which shall be my prayer for you, as for myself,

"Who am, honored Gentlemen, yours to serve,

"HENRY DUNSTER."

An appeal of this kind was irresistible; and, notwithstanding "the venom" of his heresy, and the detected coöperation with him of the "*Evil One*," the General Court consented that he should remain in the President's house till the March following.

Although the Court granted him this indulgence, their treatment of him, in other respects, was neither kind nor just. He found the seminary a school. It rose, under his auspices, to the dignity of a College. No man ever questioned his talents, learning, exemplary fidelity, and usefulness. His scanty salary had been paid, not in cash, nor in kind, but by transfers of town rates; thereby vesting him with the character of tax-gatherer, and exposing him to all the vexations, delays, complaints, losses, and abatements incident to that office. In 1643, he complained bitterly to Governor Winthrop, of the injuries he sustained by this practice. Every year he had been subjected to depreciation, delay, and loss, which he prays may be made up to him. He concludes his petition with this characteristic declaration; "Considering the poverty of the country, I am willing to descend to the lowest step; and, if nothing can comfortably be allowed, I sit still appeased; desiring nothing more than to supply me and mine with food and raiment."*

He petitions Governor Winthrop.

Neither his modesty, humility, nor virtues stood him in any stead amidst the prevailing prejudices and

* See Peirce's History, Appendix, p. 16.

poverty of the time. After his resignation, the Corporation, in May, 1655, interested themselves in his behalf, and stated to the General Court, that, "notwithstanding they have paid Mr. Dunster all that they have been able, there is still due to him nearly forty pounds, which justice and equity require should be paid; and, besides what is due in strict account, they think an hundred pounds ought to be allowed Mr. Dunster, in consideration of his extraordinary pains in raising up and carrying on the College for so many years past, and desire it may be seriously considered, and hope it may make much for the country's honorable discharge in the hearts of all, and perpetual encouragement of their servants in such public works, if it be attended."*

1655.

Dunster's treatment by the General Court.

The attempt was without success; and a committee of the Deputies treat his appeal to their humanity and justice in the following heartless way. "What extraordinary labor in, about, and concerning the weal of the College, for the space of fourteen years, we know of none, except what was the President's duty, belonging to his place; unless he can show the particulars of these labors, which were extraordinary."† The result of the whole affair was, that he obtained nothing from the General Court; and that the Corporation, after his death, paid to his widow twenty pounds, in full of the balance due to his estate.

Notwithstanding his apparent religious fanaticism, Dunster possessed a gentle heart and a noble vein of Christian charity.

In his last will, he denominates President Chauncy, who had taken his place in the College, and Mr.

* See Appendix, No. II. † Ibid., No. III.

CHAPTER I. Mitchel, the Pastor of the church in Cambridge, who thought he had the "Evil One" for his coadjutor, "my reverend," "trusty," and "judicious friends," and nominates them appraisers of his library, "some of the books of which," he adds, "being in such languages, whereof common Englishmen know not one letter." *

His death. He ordered that his body should be brought to Cambridge after his decease, and be interred near the seminary, which had been the scene of his labors, and which he had consecrated in his affections; and in the adjoining churchyard now lie the remains of as true a friend, and as faithful a servant, as this College ever possessed.

Financial state of the College. 1655. The loose and exaggerated terms in which Mather and Johnson, and other writers of that period, speak of the early donations to the College, and the obscurity, not to say confusion, in which they appear in the first records of the seminary, led Peirce, its historian, to the opinion, that "the property of the institution had increased during the time of President Dunster to at least a thousand pounds sterling, besides annuities and grants of land." The fact is, that the whole amount of the available funds of the College from all sources, during the first eighteen years of its existence, certainly did not exceed fourteen hundred, and probably was less than one thousand pounds. This had been expended in raising and repairing the building, and in providing for the current expenses of the institution. The actual state of the funds, at that period, is established beyond question by a document purporting to be "Informa-

* See his Will, in Middlesex Probate Records.

tion of the present Necessities of the College" given by the Corporation and Overseers to the General Court, signed by John Endecott, Governor, and dated the 9th of May, 1655.

After stating the lamentable condition of the College building, which, unless repaired, was not tenantable, it proceeds; "All the estate the College hath (as appears by the inventory thereof) is only its present building, library, and a few utensils, with the press and some parcels of land (none of which can, with any reason, or to any benefit, be sold, to help in the premises), and in real revenue about twelve pounds per annum (which is a small pittance to be shared among four fellows), besides fifteen pounds per annum, which, by the donors' appointment, is for scholarships."*

* See Appendix, No. II.

CHAPTER II.

Presidency of Charles Chauncy. — Previous Events of his Life. — Accepts the Office on the Importunity of the General Court. — Their Promises of Support. — Not fulfilled. — His Poverty. — Embarrassed State of the Finances of the Seminary. — Ruinous State of its Buildings. — Noble Conduct of the Town of Portsmouth. — Its Effects on Massachusetts. — Leonard Hoar chosen President. — His previous History. — Circumstances under which he was elected. — Charter of 1672. — Its Fate. — President Hoar's Difficulties. — Conduct of Oakes in respect to them. — Parallelism of the Fortunes of Hoar and Oakes. — Hoar resigns. — Urian Oakes chosen President. — His Conduct. — Difficulty in filling President's Chair. — Patronage of the General Court.

CHARLES CHAUNCY, who succeeded Mr. Dunster in the Presidency of the College, deserves particular commemoration, on account of his talents, his sufferings, and his services.

Chauncy's early life.

While in England, he was so much distinguished for his learning, as to be chosen Professor of Greek, and afterwards of Hebrew, in Trinity College, Cambridge. He seems, however, not to have possessed the stern, uncompromising, self-sacrificing spirit, which characterized his predecessor. In England, having opposed the erecting of a rail round the communion table, and the kneeling at the sacrament, and being prosecuted for schism, he recanted in open court; and acknowledged, that "kneeling at the sacrament was a commendable gesture, and "that a rail in the chancel, with a bench for kneeling, was a decent and convenient ornament;" and promised never, by word, or deed, to oppose any other of the laudable rites of the Church of England."* For this recantation he is said never to have forgiven himself. His course in this country, however, displayed a like yielding spirit. For, being conscientiously wedded to the belief, that immersion in baptism, and celebrating the Lord's supper in the evening, were true Scriptural doctrines, he refused to settle at Plymouth,† when invited, on account of the different belief of that church; and persisted in his refusal, notwithstanding that they offered, by way of compromise, that he and his colleague, Mr. Reyner, might each baptize in his own mode. Yet afterwards, on being invited to the Presidency, he made no difficulty in accepting the office on the express condition of "forbearing to disseminate or publish any thing, on either of those tenets, and promising not to oppose the received doctrines therein."

Previously to his emigration from England, Chauncy had been a settled minister at Ware. After the successes of the Republicans had subdued the persecuting spirit of the English hierarchy, he received an invitation from his former people to resume his connexion with them. This he had resolved to accept, and was preparing to return to his native country, when he was induced to abandon his intention, by "the vehement importunity" of the Overseers of the College.‡ The negotiation with him had been conducted under the auspices of the General Court, who passed several votes, indicative of their intention to give a permanent salary to the President, and of a disposition to yield an efficient support to the seminary. By the urgency

1654. Nov. 2.

Accepts the presidency.

* Massachusetts Historical Collections, First Series, Vol. X. p. 172.
† See Peirce's History, p. 22. ‡ See Appendix, No. IV.

CHAPTER II. of the agents of the Overseers, he was induced to accept the presidency.

Nothing seems to have occurred to mar the prosperous course of his official career, except, in the language of his lineal descendant and biographer, the

His scanty support. late Dr. Charles Chauncy, "his shamefully scanty support, owing, not to inability in the Province, but to the niggardly dispositions of its representatives in the General Court. A temper," he adds, "which has been too much since greatly hurtful to the interests of learning at the College."* Increase Mather, in a similar strain, says; "After he (Chauncy) was President of the College, the country was not so grateful to him, as it ought to have been; nor could he have subsisted, if he had not received supplies from England, out of estate he left there."†

1655. These censures were not undeserved. A year had not elapsed, before President Chauncy found, that his salary was inadequate to his support; and in October, 1655, he petitioned the General Court, intimating to them their promise of "a liberal maintenance," and stating, that he had already expended upwards of an hundred pounds out of his estate, in the subsistence of his family; and that his country pay, in Indian corn, could not be turned into food and clothing without great loss. He prayed, therefore, that they would provide for him according to his present necessities; that "God may not be dishonored, nor the country blemished, nor your petitioner and his family cast upon temptations, and enforced to look out to benefit his condition."‡

* See Mass. Hist. Coll., First Series, Vol. X. p. 174.
† Ibid. Vol. IX. p. 156. ‡ See Appendix, No. IV.

CHAPTER II.

The result of this application is not known. There is no reason, however, to believe that it was, in any important respect successful, since, in 1663, he again presented to the General Court his many "grievances and temptations," stating, "that his salary was not sufficient for the comfortable supply of his family with necessary food and raiment; that he had been compelled to expend his own estate, and besides had been brought greatly into debt; that the provision for the President was not suitable, being without land to keep either a horse or cow upon, or habitation to be dry or warm in; whereas, in English Universities, the President is allowed diet, as well as stipend, and other necessary provisions, according to his wants."

Petitions for relief. 1663.

The committee of the General Court on this petition, report, that "they conceive the country have done honorably towards the petitioner, and that his parity with English Colleges is not pertinent." A better spirit was, however, displayed by the Deputies, who nonconcurred the report of the committee, and voted that he should receive, out of the public treasury, five pounds a quarter. On a reference of this vote to the magistrates for their consent, they ordered to be indorsed upon it, "The magistrates consent not thereto."*

Petition rejected.

President Chauncy had then passed his seventieth year, and continued to his death, which occurred nine years afterwards, in the service of the College, laborious, faithful, necessitous, and dependent.

1672. Feb. 19.

The last page in this painful history contains the petition of Elnathan Chauncy, son of the President, presented, after his decease, to the General Court,

* See Appendix, No. IV.

CHAPTER II.

Elnathan Chauncy's petition.

in which he states, that "his father had been servant to the country, in the above trust, seventeen years, in all which time he had never received for allowance any other payment than what the country rate brought in, which had greatly impoverished his family, through the great straits they had been put into; so that, had he not had some relief in some other kind, they could not have subsisted; and now, after his decease, his children are left in a very poor condition, especially one brother, that, through the Lord's afflicting hand, is so far distempered, as to render him wholly unable to do any thing towards his own maintenance, and so will be an annual charge; and it is a great addition to this so great affliction, that his poor brothers have not in their hands to relieve him."

The petitioner asks nothing for himself, nothing for the other members of President Chauncy's family, but only that what is now due of his father's salary "may be paid in money," and that "our dear distressed brother may not perish for want of support."

On this petition, the magistrates grant, that the arrearages due should be paid in money; and the Deputies, assenting, did further grant, that ten pounds a year should be paid by the treasurer of the country to the deacons of Cambridge, for the support of the said petitioner's brother; to which the magistrates found it in their hearts to assent.

These details have been thought due to the memory of the two Presidents, Dunster and Chauncy, who, for learning, talent, and fidelity, have been surpassed by no one of their successors; who exceeded every one of them in sufferings, sacrifices, and privations; and whose fate has been little known, and of consequence had little sympathy. And yet they were both main supports of the institution for thirty years, in times when its friends were fewest and its condition humblest; and were not inferior to any of its friends, patrons, or officers, in establishing its character and perpetuating its usefulness.*

Political embarrassments.

During the greater part of President Chauncy's administration, the political embarrassments of the Colony, consequent upon the restoration of the English monarchy, materially affected the interests of the College. A political revolution, which threatened the dissolution of the colonial charter, and with it an eventful change in all the civil rights, liberties, and properties of the inhabitants, could not but have a deep influence on the prospects of the institution. Circumstances excited a peculiar anxiety about its fate. The inquiries made concerning it, in 1665, by the Commissioners of Charles the Second, indicated that its existence and importance had not escaped the searching eyes of the English Council of State. To seize upon the seminaries of education was apprehended to be the policy of the parent state, as auxiliary to that change in the religious relations of the country, which was avowedly designed by openly introducing the service and forms of the Church of England in public worship.

Financial embarrassments.

In addition to these external discouragements, the particular condition of the seminary, during the latter part of Chauncy's presidency, was critical and apparently hopeless. Its buildings were "ruinous and almost irreparable," "the President was aged," "the number of scholars short of what they had been in

* See the archives of the General Court.

CHAPTER II.

former days." All its efficient funds did not amount to one thousand pounds; without a new building its situation was desperate. The political difficulties of the Colony precluded any expectation of pecuniary aid from the General Court, who, in their best estate, had never been characterized by a disposition to give aid in money. The liberality of individuals was its only resource. Even among these, there did not early appear any active spirit for its relief.

Portsmouth, N. H., its noble conduct.

1669.

In this emergency the town of Portsmouth, in New Hampshire, first extended a helping hand to the institution. The inhabitants of that town, in an address to the General Court, dated in May, 1669, after expressing their thankfulness for the protection extended to them by Massachusetts, and saying, "that, although they had articled with them for exemption from taxes, yet they had never articled with God and their own consciences for exemption from gratitude," which "while they were studying how to demonstrate, the loud groans of the sinking College came to their ears; and hoping that their example might provoke the rest of the country to an holy emulation in so good a work, and the General Court itself vigorously to act, for the diverting the omen of calamity, which its destruction would be to New England," declare, that a voluntary collection had been made among their inhabitants, which authorized the town to pledge the payment of "sixty pounds sterling a year for seven years ensuing; to be improved by the Overseers of the College for the advancement of good literature there."

This noble example was not lost on Massachusetts. Efficient measures were immediately adopted for raising subscriptions in the Colony, and an agent was despatched to England to solicit aid from its friends there, with letters and an urgent address to them from the Overseers. These exertions produced, in the course of the ensuing year, subscriptions for more than two thousand six hundred pounds.* Under which encouragement, in 1672, authority was given for the commencement of a new edifice. Subscriptions, however, were more easily made, than collected. Great delays and delinquencies occurred. The General Court were compelled to interfere; and, after efforts for five or six years, first by urging, then by threatening, and at last, by actually authorizing the delinquent subscriptions to be collected by distress, they finally succeeded in completing the erection of a new College, in 1682, ten years after it had been commenced.

Leonard Hoar chosen President. 1672

The embarrassments of the College at this period were not exclusively pecuniary. In July, 1672, Leonard Hoar, a clergyman, and a physician, was elected President. Though not born in the Colony, he was a graduate of the College, but had been resident in England nearly twenty years. He left England, on hearing of the death of Mr. Chauncy, with the design of offering himself as a candidate for the vacant chair. For this purpose, he brought with him recommendations from thirteen clergymen, all of whom were distinguished friends of the Colony, and had been efficient agents for procuring subscriptions in that country for the College edifice. Collins, who then acted as colonial agent in Great Britain, also recommended him, for employment in the College, to Governor Leverett.

For these reasons, or some other, the General Court seem to have taken a lively interest in his election; opening their hearts so far as to add fifty pounds

* See Appendix, No. V.

CHAPTER II.

to the hundred they were accustomed annually to grant, "on condition that Dr. Hoar be the man chosen for the vacant President's place." Under these auspices, he was chosen by the Corporation, and approved by the Overseers. In the ensuing October, the General Court passed also a new College charter. By this act the name of the Corporation was changed from "The President and Fellows" to that of "The President, Fellows, and Treasurer." The number of its members was not increased. It was permitted to hold personal property to any amount whatsoever, and real estate to the value of *five hundred pounds* per annum. Ten menial servants of the Corporation were exempted from all civil and military exercises, and the personal estates of the members of the Corporation and their officers, not exceeding one hundred pounds a man, were exempted from taxes; and any three of the Corporation, of which the President was to be one, had committed to them full power to fine, sconce, or otherwise correct any officer or member of said Society, according to the laws of the country; and for this purpose, taking a constable, to enter into any house licensed for public entertainment, where they should be informed, or have reason to suspect, enormities were plotting or acting by any members of said Society.

College Charter of 1672.

Although this charter is entered at large in the journal of the General Court, it does not appear in the records of the seminary; nor is any notice taken of it in those records, nor in the general history of the times. The probability is, that it was the work of President Hoar, and had some connexion with that evanescent influence, which he seemed, in the year 1672, to have

CHAPTER II.

acquired among the members of the General Court;* and, in consequence of that unpopularity, which immediately followed his entering upon the government of the institution, its authority was never recognised by the Corporation. It is certain, that they never assumed the name given by the act, and there exists no evidence of their having, in a single instance, modified their proceedings according to its provisions. A year did not elapse, after the election of President Hoar, before there appeared "uncomfortable motions and debates" in the College; and a second year had not passed, before the General Court summoned into their presence the Corporation, Overseers, President, and students; and, after a full hearing, notwithstanding that Dr. Hoar, in consideration of the poverty of the students, voluntarily relinquished fifty pounds of his annual salary, the Court† passed this most extraordinary vote; "That, if the College be found in the same languishing condition at the next session, the President is concluded to be dismissed without further hearing." After this decisive encouragement to malcontents, it was not difficult to anticipate the result. The College continued to languish, and Dr. Hoar resigned his office in the March ensuing.

Unpopularity of Dr. Hoar.

1674.

Vote of General Court.

President Hoar resigns.

1675.

There is a studied obscurity thrown over the defects, if there were really any, in the character of Dr. Hoar. That he was a scholar and a Christian, a man of talent and of great moral worth, is asserted. Yet, for some reason, the young men of the College took a prejudice against him, and, says Cotton Mather, "did all they could to ruin his reputation." The

* See Appendix, No. LXVIII.

† See General Court Records, October, 1674.

CHAPTER II.

cause of this prejudice is unexplained to this day. "I can scarce tell how," says Cotton Mather, "but he fell under the displeasure of *some that made a figure in that neighbourhood.*"* "In a day of temptation, which was now upon them, *several good men* did unhappily countenance the ungoverned youth in their ungovernableness." It is not difficult, from the records of the College, to gather to whom Cotton Mather here alludes; and it is due to the memory of Dr. Hoar to say, that the conduct of those "good men, who made a figure in that neighbourhood," and thus encouraged the discontented youth, greatly exceeded, in dereliction of incumbent duty, any thing that appears, or was ever suggested, against him.

Dr. Hoar was, in a manner, a stranger in the country. He had come strongly recommended, seeking the presidency. The General Court had thrown their whole weight into the scale in favor of his election. His success, it was asserted at the time, had occasioned a disappointment to "*the emulation of some expecting the preferment.*" This, probably, is the clue to all the difficulties which assailed and overcame President Hoar. He was chosen in July, 1672. A year had not elapsed before the students began "*to strive to make him odious.*" In the midst of these difficulties, Urian Oakes, Thomas Shepard, Joseph Brown, and John Richardson, members of the Corporation, all resigned their seats at that Board,† leaving it without a constitutional majority, and with no *quorum* to act, and the President without support. They all fall within the description of "*good men, who made a figure in that neighbourhood,*

Urian Oakes resigns his seat in the Corporation

* Magnalia, Book IV. Part I. § 5. † See Appendix, No. VI.

and who, in a day of temptation, encouraged" the contumacious. Whether emulation, or hope of preferment, had any influence in this course of conduct, must be a matter of inference. It is certain, that no conduct of Dr. Hoar could justify, or even apologize, for such a resignation of a majority of the Corporation in the actual state of disorderly combination in the College. Their resignation occasioned an alarm in the Board of Overseers; who petitioned them to continue, or at least assist at the meetings of the Corporation, and finally warned the remaining members, that, unless their numbers were filled up, they would endanger their charter privileges. Oakes, Shepard, and the rest persisted in their resignation. The Corporation reëlect Oakes and Shepard, and they persist in not accepting the trust, until the 15th of March, 1675. On this day, Dr. Hoar sent in his resignation of the presidency. On the same day, Oakes and Shepard took their seats as members of the Corporation, and the seat Dr. Hoar had quitted was given to the Rev. Mr. Oakes. An instant acceptance of the office would have probably given rise to suspicions, which, considering the part he had taken relative to the difficulties of his predecessor, he must have been willing to avoid. Being importuned to accept the presidency, he refused, but took the superintendence of the College, with the rank and duties of President, which he held four years. During this period the Rev. John Rogers was elected President, but declined; and William Stoughton, then in England, was authorized to provide a President of the College in Europe, in which he could not succeed.

Oakes accepts the superintendence. 1675.

In February, 1679, Oakes, being again elected, accepted the office, which he held till his death,

And the presidency. 1679.

in 1681. In the mean time Dr. Hoar had died, in obscurity and sorrow, impressed with a deep sense of the wrongs he had sustained, and, as was said, with a broken heart.*

There was a singular parallelism in the fortunes of Mr. Oakes and Dr. Hoar, of a nature not unlikely to excite an "emulation" between them in respect to the presidency of the College; an office, which at that time placed the incumbent at the head of the clergy, who then possessed almost a predominating influence in the Colony. Neither of them was a native; both were brought into the country during their childhood by their parents. They had been contemporaneously members of the College; the former having graduated in 1649, the latter in 1650. Both had returned to England soon after taking their degrees. Both had been settled in the ministry there; had been ejected for nonconformity; and again emigrated to this country within a year of each other; Oakes, in 1671, on an invitation from the church at Cambridge to become its pastor; Hoar, in 1672, on a like invitation to become its pastor from the Old South Church in Boston.

The former, being settled in Cambridge, and a fellow of the Corporation, before the arrival of Dr. Hoar, and possessing qualities suited to the appointment, had probably ingratiated himself with the students and with persons of influence in the immediate vicinity of the College, and had been regarded by them as the natural successor of President Chauncy; an expectation which it is not unlikely his own heart fostered. The strong recommendations brought by Dr. Hoar,

* Eliot's Biography, articles "Hoar" and "Oakes."

and the efficient declaration in his favor by the General Court, in a manner compelled his election. The event disappointed both the students and Mr. Oakes, and led the former, in the language of Cotton Mather, to "turn cudweeds and travestie whatever he did and said, with a design to make him odious," and the latter to countenance these proceedings, by relinquishing his seat in the Corporation until Dr. Hoar had resigned. "The emulation of some seeking the preferment," to which Mather attributes the difficulties of Hoar, is applicable to no one except Oakes. It appears also, that, on some account, Oakes was suffering about this time under a great mental excitement, which, from the connexion in which it is mentioned, seems to have reference to this very subject. Governor Leverett, in a letter written in August, 1674, relating to the troubles of Dr. Hoar, after referring them to "the animosities and perverse spirit of his opposers," proceeds to state, that "Mr. Oakes hath had a distemper hang upon him, which hath much weakened him, *the greatest occasion of which is, I think, some exercise of mind.*"*

That Oakes had, or believed himself suspected to have, some agency in the discontent of the College and the troubles of Dr. Hoar, may be surmised from the following entry in the Journal of Judge Sewall, who was at this time a resident graduate of the College. "5 June, 1674. Mr. Oakes gave me to understand, that, though he respected and loved me as formerly, yet he desired that I would refrain coming to his house, and that he did it *se defendendo*, lest he should be mistrusted to discourage and dissettle me."

* Hutchinson's Collection of State Papers, p. 464.

CHAPTER II.

That, in the opinion of Sewall, the difficulties of the seminary were not exclusively attributable to Dr. Hoar, is to be gathered from another expression in his Journal, under the date of the 16th of October, 1674. "By Mr. Richardson's means I was called upon to speak. The sum of my speech was, that the causes of the lowness of the College were *external*, as well as internal." However questionable, in respect to Dr. Hoar, the course pursued by Mr. Oakes may have been, the character given of him by Cotton Mather, as "faithful, learned, and indefatigable in all the services of a President," seems to have been well deserved.

At this period, the difficulty of finding persons suitable and willing to accept that office was great. In 1681 the Rev. Increase Mather was chosen, and declined. In the same year the Rev. Samuel Torrey, of Weymouth, was chosen, and also declined. In 1683, the Rev. John Rogers was again chosen, accepted, and was inaugurated. He did not survive that event one year.

In 1684, the chair was offered to the Rev. Joshua Moody, who declined it. And on the 11th of June, 1685, the Rev. Increase Mather was requested "to take special care of the government of the College, and, for that end, to act as President until a farther settlement be made."

Increase Mather, President. 1685.

Mr. Mather retained this relation sixteen years; during eight of which he held the office of President, although non-resident at Cambridge. The period, which elapsed while the College was under his superintendence, is the most interesting, the most critical, and the most decisive of its destinies, of any in its history. The political and religious parties of

CHAPTER II.

the country were, during the whole time, in a state of excitement and struggle. The College became one of the chief arenas and objects of the contests of both; resulting in events of general and absorbing interest.

Patronage of the General Court.

Before entering upon the topics, however, which were involved in those contests, it is orderly and proper, first, to turn and examine the nature and degree of patronage the College received, during the period now under consideration, from the State; denominated, in this early time, "the country" or "the jurisdiction," afterwards the "Colony" or "Province," of which the General Court was, in every period, the organ and representative and supreme legislature. During these first seventy years of its existence, the College is indebted to the Court for many instances of countenance, encouragement, and support.

Their vote in 1636 planted the first germ of its being. Their acts, in 1642, 1650, and 1657,* gave to it an efficient corporate form and powers. They are entitled to be denominated its earliest friends and constant patrons. The character of "*founder*," the General Court never claimed. On the contrary, in the year 1661, in an address to the Commissioners of Charles the Second, they expressly concede the title of "*principal founder*" to John Harvard.

Of the General Court, and of the nature and degree of patronage which the College received from them, during its early years, justice and truth require us to speak in terms of respect and honor; although, in fact, their favor and bounty were only a refined and intelligent self-interest, supporting an institution, with whose prosperity their own, and that of their country, were inseparably identified.

* See Appendix, No. LXVIII.

CHAPTER II.

Grants of money.

In respect to grants of money, the patronage of the General Court, during this first period of seventy years, certainly never exceeded, and there is no known documentary evidence, that it ever equalled, the annual payment of £100 until the year 1673, and that of £150 during the subsequent years of this period. These payments, with the income of the Ferry, were the only resources of the institution, of a permanent character, for the support of the President and officers. The deficiency was made up by assessments on the students. With the exception of this annual stipend, there is no evidence of grants of money, or even transfers of rates, except at times, when the treasury of the Colony actually possessed an amount greatly exceeding such grant or transfer, received from private donations, on account of the College. During that whole period its officers were dependent for daily bread upon the bounty of the General Court. They always stood before the Court in the attitude of humble suppliants, destitute of the power even to enforce their rights; and found, by bitter experience, how miserable is he who hangs on a sovereign's favor, be that sovereign one or many, prince or people.

Grants of land.

In respect to grants of land, the General Court, in 1652, gave to the College eight hundred acres, and in 1653, two thousand acres. Both grants failed. In 1658 the Court attempted to indemnify the College for this loss, by granting to it two thousand one hundred acres of land, being, as they thought, a part of their share of the plunder accruing from their victory over the Pequods. The Colony of Connecticut, however, claimed these lands as their own portion of the spoils, and dispossessed the College of them; and it is not known or believed, that the College obtained any thing from that grant. In 1683, the General Court made another attempt to patronize the College by a grant of one thousand acres of land at Merriconeage. This grant, however, had the fate of its predecessors. The College gained nothing by it, but a lawsuit and a judgment disaffirming its title. During the first seventy years, the College derived no aid from the General Court towards the erection of its buildings or the increase of its funds, in consequence of any grant or donation. These were altogether the result of individual munificence. So that the whole bounty of that body, during this entire period, was limited to the annual payment, at first, of £100, and afterward £150, as above stated, and the income of the Ferry.

Neither does it anywhere appear that the original grant of £400 was ever specifically paid.* As far as can now be ascertained, the above annual grants were deemed a sufficient fulfilment of that vote.

Let not these statements lead to the conclusion, that the degree of patronage extended by the General Court was of little worth, or is intended to be undervalued. Notwithstanding the deficiency in direct donatives, the College is largely indebted to them for the actual prosperity, to which, during the period in question, it attained. The necessities of the country were extreme; its available resources scanty and precarious. The people were struggling with the parent State for their charters, and with the Indians for their existence. Their annual revenues were regularly exhausted. Surplus they had none. The power of raising rev-

* See Appendix, No. VII.

CHAPTER II.

enue by credit, either did not exist, or was extremely limited. They had only influence and authority. These they exerted largely, unsparingly, and efficiently for its support and advancement.

In respect to the patronage of the General Court, it cannot fail to be gratifying to the friends of the College to be assured, that, from unquestionable documents it is manifest, that neither the erection of its buildings, nor the creation of its funds, added any thing to the embarrassments of the country, nor were they objects of any appropriation of its revenues during the whole of this first period of its existence. On the contrary, it is manifest, that the treasury of the Colony, having been the recipient of many of the early donations to the College, was not a little aided by the convenience, which, in the poverty of the time, these available funds afforded to its pecuniary necessities. Some of those funds, although received by the treasury of the Colony in 1647, were not paid over to the treasury of the College, until 1713; then, indeed, the College received an allowance of simple interest for the delay.

There is a curious evidence of the opinion entertained, on this subject, by the Corporation of the College, in a memorial addressed by them to the General Court in 1697, having for its object to induce the Court to aid in obtaining a charter for the College from the King. "The time has been," say the Corporation in this memorial, "when the College has accommodated this Colony with a considerable sum of money, not repaid to this hour; and we would persuade ourselves, that this Province will, *in point of gratitude*, not refuse to be helpful unto the good settlement of that society, on which the welfare of the public so much depends."

With regard, therefore, to the annual allowance of £100, whereby they enabled the President of the College simply to exist, it is proper to observe, that there was not probably one year in the whole seventy, in which, by moneys collected from friends of the institution in foreign countries, by donations of its friends in this country, by moneys brought by students coming from other colonies for education here, and, above all, by furnishing the means of education at home, and thus preventing the outgoing of domestic wealth for education abroad, the College did not remunerate the Colony for that poor annual stipend five hundred fold. Well and truly did the Earl Bellamont, when Governor of Massachusetts in 1699, say to the General Court, "It is a very great advantage you have above other provinces, that your youth are not put to travel for learning, but have the Muses at their doors."

HARVARD HALL, BUILT IN 1682; DESTROYED BY FIRE IN 1764.

CHAPTER III.

Influence of the Clergy on the College. — Its catholic Spirit. — Causes of this traced to the Civil and Ecclesiastical Constitution of the Colony. — State of Religious Parties, and their Effect. — Influence of Increase and Cotton Mather on the College and the Colony. — The Administration of Andros, and its Effect. — President Mather's Agency in England. — His Influence in procuring the Charter of the Colony in 1692, and in the Appointments under it. — The Witchcraft Delusion. — The College connected with it by the Mathers. — State of Parties, which arose in Consequence of that Charter.

THE Congregational clergy next demand our notice. To them this institution is perhaps more indebted, than to any other class of men, for early support, if not for existence. Of money and lands, they had little or none, a few of them only excepted. The power which they possessed, they exerted for the College with zeal and affection. They promoted its interests by every instrument of authority, and every legitimate form of influence, at their command. It was the frequent topic of their sermons, and the constant object of their prayers. They were active for it in private solicitation, and urgent in public assemblies. Its founder was a member of their body. Those of them, who had wealth, contributed according to their means, in money or in books. Everywhere they were its unceasing and unwearied advocates. Possessing, at that day, a predominating influence in the Colony, they did not fail to associate the College with the all-absorbing passions and prejudices of the time. They denominated it "the School of the Prophets," and identified its success with all the prospects and all the hopes of religion in the Province.

Above all, we are, probably, indebted to the clergy for the catholic and liberal spirit breathed into its first, and into each successive, Constitution; in every period its vital principle and distinguishing characteristic; to which may be chiefly ascribed its success and prosperity.

Early liberal spirit of the institution.

The erection of a seminary of learning, particularly if it have for its object instruction in theology, is of all opportunities the most favorable to the establishment of sectarian tenets, if such exist at the time and have influence. Now the clergy of that early period were, not only a learned and wise, but eminently a practical body of men. They were also conscientiously imbued with certain peculiar religious opinions, which constituted the prevalent doctrines of all Protestant Christendom in that day. Their influence over the statesmen of the Colony was second to none the world ever witnessed. The religion of both was not so much coincident, as identical. Both were well apprized of the advantages resulting to worldly power from the possession and control of the seminaries of education. We expect, therefore, on opening the several charters, which form the Constitution of this University, to find it, with certainty, anchored head and stern, secure against wind, tide, and current, moored firmly on all the points which, in that day, were deemed fixed and immutable. We expect to find, in these instruments, some "form of sound words," some "creed," some "catechism," some "medulla theologiæ," established as the standard of religious faith, to which every one, entering on an office of government and instruction, shall be required to swear and subscribe, and, at the hazard of perjury and hypocrisy, under the combined temptations of loss of place, of caste, and of bread, at stated periods to renew his oath and subscription.

Yet, surprising as is the fact, there is not, in any one of the charters that form the Constitution of this College, one expression, on which a mere sectarian spirit can seize to wrest it into a shackle for the human soul. The idea seems never to have entered the minds of its early founders, of laying conscience under bonds for good behaviour. It is impossible, even at this day, when the sun of free inquiry is thought to be at its zenith, to devise any terms more unexceptionable, or better adapted to assure the enjoyment of equal privileges to every religious sect or party.

The first Constitution of Harvard College, established in 1642, in enumerating the powers granted and the objects proposed to be attained by its foundation, makes use of these simple and memorable terms; "To make and establish all such orders, statutes, and constitutions, as they shall see necessary for the instituting, guiding, and furthering of the said College, and the several members thereof, from time to time, in *piety*, morality, and learning." Nor does the charter of 1650, although it somewhat varies the expressions, introduce any thing indicative of a design to give the institution a sectarian bias. Its objects are in this charter stated to be, "the advancement of all good literature, arts, and sciences," and "the education of the English and Indian youth of this country in knowledge and *godliness*." The only terms, used in either of these charters connecting this institution with the religious principle, are "*piety*" and "*godliness*"; terms of all others the least susceptible of being wrested to projects merely sectarian.

In the conduct of the College, also, the fathers of New England evidenced a singular freedom from sectarian influence. The first two Presidents, and the only ones appointed by the early emigrants, were known unbelievers in points of religious faith to which the Congregational clergy of that time rigidly adhered.

Those emigrants were Pædobaptists; that is, believers in infant baptism as a divine rite. Dunster was, as has been stated, an avowed antipædobaptist; yet he was chosen and continued President of the seminary fourteen years; and would never have been compelled to resign, had not his excited zeal for his own sectarian faith led him, in a moment of indiscretion, to overstep the bounds of prudence, and to bear public testimony, in the church at Cambridge, against infant baptism.

The second President, Chauncy, was not less heretical than his predecessor, according to the standard of religious faith adopted by the early emigrants; and also on this very point of infant baptism. He did not, indeed, like Dunster, hold that adults were the only subjects of this rite. His heresy consisted in this, that, whereas the prevailing faith among the emigrants was, that in baptism "a sprinkling was sufficient," the faith of President Chauncy was, says the historian Hubbard, "that the infant should be washed all over." "An opinion," he adds, "not tolerable in this cold region, and impracticable at certain seasons of the year." *

* See Mass. Hist. Coll., Second Series, Vol. VI. p. 544.

CHAPTER III.

First College seal.

The original seal of the College is also illustrative of its early independence of a sectarian spirit. At the first "meeting of the governors of the College" after the first charter was obtained, on the 27th of December, 1643, a College seal was adopted, having, as at present, three open books on the field of an heraldic shield, with the motto "*Veritas*" inscribed. The books were probably intended to represent the Bible; and the motto to intimate, that in the Scriptures alone important truth was to be sought and found, and not in words of man's devising. This is the only College seal which has the sanction of any record.*

Whether this or any other indication of a liberal spirit, exhibited by the clergy, who, in that day, guided the seminary, had given offence, does not appear from history. It does however appear, that, for some cause, the Congregational clergy of that period were subjected to the charge of "dethroning Christ and setting up for themselves,"† made against them by a class of enthusiasts, who pretended to greater purity and a more evangelical spirit. Concerning which class of enthusiasts, Thomas Shepard, one of the Overseers of the College, and a man of eminent learning and piety, in one of his writings published about this time (1645), speaks with great asperity, as aiming, under these pretences, to establish worldly power, and to gratify their own personal ambition; and he calls them "Evangelical hypocrites."‡ "The

* The adjoining *fac-simile* of the original design of this seal suggested the vignette on the title-page, in which it is represented in a more regular form.

† Savage's Winthrop, Vol. I. p. 289.

‡ New England's Lamentations for Old England's Errors, in a Letter from Thomas Shepard. Dated, Cambridge, Dec. 10th, 1644. London, printed 1645.

FAC SIMILE OF A PART OF THE OFFICIAL RECORD OF THE FIRST MEETING OF THE GOVERNORS OF THE COLLEGE UNDER THE CHARTER OF 1642.

At the meeting of the Governours of Harbard Colledge, held in the Colledge-Hall this 27 of 10th — 1643

It is ordered that,

The Accounts of Mr Harbards Gift are to be finished, & Mr Pelham Mr Nowell, Mr Hibbons, Mr Syms, Mr Wilson are chosen finish it, yt an acquittance may be given Mr Allin And its agreed yt if they find things cleared in the fullfilling the will of ye dead they are to desire ye Governour of ye Colledge his hand to it as a full determination & acquittance

Mr Pelham is elected Treasurer of ye Colledge by the joynt vote of ye Governours of ye Colledge.

It is ordered that there shall be a Colledge Seale in forme following

CHAPTER III.

Epistles of James and John," says he, "are antidotes against this kind of poison; and I look upon them as lamps, hung up to discover these men." "The most subtle hypocrites," he adds, "appear, or seem to be, under grace, and their external operations are chiefly evangelical; hence I call them Evangelical hypocrites." *

Whatever was the cause, it appears that the motto "*Veritas*" was soon exchanged for "*In Christi gloriam*." † After many years there was another change. Circumstances give color to the conjecture, that this took place during the Presidency of Increase Mather, when a violent struggle was making to secure the College under the influences of the old established Congregational church.‡ At this time, there is reason to believe, that, instead of "*In Christi gloriam*," the motto now in use, "*Christo et Ecclesiæ*," was adopted. § There is, however, no authority for either of these mottos in any existing College record; nor is it known, with certainty, when either was introduced.

Cause of its liberal spirit.

There is, unquestionably, a liberality of religious principle manifested in the several charters of this College, apparently irreconcilable with the general conduct and policy resulting from predominating religious opinions in that day. But it is well known, that, among the early emigrants, there existed men, who were true disciples of the great principles of the Reformation, and who even carried them to a degree of theoretic perfection, scarcely exceeded in our time. It is possible, nay, even probable, that the reason of the entire absence of any reference to points of re-

* The Parable of the Ten Virgins, by Thomas Shepard. London, 1695. Fol.

† See above, p. 23. ‡ See App. No. VIII. § See the end of this volume.

ligious faith in the charters of the College was, that these early emigrants could not agree concerning them among themselves, and preferred silence on such points to engaging in controversy, when establishing a seminary of learning, in favor of which they were desirous to unite all the varieties of religious belief. The right of exercising private judgment in matters of religion was, at that day, in terms at least, universally recognised. It is not possible more expressly to maintain the right of every man to construe Scripture for himself, as a fundamental principle, than did some of the most distinguished and approved leaders of that period. This assertion might easily be supported by quotations from the writings of many of them. It will be sufficient, however, to refer to those of that most famous and efficient religious champion, John Robinson, whose influence, more than that of any other individual, presided over the first emigration to New England. The parting lesson he gave to his church, when about departing for this country, is familiarly known; — "To think for themselves, and not, like the Lutherans and Calvinists, stop short where their leaders stopped; but to follow their leaders no farther than they followed Christ."

It is difficult to conceive of a more catholic and liberal spirit, than that which is indicated in all his writings. He says; "God, who made two great lights for the bodily eye, hath also made two lights for the eye of the mind. The one, the Scriptures, for her supernatural light, and the other, reason, for her natural light. And, indeed, only these two are a man's own, and so is not the authority of other men. The Scriptures are as well mine as any other man's; and so is reason, as far as I can attain to it. But the authority of others is not mine, but theirs."* Again; "When we avow the Scriptures' perfection, we exclude not from men common sense and the light of nature, by which we are both subjects, capable of understanding them, and are directed in sundry manners of doing things commanded by them."† And again; "This is the first thing we are to believe, that we are to believe nothing but according to the Scriptures. All things else are human; and human it is to err and be deceived. The custom of the church is but the custom of men; the sentence of the fathers but the opinions of men; the determinations of councils but the judgments of men."‡

To such a degree of liberality had this great divine in that age attained, that, in the figurative language then common, he represents the yielding of implicit reverence to the opinions of the church or of men, to be one of the choice arts of the Devil. "In former ages," says he, "the Devil has so far prevailed, as that men, in superstitious reverence, have, as it were, pinned their faith and religion upon the sleeves of the church's authority or clergy's learning, putting out or winking with their own eyes, that their guides might lead them. And this blindfold devotion is yet affected by too many."§

The existence and the nature of this liberal spirit in many of the early emigrants, and the causes which checked and limited its developement, will be rendered further apparent from the political and religious controversies relative to the College, which occurred

* Essays, Divine and Moral, by John Robinson. 2d Edit. London, 1638. p. 118.

† Ibid. p. 100. ‡ Ibid. p. 102. § Ibid. p. 119.

CHAPTER III.

during the presidency of Increase Mather, and which constitute the most critical and eventful chapter of its history. It is impossible to understand the bearings of those controversies, which began at that time, and have not wholly ceased in our day, without recurring to the first charter of the Colony, and the powers assumed and the civil constitution established under it by the first emigrants to the Massachusetts Bay. Nor can we otherwise account for the remarkable fact in the history of this College, that a literary institution, founded for the instruction of the whole people in general science, should have been, from the first, spoken of, lauded, and conducted, as though it had been a theological seminary, destined exclusively for the benefit of one order of men; and that this language in respect to it should have been continued to be used, with few exceptions, during the whole of the century in which it was established, and have, in a degree, prevailed even in our own time.

Objects of the early emigration.

The emigrants, who, in 1630, brought with them to this country the first charter of Massachusetts, came here, to use the language of the famous John Cotton, "for the purpose of securing to themselves and their posterity, the pure and peaceable enjoyment of the ordinances of Christ, in church fellowship with his people." They were, or at least assumed that they were, in a condition, and with powers, "to mould or form a commonwealth, as should appear best to them." Being in this condition, they chose, that "religion should be the end of their civil government." "There are," says the same distinguished divine, "two administrations or polities, ecclesiastical and civil, which men commonly call the Church and Commonwealth. Both agree in this, that they have the common welfare for their scope and aim; yet the things, about which the civil power is primarily conversant are *bodies; the things of this life, as goods, lands, honors; the liberties and peace of the outward man.* The things, whereabout the church power is exercised, are *things of God; as the souls and consciences of men, the doctrine and worship of God, the communion of saints.*"

With these views and this understanding, the early emigrants deliberately adopted, as the fundamental principle of their civil constitution, that "the power of electing and being elected to office should be exclusively vested in church members;" that is, "to these alone the management of all public affairs of importance should be committed."

From this fundamental principle of their constitution, there resulted, and for the first sixty years after their emigration there was upheld, in Massachusetts, as complete an intertexture of Church and State, as perfect a church establishment, as ever existed in any country. Nor was this unknown, or unavowed. On the contrary, it was openly asserted and vindicated, as natural and necessary. The same leading divine, John Cotton, speaks to this point in language unequivocal. "In England," says he, "none but members of the Church of England are entrusted with the management of affairs. In Popish countries, none but such as are Catholics. In Turkey itself, none but men devoted to Mahomet. Yea, these very Indians, that worship the Devil, will not be under the government of any Sagamores, but such as join with them in the observance of their pawawes and idolatries; so that it seems to be a principle, imprinted in the minds of men, in the equity of it, *that such a form of gov-*

CHAPTER III.

ernment, as best serveth to establish their religion, should, by the consent of all, be established in the civil State."*

The effect of this civil constitution was, first, that none but members of the church were freemen of the state; secondly, as none could be church members whom the minister did not approve, it followed that the ecclesiastical ruler had an efficient negative on the admission of every freeman; and thirdly, as excommunication from the church created a civil, as well as ecclesiastical disability, it also followed, that both the attainment and continuance of political rights were, to all practical purposes, in the hands of the ecclesiastical rulers.†

The nature of this civil constitution is a further explanation of the cause of the liberal features of the College charters. The ecclesiastical rulers, being all-sufficient under the civil constitution, required no special provision against contumacious consciences in those charters. It also explains why a literary institution, founded for objects of general science, with no reference to particular religious opinions, was considered and permitted, by the civil authorities, to be conducted as though it were a theological seminary. For, the end for which civil government was here established being religion, all the institutions of the country, and especially those of education, were naturally to be made subservient to the great end of the civil constitution. And, above all, does it explain the origin and causes of those political and religious con-

* A Discourse about Civil Government in a Plantation, whose Design is Religion; by John Cotton. 1663.

† See Hutchinson's Collection of State Papers. Boston, 1769. p. 520

CHAPTER III.

troversies, which occurred about the College, immediately upon the dissolution of the old and the establishment of the new Colonial charter, which was granted by William and Mary in 1692.

General effects of the Colonial charter of 1692.

That charter effected in Massachusetts as perfect and thorough a revolution, as ever was produced by a similar act in any state or nation. It changed, not only the form of the government, and the relations of power among the people, but also the entire foundation and objects of the government. By making freehold and property, instead of church membership, the qualification of the right of electing and being elected to office, religion became no longer the end and object of the civil government. In the language of John Cotton, civil government in Massachusetts was no longer "exercised about the things of God, the souls and consciences of men, the doctrine and worship of God, and the communion of saints," but had exclusively for its end "the things about which the civil power is usually conversant; goods, lands, honors, the liberties and peace of the outward man."

Influence of President Mather

The direct effect of this new charter was therefore, manifestly, to deprive the clergy of the Province of that civil power, which they had, from the first settlement of the country, enjoyed. This effect was instinctively perceived by the ecclesiastical leaders, who were unremitting and vigorous in their endeavours to retain the civil authority they had so long possessed. Of these leaders, Increase Mather, and Cotton Mather, his son, were the most active, able, and indefatigable. The extraordinary influence of President Mather, during the period immediately preceding and succeeding the new charter, is inseparably identified with the history of the Province. In nothing, however, is it more apparent than in the manner in which he was permitted to manage the affairs of the College, and shape them to his own purposes. He was appointed to the superintendence of the institution in 1685, immediately afterward made Rector, and soon President. He held the relation to it of head for sixteen years; during all which time he was not resident at Cambridge (six months excepted); four of which years he was in Europe; and during eight he was perpetually assailed by votes of one or the other branch of the General Court, and required to be resident at the College. All these requisitions he found means to evade, until 1701. Being then compelled by the urgency of the General Court to reside there or resign, he considered himself extremely ill treated; and his son Cotton declares "his abdication was not brought about as fairly as it should have been," and takes credit to himself "for not telling the whole story."* Of the motives and master passions of his eventful presidency, we are enabled to speak with great certainty. There is no class of men, to whom history is under so many obligations as to those, who submit to the labor of keeping diaries. On the one hand, they enjoy a great advantage over their contemporaries, by being thus enabled to tell their own story to posterity in their own way, when there are none living to explain or contradict; yet, on the other hand, nature establishes for this advantage a compensation, in the fact, that they are often led, by vanity, passion, or inadvertence, to state facts and make records, which place their

* Life of Increase Mather, by his Son, p. 173.

own characters and views, or those of their friends, in lights which they had carefully concealed from their contemporaries;—views which the world, although it might have suspected, could not otherwise have made certain. This is remarkably the case in respect to President Mather and his son. They both kept diaries, in which they have themselves recorded their motives and purposes; so that in relation to either there can hardly be any mistake.

In June, 1685, Increase Mather was requested by the Overseers to "take special care for the government of the College, and for that end to act as President until a farther settlement be orderly made."* To this he acceded. His oversight, however, was necessarily formal and occasional. He lived in Boston, and, besides his parochial labors, was actively engaged in the absorbing politics of the period. In consequence, the annual grant of the General Court to the President for his services was, this year, placed at the disposal of the Corporation, to be applied by them "for the encouragement of *such as have done the work*."† Under that vote nothing was given by the Corporation to Increase Mather; but whatever was distributed "on account of the President's work," was given to John Leverett and John Cotton; the former of whom was, about this time, appointed fellow of the Corporation, and commenced an active fulfilment of his duties as instructor in the College. 1685.

During the period which elapsed between the dissolution of the old charter of the Colony in 1684, and the arrival of the new charter in 1692, the College partook of the embarrassments of the Colony.

* College Records, Book I. p. 68.

† Ibid. p. 69.

CHAPTER III.

The public records of the latter, for several years, are lost,* and those of the former are extremely deficient. It appears, however, from such of them as remain, that Joseph Dudley, who held, between May and December, in the year 1686, the commission of President of the Colony, and William Stoughton, who held, during the same time, that of Deputy President, availed themselves of their transitory power to place the College on a basis adapted to the uncertainty which hung over its destinies, in common with those of the Colony. On the 23d of July in that year,† they, with their Council, met at Cambridge, and appointed Increase Mather, Rector, and John Leverett and Thomas Brattle, Tutors, enjoining upon the Rector to make his "usual visitations," and vesting in the two last "the government" of the College.

Dudley's settlement of the College. 1686.

Andros.

Andros, during his short and violent rule, interfered but little, if at all, with this settlement. On the departure of Increase Mather for England, in 1688, he appointed William Hubbard temporary President or Rector,‡ for the purpose of officiating at Commencement. It appears also, by Judge Sewall's Diary, that, in July of that year, Andros attended Commencement, bringing with him Ratcliffe, a clergyman of the Church of England, who, by his orders, had a seat assigned to him in the pulpit with the President. This circumstance was sufficiently annoying, and probably was regarded as an intended insult, to the stern Congregationalists, who then governed the College. They extended, however, to Ratcliffe no professional comity; nor was he permitted to take

1686.

* Hutchinson's History of Massachusetts, Vol. I. p. 317.

† College Records, Book IV. p. 1.

‡ See Mass. Hist. Coll., Third Series, Vol. I. p. 83.

any part in the ceremonies. For Sewall carefully records, that President Mather "prayed both forenoon and afternoon, and also craved blessing and returned thanks in the Hall."

It was customary at this period for the President to make an oration on Commencement day. Sewall relates, that President Mather, after giving the degrees in 1685, made an oration in praise of academical studies and degrees. At the Commencement also, in 1688, Hubbard, when officiating as President under the appointment of Andros, "made an oration," according to Sewall, "in which he compared Sir William Phips (who had been knighted for discovering and taking possession of the wealth of a sunken Spanish galleon) to Jason bringing home the golden fleece." 1688.

President Mather's agency in England.

In the course of this year President Mather sailed for England at the instigation of the civil and ecclesiastical authorities of the Colony. The openness and boldness, with which he had resisted the tyrannical acts of Andros and Randolph, rendered him extremely popular with both those orders, and not less odious to each of these individuals. He was in Europe during the Revolution of 1688, watched its progress with solicitude, was soon appointed one of the agents of the Colony at the Court of Great Britain, and was chiefly instrumental in forming the new Provincial charter of 1692, and in persuading the people of the Colony to accept it. Being considered as the head and representative of the clergy of Massachusetts, the ministers of the crown were desirous to conciliate him; well knowing, that the ecclesiastical was in fact the predominating estate of the Colonial realm. To this end, they gave him the nomination of the Governor, the Council, and

Political influence of President Mather.

all the officers appointed under the new charter. These were of course taken from among his friends. He returned to this country in 1692, possessing the unexampled influence resulting from the fact, that all the members of the executive branch of the new government were indebted to him for their nomination. To the Mathers this was a subject of extreme exultation, and particularly the appointment of Sir William Phips as Governor.

"The time has come! the set time has come!" exclaims Cotton Mather, in his Diary under the date of April, 1692; "I am now to receive an answer of so many prayers. All the Counsellors of the Province are of my own father's nomination; and my father-in-law, with several *related* unto me, and several brethren of my own church, are among them. The Governor of the Province is *not my enemy*, but one whom I baptized; namely, Sir William Phips, one of my own flock, and one of my dearest friends."

William Stoughton.

William Stoughton also was under obligation to the Mathers for his appointment as Lieutenant-Governor. The circumstances under which it took place rendered their favor peculiarly grateful and impressive. Of all the victims of the Provincial Revolution of 1688, Joseph Dudley, next to Andros, was most obnoxious to the people of Massachusetts. That Stoughton entertained for him a strong personal attachment was well known. He had also coincided in Dudley's political course, and had accepted, with him, a seat in the Council of Andros. On these accounts he lost much of the public confidence, had been excluded from the Board of Assistants, and the state of his political influence had consequently become precarious and unpleasant. His popularity, being in these straits, took refuge under the shadow of the influence of the Mathers. He made, it appears, about this time, effectual court to Cotton Mather, who is found, accordingly, recommending to his father, then agent in Great Britain, to provide for Stoughton, as "a real friend to New England," as "willing to make amendment for all his miscarriages," and one whom he desired his father "to restore to the favor of his country."* This recommendation, if it were not the cause of the nomination of Stoughton by Increase Mather, had unquestionable weight in effecting his appointment as Lieutenant-Governor.

It cannot be doubted, that the coincidence of Stoughton's passions, prejudices, and policy, with those of the Mathers, was the cause of his immediate appointment, after the organization of the Provincial government in 1692, to the office of Chief Justice on the trials for witchcraft, then instituted under their auspices. This appointment was made in the first year of the administration of Phips, while the Mathers were in the flush of their political influence. Taking, as they did avowedly, a lively interest in the result of those trials, it admits not of a doubt, that Stoughton owed this, to him a melancholy eminence, to the agreement of his and their views. He fully justified the expectations of his patrons. The continuance and cruel destructiveness of that popular infatuation are associated so closely and disgracefully with the memory of no individual, as with that of William Stoughton. The only refuge for his character, against charges of a deeper die, is the sealed blindness of his bigotry.

* See Hutch. Hist. Mass. Edit. 1795. Vol. I. p. 365.

CHAPTER III.

Excitement concerning witchcraft.

The particulars of that excitement scarcely fall within the sphere of this History. Some reference to it, however, is required by the fact, that, as the belief in the agency of the invisible world began to lessen, and some of those, who were the chief actors in the tragedy, to feel the weight of public indignation pressing upon them, they, being members of the Corporation, brought this body into the field for the purpose of giving countenance to that belief, and of sustaining this decaying faith. In March, 1694, a paper,* purporting to be proposals made by the President and Fellows of Harvard College, prepared by both the Mathers, and signed by the whole board, was circulated throughout New England; inviting all men, and particularly the clergy, to observe and record "the illustrious discoveries of Divine Providence in the government of the world," and among others, "apparitions, possessions, enchantments, and all extraordinary things, wherein the existence and agency of the invisible world are more sensibly demonstrated."

Cotton Mather.

That both the Mathers had an efficient agency in producing and prolonging that excitement, there can be, at this day, no possible question. The conduct of Increase Mather in relation to it was marked with caution and political skill; but that of his son, Cotton Mather, was headlong, zealous, and fearless, both as to character and consequences. In its commencement and progress, his activity is everywhere conspicuous. The part he acted in that tragedy has left on his memory a stain, which time has deepened rather than

* See Robert Calef's "More Wonders of the Invisible World." Reprinted at Salem, 1796. p. 92.

removed. Belief in invisible agencies was adapted to a mind naturally active, imaginative, and ambitious. He had been early taught the power of the imagination in matters of religion, and by the precept and example of his father had been instructed in the language of excitement and alarm. No sooner was the field left open to him, by the absence, in Europe, of his father and colleague, than he entered upon it with an ardor natural to his youth, and congenial with his temperament. Regarded as the hope of the clergy, he aspired to be their champion, and, for a short time, became their idol. At the age of twenty-seven, he was raised to a seat, by the side of his father, in the Corporation of the College. A short time afterward, the General Court constituted him their preacher on Election day. He was courted and consulted by the Governor and Lieutenant-Governor, Phips and Stoughton; both of whom were conscious, that they were largely indebted to his influence for their respective appointments.

His agency in the witchcraft delusion.

Excited and emboldened by the elevated station he had obtained, in relation both to the Colony and the College, Cotton Mather seized, with a sagacity characteristic of zeal and ambition, on that popular belief in invisible agencies, which the general tenor of the preaching of that day had encouraged and made almost universal in New England. His discourses from the pulpit were passionate and exciting; and awakened perpetually into action this popular delusion. He employed himself sedulously in seeking out every case, which encouraged faith in supernatural agencies. Thus standing before his contemporaries in the light, he incurred the responsibility, of being its chief cause and promoter. In the progress of the superstitious fear,

CHAPTER III.

when it amounted to frenzy, and could only be satisfied with blood, he neither blenched nor halted; but attended the courts, watched the progress of invisible agency in the prisons, and joined the multitude in witnessing the executions. After "two hundred persons had been accused,* one hundred and fifty imprisoned, nineteen hanged, one pressed to death, and twenty-eight condemned, one third of whom were members of the churches, and more than half of good general conversation," he wrote a formal treatise, entitled "Wonders of the Invisible World," approving the proceedings of the courts, and exciting the multitude to a continuance in the belief, and the courts to a perseverance in their vindictiveness.

After the excitement had passed away, and shame had succeeded to passion, those, who had guided or submitted to its course, gave it the name of "popular delusion," or of "a visitation of Providence." But the delusion of the multitude is never general or violent, unless those, who are their natural or assumed leaders, countenance or encourage it. Nor ought human agents to be permitted to evade just responsibility, under pretence of supernatural suggestions and impulses. The guilt of the excesses and horrors, consequent on that excitement, rests, and ought to rest, heavily upon the leading divines and politicians of the Colony at that period; who had either the hardihood to uphold, or the cowardice not to withstand, the madness of the populace, of which they had been, in no small degree, the authors. Cotton Mather, however, with the singular infelicity of judgment, which constituted an

* See Calef's "More Wonders of the Invisible World." Edit. 1796. p. 233.

element of his character, while his contemporaries and coadjutors were drawing off from the delusion, and some of them, under the influence of shame and remorse, were confessing their sins, and asking pardon of Heaven and their fellow-citizens, exhibited no uneasiness, no self-upbraidings. On the contrary, he continued to avow his belief, and thus connected his name and fame inseparably with that excitement, as its chief cause, agent, believer, and justifier.

In the year 1690, Cotton Mather had been elected a member of the Corporation. His father, on his return from England, found accordingly his influence over the College increased by the introduction of his son into that board.

Effects on the College of the Colonial charter of 1692.

The new relations in the political system of Massachusetts, resulting from the charter of the Province granted by William and Mary, were of a nature strongly to influence the fortunes of the College. No sooner had it gone into operation, than the Calvinistic leaders of the Province realized, that, as a necessary consequence, the sceptre they had so long possessed, had passed from their hands; and, being desirous to secure whatever yet remained of their former authority, sought to possess themselves of such instruments of power as were yet within their grasp. Of all the institutions of the country, the College, next to the civil government, was that which they deemed the most important, and to which they thought they were best entitled, as it had been founded under their auspices, and had been at all times under their control.

At this period, however, there sprang up powerful rival and somewhat hostile influences among those citizens, who had been excluded, under the old colo-

CHAPTER III.

nial charter, from all political power, some from their attachment to the Church of England, others, though Congregationalists, because they were too conscientious to pretend to religious doctrines which they did not believe, or to religious experiences which they had not attained, for the sake of being admitted members of the church, and thus becoming freemen of the State. Such men, naturally, thought they had as much right, as the strict adherents to the Calvinistic doctrines, to have a share in the government of the College, as a literary institution. They saw no reason, why they should be excluded from such share in time to come, because they had been so in time past. And particularly were they of this opinion, since, in the qualities of "piety and godliness," the only intimated requisites in the College charters, they were not disposed to yield to any pretensions to superiority, made by others; and because, also, in their own number they were able to reckon some of its most liberal, early, and uniform friends and benefactors.

Now it appears, from the history of the controversies and events of those times, that Increase Mather, and Cotton Mather, his son, aspired to become, were best entitled to be called, and perhaps, from learning, activity, and talent, were best qualified to be, chiefs among the Calvinistic leaders. Both were members of the Corporation, and the former was President of the College. On the other hand, John Leverett and William Brattle, both tutors as well as members of the Corporation, who had been the principal superintendents and instructers of the College during the four years' absence of President Mather in Europe, though not aspiring to the character of leaders of any party, were inclined to the order of things which was coming, rather than to that which had, so far as the civil constitution had influence, already passed away.

It was, in the nature of things, so impossible for the adherents to the ancient doctrines, after having lost their power over the civil government, to retain exclusive possession of the College, the charter of which contained no handle on which the sectarian spirit could seize, that it is probable they would have yielded to the apparent necessity of the case, and have permitted the College to follow the fate of the civil government, as a literary institution, had they not been kept in a state of perpetual excitement by the two Mathers, both of whom had private objects to attain, and personal ends to answer, by the agitations they produced.

CHAPTER IV.

College Charter of 1692. — Its History and Results. — Rev. Charles Morton. — Degrees of Doctor in Divinity and Bachelor of Laws first conferred. — The General Court vote, that President Mather shall reside at Cambridge. — His consequent Conduct. — College Charter negatived by the King. — President Mather's Desire of an Agency in England. — Origin and Motive of that Desire. — Embarrassments of the College, and Settlement of it by Stoughton.

CHAPTER IV. 1692.

No sooner was the Provincial government organized under the charter of William and Mary, than a bill for a new charter for the College was introduced and passed by the General Court.* This was effected at the suggestion, and was the work, of President Mather, in pursuance of advice received by him in England, as his son Cotton asserts.†

College Charter of 1692.

The provisions of this charter were most extraordinary. It constituted a Corporation of ten persons, with the usual powers and perpetual succession by filling up their own vacancies, and vested them with authority to elect all the officers of the institution. It conferred the right to hold lands to the value of four thousand pounds per annum, and personal estate to any amount whatsoever. It exempted all the estate, real and personal, of the College and of the President

* See College Records, Book IV. p. 1. — Also, Append., No. LXVIII.

† Memoirs of Increase Mather, by Cotton Mather. Edit. 1724. p. 170.

and resident fellows from public taxes; and also the President, three of his servants, the fellows and twelve servants, from all civil and military offices and services. It gave the power of conferring academical degrees, as extensively as it existed in the English Universities. And, above all, it vested these powers in this Corporation of ten persons absolutely, without any control or responsibility; making no provision for a board of Overseers, or a visitatorial power of any kind.

All the members of this Corporation were selected by President Mather. One of them was his son, Cotton Mather.

This charter of incorporation passed the first Provincial Assembly, and received the approbation of Governor Phips on the 27th of June, 1692. It was transmitted to England for the approbation of the King, and, on the 26th of July following,* the Corporation established by it met, organized itself, and, without waiting for the decision of his Majesty, proceeded to exercise the several authorities granted by the charter. At their first meeting, all the former laws of the College were continued; the several officers of it were chosen, and their compensation was fixed. One of the members of the Corporation (Nehemiah Hobart), appointed by the charter, having declined, the Rev. Charles Morton was chosen in his place. This gentleman had been about six years in the country, having emigrated from England among the ejected ministers, and was settled at Charlestown. He was now sixty-six years of age, and enjoyed a great and just reputation, here and in England, for talents, learning, and experience. His general reli-

Rev. Charles Morton.

* College Records, Book IV. p. 5.

CHAPTER IV.

gious views coincided with those of the Mathers, and he was an active supporter of all their measures.* His original emigration was connected with the hope of being made President† of the College. But arriving in 1686, during Dudley's short administration, the expectation of the coming of Andros, and Morton's known obnoxiousness to the ruling powers in England, rendered such an appointment either impossible or unadvisable. He therefore accepted a call from the church at Charlestown to become their pastor. Morton was well qualified for the office of President. He had been a highly acceptable instructor of youth in England. On his arrival in this country, he engaged in the same occupation. His fame and success gave uneasiness to the Corporation.‡ This led him to abandon the employment. His introduction into that body was probably connected with a design of investing him with the Presidency; an office which President Mather began now to think of exchanging for an agency in England, with the hope of fixing himself permanently there. After his admission into the Corporation, no jealousy seems to have been entertained of Morton's powers, nor any disposition to diminish his celebrity. On the contrary, two of his manuscript works, "A System of Logic,"§ and "Compendium Physicæ," were received as text-books in the College, the students being required to copy them. He was often placed, out of respect to his age and acquirements, next to President Mather in the records of the Corporation, and, as we shall

* Eliot's Biog., art. *Morton.*

† Hutch. Coll. of State Papers. Edit. 1769. p. 551.

‡ Mass. Hist. Coll., Second Series, Vol. I. p. 161.

§ Mass. Hist. Coll., Second Series, Vol. II. p. 115.

soon see, was, on the first opportunity, raised to the office of Vice-President, probably as a preliminary step to his further advancement, in case the project of a European agency should be effected for President Mather. Morton, on his part, will be found earnestly pressing that appointment for the President, in which, from his influence, he would doubtless have been successful, had it not been for his death, which occurred in 1698.

The Corporation were not deterred by the fact, that the fate of the charter yet depended on the royal approbation, but proceeded at their second meeting to gratify President Mather with the degree of Doctor in Divinity, the first it had ever assumed the authority to confer. This distinction, Cotton Mather asserts, the Corporation granted from "a sense of duty"* to the President. It was certainly as well deserved, as it was acceptable both to father and son. It was not, however, a solitary instance of self-gratification, enjoyed by the members of the Corporation; since, on the same day, John Leverett and William Brattle,† both fellows of that body, had each conferred upon him the degree of Bachelor in Divinity, this being also the first instance of a grant of a degree of this class by the Corporation. As the charter, under which they now acted, required no concurrence of any other board, the process of conferring these degrees was equally easy, expeditious, and conclusive.

1692. Sept. 5.

The alacrity and adroitness with which President Mather thus availed himself of the great influence which, during the first year of the operation of the

* Memoirs of Increase Mather, by Cotton Mather, p. 171.

† College Records, Book IV. p. 5.

CHAPTER IV.

new charter, he possessed over the Governor and Council, are indicative both of talent and sagacity. The state * of the popular branch of the legislature also, which during the same period was composed chiefly of those, who had been members of the same branch under the old charter, and who probably understood and coincided in his views, greatly contributed to his success. In no other possible state of things could a charter, thus giving a permanent and independent character to the College Corporation, and setting the institution absolutely free from all legislative control, have been obtained from the colonial government. President Mather seems to have acted under the impression, that, whatever was to be done, must be effected speedily and thoroughly. He probably anticipated great alterations in the character of both branches of the government, as soon as the change of the qualification of electors from church-membership to freehold should have had time to produce its full effect. He had sufficient knowledge of human nature to apprehend, that the continuance of his own influence was, at least, precarious. He had, indeed, gratified those friends whom he had nominated to the Council. But, on the other hand, he had offended all those,† who had previously held the station of Assistants, and whom he had neglected to nominate for that body. These were neither few, nor without influence. Notwithstanding the fate of the College charter depended upon the royal approbation, he proceeded in the same spirit of vigor and expedition, which had characterized his obtaining it from the legislature, to avail

* Hutchinson's Hist. Mass., Vol. II. pp. 64–69. Boston, 1795

† Ibid. p. 69.

CHAPTER IV.

himself of the power it conferred, precisely as though it were irrevocable.

President Mather's election sermon. 1692.

That President Mather anticipated great changes in the civil and ecclesiastical influences of the Province, in consequence of the new Provincial charter, is apparent from his Election Sermon, preached before the second General Court, convened under it. This duty had been assigned to him by the preceding legislature. He selected as the topic of his discourse, "the great benefit of primitive counsellors," and took occasion to warn the legislature against "the removal of wise counsellors," as "threatening a sore judgment," and particularly not to elect "malcontent and disaffected" persons, or such as "the Governor would, though unwilling, be compelled to negative." A course sufficiently bold, considering that it was well known, that his opinion had been taken, and was conclusive, in the selection of all the members of the existing Council. The General Court, however, far from following his advice, left out *ten* of those, who owed their seats in it to him, and six of the new members were persons, who, having been Assistants in former years, had been omitted the previous year in his nomination. They also chose,* as one of them, Elisha Cooke, who, having been one of the Colonial agents with Mather in Great Britain, had opposed the new charter in every form; who, since his return, had expressed in unqualified terms his dissatisfaction with it; and who was also, on other accounts, so personally obnoxious to Governor Phips, that he immediately applied to him his official negative.

These indications of change, combined with the

* Hutch. Hist. Mass., Vol. II. pp. 69, 70.

CHAPTER IV.

calumnies to which he had been subjected in consequence of his agency in procuring the new charter, induced President Mather to prefix to his Election Sermon, on its publication, an Address to the inhabitants of Massachusetts Bay. This is a sensible, plain, and satisfactory vindication of his conduct; severe on "those ill spirits, who make it their design by slanders to disaffect others;" full of feeling and affection; at the same time in a temper of sufficient loftiness and self-esteem, of which the motto, "*Bene agere et male audire regium est*," is an indication.

In the course of this Address he states, that friends of his in England, being desirous that "he should spend the remainder of his days among them," had told him, that "the people of New England were always ungrateful towards their public servants," and that they doubted "if they would be sensible of his services." "My reply was," he adds, "that I would go to New England, and see; and, if I found their prognostications true, I should then see my call clear to return to England again."

Proceedings of the General Court.

Whatever apprehensions this narrative was calculated or designed to excite, it had little effect on the General Court. For, at their very next session, far from acquiescing in President Mather's non-residency, which, it was well known, he meant to continue, they passed a vote,* "that the President of Harvard College, for the time being, shall reside there, as hath been accustomed in time past." President Mather, adopted no measures in consequence of this vote, nor, as far as now is ascertained, took any notice of it. He undoubtedly viewed it as an in-

* Records of General Court, Dec. 2d, 1693.

dication, that his influence was on the wane; and it was one of the many intimations of this fact, which probably filled his mind with that strong desire his Diary about this time shows he felt, of returning to England. He determined, therefore, notwithstanding this vote of the General Court, to maintain his present position in respect to the College. In this determination, strange as it now seems, he had the countenance and support of the College Corporation itself. The residue of the year 1693 and the whole of 1694 passed without any further attempt, on the part of the legislature, to interfere with the relations of the President of the College. But, on the 5th of June, 1695, a vote, of a character not to be mistaken or overlooked, passed the House of Representatives. In this, they "desire Mr. Mather to go and settle at the College, that the College may not be destitute any longer of a settled President; that, if he take up with this proposal, he shall be allowed annually one hundred and fifty pounds; but, if said Mr. Mather do not settle there, then that the Corporation do propose some other meet person to the General Court, who may be treated with to settle there, that the College may no longer be destitute of a settled President."

It does not appear that the Council concurred in either of these votes. Although the former had been passed over by President Mather in silence and neglect, the latter was too pointed and personal to be treated in the same manner. Being deeply affected by it, he forthwith gave notice to the Corporation of his intention to relinquish the office of President. This drew from them the following vote,

President Mather proposes to resign.

CHAPTER IV.

which passed unanimously.* "Whereas the Reverend President (who was and is settled in his presidentship by an act of the great and general Assembly, &c.), by reason of a late vote of the House of Representatives, hath signified to the Corporation his design to relinquish his service in the College as President, the fellows of said College (though they should heartily rejoicc, if the Rev. Mr. Increase Mather could have such encouragement as might induce him to reside at the College, yet), considering how advantageous his sustaining the office and performing the work of President (as hitherto) hath been, and foreseeing how many ways it may prove detrimental to the affairs of this society, both at home and abroad, should he pursue such a design, do unanimously request the said Rev. Mr. Mather, that, laying aside such thoughts, and not too deeply resenting the matters of discouragement laid before him in said vote, he would continue his care and conduct of this society as formerly."

Proceedings of the Corporation.

In conformity with this solicitation he resolved to retain his office and continue his non-residence. To encourage and support him in which resolution, on the 6th of the ensuing April, the Corporation of the College passed a vote in the following words.† "Voted, that whereas the Reverend President has, by his manifold services to the College, laid us under deep obligations to acknowledge the same, the Corporation, out of a sense hereof, and as a testimony of their gratitude, do pray him to accept of, and hereby do order the Treasurer forthwith to pay unto the said Reverend President, the sum of seventy pounds out of the College Treasury;" and in the June following the

* College Records, Book IV. p. 11.

† Ibid.

Corporation passed another vote, "that the College Treasurer should pay to the Reverend President such money as he should need to purchase a horse with, for the better capacitating him to make his visits at the College."

College charter negatived.

The affairs of the College were thus situated when information was received, that the charter granted by the colonial legislature in 1692, had been negatived by the King on account of its omission of any provision for the exercise of a visitatorial power.

This event was probably anticipated by President Mather; possibly it was not unwelcome to him. The affairs of the College were thrown by it into a state of inexplicable embarrassment. The sense of the importance of his experience and services was greatly augmented, and the chance of his attaining the object of his returning to England on a new agency increased in consequence of it. This object, it is apparent, he began now to propose to himself, accompanied with a strong desire "to spend and end his days" in that country. Such a state of feeling was most natural. When a young man, he had visited England; and his residence and reception there had been so satisfactory,* that he would probably have never returned to this country, had he not been compelled either to give up the living, which he then held there, or conform to the established Church. He refused the latter, and returned to Massachusetts in September, 1661. Even at that time, however, he seems to have looked with a wish-

* See Notes to two Discourses, containing the History of the Second Church in Boston, delivered 20th May, 1821, by the Rev. Henry Ware, Jun., p. 46.

ful eye, perhaps with a faint hope, towards a settlement in England. For, in May, 1664, on accepting the call of the North Church, in Boston, to be its pastor, he annexed to his acceptance the following condition, among others, that "he should be at liberty, in case the Lord should call him to a greater service elsewhere, to return to England, or to remove elsewhere." During his recent four years' residence in that country, his reception and treatment had again been so flattering, that he would willingly have remained there. And, although he returned to New England with a well-earned consciousness that he had fulfilled, during his residence abroad, his entire duty to the Colony, and that, in the charter he had brought home, he had conferred on it a blessing, yet great numbers, perhaps even a majority of the inhabitants of the Province, did not coincide in his opinions on that subject; and, while by some he was received with coolness or treated with neglect, by others he was regarded in the light of a traitor. Many interests and passions combined to produce this state of feeling and conduct.

Cause of President Mather's unpopularity.

To those, who had formerly had the chief influence in civil matters, the loss of the power of appointing the Governor, Lieutenant-Governor, and Secretary, which the new charter vested in the crown, was extremely obnoxious. To those, who had possessed the chief ecclesiastical influence, the principle of toleration, and of freehold property as the basis of political power, was not more satisfactory. The recognition of judicial appeals to England, and of the royal power of negative on legislative acts, was equally unpopular with all. The privileges thus lost were deemed inherent in the old charter, the prejudices in favor of which were universal. President Mather himself had been greatly instrumental in deepening and extending these prejudices. He had gone to Europe on a special mission to uphold that charter. He had returned after having, not only consented to its abandonment, but become the open advocate of an instrument, which annihilated the basis, on which civil and ecclesiastical power had rested from the first settlement of the Colony. The opportunities he had enjoyed in England, of convincing himself of the impossibility of effecting the object of his mission, and of the necessity of acceding to the proffered charter, as well as of the advantages it secured, were not shared by his fellow colonists. The loss of the old charter and the principles of the new were known to be so obnoxious to the leading characters in the Colony, that neither Oakes nor Cooke, the agents * associated with Mather, had dared to assume the responsibility of acceding to it. One of them (Cooke) was openly opposed to its acceptance. All the odium attached to the instrument, therefore, was concentrated on President Mather. It was reported, that the other agents had said, that, "if it had not been for him, they could have saved the old charter, and that he had betrayed the country."† And, although they denied having said any such thing, yet the opinion of his subserviency to the crown and his abandonment of the interests of the Colony was very general. He had, indeed, brought with him, in the form of letters, some of them to the General Court, from the most influential friends of the Colony in England, both clergymen and laymen, ample testimonies of his zeal,

* Hutch. Hist. Mass., Vol. I. p. 361.

† See Appendix, No. IX.

talent, prudence, and fidelity; and the first General Court under the new charter had returned him "thanks for his faithful and indefatigable endeavours to serve the country."* But one branch of that legislature had been selected especially for the occasion by President Mather, and was so constituted as to dissatisfy many. All the members of the Council were, as we have seen, of his nomination, and composed of "his friends," "relatives," or "brethren of his church."† He was probably guided in this selection, not merely by personal motives, but perhaps by those he deemed patriotic. Realizing the importance of the new charter, and anticipating violent opposition to it, as well as the degree of unpopularity to which he might himself become exposed, he took care so to use his influence in constituting the Council, as to secure its acceptance. This policy, successful for the time being, sharpened the animosity of his political enemies, and probably multiplied them. It was also, unquestionably, one source of that opposition to his continuance as President, without being resident, which began the ensuing year to appear, immediately after the change in the political aspect of the Council, consequent on the new elections.

It is not surprising, therefore, that an intense desire should become fixed in his mind, to escape from a country where he had to sustain ill will and calumny, and, if possible, to establish himself in one, where he had received honors and gathered laurels, and where he had reason to hope to be kindly entertained and respected.

* Life of Increase Mather, by Cotton Mather, p. 156.

† See above, p. 60.

CHAPTER IV.

This desire appears, accordingly, in his Diary as early as September, 1693, in the form of supernatural influences and suggestions, that "to England he must go." This urgency of his will, he construed into "something divine and angelical." * In October and December following, and in January and March of the succeeding year, he had like "melting persuasions" concerning going to England. † When, in the year 1696, the news of the royal negative upon the College charter was received, he was again "wonderfully melted with the assurance, that God would return him into England." These natural cravings of an ambitious spirit, he had convinced himself were persuasions "wrought into him by the Lord," in return for "his fastings and prayers." ‡

As, on the rejection of the charter of the College by the crown, new measures for the organization of its government became indispensable, and the prospect of an agency in England on its account more distinct, President Mather's spirits revived. § He saw, in the event, "answers of God to his prayers of faith," and an assurance, that "he would not be disappointed in having an opportunity to glorify Christ in England."

When the news of this rejection of the charter by the King reached Massachusetts, Phips was no longer Governor of the Province. He had been ordered to England, to answer certain charges of misconduct, and had died there. William Stoughton had taken possession, as Lieutenant-Governor, of the executive chair of the Colony. On the 6th of July, 1696, the Corporation of the College held its last meeting under the authority of the act of 1692. From this time the

* See Appendix, No. IX. † Ibid. ‡ Ibid. § Ibid.

CHAPTER IV.

state of the institution was one of extreme embarrassment. The Corporation was bereft of all charter powers. Its former charters had been in construction of law repealed, by force of the judgment rendered against the old Colonial charter. And now the new charter, which had been devised as a substitute, was annulled by the royal negative. In the confusion, into which the affairs of the College were consequently thrown, Lieutenant-Governor Stoughton assumed the responsibility of reorganizing its government. He came to Cambridge on the 12th of October, 1696, and "desired and appointed" the former President, Fellows, and Treasurer, "to continue and proceed in the institution and government of the house, and in the management of the estate of the College, according to the late rules of said College, until his Majesty's farther pleasure shall be known, or a legal settlement of said College shall be obtained."* This proceeding, at the time, was deemed so critical and important, that it is spread in detail on the records of the Corporation, and the memory of it is carefully preserved† in the Diaries of President Mather and Chief Justice Sewall, both of whom were present on the occasion. The Corporation, however, so far as appears by their records, never held but one meeting under the appointment of Lieutenant-Governor Stoughton. This occurred on the 9th of the ensuing November, when the Corporation passed votes, declaring that "the obtaining a charter of incorporation for the College would be of singular advantage to the churches of New England, both in present and after times, and that, while it continued as at present, an unhappy

College government reorganized by Lieutenant-Governor Stoughton.

* College Records, Book IV. p. 13. † See Appendix, No. XI.

settlement of it might be feared, donations to it be obstructed, and its present stock endangered." For the obtaining of it, they vote an humble address to his Majesty, and pray the Lieutenant-Governor "to facilitate the affair"; voting at the same time an address to him, acknowledging his care and favor, and particularly expressing "their humble thanks for his late visitation and settlement of the College."

CHAPTER V.

College Charter of 1696. — President Mather discontented with it. — Takes it into a new Draft. — The Corporation ask the General Court, that he be sent as Agent to England. — Governor Bellamont arrives in New York. — The Corporation address him. — Second Application of the Corporation, that the President obtain an Agency. — Its Failure. — Project of a Vice-Presidency. — Its Failure. — The General Court again vote, that President Mather should reside at Cambridge. — Proceedings on that Vote, and its Result. — Arrival of Governor Bellamont in Massachusetts. — College Charter of 1699. — Interference of the Clergy. — Governor Bellamont objects to the Charter, and it is lost. — Cotton Mather's Disappointment.

CHAPTER V.

Bill for the charter of the College. 1696.

In conformity with the views expressed in the votes of the Corporation, as related in the preceding chapter, a bill for a charter of the College was introduced into the Council of the Province on the 27th of November, 1696;* and, after a series of postponements, critical amendments, and warm debates, it was, on the 17th of the ensuing December, passed by that branch of the legislature. The general and usual powers, included in such charters, were granted by this bill; but very material alterations were also introduced, greatly modifying the powers contained in the charter of 1692, which President Mather, in the flush of his political influence, had obtained from the first Provincial legislature. Of these the most critical, and symptomatic of legislative policy, were the following.

The number of the Corporation was increased to sixteen. — The office of Vice-President was created,

* See Appendix, No. LXVIII.

and the name of the Rev. Charles Morton inserted for the place. — Fellows were made removable for disability or misdemeanor. — Residency at Cambridge was required of the President and of all fellows receiving salary. — None was to be a fellow longer than ten years without a reëlection, and all vacancies were to be filled within twelve months. — The right to hold land was limited to two thousand pounds. — In all sales of land, or disposal of revenues, ten members were required to be present; in all other cases, a majority. — The President, fellows, scholars, steward, cook, and one servant, were exempted from civil and military services; but there was no exemption from public taxes for lands or persons. — The Governor and Council were made Visitors.

Many of these provisions were unwelcome, and some very grievous, to President Mather. While the bill was yet pending, he acquainted the General Court with his "purpose to undertake a voyage to England, for the obtaining a settlement for the College;"* indicating thereby an intention to apply to the King in Council for modifications of the legislative draft, should it prove unacceptable. No sooner had the bill passed that body, than President Mather, his son, and two other clergymen, all members of the Corporation of the College, presented to the legislature, in writing, objections to its final passage.

Clergy remonstrate.

Their remonstrance is expressed with great distinctness and boldness. In it they request, that their names may not be inserted in the bill as members of the Corporation, should it pass both branches without alteration. The discussion excited great warmth.

* See Appendix, No. IX.

CHAPTER V. "I do not know that I ever saw," writes Sewall in his Diary, "the Council so run upon with such a height of rage before. The Lord prepare us for the issue. The ministers will go to England for a charter, except we exclude the Council from the visitation; alleging this reason, that the King will not pass it, and so shall be longer unsettled."*

While the old colonial charter was in force, the clergy were consulted by the legislature in great emergencies, as though they had been an independent state of the body politic. They had been accustomed to address the General Court with a consciousness of authority. The loss of their former influence, in consequence of the provisions of the new Provincial charter, they already felt very sensibly; and a satisfactory settlement of the College began to be considered by them as intimately connected with the preservation of what yet remained of their power under the old charter. They therefore concentrated their efforts upon the attainment of this object, from combined motives of interest of caste, and of affection for the institution.

1697. The features of this bill, as it had passed the Council, being thus objectionable in the opinion of the clergy, President Mather, after an interview with Lieutenant-Governor Stoughton, drew up a new charter himself. This, being introduced into the legislature, occasioned violent debates.

President Mather drafts a new charter.

The principal alterations effected by this act, in that which had passed the Council the preceding December, were the following. — The Corporation was increased to seventeen persons. — The residency at

* See Appendix, No. XI.

Cambridge of the President, and of such fellows as received a salary, was required *after the act should be confirmed by the King*. This had reference to President Mather, in order to enable him to continue the superintendence of the seminary and yet remain in Boston, until the will of his Majesty should be known. — The right to hold lands was so far extended as to include the value of three thousand pounds. — And finally, all houses and lands, in the personal occupation of the President and fellows, were exempted from taxation; and three servants for the President, and seven for the College, were exempted from all civil and military offices.

In the passage of this bill, the first indications were publicly given of dissensions among those, who had for an uninterrupted series of years been associated in the government of the College. Only four of the Corporation joined in the remonstrance against the charter first proposed. From the Diary of Judge Sewall it appears, that in the bill drafted by President Mather, and finally substituted, after being amended, for that which had passed the Council,* the name of John Leverett was either originally omitted, or subsequently stricken out. The attempt was probably obnoxious to the House of Deputies, in which body Leverett's name was reinserted, since it appears, in the final enactment, among the other members of the Corporation.

John Leverett excluded.

Of the religious controversies of the period, the College now became the object and arena. Although the particular causes, which led to this early attempt to exclude Leverett from the Corporation are not,

* See Appendix, No. XI.

at this day, to be ascertained, it is apparent from what is known of his character and history, that his general views on many subjects did not coincide with those of the Mathers; and that even his religious opinions were, in several points, adverse to those, which they deemed important, if not essential. His connexion with William and Thomas Brattle was early and intimate. Like them, he had stood aloof during the delusions of witchcraft, which President Mather had countenanced, if not credited, and of which Cotton Mather was either a chief cause or the dupe. Leverett will be soon found, in common with both the Brattles, encouraging the foundation of a church on principles extremely obnoxious to the adherents to the old ecclesiastical doctrines. Of these both the Mathers were advocates, and aspired to be leaders in their defence. It is not unlikely also the President might find, that Leverett was not a thorough supporter of his personal views or of his official relations. Perhaps his son might, even thus early, instinctively apprehend, that Leverett's star was destined to be ascendant, and to obscure for ever his cherished hope of succeeding his father in the presidency of the College.

John Leverett and William Brattle had been associate tutors ever since 1686. They had, also, for the ten years ensuing, the principal agency in the management of the institution and the instruction of the students. In November, 1696, Brattle was chosen minister of the town of Cambridge, and gave immediate evidence of his disposition to set himself free from some customs of the established Congregational church. He preached at his own ordination, and forbade an elder, because he was a layman, to lay his hand upon his head during the ceremony. Both were deviations from the established practice of the early Congregational churches. *

In the same spirit, Brattle, during his ministry, obtained a vote of his church, that a formal and public relation of religious experiences should not be deemed necessary as a qualification for church membership ; † that the examination of the candidate should be referred to the pastor and elders ; and that the consent of the church to the admission of a member should be signified by silence, instead of a manual vote. Every one of these points was also a departure from the former usage of the churches, and was deemed important by both the Mathers and by other stern adherents to the ancient faith and discipline. To these Leverett had rendered himself obnoxious by his agreement, in religious views, with the Brattles. The records of those times show, that differences in religious opinions began to appear, with great violence, in the legislature and in the towns, and that they were brought to bear upon the College. ‡ The Diaries of Judge Sewall and President Mather evidence the existence of these dissensions, and their connexion with the questions, which arose concerning the institution.

The heavings of these theological tempests affected the condition of President Mather as well as of the College. It cannot be doubted, that the part he took in them constituted one of the elements of that opposition, which ultimately defeated his cherished project

* See Appendix, No. XI.

† See Mass. Hist. Coll., First Series, Vol. VII. p. 32.

‡ See Appendix, No. IX.

CHAPTER V.

of being sent as an agent to England, for the purpose of procuring a new charter for the College.

Petition for an agency in England for procuring a charter.

No sooner had the act of June 2d, 1697,* passed both branches of the legislature, than a direct application for the attainment of that object was made to the General Court by the persons named in it as members of the Corporation. This application was signed, "Charles Morton, with the unanimous concurrence of the rest." It expresses "the great concernment to these churches, both in present and after times, that the College should no longer labor under the unhappy uncertainties of establishment." To this end, they desire, that the Rev. Increase Mather may receive assistance and countenance from the General Court, in undertaking a voyage to England, to obtain the royal approbation of the act passed by the Assembly, and, if that "cannot be, then to endeavour to obtain such a charter as will be consistent with the constitution of the people and churches in this country.' After receiving three readings in the House of Representatives, on the 15th of June, 1697, the proposition to assist in the project received a decided negative.†

This defeat did not, however, deter the members of the Corporation from presenting a petition somewhat more formal, signed, "Charles Morton, with unanimous consent."‡ This was read on the same day the other was negatived. In it, the petitioners state their "utter despair of obtaining an establishment without a personal application to his Majesty," and that, "if the General Court discountenance that proceeding, they shall have little heart to accept the trust devolved on them." It was

* See Appendix, No. LXVIII.

† See Appendix, No. XII.

‡ See Appendix, No. XIII.

on this occasion, that the Corporation made the appeal to the "gratitude" of the General Court, for the accommodation received by the Colony from the use of their money, which has been already the occasion of remark.*

It is worthy of notice, that neither of the petitions thus signed by Morton, and stated to be "by unanimous consent," appears to have been acted upon by the Corporation. There is no record of any meeting on either of the days mentioned in them.

Agency negatived.

Nothing favorable to President Mather's agency having resulted from either of these applications, his mind was reduced to a state almost of despair. The first meeting of the Corporation, under the act of June, 1697, was holden on the 13th of the ensuing July; but their records indicate no measures touching his mission to England. Discouraged and wounded by the failure of these applications, he resolved to resign the presidency. His Diary, during the months of July, August, and September, repeatedly avows this intent.† But his affections were too intimately interwoven with his position to enable him to carry it into effect. The slightest movement in the legislature on the subject of the College revived his hopes. No sooner has he reason to expect those letters, which had been solicited from Sir Henry Ashurst, the agent of the Colony in England, recommending President Mather for the desired College agency, than his "special faith," and "the inexpressible meltings of his soul" are renewed, and his Diary indicates an ecstasy of joy and gratitude.‡

His mind was in this condition, when, about the

* See above, p. 42.

† See Appendix, No. IX.

‡ Ibid.

CHAPTER V.

Arrival of Governor Bellamont.

middle of April, 1698, the Earl Bellamont arrived in New York, bearing a commission of Governor of that Colony and of Massachusetts Bay. Two meetings of the Corporation were held in May, in which it was voted, that "a messenger should be sent to New York with an address to the Governor." The records of the Corporation indicate nothing concerning the object of the address. But the Diary of President Mather declares, that it was to "desire the Governor to encourage his going to England on the College account."* Bellamont put an end to all hopes concerning this charter by unequivocally stating, that it would never receive the royal approbation. The arrival, however, of the long-sought letters from Sir Henry Ashurst, recommendatory of President Mather's agency, raised his mind to a state of extreme delight. This was further increased, when, as his Diary asserts, it appeared on the return of the messenger, that Bellamont had expressed an opinion favorable to his wishes.

Petition for an agency in England renewed.

In consequence of this encouragement, a formal address was presented, on the 14th of June, 1698, to the General Court, signed by "James Allen, socius senior,"† in the name and with the unanimous concurrence of the Corporation, praying that President Mather might be sent to England; and stating, in detail, the importance of a charter; the danger of losing the College without it; the loss of considerable donations on account of its unsettled condition; the opinion of the Earl of Bellamont, that the royal approbation would not be given to the present charter, and that the President's presence in England would

* See Appendix, No. IX.

† The Rev. Charles Morton had died the April preceding.

be of use, an opinion to this effect being also expressed by the colonial agent, Sir Henry Ashurst; that thus the desire of a resident President at the College might be obtained; and that "no one understood, better than President Mather, the state of the College, or had a greater acquaintance and interest in England, or on whose discretion, fidelity, and integrity, more dependence could be placed, for the true interest of the College and our churches."

Petition rejected.

This memorial was read on the same day in Council, and rejected.*

In the debate on this memorial, the conduct of President Mather was the subject of severe animadversion. The pertinacity with which he pressed his mission to England had occasioned disgust. He was thought to use his ecclesiastical influence too obtrusively in the gratification of his interest or ambition. His strong desire, to transfer permanently his residence to England was known; and his zeal for the settlement of the College began to be deemed but a pretence for the advancement of other projects. A strong party appeared in both branches of the legislature, and especially in the Council, disposed to thwart his plans. His disappointment was extreme, and this state of feeling continued some months. Suddenly, however, his "glorious, heart-melting persuasions, that the Lord hath work for him in England," return in full force; and for no other reason now to be ascertained, than that a proposition had been started (November 26th, 1698), by his friends in the Corporation, for the appointment of a person to be Vice-President,† "to remove to the Col-

Project of a vice-presidency.

* See Appendix, No. XIV.

† See Appendix, No. IX.

CHAPTER V.

lege, and do the work usually attended to by Presidents resident at the College;" and also that, on a petition to the General Court for assistance and countenance in that project, "a discourse had arisen in that body, about an agent to be sent to England." On such slender encouragement he writes, "Let me turn all into prayer. Will the Lord cause me to hear out of England what will revive me? Shall I see, that faith shall not suffer an utter disappointment?"

General Court require the President to reside at Cambridge.

On the 3d of December, 1698, the project of a vice-presidency wholly failed, and the General Court renewed their vote, that President Mather "remove to the College, and take up his residence there; and for his encouragement vote a salary of two hundred pounds per annum, out of the public treasury, from the time of his removal during his residence at the College." Nothing could have been more contrary to his expectations, or adverse to his hopes, than this vote. It indicated no disposition to encourage him in his projected agency in England. He perceived, that, by acceding to it, he put an end to the gratification of that hope. His enemies in the legislature were not ignorant of the repugnancy of this proposition to his views. They anticipated, that by his removal to Cambridge his political influence would be diminished, and a new obstacle interposed to his employment in Europe. He was a man, whom it was thought, on the one hand, not desirable further to elevate, nor, on the other, politic to offend. Perhaps, under the influence of the sectarian jealousies of the age, some deemed it not safe to trust him. Their course of proceeding was therefore, at once, decided, respectful, and conciliatory. A committee of the legislature was appointed to communicate the substance of the above vote, and to urge him to concur in its views. Two detailed contemporaneous accounts of the interview between President Mather and this committee, exist; one contained in the Diary of Judge Sewall, a member of the committee; the other, in the Diary of President Mather himself.

President Mather objects to residing at Cambridge.

The interview occurred on the 8th of December, 1698.* On the one side, President Mather expressed his dissatisfaction with the limitation of the office to five years, and that his name was not inserted in the vote; his discouragement from the reduction, in the House, of the salary proposed by the Council; the unsettled state of the College charter, and the want of a President's house; urging also the unwillingness of his church in Boston to part with him, and, above all, his love of preaching, which, he said, he "preferred before the gold and silver of the West Indies."

On the other side, the legislative committee deny that any "disrespect" to him was intended by their proceedings; they flatter him as being "the object of general desire," and as "loving work rather than wages"; and, as to preaching, that he would "preach twice a day to the students, expounding the Scriptures." The interview resulted in a promise of the President to communicate his answer through the Lieutenant-Governor.

President Mather's letter to Lieutenant-Governor Stoughton.

This he accordingly did on the 16th of December, 1698, in a letter equally illustrative of his purpose and of his character;† in which he declines the proposition of the General Court, urging his health, his advanced age (being nearly sixty), the necessity it would induce of desisting from his public ministry, as other

* See Appendix, No. IX. and No. XI.

† See Appendix, No. XV.

CHAPTER V.

Presidents had been obliged to do, on account of their other work. "Should I leave preaching to fifteen hundred souls (for I suppose so many ordinarily attend our congregation), only to expound to forty or fifty children, few of them capable of edification by such exercises, I doubt I should not do well." In one paragraph he states it to be well known, that "I have had a strong bent of spirit *to spend and to end* the remainder of my few days in England." In another, he complains, that his zeal for the settlement of the College had been attributed to a desire to gratify that inclination. To put to silence, therefore, these reproaches, he resolves to resign. This he proceeds to perform in the following cautious manner, addressing Lieutenant-Governor Stoughton; "I have often (as your Honor well knows) desired to resign my relation to that society; and, *if it will not be grievous to you*, I shall to-morrow (*if you please*) deliver a resignation of the presidentship to the Senior Fellow of the Corporation, for him to call a Corporation meeting, in order for the choosing another President." This threat of resigning had been so often repeated by President Mather, that it was well understood. In the course of the discussions, arising out of this subject, he was told by one of the Council, in the presence of the Board, that "his pretence of resigning was but a flourish."*

President Mather was too well apprized of the sense entertained of the importance of his services, in the station he then held, by the predominating ecclesiastical sect of the Province, and of Stoughton's conformity to its views, to fear any decision

* See Appendix, No. IX.

favorable to his resignation from him, particularly at a moment when a great struggle was commencing, for the purpose of placing the College permanently under the management of that ecclesiastical sect. This became distinctly developed in the course of the discussions, which occurred on the passage of the next proposed charter of the institution.

The urgency of the General Court, however, on this occasion, greatly distressed him, "it being," as his Diary states, "a thing so contrary to the faith wrought into my soul, that God will give me an opportunity to glorify Christ in England."

Early in the ensuing year (1699) he consulted his church on the proposal of the legislature, and, on the 6th of February, his church unanimously refused their consent to his removal. On the 23d of this month the Council of the Province and the Corporation of the College met on the subject. "I told them," he adds, "that, if my church and my wife would consent to my removal to Cambridge, I would go. Only I put in this caution, *except some tidings from England prevent.*" *

The affairs of the College, and the negotiation with President Mather relative to his removal to Cambridge, were in this state, on the arrival of Governor Bellamont in Massachusetts, which occurred in May, 1699. In his message, at the opening of the General Court, on the 2d of the ensuing June, he introduced the subject of the College by saying, that "he would very gladly promote a charter of incorporation for the College at Cambridge, and would heartily join in an address to his Majesty for his royal

* See Appendix, No. IX.

CHAPTER V.

Bill for a College charter. 1699.

grant of such privileges and franchises, as his Majesty, in his goodness, shall think fit." In consequence of this encouragement, a bill was brought into the House of Representatives on the 8th of July following. This bill, in its general features and powers, conforms to that passed in June, 1697. The only material exceptions are contained in two provisions; the one relative to the visitatorial power; the other to a religious qualification, now for the first time attempted to be introduced into the charter of the College. The visitatorial power was reserved by this act exclusively "to his Majesty and his Governor and Commander-in-chief, for the time being, of this Province."

To compensate the Council for their loss of the visitatorial power, five members of that body were appointed members of the Corporation; and the act declared, that, "whenever any of those five die, or be otherwise removed, or dismissed, such vacancy shall be filled up out of the Council from time to time." The objections of the Council were thus obviated; and the act was so modified, as to coincide with the views of the King; which were fixed upon establishing the principle, that the visitatorial power, as a branch of his prerogative, should not be shared with the Council. It is probable that this charter would have received the sanction of Governor Bellamont, and ultimately of the King, had it not been for a new element of discord inserted at the express urgency of clergymen of the Province, with President Mather at their head. Actuated by apprehensions arising from the increase of the Episcopalian sect, and still more from the spread of liberal principles adverse to the rigorous doctrines and severe discipline of the early colonial church, while the new College charter was preparing, and on the day before its first reading, eight clergymen, of the greatest influence in the Province, all members of the Corporation, presented a petition to the General Court.*

Petition of the clergy.

In conformity therewith, and in the terms proposed by these ministers, the following proviso was inserted into this charter when it passed both branches

* "To his Excellency the Governor, and the Honorable the great and general Assembly, now met at Boston.

"The address of sundry ministers, who were members of the late Corporation of Harvard College.

"Upon consideration of the deplorable state whereunto the College is now, for want of charter settlement, reduced and threatened with no less than a dissolution and dissipation of that society (the consequences whereof would be very fatal), if due means be not used, without any delay, to prevent so terrible a calamity, we have thought it our duty, once again to address the honorable Assembly, that a charter settlement of that society may be, by them, endeavoured.

"And we do more particularly pray, that, in the charter for the College, our holy religion may be secured to us and unto our posterity, by a provision, that no person shall be chosen President, or Fellow, of the College, but such as declare their adherence unto the principles of reformation, which were espoused and intended by those who first settled the country and founded the College, and have hitherto been the general profession of New England; and that the power of visitation be so expressed, as that we may have reason to hope that the charter will be favored with the royal approbation.

"And inasmuch as the surest and the most likely, if not the only way to obtain the charter settlement, so much desired, is to send over an agent to solicit so important an affair, we pray the General Assembly to take that matter into their serious consideration.

"If these things be done, since the God of Heaven hath given us a Governor, who will improve his great interest for us, we are not without hope but that the College may again flourish, to the manifold advantage of more than this whole Province, both in present and future times.

"Increase Mather.	Peter Thacher.
James Allen.	John Danforth.
Samuel Torrey.	Cotton Mather.
Samuel Willard.	Benjamin Wadsworth."

Boston, July 7th, 1699.

CHAPTER V.

of the legislature. "Provided, that no person shall be chosen and continued President, Vice-President, or Fellow of said Corporation, but such as shall declare and continue their adherence unto the principles of reformation, which were espoused and intended by those, who first settled this country and founded the College, and have hitherto been the profession and practice of the generality of the churches of Christ in New England."

This bill passed on the 13th of July, 1699,* and, on the 18th of the same month, it appears by the records of the General Court, that "the bill for incorporating Harvard College at Cambridge was read, and His Excellency objected to one clause or paragraph therein, that none should be President or Fellow of said Corporation, but such as declare themselves, and continue to be, as to their persuasion in matters of religion, such as are known by the name of Congregationalist, or Presbyterian."

Governor Bellamont objects to the religious qualification.

"And the question being put to the House, whether they could consent to pass the said bill, leaving out that paragraph, it was carried in the negative."

"Then William Stoughton, Elisha Cooke, Samuel Sewall, Esquires, and the Secretary, were nominated and appointed to acquaint the House of Representatives, that His Excellency could not consent to the said bill, with the aforesaid clause therein, and that he rather advised to address his Majesty for a royal charter of incorporation."

From the terms of the objections made by Governor Bellamont to the obnoxious clause in this bill, it is apparent, that he apprehended it was levelled against members of the Church of England. The force of it was, however, far from being so limited

* See Appendix, No. LXVIII.

as to affect only those, who were not "known by the name of Congregationalist or Presbyterian." The criterion established in the act, being "adherence to the principles of reformation, which were espoused and intended by those, who first settled this country and founded the College," is obviously quite as effectual to exclude those persons from the government of the College, who, although Congregationalists, adopted religious principles and discipline, different from what were sanctioned by the platform and the practice of the early New England churches. That such was the intent, and that for this purpose the clause was carefully constructed, the collateral contemporaneous evidence is, perhaps, conclusive. The original petition, proposing this clause, was signed by none of the laymen of the former Corporation. Four of the twelve clergymen (Michael Wigglesworth, Nehemiah Hobart, Nehemiah Walter, and William Brattle), who composed the Corporation, were not signers of it. The names, also, of John Leverett and Thomas Brattle were omitted in the new act; and, for the purpose of excluding the last, the Treasurer was no longer permitted to be, as he had been previously, *ex officio*, a member of the Corporation. The two vacancies, thus created, were filled by "the two senior tutors resident at the College for the time being."

The religious controversies of the period, which there will be occasion to notice hereafter, and the part which Leverett and Thomas Brattle took in them, sufficiently explain their exclusion from the bill, to the framing of which the adherents of the early colonial church brought their united influences. The extreme rigor of this church, during the existence of

CHAPTER V.

the old charter, had not only given great dissatisfaction to members of other sects and to hostile churches, but had scattered seeds of discontent among those, who preferred the Congregational forms, and who even embraced the general doctrines which have obtained the name of "orthodox."

Until the introduction into the General Court of this bill for a charter of the College, nothing appears in the Diary of Cotton Mather, indicating any concurrence or interest in his father's views concerning an agency in England. But no sooner had this bill been introduced, than he enters upon the topic, and watches the progress of it with characteristic zeal and sympathy. His own "particular faith" gradually became very vivid. It was "assured to him in the spirit from Heaven, that his father should be carried into England and made there a wonderful glory and service unto the Lord, and that his own opportunities to glorify the Lord on that occasion will be *gloriously accommodated*."* Circumstances about this time concurred to excite hopes in Cotton Mather's mind, of succeeding to the presidency of the College, in case his father should be called into England. Morton, who had hitherto been regarded as the candidate for that office, was dead; and few, if any, of the clergy of the day could compare with Cotton Mather, in classical learning, extensive reading, or literary industry and reputation. These hopes were probably the "glorious accommodations," to which he alludes. The negative of Governor Bellamont to that bill put an end to these expectations. His disappointment is strongly and feelingly expressed in his Diary.

* See Appendix, No. X.

CHAPTER VI.

Temporary Settlement of the College. — Dissatisfaction of John Leverett. — Governor Bellamont recommends an Application to the King for a Charter. — Proceedings of the General Court thereon. — Features of the New Charter. — John Leverett and both the Brattles excluded from the Corporation. — Agency given to Governor Bellamont. — Disappointment of the Mathers. — The General Court renew their Vote for the Residency of the President at Cambridge. — President Mather removes, but soon returns to Boston. — His Letter to Lieutenant-Governor Stoughton. — The General Court negotiate with Mr. Willard. — Proceedings in this Negotiation. — Exclusion of President Mather.

CHAPTER VI.

1699. Temporary settlement of the College.

After the negative of the bill for a new charter by Governor Bellamont, as related in the last chapter, "a temporary settlement" of the College was made. This appears from a letter written by John Leverett to Mr. Addington, but there is no account of it, either in the College records, or in those of the General Court. In this letter Leverett complains in no measured terms of the proceedings of the Corporation at a meeting holden under that "new settlement"; doubts its validity, all the members of the former Corporation not having been summoned; and considers it "wonderful, that an establishment for so short a time, as till October next, should be made use of so soon to introduce an unnecessary addition to that society."* The language of Leverett indicates, that he was not a member of the Corporation under this new settlement; which is also

* See Appendix, No. XVI.

to be gathered not only from his exclusion from the former bill, but also from his name not appearing on the records of the Corporation among those present at that meeting. The letter sufficiently evidences his dissatisfaction with the proceedings of President Mather.

The year 1699 closed upon President Mather under circumstances well calculated to create despondency. The fourth draft of a charter had been negatived, and the favorite clause, on which the clergy relied for retaining their supremacy over the College, had been the occasion of that negative. No substitute seemed likely to be agreed upon. Governor Bellamont, although bent upon rendering himself popular with the predominant party in the country, yet dared to do nothing which should recognise or extend the superiority of the Congregational church. To secure this, and to place the College permanently and exclusively under its power, were the objects President Mather proposed to himself. The tedious drama, however, was now drawing to a close, which was destined to display to him and his son the groundlessness of their "celestial assurances" and "special faith"; and, instead of placing either of them at the head of the College, removed both from all future important influence in its concerns.

The subject of the College charter slept after the last negative of Bellamont, until the meeting of the General Court, in May, 1700. Then the Governor again revived it in his address at the opening of their first session, by expressing his regret, that "what he had proposed last May session for the advantage of the Province, in relation to the settlement of the College, had been so coldly received." "I am, in

CHAPTER VI.

Governor Bellamont recommends an application to the King for a charter.

consequence," he adds, "about discouraged from renewing my advice on this head; yet my zeal for the public service will not suffer me to pass it over in silence. The settlement of the College will best be obtained, in my opinion, by addressing the King for his royal charter of privileges."

Proceedings on a bill for a new charter.

In consequence of this suggestion, a vote passed the Council on the 11th of the ensuing June, that an application should be made to his Majesty, by way of address, for the settlement of the College. This mode of proceeding did not receive the concurrence of the House of Representatives. They preferred to prepare a charter in form, which should be "humbly solicited" from his Majesty. In the course of preparing it, the question concerning the right of nominating the members of the Corporation assumed a somewhat serious aspect. The strength of the Mathers and the ministers lay in the House of Representatives. The Council had given great dissatisfaction to both by the pertinacity it had manifested on the subject of the visitatorial power, whereby one charter had been lost. Nor were they more content with the manner in which the Council had yielded its claim to a portion of that power, by insisting upon such a modification of the last act, as that five of its members should always constitute a portion of the Corporation. In order to secure to themselves the control of the election, the House of Representatives, on the 28th of June, sent up to the Council a resolve, that "the nomination of persons for the Corporation of Harvard College be attended this afternoon, and be proceeded in, in the same manner as the election of Counsellors." As under the charter of William and Mary the General

CHAPTER VI.

Court or Assembly chose Counsellors by joint ballot in convention, the effect of this resolve was to deprive the Council of their negative upon the election of members of the Corporation. The resolve was, of course, negatived in that body; and, a conference, which was proposed and accepted, resulted in the nomination, by the House of Representatives, of President, Vice-President, and all the members of the Corporation, which, after having been "read" and "voted severally," was agreed upon in concurrence by the Council.

Exclusion of Leverett and the Brattles.

The number of the Corporation was, by the provisions of this act, as in the preceding, seventeen, but the Council no longer was to be represented by five of its members. By omitting the name of William Brattle, minister of Cambridge, and also that of "the Treasurer," (Thomas Brattle,) they were both excluded from the board. This exclusion had unquestionable reference to religious opinions; and, if not their work, was, it cannot be doubted, very acceptable to the Mathers, at that time engaged in a bitter theological controversy, in opposition to doctrines which the Brattles favored. The name of Leverett also no longer appears among the members of the Corporation, although, being at that time Speaker of the House of Representatives, his appointment might have been expected, as likely to be pleasing to the legislature, and also on account of his acquaintance with the interests of the College, and the share he had so long possessed in its government. But these considerations were outweighed by the fact, that he had identified himself with the Brattles in support of doctrines, deemed heretical by those who took the

Platform of the New England churches as the standard of orthodoxy.

Although Governor Bellamont had negatived the act which passed in 1699, on account of the association of the Council with him in the visitatorial power, yet a like provision was inserted in the act now passing; the only difference being, that, in the former, the visitatorial power was directly invested, and in the latter it was reserved. The clause containing it was as follows; "And, for preventing of irregularity in the government of the College, we do hereby reserve a power of visitation thereof in ourself, our heirs, and successors, by the Governor and Commander-in-chief, *together with our Council for the time being*, of our Province of Massachusetts Bay aforesaid, to be exercised by our Governor, or Commander-in-chief, and Council, when and so often as they shall see cause."

The clause providing for a religious qualification in the officers of the government and instruction was omitted in this act. The ancient ecclesiastical preponderance was, however, secured, by excluding the names of Leverett and of the Brattles, and by inserting in their place, and in that of the five members of the Council, the names of Peter Thacher, Samuel Angier, Henry Gibbs, Jonathan Pierpont, Benjamin Wadsworth, and John White. The seventeen members of the Corporation, with the exception of White and the Senior Resident Fellows, were thus all clergymen; of whom a great majority were of the predominating religious sect.

This act was in the form of "heads of a charter," to be presented to his Majesty for enactment. While it was in its passage, an address to Governor Bellamont, being prepared, was passed contempora-

CHAPTER VI.

neously with the act on the 9th of July, 1700.* In this address the General Court say; "It having pleased your Excellency to consent and join with us in our humble address to his Majesty, for a settlement of the College at Cambridge, within this Province, agreeably to the ends and intent of the first founders; and several articles as the heads of a charter for the incorporating the said College having been agreed to; we are bold to present the same to your Lordship, and withal humbly to pray, that your Lordship would be pleased to improve your interest with his Majesty and the ministers of state, in behalf of this Province, for the obtainment of his Majesty's grace and favor in this matter."

Agency for the charter given to Governor Bellamont.

This application to Bellamont, instead of a special agency in England, was a death-blow to President Mather's expectations. His own Diary, for this period, is missing. That of his son exists;† in which an intense desire that his father should be gratified, and his own self-delusion on the subject of his special faith, are manifested to a degree, that would be incredible, had we not his own authority in evidence of his extreme infatuation.

After a series of exciting exercises of prayer and faith, after genuflexions and prostrations and supernatural spiritual elevations, and after an angel had confirmed his special faith in the certainty of a mission to England for his father, the whole resulted in utter disappointment. In the bitterness of his anger he exclaims, that "Governor Bellamont, not without base unhandsomeness" had deceived him; and that Lieutenant-Governor Stoughton, "who had formerly

* See Appendix, No. LXVIII. † See Appendix, No. X.

been for his father's agency, now (not without great ebullition of unaccountable prejudice and ingratitude) appeared with all the little tricks imaginable to confound it."

Thus this particular faith, which had been entertained, with various interchanges of hope and fear, for more than eight years, in President Mather's mind, proved at last a delusion; excited by the natural wishes of his own heart, and encouraged by the vain promises of two or three slippery politicians, who, when their own ends were answered, were not unwilling to disappoint his expectations.

Disappointment of the Mathers.

After this sad termination of President Mather's hopes, all thoughts of an agency in England were, for the present at least, laid aside. The projected College charter was intrusted, for its negotiation, to Governor Bellamont, who died before he returned to England. With him perished all expectation of attaining it; and no subsequent attempt was ever made to obtain a College charter from the crown.

Contemporaneously with the project of transferring the contemplated agency from President Mather to Earl Bellamont, that of compelling the former either to reside at Cambridge, or to resign his presidency, was adopted by the General Court. On the 10th of July, a resolve was sent up from the House of Representatives, and was immediately concurred in by the Council and approved by the Governor, "that two hundred and twenty pounds per annum be allowed, and to be paid out of the public treasury, to the President of the College; that the person chosen President should reside at Cambridge;" and a Committee was appointed by both branches, "to wait on the Rev. Increase Mather, and acquaint him, that this

1700.

CHAPTER VI.

Court hath chosen him President of Harvard College, and desire him to accept of said office, and so expect that he repair to and reside at Cambridge as soon as may be. The said Committee to make report of said President's answer to this Court."

On the 11th of July, they reported, "That Mr. Mather could not remove without acquainting his church. If they consented to give him up to this work, he would, as to his own person, remove to Cambridge, but could not see his way clear to remove his family, until he heard of the passing of the charter in England."

The uncertainty which this answer indicated, was not satisfactory to the General Court, and a message was immediately sent to Mr. Mather by them, "to call a meeting of his church *this evening* on the said occasion." Accordingly, on the next day, it was notified to the Council by one of the members of Mr. Mather's church, that, "having had a meeting in pursuance of the directions of the Court, they had consented to his going to Cambridge, and that said Mr. Mather referred himself to his former answer."

On the next day a Committee was appointed, "to take care that a suitable place be provided at Cambridge for the reception and entertainment of the President, and to consider what ought to be done with respect to a house already built for a President's house."

President Mather removes to Cambridge.

The Committee immediately attended to their duty,* and, the necessary accommodations being prepared, President Mather, in July, 1700, apparently established himself permanently at Cambridge.

* See Records of General Court.

CHAPTER VI.

In the same session the General Court passed a vote, vesting in Increase Mather, as President, Samuel Willard, as Vice-President, and the other persons named in the last-mentioned College charter, the general care and superintendence of the College.*

President Mather continued his residence at Cambridge, however, no longer than till the 17th of October following. On this day he removed to Boston, and addressed a letter to Lieutenant-Governor Stoughton, "giving an account of his inspection of the College whilst he resided there, and containing the reasons for his removal from Cambridge, as not having his health there, and desiring that another President may be thought of."

This letter was communicated to the General Court on the 26th of February, 1701, and, on the 14th of March following, a resolve passed that body, which, after reciting, that, "forasmuch as the Constitution requires that the President reside at Cambridge, which is now altered by his removal from thence, and to the intent, that a present necessary oversight be taken of the College," proceeds to invest all the former members of the Corporation with the superintendence of the College; "and, in case of Mr. Mather's refusal, absence, sickness, or death, Mr. Samuel Willard is nominated to be Vice-President; and, with the others before named, invested with like powers and authority, in all respects."

Vice-President appointed.

On the ensuing day the General Court appointed a Committee, of which John Leverett was chairman, "to take effectual care that the President's house be repaired," the charges for which are to be allowed

* See Records of General Court.

CHAPTER VI.

by the Governor and Council, and paid out of the treasury.

President Mather's letter to Lieutenant-Governor Stoughton.

Upon this it appears, that President Mather again transferred his residence to Cambridge, and remained there until the 30th of June, 1701, when he addressed a letter to Lieutenant-Governor Stoughton,* equally illustrative of his motives and character; in which he unequivocally indicates, that his expectation and intent were to retain the office of President, and avoid the obligation of fixing his residence at Cambridge. His letter is well adapted to remove objections to his views, and to excite a spirit favorable to their attainment. He carefully limits the grounds of his unwillingness to remove his family to Cambridge, to "the unsettled state of the College;" a reason, which, as a settlement was daily expected, would be considered as temporary, and the more likely to be acquiesced in by the General Court.† In order that the spirit of sectarianism should come in aid of his views, he also takes care to sound the alarm upon points of religious controversy then in a state of heated excitement, and to warn the legislature, "how fatal it would be for the interest of religion, should one disaffected to the order of the Gospel, as professed and practised in the churches of New England, preside over the seminary."

This letter was laid before the General Court early in the ensuing August (1701), and was received and entertained by them with every outward mark of respect. They immediately appointed a Committee to "signify to President Mather that the Court desired to speak with him at 3 o'clock, *post meridiem*, relating

* See Appendix, No. XVII. † Ibid.

CHAPTER VI.

to the affairs of the College." On his attendance, the record states, that "Mr. Speaker and the Representatives were desired to come up to the Council Chamber, when Mr. Mather acquainted the Court, that he was removed from Cambridge to Boston, and as the College remained unsettled, he did not think fit to continue his residence there, and looked at it as a hardship to expect his removing his family thither; *but, if the Court thought fit to desire he should continue his care of the College as formerly, he would do so.*" *

Proceedings of the General Court.

This intimation of President Mather received no favor in either branch of the legislature. After having been for eight years foiled in their attempts to establish a resident President at the College by the pertinacious resistance of Mr. Mather, a prevalent disposition was manifested to look elsewhere for a head of the institution, and no longer to submit its welfare to the caprice of an individual, who would neither reside nor resign.

The House of Representatives immediately sent up to the Council a resolve founded upon the fact, "that the Rev. Mr. Increase Mather had acquainted this Court, that he can with no conveniency any longer reside at Cambridge, and take care of the College there," and appointed a committee to be joined by the Council "to wait upon the Rev. Samuel Willard, and desire him to accept the care and charge of the said College, and to reside in Cambridge, in order thereunto." This committee was immediately joined in the other branch.

To this application Mr. Willard having replied on

* General Court Records, August 1st, 1701.

CHAPTER VI.

the 2d of August, that "he would consider thereof and advise with his church and give his answer," the Council took such a deep interest in its success, that they appointed on the 5th of the same month a special committee, consisting of Elisha Cooke and Penn Townsend, "to attend the meeting of Mr. Willard's church, and desire their consent that he might go and reside at Cambridge to take care of the College."

Difficulties having been, however, thrown in the way of their success, the Council, on the 8th of the same month, again resolved, that "further application be made to Mr. Willard's church for their consent to his going to reside at Cambridge to take care of the College."

Negotiation with Mr. Willard, who accepts the vice-presidency.

While this negotiation with Mr. Willard and his church was in progress, the House of Representatives, in contemplation of an adjournment of the General Court, by a resolve passed on the 9th of August, devolved the whole power relative "to the settlement of the College, until the next assembling of the General Court, upon the Honorable the Council." From this resolve it is apparent, that the difficulty of obtaining a resident President was great; since it provides, that, "*if it may be*, the person, who shall have the chief government of the College reside there, and perform the duties that have formerly been discharged by the President;" thereby indicating, that success in this endeavour was dubious.

From the course of events, also, it is apparent that Mr. Willard, although he was willing to take the superintendence of the College, would not pledge himself for the present, to reside permanently at Cambridge. The cause of his reluctance thus to reside, does not appear. It threw, however, such an obstacle in the way of success in the negotiation with him, as gave the friends of Dr. Mather hopes, and a pretence for rallying in his favor. Accordingly, on the 5th of September following, no arrangement with Mr. Willard having been made, the House of Representatives, in which Dr. Mather's strength lay, passed a resolve, which they sent up to the Council for concurrence, "desiring Mr. Increase Mather to take care of and reside at the College." No sooner was this read in the Council, than that board, wholly passing over the object of the resolve of the House of Representatives, appointed their former Committee "to go, with such as the Representatives should think fit to accompany them, unto Mr. Samuel Willard, to whom this Court had made application to attend that service, to speak to him, and to receive his answer thereabout." On the same day, Mr. Cooke, chairman of the committee, "acquainted the board, that himself and the other gentleman had spoken with Mr. Willard, who declared his readiness to do the best service he could for the College, and that he would visit once or twice every week, and continue there a night or two, and perform the services there to be done by former Presidents." *

Increase Mather excluded from the presidency.

The proceedings of the ensuing day, as they closed finally the connexions of Dr. Mather with the presidency, deserve to be stated at large, as they appear on the Records of the General Court. "6th of September, 1701. The resolve, passed in the House of Representatives, and sent up for concurrence, and read yesterday, at the Board, viz., 'That Mr. Increase Mather be desired to take care of and reside at the

* See the Records of the General Court at the respective dates.

CHAPTER VI.

College,' was again read, and upon the question put for a concurrence, it was carried in the negative." "Then a resolve being drawn up in the words following, was read, passed, and sent down to the Representatives for concurrence, viz. Resolved, that the Rev. Mr. Samuel Willard, nominated Vice-President of the College, (together with the gentlemen named for the Corporation, in the order of this Court,) be desired to take the oversight of the College and the students there, according to the late establishment made by the Court, and to manage the affairs thereof as he has proposed in his answer to the Court, viz. to reside there one or two days and nights in a week, and to perform prayers and expositions in the Hall, and to bring forward the exercise of analyzing."

"Which resolve being returned from the Representatives with their concurrence thereto, the same was signed by fourteen members of the Council present at the board."

This last formality was essential, as the Council then held the Executive authority of the Province; no successor having been appointed to Bellamont, and Lieutenant-Governor Stoughton having died in the preceding July.

The eventful presidency of Increase Mather was thus brought to its close by the will and direct application of the authority of the legislature. That he was well qualified for the office, and had conducted himself in it faithfully and laboriously, is attested by the history of the College, the language of the legislature, and the acknowledgment of his contemporaries. It seems obvious, that it was honorable and useful to the institution, to have for its head an individual who had taken so large a share in the political, religious, and literary controversies of the times, and had in consequence acquired both celebrity abroad and influence in his own country. Nor does the avowed motive, "his refusal to transfer his residence to Cambridge," sufficiently account for the determined spirit with which his exclusion was pursued; particularly as it appears by the vote of the legislature itself, that the superintendence of the seminary was granted to Mr. Willard upon conditions, which did not require him to fix his personal residence at Cambridge. This he never did, although he continued more than six years the chief superintendent of the College, in the office of Vice-President. From all which it is reasonable to conclude, that the avowed were not the prevailing motives for the exclusion of Dr. Mather. That such was the fact, his son unequivocally suggests; and the circumstances of the case sufficiently indicate that this suggestion was not altogether gratuitous.

Cotton Mather, in his Life of his father, directly asserts, that "the College was taken out of his hands." The causes of this proceeding he thus recapitulates.

"There were some disaffected persons, who were for some reasons (*God knows what they were*) willing to have the College taken out of Dr. Mather's hands. To accomplish it they obtained a vote of the General Assembly, which appeared of a plausible aspect; *that no man should act as President of the College, who did not reside at Cambridge.* The leaders in this vote knew very well, that the Doctor would not remove his habitation from a loving people at Boston, to reside at Cambridge, while the College was *as it then was.* But yet his abdication was, after all,

CHAPTER VI.

brought about, I will but softly say, *not so fairly as it should have been.* I think there are thanks due to me for my forbearing to tell the story."*

Language of this temper, used two-and-twenty years after the blow had been given, sufficiently evidences, that the wound inflicted by it had been deep and immedicable. Cotton Mather saw plainly, that there were, in the General Court, persons "disaffected" towards his father. But he was not in a position to discern, or to judge accurately, of the causes of that "disaffection."

Causes of President Mather's exclusion.

These causes, however, are here proper subjects of investigation, as the exclusion of Increase Mather from the presidency was an important crisis in the history of the College. They are intimately connected with the characters of both the Mathers, and with the impressions concerning them, made upon their contemporaries by their respective religious and political courses; a general developement of which is indispensable to a just estimate of the results.

Increase Mather had scarcely passed the threshold of manhood, when he dashed headlong into the religious controversies of the period; joining ardently the side of those, who maintained the doctrines and discipline established by the early emigrants to Massachusetts in the utmost strictness and rigor.

The great question, which divided our ancestors of the second generation, and which was the chief occasion of the synod of 1662, when divested of the technicalities of the age, was, whether any children but those of parents in full communion were subjects of baptism. The decision of the synod had

* Life of Increase Mather, by Cotton Mather, p. 173. Art. 29.

been favorable to the extension of the rite to others than children of such parents. Against this decision President Chauncy came out with great learning and power, in a work entitled "Antisynodalia Americana." Increase Mather joined the side of President Chauncy, and wrote in defence of his opinion; and in opposition to his own father, who was a minister of respectable standing at Dorchester. His eagerness to engage in controversy, which seems to have been his character through life, made him obnoxious to the doubt, expressed in after times, whether his motives were "zeal for truth, or a desire to show his talents." * He had soon occasion to repent his haste, and to regret the part he had taken on this question. The side he had embraced proved to be neither popular nor prevailing. There occurred, therefore, to Mr. Mather, what his son calls "second thoughts." Availing himself of the argument of his opponent, Mr. Mitchell, he declared himself "vanquished," and, passing away from the side of President Chauncy, he joined that of Mr. Mitchell; and, with the zeal natural to new converts, in the language of his son, "obliged the church of God, by publishing to the world a couple of unanswerable treatises *in defence of the synodical propositions.*" †

President Mather's early religious course.

In a like spirit of adhesion to the "faith and order of the evangelical churches established by the early fathers of Massachusetts," he joined the party, who "would not hear of toleration," and wrote an essay full "of erudition, in favor of the power of the civil magistrate in matters of religion." This essay be-

* Mass. Hist. Coll., Second Series, Vol. I. p. 204.

† Life of Increase Mather, by Cotton Mather, p. 50. Art. 12.

CHAPTER VI.

came also the subject of "second thoughts." It "was never published." "And it was well," adds Cotton Mather, "he did not; for anon he became fully satisfied, in the declared will of our Saviour, *that the tares must have toleration*."*

These retractions of avowed opinions, adopted with more zeal than foresight, would have been visited in after times with a milder judgment, had he not, in both cases, yielded to the tide of public opinion; which the deviations in his course indicated at once an inclination to stem and an inability to resist. It is not surprising, therefore, that, among the stricter sect of his brethren, in consequence of these first essays, he became obnoxious to the charge of "*apostasy from the principles of New England*," and of having an eye to "*self-interest and self-ends*."†

Whatever suspicions of his principles his conduct in these instances might have raised, they were all dissipated by the subsequent tenor of his life and writings. For the ensuing twenty-five years he was regarded as the champion of the sternest principles of the doctrines and discipline of the fathers of Massachusetts. His zeal and boldness, combined with his position as pastor of the second church in the metropolis, placed him at the head of the clergy; a relation, which, in that day, the President of the College was, by universal consent, acknowledged to possess. In all forms of government which have, like that framed by the people of Massachusetts under the old charter, religion for their great object, the political and ecclesiastical leaders become identical in policy, if not in

* Memoirs of Increase Mather, by Cotton Mather, p. 58. Art. 13.

† Magnalia, Book IV. c. 4. § 11.

person. Under a constitution, in which none were admitted to be freemen except church members, civil and religious liberty became inseparably interwoven in the minds of those freemen. As, in a government thus constituted, the only path to influence in the state is coincidence with the received doctrines of the established church, it results, that politicians never fail to assume the aspect of divines, and divines to possess the weight, and often openly to assume the attitude, of politicians.

President Mather's early political course.

No man understood better than President Mather the nature of the constitution under which he lived. He realized the advantages he possessed, and had every disposition to avail himself of them. Happily duty to his country, religious interests, and love of distinction all united in giving a right direction to his course. In the great crisis, which then impended over Massachusetts, he gratified them all by placing himself in the front rank of those, who resisted the insidious policy of Randolph, and the unveiled despotism of Andros. Denounced and persecuted by those enemies of New England for the boldness of his opposition and the severity of his invectives, he became a favorite both of the freemen and of the clergy. So that, when the interests of the Province demanded that it should be represented in Great Britain by a confidential agent, Mr. Mather was deemed, "by the principal men of the Colony," best qualified for that office; * as uniting, more than any individual, the influence of the clergy and the confidence of the freemen. The interests of no class of men were so identified with the preservation of the old

* Hutch. Hist. Mass., Vol. I. chap. 3.

charter as were those of the clergy, and the policy of having for a representative abroad the head of that body was as wise, as in the event it proved to be happy. All the friends of the charter realized, that they possessed in him its most vigorous defender; nor can it be questioned, that he sailed for Europe with the fixed intent to relinquish none of the privileges the colonists had enjoyed under it.

When, therefore, after the lapse of four years, he returned to New England, bringing with him, not the old charter, that desire of so many hearts, but a new one, which no person sought or anticipated; when in this the appointment of Governor, Lieutenant-Governor, and Secretary of State was taken from the people, and the preëminence of the Congregational church was wrested from the clergy; a negative on the appointment of Counsellors reserved to the Governor, and on the acts of the legislature to the King; when religion was no longer the object of the frame of government, but the world and its concerns; and an independence of transatlantic control, which had been enjoyed by two successive generations, was abandoned; the agent, who, in opposition to all his colleagues, had accepted and approved an instrument so repugnant to the expectations and hopes of all, and so contrary to his antecedent opinions and promises, could not but expect to meet from his countrymen signs of deep and insurmountable discontent, if not visitations of public indignation.

President Mather's negotiation in Europe.

As Mr. Mather had, in his negotiation in Europe, conducted with exemplary fidelity, so on his return, all his measures to meet the exigency of the occasion were wise and prudent; but, though they saved the state, they caused to him the loss of popularity and influence. By letters and certificates approving his course, from clergymen known to be distinguished for their friendship to the Colony, he deadened the opposition of the clergy, or secured partially their support. By procuring the nomination of his personal friends as the first Counsellors, he filled that board with men on whom he could rely to give a right impulse to the government in its outset. By obtaining the appointment of Sir William Phips to the Governor's chair, he gratified the people among whom he was a favorite, and insured an administration likely to agree with him in policy, and to be guided by his counsels. The personal qualifications of Phips for the office of Governor being few, and some of the Council unpopular, Mr. Mather's course became subjected to censure, and his motives to impeachment. At this day, however, it scarcely admits a question, that his precautions were wise, and his arrangements justifiable. It was a case, in which the interest of the agent was identified with that of the public. He, who had taken so great a responsibility in favor of a new form of government, had surely a right to provide, that its first movements should be in the hands of his friends, and not be placed, by any false delicacy, at the mercy of its enemies. His policy was eminently successful. Whatever opinions we may be compelled to entertain concerning his measures and motives on other occasions, his conduct in this great crisis of his country entitles him to unqualified approbation. It is scarcely possible for a public agent to be placed in circumstances more trying or critical; nor could any one have exhibited more sagacity and devotedness to the true interests of his constituents. By his

CHAPTER VI.

His policy relative to the colonial charter of 1692.

wisdom and firmness in acceding to the new charter, and thus assuming a responsibility of the weightiest kind, in opposition to his colleagues in the agency, he saved his country, apparently, from a rebellion or a revolution, or from having a constitution imposed by the will of the transatlantic sovereign, possibly at the point of the bayonet.* The event, though prosperous for his country, was to him an abundant source of calumny and animosity, and ended in his loss of political influence, and his severance from all subsequent public employment.

The political and religious controversies, which ensued upon the change of influences consequent on the charter of William and Mary, were unavoidably numerous and bitter. The statesmen of the Colony, whose office Mather had assumed, and whose part he had successfully played in Great Britain, saw with little complacency a clergyman, in opposition to his colleagues in the agency, taking a lead in new modelling its constitution, selecting those who were destined to give it the first impulse, and having the boldness, in doing this, to gratify some, and to disappoint and deeply offend others. There was also a class of inhabitants, who, although able, respectable, and wealthy, had been hitherto precluded from all political power, in consequence of not being willing, though Congregationalists, to subscribe the creed, or submit to the customs and discipline, required by the church of New England. To both these classes, of politicians and religionists, President Mather had rendered himself particularly obnoxious. To the former, because, as

* Memoirs of Increase Mather, by Cotton Mather, p. 134.

CHAPTER VI.

Animosity of the politicians to President Mather.

the open advocate and the supposed author of the new charter, they attributed to him all the loss of influence and privileges consequent on that instrument. To the latter he was still more obnoxious, as the unqualified asserter and earnest defender of the doctrines and discipline of the established Congregational church. At the head of the political party opposed to him were the whole body of former Assistants, whom he had neglected to nominate to the first Provincial Council of 1692; many of whom were chosen into that Council by the legislature on the first opportunity of exerting their authority, in 1693. His colleagues in the agency saw with dissatisfaction the successful operation of the new charter. The feelings of Elisha Cooke, one of the number, were also quickened into resentment, when, after having been nominated to the Council by the legislature, he found himself negatived by Governor Phips. His friends were many, and his influence weighty; and his animosity unavoidably became directed towards Mather, who was well known to be the confidential friend and counsellor of the Governor.

The loss of influence and of place, the ultimate lot of President Mather, is not, however, solely to be attributed to his political course, or to his religious zeal. In both politics and religion, the tone of his writings was lofty and magisterial. He made no concealment of the high opinion he entertained of his own public services, and their claims to gratitude and reward. The want of delicacy with which his appointment to another agency in England was pressed, both by his personal friends and by the Corporation, of which he and his son were the guiding spirits, had a natural tendency to disgust his contemporaries, and

CHAPTER VI.

excite in them an inclination to thwart his plans and limit his power.

Character and language of Cotton Mather.

The character of Cotton Mather, his son and associate in the pastoral care of the North Church in Boston, was of a nature to repel and not to conciliate. Indefatigable, learned, laborious, but vain, opinionated, irritable, and ambitious, he held no measures with those, who crossed his own or his father's path; and was equally open and imprudent in expressing his resentments.

The Journal of Judge Sewall contains graphic sketches of the language and conduct of Cotton Mather on the proceedings in the Council relative to his father. *

Sewall agreed with the Mathers in their general views of politics and religion. As a member of the Council, he had taken an active part in those measures which preceded the exclusion of President Mather from the College chair. His expressions in the course of debate had given offence to the father and son. Their language on the occasion was characteristic of their temperament. Words and demeanor so unguarded and irritating, as Sewall records, towards men of rank and influence in the Province, must have deeply affected their popularity; nor can it be doubted, that they were among the causes, not only of the father's exclusion from office, but also of that comparative neglect and loss of influence, which were the fate of both, during the remainder of their lives.

* See Appendix, No. XI.

CHAPTER VII.

Sectarian Controversies. — Attempts to remove John Leverett and Thomas Brattle from the Corporation traced to them. — President Mather's Epistle Dedicatory to his Son's Life of Mitchell. — Its Effects. — Foundation of Brattle Street Church. — Connexion with it of Leverett and Brattle. — Conduct of the Mathers in respect to it. — Interference of Lieutenant-Governor Stoughton. — Reconciliation of the Mathers with Colman. — Dedication of Brattle Street Church. — The Mathers renew the Controversy. — Its Spirit and Consequences.

CHAPTER VII.

Sectarian controversies.

THE sectarian controversies, which at this period agitated the Province, the Corporation, and the College, were among the causes of the exclusion of Increase Mather, and, after the lapse of a few years, led to the introduction of John Leverett into the presidency.

Thomas Brattle, William Brattle, John Leverett, Ebenezer Pemberton, and Benjamin Colman, were all graduates of the College, and, with the exception of Colman, had been connected with its government while Increase Mather presided. All were men distinguished for zeal in the cause of learning and religion, and highly esteemed by their contemporaries for moral worth and intellectual attainments. None of them were adherents to the rigid doctrines of the early established Congregational church of New England, or concealed their preference of those milder and more liberal views of the Christian dispensation, which, after the charter of William and Mary had

CHAPTER VII.

deprived the clergy of their civil power, began to be openly avowed.

During the absence of President Mather in Europe, the instruction and superintendence of the College had devolved upon John Leverett and William Brattle, as tutors. Both continued in their respective offices after his return. Both were made members of the Corporation by the College charter, passed in 1692. When this charter was negatived by the King, both held that relation, and were among those, who, in 1696, were reinstated in their offices by Lieutenant-Governor Stoughton. It does not appear, that during this period they thwarted any of the views of the President relative to the College. On the contrary, they supported him in his neglect of the recommendation of the legislature to remove to Cambridge in 1693, and joined in requesting him, in 1696, not to "resent" their renewed recommendation to the same purport, and not to resign in consequence of it. They did not, however, concur in the remonstrance of the other members of the Corporation against the bill concerning the College in 1696, and, from their known religious views, could not be relied upon to support the project then contemplated, and afterwards openly attempted, to establish an absolute control of the College in the hands of the adherents to the early ecclesiastical doctrines. This contumacy of Leverett probably explains the endeavour made to exclude him from the Corporation, in the bill introduced into the General Court in 1697 by President Mather; who was of a temperament not to permit his animosities to be concealed, or their causes misapprehended. From their proceedings it cannot be doubted, that both the Mathers had determined to resist, with a strong hand,

Course of Leverett and Brattle.

the tendency to deviate from "the good old scriptural ways," which, as they thought, was countenanced in the College and the community, by the Brattles, Leverett, and Pemberton; Colman being then in Europe. The agreement of these members of the College in religious sentiment was a subject of general notoriety. In 1697, Leverett and Pemberton were tutors, Thomas Brattle was Treasurer of the College, and William Brattle had just exchanged his office of tutor for that of pastor of the church in Cambridge. In the same year Cotton Mather published his Life of Jonathan Mitchell. Availing himself of this occasion, President Mather wrote an Epistle Dedicatory for that work, addressed "to the church in Cambridge, and to the students in the College there." In this Epistle he enumerates the great lights Cambridge and the College had formerly enjoyed; and reminds them of the many countries and places, which, after possessing a faithful ministry, had become, through "young profane mockers, and scornful neuters, overgrown with thorns and nettles, so that the glory of the Lord had gradually departed." "Mercy forbid," he adds, "that such things should be verified in Cambridge." The publication of his son's Life of Mitchell, he considers "not to have been without the providence of Christ, at such a time, when there are agitations about some disciplinary questions among yourselves."

President Mather's epistle dedicatory.

The questions agitated at that time chiefly respected the qualifications and examination to be required as conditions of admission to the ordinance of the Lord's Supper.

The opinion of Mitchell, that "doctrinal knowledge and outward blamelessness were not sufficient for such admission, but that practical confessions, or some relation of the work of conversion, were necessary," President Mather applauds, maintaining, that "to admit persons to partake of the Lord's Supper, without any examination of the work of grace in the heart, would be a real apostasy and degeneracy from the churches of New England." Taking advantage of the fact, that Mitchell had been once "a tutor" in the College, he urges upon "the tutors" the example of Mitchell, and, "praying that they may have wisdom to follow it," warns them not to become "degenerate plants, or prove themselves apostate." *

The time, manner, and language of this publication could not but have been deeply offensive to the Brattles, Leverett, and Pemberton. Under the mask of advice, it was a reproof given to them before the students of the College and the world, with an evident design, in connexion with their known opinions, to load them with the reproach of degeneracy and apostasy. An address thus personal and magisterial naturally strengthened their determination to countenance, or to unite with, that sect of the Congregational church, who were preparing to vindicate their right to construe the Scriptures for themselves, and no longer to subscribe to the infallibility of the authors of the Cambridge Platform. Accordingly, that very year, Thomas Brattle took the lead in forming an association of enlightened and pious Christians in Boston, for the purpose of establishing there a new Congregational church, constituted on principles deviating from the Platform, and expressly rejecting "the imposition of any public relation of experi-

* Magnalia, Book IV. ch. 4.

ences," or any other examination, than by the pastor, as the condition of admission to the Lord's Supper. This society, in January, 1698, purchased of Thomas Brattle a lot of land, in Boston, called "Brattle's close"; and there laid the foundation of that church, which is now known by the name of the "Church in Brattle Square." *

Foundation of Brattle Street church, 1698.

Soon afterward the Rev. Benjamin Colman was elected their pastor. He was at that time preaching in England under the authority of the London Presbytery; having been absent from America more than four years. Colman accepted the invitation; and, at the suggestion of the associates, he obtained an ordination in London from the Presbytery of that city; his friends anticipating the difficulty of procuring the ceremony to be performed in Boston, in consequence of the prevailing prejudices against the new church among the clergy of Massachusetts.

The records of the church sufficiently indicate the interest taken in its establishment by the members of the Corporation and the College, who have been already named. Mr. Colman, by whom the early records were written, thus states in them the motives, which induced him to accept the election of the associates.

"This invitation was accepted by me, and the more acceptable it was, by reason of the kind and encouraging letters, which accompanied it from my excellent friends, the Hon. John Leverett, the Rev. William Brattle, Ebenezer Pemberton, Simon Bradstreet, and others."

* See Records of Brattle Street Church. Also a Sermon preached to the Church in Brattle Square, July 18th, 1824, by the Rev. John G. Palfrey; and the Notes annexed.

CHAPTER VII.

Encouraged by Leverett and Brattle.

The connexion of Leverett with the new church, and the open encouragement he gave it, are expressed in his letter to Colman, and are illustrative of the events of the time, and of the subsequent religious character of the College, in forming which he was destined to have a decisive influence.*

The church in Brattle Square was the first-fruit of that religious liberty, which the charter of William and Mary introduced into Massachusetts. The associates were, generally, men of known character and weight in the Province; and they reckoned in their number, and among their friends, individuals distinguished for learning, private worth, exemplary piety, and official station. These symptoms of revolt from the rigor of the religious dogmas, which had been transmitted in the systems established by the first emigrants to Massachusetts, were too powerful and well sustained, not to excite apprehensions of approaching innovations among all the stern adherents to its ancient ecclesiastical constitution.

As in theological, not less than in other controversies, men are apt to mistake the impulse of their passions, or their interests, for the dictates of conscience, the opponents of the new church conducted their attack, in the first instance, neither with temper nor policy. The character of this opposition is probably attributable chiefly to the Mathers, to whom controversy was not so much an incident, as an element of their natures. The chief friends and founders of the new church, also, stood toward both of them in relations, which tended to make their opposition assume a personal as well as theological character. The in-

* See Appendix, No. XVIII.

terests and future hopes of both were connected with the event of the present controversy.

Opposed by Increase and Cotton Mather.

Increase Mather, as the head of the clergy of the Colony, regarded himself and was regarded by others as the natural defender of its early ecclesiastical constitution. He had put his popularity with the prevailing sect to a severe trial in the part he had taken relative to the new Colonial charter; and he had no other way to reëstablish himself in their confidence, than by an unwavering maintenance of the fundamental doctrines of that constitution. All his hopes of future influence, of being permitted to continue head of the College and yet non-resident, of success in his earnest desire of another agency in Great Britain, rested on the same foundation.

His temper was excited, and his pride wounded, at finding the leaders in these innovations were his own pupils, members of the Corporation of which he was the head, who were indebted to him for their station in the College, and, as he probably imagined, for their influence in society. Such feelings and opinions are clearly discernible in his controversial writings at this period. After perceiving that the solemn reproof, which, in his Epistle Dedicatory to the Life of Mitchell, under the form of admonition, he administered to the contumacious "youths," had the effect to excite and stimulate, rather than to reform them, he seems to have lost all patience and self-possession.

Mr. Colman arrived in Boston on the 1st of November, 1699, and, on the 17th of the same month the new church issued a "manifesto or declaration of their aims, designs, principles, and rules, to prevent apprehensions and jealousies." This publication gave to that Society the name of "the Manifesto Church," by way of opprobrium; a designation by which it was distinguished during the succeeding half century.

The opportunity, which this exposition of principles opened for a theological combat, was too tempting for the Mathers. Both prepared to enter the lists against so dangerous an "apostasy."

The account, which Cotton Mather gives of his feelings and proceedings on the occasion, is curious and characteristic. He calls the leaders of that church "headstrong men," "full of malignity towards the holy ways of the churches," who had published a manifesto "utterly subverting them and tending to throw all into confusion." "The ministers," he adds, "who are faithful to the Lord Jesus, are driven to a necessity of appearing in defence of the churches; no little part of which falls unavoidably to my share; I have already written a large monitory letter, lovingly penned, which yet enrages their lusts to carry on the apostasy." *

Lieutenant-Governor Stoughton interferes.

The Mathers, however, began soon to be aware, that some of the pillars of the early churches of the Province were not prepared to give support to their violent and fulminatory measures. The politicians, who, in all governments, in which there is an intertexture of church and state, are always careful to guide practically the divines, readily anticipated, that persecution would strengthen rather than weaken the foundations of the new church. Lieutenant-Governor Stoughton and Chief Justice Sewall accordingly united with Willard, Clark, and Danforth, all clergymen of distinction, to still the waves of theo-

* See Appendix, No. X.

logical controversy; and their labors were so efficient, that both the Mathers were compelled to smother their resentments, and to take part in the religious services at the dedication of the new church. President Mather even preached on the occasion, from Heb. xii. 14, "Follow peace with all men, and holiness;" and thence deduced the doctrine, that peace must be followed "*so far as consists with holiness*," a reservation which opened ample scope and apology for the future attacks he meditated on the new society.

Reconciliation of the Mathers and Colman.

The account given by Cotton Mather in his Diary, of the manner and agents by which this reconciliation was effected, is singularly illustrative of his disposition to wrest every occurrence into a subject of eulogy on himself or his father.

Cotton Mather's account of that reconciliation.

In this document he states without reserve, that "the attempt to bring the people of the new church to reason," originated with him; that he "drew up the conciliatory proposal"; that he, with another minister, carried it to them; that they embraced it, and that the result filled "all hearts with joy, and caused much relenting in some of their spirits, when they saw our condescension, our charity, our compassion." "Overlooking all offences," he adds, "we kept the public fast with them. My father preached, and I concluded with prayer." *

Contemporaneous documents, however, compel the belief, that the glory of effecting the reconciliation, thus obtrusively claimed by Cotton Mather, was wholly without foundation; that he neither drew up the paper, nor had any material efficiency in producing it. In this, as in many instances in his voluminous writings,

* See Appendix, No. X.

the conviction is forced upon the mind, that he was not quite so scrupulous as might be wished, in his relation of facts, particularly in cases where his own or his father's reputation was likely to be affected.

The records of the church in Brattle Square still exist, in the handwriting of its pastor, the Rev. Mr. Colman, who thus notices the difficulties which the church had to encounter, and those who had been the chief authors of its relief.

"I omit, on purpose, the differences and troubles we had with any neighbours about our proceedings. I only am obliged to leave this acknowledgment of our great obligations to the Hon. William Stoughton, Esquire, Lieutenant-Governor of the Province, the Rev. Mr. William Brattle, of Cambridge, the Rev. Mr. Clark, of Chelmsford, and Mr. Danforth of Dorchester, for their good and kind endeavours for our peaceable settlement."

Now, if the exertions of the Mathers for this reconciliation, had been so exceedingly conspicuous and the occasion of such "wonderful joy and relentings," as Cotton Mather's Diary asserts, Colman, in his recapitulation of the authors of such a blessing to his church, obviously flowing from the fulness of a grateful heart, would certainly not have omitted to name the Mathers.

Sewall's account of the reconciliation.

There exists evidence, however, on this point, more direct and conclusive. Judge Sewall, who had no motive to induce unfairness or interpolation, also kept a Diary, to which we have already had frequent occasion to refer, and in it he enumerates the agents chiefly instrumental in effecting the reconciliation.* Sewall's

* See Appendix, No. XI.

Diary is precisely what such a record ought to be, a simple account of events, without any laudatory illustration, or specious supposition of motives. His statement is apparently irreconcilable with that of Cotton Mather.

From Sewall's Journal it appears, that this reconciliation, instead of being effected by "a proposal drawn up" by *Cotton Mather on the 21st of January*, and originating with him, as his Diary asserts, was, in truth, effected by "a paper drawn up by William Brattle on the 24th of January"; that, so far from writing the paper, it does not appear that Cotton Mather was even present, or consulted, when it was prepared; that Lieutenant-Governor Stoughton was the prime mover and leading agent in the affair, as Colman states in his Records; and that, when the Mathers were called to the conference, on the 25th of January, "there was some heat," but that afterwards an agreement took place. In whom this heat appeared Sewall does not state. From the temperature of the theological zeal of the Mathers, which was always at the boiling point, there can be little doubt to whom the "heat" is to be attributed. The account given by Sewall is natural; such as might rationally be expected in such a state of things. The account by Cotton Mather, considering the vehemence of his passions, and his and his father's violent animosity to the new church and its founders, which circumstances soon after developed, is altogether out of nature and incredible.

The immediate consequence of this reconciliation of the church in Brattle Square with the other churches of the Province is stated in the Records of the former,

CHAPTER VII.

and particularly in a very full and satisfactory manner, in Sewall's Diary. *

It might reasonably have been expected, after a reconciliation so happily effected, which, if Cotton Mather's Diary were to be credited, he had laboriously sought, and in which he heartily rejoiced, that both he and his father would have been willing to permit the churches to remain at peace. At least, that, after such pathetic prayers for Colman and his flock, they would have waited for some experience of the ill consequences of their "apostasy," before they stirred the embers of contention, which such pains had been taken to quench. They were, however, of a different opinion. They had prepared "an antidote against the infection of the churches, by the example of the new church." "They had actually put it to the press." "This they had stopped, in order to bring this people to reason." This having been done, and the reconciliation attained, both probably persuaded themselves, that it was a great pity, "an antidote" thus laboriously composed, and "so lovingly penned," † should be lost to the world, particularly, as it is not unlikely they had persuaded themselves, according to the doctrine of President Mather's sermon, that, "to follow peace with these men was not consistent with holiness." ‡

President Mather renews the controversy.

Accordingly, on the 1st of March, 1700, President Mather commenced an attack upon the new church, its friends, and founders, in a general treatise, entitled "The Order of the Gospel professed by the Churches of Christ in New England Justified," &c. The style of this publication is sufficiently indicative of a spirit

* See Appendix, No. XI.

† See Appendix, No. X.

‡ See above, p. 135.

willing no peace, except through victory and submission. In the progress of the controversy, which this work induced, President Mather was led to the exhibition of great violence and personality; partly through the excitement of his own feelings; partly through sympathy with the characteristic support given to him by his son, in a pamphlet abounding in reckless, virulent invective.

President Mather's "Order of the Gospel."

"The Order of the Gospel" was a battery erected, apparently, against the new church in Brattle Square and its founders. It was, however, so placed and played, as to bring the College, its tutors, and the innovating members of the Corporation, within the range of its missiles. This position and action, alone, connect that treatise, and the controversy it produced, with the history of this seminary. In his Epistle Dedicatory to the work, the President takes care to lament "the decay of the power of religion throughout all New England," and to intimate, as one of the causes, "universal toleration and the corruption of the schools." "In these," he says, "declension has not gone so far but that it may be stopped," and he calls upon the churches, therefore, "to pray for the College," "particularly that God may ever bless that society with faithful tutors, that will be true to Christ's interests and theirs, and not hanker after new and loose ways."

Facts, notorious at the time, and apparent in the records of the period, gave a certain personal direction and sharpness to these shafts, which, at first view, appear to be thrown into the air, without special aim, and solely for general effect. That they were felt, and their intended direction perceived, is sufficiently apparent from the answer, which, in the course of the same

CHAPTER VII.

"Gospel Order Revived."

year (1700) appeared to President Mather's "Order of the Gospel," under the title of "Gospel Order Revived"; and published by "sundry ministers of the Gospel in New England." The authors of this reply turn upon the President the same weapons of personality and insinuation, masked in like manner under generality of remark. They indicate very plainly the opinions of the time in relation to his public course and writings, and an intention to make him feel, if they could not make him desist.

"They will not guess the reverend author's secret aim, or whom, in particular, he raises his batteries against." "They charitably hope he has no private interest to bribe him in this affair." "It is well known how liberal some men are of the odious brand of apostates, for every one who cannot digest the late published 'Orders.'" They repel, as "a groundless calumny, his suggestion, that the latitude they contend for is a betraying of the liberties and privileges which the Lord Jesus Christ has given to his church;" and intimate very distinctly, that, "through the power of interest, faction, passion, and personal opposition, he had become so blinded, on a sudden, as to fight with truths, which he had learned and reverenced from his infancy." *

President Mather, in his "Order of the Gospel," having aimed one piece of masked artillery at the pastor of the new church, who had been ordained in London, † by saying, "that pastor and flock are relates, and therefore one cannot be without the other," and "that to say a wandering Levite, who has no

* Gospel Order Revived, printed in 1700, page 16.

† Page 101.

flock, is a pastor, is as good sense, as to say, that he that has no children is a father, and that the man who has no wife is a husband;" the authors of the "Order of the Gospel Revived" turn the battery with dexterity upon the President himself, by showing that he was of opinion, and had justified by his own writings and practice, "that, though there be a relation to a particular flock, yet a minister is so authorized by Jesus Christ, that he is capable, in his name, to perform ministerial acts in other places and upon all occasions;" adding, "and were not the President sincerely of this opinion, we cannot but think he would highly condemn any minister that should be absent from his flock four years together, upon any service whatsoever. Sure, if he be no way capable to act as a minister of Jesus Christ, he is all that while a stray bird, idly wandering from his nest."

Indignation of the Mathers.

This answer of the ministers excited both the Mathers to such a height of indignation, that they seem to have lost all sense of prudence and character. A pamphlet immediately appeared (1701), entitled "A Collection of some of the many offensive Matters contained in a Pamphlet, entitled 'The Order of the Gospel Revived';" not indeed having the name of Cotton Mather, but universally attributed to him, never denied, and bearing unquestionable marks of the style and temper, which characterize his controversial writings. To leave no question, however, concerning its author, it came attended with an address "to the reader," under the sign-manual of Increase Mather himself, dated December 31st, 1700.

In this pamphlet no term of vituperation, expressive of anger and contempt, seems omitted. The work of these "ministers" is characterized as "a volume

CHAPTER VII.

of invectives against the 'Order of the Gospel,'" and its author "highly scandalous and scurrilous"; as violating the third commandment by "profane scoffs, and flouts, and jeers, at the churches of the Lord, and some of their very solemn and sacred services;" as tending by its example "to bring in profaneness and atheism;" calling them "bold youths, who violate the fifth commandment, without the least spark of shame in them, to cry shame of their rude and vile threats given by them unto the aged President of the College," and reiterating charges of "impudence," "rudeness," "gross falsehoods," "injustice," "craft," "malicious flings," "deep apostasy," and "profane scurrility." This tirade of opprobrious epithets, unsurpassed for its violence and bitterness, is concentrated in a pamphlet of only sixteen pages.

President Mather, by prefixing to this pamphlet an Epistle to the Reader, not only adopts it as his own, by introducing it with words of approbation, but follows out the vituperative spirit of his son with like asperities.

The obnoxious pamphlet, he says, instead of being called "The Order of the Gospel Revived," might more properly be denominated "The Order of the Gospel Reviled"; and, instead of having been published by "sundry ministers of the Gospel," was done, some say, "by sundry underminers of the Gospel." Taking it for granted, contrary to fact, that Mr. Colman was its author, he speaks of him as "a little thing," "not worth while to notice," as "a youth, who had not feared to mock his fathers," using "rude, unmannerly, and unmanly expressions," "a scandalous scoffer," "a raw, unstudied youth, of a very unsanctified temper and spirit; his arguments nothing but scoffs and foolish jeers, without so much as one solid reason throughout his whole discourse." In the whole scope of theological and political controversy, there is scarcely an example extant, of more select, concentrated, and unmixed personal abuse, than is exhibited in this pamphlet and its preface.

It is melancholy, as well as humiliating, to trace such evidences of an ill-governed and overbearing spirit, especially in one, who, on many accounts, is worthy of esteem and approbation; but the truth of history requires, that such unquestionable characteristics of mind and manners, as this controversy presents, should not be passed over in silence. The vices, weaknesses, and passions, of those men, whose character and conduct, through the circumstances of particular times, and their connexion with them, have shaped the destinies of a city, state, or party, when apparent on the records of the period, belong to its history, and are inseparable from any just developement of it. Their nature constitutes an essential element of the judgment of after times, not only on former events, but also on the proportion of merit, or demerit, in the men who have influenced those events. The criminations and reproaches of rival interests and parties should be received at their worth, after exact analysis, and not according to their currency when first issued; but those features of character, which the writings of active men themselves display, are, of all documents explaining their minds and motives, the most unquestionable and satisfactory; and also of the minds and motives of those, whom such men have led or influenced.

It is impossible not to realize what an effect a publication of this temper must have had on the reputation

CHAPTER VII.

Effects of their language and conduct on their influence.

and influence of both the Mathers. Its connexion with the events already related cannot be mistaken. It was written in December, 1700, and issued to the world at the commencement of the year ensuing; at the very time when the legislature of the Province were insisting, and President Mather at first reluctantly yielding, and immediately after absolutely refusing, to take up his residence at Cambridge. It cannot be doubted, that such a display of mind and passions must have greatly weakened his influence in that body, disgusting some and provoking others. The part he took in this controversy is one of the causes which enable us satisfactorily to account for the obvious determination, evinced by a great and ultimately a successful party in the legislature, no longer to permit the continuance of the relation he had so long held to the College, or to gratify him in his earnest desire after another agency in Great Britain. His enemies, probably, were well aware of the fact, which his son so distinctly asserts, that "President Mather would not remove his habitation from Boston;" and availed themselves of this knowledge, to insist upon his removal, and negative his nomination on that account, and thus put an end to a presidency, from which they could reasonably anticipate nothing but violent personal quarrels and religious controversies.

CHAPTER VIII.

The Rev. Samuel Willard accepts the Vice-Presidency of the College. — His Character and that of Increase Mather compared. — Motives for Willard's Appointment. — Governor Dudley's Arrival. — His Message concerning the College. — Willard's Differences with Mather. — The Brattles reinstated in the Corporation. — The Mathers court Dudley. — Final Attempt to obtain a Charter from the Crown. — Its Failure. — Death of Vice-President Willard. — Election of John Leverett. — Conduct of a Part of the Clergy on the Occasion. — Act of the House of Representatives, reviving the ancient Charter of the College, approved by Dudley. — Responsibility of the Act. — Its happy Consequences.

CHAPTER VIII.

Vice-presidency of Samuel Willard.

THE exclusion of Increase Mather from the presidency, and the appointment of the Rev. Samuel Willard to the superintendence of the College, occurred on the same day; and were the result of the votes which passed in the legislature on the 6th of September, 1701. Mr. Willard held the station of Vice-President more than six years, and until his death. His duties were not less arduous than those of his predecessors, and his fulfilment of them was equally punctual, laborious, and successful. Under the influence of that modesty, which was a predominant feature of his character, he was content with this comparatively inferior title. Our historians have found it difficult to account satisfactorily for this anomaly in the title of the executive of the College.

Peirce, with his characteristic sagacity, intimates, that it might have been an "evasion."* Such it un-

* See Peirce's Hist. Harv. Univ., pp. 73, 78.

CHAPTER VIII.

questionably was; and resulted from the position in which the legislature found themselves placed, between the vote they had passed, that "the President should reside at Cambridge," and the determination of a majority to rid themselves of President Mather. That vote they were not willing to rescind in favor of Willard, after having for a series of years pertinaciously insisted upon it in relation to Mather. But, Willard being as unwilling as Mather to accept the office on condition of residence, and as they could not agree on a third person, they resorted to the subterfuge of continuing Willard in the office he then held of Vice-President, and vesting him with the power and duties of President. Thus, without rescinding their former vote, or any apparent inconsistency, they permitted Willard, during his life, to occupy at the same time the office of superintendent of the College and that of pastor of a church in Boston; and to perform the duties of President under the title of Vice-President, by occasional visits, without actual residence at Cambridge. These were precisely the relations Mather was desirous, and had offered, to sustain; * and, on account, apparently, of their incompatibility, he had been excluded from office.

Many circumstances united to render Willard, in the state of the religious and political parties of the time, far more generally acceptable than Mather. Both possessed the confidence of the prevailing Calvinistic sect; for they were equally learned and sound in the articles of faith by that sect deemed fundamental. But their writings and demeanor exhibited a remarkable contrast. Willard was quiet, retiring,

* See above, p. 113.

phlegmatic, and unpretending; Mather, restless, obtrusive, excitable, boastful of his public services, and complaining of neglect and ingratitude.*

The life of the former had been devoted to professional research and pastoral duties. His study was the scene of his private labors; his church the theatre of his public action. These had constituted a sphere of usefulness, to which his ambition had been limited; which he did not quit until after repeated legislative applications, for one higher and wider, and then with reluctance.

The life of the latter, on the contrary, had been one series of theological and political controversy. He was a partisan by profession; always harnessed, and ready, and restless for the onset; now courting the statesmen; now mingling with the multitude; exciting the clergy in the synod, and the congregation in the pulpit, and the people in the halls of popular assembly.

Amid the agitations consequent on that insanity of the age, denominated "the Salem witchcraft," the conduct of Willard was marked by prudence, firmness, and courage. He neither yielded to the current, nor feared to cast the weight of his opinion publicly in opposition to the prevailing delusion;† an independence the more remarkable and honorable, as Stoughton and Sewall, two of the Judges of the Court of trial, men of great influence in the Province, both his personal friends, and the latter a principal member of his

* See his "Address to the Reader," on his publication of two sermons in 1702, entitled "The Righteous Man a Blessing."

"This is the last sermon I will preach at the lecture in Boston; the ill treatment I have received from those, from whom I had reason to expect better, have discouraged me from being any more concerned in such vocation."

† See Mass. Hist. Coll., First Series, Vol. V. p. 76.

church, were deeply infected by the distemper of the times. His tongue and his pen were, notwithstanding, employed to bring back peace and reason to his country.* Increase Mather, on the contrary, although he had coöperated in that excitement with far less zeal than his son Cotton, and his course had been more prudent, yet shared, in the event, a full proportion of that odium, which attached ultimately to all the clergy and politicians, who had countenanced the infatuation.

After it had subsided, the circumspection and boldness of Willard, in that trying season, was remembered and honored, and he derived thence a weight of popularity, which President Mather had lost by his conduct during the excitement. The resulting general impressions concerning the character of each were, undoubtedly, among the causes of that preference, which the exclusion of Mather and the appointment of Willard by the legislature indicate.

Family connexion between Dudley and Willard.

The family connexion, which subsisted between Mr. Willard and Joseph Dudley, who became, the very next year, by royal appointment, Governor of the Province, might also have had some effect, in fixing attention thus strongly on Mr. Willard. They had married sisters, the daughters of Edward Tyng,† one of the earliest, wealthiest, and most influential families in the Colony. The appointment of Dudley was anticipated; and the friends of the College could

* His course was so bold and unhesitating, that he became exposed to the malignity of the "afflicted," and was actually "cried out upon" by one of them, at a period of the excitement, when "to be cried out upon by the afflicted" was regarded as sufficient evidence to justify imprisonment for witchcraft, if not conviction of it. See Hutch. Hist. Vol. II. ch. 1. p. 56.

† Mass. Hist. Soc. Coll., First Series, Vol. X. p. 181.

CHAPTER VIII.

not deem it indifferent to its interest with the new Governor, whether he should find the President's chair filled by Mather, an active leader of that political and religious party, which had imprisoned him and Andros, with whom his name and character had been an unvaried theme of abuse, or by Willard, a brother-in-law, who enjoyed at once his private confidence and personal respect.

Governor Dudley's message concerning the College. 1703.

Accordingly, Dudley, on his arrival, took an early opportunity to bring the affairs of the College before the legislature. In his message of the 11th of March, 1703, at the opening of the General Court, he thus introduced the subject.* "Gentlemen, I am often solicited and spoken to, referring to the College at Cambridge. I am sorry for the mistake of this government, at any time, in that affair. If there be any thing that imports me, referring to that affair, when it shall be communicated, I shall very freely do my duty, to lay it before her Majesty." This part of the Governor's message excited some feeling, and, on the 9th of March, a Committee of the House of Representatives † "waited on him with a message, praying him to inform the House of the mistakes committed by the government in the affair of the College, intimated in his Excellency's speech, and to desire to know what he would please to direct in that affair."

"His Excellency acquainted them, that the mistakes he referred to were, a first, second, and third draft of a charter of incorporation for the College, sent to England, and there refused." ‡

The records of the legislature indicate no further general proceedings in it, concerning the College,

* See Records of the General Court. † Ibid. ‡ Ibid.

CHAPTER VIII.

during this and the two ensuing years. But existing contemporaneous documents sufficiently evidence, that, in these years, the influences controlling it were undergoing changes, and that the government of it still continued to be an object of the ambition of both the Mathers.

As early as 1697, Willard and Increase Mather had adopted different, probably irreconcilable, views relative to the individuals, who ought to be introduced into the Corporation. The attempt made in that year to exclude Leverett from the board has been already stated. *

It appears, by Sewall's Journal, that in November, 1697, there was "a falling out" between President Mather and Mr. Willard, relative to the choosing of fellows. † This fact, with others of a general character, sufficiently show, that the views of Willard, in respect to the auspices under which the College was to be placed, were not consentaneous with those of the Mathers; and now, when the influence of his brother-in-law was paramount, Thomas Brattle and William Brattle were reinstated Fellows of the Corporation, both of whom had been excluded during the ascendency of President Mather. At the same time Josiah Willard, son of the Vice-President, was chosen a tutor. The records of the Corporation do not indicate under what circumstances, or to fill what vacancies, the Brattles were elected.

The Brattles reinstated in the Corporation. August 10, 1703.

The Diary of Judge Sewall thus supplies the deficiency. "1703. August 10th. This day is a Corporation meeting at Cambridge. Choose Mr. Thomas and Mr. William Brattle into the Corpora-

* See above, p. 87.

† See Appendix, No. XI.

tion, instead of Mr. Allen and Mr. Walter, who have abdicated, as they reckon."

By comparing the names of the seventeen members of the Corporation, chosen by virtue of the act which passed 9th of July, 1700,* with those, who, as the records show, attended its meetings during the Vice-Presidency of Willard, it is apparent, that Mr. Walter and Cotton Mather were the two, who were thus construed to have "abdicated." Neither of them attended any meeting of the Corporation after the exclusion of President Mather. But the name of Allen appears occasionally among those present at the board, quite down to the change introduced by the revival of the first charter of the College, at the time of the accession of Leverett to the presidency.

The election of the Brattles was inauspicious to the projects of the Mathers, whether they were introduced by way of filling vacancies, or increasing the number. The admission of the son of Willard to an office in the College, indicates, that the proceedings harmonized with the wishes of the Vice-President.

Influence of Governor Dudley.

Of all the statesmen, who have been instrumental in promoting the interests of Harvard College, Joseph Dudley was most influential in giving its constitution a permanent character. The Mathers, who never ceased to entertain ulterior views, in relation to the College, paid early and distinguished obeisance to this rising sun. Increase Mather, in a sermon preached on the day of general election, in 1702, at which Dudley was expected to be present, placed in high relief the topics on which the clergy

* See above, page 107.

of Massachusetts, and especially those in the superintendence of the College, were divided; "the Order of the Gospel," and "the Platform of the Churches," warning and exhorting, that such measures might be adopted, as that "the generations which were to come should not deviate from the holy ways in which their fathers had walked." As Governor Dudley was not present on the occasion, the President availed himself of the circumstance, to prefix to that sermon an "Epistle Dedicatory" to the Governor. In this he extols the father of Governor Dudley as "a principal founder and pillar of the Colony of Massachusetts, and as a nursing-father of the churches," and lauds the Governor himself as "blessed with rare accomplishments, natural and acquired," assures him of "the greatness of his soul," and that he "is, beyond all others, advantaged to serve and honor Christ, by promoting the welfare of his churches."

The Mathers laud Dudley.

Dudley reciprocates.

Dudley, who well knew the activity and influence of President Mather, reciprocated his civilities in language equally flattering; taking occasion to say, so that it came to the knowledge of President Mather, that, "if he ever had a spiritual father, Mather was the man." * Cotton Mather, not less ambitious than his father, had been even more prescient of the coming of this new political influence. While Dudley was yet in Europe, he became so assured of his success, as to write a letter in favor of Dudley's pretensions, which Dudley read to the King, and was said to have been not without effect on his appointment. †

It appears also, by Cotton Mather's Diary, that he

* See Mass. Hist. Coll., First Series, Vol. III. p. 127.

† Ibid. p. 128. Also Hutch. Hist. Mass. Vol. II. chap. 1. p. 115.

CHAPTER VIII.

was visited by Dudley immediately on his arrival as Governor. During this interview, Mather took occasion to warn Dudley against Byfield and Leverett, as those he deemed leaders in opposition to the "order of the Gospel," and "the true construction of the Cambridge Platform." Dudley was too old a politician not to discern Cotton Mather's motives, and, being inclined to the party opposed to the Mathers, did not fail to inform both Byfield and Leverett of this warning. This drew from Cotton Mather, in his Diary, the following characteristic comment. "The WRETCH went unto those men and told them, that I had advised him to be no ways advised by them, and inflamed them into an implacable rage against me."*

Notwithstanding this cause of discontent, Cotton Mather maintained a friendly intercourse with the Governor during the vice-presidency of Willard; and circumstances indicate, that neither he nor his father, during the whole period, ceased to flatter themselves with the belief, that Dudley's weight would finally be thrown into their scale.

No further movement took place in the legislature of the Province relative to the College until the year 1705, when the records of the Council contain the following statement. "2d January, 1705. His Excellency intimated to the Council, that, by letters from England, there was encouragement to hope, that a charter of incorporation might be obtained from her Majesty for Harvard College, in Cambridge, if proper application was made; and the draft, proposed in his late Majesty's reign, was ordered to be laid on the table to be read."

Dudley's message concerning the College. 1705.

* Mass. Hist. Coll., First Series, Vol. III. p. 137.

CHAPTER VIII.

No measures, however, were taken in either branch in consequence of these suggestions of Governor Dudley; and this was the last attempt ever made to obtain a charter for the College from the crown.

The circumstances of the period render it probable, that the politicians and divines of that day perceived, with certainty, that no charter could be obtained from the English sovereign, which would be acceptable to either of those ecclesiastical parties, which were then striving for ascendency in Massachusetts. Both, however differing with each other, concurred in being alike jealous of the increasing power of the Episcopal Church; which, being considered inimical as well to the civil as to the ecclesiastical liberties of Massachusetts, became equally the object of religious prejudice and of popular dislike. The root, which the Episcopal Church was now beginning to strike in the land, under the direct patronage of the English hierarchy, became a common object of fear with every class of Congregationalists. All perceived the hope to be vain, that the English monarch would permit the chief seminary of learning in the Province to obtain a charter, unless it received an ominous infusion of Episcopalian influences.

State of parties, and its consequences.

Every antecedent application for a charter had been made at the suggestion of President Mather, and was coupled with a project, avowed or understood, that he should have the negotiation of it at the British court. This, and probably this alone, rendered such an application safe, in the opinion of the stern adherents of the early New England Congregational church; since upon him they could rely, not only for resisting any attempt favoring Episcopacy, but also for securing to themselves that predominancy, which they claimed, and which was in danger of passing out of their hands, in consequence of the schisms beginning to arise among Congregationalists.

The conflict of interests and passions, which this state of things induced, made all parties unwilling to coöperate in the suggestions of Governor Dudley. It is possible, also, that a want of confidence in the sincerity of Dudley himself might have increased their hesitation to make an application for a charter under his auspices. Dudley was a thoroughly educated courtier; and the people of Massachusetts had repeatedly witnessed his willingness to serve the crown in cases contrary to their interests, or counteracting their prejudices. They had reason to anticipate, that any condition the monarch might choose to insert, however opposed to their religious views, would receive the support of a courtier equally shrewd and fearless; skilful, under every aspect of the political sky, to shape his course by his interests.

Whatever were the motives, it is certain, that Dudley's intimation received no countenance from any party, religious or political. The friends of the College now became convinced, that its satisfactory settlement, in respect to a charter, could only be effected through the instrumentality of the Provincial legislature. Of this policy, Dudley, if he was not the author, as is probable, was certainly the supporter. He gave it his countenance, possibly because that division of the Congregationalists which he favored, predominated in the Corporation, and was the least obnoxious to the Episcopal church, which he cherished, and whose worship he attended. Measures having this tendency were not developed during the life of Vice-President Willard. His death, which occurred on the 12th of Sep-

CHAPTER VIII.

Death of Vice-President Willard. 1707.

tember, 1707, gave publicity to this new policy; which was adopted and carried into effect with equal boldness and success. On the 28th of October following that event, the Fellows of Harvard College met, and chose John Leverett President. The records of the Corporation simply state, that he was "chosen President of Harvard College." In the address of the ministers, favoring this appointment, to Governor Dudley, it is said, that "he was chosen by a unanimous vote." The Diary of Judge Sewall gives a more natural, and probably an authentic account of the transaction. By his statement it appears, that fourteen members of the Corporation were present. In this he concurs with the records. His Diary proceeds to state, that *eight* votes were given for Leverett, *three* for Increase Mather, *one* for Cotton Mather, and *one* for Mr. Brattle, and that *one* member declined voting.* This, upon the supposition, which the known relations of things render almost certain, that the vote of Leverett (he being himself a member of the Corporation) was thrown for Brattle, gives a fair representation of the comparative power of the religious parties, as they were then represented in that body.

Leverett elected President.

On the 11th of the ensuing November, the election of Leverett was presented officially to Governor Dudley, by the Corporation, recommending the President "to his favorable acceptance, and praying, that he would move the General Assembly for his honorable subsistence." † The recommendation was, as the records of the Court state, "accompanied with addresses from thirty-nine ministers." This was, unquestionably, a wise precautionary measure, in a state of

* See Appendix, No. XI.

† See Appendix, No. XIX.

CHAPTER VIII.

theological controversy then extremely vivid and exciting, and one which the call of a layman to a chair, that had never before been occupied except by a clergyman, rendered not so much expedient as necessary. In this address the signing ministers express their "great joy at the choice of Leverett," "their affection and esteem for him," "their satisfaction and assurance of his religion, learning, and other excellent accomplishments for that eminent service; a long experience of which," they add, "we had while he was the Senior Fellow of that House; for that, under the wise and faithful government of him and the Rev. Mr. Brattle of Cambridge, the greatest part of the now rising ministry in New England were happily educated; and we hope, and promise ourselves, through the blessing of the God of our fathers, to see religion and learning thrive and flourish in that society under Mr. Leverett's wise conduct and influence, as much as ever yet it hath done." *

Address of the ministers in favor of Leverett

These proceedings being communicated by the Governor to the Council on the same day, the election of Mr. Leverett was accepted by them, and the vote sent down to the Representatives for their concurrence.

This branch seem not to have been prepared, however, for the measure; for they immediately non-concurred in the vote of the Council, and, adopting the policy of postponement, on the 29th of November sent up to the Council a message in writing, for "the choice of a suitable person to take care of the College until the session of the Court in May next."

The Council, on the 3d of December, after a con-

* See Appendix, No. XX.

ference with the House, refused to join in the choice of a person to take charge of the College till May.

From the subsequent proceedings of the House of Representatives it is natural to infer, that their non-concurrence in Leverett's election proceeded from a spirit of economy rather than from any objections to him, personal, religious, or political.

In July, 1700, when the friends of President Mather were desirous of removing all his objections to fixing his residence at Cambridge, a resolve had passed, "allowing the sum of two hundred and twenty pounds to the President already chosen, or that shall be chosen, by the Court, he residing at Cambridge." It was perceived, that, if Leverett's election had been confirmed, his right to this salary would have attached; and those disposed to counteract the proceedings of the Corporation availed themselves of this circumstance, first to induce the House to non-concur in the vote of the Council, and next to propose a postponement until the next General Court. After the firmness displayed by the Council in opposition to this proposition, a resolve passed the House, declaring void the resolve of July, 1700; and, as soon as this rescinding vote was known to have received the consent of Governor Dudley, another resolve, founded upon the acceptance and approval of Mr. Leverett as President by the Governor and Council, was passed in Council, proposing, that "the House of Representatives consider of and grant a suitable salary to be paid to the President annually, out of the public treasury, for his encouragement and support during his continuance in the said office, residing at Cambridge, and discharging the proper duties to a President belonging, and entirely devoting himself to that service."

To the above was subjoined the following comprehensive, substantive, and efficient clause, furnishing at once the long-sought charter for the College, and fulfilling the utmost desire of its friends, in a form not requiring the sanction of the crown, and deriving all its efficacy from the authority of the Provincial legislature.

Charter of 1650 revived.

"*And, inasmuch as the first foundation and establishment of that House and the government thereof had its original from an act of the General Court, made and passed in the year one thousand six hundred and fifty, which has not been repealed or nulled;*

"*The President and Fellows of the said College are directed from time to time to regulate themselves according to the rules of the constitution by the act prescribed; and to exercise the powers and authorities thereby granted for the government of that House, and support thereof.*" *

This charter, after having annexed to it a vote of the Representatives, establishing a salary for the President of one hundred and fifty pounds, was enacted on the 6th of December, 1707, by the official consent of Governor Dudley.†

This measure had, probably, its origin in the depths of Dudley's own mind, and is marked with boldness and sagacity, eminently characteristic of him. It is hardly probable that any other person would have ventured to propose a course so full of responsibility, and so apparently irreconcilable with the duties growing out of the relation in which he stood to the British sovereign. It was, in fact, a measure in contradiction of the avowed principles, which the government of the parent state had adopted and acted upon in relation to Massachusetts.

† See Appendix, No. LXVIII.

CHAPTER VIII.

Those principles were, that the first colonial charter was only a private act of incorporation, and gave no right to create other charters; that, by the judgment upon *quo warranto*, in 1684, the first charter of the Colony had been vacated, and that all charters granted under its authority were, on this account also, absolutely void; principles, which Dudley himself had openly asserted, and consequences, which he had publicly maintained.*

The power of granting charters was deemed by the crown one of its most precious prerogatives; and one, the infringement of which was the subject of extreme jealousy. Charters of the College, also, had been several times subjected to the consideration of the King or of his royal Governors, and had been rejected avowedly on the ground, that they did not vest the visitatorial power exclusively in the King, or in his colonial Governor.

In defiance of all these recognised principles, all these evidences of royal interests and royal claims, Dudley had the boldness to consent to revive the College charter of 1650; and thus established a charter without, and contrary to, the will of the British sovereign; including a visitatorial power, which the colonial Governors shared with a board appointed by the colonial legislature; the whole effected by the form of a simple legislative resolve, which, in its nature, did not require the sanction of the sovereign, and of course was never submitted to his inspection.

By what means the vigilance of the British statesmen was in this instance deceived, whether Dudley

* Mass. Hist. Coll., First Series, Vol. III. p. 126.

relied on their ignorance of colonial affairs or their indifference to them, or whether he took measures to satisfy the British Court of their expediency in the actual state of things in Massachusetts, does not appear from history. It does appear, however, that he took the great responsibility of the policy, and that those to whom it was obnoxious attributed it to his influence. He deserves, therefore, all the credit of its benefits and its success.

It is also certain, that the measure received the almost universal approbation of the people of Massachusetts; that the act of 1650, thus revived by a legislative resolve, has been ever since recognised as the charter of the College; that, during the continuance of the colonial relation, it received the uniform support of judicial decision and legislative sanction; and that, on the adoption of the State Constitution, in 1780, it was ratified and confirmed. Thus, by virtue of uniform judicial construction, successive legislative sanctions, and ultimate constitutional ratification, the charter of 1650 has been established on a firm and now incontrovertible basis.

CHAPTER IX.

Retrospective View of the Benefactors of the College, during the Seventeenth Century.—John Winthrop.—Sir Richard Saltonstall and his Son.—Robert Keayne.—Edward Hopkins.—Israel Stoughton.—William Stoughton.—Henry Webb.—William Brown.—John Bulkley.—Lady Moulson.—Sir Matthew Holworthy.—Theophilus Gale.—William Pennoyer.—Robert Thorner.—Joseph Glover.—College Printing Press.—Course of Studies and literary State of the College during this Century.

CHAPTER IX.

THE restoration of the early charter of Harvard College, under the auspices of Dudley, forms an era in its history. The almost universal acquiescence in the policy of the measure terminated all attempts to seek a more formal establishment from the crown. The College was thus placed in new relations, and those more literary and less exclusively theological. Gratitude demands, that we should here stay our narrative, and pay a passing tribute to those generous and public-spirited individuals, who, in times of political convulsion, amid poverty and embarrassment, by the protection and aid they extended, gave a vigor and expansion to the institution, which rendered it, in the coming age, an object of pride and patronage to the people and legislature of Massachusetts.

John Winthrop.

Next to Harvard, John Winthrop, the leader of the Massachusetts Colony, and seven times its elected Governor, deserves grateful commemoration. The loss of property, from the sacrifices he had made in support of the Colony, or from unfaithfulness in those to whom he had intrusted his affairs, deprived him, indeed, of the means of great pecuniary benefactions; but his donation of books was large and valuable. In that early day, forty volumes made an important addition to the library of the institution. A list of these is yet preserved in its archives. His name and influence were always given in its support. There is probably no one, to whose patronage the College was more indebted, during the period of its infancy, and consequent weakness and dependence. His virtues and public services have been too frequently the subject of history and eulogy, to need in this work any illustration.

Sir Richard Saltonstall.

Second only to Harvard and Winthrop, in order of time, amount of benefactions, and value of services, stands Sir Richard Saltonstall;* that "excellent knight," as he is called by Mather, that "much honored and upright-hearted servant of Christ," as he is denominated by Johnson.† He came over in 1630 with Winthrop. But soon, "wearied of this wilderness work," he returned to England; and, during a life protracted beyond the middle of the seventeenth century, continued the faithful, active, devoted friend of the Colony and the College. He defended both against the assaults and aspersions of their respective enemies, and, on all occasions, vindicated their character and interests. He was not, however, blind to the failings, nor insensible to the inconsistencies, of the ecclesiastical leaders of the Colony. His kind and catholic spirit was touched with sorrow at the persecutions they were carrying on against liberty of con-

* See Mass. Hist. Coll., Second Series, Vol. IV. p. 155.

† Ibid., Vol. III. p. 147.

science. Nor could the interest, which he took in the honor and welfare of New England, be, in any way, more strikingly manifested, than it is in that deep and solemn tone of remonstrance, in which he addresses John Cotton and John Wilson, the most powerful of all those ecclesiastical leaders, on the "tyranny and persecutions of New England."* "We pray for you," says he, "that the Lord will give you light and love." "These rigid ways are laying you very low in the hearts of the saints." "By compelling any in matters of worship, you make many hypocrites." "Do not assume to yourselves infallibility of judgment, when the most learned of the apostles confesseth he knew but in part, and saw but darkly as through a glass." During life he had contributed by his purse and influence to the foundation and advancement of the seminary. At his death he made a liberal bequest for its support.

Richard Saltonstall.

His son, of the same name, a kindred spirit, and of like moral worth, imbibed his father's attachment to the College, and displayed equal zeal and self-devotion in advancing its interests. This country being the place of his principal abode, he had opportunities of rendering frequent useful services, of which he never failed to avail himself. It appears, by the records of the College, that, of two hundred and fifty pounds sterling, subscribed in 1654 for the repairs of its buildings, by twenty-six individuals, his subscription amounted to *one hundred and four pounds.* Subsequently, being in England, he transmitted *three hundred and twenty pounds* for its benefit. Whether this was a donation of his own, or was his father's

* See Mass. Hist. Coll., Second Series, Vol. IV. p. 171.

legacy, has been made a question. It is a point, however, of little consequence. The deed belongs to the honors of the name of Saltonstall, emblazoned in every period of our history by its public spirit and its private charities.

Richard Saltonstall, not less than his father, was distinguished for fixedness of purpose and independence of opinion, and was as much in advance of his age and country in his views of civil, as was his father in his, of religious liberty. In 1637, he took the side of Winthrop in the struggle against the ascendency of Vane, and, on its success, came into the Board of Assistants, when Winthrop was elected Governor.* Notwithstanding his political predilections were in favor of Winthrop, yet his principles of liberty were so repugnant to the idea of "a standing Council, composed of members elected for life," that he wrote a book expressly against it; denominating the Council "a sinful innovation, which ought to be reformed."† The boldness and spirit which characterized the work displeased Winthrop and the ecclesiastical leaders. Deeming it an attempt to undermine the essential foundations of the government, Governor Winthrop "twice moved, that the matter of that book" should be taken into the solemn consideration of the General Court. Such, however, was the popularity of Saltonstall, and probably so congenial were the principles of the work with the views of the majority, and so satisfied were they of "the honest intentions of the writer, and that his design was in favor of popular liberty," that the Court would not even inquire into

* Savage's Winthrop, Vol. I. p. 220.

† Mass. Hist. Coll., Second Series, Vol. VI. p. 385; Vol. III. p. 147.

the subject, until they had first "voted an indemnity to the author against any censure." *

In the succeeding age we shall have occasion to dilate on the worth and the virtues of Gurdon and Mary and Dorothy Saltonstall, whose noble benefactions continue to diffuse blessings even in our own times. Nor does truth permit us to fail in remembering, that this family, distinguished in every age for intellect, faithfulness, and honor, as well as for intense attachment to Harvard College, is, at this day, especially fortunate, that the heir of their house is also the heir of their affections and virtues. †

Robert Keayne.

Among our earliest benefactors, Robert Keayne is entitled to grateful and special remembrance. He came to New England with Winthrop, and is characterized by him, as a man of "eminent parts," "an ancient professor of the Gospel," "coming over for its advancement and for conscience' sake"; as "wealthy," "given to hospitality," "very useful to the country," and a large contributor to its free "schools." ‡ He was first Captain of the Boston Artillery Company, now distinguished by the appellation of "The Ancient and Honorable"; § for several years a representative of that town in the General Court; being a firm adherent of the colonial government, and possessing its confidence in a high degree. In the civil dissensions in 1637, when the Antinomians were disarmed, his house was appointed to be the place for safe-keeping of the arms, || of which the malcontents had been deprived. Notwithstanding his usefulness and virtues, he became

* Savage's Winthrop, Vol. II. pp. 89, 116.

† See Appendix, No. XXI.

‡ Savage's Winthrop, Vol. I. p. 315. § Ibid. 254. || Ibid. 248.

obnoxious on account of the "corrupt practice" of "selling dearer than most traders." For this offence he was "convented before the incensed deputies," and, after solemn trial, "convicted," fined two hundred pounds, publicly admonished by the church, and hardly did he escape excommunication. These civil and religious persecutions did not subject him to any permanent loss of the confidence of his fellow-citizens. He was subsequently elected four times a Representative of the town of Boston, and once Speaker of the House of Deputies. In his last will he took care to interweave self-vindication with noble donations to public uses; thus compelling the officers of government to put upon the public records his defence against "the hard measures meted to him by the government of the country." This will occupies one hundred and forty-eight folio pages of the Probate Records of the County of Suffolk. After vindicating his character, with a pathos indicative of a keen sense of the injustice to which he had been subjected, and appropriating two hundred pounds sterling, to be paid to any man, who shall make it satisfactorily appear he has been wronged or defrauded by him, he speaks of the government of the country in a Christian and forgiving spirit, "as having failings," yet, on the whole, as being, he believes, "the happiest and wisest, this day, in the world." He then adds, that, "though he has suffered enough from the public to tie up both his hands," yet, "being desirous to requite evil with good, and though he cannot forget, being willing to forgive," and "deeming it a want of gratitude to God, for prosperous men to leave all to wife, children, or relatives, and nothing to the public, or to charity," and declaring his estate to be four thousand pounds sterling, he proceeds to give

CHAPTER IX.

twelve hundred pounds to objects of public use or private charity; included in which were two hundred and fifty pounds to Harvard College;* adding, with no less point than prudence and wisdom, that none of it should be spent in brick and mortar, or repairs; "for buildings and halls it belongs to the public to find."

Edward Hopkins.

Next in order of time, the noble beneficence of Edward Hopkins stands in bold relief; exceeded by that of none of his contemporaries in original value, Sir Matthew Holworthy and William Stoughton alone excepted; and, at the present day, greatly surpassing those of both, in amount and efficiency. Few, if any of the early emigrants to New England, have left a name surrounded by a purer or more unfading lustre. In the parent State, as well as in the Colony, his talents and virtues received the reward of place, preferment, and authority. After having pursued the mercantile line with success in London, and lived in that city in splendor and the exercise of hospitality until the year 1637, he emigrated to this country;† being then about thirty-eight years of age. His great estate, eminent abilities, and distinguished piety and integrity, made him a welcome visitant, and every inducement was proffered by the legislature of the Colony, the inhabitants of Boston, and the settlements in its vicinity, to induce him to fix his residence in Massachusetts, without success.‡ The fertile soil

* See Suffolk Probate Records, Vol. I. p. 116, etc.

† See Mass. Hist. Coll., Second Series, Vol. V. p. 262; Vol. VI. p. 329; Vol. I. p. 231; Vol. VII. p. 8; First Series, Vol. IV. pp. 15 and 182; Vol. VII. p. 22.

‡ Trumbull's Hist. of Connecticut, chap. VI. and VII. Savage's Winthrop, Vol. I. p. 228; Vol. II. pp. 216, 329.

on the Connecticut had charms for him, which the rock-bound shores of the "Bay State" did not possess. He was desirous of planting a Church and a State, approaching nearer to that model of perfection, which he had conceived in fancy, and to which the first settlers in Massachusetts had not, in his judgment, attained. Led by this desire, Hopkins accompanied John Davenport and Theophilus Eaton, whose views were consonant with his own, to the west. Davenport and Eaton established themselves at New Haven; Hopkins took up his residence at Hartford. There he was immediately appointed a magistrate. He soon after assisted in framing the first constitution of the Colony, and, for several years, alternated with John Haynes in the office of Governor. He was also one of the Commissioners, who formed the articles of confederation of the United Colonies of New England in 1643; the precursor of that confederation, which, nearly a century and a half afterwards, was the instrument of American Independence. He succeeded Winthrop as President of that board, which, for forty years, was the refuge and defence of the fathers of New England, and the medium of all general attempts to extend to the savages of the wilderness the knowledge of the Gospel. In 1652, Hopkins returned to England, where his integrity and talent were soon noticed and called into public service by that keen observer of human nature, Cromwell, who successively appointed him First Warden of the fleet, and Commissioner of the army and of the navy; and afterwards, through the same influence, he obtained a seat in Parliament. His spirit was not only active, but elastic; since it seems neither to have been subdued by a grievous pulmonary affection, which pur-

CHAPTER IX.

sued him during thirty years of his life, and finally brought it to a close; nor yet crushed under the weight of the severest of all domestic afflictions, the irrecoverable derangement of a wife, who, before her bereavement of reason, was distinguished for her virtues, her intelligence, and accomplishments.

His last will is an interesting monument of private friendship and public spirit; and justifies the universal language of his contemporaries, who, in eulogizing his character, never fail to celebrate his possession of those qualities, which make a man beloved. To numerous friends and domestics he bequeathed legacies, amounting to four thousand pounds sterling; to institutions in Connecticut, for the promotion of religion, science, or charity, one thousand pounds sterling. For the advancement of the same noble objects in Massachusetts, the bequest of five hundred pounds, vested in trustees, was destined to find its sphere of usefulness in Harvard College, or its vicinity.* After an unceasing flow of annual benefits for more than a century, his bounty now exists on a foundation of productive and well-secured capital, amounting nearly to thirty thousand dollars.

Thus did this lofty and intellectual spirit devise and distribute blessings in his own age, and, by his wisdom, prepare and make them perpetual for succeeding times.

Israel Stoughton.

Of the benefactors of Harvard College, during this first period of its existence, the name of Stoughton is deservedly among the most known and most honored. Two of this family were early contributors to Harvard College. Israel Stoughton was one of the early emi-

* Savage's Winthrop, Vol. I. p. 228; Vol. II. pp. 216, 329.

grants to Massachusetts. Being a member of the House of Deputies in 1634, he joined the popular party, placed himself in opposition to the magistrates, and published a book against their negative voice. The vigor of the government, at that day, did not allow contumacy of this kind to pass unpunished, even in a Deputy to the Assembly. He was disenabled by that body from holding any public office within the jurisdiction during three years, for his offence, in "affirming that the Assistants were not magistrates." The discipline had a proper effect upon Stoughton. He forthwith declared the book to be both "weak and offensive," and desired the Court to cause it to be burnt.* His humility soon restored him to favor. Taking part with Winthrop in the struggle against the ascendency of Vane, he was, in 1637, elected an Assistant. He commanded the Massachusetts forces in the war against the Pequods, and in that service gave evidence of zeal, courage, and activity, united with exemplary fidelity and eminent wisdom.† His letter to Governor Winthrop, dated "from Pequid, the 2d day of the 6th week of our warfare," while it abundantly indicates his vigor and enlargement of views, is remarkable for its disposition rather to undervalue than to exaggerate his services and sufferings;‡ notwithstanding, in that campaign, the former had been great and the latter severe.

This war having been closed with success, Stoughton was successively employed by the people as an

* See Savage's Winthrop, pp. 155, 220, 223, 233.

† See Mass. Hist. Coll., Second Series, Vol. VIII. p. 145; Vol. X. p. 59.

‡ "We do thankfully acknowledge your care and tenderness towards us, signified by your writings, and sending my provisions, &c., and desire we may deserve it. For the hardship you conceive you put us

CHAPTER IX.

Assistant, and by the government as a Commissioner to run the boundary line between Massachusetts and Plymouth. Being called to England in 1644, his love of arms, or of the cause, triumphed over his love for his adopted country, and he joined the army of the Parliament, with the rank of Lieutenant-Colonel, in a regiment of which Rainsborow was Colonel, and probably served under him, among the reserves, at the battle of Naseby;* which event he did not long survive. He had been one of the earliest contributors to the College, and, at his death in England, many years after its foundation, remembered it in a bequest of three hundred acres of valuable land in the town of Dorchester.

William Stoughton.

William Stoughton, his son, inherited his father's affection for the institution, and gave early promise of talent and usefulness. His manhood more than verified the promise of his youth. Rising gradually in rank and influence, he filled a sphere of greatness and benevolence, surpassed by none of the Colonists. After being graduated at Harvard College, in 1650, he followed, as may be inferred from events, the bias of the times and of the country, rather than of his own genius, when he selected the pulpit as the station in which he was to seek employment and distinction. He continued, however, more than twenty years in the service of the altar, was well esteemed as a preacher, although never a pastor of any particular church; declining invita-

to, and pity us for, for my part, *what I endure is so little thought of, that it is not worth pity, neither doth it trouble me, and therefore I desire that it may trouble none of my friends.* It is what I have been acquainted with, in part, before; and, if I never be more put to it for God's cause's sake, it is much less than I have expected. Whilst we enjoy part in what is there to be had, I hope we shall be satisfied."

* Harris's Life of Cromwell, London Edit. of 1772. p. 126.

tions from Cambridge and Dorchester, and other eligible offers of settlement in the ministry.

About the year 1671 he abandoned the desk, and, following probably the original bent of his mind, became a magistrate and a politician. In his new path, the extent and zeal of his Calvinism tended greatly to his advancement, under a constitution founded on religion, and in a period of society and a country, in which the influence of the clergy predominated. During that age, in all negotiations of the Colony with the parent State, one of the clergy was deemed indispensable to any agency, either for success abroad, or confidence at home. Accordingly, when Charles the Second directed Massachusetts, in the year 1676, to send over agents to make answer against the complaints of Gorges and Mason, Stoughton, though now a magistrate, was deemed sufficiently identified with the clergy, to be appointed one of the agents, as their representative, and went to Europe in that capacity, with the full approbation of the ecclesiastical leaders of the Colony. He remained in England until 1679, but attained nothing, except time and a further opportunity for the Colony to comply with the requisitions of the crown. His success did not fulfil the expectations of the colonists; who were ever too apt to expect impossibilities of their agents, and to attribute to timidity, or time-serving, a failure to obtain a recognition of their cherished principles of construction of the first charter of the Colony, notwithstanding some of them were obviously incompatible with the relations of a colony to a parent state. The claims of the sovereign to unqualified obedience, and those of the colonists to at least a qualified independence, were the source of controversies, which no agents could reconcile, and the occasion of that unpopularity, which invariably followed the return of all the agents sent to England during the first charter. Their residence in that country compelled them to take views of the reciprocal relations of Great Britain and Massachusetts, to which the inhabitants of this Colony were wholly unwilling to accede. The statement of these views was received by the people as indicative of changes produced by the influence of the British cabinet, and was often attributed to selfish motives. Early in his agency Stoughton had remonstrated by letters with some freedom on the neglect, by the colonists, of the acts of navigation, and had ventured to intimate, that, "without a fair compliance in that matter, nothing could be expected but a total breach and storms of displeasure." His urgency produced an order for the faithful obedience to those acts. Notwithstanding which they remained afterwards little more than a dead letter on the statute book. His conduct in this, and in some other respects, did not coincide with the interests and prejudices of his countrymen, and consequently gained him little popularity. On his return, he received no marks of disapprobation from the General Court, but, on the contrary, their thanks for his services. A deep and ill-concealed dissatisfaction, however, existed, on account of the result of his agency; and he became obnoxious to jealousy and censure. Of this he was well apprized; and when, at a subsequent period, a like mission was offered to him, he utterly declined it. The evidences he soon received of the confidence of the British monarch confirmed the opinion of those, who were disposed to believe, that, like his friend Joseph Dudley, he had in Europe been less active in defending colonial rights than in conciliating court favor. Like him, he was reckoned among those, who were in favor of surrendering the old charter, in preference to taking the chance of a *quo warranto*. In 1683 he was appointed by the crown one of the Commissioners to inquire into the titles in the Narraganset country, and, in 1686, on the seizure of the government of the country by the King, he was selected, next to Dudley, as one of the Council of the Colony. These appointments were deemed rewards, and, in the violence of the party feelings of the time, he was considered as one of those politicians, who change their principles with times, and shift their sails so as to catch every favorable breeze. Nor do these suspicions seem to have been wholly without foundation; since Edward Randolph thus draws his character in 1686. "Mr. Stoughton is inclined to the Non-conformist ministers, *yet stands right to his Majesty's interests*." *

The course of Stoughton had been cautious, if not timid. With Dudley he had been associated, very intimately, both in policy and friendship.† The degree to which this extended is strongly evidenced by the fact, that, when, in consequence of the state of parties, in May, 1686, Stoughton had been elected to the magistracy, and Dudley had been omitted, the former "refused to serve, out of complaisance to the latter." He was probably aware, that a commission, appointing Dudley as President and himself as Vice-President of the Colony, was then on its passage from England. This arrived before the end of the same

* Hutch. Coll. of Original Papers, p. 548.

† Hutch. Hist. Mass., Vol. I. chap. 2. pp. 206, 306, 315.

month, and was published. Although he was the avowed friend and confidant of Dudley, and shared in the honors bestowed on that politician, yet he had the address to make the people believe him not unfriendly to the civil constitution of the Colony. To the ecclesiastical constitution his attachment was regarded as sincere, both on account of his early prejudices and his present interest. Dudley in vain attempted to gain for himself a similar confidence. In the crisis of the affairs of the Colony, during the administration of Andros, Stoughton again accepted with Dudley a seat in the Council. But, being one of those against whom the charge was made, of "having more of the willow than the oak in his constitution," he did nothing either greatly to satisfy or greatly to dissatisfy the popular party. In the rising of the people, at the time Andros and Dudley were imprisoned, Stoughton had no participation. He joined, indeed, Bradstreet and the other magistrates, on the 18th of April, 1689, in their request to Andros to deliver up the fort, in order to prevent the effusion of blood. His name, however, does not appear among those, who, on the day following, formed themselves into a body, under the title of a "council of safety of the people and conservation of the peace." Nor did he return to take a share in any of the administrations that intervened, until the arrival of the charter of William and Mary, in 1692; being excluded from them by vote, in consequence of his having accepted the office of Assistant under Andros.*

When, under this charter, Sir William Phips received, by the nomination of Increase Mather, the

* Hutch. Hist. Mass., Vol. I. chap. 3. pp. 317, 337, 340.

appointment of Governor, Stoughton obtained that of Lieutenant-Governor of the Province. As has already been stated, he was probably indebted for this elevation to the assurance given by Cotton Mather,* that he "was ready to make amends for all his miscarriages," and to the knowledge Increase Mather possessed, that his appointment would be acceptable to the clergy.

To the same influence may be attributed the lamentable distinction he attained by his appointment as Chief Justice in the special commission issued for the trial of those confined on charges of witchcraft, at the time of the excitement, called "the Salem delusion." If it were possible, it would be grateful to throw the mantle of oblivion over the part acted by Stoughton in that tragedy. But the stern law of history does not permit. The high station he held for so many years in the Province, as commander-in-chief; the acceptable manner in which he conducted himself in this office; his popularity with the clergy, the chief eulogists and historians of that time; his noble donation to Harvard College; above all, the number, among the most influential in every rank and profession, implicated as actors, or as applauding or acquiescing witnesses, of that appalling drama, have been the occasion of less strictness of investigation, and a more politic tenderness of statement, than are due to truth or justice. There is no class of public men, towards whom history should be more inexorably severe than to those, who, through fear, passion, or policy, lend themselves to popular excitements, and become panders or instruments of the gross desires,

* See above, p. 61.

wayward humors, or furious rage of a multitude. The truth, painful as it is, cannot be concealed. On no individual does the responsibility of the sad consummation of that excitement rest more heavily than on William Stoughton. Cotton Mather may have had more agency in its origin and progress; but the countenance it received from the court of justice gave vitality to the epidemic rage, and deprived innocence of its security, and terminated the cruel tragedy in blood.

On the 14th of May, 1692, Sir William Phips arrived in Massachusetts, bringing with him his own commission as Governor, and that of William Stoughton as Lieutenant-Governor, of the Province.* Belief in the existence of witchcraft, which then prevailed in New England, was apparently held by no one with more solemn conviction than by Stoughton. This rendered him less qualified to hold, and, it is probable, the more anxious to obtain, a seat on the bench of justice. He was, as Lieutenant-Governor, one of the constitutional advisers of Phips, and it cannot be doubted, that the idea of a special court to try the accused, if it did not originate with him, had at least his entire concurrence; and the office of Chief Justice in that commission, if he did not seek, he certainly accepted. The union of the office of Lieutenant-Governor and Chief Justice in the person of Stoughton was calculated to give a weight to his opinion altogether conclusive. In eighteen days after he received his commission as Lieutenant-Governor from the crown, he took that of Chief Justice under

* Hutch. Hist. Mass., Vol. I. p. 367; Vol. II. p. 19.—More Wonders of the Invisible World, by Robert Calef, p. 214.

this special commission from Governor Phips, and proceeded to open a court by virtue of it, under a charter, which gave the power of constituting courts exclusively to the legislature; the appointing and commissioning of the justices and commissioners of courts, established by the legislature, being the extent of the Governor's power under the charter. Scruples of that kind did not affect Stoughton and the other judges appointed in that commission. Under an authority thus, at least, questionable, a court was suddenly organized. It proceeded hastily towards judgment, and before the ensuing October, for this imaginary crime of witchcraft, swept Massachusetts with that desolating besom, miscalled "judicial decision"; the effects of which have been already enumerated.*

The degree to which his infatuation extended, and his coöperation with Cotton Mather's popular appeals, in support of the proceedings of his court, belong to general history, and may be omitted in a work, which, as far as truth and duty permit, would touch no other chord than that which vibrates gratitude to William Stoughton.

Strange as at this day it appears, his conduct in relation to these trials for witchcraft detracted nothing from his popularity. He was chosen Assistant, though Lieutenant-Governor, "so agreeable was he to the people."† Notwithstanding Stoughton always was, in heart, attached to Joseph Dudley and his party, yet he succeeded in retaining his popularity from the time of the departure of Governor Phips, in 1694, to the coming of the Earl of Bellamont, in May, 1699.

* See above, p. 64. † Hutch. Hist. Mass., Vol. II. ch. I. p. 70.

The difficulties with the Indians and the French kept the attention of the people directed towards their external relations, and no controversy occurred between the Executive and the other branches of the legislature. So that the prejudices, which his connexion with Andros and Dudley had excited against him, gradually subsided; and the whole course of his administration in the office of Commander-in-chief was acceptable to the Province.

In March, 1698, Stoughton first intimated his design of erecting an additional building for the accommodation of the students of Harvard College, and a committee of the Corporation was appointed "to treat on that subject concerning which he had made proposals." The records of the Corporation contain no further account of proceedings on this offer. The building was erected, and the Donation Book of the University shows, that the cost was one thousand pounds, Massachusetts currency; but, as those records many years afterwards state, "being an unsubstantial piece of masonry," it grew weak with age, and, after many repairs, was taken down in 1780.

Part of the income of Stoughton Hall, and the rents of twenty-seven acres of land in the town of Dorchester, bequeathed by him to the College, were appropriated by his last will for the benefit of "a scholar of the town of Dorchester; and, if there be none such, then of the town of Milton; and, in want of such, then to any well deserving, that shall be most needy." The income from the land remains active and beneficial at the present day.

In the year 1806 a substantial brick building being erected by the Corporation, the name of Stoughton was given to it; a suitable acknowledgment for his bounty and proved affection for the institution.

Henry Webb.

Henry Webb is another benefactor of this early period, of whom, however, time has left few memorials. It is only known, that he was a merchant of great wealth, according to the standard of the time, of sagacity in business, and no less distinguished for his charities than for his opulence. He bequeathed to the College a house and land in Cornhill, now a part of Washington Street, in Boston, valuable at all times from its locality, still retained by the institution, and one of the most productive portions of its real estate; to which he added a legacy of fifty pounds, the income and interest "to be improved either for the maintenance of some poor scholar, or otherwise for the best good of the College."

William Brown.

Among the benefactors of this period, the name of Brown is honorably recorded. William Brown was the ancestor of a family distinguished in the succeeding age for munificence and public spirit. He emigrated from England in 1635, became a merchant in Salem, where he was eminent for his exemplary life and his public charities. In 1673 he paid one tenth part of the cost of a church erected in that town, and at his death left valuable bequests to the schools of Salem and Charlestown, besides large sums for pious uses. During his lifetime he contributed liberally to the support of the College, and by his last will bequeathed one hundred pounds for the benefit of poor and meritorious students.

John Bulkley.

John Bulkley, a member of the class of 1642, the first which was graduated at Harvard College, deserves respectful remembrance among our earliest benefactors. In the year 1645, he executed a deed of about an acre of valuable land, now owned by the College, and situated nearly in the centre of the town of Cam-

CHAPTER IX.

bridge. It is the earliest conveyance on the records of the College, is in Latin, and on that account curious. It is also interesting for the affection it indicates for President Dunster, and for the College. He characterizes himself as "*nuper studens Collegii Harvardini,*" gives the occupation of the land during life to Henry Dunster, "utpote eidem ob plurima atque ampla accepta beneficia devinctissimus." In case of his death or resignation, he thus directs the course of his bequest; "Tum velim ut Collegium, tanquam λεπτὸν tenue ab alumno maxime benevolo, sibi in perpetuum appropriaret."* After paying this affectionate and valuable tribute to his literary parent, he left America, and settled in the ministry in England; preaching to good acceptance, until he was ejected for non-conformity. He then studied medicine,† became duly qualified as a physician, and practised with success in the suburbs of London.

Lady Moulson.

Among the early transatlantic benefactors of Harvard College, Lady Moulson, Sir Matthew Holworthy, and Theophilus Gale, were chiefly distinguished.

Of Lady Moulson nothing is known, except that she was among the earliest of this class of benefactors, that she contributed one hundred pounds sterling for the College, and paid the amount over to Welde and Peters, the agents of the Colony in Great Britain. It appears, by the records of the Governors of the College, that her gift was known in this country as early as December, 1643, but that it was not at that time received. Welde and Peters settled for this amount, and for sums given also by others, with the

* See Appendix, No. XXII.

† Savage's Winthrop, Vol. II. p. 240.—Calamy's Account of Ejected Ministers, Vol. II. pp. 311, 312.

General Court; who kept it in their treasury, and voted to allow for it to the College an annuity of about fifteen pounds per annum. Fortunately for the College, Lady Moulson had taken a bond of Welde, that the money should not be diverted from the charitable objects to which she had devoted it. For in 1655, on a petition of the College for relief, in a state of great distress on account of the insufficiency of their buildings, the House of Deputies ordered the amount due on account of her gift to be "improved for" the repairs of those edifices. This vote the magistrates non-concurred in, "because the amount was given by the Lady Moulson and others for scholarships, annually to be maintained there, which this Court cannot alter, and therefore desire their brethren, the Deputies, to consider of some meet way for the repairing of the College;" * an instance of self-control, and of the acknowledgment of restraint by principle, as honorable as it is exemplary.

Sir Matthew Holworthy.

After considerable research, little has been discovered concerning the life and fortunes of Sir Matthew Holworthy. It is ascertained, that he was a merchant of Hackney, in the county of Middlesex, that he was knighted by Charles the Second in 1665, possessed great wealth, was distinguished for charity and piety, and that he died in 1678.

His bequest to the College was the largest pecuniary gift it received during the seventeenth century. His bounty was wise in its form and noble in its nature; expressed in terms the most useful, because the most unrestricted. He made the amount applicable at once to the wants of the institution, by placing it at the

* See Appendix, No. II.

CHAPTER IX. immediate control of its governors, indicating a confidence in them, and an elevated spirit in himself, free from all selfish and ambitious views. The simplicity and directness of his language deserves to be preserved both as an honor and an example.

"Item. I give and bequeath unto the College or University in or of Cambridge, in New England, the sum of one thousand pounds (sterling), to be paid over to the Governors and Directors thereof, to be disposed of by them as they shall judge best for promoting of learning and promulgation of the Gospel in those parts; the same to be paid within two years after my decease."

The character as well as the amount of this donation entitled him to the distinction which his name received in the year 1812, when it was given to the Hall then erected by the University; as well as to the just tribute paid to his memory by President Kirkland, in an address on laying the foundation of Holworthy Hall; who, after stating that little was known of this benefactor, observes, "We have evidence, however, that he was one of those generous spirits, who are interested in human nature and human happiness wherever found. He extended his solicitude to this seminary, then obscure and little considered by the world, and capable of adding little to the character of its benefactors, and contributed a bounty which did much to rear it to a manly strength."*

Theophilus Gale.

Theophilus Gale,† dying in 1677, devoted his whole estate, real and personal, to the advancement of edu-

* President Kirkland's Address on laying the Foundation of Holworthy Hall. Corporation Records, August 18th, 1812.

† Wilson's History of the Dissenting Churches, Vol. III. p. 163. London Edit. 1810. — Wood's Athenæ Oxonienses, Vol. III. p. 1149. London Edit. 1820. — Mather's Magnalia, Book IV. Part I.

cation and the promotion of learning. His library, one of the most select and valuable in the possession of a private individual in that day, he bequeathed to Harvard College; and it constituted for many years more than half of the whole College Library. This divine was one of the most distinguished men of his time; being justly admired for his reasoning powers, his learning, and his piety. He was a philologist, a philosopher, and a theologian. His writings, which were numerous and highly esteemed, "spread his fame," says his biographer, "throughout Europe." The fact presents a striking and instructive lesson. Where is that voice which once filled Europe with his name? It is silent. Where those glories, which assured perpetuity to his memory? What coruscations of genius now emblazon his fame? Alas! they are lost in the lapse of years; overpowered and obscured by nearer and more recent radiance. It is not his learning nor his private labors, the acuteness of his controversial nor the ceaseless activity of his intellectual powers, which lead the sons of Harvard, on days of solemn commemoration, to dwell with gratitude on his memory; but a well-directed and well-devised charity, confirming the declaration of Scripture, that, to effect an enduring remembrance, "charity is better than to have the gift of prophecy, or to understand all mysteries and all knowledge."

William Pennoyer and Robert Thorner, among our early benefactors, are next deserving grateful recognition. Both were English gentlemen of fortune, patrons of science, and eminent for their deep religious affections. But little is known of the life and fortunes of either. The former was one of the first to establish a permanent fund for those periodical

William Pennoyer.

CHAPTER IX.

distributions of money to indigent students, called "Exhibitions." By his will, dated in May, 1670, he constituted a rent charge upon an estate in the county of Norfolk, in England, of forty-four pounds per annum, for ever; of which sum thirty-four pounds were appropriated "for the education of two fellows and two scholars, for ever, in the College called Cambridge, in New England."

Robert Thorner.

Robert Thorner was also one of our noblest as well as earliest benefactors. By his will, dated on the 31st of May, 1690, he gave to Harvard College five hundred pounds sterling, to be paid after the expiration of certain specified leases. This contingency did not occur until more than seventy years had elapsed. Then the legacy was punctually paid by the trustees appointed under his will. Thorner was a maternal uncle of Thomas Hollis; and, by appointing him one of those trustees, he introduced Harvard College to the knowledge and notice of the greatest of its early patrons, and became the cause, as well as precursor, of the rising upon our horizon of that constellation of benefactors bearing the name of Hollis; the number and the value of whose bounties it will be the duty of this history hereafter to record.

Other benefactors.

To these benefactors are to be added Sir Kenelm Digby, Sir Thomas Temple, Sir Henry Ashurst, Sergeant Maynard, and John Dodderidge; men distinguished in their age and country, for their virtues, their religious and literary zeal, and the diffusiveness of their benevolence. Conjoined with these in the spirit of kindness for our institution, there exist on its records, names of benefactors,* of whom nothing is

* See Appendix, No. XXIII.

CHAPTER IX.

now known, except the example and the blessing of their bounty; men, possessing in large measure the spirit of charity, but limited in its exercise by the scantiness of their fortunes; yet, giving according to their mediocrity or poverty, they are to be cherished with a veneration and affection as deep and sincere, as the memory of those who have given us of their abundance.

Joseph Glover.

Among our earliest benefactors, "Joseph Glover," and "some gentlemen of Amsterdam," deserve notice, not so much from the amount as from the nature and consequences of their respective benefactions. That of the former was a "font of printing letters," and that of the latter was "forty-nine pounds and something more towards furnishing of a printing press with letters." Both are recorded in the Donation Book of the College as occurring in 1642, and are worthy of memory, as connected with "the first printing press established north of Mexico, and which for many years continued to be the only one in British America."*

Printing Press.

This press Glover was bringing with him to New England in 1638, but died on his passage. His widow, being possessed of considerable property, purchased an estate in Cambridge, and settled there. The press was set up in this town in 1639, under the auspices of the magistrates and elders; Stephen Daye, who had been brought over by Glover for this purpose, being the first printer. It was regarded as a public concern. President Dunster, who married the widow of Mr. Glover, had the management of it in right of

* See Peirce's Hist. Harv. Univ., p. 6.—Felt's Annals of Salem, p. 120.—Thomas's History of Printing, Vol. I. pp. 203, 224, 231.

his wife and as President of the College. It was at first placed in the President's house, where it remained until the year 1655.* Its profits were small, but constituted a part of the revenues of the College. The President superintended and was deemed responsible for its publications. The first of these was "The Freeman's Oath." To this succeeded an Almanac, a Psalm Book, a Catechism, the body of Liberties and Laws of the Colony. To works of this character it was confined while under the supervision of Dunster. In 1654 it was taken into the service of the Commissioners of the United Colonies, had its types and resources greatly enlarged by the Corporation for propagating the Gospel among the Indians; and in 1658 commenced the publication of that extraordinary result of persevering industry and pious zeal, "The Bible in the Massachusetts Indian Language, by John Eliot." In 1662 the jealousy of the clergy and magistrates was excited by some religious treatises it published, and it was subjected to a board of licensers, of which, in 1664, the President of the College was placed at the head. It attained success and celebrity, to which its connexion with the College, and the influence exerted over it by its governors, greatly contributed.

Discipline and course of study.

Touching discipline, the course of studies, and the nature and efficiency of literary instruction, in the College during the seventeenth century, our means of information are limited and unsatisfactory. Its discipline, unquestionably, partook of the austerity of the period, and was in harmony with the character of the early emigrants.† Tradition represents it to have been se-

* See Appendix, No. I. † See Appendix, No. XXIV.

vere, and corporal punishments to have been among the customary sanctions of College laws. The immediate government kept no record of their proceedings. The tutors chastised at discretion, and on very solemn occasions the Overseers were called together, either to authorize or to witness the execution of the severer punishments. Judge Sewall, in his Diary, relates an instance of the mode in which these were inflicted, illustrative of the manners of the age, and of the discipline of the College. It occurred in 1674. The offence was "speaking blasphemous words." After examination by the Corporation, the offence was submitted to the Overseers for advisement. The offender was sentenced to be "publicly whipped before all the scholars," to be "suspended from taking his bachelor's degree," and "to sit alone by himself uncovered at meals during the pleasure of the President and Fellows," to be obedient in all things, and, in default, to be finally expelled from the College. The execution of the sentence was no less characteristic than its nature. It was twice read publicly in the Library, in the presence of all the scholars, the government, and such of the Overseers as chose to attend. The offender having kneeled, the President prayed, after which the corporal punishment was inflicted; and the solemnities were closed by another prayer from the President.* There is no reason to suppose, that there was any thing revolting in this, either to the opinions or the feelings of the age or country. On the contrary, it was in strict accordance with the habits and general notions of discipline prevalent at the period. These formal inflictions gradually grew out of use;

* Peirce's Hist. Harv. Univ., p. 227.

but more than a century elapsed after the foundation of the College, before corporal punishments were obliterated from its code.

As early as 1659, "the exorbitant practices of some students," and their abuse of the "town watch," occasioned an order of the Corporation, recognising the subjection of the students to the law of the land, and providing the manner and limitations under which the watch of the town should exercise their usual power and authority within the precincts of the College.* And in 1682 the civil arm was formally recognised as the last resort for enforcing, in extreme cases, its discipline.†

A document, purporting to be the "Laws, Liberties, and Orders of Harvard College," confirmed by the President and Overseers,‡ gives the best evidence now extant, of the early principles and requisitions of the College laws; as do also the Orders of the Overseers, in 1650,§ of their progress and mode of enforcement.

In relation to the course of studies, and the degree of literary instruction in the seminary during this period, little exact and authentic information exists. "So much Latin as was sufficient to understand Tully, or any like classical author, and to make and speak true Latin, in prose and verse, and so much Greek as was included in declining perfectly the paradigms of the Greek nouns and verbs," were the chief, if not the only requisites for admission. The exercises of the students had the aspect of a theological rather than a literary institution. They were practised twice a day in reading the Scriptures, giving an account of their proficiency and experience in practical and spirit-

* See Appendix, No. XXV.

† Ibid., No. XXVI.

‡ Ibid., No. XXVII.

§ Ibid., No. XXVIII.

ual truths, accompanied by theoretical observations on the language,* and logic, of the sacred writings. They were carefully to attend God's ordinances, and be examined on their profiting; commonplacing the sermons and repeating them publicly in the hall. The studies of the first year were "logic, physics, etymology, syntax, and practice on the principles of grammar." Those of the second year, "ethics, politics, prosody and dialects, practice of poesy, and Chaldee." Those of the third, "arithmetic, geometry, astronomy, exercises in style, composition, epitome, both in prose and verse, Hebrew, and Syriac."

In every year and every week of the College course, every class was practised in the Bible and catechetical divinity; also in history in the winter, and in the nature of plants in the summer. Rhetoric was taught by lectures in every year, and each student was required to declaim once a month.

Such† were the principles of education established in the College under the authority of Dunster. Nor does it appear, that they were materially changed during the whole of the seventeenth century. Improvements were introduced but gradually, and neither their date nor their particulars are anywhere distinctly stated in the College records.

An early, systematic attempt to extend the advantages of a liberal education to the aboriginals was made by the first settlers of Massachusetts in the vicinity of Harvard College, and under the auspices of its governors. Preparatory instruction in Greek, Latin, and English, was provided, an Indian Cate-

* See Mass. Hist. Coll., First Series, Vol. I. p. 243.

† See Appendix, No. XXVII. and No. XXVIII.

CHAPTER IX.

chism, Grammar, and various religious tracts in that language were printed, and an Indian College was erected, chiefly by funds furnished by the Society for propagating the Gospel among the Indians. Daniel Gookin, the active and earnest associate of Eliot in civilizing the Indians, thus speaks concerning the project and the result. "The design was prudent, noble, and good, but it proved ineffectual."* Some of the scholars died. Some, after making good proficiency, grew disheartened, and returned to their native haunts. A few became schoolmasters and mechanics among the natives. Those, who persevered fell victims, to consumption, the effect of the "change of diet, lodging, apparel, and studies." A single individual, "Caleb Cheeshahteaumuck, Indus," stands alone on the Catalogue of the graduates of Harvard College; the only representative of the native tribes.

The number of students graduated at the College from its foundation to the presidency of Leverett, was five hundred and thirty-one, one half of whom became in after life clergymen; a proportion which that profession had maintained through the whole period.

To the general student, and such as were not destined to "the work of the ministry," the exercises of the College must have been irksome, and, in their estimation, unprofitable. The reading every morning a portion of the Old Testament out of Hebrew into Greek, and every afternoon a portion of the New Testament out of English into Greek, however it might improve their knowledge of those languages respectively, could not greatly accelerate or enlarge their acquaintance with Scripture, or tend vividly to

* See Mass. Hist. Coll., First Series, Vol. I. p. 172.

excite their piety. The exposition, required by the laws of the College to be made by the President, of the chapters read at the morning and evening services, although greatly lauded for its utility, and made the repeated subject of inquiry by active members of the Board of Overseers, seems not to have been of any material efficiency in point of instruction. President Mather himself, as we have seen in his letter to Lieutenant-Governor Stoughton, characterizes the students as "forty or fifty children, few of them capable of edification by such exercises." * And President Leverett, when assailed for neglect of it, pointedly told the Board of Overseers, that, if it was to be continued, he must be "supported"; † indicating distinctly, by this expression, that, in the state of society to which the country had advanced, this exercise was so irksome and annoying to the young men, as to subject him to disturbance or insult.

At a period when Latin was the common instrument of communication among the learned, and the official language of statesmen, great attention was naturally paid to this branch of education. Accordingly, "to speak true Latin, both in prose and verse," was made an essential requisite for admission. Among the "laws and liberties" of the College we also find the following. "The scholars *shall never use their mother tongue*, except that, in public exercises of oratory or such like, they be called to make them in English." This law appears upon the records of the College in the Latin as well as in the English language. The terms in the former are indeed less restrictive and more practical; "Scholares vernaculâ

* See above, p. 96. † See Appendix, No. XI.

CHAPTER IX.

linguâ, *intra Collegii limites*, nullo pretextu utentur." There is reason to believe, that those educated at the College, and destined for the learned professions, acquired an adequate acquaintance with the Latin, and those destined to become divines, with the Greek and Hebrew. In other respects, although the sphere of instruction was limited, it was sufficient for the age and country, and amply supplied all their purposes and wants. The best part of the education at this College, and that for which its students have, in every period of its history, been distinguished, was, that they were taught, according to the language of President Mather, in one of his public orations on Commencement day, "liberè philosophari, et in nullius jurare verba magistri."

STOUGHTON HALL, BUILT IN 1700; TAKEN DOWN IN 1780.

CHAPTER X.

Retrospect of political and religious Parties. — Their Relation to the College. — "School of the Church" established at New Haven. — Charter drafted by Sewall and Addington. — Views of Governor Dudley, in filling up the Corporation. — Disappointment of the Mathers. — Their Letters to Governor Dudley. — Vigorous Administration of Leverett. — Recovers the Legacy of Hopkins, and of Lady Moulson. — Death of Hobart. — Wadsworth elected Fellow of the Corporation. — Death of Treasurer Brattle. — John White elected Treasurer. — Death of the Rev. William Brattle and the Rev. Ebenezer Pemberton. — Election of Benjamin Colman and Nathaniel Appleton as Fellows.

To attain a correct understanding of the controversies which occurred during the presidency of Leverett, it will be useful to cast a retrospective glance on the civil and ecclesiastical history of Massachusetts. The early settlers of this Province emigrated, not for the establishment of any particular tenets, but for the enjoyment, in the modes of worship which they deemed evangelical, of those points of faith, in which, generally speaking, they all agreed. In the form of government they established, neither subscription to creeds, nor declaration of articles of belief, was required. Nor were they necessary. The principle, that none should be a freeman of the State, who was not a member of the Church, sufficiently secured the supremacy of the religious opinions of the predominant party. The inquisitorial power was vested in the church and its officers. The State thus enjoyed

CHAPTER X.

the benefit of that power, without the obloquy attached to its exercise.

Creeds and confessions of faith were equally unnecessary in the foundation of the College, either as a condition of office, or of obtaining the benefits of the institution. The magistrates of the jurisdiction, and the elders of the specified congregational churches, were the Overseers of the College. They were all necessarily church members, and, on the uniformity of the faith of the churches, they relied for the perpetuity of religious opinions, which they deemed fundamental.

State of religious and political controversies.

This security, however, was destroyed by the charter of William and Mary, which made property, instead of church-membership, the qualification for the enjoyment of civil rights. During the first forty years after this charter came into operation in Massachusetts, violent struggles occurred, inevitable at all times in states, when power is changing hands, and one party is striving to seize what another is striving to retain. Political controversy was active; theological, intense. The early New England congregational church having lost the constitutional security and power it originally possessed in the State and the College, it became the guiding principle of the policy of the clergy of that sect, in the successive schemes of a charter for the College during Dr. Mather's presidency, so to arrange its powers or its principles as to secure the institution from those great changes in religious opinions, which they had reason to anticipate, and which they called "heresies."

While the chair of state was occupied in succession by Phips and Stoughton, the early ecclesiastical influences were paramount. But seceders from their religious doctrines increased gradually in power and numbers. A natural coalition took place between them and the adherents to the Church of England, from identity of interest and a common dislike of the predominating religious opinions. Thus Governor Bellamont, in negativing the clause relative to religious qualifications in the College charter of 1699, was actuated by a perception of its bearing on the members of the Church of England; yet he negatived, perhaps unconsciously, a much more extensive power, adapted and devised to exclude all from government and instruction in the College, who seceded from the doctrines of the Reformation, as espoused and intended by the first settlers.*

In 1698, when that secession from the principles of the Cambridge Platform occurred, which eventuated in the foundation of the Brattle Street Church in Boston, an alarm was excited among all those, who claimed for themselves the character of exclusive representatives of the religious faith of the fathers of New England. This alarm was increased, when, in the course of events, the tutors of the College were reasonably suspected of being infected with this "apostasy," as it was studiously denominated.

College at New Haven founded.

The first settlers of Connecticut had emigrated from Massachusetts for the purpose of being under a stricter form of worship than they could here attain. A desire had long existed in that Colony, for the establishment in it of a "school of the prophets," constructed with reference to their peculiar religious views. To this object the crisis of affairs in Massachusetts was deemed favorable, and measures were

* See above, p. 101.

CHAPTER X. adopted for founding such an institution in the neighbourhood of New Haven. The projectors of it were aware of the advantage which would result to their seminary, should it be made satisfactory to the predominant religious party in Massachusetts, and especially if its constitution should be clear and fixed on the points by that party deemed essential. They took their measures accordingly with promptness and sagacity.

Among the firmest adherents to the doctrines of the early New England churches, were Sewall, afterwards Chief Justice, and Addington, then Secretary of State. They were both statesmen of the old charter cast, in whom the characters of politician and theologian were combined in nearly equal proportions. Both were dissatisfied with the state of things in Harvard College. Both were zealous and vigorous defenders of the doctrines of the early Congregational church. To these statesmen the clergy of Connecticut applied for a draft of a charter for their proposed institution;* and received from them an instrument, not founded, like the charters of Harvard, on "the instituting, guiding, and furthering of the said College, and the several members thereof, from time to time, in piety, morality, and learning," but on something which they, doubtless, deemed more safe and scriptural, "the reciting *memoriter* the 'Assembly's Catechism,' in Latin, Dr. Ames's 'Medulla,' and also his 'Cases of Conscience,' accompanied on the Sabbath by expositions of practical theology, and the repeating of sermons by the undergraduates; and on week days by reading and

* Trumbull's History of Connecticut, Vol. I. pp. 500, 501.

expounding the Scriptures according to the laudable order and usage of Harvard College."

Some of the points here secured were undoubtedly introduced by Sewall and Addington, on account of their being those, from which they apprehended Harvard College to be in a state of declension. The last article, although inserted in avowed coincidence with the "order and usage of Harvard," was, in fact, the one to which Sewall attached the highest importance, and about which he was most solicitous. A neglect of those expositions, notwithstanding their irksomeness and doubtful utility,* he made, a few years afterwards, the subject of a direct attack on President Leverett.

The founders of the College in Connecticut adopted, without any material alterations, the draft made by Sewall and Addington, who, in an accompanying letter, did not fail to indicate their dissatisfaction with the state of things at Harvard College, by saying, "how glad we were to hear of the flourishing schools and colleges of Connecticut, as *it would be some relief to us against the sorrow we have conceived from the decay of them in this Province.*"†

From this period the College of Connecticut began to be deemed by the stricter sect of Calvinists the strong-hold of their opinions. Their favor soon became to that institution an element of worldly prosperity and success; some of the more zealous adherents to those doctrines, who were sons of Harvard, taking it under their patronage, soliciting for it donations, and even attempting to give the tide of indi-

* See above, p. 193. † See Appendix, No. XXIX.

CHAPTER X.

vidual bounty, which was flowing towards Cambridge, a direction towards New Haven.

The success which had attended the exertions of Sewall and the leaders of the Calvinistic party in Massachusetts, in establishing a safe test of their faith in the College of Connecticut, reconciled them in a degree to the disappointment they had sustained by Governor Bellamont's negative of the clause having a like tendency in the charter of Harvard College. Willard, Stoughton, and the more prudent leaders of this party, finding that the violent attack of the Mathers on Colman, the Brattles, Leverett, and the other seceders, had no tendency to check that "apostasy," and having so far effected a reconciliation, as to induce an acknowledgment of Congregational church rights and pastoral relations with the church in Brattle Street, there resulted, and was maintained during the whole of the vice-presidency of Willard, a species of theological armistice. The animosity, however, which the controversy had enkindled, was never quenched. Circumstances prevented its appearance in the open air. The surface was, indeed, smooth, and the outside fair; but, when occasions arose to excite, or to stir, the glimmering of concealed fires might be seen under the external covering. In the nature of things it was impossible true reconcilement should take place; and that the adherents of a church which refused to inquire into the regeneration of communicants, denied the necessity of explicit covenanting with God and the church, admitted that persons, not communicants, might elect pastors, referred admission to the sacraments to the prudence and conscience of the minister, and held that admission to the pastoral relation might be valid without the approbation of neighbouring churches, and other not less obnoxious deviations from the early platform and discipline, could ever be cordially acknowledged as brethren by the strict adherents of the ancient Congregational church.

Induction of John Leverett into the presidency.

On the 14th of January, 1708, John Leverett was inducted into the office of President of the College by Governor Dudley; the Overseers, Corporation, and Resident Fellows being present on the occasion.* Conformably to the resolve of the legislature and the charter of 1650, the number of the Corporation was reduced to seven, and was thus constituted; John Leverett, President; Nehemiah Hobart, William Brattle, Ebenezer Pemberton, Henry Flynt, Jonathan Remington, Fellows; Thomas Brattle, Treasurer. In this selection of members, Governor Dudley gave a decided preponderance to those seceders from the Platform of the New England church, who had been the objects of the denunciation of the Mathers.

The election of Leverett was insupportably grievous to Increase Mather and his son. They had anticipated, that the choice would have fallen upon one or the other of them. Between them there was no rivalry. For the disappointment of both they were not prepared. Their indignation was excited against Dudley, who, as they thought, had buoyed up their hopes until he had arranged measures and agents to insure their defeat. On the 20th of January, 1707, they each addressed a letter to Governor Dudley, breathing a spirit of abuse and virulence, of which the records of party animosity contain

Letters of the Mathers to Governor Dudley.

* See Appendix, No. XI.

CHAPTER X.

but few parallels, and well deserving the character given of them by Dudley, in his reply, as "an open breach upon all the laws of decency, honor, justice, and Christianity." * "Covetousness," "lying," "hypocrisy," "treachery," "bribery," "Sabbath-breaking," "robbery," and "murder," are charged upon the chief magistrate of the Province, in terms of no dubious import. Nor was the bitterness of reproach and insinuation allayed by being made in the character, respectively assumed by each, of "spiritual father," and "faithful adviser," having "sad fears concerning his soul," and earnestly solicitous, that, "in the methods of piety, he would reconcile himself to Heaven, and secure his happiness in this world and the world to come."

The coincidence of these letters in point of time and of temper left no doubt in Dudley's mind, of their origin and motive. "I should be stupid," he says in reply, "not to distinguish between reproaches and Christian admonitions." "Every one can see through the pretence, and is able to account for the spring of these letters, and how they could have been prevented, without easing any grievances you complain of." "I desire that you will keep your station, and let fifty or sixty good ministers, your equals, in the Province, have a share in the government of the College, and advise thereabouts as well as yourselves."

The friends of the College, and of Dudley, did not fail to appear in his defence, and to express publicly their reprobation of the conduct of the Mathers. The clergy, also, took sides on the occasion.

* See Mass. Hist. Coll., First Series, Vol. III. pp. 126, 128, 135.

The pulpit, according to the too frequent custom of the period, was made the organ of crimination and recrimination. The Mathers "preached and prayed about their contest with the Governor." Mr. Pemberton "resented Cotton Mather's letter," and said, that, "if he were Dudley, he would humble him, though it cost him his head." And Colman, preaching at the lecture in Boston, treated the topics of "envy and revenge," in connexion with the question, whether "the spirit was truly regenerated or no," in a manner to be "reckoned that he lashed" the Mathers and their party.*

From this time the Mathers ceased all official interference in the affairs of the College, notwithstanding they were both members of the Board of Overseers, in virtue of their pastoral relation to a Congregational church in Boston. It appears by the records of the Overseers, that Increase Mather never subsequently attended a meeting of that board, and Cotton Mather only one during the presidency of Leverett; the occasion of which will be noticed hereafter. The breach between Cotton Mather and Dudley seems never to have been closed by concession or explanation. When, in 1712, the University of Glasgow, in Scotland, conferred on Cotton Mather the degree of Doctor in Divinity, the state of feeling known to exist between him and the Governor was the occasion of some embarrassment to President Leverett, on the question of inserting this transatlantic honor in the Triennial Catalogue of the College. Dudley, however, relieved him from his anxiety, by expressly authorizing the insertion of the title.†

* See Appendix, No. XI. † See Appendix, No. XXX.

CHAPTER X.

Vigorous measures of the Corporation.

The presidency of Leverett was distinguished for vigorous and active endeavours to increase the funds, enlarge the accommodations, and establish the neglected or dormant claims of the College. The success which attended these efforts, considering the pecuniary embarrassments of the Province, and the religious animosities, which the College had to encounter, is remarkable, and reflects great honor on the wisdom and fidelity of the President and the Corporation; which was, at that period, happily constituted for the advancement of the general interests of the seminary.

From the academic habits of his early life and his subsequent acquaintance with the world, Leverett was eminently qualified to take the management of the College. In the offices of Judge, Legislator, and Speaker of the House of Representatives, his capacity for business and intellectual labor was known, and highly appreciated. Thomas Brattle, who held the office of Treasurer twenty years, was no less distinguished for his knowledge of affairs, and for the zeal and accuracy with which he watched and enlarged the funds of the institution. William Brattle and Ebenezer Pemberton were clergymen whose acquirements and characters were well adapted to extend and strengthen the natural influences of their station and profession. Flynt was shrewd and skilful in the scholastic sphere in which he passed his life. Hobart was a clergyman highly esteemed by his contemporaries. Of Remington no particular account is preserved.

Edward Hopkins's legacy recovered.

In June, 1709, the Corporation took measures to secure the legacy of Edward Hopkins. More than fifty years had elapsed since the death of this benefactor, and his heirs interposed obstacles, which rendered the pursuit of the claim of the College troublesome and expensive, and final success dubious. Not deterred by these difficulties, the Corporation appointed Henry Newman, of London, their agent, and remitted forty pounds sterling, for the prosecution of their rights. The object was pursued with perseverance, and a favorable decree in Chancery obtained in March, 1712–13, by which eight hundred pounds sterling, the amount of the principal legacy with the accumulated interest, was vested in a Board of Trustees, and by them laid out in the purchase of an extensive tract of land, to which the name of Hopkinton was given, in honor of the donor. This purchase was subsequently enlarged by "a quantity of country land adjoining,"* which, being included within the bounds of the original act of incorporation of that town, was given by the General Court to the Trustees, "to the same good and pious uses, ends, and purposes," to which the donation of Mr. Hopkins had been appropriated.† The gratitude of the Trustees was expressed to Lord Chancellor Harcourt in very lively terms, in a letter signed by the whole body and by Governor Dudley.‡

Great losses and many obstructions, arising in later times from the nature of the investment, prevented the Trustees from attaining by that donation all the advantages, which the original rents were calculated to yield. After a long-protracted opposition from the inhabitants of Hopkinton, a final settlement was assented to by the Trustees in 1832, graduated by a

* Records of the General Court, 13th of December, 1715.

† Ibid., 1st of December, 1716. ‡ See Appendix, No. XXXI.

CHAPTER X.

scale of expediency, and not of strict right. The funds of this trust, notwithstanding the deductions to which they were subjected, now amount to nearly thirty thousand dollars.

Lady Moulson's donation obtained.

In the same vigorous pursuit of the interests of the College, Leverett, on the 25th of July, 1712, brought the state of Lady Moulson's donation before the General Court, and obtained upwards of four hundred pounds currency, being the principal and arrears of interest of her gift, which had been retained upwards of seventy years in the treasury of the Colony.

Robert Thorner's legacy secured.

The legacy of Robert Thorner was now entered upon the records of the Corporation; a measure which had an important effect in its ultimate attainment.

During the administration of Dudley the Corporation received his uninterrupted countenance and favor, until toward the end of his official career, when they incurred his resentment, for not choosing, at his urgent request, his son, William Dudley, Treasurer of the College.

Benjamin Wadsworth elected Fellow. 1712.

Until the death of the Rev. Nehemiah Hobart, in August, 1712, no event occurred bringing to a test the religious opinions of the Corporation and Overseers. On the 9th of September, the vacancy in the former board, thus occasioned, was filled by the election of the Rev. Benjamin Wadsworth. When President Leverett announced this choice to Governor Dudley, he expressed his approbation; but recommended that the meeting of the Overseers for its approval should be postponed, saying, that the Lieutenant-Governor and Mr. Sewall were about to be absent on a journey, and that he was desirous they should

CHAPTER X.

be present.* Accordingly the meeting of the Overseers did not take place until the 5th of November. Wadsworth was known to coincide in the religious opinions of Pemberton and Leverett, from which the Lieutenant-Governor and Sewall differed; but, though both were present on this occasion, no opposition occurred. It is, however, remarkable, that, at an election, having a direct bearing on the religious character of the College, out of forty members, of whom the board was composed, only ten were present, and not a single clergyman.

After the election of Wadsworth, no subsequent vacancy occurred in the Corporation until the death of Thomas Brattle, the Treasurer of the College, on the 13th of May, 1713.

The Rev. William Brattle, his brother and executor, at the request of the Corporation, took immediate possession of the funds of the College, and performed the duties of Treasurer, until another was regularly chosen. In this election great difficulties and delays occurred. Governor Dudley had † "a vehement desire," that his youngest son, Colonel William Dudley, should succeed Thomas Brattle in that office. In this wish the Corporation, for some reason not now known, did not concur. After a short delay, they chose John White, on the 13th of October, 1713. When the committee of the board ‡ waited upon Governor Dudley to inform him of this election, he expressed great dissatisfaction, recommended that White should not accept the office, and advised the Corporation not to insist upon a call of the Overseers for

John White elected Treasurer.

* Leverett's Manuscript, p. 55.

† See Appendix, No. XI.

‡ See Appendix, No. XXXII.

CHAPTER X.

their approval. The Corporation so far acceded to his recommendation, as to omit insisting upon an immediate meeting of that board. They, however, took no measures to reconsider the election of White; and, after the lapse of nearly a year, as they persisted in their choice, Dudley ordered a meeting of the Overseers in a manner altogether irregular and unsatisfactory,* on a notice of only three days. His policy, if it had in view the defeat of White's election, was unsuccessful. The friends of the Corporation and the enemies of Dudley rallied in favor of White. Among the last, Cotton Mather, not displeased to thwart the wishes of Dudley, took his seat, as an Overseer. This was the only instance of his presence at the board during the administration of Leverett. White was chosen, but circumstances, not now known, prevented his entrance upon the active duties of Treasurer until the July following (1715). During the whole period of the vacancy of that office, William Brattle managed the pecuniary concerns of the institution with the intelligence and fidelity, for which his conduct and that of his brother were distinguished. The demise of Queen Anne occurred in 1714. This event rendered the tenure of Governor Dudley's office precarious; his influence began to decline, and there is no subsequent evidence of his direct participation in any measures affecting the seminary.

Arrival of Governor Shute.

Colonel Shute, who succeeded to the Governor's chair in October, 1715, favored the party which supported the policy of his predecessor. He early received and reciprocated the civilities of the College.†

* October 7th, 1714. Leverett's Manuscript, p. 94.

† See Appendix, No. XXXIII.

Taking the oath of office on the 5th, he visited the College on the 15th of October, where he was received with the usual classic honors. One of the graduates addressed him in Latin; and the Governor replied with commendations, and assurances of his favor. President Leverett accompanied him on a tour to New Hampshire, and records, in terms of great praise, the demeanor and conversation of the Governor; who proved himself in almost every exigency an efficient supporter of the measures of the Corporation, and a firm friend of the College.

Death of Ebenezer Pemberton and William Brattle.

In 1717 the Corporation lost two of its most valued members. Ebenezer Pemberton, senior pastor of the Old South Church in Boston, died on the 13th of February; and William Brattle, pastor of the Church in Cambridge, on the 15th of that month. Brattle and Pemberton were both men in life beloved, and in death deeply lamented. "A great part of the beauty of our Israel is fallen," exclaims Colman in a funeral sermon on the occasion. "They were stars of the first magnitude. Providence set them at the head of the country for learning and usefulness. They were singular ornaments of it, pillars in the church of Christ here, and among the fathers of the College;" "alike philosophers and divines," "faithful in their trusts," "distinguished for their judgment," and "for their mutual friendship and affection."

The filling of the vacancies thus occasioned, became to each of the rival religious parties an object of solicitude; and was considered by each as a test of the religious influences under which the College was to be continued. The relations of the bereaved churches had been always intimate with the seminary. All the ministers of the Old South Church had been succes-

CHAPTER X.

sively members of the Corporation of the College. The surviving pastor, Joseph Sewall, was distinguished for his piety and doctrinal zeal. He was the son of Chief Justice Sewall, who, of all the laity, was the most earnest and active supporter of the Calvinistic faith; and was the favorite candidate of those, who were desirous that the doctrines of that sect should prevail and be established in the College. To this party Colman, the pastor of "the Manifesto Church," was more obnoxious than any other individual, who was likely to be a candidate. The pastor of the church in Cambridge, also, had always been a member of the Corporation; and it was all-important, that this church should elect a clergyman, who should be an acceptable member of that board. In the crisis of the religious character of the College, which these contemporaneous vacancies presented, the Corporation conducted with equal vigor, decision, and openness.

On the 14th of April, 1717, within two months after the decease of William Brattle, measures were taken to supply the vacancy in the Cambridge church. Among the candidates was Nathaniel Appleton, a young man, who was graduated in 1712, and on whom the wishes of the Corporation concentrated. President Leverett took an active part, as a member of the church, in effecting the election of Appleton; was moderator of the meeting, presided in all the deliberations of the church and congregation; and, when Appleton, by a great majority, was declared to be chosen, on entering the proceedings in his Diary, concludes his record with a "Laus Deo."* The Corporation having attained their wishes in thus supplying the

* Leverett's Manuscript, p. 120.

Nathaniel Appleton and Benjamin Colman elected fellows.

pastoral office in Cambridge, did not wait even for the ordination of Mr. Appleton, but immediately elected him a member of their board, in the place of Mr. Brattle. At the same time they elected the Rev. Benjamin Colman a member in place of Mr. Pemberton. These elections were approved by the Overseers without contest; although passing by Sewall, the late colleague of Pemberton and successor of Willard, was regarded by the strict adherents to the Calvinistic doctrines, as identifying the College with those heresies, which were viewed by them as sapping the foundations of the Congregational church. Opposition would have had no chance of success in the board of Overseers, in relation to clergymen of the weight of character of Colman, and of the popularity of Appleton, connected, as they both were, with churches respectable for wealth, influence, and numbers. The strength of the high Calvinistic party was then in the House of Representatives, which could not on that election be brought into the field. Those violent political passions, which disturbed the popular branch of the Provincial legislature during the whole administration of Governor Shute, had already begun to rage; and it would have been difficult to find space for a theological controversy in such an arena. Discussions concerning paper money, and private banks, and land banks, with the depreciating state of the currency, and the consequent embarrassment of individuals, were the absorbing interests of the legislature. Cooke,* the leader of the popular party, had just commenced an avowed opposition to Governor Shute, who was represented as a weak man, under

* See Hutch. Hist. Mass., Vol. II. chap. 3

the influence of the Dudleys, and inclined to principles of government dangerous to the liberties of the people. Among the rigid Calvinists these elections to the Corporation were the occasion of a deep and settled animosity to the College, malign and determined, though concealed, by the circumstances of the time, under general courtesy of language and demeanor. But means were soon discovered to embarrass, and ultimately almost to break down, the Corporation, by attempts to eject the obnoxious individuals. These endeavours would unquestionably have been successful, had it not been for the firmness of Governor Shute, and the resolved, self-sustaining spirit of the assailed members.

CHAPTER XI.

Indications of a Design to embarrass the Corporation. — Pierpont refused a Degree by President Leverett. — Appeals to the Corporation, who confirm Leverett's Decision. — Pierpont prosecutes a Tutor at Common Law. — The Case brought before the Overseers. — The Dudleys support Pierpont. — Conduct of Paul Dudley on the Occasion. — Pierpont's Case dismissed by the Courts of Law. — Judge Sewall's Attack on President Leverett before the Overseers. — Supported by Paul Dudley. — Leverett's and Sewall's respective Accounts of that Affair. — Cotton Mather's Animosity to the Corporation. — His Letter to Governor Shute in Favor of Pierpont. — His Zeal in Favor of the College at New Haven.

THE animosity to the College, excited by the election of Colman and Appleton into the Corporation, was soon manifested. A year did not elapse after that event, before the quiet of the seminary began to be disturbed, and the Corporation embarrassed, by questions undermining the authority of the board. From the nature of these questions, and the countenance given to those who agitated them by leading members of the board of Overseers, it is apparent, that other motives than those avowed were in action, and that they had their origin in external influences of more importance than the apparent agents in these troubles.

In the year 1718, a graduate by the name of Pierpont was refused his second degree by President Leverett, on the ground of allegations brought against

CHAPTER XI.

him by Mr. Sever, a tutor, "of contemning, reproaching, and insulting the government of the College, and particularly the tutors, for their management in admission of scholars." No further account of these insults is given, but the proceedings, which grew out of them, are recapitulated with minuteness in the records of the Corporation and Overseers; and also in the Diaries of President Leverett, and of Henry Flynt, senior tutor of the College. These evidence, that the attack on the government was of a very serious character. Both expressly state, that it "threatened the dissolution of the College."

In consequence of this refusal of his degree, Pierpont, with several of his friends, came before the Corporation on Commencement day, and demanded a hearing. This was granted, and, the evidence in support of the charges against him being adduced, after "long and impertinent talk," as President Leverett characterizes the speeches of Pierpont and his friends, the Corporation "declared *seriatim* their opinion, and *uno ore* voted, that said Ebenezer Pierpont ought not to be admitted to his second degree this day." *

Pierpont prosecutes Tutor Sever.

Dissatisfied with this result, Pierpont immediately prosecuted Mr. Sever at common law. This open defiance of the authority of the Corporation, in a case deemed by them wholly within their jurisdiction, led to a meeting of that body on the 11th of September following, for "consultation on the measures to be taken to secure and support the government of the College against the attack made upon it

* Records of the Corporation. — Leverett's Manuscript, pp. 144, 145.

by Pierpont, in his extraordinary prosecution of Mr. Sever."

From the proceedings of this meeting, which was informal, and from the Diaries of President Leverett and Tutor Flynt, it appears, that the Corporation had reason to believe, that Dudley, the former Governor, and his son Paul Dudley, then Attorney-General of the Province, were the origin of these difficulties.

The former, although no longer chief magistrate of the Province, retained considerable influence, which, in a degree, extended over Shute, his successor. Dudley was by nature vindictive, craving, and ambitious. By rejecting his urgent nomination of his son, William Dudley, as Treasurer of the College, the Corporation had incurred his resentment. Their election of another to that office was, probably, regarded by him as a mark of ingratitude and disrespect. Paul Dudley, his eldest son, shared the discontent of his father. In early life he had courted the favor of the crown, and openly joined those who were zealous to abridge the privileges of the Province.* He received, as his reward, in 1702, the appointment of Attorney-General, and became obnoxious to the people, as an enemy to their liberties. Being ambitious of place and political influence, he studiously endeavoured to remove those early prejudices. To this end it was then necessary to join the stricter sect of the Calvinists, and he became one of its most open and active adherents. The College owed the restoration of its early charter to Governor Dudley, and the independence of his influence, which the government of the institution now showed, excited his animosity and that of his family. Judge

Discontent of the Dudleys.

* Eliot's Biog. Dict., art. Dudley.

CHAPTER XI. Sewall, whose son had married a daughter of Governor Dudley, participated in their dissatisfaction.

Apprized of the state of feeling which existed towards them in the Dudley family, the Corporation, at this informal meeting, appointed a committee, in the language of President Leverett, "to take the first opportunity to discourse with Governor Dudley, and his son, Mr. Paul Dudley, who have been suspected to be not a little the occasion of the present disturbances given to the President and Fellows, and that they make report of their interview."*

No such report was ever made; and the conduct of Paul Dudley, on subsequent occasions, sufficiently evidences, that the "suspicions" of the Corporation were well founded.

1718. On the 15th of September the Corporation "voted to apply to Governor Shute for a meeting of the Overseers," and made a formal address to him, in writing, stating the appeal by Pierpont, from the decision of the Corporation to the courts of common law, representing "the emergency to be of great importance to the College," and apprehended by them "to be hurtful to the rights and privileges of that seminary, and tending to weaken the government thereof."

Governor Shute deemed this application for a call of the Overseers sufficiently important, to ask the advice of his Council upon granting it. They being in favor of the measure, he authorized President Leverett to call a meeting of the board, with instructions, that Sever and Pierpont should both be summoned to attend.

This meeting took place on the 31st of the suc-

* Leverett's Manuscript, pp. 142, 146, 149.

Meeting of the Overseers. 1718.

ceeding October. The general attendance on the occasion sufficiently indicates the interest felt in the result. Besides Governor Shute, Lieutenant-Governor Tailer, and President Leverett, there were present *twenty-one* lay and *twelve* clerical members. After the address of the President and Fellows to the Governor, and the act of Council, advising him to call a meeting of the Overseers, were read, the board proceeded to hear the several allegations and the evidence adduced by each of the parties. The language of Pierpont on the occasion, is represented by President Leverett to have been marked with "confusion, impertinence, and impudence"; that of Sever "with plainness, modesty, and honesty." The former adhered to his determination, "to convent Sever before his Majesty's justices of the peace," for "slandering, belying, and abusing him."*

The debate was long and animated. At length the Overseers, embarrassed by the support given to Pierpont, condescended to cause a formal draft of an acknowledgment, such as they thought Pierpont ought to make, to be prepared, expressive of his great regret at his "heat and passion," of his desire to be forgiven, and admitted to the honors of the College. This draft, having been prepared and sanctioned by the board of Overseers, a committee was appointed, of which Chief Justice Sewall was chairman, to offer it to Pierpont for his signature. After a long delay and negotiation, the committee returned and reported to the Overseers, that Pierpont utterly refused to sign any such acknowledgment. Upon which the board, without taking any further measures

* Leverett's Manuscript, pp. 149, 150.

CHAPTER XI. on the subject, broke up, in a manner equally disorderly and unjustifiable.

President Leverett gives the following account of these proceedings;

Conduct of Paul Dudley. "Mr. Paul Dudley gave himself a great liberty, to patronize Pierpont, and made sundry motions, tending to embarrass the proceedings of this meeting; and, while he endeavoured to hide, he did but the more discover his partiality; and it was to be wished he had been less indulged than he was by ——."

This blank can apply only to Governor Shute, who, as presiding officer, had alone the power to extend or deny indulgence to those engaged in the debate. His conduct at the close of the meeting is also represented as very exceptionable and undignified.

"While the Chief Justice and Mr. Gibbs," says Leverett, "were gone into the lobby, the Governor and Lieutenant-Governor withdrew, and went out from the board at the door where Pierpont's gang were waiting; Mr. Dudley having whispered the Governor. Soon after the report was made, his Excellency left his chair, followed by the Lieutenant-Governor, and, passing by, ordered Mr. Hiller, the clerk of the Council, to adjourn the Council; and so abruptly left the Overseers in some confusion and great dissatisfaction."

The Corporation, thus left by the Overseers without either support or advice, had no other resort than in the firmness and independence of the courts of law. Happily by them they were not abandoned.
1718. When, in the November following, the prosecution which Pierpont had instituted came to be heard before the justices at common law, they ordered "the complaint to be quashed, and the defendant to be dis-

CHAPTER XI.

Pierpont's complaint dismissed.

missed," upon the ground, that "the matter in difference had already had a hearing, according to the charter of Harvard College and the laws and customs thereof, before the Corporation and Overseers of said College."

The remarks of President Leverett on this decision of the courts of law indicate the critical nature of this difficulty, and that it involved more important consequences than could have resulted from a mere dispute between a graduate and a tutor.

The above determination of the justices, says Leverett, "put an end to an affair that was very troublesome, and *that which threatened the dissolution of the College;* and caused many thoughts in those that had the welfare and safety of that society, which had been so signal a blessing to New England, at heart. A particular history of the affair, may, if God directs and spirits the President thereto, hereafter be given."

This "dissolution of the College," which President Leverett and Tutor Flynt apprehended in case the result at common law had been different, can only allude to a determination, which existed among the high and honorable men who then composed the Corporation, to resign their seats in case the authority of that board were treated with the same neglect and indifference by the courts of law, as it had been by the Overseers. To effect a change in the religious influence of the board, by resignation or otherwise, was, it cannot be doubted, the policy of the ecclesiastical faction, which had the ascendency in the Province, and of which the Mathers, Chief Justice Sewall, and Attorney-General Dudley, were the leaders. Other occurrences of the period, besides this encouragement given to the contumacy of Pierpont, render this conclusion irresistible.

Circumstances of a similar character, and still more illustrative of motives, took place at succeeding meetings of the Overseers.

On the 31st of October, Governor Shute had agreed with President Leverett, that there should be a meeting of the Overseers on the 7th of November following, for the presentation of a memorial to the General Court for enlarging Massachusetts Hall, the building of which was then commenced, to the length of one hundred feet, instead of fifty, which was the first plan. As the sole end of that meeting was to agree on this memorial, to which the clerical members of the board could not possibly have any objection, they were not duly warned to appear. On the day appointed by the Governor, President Leverett, Mr. Colman, and Mr. Wadsworth waited on his Excellency and the Council board at their chamber.* After a draft of the proposed memorial had been read, Paul Dudley, who was a member of the Council, objected to further proceedings, because, as the ministers, Overseers of the College, had not been summoned, "the meeting was not regular," and because "it was not proper for the Council to address themselves." "Though these objections," says Leverett, "were accounted but frivolous ones, yet the meeting was dropped;" and the Governor appointed another on the 12th of November, ordering the attendance of the Council on that day, and desiring the President to cause the ministers to be warned.

On the day appointed there was a full meeting of

* Leverett's Manuscript, p. 153.

CHAPTER XI.

Meeting of the Overseers, Nov. 12th. 1718.

the Overseers. At the request of the Governor, President Leverett stated, that the object of the meeting was to petition the General Court to enlarge the building they were then erecting for the College from fifty to one hundred feet. He then read the draft of a memorial for that object, which, at the request of the Governor, he had prepared, and which stated, at considerable length, the general reasons for the application. After he had read the memorial, he delivered it into the hands of Governor Shute. The occurrences, which succeeded, will best be related in the words of President Leverett.

Leverett's account of it.

"When the President had read the above memorial, he delivered it into his Excellency's hand, who discoursed in short in favor of it, and seemed to be ready to put it to vote. But Mr. Dudley prayed he might look upon it, to whom it was handed; and while he was looking on it, there was an interval of silence. In which space Judge Sewall stood up, and said to this effect; 'While we are considering to enlarge the College for the receiving students, I desire to be informed how the worship of God is carried on in the Hall, and to ask Mr. President, whether there has not been some intermission of the exposition of the Scriptures of late.' The President, after a short pause, answered, 'that he thought the present business of the meeting was to be attended, and not to be interrupted by any surmise of a neglect in the administration of the affairs of the College, and that the place where the Overseers were now convened was not the proper place for such an inquiry. That if the Overseers, who are the visitors of the College, had any informations laid before them of omissions or neglects of duty, or maleadministration, by any of the persons that had the immediate administration of the College in their hands, that the Overseers should make a visitation, and inquire into those matters upon the very place, either in the College Hall or Library.' And the President added, 'he did not expect such a question should have been moved at this time, in interruption of the business before the Overseers, and for the considering and advising upon which this meeting was called; and that he was surprised, and little expected such a treatment from the honorable person that moved it, having never once suggested any thing of his suspicion or apprehension of any failure in his duty from his Honor.'

"His Excellency took up the matter, and declared, that the motion, whatever occasion there might be for it, though he knew none, was very improper, and altogether out of course; and the whole board seemed to be of the same opinion, except Mr. Dudley, who, (it may be supposed, by concert with somebody, it may be then not present,* contrived the interval of silence, by poring on the memorial, that so the zealous Judge might have the opportunity to make his impertinent, not to say, in him, invidious motion), raising his head and eyes from the paper he seemed to be intent in reading, said, — 'he, for his part, seconded his Honor the Chief Justice's motion.'

"However, this motion was put by, and the business of the meeting was reassumed. And yet sundry motions were made again by Mr. Dudley, tending to, if not designed for, a diversion; but at length the question was put, Whether it be the mind of the Overseers of Harvard College, that the General As-

* Alluding, probably, to Governor Dudley.

sembly be addressed to perfect the new building of a College in Cambridge to one hundred feet in length? Which passed in the affirmative." A Committee was then appointed to present the memorial to the General Court; and a vote, in conformity with the motion of Judge Sewall was also passed, that "the President shall entertain the scholars in the College with frequent expositions of the Scriptures."*

The account given by Judge Sewall of these proceedings does not materially differ from that of President Leverett. As a characteristic indication of the passions and policy of the factions which then agitated the Province and the board of Overseers, and as a curious illustration of this portion of the history of the College, it is worthy of preservation.†

The support given to Pierpont by some of the Overseers, and this public attack made upon Leverett in their presence, place beyond any reasonable doubt, the existence of a party in that board, ready and prepared to find fault with the measures and embarrass the proceedings of the Corporation. Nor can it be questioned, from the nature and time selected for this attack upon the President, that it had for its object to bring into public suspicion the religious state of the College, and to lead to such changes in the Corporation and government of the College, as might place both under influences more congenial to the prevailing sect in the Province.

Projects of the malecontents.

The attack made by Sewall upon Leverett seems, by the acknowledgment of both, to have been as unexpected as it was direct. The manner in which Leverett expresses himself relative to the conduct of

* Overseers' Records.

† See Appendix, No. XI.

CHAPTER XI.

the malecontent Overseers, unequivocally indicates, that there were ulterior objects in view, well understood, for the advancement of which occasions would be sought, and of the existence of which the countenance given to Pierpont, and the zeal about expositions in the Hall, were but symptoms, having their origin, however, in a settled design to effect a change in the influences which then controlled the institution.

From the religious and political relations of the period, the chance of success in this design was flattering, and all those who favored it endeavoured by zeal and activity to advance so desirable an event. Among the rest, Cotton Mather, notwithstanding he scrupulously abstained from attending the meetings of the board of Overseers, of which he was a member in right of his pastoral office, did not fail to encourage dissatisfaction, and promote discontent with the management of the College.

Cotton Mather's conduct.

As soon as Shute took possession of the Chair of State, this spirit begins to appear in Mather's Diary, his letters, and his acts. In July, 1717, he speaks of "Commencement, as they call it, as a time of much resort in Cambridge, and sorrily enough thrown away." The College he represents as being "in a very neglected and unhappy condition, and as betrayed into vile practices," so much so, that he states,* "he remained at home on that day in prayer, that it might be restored, and become a nursery of piety, industry, and all erudition."

When the attack, made upon the Corporation by Pierpont, was in discussion before the Overseers, the

* Sparks's American Biography, Vol. VI. p. 297.

CHAPTER XI.

opportunity to gratify his enmity to the administration of the College was too favorable to be passed by without an exertion, on his part, to aid in their discomfiture. He had early taken occasion to exhibit the qualities of Shute in malign contrast with those he attributed to his predecessor. "Our excellent Governor," he writes, "who has delivered the country from a flood of corruptions, which was introduced by selling places, is to be encouraged, and a course must be taken, that he may be vindicated from the aspersions of a cursed crew in this place, that traduce him."* Preparing the way for favor by language of this kind, he addressed a letter to Governor Shute on the 31st of October, 1718, being the very day on which the Overseers met to consider the complaints of Pierpont. In this, he lauds the Governor for "knowing no other interest than for the public"; speaks scornfully of "the unaccountably called Overseers of the College"; attempts to excite in Shute a prejudice against them, for not acknowledging their dependence on him, in whose "breath of favor" he intimates they exist; represents the charter under which they act as "a pretence and presumption"; calls Pierpont "the abused and oppressed"; and requests the Governor to bring "to a compendious issue the dispute between Pierpont and the *pretended President*," which he denominates a contest between a frog and a mouse ("βατραχομυομαχία"). After a course of remark thus opprobrious and hostile, he concludes with the following request, characteristic of his mind and of his motives. "Your Excellency's incomparable goodness and wisdom will easily discern

His letter to Governor Shute.

* Sparks's American Biography, Vol. VI. p. 296.

CHAPTER XI.

and approve the intention of the freedom used in this letter, and *have it and its writer covered under the darkest concealment.* And the rather, because, for some reasons, I desire to keep at the greatest distance from all the affairs of Harvard." *

Not satisfied with these exertions to embarrass the government of the College at home, Cotton Mather directed his endeavours to injure its interests abroad.

His letter to Elihu Yale.

In January, 1718, he addressed a letter to Elihu Yale, praising him for his "overflowing liberalities to objects on this side of the Atlantic," and extolling his inclination to do good; "bespeaks his favor for a people who are sound and generous Christians and Protestants, having a College at Saybrook, Connecticut;" intimates to him, that his munificence to it might "obtain for it the name of Yale College, which would be better than the name of sons and daughters. A seminary," he adds, "*from whence a good people expect the supply of all their synagogues.*" † From the temper of his mind at this time, it cannot be questioned, that he meant that Mr. Yale should understand, that Harvard College was not such a seminary. On the 25th of September of the same year, the College in Saybrook having then received the name of Yale, he writes to Governor Saltonstall, of Connecticut, telling him, "that Yale has done very little in proportion to what he will do, when once he finds the name of it;" and, taking to himself the credit both of the donation and the policy, he adds, "I confess it was a great and inexcusable presumption in me to make myself so far the godfather of the beloved infant as to propose a name for it." After saying, that "it is a thousand

His letter to Governor Saltonstall.

* See Appendix, No. XXXIV. † See Appendix, No. XXXV.

pities the dear infant should be strangled in the birth by a dissension," he thus utters his malediction upon Harvard College. "When the servants of God meet at your Commencement, I make no doubt, that they will deliberate on the interests of education and of religion, and not suffer an interview of your best men *to evaporate in such a senseless, useless, noisy impertinency, as it used to be with us at Cambridge.*"*

In the same spirit of hostility, and in a like underhand way, in which he attempted to injure Harvard College in the case of Pierpont, there is reason to believe, that he attempted, a few years afterwards, to turn the bounty of Thomas Hollis from Cambridge into the New Haven channel. The facts which lead to this conclusion claim to be recapitulated here, as they throw a strong light on the character of Hollis, and place in an interesting point of view the strength of his affection for Harvard. The connexion between Cotton Mather and Yale and Saltonstall, on the subject of favor and increased patronage of New Haven, is sufficiently established by the letters above quoted. In the former of these he refers Yale to "an excellent friend, our agent, Mr. Jeremiah Dummer, who has been a tender, prudent, and useful patron of the infant College at Connecticut, and who will doubtless wait upon you, propose to you and concert with you the methods in which your benignity to New Haven may be best expressed."

The bounty of Hollis began to flow towards Harvard College in the year 1719. In the succeeding year its friends had their expectations greatly raised by the hopes he had excited of founding in it a Pro-

* See Appendix, No. XXXVI.

CHAPTER XI.

fessorship of Divinity, and of more extensive bounties. In September of this year, Mr. Dummer, the agent for New Haven, sent for Mr. Hollis to meet him at a coffee-house, to show him a letter, and "to acquaint him about a College building at New Haven, and proposing it for his bounty." Hollis not encouraging the application, Dummer, in the February following, brought to him another letter, dated the July preceding, "handsomely worded, but no name to it, recommending to him the Collegiate School at New Haven. This letter came enclosed in one from Governor Saltonstall, of Connecticut, earnestly pressing the same affair." Hollis being neither pleased with the mode, the object, nor the agent (for he appears to have had no great respect for Dummer), utterly declined taking the subject into consideration. Dummer and his underhand mover were not, however, discouraged. In July and August, 1721, Hollis received two other "anonymous letters about Yale College." It is a curious fact, that, although one of these letters came under cover from Governor Saltonstall of Connecticut, Hollis believed the writer to be in Boston, or its vicinity, for he sends the letter to White, Treasurer of Harvard College. "I suppose him," Hollis writes, "to be urged on to it by your agent Dummer. I inclose it to you. I have no inclination to be diverted from my projected design. If you know the author, pray let him know so. I have told Dummer the same."* When we consider, that Governor Saltonstall would hardly have consented to have been the medium of an anonymous letter, unless he had known the author to be of some weight of char-

* See Appendix, No. XXXVII.

acter, — how unlikely it is, that such a person in Connecticut could have had a motive for concealment in respect to such an application to Hollis, — the connexion now established between Mather, Saltonstall, and Dummer, on this very subject of "benignity to New Haven," — Mather's avowed, new-born affection for that "dear infant Yale," and his disgust with Harvard, — the many motives Mather must have had to conceal any attempt of his to turn the bounty of Hollis away from Harvard, — the ceaseless activity which characterized him, and his capacity to resort to underhand measures to gratify his passions; the opinion, that he was the author of this attempt is forced upon the mind by a powerful concurrence of circumstances. He probably persuaded himself, that it was "an essay to serve the kingdom of God, and to beat Satan out of his quarters,"* as he denominated the College. Nor was he the only clergyman engaged in the design, of turning the bounties of Hollis away from Harvard. Thomas Prince, an alumnus, and minister of the Old South Church, in Boston, persuaded himself, also, of the wisdom or piety of that project. About this period he wrote a letter, to be communicated to Hollis, urging him to transfer his bounty to the library of the Old South Church, and suggesting to him by way of motive, that "we did not know into what hands the great library at Harvard College might fall, but that this private one would be secure to posterity."† The noble and faithful Hollis was indignant at the proposition. "I was disgusted," says he, "at the suggestion, and refused to read on, and directed Prince to be informed, that I disliked his motion, and would not be concerned."

* See Sparks's American Biography, Vol. VI. p. 329.

† See Appendix, No. XXXVIII.

CHAPTER XII.

Benefactions of Thomas Hollis. — Their Origin, Motive, and Extent. — His elevated Catholicism. — Reasons for examining a Part of his Bounties with Minuteness. — Pretensions of Increase Mather in Relation to them examined. — Commencement of his Donations. — Origin and first Form of his Professorship of Divinity. — Accepted and acted upon by the Corporation. — Edward Wigglesworth chosen Professor. — New England Scheme of the Professorship of Divinity transmitted to Mr. Hollis. — How modified by him. — Proceedings of the Overseers. — Debates on the amended Scheme. — Opposition of Chief Justice Sewall. — New Amendments proposed. — The Corporation choose Wigglesworth a second Time. — His Orthodoxy, how tested. — Discrepancy of the Test with the Statutes of Hollis. — A written Obligation to conform to his Statutes demanded of the Corporation by Hollis. — They hesitate about transmitting it. — Patience of Hollis exhausted. — He peremptorily demands it. — A written Obligation transmitted. — Liberal Character of Hollis vindicated.

CHAPTER XII.

Our narrative having arrived at the period when the first Hollis commenced his donations to Harvard College, gratitude demands they should be enumerated and acknowledged. One portion of his bounty having been forced into the service of ecclesiastical controversy, and the motives and principle of his charity called in question, a minute investigation and a strict historical statement of it will be given, in justice to the memory of the greatest of the early benefactors of the College.

In the literary horizon of Harvard the name of Hollis is applicable, not to a single star, but to a constellation. Six individuals* bearing it are entitled to rank high in the list of its benefactors. Of these, the first and greatest was Thomas Hollis, who was born in 1659, and died in 1731. Being educated by his father in the Baptist persuasion, he adhered to it through life with invincible attachment. The descendant of a family long eminent for piety and benevolence, he soon gave evidence of being heir of the faith and virtues, which had distinguished his ancestry. His attention had been directed towards Harvard College as early as 1690, in consequence of his being named one of the trustees in the will of his maternal uncle, Robert Thorner, in which it had been made the object of a noble bequest. Dr. Mather, President of the College, being about that time in England, Hollis communicated to him an account of Thorner's legacy, with a copy of the clause containing it, for the purpose of being registered in the archives of the College. He soon after named it as the object of a legacy in his own will, as we learn from a letter written by Henry Newman, the agent of the Corporation in England, to President Leverett, dated the 26th of June, 1710. Newman had been directed by Leverett to make inquiries concerning Sir Robert Thorner's legacy. In this letter, after acknowledging the full satisfaction he had received from the trustees on that subject, he adds, "Mr. Thomas Hollis, one of the trustees, at the Cross Daggers, in Little Minories, *desires his will may be inquired for after his decease.*" Thus careful was Hollis, that the College should reap the benefit of his own and his uncle's bounty, and thus early did his friendship for it commence.

* See Appendix, No. XXXIX.

CHAPTER XII.

Hollis's first donation.

After this time the records of the College indicate no intercourse with Hollis, until the spring of 1719, when, having watched the course of the seminary for many years, and satisfied himself, that the views of the Corporation were catholic and liberal, he resolved to be the executor of his own will, and to have the pleasure of witnessing the result of his own benevolence. In that year he made his first remittance of books for the College Library, and of moneys "for the assistance of pious young men, who were destined for the ministry." The motives to his bounty are thus stated by him, in a letter to Dr. Colman, whom he selected as the chief medium of his communications.* "After forty years' diligent application to mercantile business, my God, whom I serve, has mercifully succeeded my endeavours, and, with my increase, inclined my heart to a proportional distribution. I have credited the promise, 'He that giveth to the poor, lendeth to the Lord,' and have found it verified in this life."

From this time his bounty flowed towards the College in a continuous stream, enlarging its beneficiary fund, increasing its library, and at last concentrating in the establishment of two Professorships, one of Divinity, the other of Mathematics and Natural Philosophy, and amounting in the whole to nearly five thousand pounds Massachusetts currency, not including various contributions to the Library, numerous, select, and costly; a munificence, in point of value and amount, then without example in this country, and which, considering the value of money at the time, bears an honorable comparison with that of any subsequent period.

* January 28th, 1721.

CHAPTER XII.

His motives and spirit.

"The free and catholic spirit of the seminary," says Dr. Colman, "took his generous heart." Although some of its superintending powers, at that period, had little claim to this character, yet, from the influences which predominated, it was more deserving of that title than any of its contemporaries, either in Europe or America. This was perceived by Hollis, who, during life, through good report and evil report, adhered to his predilection for Harvard.

The religious spirit of Hollis was elevated and comprehensive. It is difficult to conceive of a charity more truly regulated by the principles of Christianity, than that evidenced by the whole tenor of his correspondence with the College and its officers; "envying not; vaunting not; seeking not its own; not easily provoked; rejoicing in the truth; believing all things; hoping all things; enduring all things."

Attached to his Baptist faith, with a firmness which admitted neither concealment nor compromise, he selected for the object of his extraordinary bounties, an institution, in which he knew those of his faith were regarded with dread by some, and with detestation by others, and where he had reason to think, as he averred, that the very portrait of a Baptist, though of a benefactor, would be the subject of insult. Yet he suffered neither his affection nor his charity to fail, being actuated by the elevated motive, that it was more catholic and free in its religious sentiment than any other institution existing at that period. In establishing conditions for enjoying the benefit of his bounty, he claimed no concession, he made no exclusion. He required only, that the Baptist faith should not be deemed a disqualification for partaking his bounty, or for being a candidate for his Pro-

CHAPTER XII.

fessorship. In order to place an insurmountable barrier against the imposition of artificial creeds, woven in words of men's devising, he made the simple provision, that the only articles of faith, to which the Professor on the Divinity foundation, which he established, should be required to subscribe, was, "his belief that the Scriptures of the Old and New Testaments are the only perfect rule of faith and manners."

Thus did this noble and generous spirit break away from the thraldom of sects. It is delightful to contemplate a benefactor thus divested of all that is mean, and vain, and selfish; opening the hand of his charity without the dictation of party spirit; guiding himself by the oracles of God, and not by the inventions and worldly devices of men; fixed in his own faith, yet candid in judging, and charitable in construing, the faith of others. "I love them," he writes in a letter to Dr. Colman,* "that show, by their works, that they love Jesus Christ. While I bear with others, who are sincere in their more confined charity, I would that they would bear with me in my more enlarged. We search after truth. We see but in part. Happy the man, who reduces his notions in a constant train of practice. Charity is the grace, which now adorns and prepares for glory. May it always abide in your breast and mine, and grow more and more."

His devoted charity.

The several donations of this benefactor demand, as has been intimated, an exact statement, not only on account of their extent and extraordinary character, but from the misapprehensions which have arisen concerning some of them. Singular as is the fact, a portion of his bounty has been made the occasion of

* August 1st, 1720.

an attempt to give a party bias to the institution, and to introduce an examination into articles of faith as a condition of office. One of the most catholic and liberal of men has been made to appear in the light of a sectarian to some, and of a bigot to others. A thorough investigation of the order and nature of his benefactions is, therefore, equally due to gratitude and justice.

As already stated,* the first donation of Mr. Hollis was made in the year 1719. It was transmitted to Mr. Craddock, in articles to be sold on his account, and the proceeds to be paid over to Mr. Leverett, President of Harvard College. The product, amounting to about three hundred pounds Massachusetts currency, was paid, according to this order, to the Treasurer of the College, and the thanks of the Corporation were given to Mr. Craddock, "for his generous care of managing the donation of Mr. Hollis, and not charging commissions." On the same day a vote passed that body, granting the interest of Mr. Hollis's donation, and of another by Mr. Hulton, to the son of Cotton Mather, for his support in College,† "pursuant to the desire of the Rev. Dr. Increase Mather, his grandfather, who was instrumental in procuring these donations." This claim of Dr. Mather, "founded on his instrumentality," was immediately made the subject of a question. President Leverett, who kept a duplicate of the records, thus states the counterpart in his Diary. Of Hulton's legacy he says, that "Dr. Mather was," and of Hollis's, that "he might be, instrumental in procuring it," intimating an uncertainty, without any offensive contradiction.

Claim set up by Increase Mather.

* See above, p. 232.

† College Records, Vol. IV. p. 65.

CHAPTER XII.

When Dr. Benjamin Colman informed Hollis of this claim set up by Dr. Mather, for the income of his fund, Hollis, in reply,* expresses his surprise and sorrow, that Dr. Mather's grandson should need the aid of his bounty; and adds, "I have nothing to object, rather glad he is first preferred." Concerning Dr. Mather's "instrumentality" in obtaining it he is silent, but immediately proceeds to state the real source of his good will towards the College. "I have had many thoughts of showing some liberality to it ever since the death of my honored uncle, Robert Thorner, who made me one of his trustees." By thus carrying back the origin of his good intentions to a time antecedent to any possible influence of Dr. Mather, he obviously intended to exclude any acknowledgment of it. He then proceeds to state the actual intercourse between them. "When Dr. Mather was in England, I gave him a minute out of the said will to register in your College; but the payment is yet very distant, many years. I hope it will be honestly transmitted in the time." Delicacy did not permit Hollis to say more. What he does say, however, is sufficient to show the groundlessness of Dr. Mather's claim to instrumentality in procuring his bounty, and his indisposition to recognise it. Notwithstanding this, Cotton Mather, in the year 1724, at a time when the benefactions of Thomas Hollis had already become, from their number and amount, the objects of general gratitude and admiration, in writing the life of his father, thus boldly asserts him to have been the moving cause of these benefactions. "It was *his* (Increase Mather's) acquaintance with, and

Hollis's statement concerning it.

* Hollis's letter to Colman, January 14th, 1720.

CHAPTER XII.

his proposal to that good-spirited man, and lover of all good men, Mr. Thomas Hollis, that introduced his benefactions unto that (Harvard) College; to which his incomparable bounty has anon flowed unto such a degree, as to render him the greatest benefactor it ever had in the world."* An assertion, there is reason to believe, wholly gratuitous, but in character with Cotton Mather's self-glorifying spirit.†

Cotton Mather's statement.

On the 14th of the succeeding April,‡ Hollis transmitted his second donation to the College Treasurer, amounting to about seven hundred pounds currency. The object of this and his former bounty had been previously stated by him in his letters to Colman,§ to be "the maintenance and education of pious young men for the ministry, who are poor in this world." In this letter he intimates, that his gifts may be increased, and inquires "in what manner he might best express his gift, so as to answer his intention to assist poor and pious young men in their studies for the ministry." Both branches of the College government were naturally impressed by the amount, and kind spirit indicated by these remittances, and with the propriety of fully expressing their grateful acknowledgments. On the 24th of May, the Corporation voted their thanks to him; and on the 23d of the succeeding June the Overseers appointed a Committee to prepare a letter of thanks, which, being reported and approved, they ordered, on the 6th of the ensuing July, to be signed and transmitted to him.‖

Second donation of Hollis.

Corporation and Overseers thank Hollis.

Before these proceedings had reached Hollis, he had addressed another letter to Colman, dated the

* Life of Increase Mather, by his Son, p. 170.

† See above, p. 135. ‡ 1720. § January 14th, 1720.

‖ Overseers' Records. — Leverett's Manuscript, pp. 174, 178.

CHAPTER XII.

1st of August, stating in general terms his intentions relative to his donations; reserving to himself, during life, the nomination of those students, who were to receive the income of his bounty, and after his death devolving that duty on the Corporation of the College. In this letter also, he declares his preference of adult baptism, and his spirit of catholic communion with all; and expresses the hope, "that, while he bears with others in their more confined, that they would bear with him in his more enlarged, charity."

The thanks of the Board of Overseers seem to have been couched in terms sufficiently laudatory; for, in a subsequent letter to Colman, he says, "they made him blush, that he is weary of their thanks, and begs they might cease."

This intervention of the Overseers alarmed Hollis. He well understood the prevailing bigotry of that board, and he had, by the advice of Colman, specially intrusted the Corporation with the distribution of his funds. He inquires, therefore, in a letter dated the 10th of September, 1720, apparently with some anxiety, "whether that body will have any voice in the nomination of his beneficiaries." *

Before this period, Hollis had entertained no idea of establishing a Professorship of Divinity. His plan of bounty had been limited to that most useful and effective of all endowments, the establishing funds for the education of poor, pious, and able young men for the ministry. This is evident from his next letter to Colman and Leverett, dated the 23d September, 1720, by which it appears, that they had "proposed to him to establish a suitable stipend for a Divinity

* See Appendix, No. XL.

Professor, to read lectures in the Hall to the students." In his reply, he expresses his surprise at their deficiency in this respect, and requests them "to explain more largely that matter to him, and to tell him how much will be called an honorable stipend."*

Divinity Professorship founded by Hollis.

Without waiting for an answer to these inquiries, Hollis, on the 14th of February, 1721, executed formal "orders" relative to the moneys he had sent over to New England. This instrument is the true foundation of that Professorship. In it he establishes that office in the College, and provides for the support of his Professor. And, as it is indicative of his pure intent and catholic spirit, the original document is subjoined, as it now exists in the archives of the College, subscribed by his hand.†

The foundation of the Professorship is in these words. "I order and appoint a Professor of Divinity, to read lectures in the Hall of the College unto the students; the said Professor to be nominated and appointed from time to time by the President and Fellows of Harvard College; and that the Treasurer pay to him forty pounds per annum for his service, and that when choice is made of a fitting person, to be recommended to me for my approbation, if I be yet living."

The instrument then proceeds to appoint a compensation to the Treasurer for the care of his funds; and to specify the disposition to be made of the remaining income of his bounty, in terms the most liberal and free from all words of sectarian import; the only allusion to religious opinion being, that no "candidate should be refused on account of his belief and practice

* See Appendix, No. XLI. † See Appendix, No. XLII.

of adult baptism." Being a Baptist himself, and being about to found a Professorship of Divinity, and to extend, in other ways, a helping hand to an institution under the influence of men, with whom the divine right of infant baptism was an essential article of their creed; and making on his part no condition that Baptists should be preferred, it was a fixed purpose of his mind, that Baptists, on account of their faith, should not be excluded from any of the advantages of his bounty. This fixed intent appears from the tenor of all his letters, and was the extent and the limit of the influence of religious opinion on his mind.

Its unrestricted nature.

Such was the foundation of the Hollis Professorship of Divinity, as it was first conceived and laid by this eminent benefactor; with no words of technical or theological art; with nothing mysterious, equivocal, restrictive, or doctrinal, prescribed by way of qualification of the Professor or students.

Neither does it appear from any word or intimation in his correspondence, that he asked or contemplated any other rule or restriction, except that Baptists should be regarded, in relation to the application of his funds, on the same footing as other denominations of Christians. He inquires of Colman, "how much will be called an honorable stipend for his Professor," and asks him to "explain more largely that matter" (the want of a Divinity Professor) "to him." He had indeed several times inquired of Mr. Colman, "in what manner he had best express his gift." In every instance this inquiry had relation, as appears by his letters, to the income of his funds, intended for the benefit of "poor and pious young men." His letters bear traces of his belief in those general doctrines, in which all the prevailing sects of Christians throughout Christendom at that day concurred; but they contain not a word indicative of a design or desire to use the power his wealth conferred, to establish his belief as a standard for future times.

The course of the bounty of Thomas Hollis has been thus traced to the first form in which his Professorship of Divinity appeared, and the result has shown, that the nature of the foundation was consonant to the well-known characteristics of his mind, — free from bigotry, — of a comprehensive charity, in the spirit of which he submitted, in unqualified terms, the selection of his Professor, and the conduct of his Professorship, to the decision of the President and Fellows of the Corporation, for the time being, without other rule than such as from time to time their own consciences and views of the interests of the College might dictate.

It now becomes a curious and interesting subject of investigation, how this unshackled, free condition of the first foundation of the Hollis Professorship of Divinity was attempted to be changed; how these attempts were met by the generous and catholic spirit of Hollis; and by what means words were introduced into formal statutes subsequently signed by Hollis, and a contemporaneous construction of them given, so as to make this most liberal of all minds to appear in after times, as a founder of a religious test in an institution into which such test had never been introduced, and but once attempted and then rejected; and, what is more wonderful still, how such a course of proceeding was pursued, as to make Hollis apparently acquiesce in such a contemporaneous construction of these introduced terms, as should allow a belief *in the divine right of infant baptism to be an ex-*

CHAPTER XII.

amined and required article of a Professor's faith, under statutes in which he had expressly provided, that the belief his Professor should declare, was, "that the Scriptures of the Old and New Testaments are the only perfect rule of faith and manners," and under "orders concerning the disposition of his moneys sent to New England, that none should be refused on account of his belief and practice of adult baptism."

The records of the College, illustrated by contemporary documents and well-known history, will render this investigation both easy and satisfactory.

Proceedings of the Corporation relative to the Divinity Professorship.

The "orders," dated the 14th of February, were accompanied by letters from Mr. Hollis and Mr. Neal. The letters are acknowledged to have been communicated at a meeting of the Corporation on the 25th of April, 1721, and "to relate to the setting up a Professorship of Divinity at the College, and desiring some further advice and information in that affair." As these letters are missing, the proceedings of the Corporation are the only means of ascertaining the advice and information they sought. On receiving these communications a committee was immediately appointed "to prepare a draft of such information in order to its being forwarded." On the 2d of May, 1721, the draft was reported, accepted, and ordered to be transmitted to Mr. Hollis and Mr. Neal. On the 21st of June this report was spread at large on the records of the Corporation, under the title of "minutes directory, in answer to Mr. Hollis his letters." * In these, "thanks were given for his bounty; his candor and confidence in leaving his institution open and alterable, acknowl-

* See Appendix, No. XLIII.

edged; various prudential arrangements of his funds suggested; and rules relative to the lectures of the Professor, and studies on his foundation, proposed; but not one word indicative of a design to give a sectarian bias, or to establish a religious test, was introduced. The only expressions having a tendency towards a religious qualification are conceived in a noble spirit of liberality, consentaneous with that of which Mr. Hollis had set the example, and worthy of the men who then constituted the Corporation; such as Leverett, Colman, Wadsworth, and Appleton. "As to the Professor's being in communion with a particular church, we judge it," say they, "highly expedient; and, *as to the limitation of that communion, we leave it to Mr. Hollis.*"

They choose Wigglesworth Professor.

The next step taken by the Corporation, was to elect a Professor, in strict conformity with the "orders" of Mr. Hollis, and with the most marked solemnity and formality. A special meeting of the board was held on the 28th of June, 1721. No other business was transacted. Six of the seven members of which the board was composed were present. The question of proceeding to elect a Professor to be presented to Mr. Hollis, was formally proposed and voted. Ballots were brought in, and Edward Wigglesworth was accordingly declared, and his name ordered to be sent to Mr. Hollis, as "the Professor of Divinity, chosen upon his institution."* The exact formality, with which this record is marked, becomes important to be noted, in consequence of subsequent proceedings.

Thus far the Corporation had pursued the measures

* See Appendix, No. XLIV.

prescribed in the letters and "orders" of Mr. Hollis. They had chosen a Professor. They had ordered "advice and information" to be transmitted to him. No record of the Corporation or the Overseers indicates, that "a scheme for the Professorship of Divinity" had been asked for by Mr. Hollis, or been submitted to the consideration of either board, or been authorized to be transmitted to him. It is not therefore without surprise, that, on the 8th of August, 1721, Mr. Hollis is found acknowledging the receipt of five letters (dated the 5th of April, the 5th of May, and the 6th, 9th, and 26th of June) from Mr. Colman and Mr. Leverett, accompanied by "a scheme for the Professor's work."

The motives which induced Mr. Colman and Mr. Leverett thus to change the "advice and information," authorized and voted by the Corporation in the "minutes directory in answer to Mr. Hollis his letters," into "a scheme of a Professorship," no documents indicate. It is, however, one of the symptomatic circumstances attending the early correspondence concerning this Divinity Professorship, that, while the other letters of Mr. Hollis to Mr. Colman are apparently complete and well preserved, those between the 28th of January and the 8th of August, 1721, the period of the early stage of that negotiation, have disappeared as well as all those written by Neal, Colman, and Leverett. Yet it is apparent, that many very important and critical letters must have passed.* We are left, therefore, necessarily to draw such conclusions concerning the motives of this policy, as the known relations of the religious sects of the time, and subsequent

* See Appendix, No. XLV.

CHAPTER XII.

Sectarian alarm and its cause.

unquestionable occurrences authorize. At this period of colonial history the sect of the Baptists was peculiarly obnoxions to that division of the Congregational church, which comprised the strictest adherents to the Calvinistic doctrines. To them the fact, that an avowed member of the Baptist persuasion was about to establish a Professorship of Divinity in Harvard University was a subject of great anxiety; but, when they ascertained that Mr. Hollis had reserved to himself the right of establishing, during his life, or by his will, such rules relative to his Professorship, as he might deem proper, their apprehensions were raised to the highest point of excitement and alarm. It is apparent, that the Corporation of the College did not participate in these fears, from the confidence their language indicates in Mr. Hollis, and their hitherto exact acquiescence in the course of measures he had marked out in his "orders" of the 14th of February, 1721. But the members of the Corporation themselves were, on certain points, as we have seen, deemed by some of the stricter Calvinists little better than heretics, and by others had been denounced for "apostasy."

The acceptance of Hollis's Professorship and approval of his Professor, did not exclusively depend on the votes of the Corporation. The concurrence of the Overseers was requisite in respect to both. The strength of the sectarian spirit, then existing in that board, was known to the Corporation; and it cannot be doubted, that the course of measures they subsequently adopted was intended to remove or diminish the apprehensions, which the circumstances attending the foundation of this Professorship had ex-

CHAPTER XII.

"The New England Scheme."

cited among the Overseers. New "orders" were therefore sought from Mr. Hollis, couched in language more acceptable to the adherents of the Calvinistic faith. Of the "orders" of the 14th of February preceding, nothing is said in the records either of the Corporation or the Overseers. They would not, probably, have been preserved among the archives of the College, if they had not been connected with other funds besides those appropriated to his Professorship. The "advice and information" requested by Mr. Hollis was construed to authorize the transmission of a formal draft of "rules and orders" for the Professorship. These were prepared, doubtless, with great care and consultation, and, being sent out, were denominated by Mr. Hollis, "the New England scheme for the Professor's work." Of the origin, preparation, or transmission of this "scheme," nothing is said in any record; and its existence would now be unknown, were it not for letters, and subsequent documents, transmitted by Mr. Hollis. The advantage of making the first draft of an instrument of this kind is very obvious. It gave an opportunity to introduce such terms, as, being used sometimes in a technical and sometimes in a popular sense, would render it difficult for Mr. Hollis to perceive the construction intended to be given to them; or, if he perceived it, would render it even more difficult for him either to erase, or so to qualify, as to preclude the sectarian spirit from evading them. That such was the policy of the measure, admits at this day no question. since *such words were introduced into "the New England scheme,"* and *such a construction was afterwards made of them*, notwithstanding their inconsistence with the unvaried tenor of Mr. Hollis's existing let-

Policy of the measure.

ters, and the express terms of his statutes and "orders."

Not approved by Hollis.

"The scheme," as it came from New England, was not approved by Mr. Hollis. "I have received your letters and scheme," says he, "and on due consideration I think it requires some amendments;" for which purpose, he informs Colman, that he had delivered it over to "several worthy pastors of churches here," desiring them to make alterations and remarks upon "the scheme transmitted," which, when finished, he says, "I shall send over for your more mature consideration." The spirit in which he declares this course was adopted by him is admirable, and worthy of all praise; "Believing," says he, "that you and they have nothing in view herein, but furthering of the glory of God, promoting good literature, and the true knowledge of theology and the well understanding the sacred Scriptures."*

The particular points in the "New England scheme," to which he objected, and which he thought required amendments, are not stated by Mr. Hollis, and are only to be inferred from his known sentiments, and the views he avowed in establishing his professorship. In the New England scheme the terms "sound and orthodox" were, however, of a character most adapted to excite his apprehensions. By other of his letters it appears he knew well, that, in New England, and particularly among leading members of the board of Overseers, "the divine right of infant baptism was one of the essential points of orthodoxy;" and he could not but perceive, that, under this term, by New England construction, a Baptist might be for

* See Appendix, No. XLV.

ever excluded from his professorship. It is evident there was a fixed purpose in Mr. Hollis's mind, on the one hand, that he would not require a Baptist should be chosen to his professorship, and on the other, that a Baptist, on account of his faith, should not be excluded. It can, therefore, scarcely be doubted, that these terms were among those, which he considered required amendment or modification. This his subsequent conduct evidences very clearly.

How modified.

"The worthy pastors," seven in number, to whom Mr. Hollis delivered the "New England scheme" for his professorship, returned it to him, after solemn deliberation, in due time, amended. This original paper, with the signatures of these pastors, exists at the present time among the archives of the University. It is dated, "London, August 22d, 1721," and contains eleven articles, in which the differences from the New England scheme are noted.*

It appears, that all the articles as modified by the seven pastors were acceded to by Mr. Hollis, except the eleventh, which was in these words.

"XI. That it be recommended to the electors, that at every choice they prefer a man of solid learning in divinity, of sound and orthodox principles; one who is well gifted to teach; of a sober and pious life, and of a grave conversation."

The form of this article, although it had retained the term "orthodox" only as a recommendation to the electors, and not in the form of a qualification of the Professor, it appears did not satisfy Mr. Hollis. He was obviously placed in a dilemma. He could not strike out the word "orthodox" on the one hand,

* See Appendix, No. XLVI.

CHAPTER XII.

because, in a certain sense, it belonged to him, and he recognised it. On the other hand, in a New England sense, it did not belong to him, and he rejected it. Yet he anticipated, that, if the scheme were signed as reported by "the worthy pastors," it might be construed into a test and qualification of his professor; a result, of all others, which his generous and catholic spirit deprecated. The course he adopted, as his statutes show, was to accept the eleventh article, in the terms proposed by the "pastors"; and to cause immediately to be subjoined,* and made a substantive part of his statutes, *that the only article of belief required of his Divinity Professor at his inauguration should be, "that the Scriptures of the Old and New Testament are the only perfect rule of faith and manners."* Thus successfully did Hollis, as he thought, secure his professor from the yoke of sects, which he feared might be laid upon him; and guard against such a construction of the term "orthodox," as should exclude a Baptist from his professorship. The event showed how weak are rules and statutes when they thwart sectarian interests or policy.

How farther modified by Hollis.

The "New England scheme," thus modified, was transmitted by Mr. Hollis to the Corporation, and by them submitted to the Overseers on the 10th of January, 1721-2. After voting thanks to Mr. Hollis, the Overseers unanimously resolved, "that the establishing a Professorship of Divinity at the said College, under *proper regulations*, will, by the blessing of God, very much conduce to the advancement of theology among the students there, to promote the true Christian religion throughout the whole land, and there-

Proceeding of the Overseers.

* See Appendix, No. XLVII.

CHAPTER XII.

in very much answer the great and pious end of incorporating the said College." * They then proceeded to declare, by way of preamble, that "the qualifications and regulations of the said professorship were a matter of very great importance to the religion of New England, and that the founder himself also had been pleased, in his own letter to the Corporation, to desire them duly to consider of the said rules and orders, and send over such needful amendments as should be thought fit," and after making some additional provisions relative to the duty of the professor, and some verbal alterations, they come to the eleventh article, which was the real object of all their policy. Their purpose, it appears, was twofold; first, to modify this article in such a manner as to constitute a test or qualification, and thus introduce an examination, inquisition, and declaration of particular faith by the professor; and next, to give to it such a contemporaneous construction as should exclude, if possible, a Baptist for ever from the professorship. This policy is developed by the subsequent proceedings, and is farther illustrated by the account given by Chief Justice Sewall of the nature and violence of the debates which occurred on this occasion, and of the measures in which they eventuated. His Diary states, that the debate, commenced in the forenoon, was continued through the day, and that the Governor left the board in displeasure late in the afternoon. By the records of the Overseers it also appears, that the meeting was adjourned, without completing the business before them, from the 10th to the 24th of January. The objections made are stated distinctly in Judge Sewall's

Their violent debates.

* See Appendix, No. XLVIII.

Judge Sewall's account of them.

Diary. The whole passage is sufficiently important to be given in his words. "January 10th, 1721. Overseers of the College meet at the Council Chamber, to consider Mr. Hollis's proposals as to his Professor of Divinity. Debate was had in the forenoon about the article 'He shall be a master of arts, and in communion with a church of Congregationalists, Presbyterians, or Baptists.' I objected against that article, as choosing rather to lose the donation than accept it. In the afternoon I said, 'One great end for which the planters came over into New England was to fly from the cross in baptism. For my part, I had rather have baptism administered with the incumbrance of the cross, than not to have it administered at all. This qualification of the Divinity Professor is to me a bribe to give my sentence in disparagement of infant baptism, and I will endeavour to shake my hands from holding it.'

"When it came to the vote, very few appeared in the negative. I desired to have my dissent entered. The Governor denied it with an air of displeasure, saying, '*You shall not have it.*' It was seven or eight o'clock before we had gone through the constitutions. His Excellency went away long before."

The principles on which the opposition of Sewall was founded, satisfactorily explain the motives of the Overseers in these and their subsequent proceedings. By striking out of the New England scheme, as it was returned amended by Hollis, the words "recommendatory to the Electors," and inserting those implying a qualification, the Overseers had established, as they intended, *a test.* It now only remained to give such a contemporaneous construction of that article as should form a precedent of examination, inquisition,

CHAPTER XII.

and declaration, conformable to the New England notion of orthodoxy, including particularly "faith in the divine right of infant baptism," which the statutes and "orders" of Hollis put in such eminent hazard. For this purpose, an adjournment was made by the Overseers to the 24th of January. That such was their object is apparent from the next measures of the Corporation, which, considering the eminently fair and catholic spirit of its members, can only be accounted for, on the supposition, that they acted under the direct pressure, if not absolute dictation, of the board of Overseers. The Corporation had probably ascertained, that the bounty of Hollis would be rejected by the Overseers, and his good will consequently lost, unless they complied with the course which the proceedings of the Overseers indicated that board required of them.

Overseers adjourn.

The Corporation had already reciprocated the liberal spirit of Mr. Hollis in the most unqualified terms, and expressly submitted to him the "limitation of the communion of his professor." In conformity with his "orders" of the 24th of February, 1720-21, they had in the month of June succeeding elected Mr. Wigglesworth Professor of Divinity, without applying any test, or making any examination into his faith. This election had been by ballot, in a meeting of the board at which six members were present, and his name had been, in the most formal manner, "sent to Mr. Hollis for his approbation, in a letter signed by the President and Mr. Colman."*

It is evident, that the action of the Corporation on the subject of Mr. Wigglesworth, was completed,

* See above, pp. 239-243.

and that, after the approval of Mr. Hollis was received, it only remained for them to present the election of Mr. Wigglesworth to the Overseers for their approbation.

It is not, therefore, without surprise, that we find the following statement on the records of the Corporation.

Meeting of the Corporation.

"At a meeting of the Corporation of Harvard College, at the House of the Rev. Mr. Wadsworth, in Boston, January 23d, 1721-2. Present, Mr. President, Mr. Wadsworth, Mr. Colman, Mr. Treasurer Hutchinson. The Corporation, having discoursed among themselves about choosing a Professor of Divinity on Mr. Hollis's foundation, *and having formerly their thoughts upon Mr. Edward Wigglesworth for that service*, they sent for him, and, having discoursed him in general, and put such questions unto him in particular, as by his answers gave them satisfaction about the soundness and orthodoxy of his principles in divinity, they did elect the said Mr. Edward Wigglesworth to be Professor of Divinity on Mr. Hollis's foundation."

Elect Wigglesworth a second time.

Thus, on the 23d of January, 1722, the Corporation are found in a meeting, at which only four members were present, representing an election of a Professor, made on the 28th of June preceding, at a meeting when six members were present, and which had been sent to Mr. Hollis for his approbation, as only "having formerly their thoughts upon Mr. Wigglesworth"; and then, after sending for him, and examining him as to his "soundness and orthodoxy," proceeding to declare his election, without ballot, and with the presence only of a mere quorum of the board.

The extraordinary nature of these proceedings sufficiently indicates, that they had relation to the meeting

CHAPTER XII.

of the Overseers, which had been adjourned to the day following, and had particular reference to the contemporaneous construction of those technical terms, which the objections made in that board required of the Corporation; and that the chief object of this meeting was to establish the precedent of examination into "soundness and orthodoxy."

Cause of this proceeding.

The Corporation, however, had the prudence and delicacy to leave the particular points of their examination, by which they tested Mr. Wigglesworth's orthodoxy, unspecified on their records. They had also, probably, conscientious misgivings, that some of the topics of inquiry did not altogether coincide with their implied engagements to Mr. Hollis. The acquiescence of such men as Leverett, Colman, and Wadsworth, in measures thus inconsistent with the liberal spirit, for which they were distinguished, is not, however, to be attributed solely to their fear of losing the Professorship of Divinity by the negative of the Overseers, but to the violence of party spirit, which was raging in that board and the House of Representatives against the Corporation, and which was then countenancing measures tending to remove the obnoxious members of it from their seats. The nature of these will be hereafter stated and explained.

The considerations of prudence and delicacy, evidenced in the records of the Corporation, did not answer the purposes of the Overseers. They wanted not merely a general examination into the "soundness and orthodoxy" of the candidate, but a special statement of their construction of those terms, for the guidance of future times. Therefore, at their meeting on the 24th of January, 1722, the day after the meeting of the Corporation, when the President of the College reported their choice of Mr. Wigglesworth for confirmation, stating, "that, preceding the choice, they had examined him upon several important heads of divinity; the Overseers, first approving that examination, and then confirming Mr. Wigglesworth, immediately caused the following order to be entered upon their records, under the head of "Professor Wigglesworth's creed." "Ordered by the Overseers, that a minute be taken and recorded, of the several heads in divinity, upon which the Corporation examined Mr. Wigglesworth, viz. that he appeared before the Corporation, and declared his assent, 1. To Dr. Ames's 'Medulla Theologiæ.' 2. To the Confession of Faith contained in the Assembly's Catechism. 3. To the doctrinal Articles of the Church of England. More particularly; 1. To the doctrine of the Holy Trinity. 2. To the doctrine of the eternal Godhead of the blessed Saviour. 3. To the doctrine of Predestination. 4. To the doctrine of special efficacious grace. 5. To the divine right of infant baptism."

Further proceedings of the Overseers.

By thus enumerating all the particular points on which Mr. Wigglesworth had been examined, including "the divine right of infant baptism," the Overseers unquestionably intended to fix, by contemporaneous construction, the meaning of the terms "sound and orthodox."

Their inconsistency with good faith.

These proceedings can hardly be reconciled with good faith to Mr. Hollis; first, in the attempt to establish the divine right of infant baptism as a required article of belief, under statutes established by a Baptist, which expressly provided that the professor might be of the Baptist communion; and under "orders" concerning the disposition of his moneys sent

CHAPTER XII.

to New England, "that none should be refused on account of his belief and practice of adult baptism;"* secondly, in compelling a professor to make a formal declaration of belief in all the points of high Calvinism, under statutes which expressly provide, that the only declaration required of the professor should be, "that the Scriptures of the Old and New Testaments are the only perfect rule of faith and manners."

Notwithstanding these deviations from the principles of Mr. Hollis's statutes and orders, unanimity was not obtained. *Three* out of the *fourteen* members of the board, who voted on the approval of Mr. Wigglesworth, were, according to Mr. Sewall's Diary, dissentient.† It is probable, however, that the course adopted tended to reconcile the other members of the board, and established his election.

This construction of the terms "sound and orthodox," and this required declaration of all the high points of Calvinism, were, it can scarcely be doubted, never made known to Mr. Hollis. They were in such direct opposition to the spirit and letter of his statutes and orders, that if they had been communicated to him, it is hardly possible he should not have severely commented upon them.

By Hollis's letter to Colman, of June 8th, 1722, subsequent to these measures, it appears he had notice of the acceptance of his professorship by the Overseers; that "a fair copy of his orders, with the amendments of the board of Overseers," had been sent to him; which he approved, "depending upon your (Mr. Colman's) judgment, that for the present it is best." "I am thinking," he writes, "to

* See above, p. 242.

† See Appendix, No. XI.

add some clause more binding, that my heirs and successors may have power to see my rules and orders fulfilled, according as I hinted to you last year in my letters."

It appears, also, by this letter, that Mr. Hollis had been informed of the debates in the board of Overseers on his statutes and orders, and of the part the Governor had taken in their favor; but no allusion is made to the examination and declaration required of his professor on certain articles of belief previous to his admission to the office. "I am sorry," he observes, "to hear of some men's spirits, and grieved I have occasion to say so much of my own particular persuasion about baptism, a point I am far from imposing on any, nor for writing or discoursing about unless necessarily called unto it."

"In relation to my devoted moneys," he adds, "I have confidence in the present Corporation, that they will not alter my intended purposes (which are sacred to me) without my leave, while I live, whatever changes in my rules and orders it may come into their heads to make after I am dead." His anxiety on this subject is again intimated in a postscript to the same letter. "I must pray you to have regard to the rules relating to my trust, which you have by you under my hand, till such time as I return you the fair copy, signed in form, with your amendments." These successive expressions would certainly not have been used by Mr. Hollis, had he been correctly informed of the total disregard of his statutes, in respect to Baptists, evinced by the Overseers, and of the declaration of faith they had required of his professor. These proceedings of the Overseers were confined to their records, to which Mr. Hollis had no means of

Hollis postpones signing the amended orders.

CHAPTER XII.

access. But, aware of the sectarian spirit prevalent in that board, and of the bigotry of some of its members, his fears were excited relative to the perversion of his funds, and he demanded farther security for the observance of his statutes. His letter to Dr. Colman, dated August 18th, 1722, renders this evident. "I do now, Sir, entreat you to acquaint Mr. President and the Corporation, that they should send me over some writing obligatory, that they will now, and in time following, perform this my trust, committed to them pursuant to my orders, which I have signed or shall sign with my hand and seal; which I may leave with my heirs at my decease, who may have some power to examine that your successors are faithful in the trust, and do not divert the principal nor income to other purposes." "*The late uncharitable reflections of some upon the Baptists as not orthodox*, together with the present or later motions of some to alter, by changing or increasing hands in the governing power of the Corporation, makes me think it to be needful, and I hope they will grant it me." "I have some minutes by me to strengthen my orders, as I think, but am not yet resolved, whether to add it to your present parchment writing you sent me, or to leave it sealed up with my will."

Hollis alarmed for his trusts.

Hesitates about signing the amended statutes.

"I have been prevailed upon, at your instances, to sit the first time for my picture, — a present to your Hall. *I doubt not but that they are pleased with my moneys;* but I have some reason to think, that some among you will not be well pleased to see the shade of a Baptist hung there, unless you get a previous order to admit it, and forbidding any indecency to it; which, if they do, though I am at a distance, the birds of the air will tell it, and I shall be grieved; as I have been already."

His opinion of the religious spirit of New England.

Being apprized of the temper, in which the New England religious controversies were in that day conducted, he adds, "I pray God to allay the unchristian heats, that have been among you of one sort and another. Be at peace, and continue not to divide and bite one another." As if anticipating, that the term "orthodox" was about to be abused to the propagation of an antichristian spirit, he takes occasion to advise Mr. Colman in relation to Mr. Monis (instructor in Hebrew, a converted Jew), "to instruct him a little farther in the Christian doctrine of more extensive charity, and not to judge too hastily of his neighbour, and exclude from salvation every one that differs from him in the explication and belief of the article of the Trinity. A glorious truth it is, but the manner of explaining it appears difficult; so difficult, that scarce two can say exactly alike, except they agree on a form and agree to write after it."

How little did Mr. Hollis imagine, at the time he wrote this letter, that measures had been adopted by the board of Overseers, which placed among the tests of orthodoxy a belief in the divine right of infant baptism; and that amendments and papers had been so devised, as to make him apparently instrumental in such a construction, as would for ever exclude a Baptist from a professorship, to which his statutes had made a specific provision that he might be eligible!

In a subsequent letter to Colman, dated the 14th of January, 1722–23, he thus writes, "I am not unacquainted, by books I have read, what treatment Baptists have met with in New England in former times, and been sorry for it. I am glad to see and hear by divers letters and books, that they have been better treated of late, and that a better spirit of love and charity now shows itself in Boston. But it may not be amiss to let you know, that *the speeches* of some on that head, at reading my orders, have come to the knowledge of many ministers and gentlemen in London, which have occasioned many very hard speeches against your College, in my hearing, to my sorrow."

With this clear comprehension of the difficulties and differences attending the explanation of the term "orthodox," Mr. Hollis would not have permitted its introduction into his statutes, had he not thought he had sufficiently guarded against its misconstruction by the only declaration of faith, which he required of his professor. Nor would he have confined his remarks to "*the speeches of some on that head*," if he had been apprized that the Overseers of the College had already made and acted upon a construction of the term "orthodoxy," which, if followed as a precedent, would for ever exclude a Baptist from being a professor on his foundation.

Finally signs the statutes of his Professorship of Divinity.

From this letter it appears, that his "orders" were now finally "written over fairly on vellum," and that "what relates to the Professor is verbatim as you (Mr. Colman) sent it me over." The "orders" sent by Mr. Hollis, which may be considered as the real foundation of his professorship, are dated February 14th, 1720-21. The "orders" above specified were dated "the ninth year of George the First, 10th January, 1722-23, nearly two years subsequent to the date of his first orders. So much time had this negotiation occupied.

Mr. Hollis recurs again in this letter to his "writing

obligatory." "I wait to see," says he, "your Corporation's obligation, and how you shall continue to act. If one or the other is not to my liking, I can, by the powers I reserve, add it as a codicil, or part of my will; but I have hopes I shall not need."

Hollis claims a writing obligatory.

In a letter dated on the 2d of March, 1723, he repeats his "expectation, that what I last year desired, a College obligation for performance of my trusts to me and my successors, should be sent out to me."

Corporation decline sending one.

This demand of a writing obligatory for the faithful performance of his trusts occasioned the Overseers and Corporation some embarrassment. As Hollis said, "they liked his moneys," but his "writings obligatory" were not quite so much to their fancy. President Leverett therefore replied, "that the Corporation, upon second thoughts, could not find how to bind themselves faster than they are already, in justice."

On this refusal, Mr. Hollis called a meeting, in London, of his friends, at which Governor Shute, who was then in England, was present, and submitted President Leverett's letter for their "advicc," in which, says he, "they were unanimous, that I should insist on it, to have such an obligation as strong as may be, according to your promise."

Hollis demands it peremptorily.

That this demand might be the more certainly effectual, he put the Corporation under a high pressure. "It will not be prudent," he adds, "for you to delay it" (sending the required obligation); "for, though I think I have sent enough, *yet more was designed, as I hinted, in my will, — but that it is as yet in my own power to alter, if I may not be gratified in this.**

Upon this urgency, an obligation was transmitted.

* Hollis's letter, 18th March, 1722-3. Appendix, No. XLIX.

CHAPTER XII.

Corporation transmit their obligation.

Its terms, however, were not satisfactory to Hollis. On the 15th of August, 1723, he writes to Colman; "I have now received from Mr. Treasurer a draft of a College obligation to perform my trusts. I shall return it again with some very little alteration. I think the Corporation need not be so scrupulous, and fearful of me, in coming into such a deed; I mean them no harm, no difficulty." "Since my orders are now signed and sealed with you, keep but honestly to them, and I shall be pleased, not having any design at present to alter them, unless I see some very great reason for it."

The reluctance of the Corporation was not overcome until the month of September, 1725, when they finally transmitted to Mr. Hollis a formal obligation for their faithful fulfilment of his trusts.

We have thus traced, historically, through its several stages, the foundation of the Professorship of Divinity, in Harvard College, by the first Thomas Hollis, with an exactness of investigation and a minuteness of statement, demanded by both justice and gratitude.

Result of the investigation.

The investigation, it is believed, has resulted in establishing, beyond any reasonable question, the following points.

1. That the Professorship of Divinity, as it first came from the hands of Hollis, was absolutely without restriction or qualification; and not only free from any sectarian test, but so broad and unequivocal in language, that no sectarian test could be extracted or deduced from it.

2. That the terms, out of which the attempt to establish a test has grown, were of New England invention and transmission.

3. That Hollis, by providing that the only declaration required of his professor should be, "his belief that the Scriptures of the Old and New Testament are the only perfect rule of faith and manners, and that he promise to explain and open the Scriptures to his pupils with integrity and uprightness, according to the best light that God shall give him," established his professorship upon the broad basis of a belief in the Scriptures; a foundation wholly inconsistent with a required belief in any specified sectarian points or creeds.

4. That the construction, which substituted, in place of the simple declaration required by Hollis of his professor, an examination and declaration of faith in all the high points of New England Calvinism, including a belief in the divine right of infant baptism, could not have received the approbation or consent of Hollis; and that there is no evidence, or reasonable ground to believe it was ever communicated to him, or known by him, to the day of his death.

From these points, thus established, it unavoidably results, that the suspicions of double dealing, to which an overheated zeal for sects and tests has subjected the character of Hollis, are wholly unfounded. Thomas Hollis was a man incapable of the meanness of attempting to do indirectly, by the use of a word of equivocal meaning, that which, had he done it directly, would have contradicted the whole tenor of his life, and the trait of character which he most valued,—charity. Much more was he incapable of the hypocrisy of prescribing in terms, that a belief in the sacred Scriptures should be the only declaration required of his professor, and, in the same instrument, by construction, clandestinely providing that his professor should be examined, and declare his belief, in all the high points of New England Calvinism. Above all, he was incapable of being a traitor to the faith he publicly professed, by establishing directly, in one clause of his statutes, that his professor might be of the "Baptist communion," and constructively, by the use of an equivocal word, in another clause requiring, in direct contradiction of the peculiar tenets of the Baptist faith, that, as a condition of admission, his professor should declare his belief in the divine right of infant baptism.

The negotiations relative to the establishment of the Hollis Professorship of Divinity were finally closed but a short time before the death of President Leverett, which occurred in May, 1724. Reserving the other noble donations of Hollis for the history of the presidency in which they were received, we shall proceed to narrate in the order of time the other events affecting the prosperity of the College during the administration of Leverett.

CHAPTER XIII.

Tutors Sever and Welsteed claim Seats at the Board of Corporation by Virtue of the Term "Fellows." — The Overseers appoint a Committee on the Subject. — Origin of the Term "Fellows" in the College. — History of its Introduction and Use traced through the College Records. — "Fellow of the Corporation," when first used. — "Fellow of the House," when introduced, and how used. — Distinction instituted between them. — Tenure of Tutor's Office limited to three Years. — Sever and Welsteed each elected a Fellow of the House under that Limitation. — State of Parties when their Claim to a Seat at the Board of Corporation was introduced. — Treatment of President Leverett by the General Court.

CHAPTER XIII.

WHILE the Overseers of Harvard College were carefully shaping by act and construction the statutes of the Hollis Professorship of Divinity into a form, adapted to establish in the College a creed and religious test, an event occurred, which opened a prospect of removing from their seats, those members of the Corporation who were most distinguished for the liberality of their religious opinions. On the 23d of June, 1721, in the very week the Corporation had chosen Mr. Wigglesworth Professor of Divinity, in conformity with Mr. Hollis's original orders, without any examination into his "soundness and orthodoxy," two Tutors, Nicholas Sever and William Welsteed, presented to the Overseers a memorial, claiming, under the charter of the College granted in 1650, seats at the board of Corporation, by virtue of being fellows and actual residents at the College, engaged in

Sever and Welsteed's memorial. 1721.

CHAPTER XIII.

the business of instruction, and receiving a stipend. The Overseers referred this memorial to a large committee, of which Chief Justice Sewall was chairman, with instructions to "inquire into the grounds and reasons of that memorial, to consider what is proper and necessary to be done upon it, and make report thereof to the Overseers." Although the memorial itself is not preserved, the principles upon which the claim of these tutors was founded are apparent from the records of the Overseers and from contemporary documents. From its intimate connexion with the history of the College, it requires, in this place, to be stated and illustrated with minute exactness.

By the charter of 1650, the Corporation was to consist of *seven* persons; a President, a Treasurer, and *five Fellows*. The claim of these tutors was founded upon the term "fellows" in that charter, which they maintained was technical, and to be construed according to its use in the English Universities; in which residence at the College, engagement in instruction, and receiving therefor stipend, were essential requisites to the character of "fellow."

At the time this memorial was presented to the Overseers, no vacancy existed in the board of Corporation. The seven members were, Leverett, President; White, Treasurer; and Flynt (Tutor), Wadsworth, Colman, Appleton, and Stevens, the five Fellows. According to the view of these memorialists, Flynt alone possessed the qualities essential to constitute "a fellow." The four others were neither residents, instructors, nor stipendiaries. If these qualities should be declared essential to constitute a member of the Corporation, the seats of these four would be vacated, and three of them would rightfully belong to Sever, Welsteed, and Robie, another tutor and "resident fellow," who, for some reason, did not unite in Sever and Welsteed's memorial.

Each of these tutors had accepted his appointment upon an express understanding, that he was chosen not a "fellow of the Corporation," but only a "fellow of the College or House"; a distinction, which had been sanctioned by successive votes of the Corporation, approved by the Overseers.

The claim of Sever and Welsteed rested solely on the construction of the term "fellows" in the charter of the College. They maintained that this term intended not "associates" in a general sense, but "resident instructors at the College" in an academic sense; and that it could not be satisfied, except by electing resident instructors, or by the elected persons becoming resident instructors after their election.

Meaning of "fellows" in the College charter.

Regarding exclusively the use and connexion of the term "fellows" in the charter, nothing could be more groundless than this claim; since that instrument, undeniably, gave to the Corporation the right of electing its members from the "inhabitants of the Bay" at large, without any precedent or subsequent restriction, qualification, or condition. To maintain the technical meaning of this term, it was therefore necessary to prove, either, that, antecedent to the charter of 1650, tutors and instructors in the College were designated by the term "fellows," and that the use of that term in the charter was intended to express a class of academic men then known by that name, or that the five persons named in the charter were in fact "resident instructors."

To the first position, the general history of the country, and the particular history, records, and known relations of the College, gave either no support, or such as was altogether shadowy and unsubstantial.

The name of "fellows," applied to instructors in Harvard College, is not to be found in any history, general or particular, or in any public document, or in any College record, antecedent to 1650, with one exception; and, in this instance, its use satisfactorily indicates the time and manner of its introduction.

The College, although founded in 1636, had attained, prior to 1639, notwithstanding the donation of Harvard, no higher appellation than that of "school." Eaton, its master, had assistant instructors, called "ushers." *

In the invitation given to Dunster to accept the place of President, there is no mention of "fellows." Neither is there any in the order of the General Court in 1642, which has been called the first charter of the College. There exists only a single record of any meeting of the board constituted by this act. At this meeting, on "the 27th of the 10th month, 1643,"† the settlement of the account of John Harvard's administrator was authorized, a treasurer appointed, a seal established, and two instructors were chosen "for the present help of the President to read to the junior pupils as the President shall see fit." The two Bachelors, Sir Bulkley and Sir Downing, were the persons thus chosen, and each was allowed a salary of four pounds per annum.

This is the only evidence, existing on the College records, of the appointment of any instructor by any title before the year 1650; and it appears by this record, that the persons chosen to assist the President in the

* Savage's Winthrop, Vol. I. pp. 308, 309. † See above, p. 48.

Term "Socius," when first introduced.

business of instruction, had not acquired the name of "fellows." This is farther corroborated by the circumstance, that Bulkley and Downing have never had the term "Socius" applied to them in the Triennial Catalogue; although, if at that time instructors had acquired the name of "fellows," they are as much entitled to it as any of their successors. The fact, that the first five "Socii" are those first named as such in the College Catalogue, demonstrates, that, antecedent to the charter of 1650, no one had acacquired the name of "socius" or "fellow."

Before the date of that charter, the institution was designated, and made capable of taking gifts and grants in law, by the name of the "College at Cambridge," or "Harvard College." Accordingly, all the deeds and grants to the seminary, which appear on its records, antecedent to 1650, bear that designation and none other. The deed of John Bulkley, in Latin, of the date of December, 1645, strongly corroborates the position, that the term "fellows" was not then in use in the College. "Socius," the Latin term for "fellow," is not in that deed. By it Bulkley gave to Dunster, the President of the College, two acres of land in Cambridge, therein described, for his life. The deed then proceeds; "If at any time he shall leave the presidency, or shall decease, I then desire the College to appropriate the same to itself for ever, as a small gift from an alumnus, bearing towards it the greatest good will."*

Many years afterward, this deed was inserted in the Donation Book of the College, and is there introduced as "Extractum Doni Pomarii Sociorum per

* See Appendix, No. XXII.

CHAPTER XIII. Johannem Bulkleium." But this descriptive title, which was prefixed in later times, gives no support to an argument in favor of the antecedent use of the term "fellows," inasmuch as it is not found in the deed itself. After President Dunster's resignation, the Corporation gave the income of Bulkley's donation to the tutors, who received it for many years, and hence the enclosure obtained the name of "Tutors' Pasture," or "Fellows' Orchard." On transcribing Bulkley's deed into the College records, this descriptive title was prefixed, either to give countenance to the name, or in consequence of it. Notwithstanding this descriptive title, therefore, it is evident, that Bulkley's deed adds nothing in favor of the argument, that the term "fellow" was in use in the College antecedent to 1650; but on the contrary, so far as it has any effect, it supports the reverse.

A conclusive argument, that this term "fellow" was not in use in the College antecedent to 1647, is drawn from the fact, that the first statutes on the records of the College are introduced with the following preamble; "The laws, liberties, and orders, of Harvard College, confirmed by the Overseers and President of the College in the years 1642, 1643, 1644, 1645, 1646, and published to the scholars for the perpetual preservation of their welfare and government."

In these "laws, liberties, and orders," the term "fellows" is not applied to any class of instructors or rulers, as it would have been, if any having that denomination then constituted a part of the government of the College. The term "tutor" occurs frequently, and the term "fellows" once; but in the sense of "*companions*" (being rendered in an accompanying Latin translation "sodales," and not "socii"), and is used in direct contrast with the term "tutor." — "The scholars shall attend the lectures, and if of any thing they doubt, *they shall inquire of their fellows, or, in case of non-resolution, modestly of their tutors*." A use of terms indicating almost conclusively, that "tutor" and "fellow" had not then in the College an identical meaning.

The only instance in which this term appears in the records of the College before 1650, in a sense applicable to instructors, is in an original contract, inserted in those records, and signed by one Richard Taylor. The contract is in the handwriting of President Dunster, and is dated on the 13th of January, 1646-7. In it Taylor, after declaring, that, "whereas he is in possession, on a tenancy of fifteen years, of a shop in Boston, which had been given to the College for ever by Major Robert Sedgwick," to which "*five years more had been added by Henry Dunster, President of Harvard College*," the said Richard accordeth to pay a specified rent, and leave the same in good repair, at the end of the term, "*to Harvard College, the President and Fellows thereof*."

This entry indicates very clearly two things; that the term "fellows" had not acquired any authoritative use, and that its introduction was then contemplated by Dunster. The deed of Sedgwick was "to the College." The extension of the lease, five years, was by "the President." The tenement was to be delivered at the end of the term "to Harvard College," the only name by which it was then capable of being legally contracted with. No mention is made of President and Fellows, until all the essential parts of the contract were closed. These terms were then introduced, probably, in expectation that a change would take place in the name of the society before Taylor's lease terminated. If it did, these terms would be directory to the tenant. If it did not, they would be surplusage, and could not vitiate. In fact, the change did take place.

No argument, in favor of the technical use of the term "fellow" in this country, antecedent to the charter of 1650, can be drawn from the early forms of induction of "Fellows" or "Socii." These appear upon the College records, in the handwriting of Dunster. But none of them were inserted antecedent to 1650. They are recorded in the same page with similar forms used in respect to the Overseers, and no evidence or reasonable pretence exists, that either kind of form was ever used in the College prior to the date of that charter. Such is all the light to be derived from the records of the College, on the question of the technical construction of the term "fellows," on which the claim of Sever and Welsteed was founded.

The result is, that, antecedent to 1650, no class of persons was known in the College by the general, authorized denomination of "fellows." At that early period there were two or three persons, who held the station of tutors; but the President practically concentrated in himself all the powers of the institution, and took the chief agency in the office of instruction. The probability is, that, when the charter was drafted, Dunster selected "President and Fellows," as the term most appropriate and scholastic, to become the corporate name of the government of the College, without intending to indicate any class of men as exclusively eligible, or any academic quality as essential. This seems to be the plain view common sense suggests, of the origin of these terms in the charter.

"Fellows," how used in the charter.

The general language of this instrument gives even less color to the claim of Sever and Welsteed. The selection of "President and Fellows," as the name of the Corporation, implied, in respect to either, no special qualification or duty, even upon the supposition that there had previously existed, in connexion with the College, persons to whom either designation had been applied. Either President or Fellow might be resident or non-resident, employed in instruction or not; these qualifications or duties wholly depending, by force of the charter, upon the unrestricted exercise of the authority to choose and to regulate, vested in the Corporation by that instrument.

With respect to the position, that the five persons named in the charter were resident fellows, there cannot be a question, that some were non-residents, and neither engaged in instruction nor receiving stipend; it being altogether incredible, that, at this early period, when the College was struggling with poverty, and actually dependent for its existence on charity, when the number of students had at no time exceeded *twenty-five*, and generally could not have amounted to *sixteen*, it should yet maintain a corps of five resident instructors, besides the President. In 1674, their number appears by the records to have been three, called a senior, a second, and a third fellow. Nor is there any reason to believe, that, from the foundation of the College until that time, the number of resident instructors was ever greater, or that it was increased for many years afterwards. Notwithstanding the deficiency of the early records

CHAPTER XIII.

of the College, it does not admit of a doubt, that there were always some of the five members of the Corporation, neither resident, nor giving instruction, nor receiving stipend. Those records satisfactorily show, that, as early as 1666, there were fellows, non-resident, who did not receive stipend; since they prescribe certain duties to be performed by such as are fellows of the College and receive salaries, and especially that they "shall have their constant residence in the College."* A provision, which would scarcely have been made, if there had been no fellows, except such as were resident instructors, receiving stipend.

Name, "The Corporation," how acquired.

The President and Fellows of Harvard College being the only Corporation in the Province, and so continuing during the whole of the seventeenth century, they early assumed, and had by common usage conceded to them, the name of "*The Corporation*," by which they designate themselves in all the early records. Their proceedings are recorded as being done "at a meeting of the Corporation," or introduced by the formula, "It is ordered by the Corporation," without stating the number or the names of the members present, until April 19th, 1675, when, under President Oakes, the names of those present were first entered on the records, and afterwards they were frequently, though not uniformly, inserted.

Proceedings of Dec. 11, 1674.

In the year 1674, the Corporation had been reduced by death and other causes to three members, besides Dr. Hoar, the President. These were Gookin and Thacher, both resident instructors, and Richards, the Treasurer. On the special recommen-

* See Appendix, No. L.

dation of the Overseers, the Corporation proceeded to fill up the vacancies in their body, and elected *three non-residents*, all of whom retained their seats in the board without becoming resident, or engaging in instruction, or receiving stipend. These three were Urian Oakes, minister of Cambridge, Thomas Shepard, minister of Charlestown, Increase Mather, minister in Boston. The Overseers, instead of questioning their eligibility, or requiring from them residence in the College, approved them as being orderly elected, and entreated them to accept their trust. From this time, it is apparent from the College records, that a majority of the five fellows were non-residents; and the distinction between resident and non-resident fellows is plainly and frequently to be seen in them. Sometimes they were elected under the name of "Fellows of the College," in which case they sometimes are found enumerated among the members of the Corporation, and sometimes they do not appear to have taken their seats in consequence of such election. In January, 1678, upon the death of Thomas Shepard, minister of Charlestown, the Overseers passed a vote, recommending to the Corporation to choose a Fellow in his room, "and one to officiate in the place, if they judge it needful." The Corporation, judging that one to officiate in the place was not needful, chose "Mr. John Sherman, pastor of the church in Watertown, to be a Fellow of the Corporation, all consenting." This election was approved by the Overseers; and is the first instance in which this designation, "Fellow of the Corporation," was applied to a member of that body on its records.

Jan. 15, 1675.

Proceedings in 1678.

No other light on the subject of this research is given by the College records antecedent to the judgment against the charter of the Colony, in 1684. Nothing, however, is more clear from those early records, than that, up to this time, persons, not having the character of residents, instructors, or stipendiaries, had been elected members of the Corporation, and continued members without its being required of them to take upon themselves any one of these characters. It is equally manifest by the records, that this course of proceeding received the uniform sanction of the board of Overseers.

By the revocation of the colonial charter of Massachusetts in 1684, the charter of the College was, by necessary construction, also vacated.* In relation to the future, both the Colony and the College were in a state of utter uncertainty. The officers of the seminary naturally felt reluctant to take the responsibility of managing its funds, or conducting its administration. In these difficulties,† Joseph Dudley assumed the authority, under the commission he held as Governor of the Colony, to organize the College. On the 23d of July, 1686, he appeared with his Council at Cambridge and appointed the Rev. Increase Mather Rector, and John Leverett and William Brattle Tutors. The records do not indicate the state of the Corporation after this event until June 2d, 1690, when they state, that "at a meeting of the Corporation, present Major John Richards, Treasurer, Nehemiah Hobart, John Leverett, and William Brattle, the Rev. Mr. Nathaniel Gookin and the Rev. Mr. Cotton Mather were chosen Fellows of the Corporation," which was thus composed of a Rector, two resident, three non-resident Fellows, and a Treasurer.

From this period until the year 1707, when the

* See Mass. Hist. Coll., First Series, Vol. III. p. 126.

† See above, p. 58.

CHAPTER XIII.

charter of 1650 was revived, under the auspices of the same Dudley,* the successive Governors of the Province were accustomed to assume the whole control, in respect to the organization of the College. The short, turbulent, and grasping administration of Andros had no important effect on its affairs. Dudley, Phips, Stoughton, and Bellamont were all friends of the institution. Their measures were in concurrence with the wishes of those, who had its interests at heart. In the unsettled state of the government of the Colony, and the consequent uncertainty concerning the fate of the College, its friends and officers were naturally desirous to place it under the protection of the chief magistrate.

State of things in 1692.

In all the charters, and in every organization of the Corporation occurring after the new colonial charter in 1692, a majority of the Fellows were non-resident, and neither instructors nor stipendiaries. While the number of the Corporation was *seven*, that of the resident instructors never exceeded *two*. After Lieutenant-Governor Stoughton, in 1696, took upon himself to organize the Corporation, the number of that body was increased to ten, twelve, and once even to fifteen; yet the number of resident instructors, it is believed, at no time, exceeded three. It is evident, therefore, that between the revocation of the charter of 1650, in 1684, and its revival by the vote of the General Court in 1707, the claim, on the part of resident instructors, of an exclusive right to be Fellows of the Corporation, was as groundless and without just pretence, as at previous periods.

In organizing the Corporation under this vote of

* See Hutch. Hist. Mass., pp. 159, 160.

CHAPTER XIII.

the General Court, Governor Dudley, with their approbation, as well as with that of the Overseers, had filled up the number of five Fellows, with three non-resident fellows, Hobart, Brattle, and Pemberton, and two resident, Flynt and Remington.

It appears by the records of the Corporation, that these five Fellows were at that time called "Fellows of the House." The equivocal meaning of this term, from its being also applied to instructors, who did not belong to the Corporation, was perceived by President Leverett; for, in his duplicate record of the proceedings of the Corporation and the Overseers, he designates the persons abovenamed thus, "Fellows of the House, i. e. of the Corporation." *

Flynt and Remington were tutors as well as "fellows." At the same time there was a third tutor, John Whiting, who, by courtesy, had, as well as they, the title of "Fellow of the House," or resident Fellow, and yet had no right to be a "Fellow of the Corporation"; and this indeed he could not be, without displacing one of the non-resident members of that body, inasmuch as by the charter the number of "fellows" was restricted to seven.

A year did not elapse before an attempt was made, as appears upon the records, to distinguish between these two classes of fellows. On the 14th of December, 1708, the expulsion of a student for an offence, is stated to have been done by "the President and resident Fellows, with the advice and consent of the non-resident Fellows of this House." In this vote is to be seen the first shadowing out of what at this day is called the Faculty of the College, in

Faculty of the College.

* Leverett's Manuscript, p. 8.

contradistinction to the Corporation. The same form of vote, on a similar occasion, was adopted in the March following. Nothing occurs to throw any light on the point on which this controversy turned, until the 20th of August, 1711, when, on the resignation of Remington, John Whiting was chosen "Fellow of the Corporation." On this occasion, Whiting, who had been for several years known as Tutor and "Fellow of the House," but had never, in consequence, been deemed, or pretended to be, a member of the Corporation, was admitted to a seat in that board. The circumstance probably showed the Corporation the necessity of dropping altogether the name of "Fellow of the House" as applicable to a member of that body, and establishing for themselves the more convenient, ancient, and appropriate title of "Fellow of the Corporation." From this time, therefore, the term "Fellow of the College" or "House" was restricted by their use to resident instructors, who were not members of the Corporation, by virtue of such election. Accordingly, on the 24th of December, 1711, Joseph Stevens was chosen "Fellow of the College, or House," and as such was approved by that board, in the language of the records, "to supply a vacancy in one of the Fellowships of the House."

Inauguration of a Fellow of the House, Feb. 14th. 1712.

Upon this election Stevens was inaugurated as "Fellow of the House," "secundum formam antiquitùs præscriptam;" a formality which had been discontinued since the revival of the charter of 1650, and had never been practised with regard to non-resident fellows. The proceedings on the occasion are described with minuteness by President Leverett, in his Journal; "the solemnity," he writes, "being the first of this sort that was celebrated, since the

CHAPTER XIII.

restoration of Harvard College to its first constitution." By the President's Latin address, which is transcribed at large, it appears, that these formalities were not revived solely on his suggestion, but by the express injunction of the Governor and Overseers.* The object in thus reviving the early form of inaugurating resident fellows, on an occasion when the distinction between "Fellows of the House," and "Fellows of the Corporation," was first introduced, was obviously to make that distinction plain and palpable, and to the end it might be understood, that, being chosen "Fellow of the House" conferred no right to a seat in the Corporation, and imposed a very different class of duties. Accordingly Stevens made no claim, and was never admitted to a seat in the Corporation in consequence of that election and inauguration. Upon the resignation of Whiting, Stevens was elected "Fellow of the Corporation," and on the same day Edward Holyoke was elected "Fellow of the House." Here the distinction was maintained, in direct contrast, in two elections made on the same day. It is apparent, that the Overseers knew of this distinction, and that it was adopted with their entire approbation; for on the same day (9th of July, 1712,) Stevens was presented by the President to the Overseers, as chosen "Fellow of the Corporation," and Holyoke as "Fellow of the House," and both were respectively as such approved.

On the 5th of November, 1712, Benjamin Wadsworth was presented to the Overseers by President Leverett as being chosen "a Fellow of the Corporation in the room of Nehemiah Hobart, deceased," and approved as such by that board.

* Leverett's Manuscript, p. 34.

CHAPTER XIII.

In February, 1713, Stevens, having been settled as pastor over the church in Charlestown, resigned his seat as a member of the Corporation; and, on the 7th of April following, Holyoke was chosen in his place, "a Fellow of the Corporation," and Robie "a Fellow of the House." Both were reported to the Overseers, and approved in their several stations by that board.

In February, 1715-1716, Holyoke resigned his office of Fellow of the Corporation.

Limitation of term of office of Fellows of the House.

On the 9th of April, 1716, the Corporation passed a vote, "that no Tutor, or Fellow of the House, now or henceforth to be chosen, shall hold a fellowship with a salary for more than three years, except continued by a new election."

On the same day they chose the Rev. Joseph Stevens, minister of Charlestown, "a Fellow of the Corporation," and Mr. Nicholas Sever "Fellow of the House," and presented both to the Overseers, by whom, on the 16th of April, they were "accepted in their respective stations, to which they are chosen accordingly." Robie was then also Fellow of the House. At this time Sever made no claim to be admitted as a member of the Corporation. This board was now composed of four non-resident and only one resident Fellow (Flynt). The Corporation began to perceive the inconvenience arising from the introduction into the College government of very young men without limitation of time, who, if they possessed good talents would speedily be induced to resign, and, if they did not possess the ability to become eminent in a profession, might be fixed upon the College for life. Flynt had then been a tutor for sixteen years, and Robie, who had held that office three years, they might apprehend would be equally permanent.

In order therefore to prevent unsuitable instructors fixing themselves permanently on the College, they passed the vote, limiting the continuance in office of a tutor, or Fellow of the House, to three years, except with "a new election." As nothing could be more wise than a precaution of this kind, so it could be no occasion of just complaint to Sever or any other tutor subsequently chosen, as the tenure of their office was explained to them before their election, and they knew the condition on which they accepted of it.

In September, 1717, Colman and Appleton were chosen Fellows of the Corporation, in place of Brattle and Pemberton, deceased, and were approved subsequently as such by the Overseers. Thus the proportion of non-resident to resident fellows remained unchanged, four to one.

April 28th, 1719, it appears by the records of the Corporation, that, "the three years since Mr. Nicholas Sever was chosen to be Fellow of the House being expired, he is now renewedly chosen Fellow of the House for three years."

On the 24th of May, 1720, the Corporation voted, "That a fourth Fellow of the House be now elected, there being occasion for another by reason of the great number of students now at the College."

The Corporation immediately chose William Welsteed to be the fourth fellow, and the President was desired to present him to the Overseers, "for their approbation and allowance, *as elected for three years*."

On the 23d of June, 1720, the following votes appear on the records of the Overseers. "Voted, that Mr. Nicholas Sever, having been rechosen by the Corporation a Fellow of the House for three years, be allowed and approved. 2dly. That Mr. Welsteed, having been chosen by the Corporation *a Fellow of the House for three years*, be allowed and approved."

At this time there existed in the board of Overseers and House of Representatives a party, having it for their object to effect a change in the Corporation, either by the voluntary resignation or compulsory removal of some obnoxious members of that board. The schemes of this party extended apparently to President Leverett himself, if we may judge by the nature of their attacks, and by their refusal of grants for his necessary support. At the head of this party were Paul Dudley and Chief Justice Sewall. On the 6th of December, 1720,* President Leverett addressed a supplicatory letter to the House of Representatives, stating his "difficulties, inconveniences, discouragements," and his "want of necessary support," and ending with expressing the utter "impossibility of his entertaining so much as a thought that his application would be neglected." It was, however, altogether disregarded. So that he began to infer from their proceedings, that it was their "mind to starve him out of the service." If such be "their mind," he adds, "it is but letting me know, and I will not put the House to exercise that cruelty."† This was the moment which Dudley took to assail the President with calumny. He declared openly in the House, that "the President had not given three expositions in the Hall for a twelvemonth, and that

Treatment of President Leverett by the General Court.

* See Appendix, No. LI. † See Appendix, No. LII.

CHAPTER XIII.

one of the fellows had said, he would give his oath of it."

This drew from President Leverett a letter, dated on the 15th of December, 1720,* addressed to the Speaker of the House of Representatives, declaring positively, that "it was false," protesting against the injustice of the representation, and demanding "the name of the fellow who was thus disposed to make oath to a falsehood." He had inquired of all the fellows, and all had denied the fact. "I will not pretend to say," he adds, "what the gentleman (Dudley) designed to serve by his representation; but I am sure he could not pretend to serve his country by such an averment,—our just country are not willing to be served by a falsehood." How Dudley relieved himself from the imputation cast upon him by President Leverett in his letter, does not appear. Either from principle or policy he had joined with Chief Justice Sewall in measures to introduce new influences into the Corporation. Their course of proceedings, in relation to the attack of Pierpont on that body, sufficiently indicates little delicacy as to the means, and a settled determination as to the end.

Paul Dudley's conduct in respect to President Leverett.

In June, 1721, the proposed foundation of a Professorship of Divinity in the College by a Baptist had excited an alarm, and the manner in which the Corporation reciprocated the liberal spirit of Mr. Hollis, by "leaving to him the limitation of the communion of his Professor,"† had no tendency to allay it. Such was the moment which Sever and Welsteed chose, for introducing this new element of discord; and they selected Sewall as the medium for its conveyance.

* See Appendix, No. LIII.

† See above, pp. 243-245.

President Leverett, in his Diary of the date of the 17th of June, 1721, states, "Upon the motion of Judge Sewall, to whom Mr. Sever and Welsteed had written a letter, His Excellency appointed an Overseers' meeting." But Governor Shute being satisfied that he had exceeded his powers, as a previous request of the Corporation was then necessary to authorize a special call of the board of Overseers, the meeting thus called was dissolved, and a new one was summoned on the 23d of June, 1721, the previous consent of the Corporation having been obtained.*

That two tutors, young men, who had both been chosen "fellows" under express votes of the Corporation, sanctioned by the board of Overseers, which limited their name and powers to the College, or "House," and by long known and approved practical construction excluded them from a seat in the Corporation; one of whom had held that office five years without making any claim to such seat, and both of whom had been elected to it and accepted the office under a limitation of three years, which was in itself inconsistent with that claim; should at once, and at such a moment of theological discontent, awaken into an imagination of rights withheld from them, can only be accounted for on the supposition, that they had encouragement, as the event proved, from members of the board of Overseers themselves, or from powerful influences in the legislature, prepared to second and, if possible, make good these most extraordinary pretensions.

Viewed in the calm light of history, and under the guidance of the familiar principles which common sense

* Leverett's Manuscript, p. 193.

CHAPTER XIII.

suggests, it cannot fail, at this day, to be a subject of surprise, that, under the circumstances of the College at that time, this claim should have been entertained by a board of Overseers having no personal or party interest to serve, any longer than was necessary to satisfy the memorialists that their pretensions had been fairly considered, were well understood, and intelligently decided. When, therefore, the relations of the subject strongly indicate, that the claim itself had its origin in the expectation, probably in the knowledge, that it would receive support in that board, and when we find, in fact, that it was there encouraged and sustained, and, so far as a vote of a majority of the Overseers had effect, was completely successful; and that finally it was defeated only by the firmness of the Governor of the Province; it is reasonable to conclude, that the avowed and ostensible were not the real motives which actuated a majority of the board of Overseers, in adopting the measures in which their deliberations terminated. Considering also the violence of the religious parties, which then divided the Province, each having for its object to gain or retain possession of the College, it cannot be questioned, that the opportunity a support of this claim offered, to remove at once from the Corporation three of its members, and those most obnoxious for their religious opinions, was the governing motive of their proceedings. Indeed, no possibility of doubt remains, when, in the conclusion of this long and eventful struggle, the House of Representatives, in July, 1722, are found, as we shall have occasion to show hereafter, declaring without any concealment, that their object was to remove those three "Fellows," Appleton, Colman, and Wadsworth, from their seats in the Corporation, and that Governor Shute, by making it a condition that they should not be removed, had "defeated their design and purpose."

The nature of the project was, in itself, most extraordinary, and, considering the relations of the respective individuals whom it was proposed, on the one hand to remove, and on the other to introduce, altogether irreconcilable with any true regard to the interests of the College.

At the moment this design was avowed by the House of Representatives, Wadsworth had been ten years, Appleton and Colman five years, members of the Corporation, elected according to early and, until this time, unquestioned practice. They were all of mature age, clergymen of great learning, weight, and influence in the Province; active, able, and successful in advancing the prosperity of the institution. One of them (Colman) was the confidential friend and correspondent of Thomas Hollis, and the selected medium of that unparalleled series of bounties he was then bestowing on the College. These three were the individuals the House of Representatives claimed of the Governor the right to remove, for the purpose of introducing three tutors, comparatively young men, little known, and without personal weight, influence, or experience.

The evidence upon this point of controversy has been thus traced through the College records with the more minuteness, because the utter want of a colorable pretence for the exclusion of all these non-resident Fellows from seats in the Corporation, by force of either the terms of the charter of 1650, or of more than seventy years' construction and practice under it, renders the conclusion unavoidable, that the at-

CHAPTER XIII.

tempt, in 1722, to sweep all the non-resident fellows from their seats in the Corporation, had no foundation either in expediency or sound principle; but was a spasmodic exertion, made under the influence of strong interests or strong passions, which, when they prevail in political or religious assemblies, seldom fail to create a regard for the end, and a disregard for the means; and, in eagerness for success, to cause to be trampled down every moral, social, and even religious obligation, which impedes their progress.

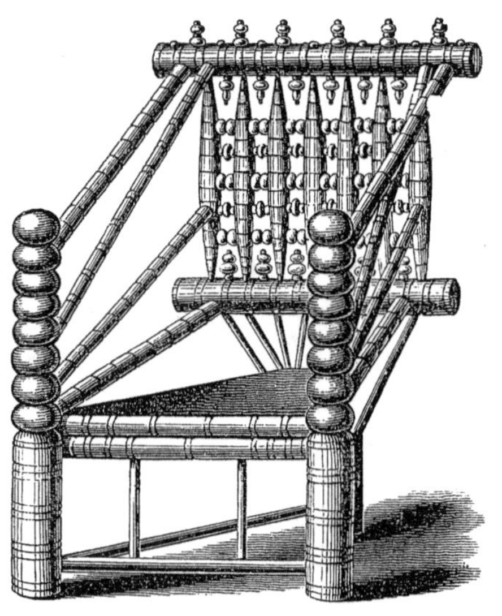

PRESIDENT'S CHAIR.*

* See Appendix, No. LIV.

CHAPTER XIV.

Proceedings of the Overseers on Sever and Welsteed's Memorial. — The Rev. Joseph Sewall chosen Fellow of the Corporation. — Overseers do not approve this Choice, and recommend the Election of a Resident Fellow. — Corporation choose Tutor Robie. — Overseers postpone their Approval of this Choice. — Corporation declare Sever no longer Fellow of the House. — Overseers declare him still to be Fellow of the House. — Corporation reinstate Sever. — Overseers apply to the General Court to enlarge the Corporation. — General Court refuse, but resolve that Fellows of the Corporation should be resident Fellows. — Governor Shute conditionally consents. — House of Representatives request him to make his Consent absolute. — Shute refuses. — A fifth Tutor chosen by the Corporation. — Negatived by the Overseers, who approve the Election of Robie and negative the Limitation of a Tutor's Office to three Years. — House of Representatives revive their Resolve, and intimate that the Corporation have not kept within their Charter. — Corporation claim a Hearing. — Denied by the General Court. — Attempt to make Members of the Corporation resign. — Its Failure. — Professor Wigglesworth chosen Fellow of the Corporation. — Negatived by the Overseers. — House of Representatives again revive their Resolve. — The Council give a Hearing to the Corporation. — Final Defeat of the Project of the House of Representatives. — Tribute to the Spirit of the Corporation.

CHAPTER XIV.

At a meeting of the Overseers on the 23d of June, 1721, a committee was appointed to inquire into "the grounds and reasons of the memorial of Mr. Nicholas Sever and Mr. William Welsteed, and consider what is proper and necessary to be done upon it, and make a report thereof to the Overseers in August next." The committee were, Judge Sewall, Mr. President Leverett, Judge Davenport, Colonel

Fitch, Colonel Quincy, the Rev. Mr. John Danforth, and the Rev. Mr. Joseph Sewall. Previous events indicate the views of Judge Sewall and his son, but at this day we have no means of ascertaining the other members of the committee who favored the claims of the memorialists.

The Overseers adjourned to the second day of August, for the special purpose of receiving the report of this committee. A meeting of the board did not take place on that day, and there is no notice of further proceedings on this memorial before March, 1722. The intermediate meetings of the Overseers, in December and January, were occupied with the election of Edward Hutchinson, Treasurer, in the place of White, deceased, and with those agitating questions and altercations concerning the Hollis Professorship of Divinity, which have been already related.

Joseph Sewall chosen fellow of the Corporation.

In November, 1721, the Rev. Joseph Stevens, minister of the church in Charlestown, and fellow of the Corporation, died; and, on the 23d of January ensuing, the Rev. Joseph Sewall, pastor of the South Church, in Boston, was chosen by the President and Fellows to supply the vacancy thus occasioned. The Corporation probably expected to conciliate Chief Justice Sewall by this election of his son, and, by thus introducing a clergyman of eminent piety, and a peculiar favorite of the zealous adherents to the Calvinistic doctrines, to defeat the scheme of the resident fellows. That scheme was, however, too promising, and the prospect of removing at once, from the Corporation the three obnoxious individuals, too flattering, to be abandoned by the Overseers for the sake of either individual or party gratification.

Not approved by the Overseers.

The choice of Mr. Sewall was presented to the Overseers by President Leverett on the next day (January 24th, 1721–2) for their approval. That board suspended their answer until the committee on the memorial of Sever and Welsteed should make their report. For a knowledge of this fact, we are solely indebted to the records of the Corporation. Those of the Overseers take no notice either of the presentation of Mr. Sewall at that meeting, or of the postponement of their approval. Both these occurrences took place at the meeting when the Overseers were actively engaged in defeating the provision in Mr. Hollis's statutes, which rendered a Baptist eligible to his professorship, and in substituting, in place of the belief in the Scriptures of the Old and New Testament, required of his professor, a declaration of faith in all the high points of New England Calvinism. Either the absorbing interest excited by this enterprise occasioned the omission of a notice of the election of Mr. Sewall on the records of the Overseers, or it was designed to keep from those records a statement of the fact, that Mr. Sewall had been presented as an elected member of the Corporation, and not accepted by the Overseers.

Proceedings on Sever and Welsteed's memorial.

From President Leverett's Diary alone, we derive an account of the proceedings of the committee on the memorial of Sever and Welsteed. By this it appears, that they met on the 19th of July, 1721, but came to no result, and, after "some altercations between President Leverett and the Rev. Mr. Danforth and Mr. Sewall, concerning the state of the College," * they adjourned. This committee did not

* Leverett's Manuscript, p. 202.

CHAPTER XIV.

meet again to any efficient purpose, until the 20th of February, 1722. The proceedings on this occasion are thus stated by President Leverett in his Diary. "The committee formed their report to this purpose; 'That they are of opinion, that it is proper for the Corporation to choose one of the Resident Fellows of the House, or Tutors, to be a member of the Corporation in the place of the Rev. Mr. Joseph Stevens, deceased;' whose report was signed by the chairman of said committee, the Honorable Judge Samuel Sewall.

"Mem. The President, being one of the committee, was asked, whether he consent to the said report; answered, that he could not consent thereunto, because that the Corporation had chosen the Rev. Mr. Joseph Sewall to fill up the vacancy in the Corporation by the death of the Rev. Mr. Joseph Stevens, and had presented him to the Overseers, who had not declared themselves thereupon, so that as to him the Corporation was full." *

On the 9th of March ensuing, this committee made their report to the Overseers, who, without noticing the previous election and presentation of Mr. Sewall by the Corporation, accepted it, as appears by their records in these words, "That they judge it proper, that the vacancy in the Corporation, made by the decease of the Rev. Mr. Stevens, be filled up by the election of a resident fellow in his stead." Thus the Overseers negatived, by construction, the election of Mr. Sewall, without its appearing on their records, that such election had been ever made, or presented to, or acted upon by, their board. Nor should we, at this day, be able to trace the course

Overseers recommend that a resident fellow be chosen Fellow of the Corporation.

* Leverett's Manuscript, p. 216.

of this policy, and the nature of their proceedings, had not the Corporation wisely and faithfully spread the whole transaction at length upon their own records.

At the next succeeding meeting of the Corporation (3d of April, 1722), the vote of the Overseers came under consideration. Their proceedings were firm and conciliatory; and their importance requires a statement of them in the words of the record.

"At a meeting of the President and Fellows of Harvard College, in Cambridge, April 3d, 1722. Whereas at a meeting of the President and Fellows of Harvard College, January 23d, last past, the Rev. Mr. Joseph Sewall, pastor of the Third Church, in Boston, was chosen a Fellow of the Corporation, and, on the 24th day of the same January, the President presented the said Mr. Sewall to the Overseers for their acceptance and allowance; and whereas the Honorable and Reverend the Overseers pleased to suspend their answer to the said presentation to a further meeting, having a committee appointed to consider of a memorial laid before the said Overseers, and until the said committee should make their report thereupon, who made their report March 9th, 1721-2, in these words, 'That they judge it proper, that the vacancy in the Corporation, by the decease of the Rev. Mr. Joseph Stevens of Charlestown, be filled up by the election of a resident fellow in his stead,' which being read, was accepted by the Overseers; by the acceptance of which report the election of the Rev. Mr. Joseph Sewall, made by the Corporation as aforesaid, was, by implication, plainly not allowed of, though it was declared, that it was not designed that any disrespect to the Rev. Mr. Sewall should be conceived to be offered by the Overseers, however it

CHAPTER XIV.

may seem to be a more than ordinary determining upon the Corporation: Wherefore it is voted, That the Corporation, saving to themselves the right of electing members of the Corporation, upon any vacancy, according to the powers vested in them by the College charter, they will proceed to fill up the vacancy occasioned by the decease of the Rev. Mr. Stevens, by electing one of the Fellows of the House. But yet this shall not, for the future, be brought into example to limit the right of the Corporation in the election of their members. Hereupon the President desired the Fellows of the Corporation to bring in their votes for the election of a Fellow to fill up the vacancy in the Corporation, occasioned by the decease of the Rev. Mr. Joseph Stevens; and accordingly the fellows brought in their votes in writing. And Mr. Thomas Robie, one of the Fellows of the House, was chosen unanimously a Fellow of the Corporation; and the President was desired to present the said Mr. Thomas Robie to the Overseers for their approbation and allowance."

Thomas Robie chosen Fellow of the Corporation.

The result of this election was equally unexpected and unwelcome to the malecontents in the board of Overseers. Neither Sever nor Welsteed had obtained the object of their memorial. Robie, who was also a "resident fellow," and of elder appointment than either, had obtained the distinction they solicited, and for which he had not memorialized. The vote of the Overseers was thus complied with; the proportion of resident to non-resident fellows, which Governor Dudley, in 1707, had sanctioned, in the reinstatement of the charter of 1650, with the approbation of the Overseers and the General Court, and which the practice of sixty years, if not of the whole period since that charter, justified, was restored. Had the object of the Overseers been limited to a restoration of the early proportion of resident and non-resident fellows, it was attained, and they had every reason to be satisfied; but their proceedings show that their object was very different.

When, on the next day (4th of April, 1722), the election of Robie was presented to the Overseers for approbation, it appears by their records, that "it was not agreed to, it being proper first to consider a memorial still depending before the Overseers, formerly exhibited by Mr. Nicholas Sever and Mr. William Welsteed."

President Leverett gives a more graphic account of this meeting in these words.

"At a meeting of the Overseers, in the Council Chamber, Boston, April 4th, 1722, Mr. Thomas Robie was presented to the Overseers in proper form and order by the President; but, it being moved (after a vote upon the presentation of Mr. Robie was called for) that a memorial was depending; not without great debate and some heat, this order was broke in upon, and it was overruled, that the memorial should be considered, and the vote upon Mr. Robie suspended. The memorial was read, and long debate thereupon. The meeting concluded by a resolute adjournment by His Excellency the Governor, to April 11th, 10 o'clock, A. M. The Governor and the President left them; and the rest continued, and unwillingly and murmuringly agreed." *

Strictly speaking, the memorial of Sever and Welsteed was not "depending." The committee had finished their deliberations and reported their opinion;

* Leverett's Manuscript, p. 220.

CHAPTER XIV.

their report had been accepted by the Overseers, and acceded to by the Corporation, who had, in conformity with the report, elected a resident fellow to fill the vacancy in their board. The memorial had attained its purpose, and the action of both boards was completed. The revival of that memorial, therefore, proved that the design of those Overseers, by whom Sever and Welsteed were countenanced, if not instigated, was not to restore the former proportion of resident fellows in the Corporation, but to remove certain obnoxious individuals from their seats in that board.

In pursuance of the policy, which dictated this memorial, it was therefore determined to consider it yet "depending," and thus revive the discussion.

Second memorial of Sever and Welsteed.

Sever and Welsteed immediately followed up, as we learn from the records of the Overseers, their memorial with another paper subscribed by the memorialists, entitled, "An extract from the College charter of 1650, the English laws," &c.

No such paper is now extant on the records. It appears, however, by those of the Overseers, that, at this period of the proceedings, Governor Shute interposed, ordered the meeting to be adjourned, and the books and records of the College to be brought, and all the members of the Overseers to be specially summoned to attend on the 11th of April. At this meeting, the records of the Overseers state, that "after a great deal of debate upon the subject of Mr. Sever and Mr. Welsteed, nothing was concluded;" and that an adjournment took place to the 2d of May ensuing. On this day a meeting was held, but nothing conclusive was done; and it was adjourned to the 23d of May.

CHAPTER XIV.

Sever declared by the Corporation to be no longer Fellow of the House.

About this time the three years, for which Mr. Sever had been elected a Tutor, or "Fellow of the House," expired. This "occasioned a question to be moved," at a meeting of the Corporation on the 30th of April, 1722, "and put, whether the said Mr. Sever is to be deemed as a Tutor, or Fellow of the House, or can act as such? Upon which the members of the Corporation declared themselves *seriatim*, and said, that they deem the said Mr. Nicholas Sever to be no longer a Tutor or Fellow of the House, nor may he act as such unless he be reëlected by the Corporation." In consequence of this resolve, the class formerly taught by Sever was immediately placed under the instruction of another fellow.

This decisive step, which the Corporation probably deemed necessary for the vindication of their authority, and the peace and order of the seminary, which Sever had shown himself well inclined to disturb, became immediately a new element of trouble, and source of discord between that board and the Overseers. At their meeting on the 23d of May, holden according to adjournment, the records of the Overseers state, that, "upon Mr. Nicholas Sever's representing to the Overseers a matter of importance referring to the College, the Overseers deferred the consideration of it until it be offered in writing at their next meeting." On the 6th of June ensuing, Sever's memorial being accordingly read, President Leverett moved, that the Corporation might be furnished with a copy, for the purpose of making an answer. The motion was sustained, and, after "several papers were read, some for, others against, the design of the memorial, and things were largely debated," the Overseers "voted, that a committee be appointed to draw up a memorial to the

CHAPTER XIV.

General Court respecting the enlargement of the number of the Corporation, by adding the resident tutors to it." Of this committee Judge Sewall was appointed chairman, and the farther consideration of the subject was postponed to the meeting of the Overseers on the 13th of June.

At this meeting both of the contending parties appear to have rallied their whole strength. Besides the Governor, Lieutenant-Governor, and the President, there were present *nineteen* civil and *twelve* clerical members.

Proceedings of the Overseers thereon.

The committee appointed at the last meeting presented the memorial they had prepared, respecting the enlargement of the Corporation by adding the resident tutors, which was read, and ordered by the Overseers to be presented to the General Court by the committee that had drafted it. The meeting was then adjourned to the afternoon, when "Mr. Sever's memorial respecting his dismission from his fellowship was read, as also a reply to it by the Corporation; and, after large debate on the matter," it was voted, that "Mr. Nicholas Sever still continues a Fellow of the House, notwithstanding what has been done with reference to him by the Corporation upon a by-law not approved of by the Overseers." After these proceedings the meeting was adjourned.

The Appendix to the College charter, passed in 1657, had expressly authorized the Corporation "to make such orders and by-laws, for the better ordering and carrying on of the work of the College, as they shall see cause, *without dependence upon the consent of the Overseers, foregoing*." And although, by the same act, orders and by-laws passed by the Corporation were alterable by the Overseers at their discretion;

yet, until they were altered, they were of consequence valid and obligatory.

The by-law, referred to by the Overseers as not approved by them, had been passed by the Corporation on the 9th of April, 1716, and was in these words; "No tutor, or Fellow of the House, now or henceforth to be chosen, shall hold a fellowship, with salary, for more than three years, except continued by a new election."* It had not, indeed, been formally presented to the Overseers for their approbation; but after that by-law had passed the Corporation, and on the same day, Nicholas Sever was chosen by that board, and on the 1716. 16th of April was approved by the Overseers as Fellow of the House, and when those three years had expired, he, being rechosen by the Corporation, and presented to the Overseers on the 23d of June, 1720, was approved by them as "rechosen Fellow of the House for three years," and on the same day William Welsteed was approved also by the Overseers as "chosen Fellow of the House for three years."† Whatever course therefore the Overseers might choose to pursue relative to the alteration of this by-law, as it respected Sever and Welsteed it was valid and unobjectionable. The Overseers could not aver that they had not approved of this limitation of their term of office, without contradicting their own records. The declaration of the Overseers, that Sever "was yet a Fellow of the House," notwithstanding the term for which he had been elected with their approbation had expired, was of consequence a gratuitous assumption of power, strongly indicative of the violence of party spirit in the board.

* See above, p. 281.

† Ibid., p. 283.

CHAPTER XIV.

On the 30th of July, 1722, the proceedings of the Overseers came under the consideration of the Corporation. Their vote on this occasion, from its importance, deserves also to be stated at large.

"Whereas the Corporation, at a meeting, April 30th, last past, gave their sense concerning Mr. Nicholas Sever, who was twice chosen a tutor, or Fellow of the House, for three years, and the last time confirmed as such by the Overseers, which last three years ended on the 28th of April this present year; that the said Mr. Sever no longer continued a tutor, nor could act as such unless reëlected by the Corporation, which sense or apprehension the Corporation are more confirmed in, by an Appendix made to the College charter of 1650, by the General Court, on October 14th, 1657; and whereas at an Overseers' meeting, June 13th, 1722, they signified by vote, that the said Mr. Sever still continues a fellow, notwithstanding what has been done with reference to him by the Corporation; we agree as follows, that, saving the proper rights and privileges of the Corporation, and to prevent further debates and contentions (which we look on as threatening to the welfare of the College), that the said Mr. Sever again act as a tutor, or Fellow of the House, and that he take care of the classes formerly under his tuition."

Sever reinstated by the Corporation.

The Corporation then, "in consideration of the President's indisposition," desired Mr. Wadsworth to present the above votes to the Overseers, and to revive the presentation, that had been made of Mr. Robie as an elected "Fellow of the Corporation," in that board. In these proceedings the firm, faithful, and conciliatory spirit of the Corporation are strikingly manifested.

A memorial, praying for an enlargement of the Corporation, was presented to the General Court on the 13th of June, 1722, being the same day it was voted by the Overseers. That board gave no official notice of their design to the Corporation, whose records afford no evidence of their having been consulted on this memorial. It was received and entertained by the General Court with a like indifference to their interests and disregard to their relation to the subject. The only reasons given in this memorial, for the alteration it proposed, were, that the number of students, and the business of the College, had greatly increased, which rendered it expedient, in the apprehension of the Overseers, that the Corporation should be enlarged. And their prayer was, that the General Court would make a "convenient addition to the Corporation, and therein to have regard to the resident fellows, or tutors, that they may be of that number." This memorial was referred to a joint committee of both branches of the legislature, composed of five members of the Council and five of the House of Representatives.

Memorial of the Overseers to the legislature, to enlarge the Corporation.

It is obvious from the course of these proceedings, that the proposition for an enlargement of the Corporation was the result of a compromise in the board of Overseers. To the project of those who supported or had instigated Sever and Welsteed's memorial it was not conformable, as it would only introduce the resident tutors into the Corporation, but would not remove the obnoxious members. There was no ground for the pretence, that for all the objects within the powers of the Corporation, seven were not an adequate and, in fact, a much more efficient board than a larger number. The real project of the malecontents among the Overseers was well understood by the committee to whom their memorial was referred, five of them being members of that board, and of these some were the most decided opponents of the Corporation. They accordingly voted, that an enlargement of the number of the Corporation was inexpedient, and adopted resolutions, which, if carried into effect, would sweep all the non-resident, and consequently all the obnoxious, members from the board of Corporation. In conformity with these views, on the 28th of June, 1722, they reported, that, having taken the subject into consideration, and perused the charter, the present constitution of the College, and the memorial, they "came to the following resolutions, which, being put in practice, would answer the end of the memorial, and be more beneficial to that society than enlarging the number of the Corporation."

Proceedings of the legislature on that memorial.

"First, that it was the intent of the said College charter, that the tutors of the said College, or such as have the instruction and government of the students there, should be Fellows and Members of the Corporation of said College, provided they exceed not five in number.

"Secondly, that none of said Fellows be Overseers.

"Thirdly, that the President and Fellows of the said College, or the major part of them, are not warranted to fix or establish any salary or allowance for their service, without the approbation and consent of the Overseers."*

This report was accepted in the House of Representatives, and concurred in by the Council.

Governor Shute, well aware that this measure did

* See Records of the General Court.

not originate in just views of the interest of the College, and that the avowed were not the real motives, adopted a course of policy which gave an instantaneous developement to the whole project. Instead of giving the resolutions his official negative, on the 2d of July he returned them signed, with this conditional approval. "I consent to these votes, provided the Rev. Mr. Benjamin Wadsworth, and the Rev. Mr. Benjamin Colman, and the Rev. Mr. Appleton are not removed by said orders, but still remain Fellows of the Corporation." By the tenor of the Governor's concurrence, the concealed design of the House of Representatives, as if touched by the spear of Ithuriel,

Governor Shute consents conditionally.

> . . . . "returned
> Of force to its own likeness, ...
> Discovered and surprised!"

Although nothing could have been more easy than a temporary arrangement, which would have complied with the conditions proposed by the Governor, had the motive really been the permanent interest of the institution, the House of Representatives lost their prudence in their passion, and their project with their temper. They avowed, without qualification, their design, and demanded of the Governor an unconditional approval.

Remonstrance of the House of Representatives.

On the 5th of July, 1722, they voted, "That a message be sent up to His Excellency the Governor, to acquaint him, that, whereas he has been pleased to make a proviso in his consenting to the votes, passed by both Houses, relating to Harvard College, *which has a tendency entirely to defeat the design and purpose of those votes*, therefore to desire His Excellency to pass absolutely thereupon, according to the constant

CHAPTER XIV.

usage and practice ever since the present happy constitution."

An avowal of this kind had the effect it was naturally calculated to produce. The Governor became more fixed in his purpose, and returned at once by his secretary the following decided and well-considered reply.

Reply of Governor Shute.

"Gentlemen, I received your message relating to the affairs of the College; and, although I am not obliged to give my reasons for my manner of signing, or my refusing to sign, any vote, yet I think it proper so to do upon this occasion; and therefore I do now inform you, that the limitations, with which I signed the resolve, were agreeable to the explanations made to me by the Council at the time of my signing, and also agreeable to the intention of the Overseers, in their address to the General Court; wherefore I cannot consent to these votes upon any other terms than what I have already done, until I have appointed an Overseers' meeting for their further opinion in that matter."

Governor Shute had unquestionably ascertained, that an enlargement of the Corporation was not the real wish of either of the parties which divided the board of Overseers, but was the result of a compromise between them founded upon the basis, that the resident fellows should be admitted and the non-resident not removed from the board. At that period, the strength of the stricter sect of the Calvinists was concentrated in the House of Representatives. Although church members were not, as under the old charter, exclusively freemen of the Province, yet from the impulse and direction, which that charter, by its long continuance, had given to the religious sentiments of the people, the influence of church members retained a decided ascendency. Belief in the predominating religious opinions continued to be an essential requisite to political advancement, and the influential men in each town represented the prevalent faith of the church or churches, of which it was composed. The House of Representatives, therefore, were resolved not to lose, by any compromise, the opportunity they now possessed of changing the influences then ascendant in the Corporation. They, therefore, immediately responded to the message of the Governor in the following terms; "In the House of Representatives, voted, that the explanations made by the Council to His Excellency, seem inconsistent with their own vote upon the resolves; and therefore this House insists upon their desire, that His Excellency would pass upon it absolutely, without any proviso or limitation."

Proceedings of the House of Representatives.

No notice appears to have been taken by the Governor of this vote; and the subject was not again called up for consideration in that session.

During the ensuing recess of the legislature the Overseers continued to thwart the measures of the Corporation, and to indicate towards that board a spirit of determined hostility. The health of President Leverett became at this time precarious. In the instruction of the undergraduates he had been accustomed to take a part, but was now compelled to allow the whole of this labor to devolve on the tutors. The Corporation, in this exigency, deeming a fifth tutor necessary, elected William Cook to that office. When this choice was presented to the Overseers for approval, they at once negatived his election,

CHAPTER XIV. 1722. Aug. 14. and voted, that "four tutors were sufficient at present for the instruction of the scholars." The Corporation made a deliberate declaration, that a greater number of tutors was necessary for the inspection and instruction of the students, and passed a vote, requesting a conference on the subject with the Overseers. To this request it does not appear that this board ever acceded. It is certain, that Cook was never approved by them as a tutor, nor did he ever officiate in that capacity.

Sept. 5.

Aug. 14. About this time the nomination of Robie as a member of the Corporation came under the consideration of the board of Overseers. They passed a vote in the affirmative, annexing this proviso, "during his residence as a tutor at the College;" a limitation wholly unauthorized by the College charter.

Aug. 30. The Overseers next proceeded to order, that the act of the Corporation for the choice "of tutors every three years should be laid before them for their consideration." This was accordingly done at the next meeting by the Corporation, and the act received a decided negative from the Overseers.

Nov. 21.

House of Representatives renew their attack on the Corporation.

The House of Representatives, in a like spirit of animosity, passed, on the 22d of November, 1722, a resolution intimating, that the Corporation had not kept strictly within the rules prescribed by the charter of the College; and, after expressing their concern thereat, recommended "a greater caution, lest they endanger the early privileges of the institution."

This resolution drew forth from the Corporation a formal memorial on the 10th of December, 1722, to the Governor and legislature, in which they aver, that they are not sensible of having done any acts not warranted by their charter, and praying, "that they

CHAPTER XIV.

may be admitted to a hearing in the premises, the Corporation not having as yet been heard thereupon."

Corporation request a hearing.

This memorial was read on the 12th of December in the House of Representatives, who immediately voted, "that it be dismissed, for that the prayer of the memorial is altogether groundless, and no ways to be justified;" * and, in the course of that session, they took up the resolves, which had been passed at the previous session, and which had been lost in consequence of the conditional consent of Governor Shute; and, after recapitulating those resolves, in their very terms, they passed an additional resolve, "that the same be and hereby are revived and declared to be the rule for the future proceedings of Harvard College." †

Their petition is dismissed.

1723. Jan. 18.

In this resolve a majority of the Council refused to coöperate; and the House of Representatives, being thus defeated in their project, made no farther attempt to renew the controversy during that session. This attack on the Corporation was probably encouraged by the absence of Governor Shute, who had sailed for England on the 1st of January, 1723. From Lieutenant-Governor Dummer the House of Representatives probably expected greater complacency towards their policy, or less ability to resist it. But their design had been anticipated by Governor Shute, who had a great personal respect for Colman, Wadsworth, and Appleton; and, in 1723, when in London, he assured Mr. Hollis, that, if the vote to remove the three non-resident members succeeded in the House of Representatives, it should not receive the concurrence of the executive authority.‡

* See Appendix, No. LV. † See Records of the General Court.
‡ See Appendix, No. LVI.

CHAPTER XIV.

Attempts to induce members of the Corporation to resign.

The Overseers continued to seize every opportunity to excite and keep alive a spirit of opposition to the Corporation, and their proceedings render the conclusion unavoidable, that a majority had determined, that, if they could not remove the obnoxious members of that board from their seats by the arm of power, they would compel them to resign by the treatment to which they subjected them.

In conformity with this policy, one of the Dudleys informed the House of Representatives, that "Mr. Colman and Mr. Wadsworth would resign their places, and then the way will be cleared." His wishes were the parents of that prophecy. It indeed appears from Hollis's letters, that, in October, 1722, Colman had thought of resigning his seat in the Corporation, which probably had been communicated to Dudley, who hoped, by this public annunciation, to induce the act. But it had a contrary effect; for, no sooner had Leverett notice of Dudley's speech, than he addressed a letter to Mr. Colman, dated November 26th, 1722,* expressing "his hope of better things" from him and Mr. Wadsworth; and intimating that his own situation would be much more difficult should they withdraw. The violent spirit which actuated the House of Representatives is indicated by this letter, in which Leverett states, that he is informed, that the House intend "to refuse the Governor's allowance, unless he come into their scheme, without reserve, of alterations in the Corporation." He adds; "His Excellency has told me, that he is so well satisfied, that the project will be fatal to the College, that he will never come into it, let what will come."

* Peirce's Hist. Harv. Univ., p. 119.

CHAPTER XIV.

Conduct of the Corporation on the occasion.

There is no reason to believe, that any serious intention to resign ever existed in the minds of those firm and conscientious men, whose removal from the Corporation was the object of the House of Representatives. The true and elevated spirit by which they were actuated is feelingly expressed in the close of that memorial, which the Corporation addressed to the Lieutenant-Governor and Council on the 23d of August, 1723.* "We thank your honors for this opportunity granted us faithfully to discharge our consciences, in what we really think would be for the good of the College; making this representation not for any by-ends or self-interest. Those of us, whose ejectment is so earnestly sought for, neither seek nor find any reward for all that time we spend or pains we take, as members of the Corporation. If we have served the College in any kind and degree, we thank God for the time and assistance. We heartily wish and pray for its welfare, and for the flourishing of religion and good literature in it, to the glory of God, and the good of this people, even to the latest posterity; if it may be the divine pleasure so to order it. We wish its enemies may not find nor take any occasion against it by its late unhappy discontents and differences; the fault whereof lies at their door, who have contrived and fomented them. A house or city divided against itself, — what is likely to come of it? God avert the omen!"

Robie resigns his seat in the Corporation.

In February, 1722-3, Thomas Robie, the senior resident tutor and Fellow of the Corporation, resigned both those offices. Robie had joined Sever and Welsteed in none of their cabals, and had fulfilled all his

* See Appendix, No. LVII.

CHAPTER XIV.

duties, to the entire acceptance of the Corporation. The President accordingly returned him thanks for his good services both as a tutor and a Fellow of the Corporation, and made the following entry in his Diary. "It ought to be remembered, that Mr. Robie was no small honor to Harvard College, by his mathematical performances, and by his correspondence thereupon with Mr. Durham and other learned persons in those studies abroad." *

The vacancy occasioned by Robie's resignation was immediately filled by the election of Nathan Prince, to be a tutor for three years. As this limitation might be considered by the Overseers a defiance of their authority, the Corporation passed a vote, declaring it was not done "in contradiction to the Overseers, nor in any disparagement of the person elected, but as what, upon mature deliberation, they esteem most for the good of the College. And, if the election shall not be acceptable to the Overseers, they direct that it should then be presented as if it were made without limitation of time."

When Mr. Prince was presented to the board of Overseers, as a tutor for three years, they negatived his election. Being then presented to them as tutor, without limitation of time, they passed a vote in the affirmative.

Third memorial of Sever and Welsteed.

Sever and Welsteed, on the 7th of June, 1723, presented another memorial, complaining of their salaries. Although an interference of the Overseers with the Corporation in relation to salaries had been altogether unprecedented since the revival of the charter, the Overseers made no scruple on the subject, but

* Leverett's Manuscript, p. 252.

declared the salaries of both insufficient, and "advised the Corporation to make further and suitable addition to the yearly salaries of both." This vote was passed without calling upon the Corporation for any explanation on the subject. It does not appear, however, that the Corporation took any notice of this interference.

Professor Wigglesworth elected Fellow of the Corporation.

On the 4th of June, 1723, Professor Wigglesworth was unanimously elected a Fellow of the Corporation. Every consideration of age, permanent relation to the College, and literary qualification, were in favor of this selection; but to Sever and Welsteed it was a signal, that their hopes of admission to that board were again about to be foiled. Their friends rallied in their favor; but, to defeat this nomination, they had a peculiar difficulty to encounter. Mr. Hollis, whose bounties were at this time flowing, in full tide, towards the College, had expressed in his letters a strong desire, that his professor should be admitted to a seat in the Corporation. The fear of offending this benefactor was not strong enough, however, to arrest the determined spirit of party in its course. The Overseers negatived the election of Mr. Wigglesworth, and appointed a committee "to prepare a letter, setting forth to Mr. Hollis the grounds upon which the Overseers have disapproved of the choice of Mr. Wigglesworth as a Fellow of the Corporation."

Negatived by the Overseers.

During the session of the General Court in June, 1723, the theses of the Bachelors to be graduated at the Commencement in July were published according to custom; and the House of Representatives, for some reason not to be ascertained from their records, took offence "at the dedication of them as not properly addressed," and passed a formal vote, "That it

CHAPTER XIV.

is derogatory to the honor of the Lieutenant-Governor, who is now Commander-in-chief of the Province, and the head of the Overseers of the College, to have the impression of these theses go out as they now are; and therefore ordered, that the printer, Mr. Bartholomew Green, be, and is hereby, directed not to deliver any of the theses till they shall be properly addressed." *

The Council non-concur.

The Council again put a check on the temper of the House, and non-concurred the order.

House of Representatives revive their resolve against the Corporation.

In the August ensuing the House of Representatives took up for the third time their former resolves, which had been lost by the conditional consent of Governor Shute, and sent them to the Council for concurrence. This was done without any notice being given to the Corporation, notwithstanding their solicitation to be heard at the preceding session. They were, however, not deterred by the chilling repulse their former re-
1723. quest had received. On the 9th of August the Corporation again met, and prepared a formal address to the Lieutenant-Governor, Council, and House of Representatives, declaring it to be, in their apprehension, their bounden duty, although their former application had not been successful, humbly to petition for a hearing, before further proceedings should be had on the subject of those resolves. The address was presented to the Council, before whom the resolves of the House were then pending for concurrence. The hearing requested by the Corporation was granted by the Council on the 23d of August, 1723, and the result was effectual and final.† The Council again non-concurred in the resolves of the House, and they were never after revived in that or any succeeding legislature.

* See Records of the General Court. † See Appendix, No. LVII.

CHAPTER XIV.

Thus at last this reiterated and violent attempt to change the charter of the College terminated in the complete triumph of the Corporation.

Tribute to the spirit of the Corporation.

History has seldom to record a firmer or better principled spirit of resistance to attempted encroachments on charter rights, than that displayed in this exigency by Colman, Wadsworth, and Appleton. The circumstances in which they were placed were full of trial and discouragement. Party spirit had no path to its object, but by making them its victims; and their removal became, therefore, its settled policy, at first covertly, at last openly. They as well knew, that Sever and Welsteed's attack was levelled at them personally on the day their memorial was offered, as they did two years afterwards, when the House of Representatives unequivocally avowed their object. They had no motives to maintain the struggle, but a sense of duty, and a deep conviction that this attempt, if successful, would be fatal to the interests of the College. Their places in the Corporation were offices of mere labor and responsibility, with no emolument. They had to resist a numerous, active, prejudiced, and powerful class of individuals in the Province, occasionally able to command the superior vote, both in the board of Overseers and in the Council. In the House of Representatives there was at that time a majority, actuated by as overbearing a spirit of party, as at any previous period had existed in the Province; possessing a predominating popularity; active and fearless, with no delicacy as to its means, and determined as to its objects. The whole administration of Shute was tempestuous; and the affairs of the College were affected by the passions and interests which embarrassed the Colonial government.

CHAPTER XV.

Increasing Influence of the Episcopal Church. — Alarm of the Congregationalists. — Relations of the College to both. — Discontent with the general State of the College. — Visiting Committee appointed by the Overseers. — Their Report. — Its Result. — Death of President Leverett. — Professor Wigglesworth approved by the Overseers as Fellow of the Corporation. — Review of the Administration of Leverett. — The Deficiency of his Salary for his Support. — Application to the General Court for the Relief of his Family. — Its Result.

CHAPTER XV.

Increase of the Episcopal church.

In the party spirit which characterized and embarrassed the Massachusetts House of Representatives during the administration of Governor Shute, the elements of civil and ecclesiastical policy were intimately combined. Political jealousy and theological zeal reciprocally stimulated each other. The fears of the politicians were excited by the increasing influence of the English crown; those of the clergy, by the proselyting spirit of the English hierarchy. Both divisions of the Congregational church saw, with undisguised anxiety, Episcopacy daily gaining strength and gathering converts, by the aid of transatlantic funds and missionaries. But the feelings and conduct of the parties were modified by their respective characters and religious opinions.

Brattle, Colman, Pemberton, Wadsworth, and Appleton, belonged to a class of divines, which first appeared, when the civil power the clergy had wielded under the old charter was beginning to be dissolved by the influence of the new principles introduced by that of William and Mary. They were eminently liberal in their religious views, and, although not friendly to the influence of the Church of England, they regarded the introduction of Episcopacy as unavoidable, considering the relation of the Province to the parent State. Thomas Brattle, Treasurer of the College, and for more than twenty years an active member of the Corporation, made no concealment of his decided preference for the Episcopalian forms of worship.

Relation to it of the governors of the College.

As the College was, in that day, dependent on the favor of the General Court for the support of its President, it was the policy as well as the duty of its governors to conciliate the Chief Magistrate of the Province, and as far as possible to harmonize with a church, which, from his official relations, if not from principle, he was compelled to patronize. Colman, the leading member of the Corporation, was highly esteemed by some of the dignitaries of the English hierarchy. He was a correspondent of the Bishop of Peterborough, who was disposed to consider "the catholic spirit," for which the College was distinguished, as attributable to his influence; and even expressed a wish that he should therefore be advanced to the President's chair, when a vacancy occurred by the death of Leverett.*

The policy and spirit, thus manifested by leading members of the Corporation, was equally offensive to the political and religious zealots of that period. The one considered the College as inclining to the side of prerogative; the other, as verging towards here-

* See Turell's Life of Colman, p. 136.

CHAPTER XV.

Its effects on the character of the College.

sy, and not sufficiently inimical to the English hierarchy. With both parties it became an object of severe scrutiny and some misrepresentation. Its moral and religious condition was canvassed with asperity, and its character assailed by general suggestions of declension, easily made, and difficult wholly to refute, but, in the degree insinuated, utterly devoid of probability.

Thus Cooke, the leader of the patriotic party in the House of Representatives, being in England in the spring of 1724, is found representing to Mr. Hollis the very bad state of the College, and attributing it to the fact, that "the Corporation was not composed of resident fellows," yet at the same time acknowledging, that "the present non-resident fellows were as worthy persons as the country afforded, or as could be chosen."* As if three or four tutors, mostly young men just out of College, whose connexion with the seminary was usually short and precarious, without experience, and having no external influence, were likely to manage its concerns better than such men as Colman, Wadsworth, and Appleton.

Overseers take measures indicative of discontent.

On the 18th of January, 1723, the House of Representatives revived the resolves they had passed at the previous session, on the memorial of Sever and Welsteed, and which Governor Shute had negatived, and, passing them a second time, sent them to the Council for their concurrence. This body referred the subject to the ensuing May session; and, in the month of August, the resolves were taken up for discussion. While the project of removing the obnoxious members of the Corporation was in progress,

* See Appendix, No. LVIII.

the moment was thought favorable to commence in the board of Overseers measures strongly indicating discontent with the state of the College. Accordingly, on the 9th of August, a formal vote was passed by the Overseers, "that a visitation of the College would very much serve the interests of religion and learning in that society," and should be made accordingly; and a committee, of which Judge Sewall was chairman, was appointed "to prepare and lay before the Overseers at their next meeting, such heads or articles which may be thought proper for the aforesaid visitation of the Overseers to proceed upon." This committee made a report, which on the 30th of September was read, and the several articles proposed were voted in the board of Overseers.

1723.

Heads of inquiry.

These articles were *ten* in number, of which three had reference to the general conduct of the College; and seven, exclusive reference to its religious and moral condition; indicating very distinctly the points on which there existed, or there was a disposition to create, suspicions. These articles of inquiry were;

1. "What are the stated exercises enjoined on the students, and how attended by them.

2. "What are the books in Divinity, which are most used, and more particularly recommended to the students.

3. "How are the Saturday exercises performed, and are the great concerns of their souls duly inculcated on the youth.

4. "What is the state of the College as to the morals of the youth.

5. "Whether the Holy Scriptures be daily read in the Hall, and how often expounded.

6. "Whether the tutors and students do duly give

their attendance on the public prayers and readings of the Holy Scriptures in the Hall, morning and evening.

7. "Whether many of the students are not allowed to be too often and too long absent from the College.

8. "Whether the tutors duly visit their pupils' chambers and oblige them to their proper hours.

9. "How the Lord's day is observed, and the public duties of it attended by that society.

10. "How the lectures and other exercises of the Hollis Professor are performed and attended by that society."

Report of the committee of inquiry.

The report of this committee of visitation, made on the 9th of October, 1723, breathes a spirit of subdued discontent with the College, yet its sharpness is sufficient to give color of justification for antecedent apprehensions. Did we not know the violence of the times, and the natural tendency of party spirit to exaggerate, we should be led to lament the moral degeneracy of the institution, and to make no favorable conclusions concerning its management. But the scrutiny had been commenced when there were vivid expectations of success in the project connected with the revival of the resolves, in which Sever and Welsteed's memorial had resulted. The report was made after the malecontents with the Corporation in the board of Overseers and the House of Representatives had been defeated by the firmness of the Council, who admitted the Corporation to a hearing which the House had denied, and afterwards finally non-concurred in the resolves. A course suited to the actual state of things was adopted. The governors of the College were passed over without censure; but a minute detail was given of crimes and offences, sufficient to justify the insinuations which had been made concerning the moral and religious declension of the institution.

To the first inquiry the committee report, "That the stated exercises in the College are generally the same which they have formerly been; and that there is too common and general a neglect of the stated exercises amongst the undergraduates, and that the Masters' disputations and Bachelors' declamations, enjoined by the laws of the College, have been a long time disused."

As to the second inquiry, "That there does not appear to have been any great recommendation of books in Divinity to the students, but that they have read promiscuously, according to their inclinations, authors of different denominations in religion; and, by some information given, the works of Tillotson, Sherlock, Scott, and Lucas, are generally most used."

As to the third inquiry, "That the Greek Catechism is recited by the Freshmen without exposition. Wollebius' and Ames's Systems of Divinity by the other classes, with exposition on Saturdays; and repetitions of the sermons of the foregoing sabbath are made by the students on Saturday evenings, when the President is present."

As to the fourth, "That, although there is a considerable number of virtuous and studious youth in the College, yet there has been a practice of several immoralities; particularly stealing, lying, swearing, idleness, picking of locks, and too frequent use of strong drink; which immoralities, it is feared, still continue in the College, notwithstanding the faithful endeavours of the rulers of the House to suppress them."

CHAPTER XV. As to the fifth, "That the Scriptures are read in the Hall, on Mondays, Tuesdays, Wednesdays, and Thursdays, when the President is present, and once a week expounded by the President."

As to the sixth, "That the tutors and graduates do generally give their attendance on the prayers in the Hall, though not on the readings; and that the undergraduates attend both prayers and readings; but they attend in greater numbers at prayers when there are no readings."

As to the seventh, "That the scholars are, many of them, too long absent from the College; but their long absence is not with allowance."

As to the eighth, "That the tutors do duly visit their pupils' chambers, and oblige them to their proper hours."

As to the ninth, "That there are prayers, and a psalm sung, in the Hall on the Lord's day mornings; and repetition of the sermons by one of the scholars; and a psalm and prayers in the evening; and that the scholars do generally attend the public worship; and that the scholars too generally spend too much of the Saturday evenings in one another's chambers; and that the Freshmen, as well as others, are seen, in great numbers, going into town, on Sabbath mornings, to provide breakfasts."

As to the tenth, "That the public lectures of the Hollis Professor are well performed, and are attended by the scholars; but the private lectures are very much neglected by the scholars."

No direct action upon this report appears to have been had, not even an acceptance of it by the Over-
1723. seers. On the 18th of the ensuing November, indeed, a committee was appointed, to revise the laws

of the College, and with instructions to consider "what farther is requisite to be done, beyond what has been done, in pursuit of the Overseers' inquiry." It does not appear by the records of either the Corporation or the Overseers, that this committee ever made a report.

Result of the inquiry.

The death of President Leverett, in May, 1724, gave an entirely new direction to the views and interests of parties. The Overseers met on the succeeding day, and, Professor Wigglesworth having been rechosen on the 25th of December a Fellow of the Corporation by that board, the Overseers now "reconsidered their reasons for their former non-acceptance of him," and concurred in his election. Yielding either to the arguments or the authority of the Council of the Province, the House of Representatives took no farther measures on the claim of Sever and Welsteed, which was never afterwards renewed. The three obnoxious members of the Corporation were permitted to retain their seats unmolested, and the vacant chair of the President concentrated the attention of all parties.

1723.

The administration of President Leverett was laborious, difficult, and eventful. By the very force of the factions, which divided the politics and religion of the country, the prosperity of the College had been advanced, and its usefulness extended. Institutions amid the tumults of party discord, like ships amid the strife of warring elements, are often urged onward with accelerated force by the tempest, which at first retarded their progress, and even threatened their destruction. Success in both cases depends on the firmness and skill of the pilot.

During the administrations of Governors Dudley and Shute, the affairs of the Colony were subjected

CHAPTER XV.

Financial embarrassments of Massachusetts.

to great pecuniary embarrassment. The wars of Queen Anne had created a considerable public debt. Taxes were heavy. The population of Massachusetts was increasing, but in a smaller ratio than formerly. Its finances were depressed in consequence of the practice of issuing paper money without adequate funds for redemption. Yet in times thus unpropitious the Corporation of the College, under the auspices of Leverett, obtained from the legislature of the Province a succession of efficient grants unparalleled in the previous history of the institution. All their donations to it in land had hitherto failed, either from want of title or of means to enforce it. With the exception of the profits of the ferry over Charles River, the patronage of the Province had been limited to an annual grant for the support of the President, and this had been the only direct pecuniary aid the College had received from the treasury. But in November, 1717, on the memorial of the Corporation, stating that "a considerable number of students were obliged to take lodgings in the town of Cambridge for want of accommodations in the College, and praying the assistance of the General Court for erecting a suitable building," the legislature took the subject into consideration, and in May, 1718, ordered an edifice three stories high, fifty feet in length, and of the same breadth with Harvard Hall, to be erected at the expense of the Province. In 1719 this building was extended in length to one hundred feet, and was completed in 1720, at a cost of about three thousand five hundred pounds, currency of the Province. This edifice received the name of Massachusetts Hall, and continues in good preservation to this day. For the liberality of the General Court on this occasion, the College was chiefly indebted to the influence of Gov-

General Court erect Massachusetts Hall.

ernor Shute, who made two special recommendations on the subject in public messages. Notwithstanding the embarrassed state of their finances, it was not easy for the General Court to resist the zeal and urgency of the chief magistrate, in aid of an institution, which had been the object of the favor of the people of the Province from its first settlement, and which was evidently in extreme want of the accommodation solicited. The disposition manifested about this period, by wealthy individuals among the Dissenters in Great Britain, to patronize and endow the College, also tended to excite the legislature to aid its advancement. In concurring with the recommendations of Governor Shute, the House of Representatives expressed their thanks for "his care to promote good literature, without which religion will not be upheld among us." *

Death of President Leverett.

The death of President Leverett was sudden, unexpected, and deeply lamented. On the morning of the 3d of May, 1724, he was found dead in his bed, to which he had retired the night before, suffering under what was considered a slight indisposition. The funeral sermons delivered on the occasion, by his friends Colman, Wadsworth, and Appleton, are replete with sorrow and eulogy. Chief Justice Sewall also, in an address to the Grand Jury, spoke of President Leverett, "as one, who had been an ornament to the Bench of Justice and Court of Probate, full of sweetness and candor, displayed in the government of the College, tempered by convenient severity."

The abilities of Leverett seem to have been of a superior order, which the events of his life had en-

* See Records of the General Court, 14th of February, 1718.

CHAPTER XV.

Character of President Leverett.

abled him to improve and refine by an extensive intercourse with books and mankind. His talents were eminently practical. He knew better than most men what course to shape in difficult times, and how political and religious factions were to be managed or controlled. To these characteristics the College owed much of the prosperity it enjoyed at that period; and these conferred the reputation for success, which has ever since rested upon his administration. In all his official relations, his industry, vigor, and fidelity were conspicuous and exemplary. He was a man more actuated by a sense of duty than by desire of fame, and no important monuments of his literary or scientific attainments remain, except such as are identified with the prosperity of the College while under his care.

The religion of President Leverett was enlightened and catholic. In a country, and at a period of society, when the sectarian spirit was strenuously contending for power and supremacy, he maintained his integrity, and preserved the College in that independence of religious sects, which was established by the terms of its first charter. To his firmness, and that of his associates, under circumstances of great trial, and in opposition to an almost overwhelming power, the institution is, probably, in a great measure indebted for its religious freedom at this day.

His poverty.

While he was able to maintain the College in the independence of its early constitution, he was compelled himself to become the victim of poverty and disappointment; a fate he might probably have avoided, had he been more subservient to the times, and less conscientiously scrupulous. For his own support and that of his family, he was chiefly dependent on grants from the General Court. These had not been enlarged in proportion to the increase of the expense of living, and the depreciation of money consequent on a paper currency. As early as November, 1711, he addressed a letter to the General Court, in which he stated that he had been "invited to the cares and services of the office of President of the College, by the votes of that Court, and with a demand of devoting himself entirely to those cares and services," which he had done without any diversion; that the insufficiency of the salary was at the time of his appointment universally known and acknowledged, even by the General Court itself, who had "declared that it must be and should be seasonably advanced"; that, relying on the justice and honor of the Court, and at the instance of well-wishers to the public as well as to himself, he was persuaded to accept the office without insisting on the insufficiency of the salary; that he had been four years President, and had found by experience that his salary had fallen far short of his maintenance. He therefore petitioned, that he might be indemnified for the loss he had sustained, for, unless this should be done, "the damage would prove insupportable, not to say irreparable." The urgency and justice of this petition drew nothing from the General Court except a resolve, "that the sum of thirty pounds be added to the allowance of the memorialist *for the year next coming*." And a like sum, which sometimes was increased to forty, and once to fifty, pounds, was granted in subsequent years, "in consideration of the extraordinary scarcity and dearness of provisions and other necessaries of housekeeping." In December, 1720, President Leverett addressed a supplicatory letter to the General Court, praying for an indemnification for the diminution of his subsistence by reason of the

CHAPTER XV.

"demolition of the President's House," and the inadequacy of his support.* This application having produced no effect, two of the Fellows of the Corporation, Mr. Wadsworth and Mr. Colman, in the ensuing May addressed the legislature on the subject, wholly, as they assert, "from their own mere motion, and without any agency of President Leverett's," stating the utter insufficiency of his salary for his necessary annual expenses, and urging, with great pathos, the reasonableness and necessity of some addition to his present allowance.† The memorial was treated by the legislature, as far as its records indicate, with total neglect. The President was left to struggle with poverty and embarrassment. The result was, that, after sixteen years of faithful and laborious service, on a salary of one hundred and fifty pounds per annum, exclusive of the abovementioned grants, his estate, at his death, was found bankrupt; being in debt upwards of two thousand pounds, for the payment of which sum his children were compelled to sell the mansion-house of Governor Leverett, which had descended to them from their great-grandfather. These circumstances appear on the records of the General Court, in a memorial presented by the daughters and heirs of President Leverett, in the year 1726, in connexion with this further statement, that their father had been "necessitated, for the decent support of his family, to sink the yearly rent of his own estate, and to fall in debt one hundred pounds every year during his presidency," and that, the President's house having been pulled down to make way for the new College, their father had been subjected for four years to the additional

Memorial of his daughters for an allowance.

* See above, p. 283.

† See Appendix, No. LIX.

expense of twenty pounds annual rent; and that rent for two months was due for their house while occupied by President Wadsworth.

Proceedings thereon of the Council;

This memorial was first presented to the Council of the Province, and was by them transmitted to the House of Representatives, with a special and earnest message, recommending it to their favor, accompanied by a solemn declaration, that, "in the opinion of that board, the justice and honor of this Court are much concerned in making compensation to the heirs of President Leverett for the loss accruing to his estate through the insufficiency of his allowance."

and of the House of Representatives.

This message and the memorial were received and acted upon by the House of Representatives, in the cold spirit of calculation, or under the influence of the vindictive spirit of party. They voted "thirty pounds to the petitioners in full satisfaction of and in answer to the petition," declaring, that of this sum twenty pounds were for the arrearages of salary occurring in the month antecedent to the President's death, and ten pounds for the two months' rent remaining due, as stated in the memorial.

It would have been grateful to have left this last-mentioned feature of the period in the oblivion, to which it well deserves, from its character, to be consigned. But public bodies, acting in subserviency to the corrupt propensities or party passions of the day, are only amenable to a returning sound state of public opinion. And the sole principle of control upon such bodies is identified with the certainty, that, sooner or later, History, in the exercise of an inexorable fidelity, will drag the meanness or injustice of power, whether of one or of many, to receive its ultimate reward of disgrace from her tribunal.

CHAPTER XVI.

Difficulties attending the Selection of a President. — Cotton Mather, Wadsworth, Colman, and Joseph Sewall, Candidates. — Election of Sewall. — Dissatisfaction of Cotton Mather. — Sewall declines the Appointment. — Election of Colman. — Overseers apply to the General Court for a sufficient Salary for him. — Vote of the House of Representatives on the Application. — Colman makes a fixed Salary the Condition of his Acceptance. — House of Representatives refuse it. — Colman declines the Presidency. — Wadsworth chosen President. — Accepts. — General Court grant a Salary. — Cotton Mather attacks the Character of Leverett. — Comparison of the Lives of Mather and Leverett.

CHAPTER XVI.

Difficulties in choosing a President.

AFTER the death of President Leverett the attention of the friends of the College was concentrated on the choice of his successor. The relations of the religious and political parties of the Province, and the dependence of the College on annual grants from the legislature for the support of the President, rendered a satisfactory selection among the candidates for the office unusually difficult, and gave intensity to the interest of the occasion.

The independent and successful stand made by the Corporation against the attempt to remove three of their number, on the claim of Sever and Welsteed, had no tendency to conciliate the favor of the House of Representatives. That conclusive defence of the chartered rights of the Corporation had been chiefly the work of Colman and Wadsworth. The talent and fidelity they had thus manifested had endeared

Comparative claims of Colman and Wadsworth.

both to the friends of the institution; to whom the elevation of either to the President's chair would have been, perhaps, equally acceptable. The claims of Colman, though the younger of the two candidates, were, from his more extensive acquaintance with life and the world, higher than those of Wadsworth. But, as the first pastor of the Manifesto Church, and as the leader of that ominous secession from the doctrines of the early Platform, he was peculiarly obnoxious to the stricter sect of the Calvinists. His spirit was more active than that of Wadsworth; his temper, bolder and more ardent. The Corporation, aware of the relations of individuals and parties, were unwilling to choose a member of their own board, and, in a spirit eminently catholic, gave a pledge of their desire to soften the asperities of religious controversy, by selecting a President from the ranks of their opponents.

The Rev. Cotton Mather and the Rev. Joseph Sewall at that time were held in high esteem by the Calvinistic party. Both were clergymen holding pastoral relations to churches in Boston. Both had given unequivocal evidence of their discontent with the religious influences and literary state of the College.

Claims of Cotton Mather.

In favor of Mather, Dr. Eliot asserts,* "The voice of the people cried aloud, and it was declared even in the General Court, that he ought to be President; but it was decided otherwise by the Corporation." This assertion is considered by Peirce,† as "a charge made against the Corporation, of disregarding the voice of the people," which he examines and seriously refutes. But probably it was the intention of Eliot

* Biography, art. *Cotton Mather.*

† See Peirce's Hist. Harv. Univ., p. 135.

CHAPTER XVI.

only to state, that it was the opinion of many individuals that Cotton Mather should be selected, with whom, as the result showed, the Corporation did not coincide.

The learning and industry of Cotton Mather, his voluminous writings, and his theological zeal, gave him popular and ostensible claims to the presidency of the College; a station to which, it is well known, he had long aspired. But violence of passion, frequent coarseness of language, and deficiency in judgment, to a degree at times scarcely reconcilable with common sense, rendered him obnoxious to those who disagreed, and little acceptable to those who coincided with him, in their view of church discipline and religious doctrines. By the former his election would have been considered as a positive evil, and by the latter as a very uncertain good. His pretensions were, therefore, passed over by a general consent, and, on the 11th of August, 1724, the Rev. Joseph Sewall was elected President of Harvard College by the Corporation, and on the 26th of the same month was approved by the Overseers. Cotton Mather notices this appointment in his Diary with one of those bitter sarcastic sneers, in which he was accustomed to indulge. "This day," he writes, "Dr. Sewall was chosen President *for his piety*."*

The Rev. Joseph Sewall chosen President.

In another place he thus gives scope to his feelings; "I am informed that yesterday the six men who call themselves the Corporation of the College met, and, contrary to the epidemical expectation of the country, chose a modest young man, of whose piety (and little else) every one gives a laudable character.

* Peirce's Hist. Harv. Univ., p. 141.

CHAPTER XVI.

"I always foretold these two things of the Corporation; first, that, if it were possible for them to steer clear of me, they will do so; secondly, that, if it were possible for them to act foolishly, they will do so.

"The perpetual envy *with which my essays to serve the kingdom of God are treated among them, and the dread that Satan has of my beating up his quarters at the College, led me into the former sentiment;* the marvellous indiscretion, with which the affairs of the College are managed, led me into the latter."*

Cotton Mather well understood, that, by the election of Sewall, the Corporation sought to conciliate the predominating religious influences of the Province. Sewall, though not deficient in other qualifications for the President's chair, besides piety, was not distinguished for possessing them. The office was not suited either to his character or his views. Amiable, faithful, and affectionate, he was peculiarly adapted to the office of teacher and pastor. He had the good sense to realize the advantages he possessed; and his church, by refusing their assent to his removal to the College, expressed the wishes and affections of their pastor not less than their own.

Mr. Sewall declines the presidency.

Mr. Sewall having declined the appointment, the selection of a President devolved again on the Corporation, who, on the 18th of November, 1724, fulfilled that duty by the election of the Rev. Benjamin Colman. This eminent divine, though, to use his own expression, "long disused to academical studies and exercises," possessed, in a high degree, the confidence of the best friends of the College, and his qualifications for the office were many and important. His

The Rev. Benjamin Colman chosen President.

* Sparks's American Biography, Vol. VI. p. 329.

CHAPTER XVI.

talents were unquestionable, and his industry exemplary. As a member of the Corporation, his zeal for the advancement of learning and the interests of the College had been evidenced by a series of persevering and successful efforts. He was the correspondent of Thomas Hollis, of many other friends of the College among the Dissenters in England, and of White Kennett, afterwards Bishop of Peterborough, to all of whom he was endeared by his catholic spirit. No individual in the Province possessed higher qualifications for the office than Mr. Colman.

His election was undoubtedly not acceptable to many of the Overseers, but they had no candidate to interpose with any hope of success, and his appointment was consequently approved by that board on the 24th of November, 1724. Cotton Mather, who had continued to cherish hopes that the influences of the predominating religious party in the Province would eventually effect his election, thus indicates the disappointment he experienced, in his Diary, on the 22d of November, 1724; "The Corporation of the miserable College do again (on a fresh opportunity) treat me with their accustomed indignity."

Financial embarrassment of the College.

At this period the prospects of the College were affected by pecuniary embarrassments. Its funds were scanty and, almost the whole of them, specifically appropriated. The support of its President, even in the humble style which the simple state of society then required, was dependent upon the favor of the General Court, who made an annual grant of one hundred and fifty pounds, Massachusetts currency, generally without regard to the depreciation of the circulating medium. The insufficiency of this grant had been strikingly manifested by the fate and fortunes of Leverett; and the friends of the College now resolved to attempt, if possible, to enlarge the amount, and, by connecting it with the acceptance of the office, to give the transaction the aspect of a contract, and thus place it upon a surer basis than the precarious favor of the General Court. To this end the Overseers, at the same meeting in which they approved the election of Mr. Colman, having appointed a committee to give him notice of the choice, and to apply to his church for his discharge from their service, directed the committee to wait upon the General Court, to inform them of his election, and to "move for a proper salary for his encouragement." The committee accordingly presented to them a memorial, on the 11th of December, 1724, praying that they would "appoint a larger salary than has been usually allowed, for the honorable maintenance of the President," on which the following vote was passed. "In the House of Representatives read, and forasmuch as at present it is uncertain whether the church, of which the Rev. Mr. Colman is pastor, can be persuaded to part from him, or whether Mr. Colman is inclinable to leave his church and undertake the office of President of Harvard College, and this being a matter of great weight and importance, especially to the establishment of the churches in this Province, as well as to the said College; Therefore voted, that the further consideration of this memorial be referred until the said Mr. Colman's mind, as well as of the church of which he is pastor, be communicated to this Court, and made certain, whether he and they are willing he should accept of the choice and undertake the office

House of Representatives refuse a grant to Mr. Colman.

CHAPTER XVI.

of a President of Harvard College, to which he is chosen as aforesaid."

This vote having been passed in the House of Representatives was not concurred in by the Council.

The disposition of the House of Representatives in relation to the election of Mr. Colman, was indicated by the debate and their proceedings. One of the members of the House of Representatives from Boston declared in his speech, that "Dr. Colman was a man of no learning compared with Dr. Mather." The tenor of their vote gave no evidence of a desire to encourage the former to accept the appointment, and a settled determination was apparent, that their proceedings should be such as not to admit of being construed into a contract for a fixed salary.

The state of feeling towards Mr. Colman in the House of Representatives, thus indicated, was far from being propitious; and he had too much spirit and wisdom, voluntarily to trust the fortunes of his life to their future favor. The history of the Province was full of evidence touching the nature of the regard paid by the General Court to the wants of the Presidents of the College; and Mr. Colman was determined, that he would not add another to the list of their disappointed dependants.

Mr. Colman's resolve to be independent of the favor of the General Court, and why.

He knew that Dunster,* after long, faithful, and most successful services, had been compelled to resign by the prevailing Pædobaptist fanaticism, under circumstances of great pecuniary embarrassment; and the application of the Corporation for his relief, rejected by the General Court with a cold and somewhat contemptuous denial. He knew that Chauncy, after

* See above, pp. 18-21.

accepting the office of President on a promise of liberal maintenance by the General Court,* had been stinted in his resources, and his touching appeals to their humanity and good faith neglected; and that, after a long, laborious, and useful life, he left a helpless family, who were compelled to expose to the world their utter poverty, in order to awaken that body to the performance of a simple act of retributive justice. He had seen Mather and Willard, dependent for their compensation upon annual grants, and chiefly indebted for their support to their pastoral relation. And last of all, he had witnessed Leverett, after entering upon the presidency, and resigning all his other offices under full assurances of a liberal maintenance, neither supported adequately to his station, nor even requited according to the depreciation of the currency, and, after services which have rendered his presidency an era in the history of the College, dying bankrupt, and his children compelled to sell the estates of their ancestors to pay the debts of their father; the General Court regardless of all solicitations for sympathy, and of all claims but those of strictly legal obligation.† Had Colman, therefore, deemed them favorable to his election, the past gave him no reason to rely on their sense of justice, or their generosity. He knew well, also, that he was particularly obnoxious to a majority of the members of the House of Representatives, among whom, from circumstances already explained, theological zeal had concentrated the high Calvinistic influences of the Province. Of all persecutors, politicians whose power depends upon a display of religious zeal, are naturally the most bitter. Colman

* See above, pp. 25–28.

† Ibid., p. 327.

CHAPTER XVI.

thus writes to the Bishop of Peterborough on this subject, "I am not well in the opinion of our House of Representatives of late years, on whom the President depends for his subsistence, and they could not have pinched me without the chair's suffering with me, which I could by no means consent it should do for my sake."* For this ill opinion there existed no cause but his theological course and his fidelity to the interests of Harvard College. Colman was the recognised leader of the most liberal religious party of the Province, and had dared openly to declare, in defiance of the adherents to ancient creeds and platforms, that "the Bible was his platform."†

With a perfect understanding of the existence and the causes of that "ill opinion" entertained for him by the General Court, Mr. Colman determined to bring to a quick decision the question pending before them, respecting his support. After receiving private information of the vote, which passed the House of Representatives on the 11th of December, and of the rejection of it by the Council, he immediately addressed a letter to the Honorable Samuel Sewall, chairman of the committee, "fearing lest on my account there may be like to ensue any difficulty to the honorable government, or detriment to the College, for want of an honorable allowance or salary to the President."‡ In this letter, after stating his disinclination to accept the office of President, his reluctance to leave his church, and the zeal with which he had served the College as a member of the Corporation, he supplicates the General Court to enable any one who may be elected to that station,

His letter to Chief Justice Sewall.

* Turell's Life of Colman, p. 136. † Ibid., p. 96. ‡ Ibid., p. 56.

CHAPTER XVI.

to apply himself to the studies and exercises appropriate to the office, by granting a sufficient and honorable support; and he proceeds to declare, that, "for the Honorable Court to insist on those terms, of knowing my mind, whether I am willing to accept of the choice, and to undertake the office of President, to which I am chosen, and also of knowing my church's mind, whether they can part from me, before they will fix any salary for me in the said office, must determine me to give my answer in the negative to the Honorable and Reverend Overseers of Harvard College, which in that case I now do."

On the 17th of December, 1724, this letter from Mr. Colman was read before the board of Overseers, who directed a committee to wait on the General Court with Mr. Colman's answer, and to pray, "that the matter of a salary may be considered by them, and so acted upon as may be most for the speedy settlement of a President in the said College, and therein for the good of the whole Province."

The proceedings of the House of Representatives on this petition are thus stated on their records.

"18th December, 1724. A vote of the Overseers of Harvard College, for applying to the General Assembly for the settling a salary on the President of the said College.

House of Representatives refuse to fix a salary.

"In the House of Representatives read, and the question was put, whether the Court will establish a salary or allowance for the President of Harvard College, for the time being, before the person chosen for that office has accepted the duty and trust thereof; it passed in the negative, *nemine contradicente.*" The Council, indeed, non-concurred in the vote of the House; but the symptoms of hostility were too strong,

CHAPTER XVI.

and Mr. Colman had too much spirit and experience to trust the future support of himself and family to favor so precarious. On the 26th of December, therefore, in reply to another application from the board of Overseers, he transmitted his final answer, declining the presidency of the College.

The difficulties attending the selection of another candidate were numerous and agitating, and further action on the subject was postponed for nearly six months.

During the intervening period, the wishes of the friends of the College had united in favor of the Rev. Benjamin Wadsworth, pastor of the First Church in Boston, who was elected by the Corporation on the 8th, and approved by the Overseers on the 10th, of June, 1725. From his Diary it appears, that his reluctance to accept the office was extreme. After the application made by the Overseers to his church, "for their consent to part with him for that service," on being called upon officially, "by the three deacons of his church, to know his mind about the call given to him to be President," he thus writes; "I told the messengers from our church, that I had kept off my own being chosen as long and as far as I dared to do, and had heartily desired and endeavoured to have the vacancy filled up otherwise; that, as to my own desires and inclinations, I had much rather stay with the church than go to Cambridge; yet, considering of how great weight and importance the College is for the welfare of the country, so far as concerned myself, I dared not negative the call given me to be President." His church having "resolved (after serious consideration and prayer to God for direction) that, if our Reverend pastor, Mr. Wadsworth,

The Rev. Benjamin Wadsworth elected President.

judges it to be his duty to accept of the call given him, we will humbly submit, and say 'The will of the Lord be done,'" he addressed a letter to the Overseers, accepting the office. In this letter he declares how sensible he is of his "insufficiency to the weighty and important service to which he was called." "If I had consulted flesh and blood," he adds, "I think I should have returned a speedy and peremptory negative to this call. So far as I know my own heart, no carnal or worldly views have at all moved me to think of an affirmative answer; yet, considering the glory of God, the interest of religion in the present and succeeding generations, the good of the whole Province in various regards, are deeply concerned, as I humbly conceive, in the settlement of the College; and sundry essays for its settlement having proved abortive and unsuccessful; I say, seriously considering these things, I dare not (for fear of offending that God, whose I am and whom I serve,) give a negative answer to the invitation I have to be President of the College."

The refusal of Mr. Colman to accept the station of President, until some specific engagement was made by the General Court, sufficiently and publicly indicated a want of confidence in their indefinite promises of support, and awakened them to an earnest and active exhibition of interest in the College.

On the 18th of June, 1725, being the day after Mr. Wadsworth had declared his acceptance of that office, the General Court granted him one hundred and fifty pounds "to enable him to enter upon and manage the great affair of that presidency;" and a committee of the House of Representatives was appointed to inquire into the revenues, appropriations, and expenditures of the College, with powers "to look

CHAPTER XVI.

out a suitable house for the reception of the President," and make report at the next session, "that so an honorable settlement and support may be allowed to the Rev. President of Harvard College, which is the full intention of this Court."

Although Mr. Wadsworth belonged to the liberal class of the clergy, he was less obnoxious than Colman to the predominating religious sect in the Province. He was of a temperament less bold, ardent, and active, than Colman, and his church had been formed on the early synodical Platform, and not, like that of which Mr. Colman was pastor, in opposition to some of the cherished principles of the adherents to that instrument. Even Cotton Mather derived a qualified consolation for his own disappointment, from the fact, that Mr. Colman had not succeeded. In a letter to Mr. Hollis, he expressed a favorable opinion of Mr. Wadsworth. But he could not omit the opportunity to display his malevolence towards President Leverett, although he had now passed that "bourn," at which envy withdraws from its victim, and hatred usually listens to the suggestions of humanity.

Although Cotton Mather pretended "to keep at the greatest distance from all the affairs of Harvard,"* yet he eagerly seized every occasion to excite suspicions concerning both its literary and religious character. When, in August, 1723, the Overseers instituted a committee of inquiry into the state of the College, under circumstances indicating doubts upon that subject,† his never-sleeping animosity was roused into immediate action. Among his papers

* See above, p. 226.

† See above, p. 317.

there is yet preserved a document in his own handwriting, purporting to be "points needful to be inquired into relating to the education at Harvard College." It is without date, but by its referring to "*some newly passed through the College*," and to "*the performances of a deceased person of distinguished industry and fidelity to the churches*," the period at which it must have been written is sufficiently indicated, as Cotton Mather undoubtedly referred to his own son, who was graduated in July, 1723, and to Increase Mather, who died in August of the same year. In this month the labors of the investigating committee of the Overseers commenced, and they reported in October. It hardly admits of a doubt, therefore, that this writing was prepared with reference to that committee, and was intended to excite and direct their inquiries. It carefully enumerates "the points needful to be investigated," and breathes a spirit of settled animosity to the government of the College, and discontent with its state; intimates that "learning is there notoriously on its decay," that the speaking of Latin is neglected; the authors allowed to be read are "unprofitable and of little regard"; the students are compelled "to get by heart a deal of insipid stuff, of which the tutors teach them to believe nothing;" the scholars' studies are filled with books, "which may truly be called Satan's library"; books having "the spirit of the Gospel" are not recommended, but those "erroneous and dangerous"; the tutors, having no regard "to the doctrines of grace," set themselves to instil contrary principles, and grievously neglect the souls of their pupils; children, who left home "with some gospel symptoms of piety, quickly lose all;" and "young ministers, who are the gifts of Christ in the

CHAPTER XVI.

service of our churches, declare, that, before they came to be what they are, they found it necessary to lay aside the sentiments which they brought from the College with them."*

The ill impression concerning the seminary this paper was calculated to excite, is the more worthy of notice because it stands in singular contrast with the impression conveyed in letters written to President Leverett but a few years before by this same Cotton Mather, in which he expresses his satisfaction at the number of the sons of the church who were educating at the College, and of its "flourishing state under Leverett's sway."

During the last years of Leverett's life and presidency, a son of Cotton Mather was a member of the College, and had received from him a letter of introduction to Leverett, in which he expresses "a full persuasion that the President would be a father to him." This confidence was not misplaced; for, in a subsequent letter to Leverett, Mather expresses his obligations to him, and the Corporation "under your influence, for the generous allowance to assist the education of my son," declaring that it ought to be most gratefully acknowledged, and shall be so. He adds, "Your own more particular kind aspect upon the child obliges me to be very thankful for the kindness of God therein shown unto him; and I am so. His delight in the College, which, indeed, is in a singular manner owing to your smiles upon him, and the acceptance he finds with his superiors there, is to me no little consolation. *And it is no less a satisfaction that I can reckon sixteen or seventeen sons*

* See Appendix, No. LX.

of the church whereof I am the servant, who belong at this time unto the College. Your paternal wisdom and goodness is what I much rely upon." He concludes with "hearty prayers, that the Lord would prosper you, and grant his blessing on your *whole society flourishing under your sway*, and make you a rich blessing to them and all of us."

Mather's son was graduated at the College but a few months before Leverett died. Notwithstanding the obligations these expressions imply, a year probably did not elapse, before he made the following unwarrantable attack on the memory of President Leverett, as stated in a letter preserved in the archives of the College, from Thomas Hollis to Mr. Colman, dated on the 10th of February, 1726. "I have received a letter from Dr. Cotton Mather, which gives me a good account of Mr. President Wadsworth, with hopes of his being very useful to the College, preferring him much to the *infamous drone, his predecessor.*"

Cotton Mather's attack on the character of Leverett.

The kind-hearted Hollis was struck with astonishment at this wanton calumny sent across the Atlantic with intent to depreciate a distinguished head of the College in the opinion of its most eminent friend and benefactor.

"I have written," continues Hollis, "to Cotton Mather, desiring an answer by the first opportunity, why he brands the memory of that man, now dead, with such a character. You have, in years past, represented him to me, as a gentleman deserving a much better character, and I am surprised at it."

A mind like Cotton Mather's could neither thoroughly understand, nor justly appreciate, the character of Leverett. His election in 1707, as President of the College, had interfered with Mather's long-cherished hope of succeeding his father in that office. And it was Mather's custom to speak and to write, in moments of passion, with great license, concerning any one, whom it was his interest or will to disparage.

Injustice of this attack.

Judging by all that is known of the life, actions, and thoughts of Leverett, the epithet "infamous" was never applied with less color of truth or show of reason. That of "drone" was equally gratuitous and unjustifiable. The history of Leverett's presidency is one continuous testimony to his active and laborious fulfilment of every official duty.

Leverett's life was now ended, and that of Mather drawing swiftly to a close. He survived the writing of this letter only two years, and it appears to have been the last of his acts affecting the character of the College or its officers. Mather and Leverett both held a high place among their contemporaries. They were within two years of the same College standing. Their lives were passed in the same vicinity, and their talents and qualities excited and put to trial by the same influences and events. Both were learned men, and sufficiently, though differently, qualified for the office of President of the College, which the one eagerly sought but failed to attain, and which the other reluctantly accepted. The conduct and events of their lives exhibit their characters in remarkable contrast. The spirit of Leverett was calm, chastened, disinterested, not indifferent to fame, but seeking it solely by the path of well-discharged duty. That of Mather was restless, violent, selfish, and passionate, craving distinction, and claiming it by every form of self-illustration and display. The former, in the unwavering confidence and honor of his fellow-citizens, received through life the reward due to his fidelity, judgment, and integrity. The latter, possessed of a mind wayward and ill-regulated, disgusted his contemporaries by the unrestrained license of his tongue and his pen, and became the frequent subject of ridicule and derision.* The clergy of the period, admiring the variety of Cotton Mather's attainments, the extent of his learning, his ready invention, ceaseless activity, and invincible industry, and, above all, honoring his professional zeal, threw the broad shield of their authority, or the more becoming mantle of their charity, over his frailties.

"Could I imagine," exclaims the Rev. Joshua Gee, in a funeral sermon preached on the occasion of his death, "that any in this assembly belong to that herd of abandoned mortals, whose sport it has been to wreak their venom upon a faithful servant of God, in profane and ungodly scorn and derision, I would, in compassion to their poor souls, turn my discourse to them, and say, 'Mourn, O forsaken wretches, mourn at length the death of that saint, who endeavoured, by his holy exhortations and fervent prayers, to keep you from the damnation of hell fire, and turn you to the wisdom of the just, while he lived above the reach of your envy and malice, and, in imitation of his great Master, Jesus Christ, was grieved for the hardness of your hearts. If you will not mourn his death, God only knows how soon, if he have mercy on you, you will be constrained to it at your own; like some others, already, who have found it impossible to take comfort in the hopes of the mercy of God till they had repented and bewailed their abuse of his servant.'"†

* See Sparks's Amer. Biog., Vol. VI. p. 334.

† See "A Sermon preached on the Lord's Day after the Death of the very reverend and learned Cotton Mather, D. D., F. R. S., Pastor

CHAPTER XVI.

The Rev. Mr. Colman, on the other hand, who had more than any other clergyman been the object of Cotton Mather's attacks, after repeating, in a funeral sermon, the usual topics of eulogy on his character, declares his wish "to draw a veil over every failure," and intimates to "his brethren, the prophets, that they have the mantle of Elijah wherewith to cover his defects and infirmities." * Time, however, has unavoidably lifted that "veil," and thrust aside that "mantle," which the tenderness of his friends and professional interest desired to spread. Letters and diaries of his contemporaries, as well as his own, have cast a light upon his character, of which it is impossible for History, with any regard to truth, not to avail herself.

Through her faithful medium Cotton Mather must be transmitted as an individual of ungovernable passions and of questionable principles; credulous, intriguing, and vindictive; often selfish as to his ends, at times little scrupulous in the use of means; wayward, aspiring, and vain; rendering his piety dubious by display, and the motives of his public services suspected by the obtrusiveness of his claims to honor and place; whose fanaticism, if not ambition, gave such a public encouragement to the belief in the agencies of the invisible world, as to have been one of the chief causes of the widest spread misery and disgrace, to which his age and country were ever subjected.

of the North Church in Boston. By Joshua Gee, M. A., Pastor of the same Church." p. 20.

* See "A Sermon preached at the Lecture in Boston, two Days after the Death of the very reverend and learned Cotton Mather, D. D., F. R. S., by Benjamin Colman." p. 24.

In the character of Leverett, there was no obtrusive display, and no subsequent disgrace and disappointment. He studied not to gratify vanity, but to enable himself better to perform his duty. His labors were practical, and in the shades of the Academy he prepared himself for the various and important stations, to which he was called by the voice of the community. A perfect fulfilment of whatever he undertook was the object to which he limited his endeavours. At this he aimed; in this he succeeded. His administration of the affairs of the College, in circumstances of great delicacy and difficulty, reflected an honor on his name and character, which his contemporaries almost unanimously acknowledged, and which has been confirmed by the judgment of posterity.

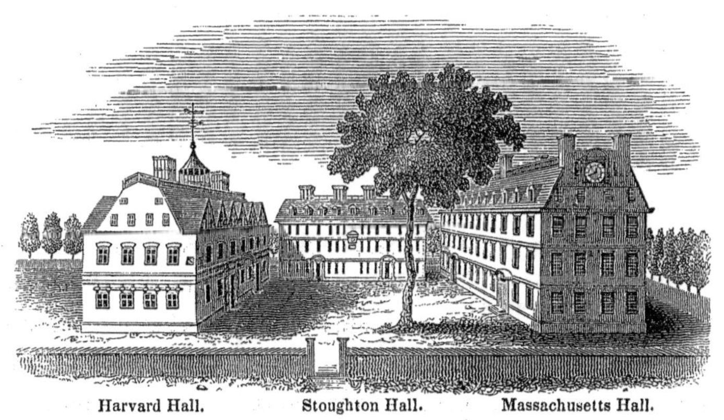

Harvard Hall. Stoughton Hall. Massachusetts Hall.

MASSACHUSETTS HALL; BUILT IN 1720.

CHAPTER XVII.

Change in the political Relations of Massachusetts. — Its Effects on the College. — Nicholas Sever elected Fellow of the Corporation. — English Crown and Hierarchy patronize the Episcopal Church. — Its Clergy claim Seats at the Board of Overseers. — Alarm of the Congregational Church at the Progress of Episcopacy. — Origin of the Puritans. — Spirit and Policy of the first Emigrants to New England. — Edmund Randolph founds the first Episcopal Society in New England. — Arrival of Edmund Andros. — His violent Seizure of the South Church for Episcopal Worship. — Progress of the Episcopal Church after the Revolution of 1688. — "Society for propagating the Gospel in Foreign Parts" established in its Aid. — Mr. Colman's Correspondence with the Bishop of Peterborough on the Proceedings of that Society. — Timothy Cutler, Rector of Yale College, and Six other Clergymen of Connecticut, converted to Episcopalianism. — Honors and Rewards bestowed on Cutler in England. — He is chosen Rector of King's Chapel in Boston. — Claims a Seat at the Board of Overseers. — Grounds of his Claim. — Rejected by the Overseers. — He appeals to the General Court. — Overseers reply to his Appeal, which is rejected by the General Court. — He renews his Claim before the Overseers. — Final Rejection of it by that Board.

CHAPTER XVII.

About this period many circumstances indicate the advance of a new era in Massachusetts. More than thirty years had elapsed since the Charter of William and Mary had changed the political relations of the Province. All those individuals, whose characters and opinions had been formed under the "Old Charter," had passed, or were rapidly passing, away. The concerns of the Province were now governed by the general rules of political wisdom. The Clergy began to perceive, that their influence on public affairs, although yet great, was diminishing. By the events of the last thirty years they had become convinced, that neither the power of the Gospel nor their own was advanced by those violent doctrinal dissensions, which had been excited and perpetuated chiefly by the Mathers. The several divisions of the Congregational church began to evince towards each other a more catholic spirit, and the character and prospects of Harvard College were favorably affected by the gradual cessation of their controversies. By silent though apparently common consent, its theological character was by degrees modified, and it was encouraged to assume more decidedly the aspect of a literary institution.

Nicholas Sever chosen into the Corporation, 1725. Sept. 13.

The acceptance of the President's chair by Mr. Wadsworth occasioned a vacancy in the Corporation, which was immediately filled by the election of Nicholas Sever, a tutor, and one of the individuals, whose claim to a seat that board had resisted with firmness and success. A seat, which the Corporation would not concede to a claim of right, they now voluntarily gave by election. The pretensions of Sever had been supported in their full extent by the House of Representatives. His election, having the appearance of submission to their authority, was very acceptable to that body, as also to the high Calvinistic clergy, who had uniformly and zealously advocated his claims to a place in the Corporation. By the election of Sever, and that of Mr. Sewall as President, the Corporation were regarded as giving evidence of a disposition to coalesce with the predominating religious influences of the Province. The increasing favor with which the College was viewed by the General Court was evinced the succeeding year by an extraordinary dis-

1726. Jan. 1

play of liberality in their provision for the support of President Wadsworth, and for the erection of a President's house.

Alarm of the clergy at the progress of Episcopacy.

The wisdom of terminating their disputes, and of softening asperities, began about this time to be impressed on both divisions of the Congregational clergy by very ominous events. Since the commencement of the eighteenth century they had seen the Episcopal church establishing itself in almost every important settlement of New England, aided by the bounty and upheld by the authority of the English crown and hierarchy. The fears and antipathies of the politicians harmonized with those of the divines. Both viewed with equal jealousy these encroachments of transatlantic power. The ecclesiastical and monarchical influences of the parent state were, in their apprehension, identical in interest and policy, and alike opposed to the civil and religious establishments of New England.

Early in the presidency of Wadsworth the Episcopal clergy of Boston claimed seats in the board of Overseers as "teaching elders" of one of the six towns enumerated in the College charter. Their attempt thus to obtain an introduction into the government of the College occasioned one of the most agitating controversies of that period. To form a correct estimate of the motives and passions it involved, a brief statement will be given of the causes and events, which had excited throughout New England a determined opposition to every form of Episcopal influence.

Origin of the Puritans.

The sect of the Puritans originated in Germany about the year 1556, among the English reformers, who fled from the persecutions of Queen Mary. One congregation, which had taken refuge at Strasburgh, determined on the use of the service-book of King Edward, while another, established at Frankfort, rejected not only the English Litany, Liturgy, and surplice, but also the practice of answering aloud after the minister, and that of reading portions of Scripture in the public worship of the Sabbath. The disputes on this subject between these societies becoming serious, they applied for advice to John Calvin, who was esteemed an oracle on such occasions. In reply, Calvin characterized the English liturgy as "the leavings of Popish dregs," and recommended to them "to enterprise a farther reformation, and to set up something more filed from rust, and *purer*." *

From this language of Calvin, and from the object at which their reformation aimed, the Puritans derived their name and characteristics.

When life was restored to the Reformation by the accession of Queen Elizabeth, those exiles returned to England, and brought with them a rooted animosity to the English hierarchy, and a settled determination not to conform to the service, customs, and discipline of the English Church. The persecutions they and their proselytes subsequently suffered, during the reigns of Elizabeth and James the First, fixed in the minds of their descendants an utter detestation of the English hierarchy, Church service and discipline, and occasioned the emigration to New England. Though compelled by circumstances sometimes to conceal, and sometimes to deny, this antipathy, it was, in truth, one of the master passions in the breasts of those early emigrants, and constitutes a principal clue to their language, conduct, policy, and laws.

* Neal's History of the Puritans, Vol. I. chap. iii. p. 72.

CHAPTER XVII.

Antipathy to Episcopacy in New England.

The form of government they adopted in Massachusetts had for its object the supremacy of the Congregational church, and the exclusion of the Episcopal and all other sects from political power and influence. During the thirty years in which the first emigrants conducted the affairs of Massachusetts, the civil wars which harassed the parent state, and the coincidence in religious and political views of the chiefs of the English Commonwealth and the leaders of the New England colony, gave this antipathy to Episcopacy a fixed root among the people of New England; the fibres of which were spread throughout the whole settlement. The language and writings of the early divines were carefully calculated to keep alive these passions, and to inspire a universal dread of the English church and hierarchy.

A generation of men, for the most part born on the soil of New England, and educated under the prejudices and antipathies of the first emigrants, began to take a lead in the concerns of the colony, about the time of the restoration of the English monarchy under Charles the Second. At this period the English malecontents studiously endeavoured to establish at home, and to propagate through the English colonies, an opinion that the English monarch was a Papist at heart, and that his policy had for its object the reconcilement of England to the See of Rome. The apprehensions thus excited were strengthened by the avowed determination of the government of the parent state to change the principles of their charter, and with it the foundation of their civil and ecclesiastical rights and privileges.

The disadvantageous light in which professed Episcopalians were thus viewed, and the real inconveniences they suffered, prevented their erection of a church, or any public observance of their forms of worship, for the first fifty years after the settlement of Massachusetts; so that in 1686 a majority of its inhabitants had never seen an assembly in which religious service was performed according to the rites and ceremonies of the Church of England.*

Edward Randolph, who, during the reign of Charles the Second, was the most active emissary of the crown, suggested, as early as 1682, the plan of propagating Episcopacy in New England, by means of funds derived from the parent state. In letters to Sancroft, Archbishop of Canterbury, after stating that the Episcopalians in Massachusetts were compelled to pay rates for the support of the Congregational clergy, and also to maintain their own ministers by contribution, Randolph proposed, "that able ministers might be appointed to perform the offices of the Church with us, and that for their maintenance *a part of the money sent over hither and pretended to be expended amongst the Indians should be ordered to go towards that charge.*"†

A more gross perversion of funds can scarcely be imagined, than that included in the proposition of Randolph. It was, however, in unison with the violence of his character, and the utter disregard of private rights and public morals, which characterized the reigns of Charles the Second and his successor, James.

The funds which Randolph thus proposed to seize and devote to the establishment of the Episcopal

* See Hutch. Hist. Mass., Vol. I. chap. iii. p. 318. Edit. 1785.

† See Hutch. State Papers, p. 531.

CHAPTER XVII.

Church in New England were the product of subscriptions collected among private individuals for the purpose of instructing the heathen natives, and were limited to that object by the constitution of the Society intrusted with their management and distribution.

First Society for propagating the Gospel in New England.

The first of these societies was incorporated in 1649, by the English Parliament, in the time of the Commonwealth. It was denominated "The President and Society for the Propagation of the Gospel in New England." It was authorized to collect moneys and receive donations, and transmit them to the commissioners of the United Colonies, by them to be disposed of so as "shall best and principally conduce to the preaching and propagating of the Gospel among the natives, and for maintenance of schools and nurseries of learning for the education of the children of the natives."*

On the restoration of Charles the Second, in 1660, this Society, having derived its existence from the Commonwealth, was deemed dead in law, and attempts were made to seize upon their funds and convert them to private use.

Second Society for propagating the Gospel in New England.

Through the agency of Robert Boyle, Sir Henry Ashurst, and other friends of the settlement, a new Company was formed, denominated "The Company for the Propagation of the Gospel in New England, and Parts adjacent, in America." By this charter the objects of this Society and the application of its funds were as strictly limited, as those of the former, "to the civilizing, teaching, and instructing the heathen natives and their children, in religion, morality, and

* Hazard's State Papers, Vol. I. p. 635, where this charter is given at large.

the English tongue, and in other liberal arts and sciences." *

There is no evidence, that the proposal of Randolph to pervert these funds received at the time any encouragement; but it appears from one of his letters to the Archbishop of Canterbury, that he renewed those suggestions in 1686, and that Sancroft had been so far influenced by them, as to express his desire, that "the moneys in the hands of the Corporation for evangelizing the Indians should be inquired after, and applied to build a church for Episcopal worship, and a free school, that our youth may be no longer poisoned by the seditious principles of New England." †

First Episcopal society in Boston.

Either this Corporation was found to be unmanageable, or the scheme itself was deemed too great an outrage upon the rights of corporate property; since it does not appear, that the proposed perversion of the funds was ever effected. Randolph saw plainly, that the influence of the English crown could never become predominant in the colony unless in connexion with the English hierarchy. Bold, active, and intelligent, he directed all his efforts to this object, and incessantly urged its importance upon the Lords of the Council and the dignitaries of the Church. ‡ He was the chief founder of the first Episcopal society in New England; and in June, 1686, he associated himself with Ratcliffe, and nine other individuals, for that purpose. Although they were few in number, poor

* Life of Robert Boyle, fol. edit. London, 1744, p. 98, where this charter is given at large. — Neal's Hist. of New England, Vol. I. p. 260.

† Hutch. State Papers, p. 551.

‡ Greenwood's History of King's Chapel, p. 16.

CHAPTER XVII. in revenue and resources, and discountenanced by all the predominating colonial powers, yet their proceedings indicate a spirit sufficiently lofty and determined. Excluding from their records all recognition of the authorities of Massachusetts, not even referring to the colony by name, they laid hold of the horns of the transatlantic altar, placed their society under the shadow of the sceptre of the monarch, and denominated themselves "the members of the Church of England by law established, under the gracious influences of the most illustrious Prince, our sovereign Lord, James the Second, by the grace of God, of England, Scotland, and Ireland, King, Defender of the Faith, &c., Anno Domini, 1686, and in the second year of his said Majesty's reign, at Boston, within his said Majesty's territory and dominion of New England, in America."*

Among their acts at this first meeting were an humble address to his Majesty, and letters to the Archbishop of Canterbury and the Bishop of London, imploring their favor. Edward Randolph was also appointed chairman of a committee "to wait on the President and Council about our Church affairs." In the July ensuing they made application to the chief authorities of Massachusetts, for a brief to pass through the whole of New England, to collect and receive "voluntary donations towards the building of an Episcopal church in Boston, to be erected for the service of God, and for the use of the Church of England by law established."

The administration of the colony was, at that time, in the hands of Dudley as President, and the Council,

* Greenwood's History of King's Chapel, p. 22.

temporarily established by a commission from King James. The application, however repugnant to their prejudices, was too reasonable to be denied. The "brief" was granted, and also a room in the Town House, where public worship was first commenced in the capital of New England, under a license from the colonial authority, according to Episcopalian forms.

Violent proceedings of Andros.

Andros, the royal Governor, on his arrival in 1686,* determined to obtain, by favor or force, a more suitable and commodious place for the Episcopal service. Sancroft, Archbishop of Canterbury, had suggested, that one of the Congregational meetinghouses might be obtained for Episcopalian worship by way of compromise with the clergy of that sect, in exchange for liberty of conscience. In accordance with this suggestion, Andros, on the day of his arrival, in a conference with three Congregational clergymen of the place, intimated, that one church might admit two assemblies, and thus the Episcopal service be accommodated without interfering with the Congregational. This proposition was, in the opinion of these divines, equivalent to an assent to the desecration of the church which should accede to it; and they answered with one voice, that they "could not consent, that any of their meetinghouses should be used for Common Prayer worship." Being desired to permit their bell to be tolled at nine o'clock on Wednesdays and Fridays for the Episcopal meeting for prayers, they replied, that "they could in no wise assent, it intrenching on their liberty of conscience."†

Andros waited until the March following, in the

* Hutch. State Papers, p. 550. — Greenwood's History of King's Chapel, p. 37. — Sewall's Diary.

† Hutch. State Papers, p. 553.

CHAPTER XVII.

Violent seizure of the South Church for Episcopal worship.

hope of effecting his object by negotiation. Being disappointed in this expectation, he commanded on Good Friday the doors of the South Church to be opened, and the bell to be rung for the Church of England service; which continued to be performed there during the whole period of his administration. This violent invasion of the rights of private property, and open defiance of the religious prejudices of the colony, deepened the hereditary fear of the Episcopal church. The alarm was strengthened by the well-founded apprehension, that the English monarch designed to seize on the seminaries of education.* These were probably among the causes of the little civility paid to Ratcliffe, the Episcopalian clergyman, when, by the authority of Andros, he took his seat in the pulpit, and attended the services on Commencement day.†

The antipathy of the clergy to the Episcopal church was shared by the laymen of the Congregational persuasion. When, in 1688, the same Ratcliffe, for the purpose of building an Episcopal church, applied to Judge Sewall for the purchase of an estate on "Cotton Hill" in Boston, formerly belonging to the Rev John Cotton, Sewall replied, that "he would not put Mr. Cotton's land to such a use, nor be concerned in setting up that, which the people of New England came over to avoid." In the same spirit, more than thirty years afterwards, when Governor Shute proposed to adjourn the Court on account of Christmas, Judge Sewall, being one of the Council, told the Governor, that "the Dissenters had come a great way for their liberties, and now the Church had theirs, yet

* See above, p. 29. † See above, p. 58.

they would not be contented except they might tread all others down." *

After the deposition of Andros by a popular insurrection, in 1688, a small wooden building was erected on the site of the present King's Chapel, in Boston, with funds gradually collected from voluntary donations, and the service of the Episcopal church was henceforth tolerated but not encouraged. When the arbitrary rule of the Stuarts terminated, by the accession of William and Mary, Episcopacy was viewed with a subdued animosity, but it never obtained either the confidence or favor of the Congregational church.

From this time the patronage of the crown and hierarchy was extended to the infant Episcopal church in New England. Aware that it was a ready path to royal favor, Joseph Dudley, when he came as Governor of the Province, in 1702, joined himself to that Society, and with Lieutenant-Governor Tailer became one of its active vestrymen.

Episcopacy, having taken such strong hold of the soil of New England, wanted nothing to secure its permanency and expansion, except pecuniary funds for its support and encouragement. These were soon supplied by an association, denominated the "Society for propagating the Gospel in Foreign Parts." The incorporation of this Society constitutes an era in the progress of Episcopacy in New England, and was the precursor and cause of that controversy, which connects the history of the Episcopal church with that of Harvard University.

The funds of the "Company for the Propagation of the Gospel in New England and Parts adjacent

* Sewall's Diary.

CHAPTER XVII.

in America," incorporated in 1660, had fallen under the agency of Presbyterians or Congregationalists, and of men attached to the dissenting interests.*

It became, therefore, apparent to Tillotson, who succeeded Sancroft in the See of Canterbury, that the attempt to divert the funds of that Society to the establishing Episcopacy in the settled parts of North America, and especially in New England, could not be carried into effect. The plan recommended by Randolph, and acceded to by Sancroft, was accordingly abandoned as impracticable.

Episcopal Society for propagating the Gospel in Foreign Parts.

These circumstances led to the formation of a Society under Episcopal influences, which was ultimately incorporated by William the Third, in 1701, and denominated "the Society for the Propagation of the Gospel in Foreign Parts." The chief dignitaries of the English hierarchy were constituted members, and all the individuals named in the act were of the Episcopal persuasion. In the enumeration of the objects of that Society all reference to the instruction of the heathen or of the Indian nations was carefully avoided. And to the end that there might arise no embarrassment in the application of its funds, those objects were declared to be "to instruct our loving subjects in our plantations, in the principles of true religion," "to supply them with the administration of God's word and sacraments," and "to provide a sufficient maintenance for an orthodox clergy, the provision for ministers being in some of those plantations very mean, and in others wholly wanting."†

* Hutch. State Papers, pp. 552.

† See the act given at large in Dr. Humphrey's "Historical Account of the incorporated Society for the Propagation of the Gospel in Foreign Parts," p. xv.

Considering the phraseology of this act and the tendency of all religious sects to restrict the term "true religion" to their own forms of worship, doctrines, and observances, the New England clergy had no doubt that the real purpose of this Society was the establishment and extension of Episcopacy in the colonies. It became, therefore, an object of their extreme jealousy and animosity.

Proceedings of the Society for the Propagation of the Gospel in Foreign Parts.

The proceedings of this Society did not tend to calm these apprehensions. Instead of applying their funds to those colonial districts where there was no religious instruction, their efforts were chiefly directed to the ancient towns of New England, where only a few Episcopalians existed. Here they established Episcopal ministers, with salaries greater and better paid than those of a majority of the Congregational clergy.* At Stratford in Connecticut, at Braintree and Marblehead in Massachusetts, and in other principal towns, their missionaries were stationed, and their labors and resources apparently applied, not to furnish destitute places with Christian ministers, but to make converts from Congregationalism to Episcopacy; so that at the end of fifty years from the incorporation of this Society it was estimated, that the Society had "laid out one hundred thousand pounds sterling under the notion of propagating the Gospel in America," of which "twenty thousand pounds had been expended in supporting Episcopacy in the single town of Stratford in Connecticut.†"

These proceedings early excited animadversion among the sects into which the Congregational church

* Turell's Life of Colman, p. 124.

† Hobart's "Address to the Members of the Episcopalian Persuasion in New England," pp. 53, 129 - 134.

CHAPTER XVII.

began to be divided. The Rev. Mr. Colman, although he was himself obnoxious to the stricter sect of Congregationalists for so far conforming to the practice of the Church of England, as to use the Lord's Prayer and read the Scriptures in public worship, and for enlarging the freedom of coming to the sacrament, was also alarmed and indignant at what he deemed an abuse and manifest perversion of the funds of the Society. In November, 1712, he addressed a letter on the subject to White Kennett, then Dean, afterwards Bishop, of Peterborough. Colman was, at that time, one of the Corporation of Harvard College, and, for the purpose of impressing Dean Kennett with his impartiality and freedom from prejudice, he states, that, while in England, he had been strengthened "in the generous principles of an enlarged catholic spirit, cherished in me by my tutor, Mr. Leverett, now President of Harvard College; and, if I am able to judge," he adds, "no place of education can well boast a more *free air* than our little College may."* After acknowledging the project of sending the Gospel to the heathen, "and settlements void of the form of religion," to be a noble charity, he complained, that its funds had been perverted to encourage discontent, and to create divisions, in towns where the Gospel was already preached and the sacraments administered, and, instead of spreading, had actually obstructed, the success of the Gospel. By the hope of a better salary for the minister, out of the funds of the Society, than the Congregationalists gave, and by the expectation of a lighter church rate for the parishioner, the Church of Eng-

Mr. Colman's letter to Dean Kennett.

* Turell's Life of Colman, pp. 123, 125.

land had been planted under the auspices of that Society, and the Congregational churches had been either divided or embarrassed.

Dean Kennett's reply. Sept. 15, 1713.

In reply, Dean Kennett states, that, if abuses had occurred, the Society had been imposed upon, and their proceedings in such cases had been the result of mistake. To obviate the effects of future misinformation, he intimates the design of some members of the hierarchy to settle bishops in the Province; a remedy, in the opinion of the Congregational clergy, somewhat worse than the disease. In this letter, however, Kennett unequivocally acknowledges, that the general aim of the Society was, "to plant Christianity according to the Church of England," and that, not only in places where there was no settled ministry, but also in those where there was a settled ministry,* "if numbers were there, who could not in conscience conform to the ways of worship different from the English established Church." To establish schools and universities, under the influence of bishops appointed by the English hierarchy, was avowed to be a project connected with the general plan of appointing bishops in New England. The design relative to the seminaries of education excited peculiar alarm in the Congregational church, as it was obviously directed to enlarge the boundaries of the Episcopal church by influencing the rising generation to quit the faith of their fathers.

Dean Kennett, in another letter to Mr. Colman, dated on the 28th of July, 1716,† admits that these designs were among the known and unquestionable objects of the Society for propagating the Gospel in Foreign Parts.

* Turell's Life of Colman, p. 127.

† Ibid., 130.

CHAPTER XVII.

During the first twenty years of the operations of this Society the gradual increase of Episcopacy was perceptible, but no very distinguished convert had as yet been made from the ranks of the Congregational clergy. In September, 1722, an event occurred in Connecticut, equally unexpected and alarming. Seven clergymen of the Congregational order, at the head of whom was Timothy Cutler, Rector of Yale College, openly avowed, before the trustees of that seminary, their doubts concerning the validity of Presbyterian, and their belief in the validity of Episcopalian ordination.* This event shook Congregationalism throughout New England like an earthquake, and filled all its friends with terror and apprehension. The effect of the direct operations of the "Society for the Propagation of the Gospel in Foreign Parts" was seen and recognised in these conversions. They had occurred in Stratford, or its vicinity; a place in which the funds of the Society had been most lavishly expended; and the fact, that the head of one of the most cherished seminaries of learning in New England had yielded to its influence, was indicative of its power and ominous of Episcopal success.

Mr. Cutler's conversion to Episcopacy.

Cutler had been graduated at Harvard College in 1701, been settled over the Congregational society in Stratford,† Connecticut, in 1709, and made Rector of Yale College in 1719. In consequence of his avowed conversion to Episcopacy, he was "excused from all further service" by the trustees of Yale College; and he immediately sailed for England, where honors and

* Eliot's Biog., art. *Cutler, Timothy.* — Dr. Humphreys' "Historical Account of the Society for the Propagation of the Gospel in Foreign Parts," p. 339.

† Allen's American Biography.

reward awaited him. In the following January (1723), being in London, he was invited by the honest and zealous Hollis to a conference, in the hope of converting him from Episcopalianism. To this invitation Cutler acceded. The conference, however, never took place. "I am no doubter," said Cutler to Hollis, "I am resolved.* I hope to be speedily ordained. I may with as much reason hope to bring you over to me, as you can hope to bring me over to you. I have a wife and seven children, am not yet forty years old. I have lost all my old friends. I am turned out of all. And if I should do any thing now that looked like doubting, it were the way to lose my new friends." "I was never in judgment heartily with the Dissenters, but bore it patiently until a favorable opportunity offered. This has opened at Boston, and I now declare publicly what I before believed privately." "After such positive barring cautions, I thought," says Hollis, "the proposed conference would be of little service."

Mr. Cutler's reception in England.

Cutler was received with great distinction by the dignitaries of the Church, episcopally ordained, and gratified by a degree of Doctor in Divinity both at Oxford and Cambridge. In the mean time a society was formed for him in Boston, and he returned to America under an allowance, as missionary, of sixty pounds sterling per annum.

Such was the general state of feeling in New England relative to the Episcopalian power and policy when Dr. Cutler arrived in Massachusetts, in 1724. In concurrence with Mr. Myles, the Rector of King's Chapel, he soon commenced prosecuting a claim on

* Hollis's letter to Colman, January 14th, 1723.

CHAPTER XVII.

Mr. Cutler claims a seat at the board of Overseers.

their part to be admitted of right, as ministers of the Episcopal Church in Boston, to the board of Overseers of the College. This claim was deemed inseparably connected with the prospects of Episcopacy in New England, and as such received the support of all its powers. As early as August, 1725, the vestry of King's Chapel authorized the churchwardens of that society "to sign a memorial to the General Court, in relation to the ministers of the Church of England, in Boston, being Overseers of the College in Cambridge." And at a subsequent meeting these officers were authorized to expend "out of the contingent charges of the church, for the purpose of prosecuting to effect the memorial of the Rev. Dr. Cutler and Mr. Myles, and of maintaining their right to a seat at the Overseers' board."* The attempt was sufficiently bold, considering that the right to such seat was restricted by the charter of the College to "teaching elders," and that this term was exclusively of Dissenting, if not Congregational, origin and use, and neither authorized nor acknowledged by the Church of England. The auspices under which the College had been established and hitherto conducted, and the opinions and influences predominating among the Overseers and in the General Court, rendered success in this claim improbable, if not hopeless. After Dr. Cutler's return from England, he was regarded in Massachusetts in the light of a pensioner on the English hierarchy; and this attempt was naturally deemed to be made in coincidence with their views, and to be an evidence of a design to introduce Episcopalian influences on an equality with Congregational, into the great seminary of learning in the Province.

* See Records of King's Chapel, of this date.

A color for this claim.

This claim derived some color from the fact, that Mr. Harris, who had been sent out in 1709, by the Bishop of London, as Assistant to Mr. Myles, the Rector of King's Chapel, had been summoned about the year 1720, and permitted to take his seat at the board of Overseers, as appears by their records, several times during the years 1720, 1721, and 1722. It does not appear, that either Cutler or Myles ever took a seat at that board, or attempted to do it, although in their memorial it is asserted that they had been summoned to attend. The two facts, that Harris had been permitted to take a seat, and that Cutler and Myles had been summoned to attend, are not accounted for by the records of the College, or the history of that period. It is probable, that under the influence of the Governor and Lieutenant-Governor of the Province, who worshipped with Episcopalians, and were, *ex officio*, at the head of the Overseers, Harris had been summoned and admitted without question to take a seat at the board. But, with the apprehensions consequent upon the "apostasy" of Cutler from Congregationalism, a rigid inquiry into this right was determined upon, for the purpose of preserving the College from Episcopalian influences. The attempt of Cutler and Myles thus to introduce themselves into the board excited a sensation throughout the Province somewhat proportionate to the greatness of the anticipated consequences. The defection of Cutler from Congregationalism was openly avowed by him at New Haven, in September, 1722, and in December of that year is the last record of the presence of Harris at the board of Overseers. He was, probably, from that time omitted to be summoned, in conformity with the policy

CHAPTER XVII.

of excluding Episcopalians, then resolved upon. Although it appears by the records of King's Chapel, that, as early as August, 1725, a memorial had been presented either to the General Court or to the board of Overseers, yet the records of neither take any notice of the presentation of any such memorial antecedent to the 18th of May, 1727. On that day the records of the Overseers state, that "His Honor, the Lieutenant-Governor, informing the board, that application had been made to him by the Rev. Dr. Cutler, that he might be notified to be present at the meetings of the Overseers, after a debate had thereon, the question was put, whether he, the said Dr. Cutler, be notified accordingly, and it passed in the negative; the board apprehending that he is not entitled thereunto." On the 25th of May following, a copy of the above vote was ordered to be delivered to Dr. Cutler, and at a meeting on the ensuing 8th of June, an adjournment took place to that day sevennight; and the clerk was ordered "to make Dr. Cutler acquainted with the time and place of this adjournment." Accordingly, on that day, the records of the Overseers state, that, "a motion being made to this board by the Rev. Dr. Timothy Cutler, in writing as follows, viz. Whether he was not entitled to be present at the meetings of the Overseers of Harvard College, when he was notified by their clerk to be present at one of said meetings, nor at any time since he has been an Episcopal minister of the town of Boston, or whether he has forfeited that title since, and by what means? — the Overseers having taken said motion into their consideration, and maturely considered their constitution, are of opinion, that the Rev. Dr. Timothy Cutler has not, nor ever had, by the said

His claim rejected by the Overseers.

constitution, a right to sit as Overseer of Harvard College.

"To which vote the Honorable William Tailer, Esquire, entered his dissent."

A copy of the above vote was ordered to be delivered to Mr. Cutler.

On the same day "the Rev. Mr. Samuel Myles presented his desire in writing to the Overseers, that he might be notified as formerly to sit at the meetings of the Overseers of Harvard College, and, if that be denied, he humbly craved of the honorable board that he might be favored with the reasons of it." Upon which a vote was passed by the Overseers similar to that passed in the case of Dr. Cutler.

Memorial of Dr. Cutler and Mr. Myles.

Immediately on this rejection of their respective applications by the board of Overseers, Dr. Cutler and Mr. Myles memorialized the General Court, stating the terms of the act of 1642, the general grounds of their application to the Overseers, and the rejection of their petition; and asking redress from the legislature for the wrongs they have sustained, in being "excluded, as ministers of the Church of England, from the inspection and ordering of Harvard College." They aver that "the orthodoxy of that church is questioned by no sound Protestant," that "its members in this government bear an equal proportion in all public charges to the support of said College," that "its ministers are equally with any others qualified and disposed to promote the interests of religion, good literature, and good manners," and that, by their ordination and induction into their respective churches of the town of Boston, they are fairly included within the denomination of "teaching elders," and as such

CHAPTER XVII.

entitled to a seat at the board of Overseers of Harvard College.*

Petition of the members of the Episcopal Churches.

This memorial of Dr. Cutler and Mr. Myles was supported by a contemporaneous petition, signed by about seventy persons, embracing all the principal members of the several Episcopal churches in Boston and the vicinity. These petitioners assert, that "the ministers of the Church of England in Boston have been, by force of the first constitution of Harvard College, deemed and taken to be Overseers of the College, and from time to time ever since have assembled and met together, and ordered and disposed the affairs of said College as the Overseers;" that within the last three years they have been "neglected and not called to their meetings"; and that, on application made by Dr. Cutler and Mr. Myles, two of the ministers of the Church of England, to the Overseers, they had "voted, declared, and recorded their opinion, that the said Dr. Cutler and Mr. Myles have not, nor ever had, by the constitution of Harvard College, a right to sit as Overseers." The petitioners then proceed to state, that "they consider that College as the common nursery of piety and learning to New England in general, as well to those that are of the order of the Church of England as to them that are of the order of the churches of New England; that it is the common interest of both to support it, and a blessing to both when it flourisheth; and therefore they apprehend it is a pity those different orders should be made different parties, not only in the churches where they are different, but in the College, where they are entirely one; which will tend to discourage those of the order

* See Appendix, No. LXI.

of the Church of England from doing those services to the College, or receiving that benefit from it, as otherwise they might;" that it is impossible to imagine the admission of these two gentlemen can "serve any secret designs or separate interests, and that the petitioners only seek that all especial notes of groundless distinction and disesteem may be abated, and a universal good understanding established." As the rejection of the claim of these ministers seemed to imply that they were not regarded by the Overseers as "teaching elders," the petitioners aver, that both Dr. Cutler and Mr. Myles were "ordained as such by the Bishop of London, and were sent to execute that their function in Boston, and that their being such had never before been questioned by those of the order of the churches of New England, as they have heard of;" and they pray, therefore, the General Court, as their last resort, and as the best expositors of their own acts, would declare these Episcopal clergymen to be, according to the original fundamental constitution of the said College, two of its Overseers.*

Answer of the Overseers.

The General Court, in August, 1727, referred the subject of these memorials to its next autumn session for consideration, and caused the Overseers to be served with copies of them, who, in October, appointed a committee "to draw up an answer," and, in December following, made a formal reply to them, justifying their vote, refusing to summon the memorialists to attend the meetings of the board, and denying utterly their right to a seat by force of the terms "teaching elders," in the first charter of the College. They contended, that, by known rules of

* See Appendix, No. LXII.

construction, the signification of those terms must be decided by the established and general acceptation of them in the places and at the times in which they were used; and that "the known construction of these terms in this country from the very beginning is this, namely, the pastors and teachers of a complete Congregational church, who have the full power both of teaching and administering the sacraments, and of ruling in the said church, being the very same which the Scriptures call bishops." They maintained that this signification had been given in all former times to those terms, in all public and controversial writings, in the judgments of synods, in the General Court, and in the laws of the jurisdiction; that "this is the known use and signification of them at the present day"; and "that for above fifty years after the settlement of the colony there was no minister, magistrate, or representative, in the General Court, professedly of the Church of England, and, for above forty years after the act constituting the College, there were no other teaching elders, except those of Congregational churches, then in being in this country." To such teaching elders alone, therefore, they maintained that these terms could be applied; and, from the laws of the jurisdiction, from the declarations of magistrates, ministers, churches, courts, synods, and people, they "draw the undeniable conclusion, that the reverend memorialists neither have, nor ever have had, a right to sit among us as Overseers of Harvard College." By way of corroborating this opinion, they state, that "all the insinuations of the memorialists, about their being teaching elders, are groundless and vain, because no such denomination as 'teaching elder' can ever be found attributed to ministers of the Church of England, either abroad or here, but is only now assumed to serve their present turn, and to break in upon our ancient constitution;" that even the memorialists carefully avoid styling themselves "teaching elders," but call themselves "incumbents" of Christ Church and King's Chapel; and, further, that "they never pretended, nor may they pretend, to assert themselves to be bishops, and to have the full and unsubordinate power to teach, feed, and govern their particular churches." As it respects the fact, that the memorialists had been summoned to attend the meetings of the board, they state, that the occurrence had taken place without the direction of the Overseers, through error, which was corrected as soon as noticed; that the notification had been of recent occurrence, and that ministers of the Episcopal church had for many years existed in Boston, yet had never been summoned to attend those meetings, nor deemed Overseers, nor ever had complained on this account; and that notification through error could give no right, where no right previously existed; that neither of the memorialists, if they had been summoned, had ever personally attended, or on any occasion had acted as Overseers. As to the "argument from the College being a nursery of piety and learning" as well to those of the Church of England as to others, they answer; "We account it the distinguishing honor of our College, that education there is free, without oaths or subscriptions to any particular sort of church order or discipline; and that, though the government of the College be of the Congregational order, yet, agreeably to their known principles of liberty, the sons of the Church of England are as welcome to the learning and academical honors there as any of our own children; and this is as much as the memorialists can in

CHAPTER XVII.

honor or justice desire, of those who are intrusted with a constitution settled for above fourscore years, before any of their order pretended to a right to come among us, and even above forty years before any of the said reverend order was settled in this country." Considering "the said act and constitution a sacred deposit, put into their hands to keep inviolate by the excellent and ancient fathers of the country," they pray the General Court to adhere to the said ancient constitution, and not adjudge the reverend memorialists to be such "teaching elders" as the act constituting the College intends, nor declare them to be of the number of the Overseers of Harvard College.*

Reply of Dr. Cutler and Mr. Myles.

The reply of Dr. Cutler and Mr. Myles, to this answer of the Overseers, was prepared and signed by their counsel, John Read, one of the most eminent lawyers of that period in New England; and their right to a seat in the board was maintained on the following grounds.

1. That Episcopal ministers, by force of ordination, institution, and induction, are in fact proper teaching elders.

2. That these ministers were meant and intended to be included in that act, by the plain force of its terms.

3. That they have the same right now as they would have had in case they had applied for it forty years before.

4. That the liberty of individuals to form churches, under the New England ecclesiastical law, did not deny to members of the Church of England the right to have their ministers ordained by bishops, nor in-

* See Appendix, No. LXIII.

tended to refuse ministers so ordained the character of teaching elders.

5. That, by the ecclesiastical law of Massachusetts, the whole power of ordaining, expelling, and disposing of the pastors is vested in the fraternity; so that the teaching elder of a Congregational church has no more an unsubordinate, and is no more a ruling, power, than are ministers of the Church of England; and, of consequence, has no more right to regard himself in the light of a bishop than they; both being officers to teach and to feed the flock; and both, having the same office and faculty, were equally entitled to the denomination of "teaching elders"; so that ministers of the Church of England in Boston have as much right to call the College theirs, and the said act their "depositum," as had Congregational ministers; they therefore pray, that their right to a seat at the board of Overseers may be confirmed, whereby the Congregational minister would not have the less benefit of the institution, and the Episcopalian have the more charity, and the better title to confer a blessing on it.*

Result.

The result of these memorials was such as, from the temper of the times and the predominating influences in the legislature, the memorialists probably anticipated. On the 28th of December, 1727, the memorials, with the answer of the Overseers, and the reply of the memorialists, were taken into consideration by the legislature, and largely debated; and upon the question, "whether it is within the intent and meaning of the charter granted to the said College, that the reverend memorialists ought to be deemed members of the Overseers," it passed in the nega-

* See Appendix, No. LXIV.

tive. This vote was concurred in by the Council, and approved by Lieutenant-Governor Dummer.

On the 11th of January, 1728, the House of Representatives revived, and "entered further into consideration of the subject matter of, these petitions, and the following question was thereupon put, viz. Whether it is within the intent and meaning of the act of the General Court, anno 1642, and referred to in said memorial, constituting the board of Overseers, that the reverend memorialists, the said Dr. Timothy Cutler and Mr. Samuel Myles, ought to be deemed members of the board of Overseers? It passed in the negative. In Council read and concurred. Consented to, William Dummer."

Dr. Cutler seems not to have been content with this decision, publicly and deliberately as it had been made. On the 16th of June, 1730, he again memorialized the Overseers upon the subject of his right to a seat at their board, on which they passed a resolution as follows, viz. "A memorial of Dr. Timothy Cutler, bearing date the 11th of June, 1730, was this day read, and, inasmuch as the affair referred to in this memorial has been once and again maturely considered by this board, and afterwards by the General Court, upon his own appeal to them, and at length by them determined, voted, that the said memorial be dismissed." A copy of this vote was ordered to be delivered to Dr. Cutler, which closed for ever his further pursuit of this fruitless and agitating claim.

CHAPTER XVIII.

Wadsworth inaugurated. — General Court establish a Salary, and take Measures towards building a House for the President. — Thanks of the Corporation. — Difficulties of President Wadsworth. — Application of the Corporation to the General Court for Assistance. — Rejected. — Address of the Corporation to George the Second on his Accession. — Disorders at the College. — Commencements made private. — Overseers appoint a Committee to examine into the State of the College. — Their Report. — President and Tutors first form a distinct Board. — First Code of Laws passed according to existing Forms. — Dancing restrained. — Longloissorie prohibited teaching French. — A Tutor refuses to be examined concerning his Religious Opinions. — Proceedings of the Overseers. — Public Commencements renewed. — Hartshorn denied a Degree. — He appeals to the Overseers. — Their Conduct in relation to it. — Thomas Hollis founds a Professorship of Mathematics and Natural Philosophy. — State of the College. — Corporation fail in their Suit for Lands at Merriconeag. — Colman resigns his Seat in the Corporation. — Cotton's Donation, and Colman's Conduct in relation to it. — Death of President Wadsworth. — His Services and Character.

CHAPTER XVIII.

Inauguration of President Wadsworth.

THE inauguration of President Wadsworth took place on Commencement day, the 7th of July, 1725. The records of the Corporation state, that there was a procession, as had been usual on such occasions, from the College to the meetinghouse. "The Bachelors of Art walked first, two in a rank, and then the Masters, all bareheaded; then followed Mr. Wadsworth alone as President; next the Corporation and Tutors, two in a rank; then the Honorable Lieutenant-Governor Dummer and Council, and next to them the rest of the gentlemen." After prayer by the Rev. Mr. Colman, the Governor, on delivering the keys, seal, and records of the College, to the President elect, as badges of authority, addressed him in English, investing him with the government thereof, to which the President made a reply, also in English, after which he went up into the pulpit, and "pronounced *memoriter* a Latin oration"; and afterwards presided during the usual exercises on Commencement day.*

The report of the committee appointed by the General Court on the 18th of June, 1725, was made in the ensuing December; and, after considerable debate and interchange of amendments between the two branches, resulted in a vote establishing the salary of the President at four hundred pounds annually, which the General Court declare to be, "in their opinion, a sufficient and honorable maintenance for him, the President, for one year." To this object they appropriated the future rents and income of Massachusetts Hall, and expressed a "hope, that there will not be like occasion, in future, to make such drafts on the public Treasury, but that the Corporation will be able to support the President, in a great measure, out of their unappropriated rents and incomes." And, "further to encourage Mr. Wadsworth cheerfully to go through the momentous affairs of his office, they resolved, that one thousand pounds should be paid to the Corporation by them, to be used for the building a handsome wooden dwellinghouse, barn, and outhouses, on some part of the College land, for the reception and accommodation of the President of Harvard College for the time being."

Liberality of the General Court.

* See Records of the Corporation. — Peirce's Hist. Harv. Univ., p. 146.

CHAPTER XVIII.

Address of thanks by the Corporation.

In consequence of this unprecedented act of liberality, the Corporation prepared a formal address to the General Court, in which they declare, that "the Court had shown themselves kind and bountiful patrons of the College, by the steady and constant care they have taken of it, and the salary they have given out of the public treasury for the support of the successive Presidents, and at sundry particular times by expending considerable sums for the accommodating scholars and furthering the good purposes for which the College was founded."

The style of this address of the Corporation is sufficiently humble and laudatory, considering that both bodies were servants of the Province, and that the bounty thus praised was necessary to the existence of a public institution, which, the address proceeds to state, the Honorable Court themselves must "esteem to be one of the greatest blessings of the whole Province; for, besides the good supply which most of the pulpits through the land have from thence, many of your own honorable members have had the benefit of an education there, and attained those desirable accomplishments which make our country justly esteem them the more fit to serve the public in sundry of the most important posts."

1726. Jan. 18.

By way of reply to the hope expressed in the resolve of the legislature, that the Corporation would be able to support the President out of the College stock, they, in this address, proceed to state, that, though "we are heartily willing to do what we can towards the annual support of a President, yet we shall not be able to do any thing considerable therein without diminishing the College stock or principal."

Anticipating probably the inadequacy of the sum

CHAPTER XVIII.

granted for the building of a President's house, the address expresses "a willingness to employ it for that purpose as well as we can, unless the General Court should see meet to entertain a new thought, and build it by a committee of their own choosing, which would be no way unacceptable to us." A suggestion, however, which the General Court did not "see meet to entertain."

This address was delivered by the President and a committee of the Corporation to Lieutenant-Governor Dummer and the Council in the council-chamber, and by them communicated to the House of Representatives.

Difficulties of President Wadsworth.

Notwithstanding these flattering appearances accompanying the commencement of this presidency, Wadsworth, like his predecessors, soon found other thorns in his path besides those strewed by official duty and College discipline. By the appropriation of the rents of Massachusetts Hall, the legislature had indeed placed a portion of his compensation upon a somewhat more solid foundation, than former Presidents had enjoyed; but the unappropriated funds of the College were wholly inadequate to supply the residue, and the precarious favor of the General Court continued to be the sole dependence of the President for an important part of his maintenance. The pecuniary embarrassments of the period also did not cease, and, with the depreciation attendant on a currency chiefly paper, soon reduced his efficient income nearly to the same level with that of his predecessors; and Wadsworth, although not compelled like Leverett to incur debt, derived only a scanty support from his office.

In other respects the difficulties he had to encounter

were annoying and painful. After the lapse of a year, the building erecting for the President's house was not in a tenantable condition. The sum granted by the General Court, as had been anticipated, proved insufficient, and, being expended, the Corporation had no other resource than to apply to them again for relief. Accordingly, in August, 1726, they addressed a memorial to the legislature, acknowledging thankfully their bounty in granting a thousand pounds, which although they had expended with "the utmost care and frugality," the President's house was not yet finished; and, after proffering an exhibition of their accounts to whomsoever the General Court should appoint, they "humbly entreat the Court to enable them to obey their former order, viz. to build and finish a handsome house for the President;" and they terminate their urgent request for an additional grant with the following graphic account of the difficulties in which President Wadsworth and his family were involved. "He can nowhere hire a convenient house for himself, and his family is divided, some dwelling in one house and some in another. His household goods are disposed of in several houses and barns. These difficult circumstances render the speedy finishing a house for his reception very necessary, which have obliged us to take the first opportunity to lay this representation before the Honorable Court, which we do in all humility."

Corporation apply for relief to the General Court;

A statement of difficulties like these had not the power to open the purse, or soften the heart, of the General Court. The request of the Corporation being refused, they immediately called a special meeting of the Overseers, to ask their advice as to the further

which is refused.

CHAPTER XVIII.

steps to be taken for the speedy finishing of the President's house.

1726. Oct. 6.

The Overseers at their meeting recommended the Corporation to proceed to finish the house "with all convenient speed and frugality, so as to receive the President before winter, and prepare their accounts to be laid before the General Court."

On this recommendation the Corporation proceeded to finish the house upon "credit, as far as might be without a present advance of money to the workmen, and agreed with the workmen accordingly."

The inconveniences to which President Wadsworth and his family were subjected from the want of a comfortable residence were so intolerable, that, as appears by his Diary, they took possession of the house on the 4th of November, 1726, "when not half finished within."

Corporation apply again for relief, and the result.

It being completed in the ensuing January, a meeting of the Corporation was called, and a memorial to the General Court prepared, stating the debt they had incurred on the recommendation of the Overseers, and the urgency of the workmen for their pay, and entreating a farther grant for their relief. The application received from the legislature a decided negative. The Corporation had therefore no other resource than to order their treasurer to pay the amount out of the College treasury, "as far as the state of it will allow"; and the General Court, by paying one thousand out of eighteen hundred pounds* of the cost, have enjoyed the credit, ever since, of building a house for the President of the College.

The accession of George the Second to the British

* Peirce's Hist. Harv. Univ., p. 151.

Address of the Corporation to George the Second, on his accession.

throne occurred in June, 1727. It was deemed by the Corporation a fit occasion to express their loyalty and patriotism by an address to the King, which was carefully prepared, and "sent over to Mr. Thomas Hollis and Mr. Henry Newman, to be presented by them and such as they should choose to go with them." In this address they set forth the zeal of the College "for the Protestant succession in your Majesty's person," their "tears over the grave of the great king your father," and say, that they "bring hearts full of joy for your Majesty's peaceful accession." They proceed; "Our fathers were some of the old Puritans, so called from their purer church state and way of worship, and manner of godly discipline, which, in their apprehensions, they sought and practised. To their immortal honor it must be remembered and recorded, that, as they sought a quiet seat and retirement for themselves and their posterity in the deserts of America, so they were likewise animated with a prospect of enlarging the English empire in regions not known to former ages. And as, under the encouragement of royal charters granted them, they cheerfully planted and subdued a vast wilderness at their own expense, and not without many hardships and hazards, so religion was always their first and chief care, and, in order to that, learning. In this they were singular among the Provinces, and we their posterity reap the honor and happy fruits of it. In one of their first towns they planted a seminary for learning, and called it by the worthy name of Cambridge. In this College are taught the learned languages, the liberal arts and sciences, unto this day, and from it our many churches have (through the favor of God) been supplied with pastors, and the highest chairs of honor among us

CHAPTER XVIII. have been sometimes laudably filled, to the service of the King and the good of the country.

"Nothing but learning and good morals are here required to qualify persons for the honors and favors of the house, but they are equally dispensed unto Protestants of all persuasions. The principles of loyalty and religion are here taught and instilled into our youth; and our many churches are, at this day, famous for their zeal for the true Protestant religion, according to the doctrinal articles of the Church of England, which divine truths we see with joy secured to us in your Majesty's possession of the throne of your ancestors."

The address concludes with a prayer, that the College may find favor and protection with his Majesty, and also "grace in the eyes of her Majesty, your royal consort, who, with her royal offspring, are to us as the light of our eyes and the breath of our nostrils."

1723. Feb. 5. The body of the address above quoted, had been prepared four years before, on occasion of the detection of a conspiracy against the person and government of George the First, in favor of the Pretender, and sent to England, to Mr. Hollis, for presentation; but, arriving after the death of that king, it failed of its object. Having been read at that time "paragraph by paragraph, and approved of," it was thought too good to be lost; and, after changing the beginning and the end, to suit the new occasion, it was inserted bodily into an address to George the Second, congratulatory upon his accession.

Its style and topics were, it is very obvious, better suited to the atmosphere of New than of Old England, and adapted rather to that of a synod than of a court. Mr. Hollis, to whom it had been sent when designed for George the First, perceived the inaptitude of the address, and, in a letter to Mr. Colman, dated the 22d of July, 1727, he thus expresses himself concerning it.

Remarks of Thomas Hollis on the address.

"I have showed your address to sundry persons, who say your compliments to our court now are fifty if not one hundred years too ancient for our present polite style and court. If you reassume the thoughts of addressing the new King, let me recommend to your reading over the addresses of the London Dissenting ministers, the University of Cambridge, and the Quakers, all of which are printed, with many more good ones, in our *London Gazette*, from which you may make one that will be better accepted at St. James's. This is now flirted at, as 'a Bible address,' says one; 'a Concordance address,' says another; though I think it an honest-meaning, Christian address. Plain dealing will not go down among flatterers. I have not seen the Governor (Shute) lately, nor had opportunity to show it unto him for advice. Perhaps he may be displeased, if I should, because you have not mentioned his name. What have courts to do to study Old-Testament phrases and prophecies? It is well if they read the Common Prayer Book and Psalter carefully."

In a subsequent letter he repeats his advice as to the models for an address, but declines the honor of presenting it. "I have no acquaintance with the great ones at the court. I live privately among my own family, and decline the public show."

The state of the institution during the presidency of Wadsworth was troubled and disorderly. If records and diaries are to be credited, there is cause for the

CHAPTER XVIII.

consoling exclamation of the Preacher; "Say not thou, What is the cause that the former days were better than these? for thou dost not inquire wisely concerning this."*

Disorders at Commencement.

Great excesses, immoralities, and disorders occurred about this period. These were peculiarly annoying at the Commencement season. Five years before, on the 11th of June, 1722, a check upon them had been attempted by a vote of the Corporation and Overseers, prohibiting Commencers from "preparing or providing either plumb cake, or roasted, boiled, or baked meats, or pies of any kind," and from having in their chambers "distilled liquors, or any composition made therewith," under penalty of being "punished twenty shillings to be paid to the use of the College," and of forfeiture of the provisions and liquors, "to be seized by the tutors." On Commencement day the President and Corporation were accustomed to visit the rooms of the Commencers, "to see if the laws prohibiting certain meats and drinks were not violated."† But, the disturbances incident to the day not being prevented by these measures, a vote, in April, 1727, passed both boards, that "Commencements for time to come be more private than has been usual; and, in order to this, that the time for them be not fixed to the first Wednesday in July, as formerly, but that the particular day should be determined upon from time to time by the Corporation, and that the Honorable and Reverend Board of Overseers be seasonably acquainted of the said day, and be desired to honor the solemnity with their presence."

Neither the penalty of the law, nor the vigilance

* Ecclesiastes, vii. 10,

† Wadsworth's Diary, pp. 45, 63.

CHAPTER XVIII.

of both boards, was effectual to restrain the tendency to expense at Commencement; and, on the 12th of June, 1727, a vote passed the Corporation, and was subsequently approved by the Overseers, declaring, that "if any who now do, or hereafter shall, stand for their degrees, presume to do any thing contrary to the act of 11th of June, 1722, or *go about to evade it by plain cake*, they shall not be admitted to their degree, and if any, after they have received their degree, shall presume to make any of the forbidden provisions, their names shall be left or rased out of the Catalogue of the graduates."

1728. June.

To prevent disorders, at the suggestion of the immediate government, a formal request also was made by the President, to Lieutenant-Governor Dummer, praying him to direct the sheriff of Middlesex to prohibit the setting up of booths and tents on those public days.*

Some years afterwards, in June, 1733, "an interview took place between the Corporation and three Justices of the Peace in Cambridge, to concert measures to keep order at Commencements, and under their warrant to establish a constable with six men, who, by watching and walking towards the evening on these days, and also the night following, and in and about the entry at the College Hall at dinner time, should prevent disorders."

Disorders in the College.

Circumstances indicate that offences incident to College life were, from some cause, greatly multiplied, and that insubordination was not confined solely to students. At the Commencement in 1731, President Wadsworth states in his Diary, that "three of the tutors were absent (two of them purposely, a thing never

* Wadsworth's Diary, p. 63.

CHAPTER XVIII.

known before); a third, though he stayed at College, and went to the meetinghouse, yet did not appear to act as fellows used to do, in keeping good order in the Hall at dinner time, nor in walking in the procession as usual."

Overseers appoint a committee of inquiry, who report.

The general state of the College attracted the attention of the board of Overseers in November, 1731; at which time a committee was appointed, to inquire into its condition, and "to report proposals for its benefit." Neither the President, nor Mr. Colman, nor any of the Corporation, although several of them were members of the board of Overseers, was included in this committee; and, as the result proved, it was composed of individuals not unwilling to find faults, and little scrupulous about giving them publicity.* After an investigation of eight months, in September, 1732, the committee made a report, "that the government of the College is in a weak and declining state, partly through a deficiency of laws, partly by reason of some disputes and difficulties which have arisen respecting the execution of the laws in being; that religion, one great end of that society, is much upon the decay; a manifest evidence of which is, that the worship of God in the Hall is scandalously neglected, or but partially and not seasonably attended by many; that great disorders have of late appeared amongst the students; some gross immoralities are growing, and many customs, that have a bad influence, indulged; that the long-accustomed method of instruction requires alterations, and that the general condition of the College calls loudly for the interposition of the wisdom and authority of the Overseers."

* See Appendix, No. LXV.

By way of remedy for these evils the committee made seven proposals.

Proposals for a revision of the laws.

First Proposal. That the laws should be revised and adapted to the present circumstances of the society; that all be in Latin, and each student have a copy.

Under this head the committee made the following specifications of laws. 1. That pecuniary mulcts or fines be specified in the quarter bills and sent to parents. 2. That mulcts for absence from chapel prayers, from public worship, and divinity lectures, be raised, and followed up by admonitions, degradation, and expulsion. 3. Students sick on the Lord's day, to give notice to the President or fellows, before meeting, that their case may be inquired into. 4. That tutors take care, that students early retire to their chambers on Saturday evening, and that disorders on Sabbath evening be punished like those on the Sabbath. 5. That students remiss in attending College exercises be punished by fine, admonition, degradation, or expulsion. 6. That the tutors, to quicken diligence, visit chambers in the day, in study hours, and at night after nine o'clock. 7. That Hollis scholars be deprived of his bounty, unless they attend the instructions of his Professor. 8. That students should not allow strangers to lodge in their rooms without leave of the President or a tutor. 9. That students and graduates be prevented from using punch, flip, and like intoxicating drinks. 10. That laws with severe penalties be made against immoralities, particularly against profane swearing, cursing, taking the name of God in vain, sabbath-breaking, light behaviour, playing or sleeping at public worship or prayers; against drunkenness, uncleanness, lying, and stealing; breaking open chambers, studies, letters, desks, chests, or any place under lock and key; and having picklocks. 11. That graduates, bachelors, and masters, who set a bad example to the undergraduates by idleness, extravagance, neglect of public worship, or disorders in their chambers, or by showing contempt to the authority of the College, be subject to be admonished, to be deprived of their chambers and residence, and to have their rooms visited by the President. 12. That fellows and graduates, who have chambers in the College, board in commons. 13. That commons be of better quality, have more variety, clean tablecloths of convenient length and breadth twice a week, and that plates be allowed. 14. That students discontinuing the occupation of a study three months be deprived of it. 15. That the annual vacation after Commencement be only six weeks, and students staying away beyond that time be punished.

Second Proposal. That the salaries of the tutors and instructors be paid quarterly.

Third Proposal. That the Overseers reassume their ancient right of consenting to and allowing salaries.

Fourth Proposal. That the Corporation, in the election of President and Fellows, procure the presence of the Overseers.

Fifth Proposal. That the Fellows be all resident in Cambridge, and be such as are employed in the instruction of the College.

Sixth Proposal. That tutors be chosen for a term of years, at the expiration of which a new election shall be made.

Seventh Proposal. That the Overseers have two stated meetings at the College, of the nature of visitations.

That there was cause for dissatisfaction with the moral conduct of some of the students, about this time, is certain; but whether greater than at former periods, considering the relative numbers, is questionable. On this point we have no means of comparison; since no records are extant of the proceedings of the President and tutors acting as a distinct board previous to the presidency of Wadsworth. Under his auspices the immediate government first assumed the character, and adopted the forms, of an independent board, on all subjects of discipline. This had been administered before by the tutors, who, on their personal authority, inflicted fines, or "boxed" the students at discretion, provided only that it was not "immoderate or inhuman." Great offences, requiring admonition, degradation, or expulsion, were punished by the President after consulting the tutors, but no systematic account was kept of their proceedings.

President and tutors first form a distinct board.

The records of the immediate government, which commence in September, 1725, not only indicate that a disposition to commit the offences incident to Colleges was then sufficiently active, but prove also, that the will and the power to punish existed in that board. From increasing wealth, population, and intercourse with Europe, the strictness of ancient manners had been greatly relaxed about this period in the Province, and the College was naturally the point at which the effects of this change would appear. Causes enough existed for a revision of its laws, but apparently none sufficient to justify the broad denunciations and intimations contained in the report of this committee.

The charges thus brought, in no very measured

CHAPTER XVIII.

terms, against the government of the seminary, as being "weak and declining," and the lamentations concerning "the decay of religion," were probably understood at the time to be the exaggerated expressions of a sectarian party of considerable power, then struggling to regain their ancient ascendency, both in the College and in the Province; and who were willing to attribute the disorders, incident to the period, to the influences of the liberal religious spirit, in which its administration was conducted. From this party the celebrated Methodist, Whitefield, unquestionably derived the opinion, which he expressed some years afterwards in his Journal, that the College was "not far superior to the University of Oxford in piety and godliness."

Report recommitted.

On the reading of this report, the friends of the institution and of its administration rallied; and the first proposal, and all its specifications, were referred to the committee which made the report, after adding to it the President and two members of the Corporation; thus giving to this body an efficient voice in the committee upon all questions arising out of those specifications.

The second proposal was so far accepted as to order a draft of a law in conformity to it to be prepared.

The third was adopted, and a copy ordered to be delivered to the Corporation.

The fourth was then so modified, as to declare, that "a meeting of the Overseers should be equivalent to their presence."

The fifth was negatived.

The sixth was accepted, and the term for which the tutors should be chosen fixed at three years.

The seventh was accepted, and the times fixed for

the meetings of the Overseers were the last Tuesday in March and the last Tuesday in September.

Thus both the points, on which the controversies started by Sever and Welsteed turned, were, after a struggle that continued nearly ten years, deliberately and finally settled on the basis asserted by the Corporation. The election of tutors was limited to three years, and Fellows of the Corporation were not required to be resident instructors.

The committee on a revisal of the laws reported, in May, 1733, to the Overseers, who, instead of acting upon the report, referred the whole subject to the Corporation, recommending a revision of the laws, and that the result be laid before the Overseers for their consent. The Corporation proceeded accordingly, and, on the 26th of March, 1734, presented the revised code to the Overseers, who consented to it with certain amendments. These were also referred to the Corporation, who, after consideration, having adopted them, presented the laws thus amended to the Overseers, for their final sanction. On the 24th of September, the laws thus laboriously framed, were published in the College Hall, in the presence of the Overseers, the Corporation, and the whole body of students.

Laws of the College revised, and published in the College Hall.

This was the first code of laws known to have been passed by both boards, with the observance of all the forms of proceeding in making laws, which afterwards prevailed, and which continue to this day.

On one occasion during the process of forming this code of laws, the Corporation and Overseers appear to have met in the College library, for the purpose of mutual explanation, and facilitating the progress of the work. The forms of proceeding in the inter-

CHAPTER XVIII.

course between the two boards were, notwithstanding, scrupulously observed. The amendments proposed by the Overseers were first recommended by them to the Corporation for consideration, and all farther action was suspended until "the law so amended was again presented to the Overseers for their consent." This course was pursued "until the whole body of laws was agreed to both by the Overseers and Corporation." *

An inquiry into obnoxious opinions of instructors.

In April, 1735, a vote passed the Overseers, recommending the Corporation "to restrain unsuitable and unseasonable dancing in the College." A committee was also appointed to inquire into certain dangerous errors, said to have been disseminated in the College by a Mr. Longloissorie, a Frenchman, employed under the authority of the President and tutors as an instructor in the French language; and the committee were directed to report how far his errors had been propagated and received.† The committee, in May, 1735, reported, "that it did not appear that Mr. Longloissorie had vented any of his dangerous errors among the undergraduates; but that he had freely communicated them to the graduates, by none of whom, however, had they been embraced." Popular reports upon this subject having been circulated concerning Mr. Rogers, one of the tutors, the committee extended their inquiries to him. This officer declined making a satisfactory answer to the committee, replying, that he thought it a hardship to be examined as to his particular sentiments on the said heads, when no express charges had been made against him, and the committee therefore did not deem them-

* Overseers' Records.

† See Appendix, No. LXVI.

selves enabled to report him to be "free and clear of the obnoxious opinions."

Vote of the Overseers thereon

Upon this report, after considerable debate, the Overseers voted;

"That the President and tutors have not power by any law to introduce or permit any person to instruct scholars in arts or language in this society; and therefore the permission, some time since granted to Mr. Longloissorie, to teach the French tongue, is in itself void; and, inasmuch as this board judge it not consistent with the safety of the College that Mr. Longloissorie should continue to teach the French tongue there any longer, it was further voted,

"That the President and tutors be directed to forbid the students, whether graduates or undergraduates, from attending his instructions, either within the College walls or elsewhere."

The board took no further notice of the refusal of Mr. Rogers to be examined by their committee, but "thought it proper to assert and declare their right to examine into the principles of all those that are employed in the instruction of the students of the College, upon any just suspicion of their holding dangerous tenets, although no express charge be laid against them."

The Overseers also proceeded to recommend to the Corporation to "take due care as to the principles of such persons as shall from time to time be chosen by them into any office of instruction; and that no person, chosen into such an office, shall be accepted or continued, who refuses, when desired, to give satisfaction to this board, as to his principles in religion."*

* Overseers' Records.

CHAPTER XVIII.

Private Commencements unpopular, and why.

For several years during the administration of Wadsworth, by a vote of the Overseers the time of Commencement was concealed, only a short notice being given to the public of the day on which it was to be held. In the Diary of President Wadsworth it is stated, that Friday was fixed on, for the reason "that there might be a less remaining time of the week spent in frolicking." At that period Commencement was considered a great holiday in Boston and its vicinity. This attempt, therefore, to deprive the people of their chief and most cherished season of hilarity was very ill received by the multitude. The clergy of the Province, who almost universally assembled on that occasion, were also dissatisfied, complaining, that they were prevented from attending by not knowing the day;* and that, by fixing it on Friday, those of them who lived at a distance from Cambridge, were subject to great inconvenience. Accordingly in 1736 this practice was abandoned, and Commencement, as formerly, was held on Wednesday, to general satisfaction.

On this day an event occurred indicative of the unsettled state of the practice of the two boards which composed the government of the College, and the uncertainty which existed concerning the boundaries of their respective authorities.

Ebenezer Hartshorn claims, and is refused, a Bachelor's degree.

One Ebenezer Hartshorn, who "had formerly resided at the College for some time," had requested, in June, 1733, to be admitted to the degree of Bachelor of Arts. The Corporation, after taking the request into consideration, decided, that he had "no just claim to a degree according to the laws of the College, and that it would not be for the honor of the

* Wadsworth's Diary, p. 135.

society to admit him to it, unless he offer himself for examination, and be found to have made such attainments in academical learning as might render it proper to confer such a degree upon him." Hartshorn declined offering himself for examination, declaring, "that he knew nothing of Hebrew, not even the letters; that he had never read any system of Natural or Moral Philosophy; that he was unacquainted with Mathematics, and could not pretend to answer in Logic; that he chose not to put himself on examination, if he must be examined in those parts of academical learning; and that all he could consent to be examined in was Latin classic authors, the Greek Testament, and his profession of physic."* In June, 1736, Hartshorn applied for a Master's degree, although he had never yet obtained a Bachelor's. The Corporation having voted, that it was "inconsistent with the laws and interests of the College that he should be favored with a degree," Hartshorn, dissatisfied with this decision, presented a petition to the Overseers for a Master's degree on Commencement day, when it was long debated; and, although those members of the Corporation, who were also members of the Overseers, showed that the Corporation had already negatived the petition, and how the College laws expressly declared, that "*no academic degrees should be given but by the Corporation with the consent of the Overseers*," yet the Overseers proceeded to vote Hartshorn his degree.† This vote occasioned President Wadsworth great embarrassment; for he was obviously reduced to the dilemma of giving a degree contrary to the College laws, or of refusing it in oppo-

He claims a Master's degree, and is refused. 1736.

* Records of the Corporation, Vol. IV. pp. 166, 167.

† Wadsworth's Diary, p. 136.

CHAPTER XVIII.

sition to the vote of the Overseers. At that time, the performances of Commencement day were attended both in the forenoon and afternoon. The President, during the recess, proposed to several of the Corporation to have a meeting on the subject, which was opposed; and, one of them being asked what was proper to be done, he explicitly refused to give any advice. In this perplexity the President had resolved "to yield to the torrent, and graduate Hartshorn." But when he was conferring the Masters' degrees in full assembly, three of the Corporation (six of them being present), Dr. Sewall, Dr. Wigglesworth, and Mr. Appleton, came forward and opposed Hartshorn's being graduated. The President then declared publicly, that it was directly against the College laws that he should be graduated. Whereupon the Governor arose, and declared publicly that he ought to be graduated. The debate continued long, and at last the Governor left the meeting. The President then proceeded to give the degrees, and refused to graduate Hartshorn, though he presented himself.

Proceedings thereon of the Corporation.

A degree granted to Hartshorn. 1737.

The next year Hartshorn again renewed his petition to the Corporation, who, after declaring that "the Honorable and Reverend Overseers of the College, since the last vote of the Corporation upon that affair, had manifested their disposition that such a favor should be conferred upon him," proceeded to vote, that he should be admitted to a Master's degree at the then ensuing Commencement.

Foundation of the Hollis Professorship of Mathematics. 1727.

During the early part of Mr. Wadsworth's administration, that unwearied friend, the first Thomas Hollis, laid the foundation of a Professorship of Mathematics and Natural Philosophy in Harvard College. He had long meditated the subject, and thus wrote upon it to Mr. Colman; "Though jeered and sneered at by many, I leave the issue to the Lord, for whose sake I perform these offices and services, and hope I shall be enabled to continue firm and finish this affair, which I call a good work." He was as careful that the principles, on which the Professorship was founded, should be wise, as he was liberal in establishing it. He called upon his educated friends for plans, and received five, all of which he transmitted to the Corporation for their selection and approval of the best. They were written respectively by Isaac Watts, Daniel Neal, Jeremiah Hunt, and Professor Emms, all eminent for their scientific attainments and religious zeal; and by Isaac Greenwood, the individual, whom he had selected, and who was afterwards chosen by the Corporation and Overseers, first Professor on this foundation.

State of the College funds in 1732.

By the report of the investigating committee in 1732, it appears, that "the annual income of the estate of the College, not appropriated specifically by the donors, amounted to £728 7*s*. currency; and that the stated and incidental charges have been such for these ten years past that the estate of the College had increased about £100 per annum."

The funds of the College were diminished, during Mr. Wadsworth's presidency, by the expenses and result of a lawsuit, instituted for the purpose of getting possession of a tract of land in Maine, called Merriconeag Neck. This tract had been granted by the General Court to the College in 1682. But the Indian wars, which soon after took place, had prevented the legislature from bounding out the tract; so that the College had never obtained possession. The Corporation were very reluctant to enter upon the pursuit

CHAPTER XVIII.

of their title; but, the advice of the Overseers being asked in November, 1731, they recommended employing counsel, and putting measures in train to prosecute their title to effect. This advice the Corporation proceeded to follow in 1732. Being soon doubtful of success, they applied twice to the Overseers, submitting it to their judgment, whether the College had not better endeavour to make a compromise with the claimants, but to both propositions the Overseers opposed a decided negative.

Title of the College to Merriconeag tried and defeated.

The Corporation, out of respect to the opinion of the Overseers, persevered in their suit, which, in 1733, was finally decided against the College, to its loss of the lands and costs. It derived therefore no more benefit from this grant of 1682, than it had previously from the grants of two thousand acres in 1653, and two thousand acres in the Pequod country, in 1657, both of which failed; yet, in all succeeding times, when a question has arisen in the General Court concerning "what that Court has done for the College," not only have both these grants been carefully enumerated, but, to these ideal bounties, there has ever been added "*Merriconeag Neck, in Casco Bay, with a thousand acres adjacent.*"

Benjamin Colman resigns his seat in the Corporation.

In the third year of Wadsworth's presidency the Corporation lost, by resignation, the services of the Rev. Benjamin Colman, who, during twelve years, had been an active, faithful, and able member of the board. In February, 1728, he gave notice of his intention to resign. The Corporation, anxious to retain his services, immediately passed the following vote; "Whereas the Rev. Mr. Colman has, by word of mouth and letters to the President, expressed his desires to resign his place in the Corporation, the

CHAPTER XVIII.

said Corporation, being sensible of his good services past, and of the importance of his future service to the College as a member of the Corporation, are very desirous of his continuing his place therein; and accordingly voted, that the President be requested to write a letter in the name of the Corporation, signifying their sentiments and desires." Colman having in a letter to the President avowed his intention to be unaltered, the Corporation, on the 30th of August, passed a second vote, "that it would tend much to the peace and service of the College, if he continue his standing in the Corporation, notwithstanding his former desires to be dismissed from it." The purpose of Mr. Colman, however, was not changed. He left the board finally in December, 1728, and the Rev. Joseph Sewall, minister of the South Church in Boston, was chosen in his stead. Mr. Colman had several years contemplated this resignation, but, out of respect to his friends and their urgency, he had reluctantly retained his position at the board. Among these, Thomas Hollis had probably the most influence. He was anxious that Mr. Colman should continue in the Corporation, and that he should be made President of the College. In 1724, on receiving information that he had been elected to that office, but that he hesitated accepting it on account of the insufficiency of the salary, Mr. Hollis communicated the fact to the Rev. Mr. Cotton, a gentleman of fortune, who had known Mr. Colman when in Europe. That gentleman immediately placed in the hands* of Mr. Hollis *one hundred pounds sterling*, "for Mr. Colman, President of

* Letter of Thomas Hollis to Colman, February 23d, 1724.

the College, as an augmentation of his salary, and as an encouragement to him to accept it, and for the purpose of removing difficulties towards such acceptance." Mr. Cotton also placed in Mr. Hollis's hands three hundred pounds sterling more, to be laid out for the College in books or charity, according to the advice of Mr. Colman. This donation was the occasion of putting to trial Mr. Colman's delicacy and disinterestedness. The first hundred pounds had been bestowed in terms which authorized him to consider the sum as a gift to him individually. But it had been also stated to have been designed as an encouragement for him to accept the presidency. No sooner, therefore, had he declined that office, than he applied the whole amount of Mr. Cotton's bounty to the use of the College. This appears by a letter to Mr. Colman from Mr. Hollis, dated August 12th, 1725, who treats the subject in this kind and friendly way; "With reference to the account you give me of the proportioning the four hundred pounds Mr. Cotton has ordered for bounty and charity, I do nothing to contradict your agreement, and I believe my good friend Mr. Cotton will also, save in one particular. I think Mr. Colman is over-righteous. Mr. Cotton told me, it was a present to Mr. Colman, from a long-contracted friendship; and, as he was now chosen President, it might be a small inducement to encourage his accepting the chair, believing him a fit person to fill it; but it is not to Mr. President, but to Mr. Colman, the present is made, as I understand it. If Mr. Colman's circumstances need not such a gift, it is at your liberty to do what you will with your own; *but it must be Mr. Colman's gift, and not Mr. Cotton's.*"

Notwithstanding this kind remonstrance Mr. Colman adhered to his purpose. In a subsequent letter Mr. Hollis acknowledges having received an account of "the hundred pounds, Mr. Cotton's gift, and his satisfaction with its distribution."

Mr. Colman survived the dissolution of his connexion with the Corporation nearly twenty years; and died, at the age of seventy-three, in August, 1747; to which period is postponed the tribute due to his character and services.

Death and character of President Wadsworth.

The death of President Wadsworth occurred on the 16th of March, 1737, and was lamented with more than ordinary demonstrations of sorrow. Appleton, Sewall, Wigglesworth, and Foxcroft, all divines of celebrity, delivered funeral sermons on the occasion; and Flynt, the oldest tutor of the College, a Latin oration. In those testimonies of contemporaneous respect and affection, the general features of his character are sketched with a truth and accuracy, which are justified by the impressions derived from the history of the times and of the College.

President Wadsworth was born in 1669, and was graduated at Harvard College in 1690. He selected the ministry for his sphere of usefulness, and held the relation of pastor of the First Church in Boston from 1696 until his transfer to the College, in 1725. His talents were solid rather than brilliant, and adapted for service more than display. Many of his sermons were published, and remain to evidence the character of his intellectual efforts. They are plain, practical, and scriptural. Being argumentative and without ornament, their interest is the effect of the truth, earnestness, and zeal they display. Neither a bigot nor an enthusiast, and destitute of all ambition to shine or to lead, he avoided controversy. While he thought and acted with the liberal part of the clergy, he was lauded during his life, and claimed, after his death, by the stricter sect; a fate common to those who are not ardent in temperament, and free from the spirit of party proselytism. In religion, as in politics, zealots ever reckon men of this character among their number, especially "after death has opened the gate of fame and extinguished envy."

President Wadsworth was fifty-six years old when he accepted, reluctantly, the chair of the College. His health began to fail soon after he entered upon its duties, which were performed, however, to general acceptance, under all the disadvantages of bodily infirmity. His conduct in their discharge was marked by firmness, prudence, and judgment. Faithful to every trust, kind to all, calm, cautious, moderate, self-possessed, and affectionate, he left a name precious to his own, and appreciated highly by after times.

PRESIDENT'S HOUSE, BUILT IN 1726.

CHAPTER XIX.

Benefactors of the College. — John Hull. — Samuel Sewall. — Richard Sprague. — Thomas Brattle. — William Brattle. — William Brown. — Joseph Brown, William Brown, and Benjamin Brown. — Samuel Brown. — John and William Brown. — Edmund Brown. — Gurdon Saltonstall. — Mary Saltonstall. — Dorothy Saltonstall. — John Frizell, and John Frizell, his Nephew. — John Walley. — Ephraim Flynt. — Henry Gibbs. — Ezekiel Rogers. — Thomas Cotton. — Thomas Hollis. — John Hollis. — Nathaniel Hollis. — Thomas Hollis, the second Benefactor of that Name. — Exercises, Studies, Discipline, and Customs of the College, during the Presidencies of Leverett and Wadsworth.

We have now arrived at a period of colonial history, when extended commerce, increased population, and consequent wealth, changed materially the general character of New England. The severity of manners, the staid demeanor, and the scriptural phraseology of the early emigrants of the Puritan sect disappeared. But their principles and institutions, their love of liberty, and their stern resistance to oppression still continued to influence the character and fortunes of their descendants. In politics, the jealousy of the clergy as to the measures of the English hierarchy, and that of the statesmen as to the designs of the English ministry, raised the dread of transatlantic control into a master passion. In religion, although sects multiplied, controversy diminished and its bitterness moderated. Before tracing the influence of this change on Harvard College, gratitude demands that we again

CHAPTER XIX.

turn our thoughts towards those generous spirits, not yet commemorated, who encouraged or aided the progress of the institution by their bounty.

John Hull.

The earliest of these benefactors was John Hull, who, in 1681, gave to the College one hundred pounds, Massachusetts currency. This donation was probably made in his lifetime, as he died intestate in 1683.* By persevering industry, great talents for business, and strict integrity, he acquired the confidence of his contemporaries, rose from poverty and a low estate to great affluence, was elected Treasurer of the colony in 1676, and an Assistant from 1680 to 1683. In 1652, when the government of Massachusetts determined to assume the prerogative of the crown, and coin money for the currency of the country, Mr. Hull was appointed master of the mint; which was built upon his land. The General Court, inviting all the inhabitants to bring in Spanish coin, bullion, and plate, contracted to allow Mr. Hull one in every twenty shillings for his services in coining.† Perceiving afterwards that he had too advantageous a contract, they offered him a considerable sum of money to relinquish it, which he refused, and soon accumulated a fortune, second to none of domestic creation in that age, in New England. His only child married Samuel Sewall, afterwards Chief Justice, and brought to him in dowry, as was commonly reported, says Hutchinson, "thirty thousand pounds, in New England shillings."‡ By this marriage Sewall became one of the most wealthy inhabitants of the colony.

* Farmer's Genealogical Record of the first Settlers in Massachusetts, art. *Hull.*

† Records of the General Court.

‡ See Hutch. Hist. Mass., Vol. I. p. 164, note.

CHAPTER XIX.

Samuel Sewall.

On the 24th of June, 1696, Samuel Sewall, and Hannah, his wife, gave by deed to Harvard College, a farm of five hundred acres, being a portion of a large tract of land purchased by John Hull in the Narragan-set country, and called the Petaquamscot purchase;* the incomes or profits of which he appropriated to "the support and education at the College, of youths, whose parents may not be of sufficient ability to maintain them there, especially such as should be sent from Petaquamscot, English or Indians."

In recent times it has been sold, and the interest of the proceeds constitutes an important part of the funds of the College for the benefit of needy and meritorious students, to which object it is scrupulously applied.

Samuel Sewall was born in England in 1652, came with his father to Massachusetts, in 1661, and was graduated at Harvard College in 1671. He studied divinity, became a tutor at the College in 1674, and a candidate for the ministry. In 1676, after acquiring a fortune by marriage, he quitted both employments, and entered the career of politician and jurist; a transition not violent under a constitution founded upon religion. In 1684 he was chosen a magistrate, and in 1690 was appointed one of the commissioners with William Stoughton, to meet those of the United Colonies at Albany.†

By the nomination of Increase Mather he became, in 1692, one of the first Council under the charter of William and Mary; an office which he retained, by successive annual elections, until he declined it in 1725. He was constituted one of the special justices in the commission for the trial of witchcraft, of which

* See Mass. Hist. Coll., First Series, Vol. V. p. 217.

† Ibid., Vol. VIII. Second Series, p. 238.

William Stoughton was Chief Justice. Having been deeply implicated in the transactions consequent on that delusion, he was awakened to a conviction of the guilt of those proceedings by the returning sense of the community, and reduced his sorrow and repentance into the form of a confession, which, agreeably to the church discipline of the period, his clergyman, Mr. Willard, read publicly in full assembly at the South Church, on fast day, Mr. Sewall standing up in his pew during the ceremony. A species of humiliation, to which William Stoughton, being chief magistrate of the Province through favor of the crown, and less affected by the vibrations of popular opinion, refused to submit, saying, "that he saw no cause for any public acknowledgment of error, as, when he sat in judgment, he had the fear of God before his eyes, and gave his opinion according to the best of his understanding."*

In 1715 Mr. Sewall was made Judge of Probate for the County of Suffolk, and in 1718 was raised to the office of Chief Justice of the Province, which he satisfactorily sustained until his resignation in 1728, two years before his death.

Chief Justice Sewall was learned, according to the colonial standard, being well acquainted with the Latin, Greek, and Hebrew, assiduous in fulfilling the duties of a Christian and a citizen, liberal, hospitable, sympathetic, and practically wise in the affairs of the world. He was an active member of the Company for the Propagation of the Gospel among the Indians; built for their worship, at his own expense, a church at Natick; and made some laudable exertions to ren-

* See Hutch. Hist. Mass., Vol. II. p. 62.

CHAPTER XIX.

der the practice of enslaving negroes odious, writing a pamphlet against it, and publicly protesting against the lawfulness of the traffic. A diligent and careful observer of passing events, he kept a diary for more than forty years of a life spent chiefly in the public service. This curious document often lifts the veil of time from the motives of men and parties, and affords means of estimating the actual state of learning, morals, and piety in New England at that period, far superior to those furnished by general history.

Judge Sewall's doctrinal faith was conformed to that of the strictest sect of Calvinists; and, although constitutionally of a candid and conciliatory spirit, he firmly adhered to ancient customs, manners, principles, and doctrines, and resisted every innovation with earnest and unquenchable zeal. Among the active politicians of his age, no one attained higher or more unvaried tokens of public confidence, and time has disclosed no circumstance to qualify the favorable opinion his contemporaries formed of his worth and his virtues.*

Richard Sprague.

Richard Sprague, an inhabitant of Charlestown, is entitled to rank high among the benefactors of Harvard College. He was the son of Ralph Sprague, who came with Governor Endecott to Salem in 1628, and the next year commenced a settlement at Charlestown. Few traces remain of his course and character. It is only known that he was among the most active and useful men of his place of abode, employed on all important committees of the town, and for many years was its Representative in the General Court. He died childless in 1703, and bequeathed

* Allen's and Eliot's Biographical Dictionaries.— Prince's Funeral Sermon on the Death of the Honorable Samuel Sewall.

CHAPTER XIX.

to the College three hundred pounds, Massachusetts currency. He also left to the town of Charlestown the reversion of a house and land, and a portion of his personal estate, the proceeds of which now constitute an important part of the Fund for the Poor in that town.

Thomas Brattle.

Among those entitled to grateful remembrance for services and bounties to Harvard College, the name of Thomas Brattle is conspicuous. He was a merchant of Boston, distinguished for opulence, activity, and talent, and for the zeal and readiness with which he devoted his time, wealth, and intellectual power to objects of private benevolence and public usefulness.

He was born in 1657, was graduated at Harvard College in 1676, and died in 1713, at the age of fifty-six. He was chosen Treasurer of the College in 1693, and held that office twenty years, until his death. In the July preceding that event, he caused the settlement he had made with his predecessor, in 1693, and his own account of receipts and expenditures during the intervening period, to be entered on the records of the Corporation; carefully specifying the particulars of the real and personal estate of the College, with the incomes of both; thus giving the most authentic and satisfactory developement of its property and pecuniary relations at that early period. Two years elapsed after his death before a successor was appointed. During the interval, his brother and executor, the Rev. William Brattle, at the solicitation of the Corporation, took upon himself the superintendence of the finances of the College. By the accounts of these treasurers it appears, that Thomas Brattle received, in 1693, from John Richards, his predecessor, upwards of one thousand five hundred and fifty pounds, lawful money, personal estate of the College, and a real estate yielding one hundred pounds annual income; and that William Brattle, his executor, delivered over to John White, his successor, in 1715, nearly three thousand eight hundred pounds, personal estate, and a real estate, yielding two hundred and eighty pounds. Such was the accumulation of the property of the College, while its finances were under the management of these brothers.

Thomas Brattle was not unmindful, at his death, of the institution, to whose prosperity he was so assiduously devoted during his life. He bequeathed to the College two hundred pounds, Massachusetts currency, and devoted its income to the advancement of Mathematical science in the institution. His independence of the strong and universal prejudice, existing at that day in New England, against the use of instrumental music in public worship, is strikingly evidenced by the following clause in his last will. "I give, dedicate, and devote my organ to the praise and glory of God in the said Church (Brattle Street), if this shall accept thereof, and within one year after my decease procure a sober person that can play skilfully thereon with a loud noise." If that Church refuse to accept the gift, he then bequeaths the instrument on similar terms to the Church of England in Boston. If this refuse, he then gives it to Harvard College, on the same condition. If the College refuse the organ, he bequeaths it to his brother, the Rev. William Brattle. His affection for the College is also indicated by his giving "half a crown to every student belonging to it, who should attend his funeral."

Thomas Brattle was distinguished among his contemporaries for his intellectual powers and scientific attainments. Judge Sewall thus writes concerning him, in a letter dated on the 18th of May, 1713, it being the day of Mr. Brattle's death. "We are in danger of losing Mr. Thomas Brattle, who is a great ornament to our College, on account of his eminent learning, especially in the Mathematics. He is also very useful as their treasurer, very serviceably and excellently performing that office." Among the transactions of the Royal Society, in London, is a communication, entitled "Observatio Eclipsis Lunaris peracta Bostonii Novanglorum, die quinto Aprilis, vespere, A. D. 1707, a Tho. Brattle." Bailey, in his supplement to the account of Flamsteed, states, that "Mr. Thomas Brattle, of Boston in New England, is the anonymous person alluded to by Newton, in his Principia, as having made such good observations of the comet of 1680."

The views of Mr. Brattle were enlightened and enlarged, and in his religious opinions he was catholic and liberal. His connexion with the Brattle-Street Church is indicated by its location and name. He was one of its earliest founders, continued through life among its firmest supporters, and was of consequence involved in the ecclesiastical controversy, which originated in the secession of that church from the Cambridge Platform. Like other congenial minds, he was stigmatized in the party heats of the time, as an "apostate" and "infidel"; but his mind and labors, devoted to science and religious liberty, have shed upon his memory a light, which has survived all record and tradition of the calumnies which assailed his name and influence.

The account written by Mr. Brattle of the "witchcraft delusion," and of the judicial trials and executions at Salem for that pretended crime, is one of the most interesting and illustrative productions of the period, and highly honorable to his sagacity and foresight. It was written in October, 1692, at the very moment, when that destructive delusion was at its height, and the terror of being "accused by the afflicted," in full sway; when the special commissioners had just finished their first tragic session;* when fifty, confessing themselves guilty of witchcraft, besides many others accused of it, were in prison, and another session of the commissioners was approaching, in which a renewal of the same appalling scenes was anticipated; when the writer himself could not express his opinion upon the passing events without "fear lest his freedom should bring him into a snare."† Under circumstances thus critical, Thomas Brattle wrote a letter, in which he declares his determination to make "a very open communication of my thoughts, and in plain terms to tell what my opinion is of these proceedings."‡ He then with great clearness exposes and reprobates the nature of the examination, the form of the indictment, the irrelevancy of the admitted evidence, the guilt of the accusers, the innocency of those already condemned and executed, and the madness and iniquity of the course pursued. His remarks are acute and conclusive, exhibiting firmness and self-possession, and a mind elevated above the agitated chaos of the time. He comments severely on the partiality of the judges, and on the infatuation of "the civil leaders and spiritual teachers,

* See above, p. 64.

† See Mass. Hist. Coll., First Series, Vol. V. p. 61.

‡ Ibid., p. 62.

CHAPTER XIX.

and of those who profess high, and pass among us for some of the better sort; who, instead of punishing and preaching down such sorcery and wickedness, do allow of, encourage, yea, practise this very abomination." *

He then proceeds to foretell, what soon became history, that "the justices and judges, or any else concerned in these matters, will not be able soon to look back upon these things without the greatest sorrow and grief imaginable." † He does not hesitate to speak, in terms implying reprobation, of "the zeal and impatience" displayed by "the Chief Judge" (Stoughton) in these trials, and to express his "fear, that wisdom and counsel are withheld from him in this matter." Although this letter was not published at the time it was written, it is an honorable testimony to the clearness and independence of his judgment, and his regard for justice and truth.

William Brattle.

William Brattle, the younger brother of Thomas, was alike eminent for liberality, talent, and literary acquirements. He was born in Boston in 1662, and was graduated at Harvard College in 1680. In 1686 he was appointed tutor in the College, at the same time with John Leverett. They were the principal instructors in the institution for ten years succeeding, during four of which President Mather was absent in Europe. Mr. Brattle was chosen pastor of the Church in Cambridge in 1696, and, the Corporation of the College carefully state on their records, that "they unanimously concurred with the Church of Cambridge in their invitation of the Rev. William Brattle to the work of the ministry in that church." When Lieu-

* Mass. Hist. Coll., First Series, Vol. V. p 70. † Ibid., p. 74.

tenant-Governor Stoughton reorganized the government of the institution in October, 1696,* on the occasion of the negative of the College charter by the King, he appointed William Brattle a member of the Corporation. He held his seat in that board until July, 1700, when he was excluded by the act passed under the influence of President Mather.† In August, 1703, he was reinstated by the influence of Governor Dudley and Vice-President Willard,‡ and retained his place until his death, which occurred in the year 1717, in the fifty-fourth of his age.

William Brattle was alike respected as a man, a scholar, and a divine. His manners were urbane and polished; and, although his habits of life were studious and retired, he was yet skilful in business, and devoted to the duties of his profession. After the death of his brother, at the request of the Corporation, he took the office of Treasurer, and during two years managed the financial concerns of the College with fidelity and success. While engaged in the superintendence of the seminary, he blended a tutor's discipline with a parent's tenderness. At that period the small-pox was an object of universal terror. Inoculation had not then been introduced, and flight was the only refuge of those who were liable to the disorder. Mr. Brattle, though not secure from the disease when it appeared in the College, instead of abandoning his post, remained firm and unterrified; visited the sick students, administered to them, and personally contributed to their comfort and convalescence. When suffering himself under the disease, the fearlessness of his mind proved the best preservative

* See above, p. 82. † Ibid., p. 106. ‡ Ibid., p. 150.

from its malignity, and he was soon restored to health and his duties. This heroism endeared him to the students, and he received from them, by common consent, the name of "Father of the College." At his death he bequeathed to the beneficiary fund of the institution two hundred and fifty pounds, Massachusetts currency. His other bounties were numerous. Charity was with him a principle rather than an impulse, his fortune being large and his liberality proportionate. He was not merely a patron of literature; he was himself a man of science, and as such was admitted a Fellow of the Royal Society of London, a distinction not easily obtained by a colonist. His publications were few. The only one now known is a treatise upon logic, written originally in Latin, which was used many years in the College as a text-book, and came to a second edition in 1758.*

Few divines of that period have obtained a purer or more desirable reputation. He mingled little in controversy, and never troubled himself or others with unprofitable speculations, or with metaphysical theology. Deeply impressed with the truth of the Scriptures, he sought in them the rule of life and duty; led in the way of religion by the force and attraction of his example; and stood aloof from words which darken counsel and obscure the simplicity of the Gospel.

He early deviated from some of the ancient practices of the churches in New England. Under his influence, and soon after his settlement, as we have already stated,† a formal, public relation of religious experiences ceased to be required in the church at

* Mass. Hist. Coll., First Series, Vol. VII. pp. 32, 55.

† See above, p. 89.

CHAPTER XIX.

Cambridge, as a qualification for membership, the examination of the candidate was intrusted to the pastor and elders, and the consent of the church to admission was signified by silence instead of a hand vote. These were all deemed dangerous innovations by those attached to the early order and practice of the New England churches, and were in fact precursors of that schism, which, under the auspices of his elder brother, eventuated in the foundation of the Brattle-Street Church in Boston, and the divisions which ensued among the Congregational clergy.

For more than half a century, the family of Brown stands distinguished among those, whose continued bounty to Harvard College assumes the aspect of an inheritable quality. Eight of that name are entitled to grateful remembrance. Seven of them were inhabitants of Salem, and held the relation to each other of father, sons, grandsons, and great-grandsons. William Brown, the head of the family, has been already the subject of notice.* He emigrated in 1635, from Brandon, in Suffolk, England, to Salem, where he acquired wealth, public confidence, and general esteem. For several years he was Representative from Salem in the General Court, afterwards was appointed an Assistant, and finally one of the Council, in 1687, during the administration of Andros. He died in 1688, highly esteemed for his usefulness and example as a private citizen, and honored in his public station for his judgment and knowledge in commercial affairs, and for his practical political skill. His charities were his crowning glory. To Harvard College he gave forty pounds in his lifetime, and one hundred pounds

William Brown.

* See above, p. 181.

CHAPTER XIX.

by bequest. The public institutions of Salem and Charlestown were also largely indebted to his bounty.* In this munificence he was emulated by his descendants.†

Joseph Brown.

Joseph Brown, son of the preceding, was graduated at the College in 1666. He died in early manhood, before his father, in the year 1678. Partaking of his spirit, he bequeathed for the use of his *alma mater* one hundred pounds, and also fifty pounds in books for the library. He was destined for the sacred desk, and had received, just before his death, an invitation to the pastoral care of the church in Charlestown.

William Brown.

His brother, William Brown, was born in 1639, survived his father, and, treading in his steps, was successful as a merchant, and in attaining public confidence as a Representative in the General Court, a member of the Council of Safety in 1689, and a counsellor under the charter of William and Mary. After a long life of honor and usefulness, he died in 1716, at the age of seventy-seven, leaving to the College a legacy of one hundred pounds, currency of Massachusetts.

Benjamin Brown.

Benjamin Brown, a younger brother, was born in 1648, and died in 1708, at the age of sixty, concerning the course of whose life and fortunes no record remains. By his last will he also bequeathed a legacy of two hundred pounds to Harvard College.

Samuel Brown.

Samuel, son of William Brown, last mentioned, was born in 1669, and died in 1731, at the age of sixty-two. He emulated the beneficence of his father, uncles, and grandfather, and, enlarging the measure of

* Donation Book, Vol. I. pp. 15, 23.

† Mass. Hist. Coll., First Series, Vol. VI. p. 287.

his bounty to the College, bequeathed, in aid of its beneficiary funds one hundred and fifty pounds, and for general purposes sixty pounds, and, in addition, a house and a valuable, well-stocked farm in Hopkinton, consisting of two hundred acres.*

John and William Brown.

In a later period, John Brown and William Brown, great-grandchildren of the first benefactor of that name, were among the liberal subscribers in books and money for repairing the loss sustained in 1764, by the burning of Harvard Hall, and the destruction of the library it contained.†

Edmund Brown.

Edmund Brown, another benefactor, who bequeathed a legacy of one hundred pounds to the College, is not known to have been related to the Salem family of that name. He emigrated from England to Massachusetts in 1637, became the first minister of Sudbury in 1640, and died in 1677. He was exemplary in his life, and attained professional distinction. There is some doubt whether the College ever derived any benefit from this legacy; but the debt of gratitude to his memory is not the less due, since the intention was direct, and his property ample. He adopted one Samuel Goffe as his son and heir, and made him his executor. To him Mr. Brown bequeathed a large real estate, on the condition of paying to Harvard College, within two years after his decease, one hundred pounds, current money of New England. This condition Goffe failed to fulfil. A suit in chancery was the consequence, and the College obtained and levied an execution on the land, but, for some cause, without any beneficial result.

* College Book, No. IV., pp. 6, 9, 12.

† Donation Book, Vol. I. pp. 23, 65, 67.

CHAPTER XIX.

Gurdon Saltonstall.

The family of the Saltonstalls we have already had occasion to number among the earliest and most liberal patrons of the College.* Gurdon, great-grandson of the first Sir Richard Saltonstall, supported the character of the family, and extended the obligations of the institution to this distinguished name. Gurdon Saltonstall was born at Haverhill in 1666, graduated at Harvard College in 1684, became a popular and successful preacher, and in 1691 was ordained pastor over the Congregational church in New London, Connecticut. On all momentous occasions he was resorted to as an oracle, and on the death of Fitz John Winthrop, in 1707, both clergy and laity united to call him from the care of a church to the chair of state. By the law of Connecticut the people were restricted in the choice of Governor to the magistrates then in nomination. To remove this obstacle to his election, the Assembly of the colony, in 1708, repealed the restrictive law, and the ensuing year Gurdon Saltonstall was chosen Governor, and was continued in that office by successive elections for sixteen years, until his death in 1724. In all the relations of public and private life he was faithful and exemplary. In the attributes of public spirit and benevolence he was not surpassed by any of his contemporaries, among whom he attained the highest rank as a divine, orator, and statesman.

Gurdon Saltonstall bequeathed by will one hundred pounds, lawful money, to Harvard College ; thus emulating the example of Mary Saltonstall, his wife, who, the year previous, had made a donation of a like sum from her own private estate.

* See above, p. 163.

Mary Saltonstall survived her husband six years, and by her last will bequeathed, in 1730, one thousand pounds to the College, for educating young men "of bright parts and good diligence for the service of the Christian church." By the same instrument she made noble and judicious legacies for the advancement of learning and religion, and for charitable purposes.

Mary Saltonstall.

Uniting exemplary piety and enlarged charity with a highly cultivated mind, she filled the high station, to which she was called, with prudence and dignity. By her contemporaries she is celebrated for the graces which adorn, and the virtues which are the honor of, human nature.*

Dorothy Saltonstall.

To Dorothy Saltonstall, who died in 1733, the College is indebted for a liberal bequest. This lady derived her fortune from her first husband, John Frizell, an eminent merchant of Boston, who was himself a benefactor to the institution. The donation books of the College acknowledge the receipt of one hundred and fifty pounds as a legacy from him; but some obscurity rests upon his bounty, as no record has yet been found of a will, nor is there any account of the authority under which the donation was received. His widow married Nathaniel Saltonstall, and, having by her marriage contract reserved to herself the power of disposing of her own estate, bequeathed three hundred pounds to Harvard College, and other legacies to pious and charitable uses. Her benevolence and intellectual power are respectfully and honorably noticed in the records of that period.

John Frizell.

John Frizell, nephew of the last-mentioned benefactor, was a successful merchant of Boston, and

John Frizell.

* Allen's Biog. Dict.—New England Journal, 26th January, 1729–30.

CHAPTER XIX.

is also entitled to grateful remembrance. He died in 1730, and by his will left two hundred and fifty pounds to the College. There remains no record or tradition concerning his life, except of his wealth and his bounties.

John Walley.

John Walley, by a bequest of one hundred pounds to the College, became another benefactor, and directed the amount to be applied to the support of "scholars devoted to the ministry." He came to this country in 1662, with his father, the Rev. Thomas Walley, a clergyman, ejected for non-conformity, and was continually employed in offices of honor and trust during the residue of his life. In 1671 and 1684 he was a member of the committee appointed to codify the Plymouth Colony laws. In 1687 he was member from Plymouth, in the Council of Andros, and in 1697 had the command of the land forces in the unsuccessful expedition against Canada. His Journal is preserved by Hutchinson,* and is the most authentic account, now extant, of the transactions of the invading force. Under the charter of William and Mary he was appointed Counsellor in 1692. In 1700 he received the appointment of Associate Justice of the Supreme Court of the Province, which he resigned in 1711. He died in 1712, at the age of sixty-eight. The constancy and importance of his public employments indicate the confidence of his contemporaries in his talents and virtues. He was subjected, like all unsuccessful commanders, to the suspicion of misconduct. But, although he solicited an investigation, none was granted. Public opinion finally settled into a firm conviction, that the causes of the failure were in-

* Hutch. Hist. Mass., Vol. I. p. 470.

sufficiency of preparation, and ignorance of the difficulty of the attempt, rather than want of courage and talent in the commander.

Ephraim Flynt.

Ephraim Flynt of Concord, by his last will, bequeathed to the College one hundred pounds, Massachusetts currency, the income to be applied for the benefit of scholars, "who are studious, well disposed, and need help."* He was the son of the Rev. Thomas Flynt, of that place, was born in 1642, and died in 1723, at the age of eighty-one. Of the particulars of his life nothing has been ascertained.

Henry Gibbs.

The Rev. Henry Gibbs, pastor of the church at Watertown, also gave, by his last will, dated on the 26th of December, 1722, one hundred pounds to the College. He was born in 1668, was graduated at Harvard in 1685, ordained at Watertown in 1697, and died in 1723. He was regarded by his contemporaries among the eminent clergymen of the period; and he is ranked by Dr. Barnard among those, who were "men of learning, pious, humble, prudent, faithful, and useful, in their day."†

Ezekiel Rogers.

The Rev. Ezekiel Rogers, of Rowley, is entitled to remembrance, among the earliest benefactors of Harvard College; but his donation was contingent, and the event on which it depended did not occur until many years after his decease. His father, the Rev. Richard Rogers, was a distinguished Puritan minister at Wethersfield, in Essex, England, at which place Ezekiel Rogers was born in 1590. After being graduated at Cambridge, he entered the family of Sir Francis Barrington, as chaplain, and from his in-

* Donation Book, Vol. I. p. 243.

† Mass. Hist. Coll., First Series, Vol. X. p. 170.

CHAPTER XIX.

fluence obtained the benefice of Rowley, and became eminent for his professional zeal and oratorical talents; but, soon rendering himself obnoxious, he was persecuted for his non-conformity, and emigrated with a portion of his congregation to Massachusetts in 1638. Here they purchased a tract of land from the towns of Newbury and Ipswich, and gave the name of Rowley, the place of their former residence in England, to their new plantation.

In the early struggle between the magistrates and ministers for power and influence, Mr. Rogers joined the party of the latter, and became obnoxious to Winthrop and Dudley, by telling the people, that no governor ought to be continued more than a year, and by coinciding in the views of John Cotton, who endeavoured to prove from Numbers xxvii. 21, and other texts, that "the priesthood ought to be consulted by the magistrates, not only before they went to war, but in every thing appertaining to the affairs of the Commonwealth."*

He is characterized by Johnson, in his "Wonder-working Providence," as a "judicious and zealously affected servant of the Lord"; and his people, who came with him, to the number of threescore families, as "holy, humble, and industrious; as being the first who set up the making of cloth in this western world, building a fulling-mill, and causing their little ones to be very diligent in spinning cotton wool."†

He is represented by Cotton Mather, as "very acceptable" as a preacher, "exceedingly successful," "marvellously profitable to the young," "being a tree

* Mass. Hist. Coll., First Series, Vol. IX. p. 46.

† Ibid., Second Series, Vol. VII. p. 12.

of knowledge, so laden with fruit, that he stooped for the very children to pick off the apples, ready to drop into their mouths."*

In his old age Mr. Rogers entertained very melancholy anticipations concerning the degeneracy of the times. "I tremble to think," he writes to his brother, "what will become of the glorious work we have begun, when the ancients shall be gathered unto their fathers. I fear grace and blessing will die with them. We grow worldly everywhere. Methinks I see little godliness, but all in a hurry about the world; every one for himself, little care of the public good."†

Mr. Rogers was distinguished for his piety and zeal. In the latter part of his life he was subjected to great suffering, and died, after a lingering illness, in January, 1661. His last will, dated in April, 1660, is an extraordinary document, and contains an outline of his life and fortunes. Among the blessings he enumerates as causes of thankfulness, are his being "called to be a minister of the Gospel, the most glorious calling in the world, in the time of the hottest persecution of that bloody hierarchy, and that, being enlightened concerning the evil and the snare of subscriptions and ceremonies, I was mercifully prevented from betaking myself, as I was advised, to the practice of physic; which," he adds, "although it be a good and necessary calling, I have observed that the most, through their corruptions, have made to themselves the very temptations to covetousness." The will then proceeds with a sketch of his life, until, "being suspended for refusing to read that accursed book, that allowed sports on God's holy Sabbath, I

* Magnalia, Book III. chap. 13. § 9.

† Ibid., § 13.

was driven into New England, to seek that rest and comfort in the way of the churches here, which I believe to be, according to the present light that God hath given, the purest in the whole world."

"Now," he continues, "age and infirmities calling upon me to look daily for my change, I profess myself to have lived and to die an unfeigned hater of all the base opinions of the Anabaptists and Antinomians, and of all other frantic dotages of the times that spring from them. I do also protest against all the evil fashions and devices of this age, both in apparel and that general disguisement of long, ruffian-like hair, a custom most generally taken up at that time, when the grave and modest wearing of hair was a part of the reproach of Christ, as appeared by the term 'round head,' and was carried on with a high hand, notwithstanding its known offence to so many godly persons."

After this preamble, and bequests to his wife and other relatives and friends, he gives all his Latin and some English books to Harvard College; and to the town of Rowley several large portions of his real estate, upon condition, that they should maintain two teaching elders in the church for ever; and, if they failed in providing themselves at any time within four years after any vacancy, with two teaching elders, then "the abovesaid housing and lands shall be to the use of Harvard College."

After 1696 the church and town of Rowley continued more than four years without two teaching elders, and the Corporation of the College took possession of the lands, and after some trials at law maintained their title. The property thus acquired was sold in 1735, and the proceeds vested in an estate in Waltham, which has recently been sold for five thousand dollars.

Thomas Cotton.

Of the transatlantic benefactors of the College at this period, next to Thomas Hollis, the Rev. Thomas Cotton of London was the most distinguished. His gift, in 1724, of four hundred pounds sterling, transmitted through the agency of Mr. Hollis to Mr. Colman, to be appropriated at his discretion,* for the benefit of the College, has been already noticed. In a letter dated on the 26th November, 1726,† his approval of the application of that donation is expressed. In February, 1727, he added another gift of one hundred pounds sterling, from himself and Bridget his wife, directing its income to be appropriated to the "augmentation of the President's salary for the time being."‡

The Rev. Thomas Cotton was born in 1653, at Workley, a village in Yorkshire, England, and educated at the University of Edinburgh, from which he received a degree of Master of Arts. After preaching for a short time with great acceptance in Liverpool, being prevented from farther exercising his talents in the ministry by the persecution against non-conformists, he passed several years in travelling through Europe. On his return to England he had great offers made to him, if he would join the national church. But, "upon the maturest consideration, he chose to take his lot with the Protestant Dissenters."

He soon after married a lady of good family, who

* See above, p. 402.

† Preserved among Judge Sewall's Papers.

‡ Receipt of Treasurer Hutchinson, among Judge Sewall's Papers.

CHAPTER XIX.

had lately come from New England, being the granddaughter of Lord Lisle, and the daughter of Leonard Hoar, President of Harvard College. To this connexion may be attributed the deep interest taken by Mr. Cotton in the seminary, and to the harmony of its catholic and liberal spirit with his own.

He was settled in London, and in 1709 he suffered great pecuniary loss by a mob, excited by Dr. Sacheverell's trial, for which he could obtain no redress. Upon the revival of the disputes in the west of England, in 1718, relating to the doctrine of the Trinity, and the subsequent transactions which led to the famous synod in Salters' Hall, he became one of the non-subscribing ministers, and received, on account of his liberality and catholicism, very unkind and censorious treatment. He strongly maintained that great Protestant principle, the right of private judgment, and was an enemy to all needless subscriptions to human forms in matters of religion. When some of the Dissenters used him ill on this account, and discovered an intolerant disposition towards one another, he used to say, "they had not seen the dragoonings and persecutions to make all of one way, in France, as he had done," intimating, that, if they had, they would be more candid towards each other. The self-command, which he thus evinced, caused him to be respected and esteemed by those who continued to differ from him He died in 1730, at the age of seventy-seven.*

Hollis.

At this period the name of Hollis stands preeminent on the records of the College, for active endeavours to

* Wilson's History of the Dissenting Churches, Vol. IV. p. 376.

promote its prosperity, and an uninterrupted succession of judicious benefactions.

CHAPTER XIX.

Thomas Hollis.

The earliest donations of Thomas Hollis have been already the subject of notice,* and other evidences of his noble and faithful spirit, justly denominated "unparalleled and unceasing munificence,"† will be adduced hereafter in connexion with the Hollis Professorship of Mathematics. But it is due to the number and character of his benefactions, and to their happy influence in exciting other individuals to like acts of bounty, to relate such circumstances of his life, as are not elsewhere recorded in this work.

Thomas Hollis, the father of our benefactor, was born in the year 1634, and died in 1718, at the age of eighty-four. In his social and religious affections, and in the spirit which characterized his benevolence, we see the archetype of those qualities which distinguished his son, "not delaying doing good till his death," "not confining his charity to a party," "living frugally, that he might have wherewith more extensively to express his goodness," "in various methods being publicly useful, by distributing books to encourage religion and virtue, by promoting schools for the instruction of the poor, by erecting and founding two churches, an almshouse, and two schools, contributing liberally to their maintenance during life, and bequeathing for their encouragement at his death." Such is the character of his virtues drawn by a contemporary.‡ His son caught and wore the paternal mantle with a ready and enduring spirit. The bene-

* See above, pp. 186, 230.

† Treasurer White's Letter to President Leverett, June 10th, 1721.

‡ The Rev. Jeremiah Hunt's Sermon occasioned by the Death of Thomas Hollis, p. 33. London, 1718.

factions of Thomas Hollis to Harvard College, commenced the year succeeding his father's death. Being then about sixty years of age, he had quitted business, and lived in the vicinity of London in retirement, frugally but hospitably. Regarding himself as an almoner of Providence, and his wealth as a trust, he constantly sought objects of just and useful charities. His appointment as trustee of the legacy of Robert Thorner to Harvard College,* first turned his thoughts to this institution; and, once fixed, they were never afterwards withdrawn. The interest he took in its prosperity was general, constant, and unwavering. Scarcely a ship sailed from London, during the last ten years of his life, without bearing some evidence of his affection and liberality. In addition to his greater bounties, he was in the practice of transmitting, almost every year, trunks of books, generally well selected and valuable, with directions to his correspondent, Dr. Colman, "to examine them, take out for the College such as its library had not already, and to give the rest to specified individuals, or to such young ministers, who may need and make a good use of them."† His zeal for the increase of the College library was intense. He contributed to it liberally himself, and was urgent in soliciting his friends for their assistance. Through his instrumentality the College received donations of books from Isaac Watts, Daniel Neal, William Harris, John Hollis, and others. He first suggested to the Corporation the want of a catalogue, which, he writes,‡ if he possessed, he should be able materially to serve

* See above, p. 231.

† Letter, January 14th, 1721

‡ February 2d, and September 1st, 1722.

the College, since many were deterred from sending books, through fear that they might be already in the library. The Corporation immediately ordered a catalogue to be prepared, and, when it was completed, sent eight dozen copies to Hollis for distribution, who, in a postscript to a letter acknowledging the receipt, gives the names of the persons to whom they had been sent. Finding, on perusing the catalogue, that "numbers of useful books fitting for such a library were wanting," he proposed to the Company for the Propagation of the Gospel in New England, of which he was a member, to apply a hundred pounds sterling for the "valuable purpose of supplying those books." "I have read over the charter," he said to that society, "and I think you may. You send books to the Indians, you pay masters and ministers to instruct them, you send out orders to seek out Indian youth fitting to send to College at the Corporation's expense. I argue, How shall youth be instructed, if such books as are necessary are wanting in the library?"* This proposition was not successful. And it appears by a subsequent letter, that he adopted a course which others could not obstruct. "I forward you," he writes, "about a hundred pounds sterling, in books, for your library; there is room to lay out five hundred pounds sterling more, to furnish it well for a public library."†

About this time he calls for additional catalogues of the College library, that "I may know what you most want;" and adds, "If some of your New England merchants had the good of your College at heart, you might have a great number of books sent

* Letter, May 16th, 1724.

† Letter, August 1st, 1724.

to you in a little time." By this letter it appears, that the spirit of misrepresenting the state of the pecuniary resources of the College, was of an earlier origin than our own times; for he writes, "A person in my neighbourhood has discouraged one I expected a present from, by telling him how rich and flourishing you are, to buy books yourselves, if you want them. I have been discoursing the great bookseller, Mr. Guy, for some valuable books, and to settle a Professor of Mathematics among you, which I also discoursed him upon, with some expectation; but he died after a short indisposition, and that motion is sunk."*

His zeal and friendship was not limited to contributing himself, and soliciting donations for the library from others. They extended to its care and management. In June, 1725, he thus writes to Colman; "Your library is reckoned here to be ill managed, by the account I have of some that know it. You want seats to sit and read, and chairs to your valuable books, like our Bodleian Library, or Sion College, in London. You know their methods, which are approved, but do not imitate them. You let your books be taken at pleasure, to men's houses, and many are lost; your boyish students take them to their chambers, and tear out pictures and maps to adorn their walls. Such things are not good. If you want room for modern books, it is easy to remove the less useful into a more remote place, *but not to sell any; they are devoted.* Your goodness will excuse me, if I hint to you what I think faulty, if you are convinced my hints are just. Your own prudence will rectify what is amiss as far as you can."

* Letter, January 6th, 1725.

The views of Hollis concerning the nature of the works were as wise and liberal as was the spirit in which he bestowed them. The Corporation had written to him "about exchanging Bayle's French Dictionary for an English one." "That set of books," he replies, "are very valuable. It is very easy for one versed in Latin to read French. Our students, in London, who sincerely endeavour after knowledge, easily attain to read French. However, upon your notice, I may discourage any more French books by my hand, though I should think such ought to be esteemed in a public library. Mr. Hunt tells me, that Bayle's Dictionary in French is worth two in English. He blames me for sending Montfaucon's Antiquities in English; he would have had the French sent you. But, according to your remark upon Bayle, I perceive you like what you have best, as it is in English." *

In the same spirit, writing of his "expectation of sending out another parcel of books," he adds, "If there happen to be some books not quite orthodox, in search after truth with an honest design, don't be afraid of them. A public library ought to be furnished, if it can, with *con* as well as *pro*, that students may read, try, judge; see for themselves, and believe upon argument and just reasonings of the Scriptures. 'Thus saith Aristotle,' 'Thus saith Calvin,' will not now pass for proof in our London disputations."

Hollis took an affectionate interest in whatever affected the College or the Province. In consequence of the uncertain foundations of the charter, frequent suggestions were made during the administration of

* Letter, January 6th, 1724.

Leverett concerning applying, in behalf of the College, to the crown for a charter. Among others the opinion of Hollis was asked concerning its expediency. He replied; "I am not capable of advising you about the success of a new charter. If you resolve to attempt it, your Governor Shute and Mr. Barrington, his brother, can best advise you in it. But this I believe, if you come over, there will be needful a long purse and a large degree of patience." *

The importance of a learned ministry was not, at that period, generally recognised by the Baptist Church; and the fairness of Mr. Hollis's mind is evinced by the freedom with which he acknowledges the deficiency, in this respect, of those of his persuasion, and his anxiety that their wants should be supplied. It is also highly honorable to him, as it shows that he was in advance of those with whom he was united in faith. In January, 1721, he thus writes concerning the son of a Baptist, who had been recommended for education at Harvard College. "It is a pleasure to me, because so rare in England or elsewhere, Baptists devoting their children to the ministry and qualifying them for it, by training them up in arts and sciences. I would encourage it as a method to correct mean and ignorant explications and applications of Scripture, attended with a little enthusiasm too often, which narrows that catholic charity among all Christians, recommended by the apostles of our Lord Jesus."

In the same spirit he writes in a subsequent letter, "I should rejoice to see or hear your College was well furnished with Professors in every science, over and above your resident Fellows or Tutors, that young

* Letter, August 18th, 1722.

students might be completely instructed in the ministry, and our ministers at London encourage the sending such like youth so designed, to Harvard College, instead of Leyden or Utrecht, our present practice, which would bring some money or money worth into New England, and perhaps, notwithstanding the charge of the voyage, would be as easy an expense as they are now at in Holland.

"I have given some intimations to the Baptist churches in Pennsylvania and the Jerseys of my design in your College for promoting learning. They have many churches and preachers among them, by the accounts sent me; but I find not one preacher among them that understands the languages. If any from those parts should now, or hereafter, make application to your College, I beseech the College to show kindness to such, and stretch their charity a little. It is what I wish the Baptists would do, though I have no great expectation; as what I think would be for the advantage of the Christian faith, especially while there are so many Quakers among them."

The interest Hollis took in Harvard College led him to watch with attention the political relations of the Province and Great Britain, and to keep his correspondent, Colman, informed of the prevalent opinion in the parent State in respect of the conduct of the Colony. Governor Shute, tired and indignant at the nature and violence of the opposition made to his administration by the House of Representatives of the Province, had suddenly and secretly sailed * for England, to carry his complaints personally to the foot of the throne. He was followed immediately by

* See above, p. 307.

CHAPTER XIX. Elisha Cooke, the leader of the popular party, who was sent out by the legislature as agent of the Province to counteract the representations of Governor Shute.

Hollis entertained very favorable views of the character of Shute, whom he represents as faithful in his endeavours to serve New England, and as willing to return, if he can do it with honor, and be suitably maintained in his government.* He laments the party divisions, which then distracted the councils of Massachusetts, and which he deprecates, as driving the Province into the hands of men, "whose resentments will be found cruel." "You have enemies," he adds, "in London and at court, who greatly aggravate your faults, and would rejoice in the ruin of your civil and religious liberties, and who say, that some of your actions are high treason."† "Boston is represented as though in actual rebellion, and some speak of sending over regular troops to keep you in subjection."‡ His statements concerning the feeling towards the Province, among certain parties in Great Britain, are supported by the complete triumph of Shute, on the hearing of his memorial before the Lords of the Committee of the Privy Council, who, after applauding his zeal and probity, declared that he had made good his charge against the House of Representatives, of "invading and encroaching on your Majesty's prerogative," and intimated that, if the explanatory charter of the Province, which they recommended, should not be accepted by the House of Representatives, "*further provision may be necessary to support and preserve*

* Letter, May 10th, 1723. † September 5th, 1723.
‡ July, 1724.

your Majesty's just authority in that Province, and to prevent such presumptuous invasion for the future."*

Hollis, who regarded the power of the crown with the loyalty of an Englishman, and New England with the affection of a friend, urges upon his correspondents to promote submission, the disannulling of all offensive acts, asking pardon of the King, and promising more regular proceedings in future, as the only mode of preserving the provincial charter.

The advice was not suited to the temper of those whom it was intended to influence, or to the state of the times. His letters to Mr. Colman are honorable and continuous testimonies to the action of a generous mind, excited solely by a desire to do good. The disinterested zeal, the earnest, active, and undeviating affection, exhibited by Thomas Hollis for the service of the College, justly render his name dear to the sons of Harvard, and entitle him for ever to their grateful remembrance.

John Hollis.

John Hollis made several donations to the College, and, in the year 1724, contributed sixty-five pounds sterling, in books, for the library. He was an active and successful merchant in London, the brother and partner in business of Thomas Hollis. Both were actuated by a kindred spirit of benevolence, but the munificence of John Hollis was controlled by considerations of duty to a family of eight children.

Nathaniel Hollis.

Nathaniel Hollis, the youngest of these three brothers, although possessed of an inferior estate, also extended a vigorous hand in aid of Harvard College. He transmitted, in 1733, three hundred and fifty

* See the Report of the Lords' Committee upon Governor Shute's Memorial, June 1st, 1725.

CHAPTER XIX.

pounds sterling, for the establishment of two scholarships in the College, to be subjected to the general rules and provisions established by his elder brother, Thomas Hollis, for the ten scholarships he founded.

Thomas Hollis.

Thomas Hollis, the son of Nathaniel Hollis, was the favorite of the great benefactor of Harvard College, whose name he bore, and became, in 1731, the heir of his whole estate. He survived his uncle only four years; but during that short period he diligently followed his example, and in 1732 accompanied his father's donation of three hundred and fifty pounds, with a gift from himself, of seven hundred pounds, with orders to have it "placed out on good security, and that twenty pounds be added to the salaries of each of the two Professors on my uncle's foundation for ever, towards their more comfortable subsistence."* By this noble benefaction the Corporation were enabled to raise the salaries of the Hollis professorships from eighty pounds, as established by the founder, to one hundred pounds per annum.† This donation was not the only evidence given by Thomas Hollis, of inheriting, with the estate of his uncle, his liberal disposition and affection for the College. In July, 1732, he transmitted "a sphere, a newly-invented machine, called an Orrery, and a double microscope;" and in 1733 he made a donation to the library, of a valuable collection of books. This gift closed the bounties of two generations of the Hollis family to Harvard College. The total amount of their munificence exceeded six thousand pounds currency of Massachusetts, which, considering the value of money at that period, and the disinterested spirit by which

* Hollis's Book, p. 26. † Memoirs of Thomas Brand Hollis.

their charities were prompted, constitutes one of the most remarkable instances of continued benevolence upon record. Thomas Hollis died in 1735, his father in 1738, and their fortunes concentrated upon his son, who bore his name. The bounties of the other branches of the Hollis family will be mentioned in connexion with the succeeding period of the history of the College.

The Diaries of Leverett and Wadsworth, and the records of the Corporation and of the College Faculty, contain many, though incomplete accounts of the required exercises, studies, discipline, and customs of the College at this period.

Previous to the accession of Leverett to the presidency, the practice of obliging the undergraduates to read portions of the Scriptures from Latin or English into Greek, at morning and evening service, had been discontinued. But in January and May, 1708, this "ancient and laudable practice was revived" by the Corporation.* At morning prayers all the undergraduates were ordered, beginning with the youngest, to read a verse out of the Old Testament from the Hebrew into Greek, except the Freshmen, who were permitted to use their English Bibles in this exercise; and, at evening service, to read from the New Testament out of the English or Latin translation into Greek, whenever the President performed this service in the Hall.†

Early in the presidency of Wadsworth this exercise was again discontinued, and ordered to be performed by the classes at the chambers of their respective tutors.

* Leverett's Diary, pp. 12, 13.
† Neal's History of New England, Vol. I. p. 203.

The morning service began with a short prayer; then a chapter of the Old Testament was read, which the President expounded, and concluded with prayer. The evening service was the same, except that the chapter read was from the New Testament, and on Saturday a psalm was sung in the Hall. On Sunday exposition was omitted; a psalm was sung morning and evening; and one of the scholars, in course, was called upon to repeat, in the evening, the sermons preached on that day. On the Sabbath, public worship was attended in the parish church, where the undergraduates occupied the front gallery; and none were excused on account of difference in religious sentiment.

President Wadsworth in his Diary states, that he expounded the Scriptures, once eleven, and sometimes eight or nine times, in the course of a week. The President's duty embraced these exercises, general inspection of the conduct and morals of the students, presiding at the meetings of the Corporation and immediate government, recording their proceedings, and attending the meetings of the Overseers. He was occasionally present at the weekly declamations and public disputations, and then acted as moderator; an office, which, in his absence, was filled by one of the Tutors.

The College course occupied four years, and the undergraduates were divided and distinguished as at present, into four classes, Senior Sophisters, Junior Sophisters, Sophomores, and Freshmen. The Freshman class were servitors to the whole College out of study hours, to go on errands. Every student, on admission, was required to copy out and subscribe the College laws.

The regular exercises are thus stated in an official report, made in 1726, by Tutors Flynt, Welsteed, and Prince.

"1. While the students are Freshmen, they commonly recite the Grammars, and with them a recitation in Tully, Virgil, and the Greek Testament, on Mondays, Tuesdays, Wednesdays, and Thursdays, in the morning and forenoon; on Friday morning Dugard's or Farnaby's Rhetoric, and on Saturday morning the Greek Catechism; and, towards the latter end of the year, they dispute on Ramus's Definitions, Mondays and Tuesdays in the forenoon.

"2. The Sophomores recite Burgersdicius's Logic, and a manuscript called New Logic, in the mornings and forenoons; and towards the latter end of the year Heereboord's Meletemata, and dispute Mondays and Tuesdays in the forenoon, continuing also to recite the classic authors, with Logic and Natural Philosophy; on Saturday mornings they recite Wollebius's Divinity.

"3. The Junior Sophisters recite Heereboord's Meletemata, Mr. Morton's Physics, More's Ethics, Geography, Metaphysics, in the mornings and forenoons; Wollebius on Saturday morning; and dispute Mondays and Tuesdays in the forenoons.

"4. The Senior Sophisters, besides Arithmetic, recite Allsted's Geometry, Gassendus's Astronomy, in the morning; go over the Arts towards the latter end of the year, Ames's Medulla on Saturdays, and dispute once a week."*

By a vote of the Overseers, "all who had actually studies at College and resided there, were ordered to

* Wadsworth's Diary, p. 27.

be in commons, except waiters, transient preachers, and such whose bodily infirmities the President and major part of the Tutors should think would not admit of it."* The Tutors were also required to attend "in the Hall at meal times, to prevent disorders."

All the students, except the freshmen, were obliged to attend, four days in the week, the exercises of Judah Monis, a converted Jew, who was instructor in Hebrew, unless specially exempted. Every student was to have a Hebrew Bible or Psalter, and a Hebrew Lexicon, and the prescribed exercises were as follows; "One exercise in a week shall be the writing the Hebrew and Rabbinical, the rest shall be in this gradual method. 1. Copying the grammar and reading. 2. Reciting it and reading. 3. Construing. 4. Parsing. 5. Translating. 6. Composing. 7. Reading without points."†

The discipline of the College was enforced and sanctioned by daily visits of the Tutors to the chambers of the students, fines, admonition, confession in the Hall, publicly asking pardon, degradation to the bottom of the class, striking the name from the College lists, and expulsion, according to the nature and aggravation of the offence. The manner in which this last punishment was inflicted is thus minutely stated by President Leverett.‡ "In the College Hall the President, after morning prayers, the Fellows, Masters of Art, and the several classes of undergraduates being present, after a full opening of the crimes of the delinquents, a pathetic admonition of them, and solemn obtestation and caution to the scholars, pronounced

* Wadsworth's Diary, p. 21.

† Leverett's Diary, p. 226.

‡ Diary, p. 96.

the sentence of expulsion, ordered their names to be rent off the tables, and them to depart the Hall."

Mr. Flynt, in his commonplace-book, thus records an instance of College punishment for stealing poultry.

"Nov. 4th, 1717. Three scholars were publicly admonished for thievery, and one degraded below five in his class, because he had been before publicly admonished for card-playing. They were ordered by the President into the middle of the Hall (while two others, concealers of the theft, were ordered to stand up in their places, and spoken to there). The crime they were charged with was first declared, and then laid open as against the law of God and the House, and they were admonished to consider the nature and tendency of it, with its aggravations; and all, with them, were warned to take heed and regulate themselves, so that they might not be in danger of so doing for the future; and those, who consented to the theft, were admonished to beware, lest God tear them in pieces according to the text. They were then fined, and ordered to make restitution twofold for each theft."

The Diary of President Leverett, of the 20th of March, 1714, contains an interesting account of the effects of the College discipline upon a student belonging to one of the native tribes, which deserves to be recorded as a tribute to his character. Larnel, an Indian student belonging to the Junior Sophister class, had been guilty of some offence, for which he had been dismissed from the College. "He remained," says President Leverett, "a considerable time at Boston, in a state of penance. He presented his confession to Mr. Pemberton, who thereupon became his intercessor, and in his letter to the President expresses himself thus; 'This comes by Larnel, who brings a confession as good as Austin's, and I am charitably disposed to hope it flows from a like spirit of penitence.' In the public reading of his confession, the flowing of his passions were extraordinarily timed, and his expressions accented, and most peculiarly and emphatically those of the grace of God to him; which indeed did give a peculiar grace to the performance itself, and raised, I believe, a charity in some, that had very little I am sure, and ratified wonderfully that which I had conceived of him. Having made his public confession, he was restored to his standing in the College." *

On the 22d of the ensuing July, Larnel died, and was buried in Boston. "He was," says Leverett, "about twenty years old, an acute grammarian, an extraordinary Latin poet, and a good Greek one."†

It was the custom, during the presidency of Wadsworth, on Commencement day, for the Governor of the Province to come from Boston through Roxbury, often by the way of Watertown, attended by his body guards, and to arrive at the College about ten or eleven o'clock in the morning. A procession was then formed of the Corporation, Overseers, magistrates, ministers, and invited gentlemen, and immediately moved from Harvard Hall to the Congregational church. The exercises of the day began with a short prayer by the President; a salutatory oration in Latin, by one of the graduating class, succeeded; then disputations on theses or questions in Logic, Ethics, and Natural Philosophy commenced. These were generally three, and were printed, and distributed on

* Leverett's Diary, p. 88.

† Ibid., p. 89.

Commencement day. Each question was maintained and defended by a respondent, and every member of the graduating class, the respondents and orators alone excepted, was obliged to adduce publicly at least one opposing argument. When the disputation terminated, one of the candidates pronounced a Latin "gratulatory oration." The graduating class were then called, and, after asking leave of the Governor and Overseers, the President conferred the Bachelors' degree, by delivering a book to the candidates (who came forward successively in parties of four), and pronouncing a form of words in Latin. An adjournment then took place to dinner, in Harvard Hall; from thence the procession returned to the church, and, after the Masters' disputations, usually three in number, were finished, their degrees were conferred, with the same general forms as those of the Bachelors. An occasional address was then made by the President. A Latin valedictory oration by one of the Masters succeeded, and the exercises concluded with a prayer by the President. The students then escorted the Governor, Corporation, and Overseers, in procession, to the President's house, and thus closed the ceremonies of the day.

In July, 1728, when William Burnett arrived as Governor of Massachusetts, he was "waited upon by the Corporation, to salute him, wish him assistance and prosperity in his government, to ask his smiles on the College, and the honor of waiting upon him there." On the 21st of August ensuing he accordingly visited the College, accompanied from Boston by two members of the Corporation; and, being met by two others, the Professors and Tutors, and Masters of Arts, a mile from the College, he was received by the President and the two remaining members of the Corporation at the library. The Governor was there addressed in Latin by a Senior Bachelor, and made a short answer in the same language; and, after having gone to Tutor Flynt's chamber and "the Mathematical Professor's, where he saw an experiment," he dined, with about fifty other guests, in the library, with the President and Fellows.

The visit of Governor Belcher to the College appears, according to its records, to have been attended with like ceremonies. He was, on the 9th of September, 1730, escorted to Cambridge by "a military troop, then waited on by two companies of foot." When he arrived at the College, after "having been awhile at Mr. Flynt's chamber, the bell tolled, and the scholars assembled in the Hall, into which the Governor and Corporation having entered, Mr. Hobby made a Latin oration, and his Excellency made a very handsome answer in Latin. This done, and his Excellency the Governor, his Majesty's Council, the Tutors, Professors, and sundry gentlemen, who came on the occasion, dined together in the library, with the Corporation."

These forms and ceremonies of the last, and of the preceding age, are interesting as characteristic of the customs and manners of Massachusetts under the Colonial and Provincial governments.

APPENDIX.

APPENDIX.

No. I.—See pp. 11, 188.

EARLY RECORDS OF THE COLLEGE.—HARVARD'S LEGACY.

APPENDIX, No. I.

Early records of the College.

THE ancient records of the College are defective, and leave in obscurity points of its early history, on which questions have arisen. Some account of those records, and of their present state, may properly be given here; to which will be added such portions of their contents as have been the occasion of doubts, and such contemporaneous evidence as may enable the friends of the College to form for themselves a judgment concerning them.

The early records of the College, which embrace the occurrences of the first century after its foundation, are contained in three books, denominated College Books, Nos. I., III., and IV. There is none extant denominated No. II.; but that which is now called No. I., and by President Wadsworth is referred to as such, is sometimes in later College Books referred to as No. II.

College Book, No. I., is a collection of old accounts, records, and papers. One of its earliest entries is in the handwriting of President Hoar, and has the signature L. H., whence it has been conjectured, that this book was collected and bound together in his time, or about 1673. Its earliest pages contain only old accounts of repairs and expenditures on College chambers and studies, of the date of 1640 and 1644.

On the 23d page of this collection a double paging commences, showing, unquestionably, that page 23 was page 1 of a more ancient book. This page contains an account of "the studies in Harvard College, with their incomes and quarterly rents." The 25th, or 3d page of the ancient book, contains that record of a "meeting of the Governors of Harvard College," of a part of which there is a *fac-simile* opposite to the 48th page of this volume.

Page 28th, anciently the 5th, contains the account of the re-

APPENDIX, No. I.

Early records of the College.

ceipts and expenditures of Samuel Shepard, who succeeded Nathaniel Eaton as superintendent of the building then erecting for the College.

In page 33d, anciently the 9th, the account of Tyng, the Treasurer of the country in 1644, with Harvard College, is also preserved.

The residue of the book contains the early laws, orders, forms of admission, records of gifts, deeds, proceedings of the Corporation, and a few proceedings of the Overseers. All these are unquestionably original records, as indicated by the variety and nature of the handwriting.

The last regular entry in this book is in the handwriting of President Mather, and is dated July 8th, 1686.

At this period the College Book, No. IV., being opened, No. I. ceased to record the proceedings of the Corporation. On its blank leaves had been inserted, in early times, a list of the books given to the College by John Harvard, John Winthrop, and Sir Kenelm Digby, and in later times were added, a copy of the code of College laws, passed in 1735, and a catalogue of the names of the graduates from 1642 to 1795. This catalogue is thus prefaced in the handwriting of President Wadsworth.

"Nomina Graduatorum. — Having observed that the names of the graduates in Harvard College are not recorded in any of the College Books, I thought such an omission ought not to be continued. Therefore I (Benjamin Wadsworth, President) think meet now, January 23d, 1733-4, to insert in this College Book the following catalogue of graduates, printed An. Dom. 1733."

His example was followed by his successors until 1795. It appears conclusively from this entry, that nearly one hundred years had elapsed before any catalogue of graduates was entered in the College Books.

College Book, No. III., is a compilation, consisting chiefly of extracts from College Book, No. I., with some additions. It was probably made by Thomas Danforth, who resided in Cambridge, and was Treasurer of the College from 1650 to 1669, when John Richards was appointed to that office. Danforth then took, by desire of the Overseers, the office of "Steward and Inspector of the economical affairs" of the College, which he held until April, 1682, when Richards sailed for Europe. He then had "all the accounts and papers concerning the College" placed in his hands. These he held until January, 1683. Until this date, Book No. III. is apparently all in his handwriting, with the exception of some marginal insertions in the handwriting of John Leverett, then tutor, afterwards President, in which all entries subsequent to this date appear.

Early records of the College.

This book has therefore no claim to the character of an original record. It commences with a statement of the vote of the General Court in 1636, granting four hundred pounds for the building of the College, of which the account is short and general. Concerning Harvard's legacies its statement is as follows, in p. 1.

"The Rev. Mr. John Harvard, sometime minister of God's word at Charlestown, by his last will and testament, gave towards the erecting the abovesaid School or College, the one moiety or half part of his estate, the said moiety amounting to the sum of seven hundred and twenty-nine pounds, seventeen shillings, and two pence."

This book then narrates, historically, other donations. It also contains the accounts, at large, of Eaton and Dunster, and of the other Treasurers antecedent to 1693, but omits those of Shepard and Tyng. Its regular entries terminate, like those in No. I., with a record of the meeting of the Corporation, dated the 8th of July, 1686.

This book was superseded by College Book, No. IV., after the above date. Its blank leaves were subsequently made the receptacle of forms of diplomas, copies of deeds, and plans of land belonging to the College.

College Book, No. IV., commences with the record of "a meeting of the Honorable President and Council, at Cambridge, July 23d, 1686." This occurred during the short administration of Joseph Dudley. The entries are few antecedent to the charter of the College granted by the first legislature under the Provincial charter of William and Mary. The last of these entries is dated, "Boston, 24th of December, 1691." When the College charter of 1692 was about to be carried into effect, this book, No. IV., was reversed, without changing its denomination, and that charter was inserted at length in the first, formerly the last, page, and the first meeting under it was recorded July 26th, 1692. From this time the records of the Corporation are preserved in this volume, with occasional interruptions, until January, 1708; and after this date they were kept in it by President Leverett, with great care and accuracy, until his death; and subsequently by the successive Presidents, in their own handwriting, until September, 1750, when this volume closes.

The preceding are all the books that have any claim to the

APPENDIX, No. I.

Early records of the College.

character of "early records" of the College. There is a book of recent origin, denominated "Donation Book," which contains "an account of grants, donations, and bequests, to Harvard College from the foundation of that society to the year 1773," to which a second volume has been added, of donations since that period. This is a mere abstract of Books No. I. and No. III., with a few additions, and is stated to be "collected by order of the Corporation."

In Books No. I. and No. III., are contained the accounts of Nathaniel Eaton, Samuel Shepard, and Henry Dunster, the three individuals who acted as agents for the building of the first College, and received and disbursed all its moneys; and also the account of Tyng, the Treasurer of the country, with the College as stated in 1644. From these accounts is derived all that at this day is known officially of the receipts and expenditures of the College during the first eighteen years of its existence, from 1636 to 1654. As they are few, are illustrative of the period, and have been the occasion of doubts concerning the accuracy of some statements relating to the College, made in popular and general histories, it has been deemed proper to insert them here at length, as they stand in the abovementioned records.

The account of Eaton's agency is thus stated in College Book, No. III., p. 2.

"Mr. Nathaniel Eaton was chosen Professor of the said school in the year one thousand six hundred and thirty-seven, to whose care the management of the donations before mentioned were intrusted, for the erecting of such edifices as were meet and necessary for a College, and for his own lodgings; an account of his management whereof is as followeth.

"*Mr. Nathaniel Eaton's Account under his own hand.*

		£.	s.	d.
Imprimis.	The frame in the College yard, and digging the cellar, carriage, and setting up, . .	120	00	0
Item.	Fencing the yard with pales, 6½ feet high, .	30	00	0
"	To the mason, Thomas King, for chimneys, .	6	00	0
"	To the smith, paid for iron casements, . .	2	00	0
"	Part of the frame for an outhouse, . . .	5	00	0
"	Felling, squaring, and loading lumber, to be added,	4	00	0
"	Loading stone and clay for the underpinning, .	1	10	0
"	For thirty apple trees, and setting them, . .	6	00	0
"	For bricks provided and laid in place, . .	3	10	0
"	Paid by me to the carpenter for additions to be made to the frame already raised, besides the £20 received by virtue of a note from yourself to Mr. Allen,	108	00	0

APPENDIX, No. I.

Early records of the College.

Item.	In part payment for lime to be burnt for the College,	1 00 0
"	Unloading the lumber prepared for the addition, .	3 10 0
"	For 250 cedar boards, with the carriage of them,	10 10 0
		£ 301 00 0
	Received of Mr. Allen, . . .	200 00 0
	Remains due, ...	£ 101 00 0"

College Book, No. III., p. 3, after stating, that Nathaniel Eaton, having been convicted of sundry abuses, was, in September, 1639, removed from his trust, proceeds thus; "The charge of carrying on the building begun by Mr. Eaton was then committed to the management of Mr. Samuel Shepard, and the College Book was put into his hands."

Shepard's accounts are preserved in College Book, No. I., p. 5, where they appear as follows.

"*Mr. Samuel Shepard's Account.*

			£. s. d.
1639.	Received	imprimis Cambridge rate, . .	20 00 0
"	"	of the Ferry, ...	50 00 0
"	"	Mr. Sparrawk and Mr. Gourdon, .	55 00 0
"	"	Mr. Willowby, ...	25 00 0
1641.	"	Mr. Angier, corn at 4*s*. per bushel, .	40 00 0
1639.	"	Watertown rate, ...	30 12 0
"	"	Mr. Norton, ...	7 2 8
"	"	in clapboards, ...	1 13 0
"	"	in work of Jo. Friend, ...	7 8 0
"	"	of Mr. Nowell, ...	2 00 0
"	"	Mr. Peters and Mr. Weld, . .	10 00 0
			£ 248 15 8
"	"	Mr. Allen, paid by Goodridge. Tho particulars cannot be produced. .	3 00 0
			£ 251 15 8

Disbursed for the College, as follows.

	£. s. d.
1. Money disbursed by Mr. Eaton, £ 12 10*s*. and to Finch, Eliot, Winter, and Symonds, carpenters, and Goodman Harding, as appears, ...	20 17 4
2. For work and materials for the College, all I received for the Ferry, ...	50 00 0
3. Mr. Sparrawk to the workmen, as appears, . .	55 06 0
Mr. Willowby paid the workmen in commodities as appears,	21 10 0
4. Lost by paying out the corn received at 4*s*. the bushel, and paid out at 2*s*. 8*d*., little at 3*s*., and some at 2*s*. 6*d*. In the whole my old account is but lost £ 9, 8*s*. 9*d*. I doubt it was more, and paid, ...	29 11 3

APPENDIX, No. I.

Early records of the College.

	£. s. d.
5. Paid for carting and other businesses and materials for the College, as appears in particulars,	33 10 4
6. Paid for John Friend by Mr. Norton, £ 3, 10*s*. To other workmen £ 3, 12*s*. 8*d*. In all,	7 2 8
Mr. Nowell paid for lime,	2 00 0
Mr. Dunster discounted with John Friend	10 00 0
	£ 229 17 7

	£. s. d.
Paid Captain Gibbons,	10 10 4
" Mr. Storer for John Friend,	5 3 0
" to Mr. Ford for John Friend,	1 15 0
" to Thomas, the smith,	1 5 6
" to Nash, for meat to the workmen,	2 0 0
" to bricklayers,	1 15 0
" to Mr. Russell for John Friend,	2 2 0
" for Rich, the plasterer,	0 13 0
" for the commodities the workmen had of him,	2 6 0
" to Stetson, for cleaning the house,	0 1 6
" to Mr. Sparrawk,	1 0 0
" to brickmakers,	2 15 0
" to Goodman Goff,	1 18 3
" to Goodman Freem, for hair,	0 2 8
" to John Stedman,	3 0 0
" to Mr. Eldred, for stones,	2 2 6
	£ 38 9 9

Due to him by this account, . . £ 14 11 8

Received a goat, 30*s*., of plantation of Watertown rate, which died; writ on the other side of the said paper as follows.

	£. s. d.
Paid Mr. Weld for Richard Harrington, a plasterer,	3 10 0
Paid him in corn,	0 14 0
Put off Watertown rate, loss,	2 0 0
In another column, thus.	
To a horse and charges to Linn,	0 5 0
To Salem, twice,	0 10 0
At Boston and Charlestown,	1 0 0
	£ 7 19 0"

By the above accounts Shepard disbursed,	229 17 7
	38 9 9
	7 19 0
Total of Shepard's disbursements,	£ 276 6 4
Total of his receipts,	£ 251 15 8

Early records of the College.

In College Book, No. I., p. 9, Tyng's account is thus stated.

"*Mr. Tyng, the Treasurer for the country, has given in the following account.*

Month 3d, 16th day, 1644.	£. d. s.
The country debtor to the College for Mr. Harvard's estate, lent to it, ...	175 . 3 0
Item for insufficient pay made to Mr. Samuel Shepard, which he abates the College, ...	11 8 9
Item for whatever is due to the College of that which was sent by Mr. Weld and Mr. Peters,	
Item, by the country's gift by Court act, held at Boston, 8th of the 7th, 1636. See Register, p. 131. . .	400 0 0
	£ 586 11 9

The country hath paid the College as followeth.

		£. s. d.
1639.	To Mr. Eaton and Mr. Samuel Shepard, by Mr. Bellingham, Treasurer of the Cambridge rate, . .	20 0 0
1640.	To Mr. S. Shepard of Watertown, . .	30 12 0
1641.	To Mr. Shepard from Edmund Angier, of Cambridge rate, ...	40 0 0
	Memorandum. That of this £ 90 12*s.* Mr. Samuel Shepard abates the College, £ 11 8*s.* 9*d.* for insufficiency of pay, so that the College hath but received by his account from the country, £ 79 3*s.* 3*d.*	
1642.	Henry Dunster received £ 9, of which 12*s.* 6*d.* for printing the laws; — for the College received, .	8 7 6
	Item of Cambridge rate, first and last, H. Dunster received, ...	62 12 6
	Mr. Sedgwick £ 40, from Mr. Stoughton £ 16, of them both, ...	56 0 0
	Item, the country has paid Mr. Allen of Hingham, for 4000 of the boards, ...	10 0 0
		£ 227 12 0"

College Book, No. III., pp. 6 and 10, contains the account of the receipts of Mr. Dunster, as follows.

"*A particular account of the contributions made in the space of eight years, for the benefit of the scholars, by the several Colonies of Massachusetts Bay, Plymouth Hartford, and New Haven.*

MASSACHUSETTS.

	£. s. d. f.
Boston, . . .	84 18 7 2
Salem, . . .	0 0 0 0

APPENDIX, No. I.

Early records of the College.

	Charlestown,	37 16 2 0			
	Watertown,	0 0 0 0			
	Lynn,	1 0 0 0			
	Ipswich,	5 0 0 0			
	Dorchester,	4 6 0 0			
	Concord,	8 17 4 0			
	Dedham,	4 6 6 0			
	Cambridge,	2 15 3 2			
	Brantrey,	5 4 3 0			
	Glocester,	0 12 0 0			
	Maulden,	0 12 6 0			
	Rowley,	7 8 7 2			
	Roxbury,	16 18 3 0			
	Springfield,	3 0 0 0			
	Newbury,	1 10 0 0			
	Woburn,	5 13 7 2			
	Sudbury,	1 4 3 0			
	Weymouth,	0 0 0 0			
	Hingham,	0 0 0 0			
	Salisbury,	0 0 0 0			
	Hampton,	0 0 0 0			
	Andover,	0 0 0 0			
	Haverhill,	0 0 0 0	191 3 5 0		
Hartford,					
	Hartford,	30 17 0 0			
	Saybrook,	2 9 0 0			
	Windsor,	5 15 0 0	39 1 0 0		
New Haven,					
	New Haven,	17 11 9 0			
	Millford,	10 15 6 0			
	Stratford,	6 14 0 0	35 1 3 0		
Plymouth,					
	Plymouth town,	4 13 0 0	4 13 0 0		
			£269 18 8 0"		

In College Book No. III., p. 11, the account of Mr. Dunster's disbursements is thus stated.

" *The distribution made of the moneys for the several Colonies now followeth.*

	£.	s.	d.
To Mr. Bulkley and Mr. Downing,	8	18	6
" Samuel Mather, during his fellowship,	9	8	6½
" Samuel Danforth, Reader and Fellow six years,	56	13	8
" Jonathan Mitchell, Fellow three years,	26	0	0
" Comfort Star, Fellow part of two years,	11	0	0

APPENDIX, No. I.

Early records of the College.

	£	s.	d.
To Mr. Samuel Eaton, Fellow two years and a half,	34	7	6
" Urian Oakes,	10	16	0
" John Collins,	18	0	0
" Wigglesworth, Fellow half a year,	4	0	0
" White,	6	0	0
" Elija Corlett,	2	0	0
Sir Ames,	22	8	0½
John Ames,	11	5	3½
Mr. John Brock,	3	7	6½
Mr. Stirk,	2	6	8
Sir Hollett, steward,	2	16	6
Sir Phillips, steward,	6	10	0
Sir Ince,	9	13	4
Bowers,	9	12	0
Thompson,	18	11	6
James, by order from New Haven,	10	7	10½
Six students, for writing for the churches,	2	7	6½
Mr. Jenner's sons,	11	14	8½
	£298	5	2½

"Memorandum. The several donations made to the College during the time Mr. Dunster was President of said College, were by said Mr. Dunster received and distributed according to the appointment of the Overseers, and, on the balance of account by him made at the resignation of his place, said Mr. Dunster was creditor to the College, as appeareth, page 18," in which this subject is thus stated.

"Mr. Dunster's account presented to the College, January 15, 1654, wherein he makes himself debtor £110, 19*s.* 2½*d.* and gives himself credit for £119, 4*s.*"

Beneath the above account in page 18, Book III., is the following record.

"By order of the Overseers, paid to Mrs. Elizabeth Dunster, the relict widow of the abovenamed Henry Dunster, deceased, in full of the balance of account, as above, and for all other demands, by Thomas Danforth, Treasurer, twenty pounds."

Neither the account of Eaton, nor of Shepard, nor of Dunster appears as settled on these books.

From the preceding accounts, it is apparent, that Eaton received from Allen, John Harvard's administrator, £200 0 0 and, if the £20 specified in the 10th item of his account was

APPENDIX, No. I.

Early records of the College.

additional to this sum, he then received also			20 0 0
making a total received by Eaton from Harvard's estate,			220 0 0
That Shepard received from the town-rates of Cambridge and Watertown, or from "the country,"	£ 90 12 0		
from which deduct "insufficient pay," as acknowledged in Tyng's account, .	11 8 9		
	£ 79 3 3		
He received from the Ferry, .	50 0 0		
and from various subscriptions not otherwise appearing in the donation books of the College, ...	122 12 5		
Shepard's receipt, ...			251 15 8
Dunster received from the contributions of the several Colonies as stated in College Book, No. III., p. 10, and which is extracted into Donation Book, Vol. I. p. 6, in exact terms,			269 18 8
Total of the receipts of Eaton, Shepard, and Dunster, ...			£ 741 14 4

In addition to the above the following cash gifts are stated in College Book, No. III., pp. 5, 6, as of the year 1642, and which do not appear in either of the above accounts. They were probably applied to the erection of the College buildings, by whomsoever received. To this object many of them appear to be specifically appropriated, viz.

Henry Pool, ...	10 0 0
Theophilus Eaton, . . .	40 0 0
Richard Russell, ...	9 0 0
Edward Jackson, ...	10 0 0
Mr. Wory, ...	4 0 0
Mr. Parish, merchant, . . .	3 0 0
Mr. Holbrook, ...	22 0 0
Mr. Greenhill, minister of God's word at Stepney,	7 0 0
Mr. George Glover, ...	2 0 0
A person not willing his name should be known,	50 0 0
Willis, merchant at Boston, . . .	7 0 0
Wells, of Roxbury, ...	10 0 0

Early records of the College.

Israel Stoughton, of Dorchester,	5	0	0			
Richard Parker, of Boston, woollen draper,	4	0	0			
John Pratt, of Hartford,	4	0	0			
				187	0	0
Total of all cash receipts by the College, so far as these books and accounts evidence, previous to 1654,				£928	14	4
By the accounts of those agents it appears that Eaton expended,	£301	0	0			
Shepard "	276	6	4			
Dunster "	298	5	2			
				875	11	6

It is sufficiently apparent from the above accounts, that the statement made by Governor Endecott, in 1655, must have been perfectly correct.

It appears by College Book, No. III., that during these first eighteen years, besides these cash donations, there were others, either of specific articles or in money appropriated to other objects than those of the building, viz. £200 by the magistrates in books. — A font of printing letters by Mr. Glover. — £49 and something more by gentlemen in Amsterdam, for furnishing the press with letters. — (" Benefactors to the first font of letters for printing in Cambridge, their names collected by L. H. [Leonard Hoar] in 1674: Major Thomas Clarke, Capt. James Oliver, Capt. Allen, Capt. Lake, Mr. Stoddard, Mr. Freake, Mr. Hues." — *College Book*, No. I. p. 32.) — £20 in utensils, by Mr. Bridges, Mr. Greenhill, and Mr. Glover. — £150 from divers gentlemen and merchants in England, by William Hibbons, Thomas Welde, and Hugh Peters, towards furnishing the Library with books.

There exists no distinct book of records of the Overseers antecedent to Leverett's administration. Their meetings are found occasionally entered in College Books, Nos. I., III., and IV., among those of the Corporation.

The Books denominated " Records of the Overseers," commence with the act of the General Court, passed in December, 1707, reviving the College charter of 1650, and have been kept regularly since that time. They had no official sanction from the Overseers until Nov. 1718, when the following vote passed that board.

" 1718, 12th of November. It was voted, that the votes of the Overseers should be written in a book by themselves, and that the book should be produced at the Overseers' meetings."

APPENDIX, No. I.

HARVARD'S LEGACY. — See p. 11.

Harvard's legacy.

The doubt concerning the amount received from Harvard's bounty arises from the fact, that only two accounts of that period contain any acknowledgment of receipts from that source.

Eaton acknowledges (See above, p. 410 and p. 411).	£220	0	0
and Tyng, the country treasurer (See above, p. 413).	175	3	0
	£395	3	0

This is about half of his estate, in case the whole did not exceed £800.

The contemporaneous statements, which represent his whole estate as double that sum, are the following.

The earliest account of Harvard's legacy is that of Governor Winthrop (Savage's Winthrop, Vol. II. p. 342), who states, that "Mr. Harvard gave to the College about £800." Now as Harvard's bequest was not specific, but only "the half of his estate," this statement by Winthrop must have been grounded on report; for it was made before 1641, and it appears by College Book, No. I., p. 3, that Harvard's estate had not been settled in 1643. A committee was then appointed by the governors of the College to give Mr. Allen an acquittance. This appears to have eventuated in paying over the balance to Tyng, Treasurer of the Colony, who credits the College with £175 3*s*. as received from Harvard's estate, and lent to the country in 1644.

The next statement of the amount of Harvard's legacy is in the Almanac of the Rev. Samuel Danforth for 1648, which states as follows.

"7 m°. 14 day, 1638. John Harvard, Master of Arts, of Emanuel College in Cambridge, deceased, and by will gave the half of his estate (which amounted to about 700 pounds), for the erection of the College." — See Savage's Winthrop, Vol. II. p. 88.

The form of expression here used may imply, that the whole of Harvard's estate was £700.

The next early statement of this legacy is contained in the autobiography of the Rev. Thomas Shepard,* and is in these words.

"The Lord put it into the heart of one Mr. Harvard, who died worth £1600, to give half of his estate to the erecting of the school.

* Edited by the Rev. Nehemiah Adams, in 1832; p. 64.

APPENDIX, No. I.

Harvard's legacy.

This man was a scholar, and pious in his life, and enlarged toward the country, and the good of it, in life and death, but no sooner was this given, but Mr. Eaton (professing valiantly, yet falsely and most deceitfully, the fear of God), did lavish out a great part of it."

Thomas Shepard died in 1649. His work is historical, and written probably from general recollection. Facts are brought together in it without regard to the order of events. Thus the death and legacy of Harvard are mentioned antecedent to the date of October, 1637, which was nearly a year before Harvard's death occurred. What he states may be regarded as the popular opinion at the time his Memoirs were written. Harvard died in September, 1638, and Eaton was dismissed in September, 1639. Eaton acknowledges the receipt of £220, of Allen (Harvard's administrator). That he should have received an additional sum of £400, and thus "lavished" upwards of £600 in the course of one year, should credit only £200, and bring the College in debt £100, is incredible, especially as no intimation of such receipt anywhere appears.

The only specific statement is that contained in College Book, No. III. p. 1, where the moiety of Harvard's estate is stated to have been £779 17*s.* 2*d.**

John Dunton, who wrote in 1686;† Cotton Mather,‡ who wrote in 1696; and the College Donation Book, No. 1, all state the above to be the amount. Hubbard, who wrote about the year 1680, states it at £700. These probably all derived their authority from College Book, No. III.

For all general purposes the statements in this book may well be considered as authentic. But it has been doubted whether, considering the date when it was compiled, its referring to no authority for its statements, and its general historical character, this statement can countervail the presumption arising from the fact, that the only known receipts from Harvard's estate, appearing on any of the College Books, are those of Eaton, amounting to £220, and of Tyng, the College Treasurer, amounting to £175 3*s.*, making in all £395 3*s.*, about one half, supposing the whole estate was "about £800"; and from this farther extraordinary circumstance, that, upon the supposition the half of his estate was "about £800,"

* See above, p. 409.

† Mass. Hist. Coll., Second Series, Vol. II. p. 106.

‡ Magnalia, Vol. IV. p. 1.

APPENDIX, No. I.

so great a sum as nearly £400 should have been received, and no mention of it appear in the accounts of Eaton or Shepard, Dunster or Tyng, or in any other contemporaneous document.*

No. II. — See pp. 21, 183.

INFORMATION GIVEN BY THE CORPORATION AND OVERSEERS TO THE GENERAL COURT, 9 MAY, 1655.

Information to the General Court in 1655.

"May 9th, 1655. A brief information of the present necessities of the College, which the Corporation do desire may, by the concurrence of the Overseers, be presented to the consideration of the General Court, with earnest desires of their speedy and effectual help for supply.

"First. We are indebted to Mr. Dunster, as expended upon account, near £40, notwithstanding that he hath all that we have been able to pay or assign him. Justice and equity requires that this be paid him, being due debt, and apparent upon diligent examination of accounts. Also, besides what is due upon a strict account, that former motion sometimes made by the committee of a hundred pounds to be allowed Mr. Dunster in consideration of his extraordinary pains in raising up and carrying on the College for so many years past. We desire it may be seriously considered, and hope it may make much for the country's honorable discharge in the hearts of all, and perpetual encouragement of their servants in such public works, if it be attended.

"Secondly. The College building, although it be new groundsilled by the help of some free contributions the last year, yet those

* The Honorable James Savage, the learned and laborious commentator on the early history of Massachusetts, has suggested to the author, that the discrepancy between the popular estimate of Harvard's estate and the amount found acknowledged to have been received from it on the books of the College, may have arisen from the circumstance, that Harvard, who had at the time of his death resided only a year in the country, left probably a considerable part of his estate in England, which his administrator was prevented from obtaining, by the distracted state of the times, and the civil wars which ensued. The same suggestion may account for the fact, that no trace of Harvard's will, or of administration granted on his estate, can be found on the public records of the Colony.

APPENDIX, No. II.

Information to the General Court in 1655.

ceasing, and the work of reparation therewith intermitted, it remains in other respects in a very ruinous condition. It is absolute necessity that it be speedily new covered, being not fit for scholars long to abide in as it is. And without such reparation some time this summer both the whole building will decay, and so the former charge about it will be lost, and the scholars will be forced to depart. So that either help must be had therein, or else (we fear) no less than a dissolution of the College will follow. And it is conceived that it will need a hundred pounds to set it in comfortable repair. All the estate the College hath (as appears by the inventory thereof) is only its present buildings, library, a few utensils, with the press, and some parcels of land (none of which can be with any reason or to any benefit sold to help in the premises), and in real revenue about twelve pounds per annum (which is a small pittance to be shared among four Fellows), besides fifteen pounds per annum, which, by the donor's appointment, is for scholarships.

"The steward's stock is indebted for studies, and for diet of former Fellows, and to the Steward's personal estate, and otherwise, near as much as it is.

"Though we have the Ferry, yet what the produce of it will be we have no certainty, and, whatever it be, it had need to go to the Fellows, until there be some other provision for them.

"The revenue of the press (which is but small) must at present be improved for the finishing of the print-house, its continuance in the President's house being (besides other inconveniences), dangerous and hurtful to the edifice thereof.

"The study rents, until December last, were discounted with Mr. Dunster. Since that time they have been inconsiderable. And there are other smaller charges (not here mentioned), more than will be answered by the study rents, though they were more than they be.

"Hence it appears, that the Corporation have nothing under their hands which they can make use of, either for payment of debts or for the repairing of the College.

"There are other things we might mention, for which there is much need of help, as, viz., for some way of maintaining College affairs and servants by public stock, that so the scholars' charges might be less, or their Commons better; provision of utensils wanting in the kitchen and buttery, accommodations for the scholars' tables; also some fitter way of maintenance for the Fellows.

"But we are not willing to trouble or press the General Court, or

APPENDIX, No. II.

Information to the General Court in 1655.

others, with any thing that we can make shift either to bear, or for the time to wrestle through. These two things above mentioned, viz. payment of debts and repairs of the College, are of present absolute necessity; and it cannot be conceived or expected, that particular persons, out of their own estates, much less that those who are (as most of us in the Corporation) without estates, can carry on these things of themselves.

"If this work of the College be thought fit to be upheld and continued (as we hope that considerations of the glory of God, the honorable interest of the country, the good of posterity, and experience of the benefits and blessings thereof, will constrain all men to say it is), then something must effectually be done for help in the premises.

"We are loth to seem burthensome to the country by such motions as these; but the considerations foregoing have called upon us (whom the country have been pleased to employ as their servants in this society) to make this faithful representation of the condition and necessities thereof, that, if any decay or ruin to so good and important a work as this is, should ensue (which we hope and desire may never be), we might not afterwards fall under blame for our silence.

"We confess sundry petitions have been presented to the General Court in the College's behalf heretofore, and we are not so unthankful as not to remember, and acknowledge, that sundry efforts for our help have been used, and that a considerable matter hath been granted for the President's maintenance.

"But we hope all will consider, partly, not so much what hath been said or attempted, as what hath been done, and partly, that the things above mentioned are distinct from that particular of the President's future maintenance, and that unless this, of repairing the College building, be added thereto, the work cannot stand.

"Also, concerning the promised maintenance of the President, we desire it might be clearly settled in some such way as may be comfortable, and that it may be commended to the General Court to take order thereabout."

"The Magistrates desire that their brethren, the Deputies, consider first of this present information. It is a matter that will require serious agitation and speedy action.

"JOHN ENDECOTT, Governor."

"In answer to what hath been represented to this Court by the

Informa-tion to the General Court in 1655.

Overseers of the College, in reference to what is necessary to be done there, the Deputies, understanding that there is due to the College from the country about an hundred and fifty pounds, for which we pay interest, do find it meet that the said £150 be added to the next country rate, and collected by the constables, to be paid to the country treasurer, and by him to the College treasurer, or whom else this Court may or shall appoint, to be improved for the repairing of the College, and to satisfy Mr. Dunster what shall be truly due to him on account, and for an equal distribution of the same upon the several towns. It is ordered, that for this present year there shall be an addition of one fourth part more to the country rate, payable from each town for the use and ends above mentioned. The Deputies have passed this, and desire our honored Magistrates' consent thereto.

"WILLIAM TORREY, Clerk.

"25 3d mo., 1655."

"The Magistrates cannot consent thereto because the £150 was given by the Lady Moulson, and others, for scholarships annually to be maintained there, which this Court cannot alter; and therefore desire their brethren, the Deputies, to consider of some meet way for the repairing of the College, which is at so great hazard.

"The Magistrates desire their brethren, the Deputies, to send answer to their return.

"EDWARD RAWSON, Secretary.

"JOHN ENDECOTT, Governor,
21 June, '55."

No. III. — See pp. 21, 23.

ANSWER TO MR. DUNSTER'S PETITION.

Answer to Dunster's petition.

"In answer to the particulars of Mr. Dunster's petition,* besides what is agreed by the Court, viz. That no petition is to be received after the first week of this Court, followeth, viz.

* President Dunster's petition, to which this document refers, is printed at large in Peirce's History of Harvard University, Appendix, p. 151.

APPENDIX, No. III.

Answer to Dunster's petition.

"1. In answer to that section, figure 1. What extraordinary labor in, about, and concerning the weal of the College, for the space of fourteen years we know of none, but what was the President's duty belonging to his place; unless he can show the particulars of these labors which were extraordinary.

"2. In answer to the second. It is most unreasonable. For he may protract the making up of his accounts some years, and thereby hinder the comfortable being of him who is chosen to the work of the College. What the President can make justly to appear to be his due, it must be paid him with convenient speed.

"3. This Court doth not think it meet, for reasons (whereof Mr. Dunster is not ignorant), and well known to this Court, to grant this part of the petition. What other laudable or liberal calling, besides preaching, and education of youth, is intended, Mr. Dunster is to explain himself.

"4. We see no ground to reverse that vote referring to the examination of the accounts of Mr. Glover's estate. And we judge it necessary, seeing Mr. Dunster made himself administrator, *de facto*, of all that estate, and never presented an inventory of the same to the General Court, in so many years past, that he satisfy all due debts. And therefore judge it unmeet to make Mr. Dunster administrator *de jure*.

"Agreed on by the Magistrates, with further reference to our brethren, the Deputies.

"R. BELLINGHAM, Governor."

No. IV.—See pp. 25, 26, 27.

PRESIDENT CHAUNCY.

See p. 25.

President Chauncy.

"At a meeting of the Overseers, 24, 8th, 1654. It is agreed by the Overseers, that the Rev. Mr. Richard Mather and the Rev. Mr. John Norton speak with the Rev. Mr. Chauncy, and, as they shall see cause, encourage him to accept of an invitation to the presidency of the College, in case the Overseers give him a call thereto.

APPENDIX, No. IV.

President Chauncy.

"The Magistrates having lately consulted with the rest of the Trustees of the College concerning a fit person to be President there, have fixed their thoughts on the Rev. Mr. Chauncy, who, though he is returning to England, yet, if this Court will give him some small addition, by way of encouragement, to the President's stipend, as might be honorable and comfortable, he might be stopped, and therefore they judge it meet to commend it to the consideration of their brethren, the Deputies, in the first place, to declare what they judge meet to allow him in that respect,

"Edward Rawson, Secretary.

"30 Oct., 1654."

At the General Court holden at the time of the above application from the Magistrates (October, 1654), an order was passed, that, "besides the profit of the ferry formerly granted to the College, which shall be continued, there be yearly levied by addition to the country rates, one hundred pounds to be paid by the Treasurer of the country to the College Treasurer for the behoof and maintenance of the President and Fellows, to be distributed between the President and Fellows, according to the determination of the Overseers of the College, and this to continue during the pleasure of the country."

General Court Records, Vol. II. p. 231.

"At a meeting of the Honorable and Reverend Overseers of the College, 2, 9, 1654.

"Mr. Mather and Mr. Norton are desired by the Overseers of the College to tender unto the Rev. Mr. Charles Chauncy the place of President, with the stipend of one hundred pounds per annum, to be paid out of the country treasury, and withal to signify to him, that it is expected and desired, that he forbear to disseminate or publish any tenets concerning the necessity of immersion in baptism, and celebration of the Lord's Supper at evening, or to oppose the received doctrine therein."

"General Court, May 23, 1655.

"The Court doth grant the present President, Mr. Chauncy, five hundred acres of land, free of former grants, and not hindering a plantation, so as he continue in the place three years."

Ibid., Vol. IV. p. 205.

APPENDIX, No. IV.

President Chauncy.

"General Court, May 23, 1655.

"In answer to the petition of Mr. Charles Chauncy, President of Harvard College, the Treasurer is desired to disburse the sum of £30, to furnish his necessary occasions, to be repaid out of the first rents of the ferry."

See p. 26.

"Mr. Chauncy's Petition, 25th 8 mo. '55.

"To the Honored Governor of the Massachusetts, Mr. John Endecott, and the rest of the Honorable Bench and Honorable General Court, the petition of Charles Chauncy, President of Harvard College.

"First of all thankfully acknowledging God's gracious providence in so disposing your hearts to call your petitioner to this place, with promise of your liberal maintenance, allowing him £100 per annum, which also, in regard of the manner of the payment hath been ordered to be amended somewhat at your last session. Yet withal, judging himself bound further to acquaint the Honorable Bench and whole Court with his condition in the particulars following:

"1. That the former allotment and portion of English corn designed to your petitioner at the last session hath been expended for the payment of debts due for necessaries requisite for your petitioner's fitting and supply in the College, with much more afforded by the kindness of the worthy Treasurer, and also the expense of an £100 or thereabout of your petitioner's own estate, since his entrance into this place.

"2. That the residue of the country pay, being Indian corn, will neither pass for food nor clothing.

"3. That if any part thereof by entreaties be put off, twelve pence or eight pence in the bushel must be lost.

"4. That there is no ground belonging to the President to keep any cattle upon, so that neither milk, butter, nor cheese, can be had but by the penny.

"5. That the country's allowance is and must be your petitioner's whole means of subsistence, having no other means of farm or rents which the former President had, and others have, that have any allowance made them by the country.

"6. That what benefit your petitioner may be supposed to receive by the Commencement is hardly sufficient to defray the charges thereof.

"7. That your petitioner's family consists necessarily of ten persons, that must needs be very chargeable.

"8. That the greatness and multitude of College businesses doth require the whole man, and one free from other distractions.

"In regard of all which, though your petitioner be not desirous to put the country to further charge, yet he desires the Honored Bench and Court in their wisdom to provide for him according to the pressing exigency of his condition, to remove his grievances that God may not be dishonored, nor the country blemished, nor your petitioner and his family cast upon temptations, or enforced to look out to alter his condition.

"Your unworthy servant, to my power,

"CHARLES CHAUNCY."

See p. 27.

"President Chauncy's Petition, May 27th, 1663.

"To the Honored Governor of Massachusetts, John Endecott, Esq., with the residue of the Honored Bench of Assistants, and the Honored Court of Deputies.

"The humble petition of Charles Chauncy, President of Harvard College, in Cambridge, as followeth.

"Whereas your petitioner hath continued, with much toil and many grievances and temptations, in the College about eight years; all which time, his family being great, the stipend allowed him by the Honored Court hath been insufficient for his comfortable subsistence, and the maintenance of his family with necessary supplies of food and raiment; for want whereof he hath been forced both to expend his own estate that he brought with him, and is besides by this means run far into debt.

"And in respect that the President hath no fit provision either of land to keep so much as one cow or horse upon, or of habitation to be dry and warm in. Also seeing that there are no Colleges in our English Universities (wherein the petitioner hath continued long), but that the Presidents thereof, beside their yearly stipend, are allowed their diet, with other necessary provisions according to their wants.

"Your petitioner, with all due observance, entreats the Honored Court not to take offence, if necessity constraining, no redress being made of such intolerable grievances and temptations now suggested,

APPENDIX, No. IV.

President Chauncy.

he shall take his liberty upon other opportunities presented to embrace them, though notwithstanding his President's place in the College.

"He desires also, that this petition may not be put by as unseasonable, some other disappointments hindering before; so shall your petitioner be further engaged to pray for the peace of Jerusalem.

"Your Worships' humbly devoted in the Lord,

"CHARLES CHAUNCY."

"June 9th, 1663.

"We conceive the country have done honorably towards the recompense and encouragement of the Petitioner both for annual allowance and grant of land, and that his parity with English Colleges is not pertinent, and as for other things respecting his removal, that it properly belongs to the feoffees of the College, and that it be referred unto them.

"RICHARD RUSSELL.
"EDWARD JOHNSON.
"JOSEPH HILLS."

"The Deputies do not concur with the committee in answer thereunto, but in regard to the urgent necessities of the Petitioner, do judge meet that there be allowed five pounds a quarter out of the country treasury to supply his wants, and this to be and continue during the country's pleasure, with reference to the consent of the Honorable Magistrates hereto.

"WILLIAM TORREY, Clerk.

"June 13th, 1663."

"The Magistrates consent not thereto.

"EDWARD RAWSON, Secretary."

No. V. — See p. 31.

SUBSCRIPTIONS FOR BUILDING HARVARD HALL.

Subscriptions for building Harvard Hall.

The voluntary contributions made on this occasion by the towns in Massachusetts, with the amount subscribed by each, may be found at large in Appendix, No. XXIII.

No. VI. — See p. 34.

PRESIDENT HOAR AND PRESIDENT OAKES.

President Hoar.

Dr. Hoar was elected July 30th, 1672, and inaugurated September 10th, 1672. — *College Book*, No. I. p. 49.

President Oakes.

"September 15th, 1673. At a meeting of the Overseers at the College in Cambridge, Mr. Urian Oakes, Mr. Joseph Brown, and Mr. John Richardson declared that they resigned up their places of Fellows in the College." — *College Book*, No. III. p. 62.

"October 2d, 1673. It was voted, that Mr. Urian Oakes and Mr. Thomas Shepard be requested to continue their assistance to the College as Fellows, according as they were formerly appointed thereto, and that Captain D. Gookin and the President are desired to acquaint them with the mind of the Overseers thereon." — *Ibid.*, p. 62.

"At a meeting of the Honorable and Reverend Overseers of the College, at Boston, December 3d, 1674. The Overseers do commend it to the President and Fellows, now remaining, that they take care speedily to fill up their number, according to their charter, that so their power and privilege, granted them by the General Court, may not be weakened nor abated in any kind. — Taken out of the Old Overseers Book, p. 62." — *Ibid.*, p. 64.

"December 11th, 1674. Present, the President, Mr. Gookin, Sir Thatcher, Mr. Richards. The Rev. Mr. Urian Oakes, Mr. Thomas Shepard, and Increase Mather, chosen Fellows of the College, to fill up the Corporation in its number of seven, which vote the President is to acquaint them with, and to receive their answer in order to their instalment." — *Ibid.*, p. 64.

No answer was given by any one of the above elected persons, until after the resignation of Dr. Hoar, as appears by the following vote and record.

"At a meeting of the Honorable and Reverend Overseers of the College, at Cambridge, 15, 1, 1674-5, Mr. Urian Oakes and Mr. Thomas Shepard being orderly elected Fellows of the College, and presented by the Corporation for their allowance, they were accordingly accepted and entreated to accept that trust.

"Dr. Leonard Hoar made a resignation of his presidency of the College." — *Ibid.*, p. 66.

APPENDIX, No. VI.

President Oakes.

The remaining votes concerning the election of Mr. Oakes are the following.

"At a meeting of the Corporation, 7th April, 1675. Mr. Urian Oakes was desired to give his answer to a former motion of the Overseers to accept of the place of President of the College *pro tempore.*

"In answer whereto he declared a deep sense of his unfitness for the work, yet, considering the present exigency the society was now in, and confiding in the Overseers seasonably to endeavour the settling a fit person for that work, manifesting his willingness to accept of that place for a time, God enabling by health and strength, and so far as his church consented." —*Ibid.*, p. 66.

From this time the records show that he was present and acted as President of the College.

"Overseers' meeting, 27th, 8th, (October) 1675. Mr. Urian Oakes is elected President of Harvard College, and by the Overseers importuned to accept said place and trust." — *Ibid.*, p. 67.

"14, 3d (June) 1677. Mr. John Rogers of Ipswich then chosen President of the College *nemine contradicente.*" — *College Book*, No. I. p. 55; also No. III. p. 67.

"At a meeting of the Corporation at Cambridge, June 30, 1679, voted, That the Worshipful Mr. Stoughton be desired and empowered to provide a President of the College, and that, the Honorable Overseers concurring herewith, the Rev. Mr. Oakes be entreated to write to Mr. Stoughton accordingly in the name of the Corporation." — *College Book*, No. I. p. 55; No. III. p. 69.

"At a Corporation meeting, 2d day, 12 mo. (February) 1679, Mr. Urian Oakes was chosen President of Harvard College, by the unanimous consent of the Fellows of said College, desiring the approbation of the Honorable and Reverend Overseers." — *College Book*, No. I. p. 56; No. III. p. 70.

"February 9th, 1679. The Overseers approve of the choice of the Rev. Mr. Urian Oakes to the office of President in the College, and request the Worshipful William Stoughton, Joseph Dudley, and Peter Bulkley, Esqrs., and the Rev. Mr. John Eliot, and Mr. Increase Mather, to present their desires to Mr. Oakes and the church at Cambridge, for his acceptance of said trust, and their concurrence therein."

"The Rev. Mr. Urian Oakes was installed President of Harvard College by Governor Bradstreet in the College Hall, on the Commencement day in August, 1680." — *College Book*, No. III. p. 71.

Several of the above records are inserted in the margin of College Book, No. III. in the handwriting of John Leverett, afterwards President of the College, and are stated to be from "the Old Overseers' Book," which is now lost.

President Oakes.

No. VII. — See p. 41.

ORIGINAL GRANT OF THE GENERAL COURT.

Original grant of the General Court.

By Tyng, the country Treasurer's account,* it is evident, that the original grant of £ 400 was in 1644 acknowledged to be a debt on account, and that, after the charge of all rates received, a balance of upwards of £ 350 is apparently due. That it had not been paid on the 13th of the ensuing November, appears also by the following vote, passed on that day by the General Court.

"The 13th of the 9th mo. A. 1644. It was ordered that Mr. Dunster, President of the College at Cambridge, shall have £ 150 assigned to him (to be gathered by the Treasurer for the College) out of the money due for the children sent out of England, to be expended for a house to be built for the said President, in part of the £ 400 promised unto him for his use, to belong to the College."

That no part of the above £ 150 was ever paid, is concluded from this, that Mr. Dunster, in his petition in November, 1654, to the legislature, speaks of the President's house as "the place, *which, upon very damageful conditions to myself, out of love to the College, I have builded.*" Now if the General Court had paid towards his house so great a sum, it can hardly be imagined he would have failed to notice it, or would have ventured to take all the credit of building it to himself. Besides, it appears by the vote, that this £ 150 was to be paid out of a particular fund, viz. "*the money due for the children sent out of England,*" and from their agent's (Mr. Welde's) account. This was not settled until 1651, as appears by the language of a committee of the General Court. "The committee had little benefit from those moneys, the entire balance of Welde's account not exceeding £ 200; which, after payments of sums enumerated below, subscribed and included in that account,

* See above, p. 455.

APPENDIX, No. VII.

Original grant of the General Court.

as belonging to the College, did not leave but little more than £40 received on account of the children, and probably, considering other deductions, did not leave any thing."

The above appears on a settlement of Welde's account, made on the 25th of the 8th month, 1651, and is signed,

Increase Nowell.
William Tyng.
Edward Jackson.
Nathaniel Duncan.

The enumerated sums are,

Lady Moulson's gift for the College, . .	£100	0	0
Mr. Bridge's " . .	50	0	0
Other small gifts " . .	12	16	4
	£162	16	4

From no evidence now known does it appear, that the sum of £400 was ever paid over specifically to the College, so as to constitute a part of its available funds, except to the amount stated in Tyng's account.

The General Court probably deemed their obligations sufficiently performed by the grant of the Ferry between Charlestown and Boston, and by the annual grants made for the support of the President.

No. VIII. — See p. 49.

COLLEGE SEAL.

College seal.

This conjecture is founded on the following records, the only ones extant concerning the College seal and arms except that stated in page 48.

"At a Corporation meeting at Harvard College, June 11th, 1694.

"Memorandum. That Mr. Newman's proposal about procuring the College arms at Bilboa is left to the President's consideration and determination." — *College Book*, No. IV. p. 3.

That the College arms were at this time procured, and from Mr. Newman, is proved by a record in the same College Book, p. 49. In Treasurer Brattle's account, there stated, is the following item.

"1694, July 20. To cash paid Mr. Newman to get the College arms cut, £5."

No. IX.* — See pp. 79, 81, 85, 89, 91, 92, 93, 95, 96, 97.

EXTRACTS FROM PRESIDENT MATHER'S DIARY.

See p. 79.

Extracts from President Mather's Diary.

"1693. *June 30th.* At the Governor's, where, in discourse with Dr. Cook, and Oakes, they both denied that they ever said, that they could have saved the old charter if it had not been for me, and that I had betrayed the country, I declared I was willing to forgive the wrongs they had done me."

See p. 81.

"1693. *September 3d.* As I was riding to preach at Cambridge, I prayed to God, — begged that my labors might be blessed to the souls of the students; at the which I was much melted. Also saying to the Lord, that some workings of his Providence seemed to intimate, that I must be returned to England again; and saying, 'Lord, if it will be more to your glory, that I should go to England than for me to continue here in this land, then let me go; otherwise not.' I was inexpressibly melted, and that for a considerable time, and a stirring suggestion, that to England I must go. In this there was something extraordinary, either divine or angelical."

"*October 29th.* As I was riding thither (to Cambridge), all the way between Charlestown and Cambridge I conversed with God by soliloquies and prayer. I was much melted with the apprehension of returning to England again; strongly persuaded it would be so; and that God was about to do some great thing there, so that I should have a great opportunity again to do service to his name."

"*December 30th.* Meltings before the Lord this day when praying, desiring being returned to England again, there to do service to his name, and persuasions that the Lord will appear therein."

"1694. *January 27th.* Prayers and supplications that tidings may come from England, that may be some direction to me, as to my returning thither or otherwise, as shall be most for his glory."

"*March 13th.* This morning with prayers and tears I begged of

* Under this number of the Appendix are arranged all the passages from President Mather's Diary, referred to in this work; except such as are quoted at length in the text.

APPENDIX, No. IX.

Extracts from President Mather's Diary.

God that I might hear from my friends and acquaintance in England something that should encourage and comfort me. Such tidings are coming, but I know not what it is. God has heard me."

"1696. *April 9th.* This morning as I was reading in course Matt. viii. 13, it was with a strong hand impressed upon my spirit, as I had believed, that God would return me to England, and there give me an opportunity greatly to glorify the Lord Jesus Christ, so it shall be done unto me. I was wonderfully melted with assurance that so it will be. And after that, again, as I was praying in my study. In the mean time the Lord help me diligently to improve my time, to do all the good I can in New England; which, oh! how little it is that I am capable of doing, because I want wisdom and grace."

"*April 19th.* (Sabbath.) In the morning, as I was praying in my closet, my heart was marvellously melted with the persuasion, that I should glorify Christ in England. So again, as I was praying and using soliloquies with the Lord in my study between the public meetings."

"*April 26th.* The persuasions which have been in my heart concerning that matter (going to England), I cannot help. They were wrought in me with fastings and prayings by the Lord. Also on Lord's day, when I have been most in the Spirit; and I have left that matter wholly with God."

"*May 2d.* I was wonderfully affected this day with suggestions and impressions on my spirits, that tidings are coming from England which will revive me, and let me see, that my prayers are heard, and that my faith shall not suffer a disappointment."

"*June 18th.* God has given me to see answers of prayer and faith, which I have made with respect to my having an opportunity to glorify Christ in England, shall not be disappointed. Bless the Lord, O my soul!"

See p. 85.

"1696. *December 11th.* I was with the Representatives in the General Court, and did acquaint them with my purpose of undertaking a voyage for England in the Spring (if the Lord will), in order to the attainment of a good settlement for the College."

"*December 28th.* The General Court have done nothing for the poor College. Only the Council has undone what was by the advice of the ministers consented unto by the Representatives. The

Extracts from President Mather's Diary.

Corporation are desirous that I should go to England on the College's account."

See p. 89.

"1696. *October* 3*d*. Things are in a great confusion in New England. Divisions in the General Court. The College unsettled. The Representatives have assented to a resettlement. The Council obstructs."

"1697. *March* 20*th*. There are miserable confusions and divisions in Watertown, Cambridge, Charlestown, and at the South Church in Boston. The College still is unsettled. Humble request to God in Jesus Christ, that he would order the resettlement of the College in mercy, direct the General Court, now sitting, as to that matter, and me also how to act therein."

"*March* 24*th*. This morning I was sent to Watertown, where was a Council of five churches, and an ordination of two ministers (Mr. Angier and Mr. Gibbs) intended, but, because of dissensions in the church, there was no ordination. The like not known in New England."

See p. 91.

"1697. *June* 7*th*. Discourse with ministers about the College, and the Corporation unanimously desired me to take a voyage for England on the College's account."

"*June* 12*th*. As to personal concerns, the Corporation has this week desired me to undertake a voyage to England on the College's account. Also the Representatives and the Governor have voted a concurrence therein. The matter is now before the General Court. The Lord appear and direct therein to his own glory and my rejoicing in the day of its still preventing my going for England, except that will be for the best."

"*June* 15*th*. The Representatives this day undid their votes."

"*July* 3*d*. The College is in a ticklish state because of the spirit in the General Court; the Representatives there having voted and unvoted what concerns the settlement of the College."

"*July* 17*th*. I am discouraged about the College, and inclined to resign the Presidentship. The Lord help me to set aside all selfish respects, and so do what shall be most pleasing to him.

APPENDIX, No. IX.

Extracts from President Mather's Diary

"*Mem.* A special ground of my setting apart this day by fasting and prayer to serve the Lord, was because of my being much distressed in my spirit, lest my faith as to an opportunity to do service and promote the glory of Christ in England should suffer a disappointment, since it has been so long a time delayed. But, in prayer, as I was before the Lord, I was melted with hopes of receiving tidings coming from England."

"*August 7th.* I am determined (with the Lord's leave) to resign my relation to the College the next week, having desired a Corporation meeting for that end. The Lord guide and supply the College with a better than I am; pardoning my many defects, and that I have done no more good for the poor College."

"*August 12th.* Corporation meeting at Mr. Allen's about College affairs, when I desired to resign the Presidentship; but they urged me to continue still to preside, expecting a Governor from England."

"*September 3d.* In the College, matters are uncomfortable. There is a difficulty as to choosing new Tutors. My discouragements are such, that I am fully purposed to resign the Presidentship."

"*September 15th.* At College to attend a Corporation meeting, when I intended to resign the Presidentship; but, it being a stormy day, there wanted one to make a sufficient number for a Corporation meeting."

"*September 26th.* Surely this Lord's day the Spirit of the Lord melted my heart, that he has work for me to do in England, and that there I shall glorify the Lord Jesus Christ, and do service for his name, interest, and kingdom, in the world."

"*November 7th.* This evening again melting persuasions that I shall have an opportunity and advantage put into my hands to glorify Christ in England."

"1698. *January 29th.* This day again my soul was inexpressibly melted with persuasions that there is work for me to do in England by-and-by, and that there I shall glorify Christ."

"*March 19th.* As to my ever being returned to England, there to glorify the name of Christ, which I have so often with tears believed, the Lord order that important affair in much mercy! and, if any letters are sent to me that may be directory in that matter, let the gracious providence of God cause them to come safe to my hands!"

See p. 92.

Extracts from President Mather's Diary.

"1698. *April* 16*th*. The expected Governor is arrived at New York. Let me turn all into prayer."

"*April* 18*th*. This morning I experienced inexpressible meltings of soul, with persuasions that God has work for me to do in England, and that there I shall glorify the dear name of Jesus Christ. It may be, the next vessel from London will give me to understand that which will make me wonder at the infinitely condescending grace of God, who has vouchsafed to deal familiarly with a poor sinful creature."

"*May* 5*th*. The Corporation of the College met, and unanimously concurred in an address to the Governor, desiring him to encourage my going to England on the College account."

"*May* 12*th*. The Corporation met at Mr. Willard's, and appointed a messenger to go to the Governor, desiring him to assist my going to England on the College's account. This day also a letter came from Sir H. Ashurst to the Council, desiring them to encourage me therein. These things are astonishing to me. What shall I do for God and Jesus Christ!"

"*May* 14*th*. The Fellows of the College are sending an address to the Governor, praying him to encourage my undertaking a voyage for England on the College's account. Also this week a letter has come to the Governor from Sir H. Ashurst to encourage them therein. Turn this into prayer."

"*May* 28*th*. And whereas one of the fellows of the College has sent in an address to the Governor about my going to England, on which account probably the matter will come before the General Court, now sitting, the Lord in mercy appear in this, and overrule all matters so that I may see the Lord directing us."

"*June* 11*th*. The Governor has written from New York, that the act of the General Court about the College will not obtain the Royal approbation in England; that the College sending me to England will be of use. The matter is now under consideration in the Assembly. The Lord overrule this affair to his own glory, and so as that I may see his holy hand pointing to me what I should do."

"*June* 26*th*. This Lord's day I had such communion with God, and received soul-melting persuasions that the Lord had work for me to do for his name in England. The Lord prepare me for what I may hear from thence."

"*June* 28*th*. Troubled at what I was told yesterday, that I had

APPENDIX, No. IX.

Extracts from President Mather's Diary.

been severely animadverted on in the Council, and that some said I deserved a year's imprisonment. Is this my reward for taking so much pains to serve and save New England?"

"*July* 1*st*. At this time, in special I humbly cry to Heaven (among other things), that the Lord will sanctify what has lately happened in the General Court respecting my intentions for England, whereby that affair is delayed. What is the meaning of Providence? for when that matter has come to the birth, there has not been strength to bring forth. The Lord direct me what to do, as to a resignation of my relation to the College; and be with me on the Commencement approaching; prepare me for what his Providence shall cause me to hear from England."

"*September* 25*th*. This day as I was wrestling with the Lord, he gave me glorious and heart-melting persuasions, that he has work for me to do in England, for the glory of his name. My soul rejoiceth in the Lord."

See p. 93.

"1698. *November* 26*th*. There is a motion about a Vice-President at the College, there to reside. That matter is before the General Court, now sitting. There is a discourse of an agent to be sent to England. Let me turn all into prayer. Will the Lord cause me to hear out of England what will revive me? Shall I see that faith shall not suffer an utter disappointment?"

"*December* 1*st*. Corporation had conference with the Council about the College."

"*December* 1*st*. Marvellous meltings of the soul I did this morning experience with respect to tidings from England."

See p. 95.

"1698. *December* 8*th*.* This evening some from the General Court came to me, viz., Mr. Sewall, Mr. Addington, Col. Byfield, &c., desiring me to accept of the Presidentship, and remove to Cambridge; and pressing me to receive the new salary. I told them that I was discouraged, in that the Representatives had nega-

* For Judge Sewall's account of this interview, see p. 490.

APPENDIX, No. IX.

Extracts from President Mather's Diary.

tived the vote of the Council, and sent another vote, in which my name was left out. Col. Byfield (the Speaker) said, it was not out of disrespect to me, for every one in the House desired that I should be the President, &c. I objected, that I was not willing to leave my preaching work. Mr. Sewall's reply was, I might preach to the scholars by expositions every day. I told them, I could not go till the church spared me."

"*December* 10*th.* The General Court having desired me to go and reside at the College, I am in great distress concerning it; being, in my spirit, exceedingly against complying with the motion, yet desirous to do what God would have me to do. I have set apart this day to cry to Heaven for direction in this matter, and that God will incline my heart to do what shall be pleasing in his sight. But oh that God would accept of service for me in England according to my faith!"

See pp. 96, 97.

"1699. *January* 21*st.* I am still distressed about the College and my removal to Cambridge. How does that consist with the faith I have had concerning my doing service for the name of Christ in England?"

"*February* 4*th.* Being still distressed in my spirit about the motion of the General Court concerning my removal to Cambridge, which is a thing contrary to the faith marvellously wrought into my soul, that God will give me an opportunity to serve and glorify Christ in England, I set the day apart to cry to Heaven about it. And, considering that the Council is to meet next week, to consider the affair of the College, the Lord be with me, and direct me what to do and say to them."

"*February* 5*th.* At a church meeting of the brethren, I mentioned to them the proposal of the General Court about my removal to Cambridge. The vote I read to them was in the words following; 'Whether do you consent, that the Pastor of this church be dismissed from his relation unto, and his work in, this congregation, that he may wholly devote himself to the service of the College, and that in order thereunto he remove his habitation from Boston to Cambridge?' When the vote was put in the affirmative, not one man would lift up his hand; when in the negative, every one of the brethren lifted up his hand."

APPENDIX, No. IX.

Extracts from President Mather's Diary.

"*February* 17*th.* In New England the College is in an uncomfortable state. I am still distressed about my removal thither. The Council and Corporation are to meet next week about the affair. The Lord prepare me for what I may hear from England, and let me once more see that the prayer of faith shall not suffer another disappointment."

"*February* 23*d.* The Corporation met with the Council about the College. I told them, that, if the church and my wife would consent to my removing to Cambridge, I would go. Only I put in this caution; 'except some tidings from England did prevent.' They generally seemed satisfied. Only Mr. Torrey said, 'All I said was nothing.' He then said to me, that '*my pretending to resign was but a flourish.*'"

"*February* 24*th.* Discoursed with Mr. Torrey, who desired me not to resign the Presidentship, and expressed entire respect to me."

"*February* 26*th.* Why should I be so distressed in my spirit about my removing to Cambridge? Has not God told me this very day, that he has work for me to do?"

No. X.* — See pp. 102, 108, 134, 135.

EXTRACTS FROM COTTON MATHER'S DIARY.

Extracts from Cotton Mather's Diary.

"1699. *7th d. 4th m.* (*June.*) The General Court has, divers times of late years, had under consideration the matter of the settlement of the College, which was like still to issue in a voyage of my father to England, and the matter is now again considered. I have made much prayer about it many and many a time. Nevertheless, I never could have my mind raised unto any particular faith about it, one way or another. But this day, as I was (may I not say) *in the Spirit,* it was in a powerful manner assured me from Heaven, that my father should one day be carried into England, and that he shall there glorify the Lord Jesus Christ; and that *the particular faith* which has introduced it, shall be at last made a matter of wonderful

* Containing all the extracts from the Diary of Cotton Mather, referred to in this work, except such as are quoted at large in the text.

APPENDIX, No. X.

Extracts from Cotton Mather's Diary

glory and service unto the Lord. And thou, oh Mather the younger, shalt live to see this accomplished!"

"16*th d.* 5*th m.* (*July*). Being full of distress in my spirit, as I was at prayer in my study at noon, it was told me from Heaven, that my father shall be carried from me unto England, and that my opportunities to glorify the Lord Jesus Christ will, on that occasion, be *gloriously accommodated.*"

"18*th d.* 5*th m.* Both Houses, in our General Assembly, have so passed their bill for the incorporation of the College, that there appears a necessity of sending an agent to White Hall, to solicit the royal approbation for it. The agency will doubtless fall upon my father, and this prove the time for its being one way or the other determined. I therefore set apart this day for prayer, with fasting, in my study before the Lord, especially on this occasion. And when it was about noon, crying to Heaven, that the matter of my father's voyage to England might be well ordered, it was (in a manner that I may not utter) assured unto me, from Heaven, that my father shall be carried into England, and that I should live to see the glory of the Lord in this matter, and that, at this very time, there was occurring that which should one day accomplish it.

"And now behold a most unintelligible dispensation! At this very time, even about noon, instead of having the bill for the College enacted, as was expected, the Governor plainly rejected it, because of a provision therein, made for the religion of the country. But, at the same time, he told them he believed the King would grant them that very provision, and security for our religion, and urged them to address the King for it, and send an agent with an address, and choose my father for their agent; and added, that he would heartily join with them in their doing so. The Assembly was now all in confusion, and had sat many weeks, and were grown impatient to be at home, and many of their members had already gone home, so that no importunity of the Governor could prevail with them to be willing to do any thing in this matter, until their next session in October.

"Lord, preserve my faith, and assist me to wait with an holy and humble patience for the issue of these mysterious things!"

"31*st d.* 10*th mo.* (*Dec.*) Observing my father, in discourse with him yesterday, to be under some discouragement about the accomplishment of the particular faith which had seemed so often infused from Heaven into our minds, about his yet having an opportunity to glorify the Lord Jesus Christ in England, I did, this day at noon, in my

APPENDIX, No. X.

Extracts from Cotton Mather's Diary.

study, lay that matter before the Lord; and, as I was concluding my petitions about it, without any special operation from Heaven upon my mind, and just ready to conclude I should have none, my mind suddenly felt a strange and strong operation from Heaven upon it, which caused me to break forth into expressions of this importance; 'The Lord will do it! The Lord will do it! My father shall be carried into England, and he shall there have a short but a great opportunity to glorify my Lord Jesus Christ. In a most wonderful way it shall be brought about, and it shall at last appear, that the faith which there has been concerning it was the wonderful work of Heaven, and the Lord shall have revenues of glory from it.'"

See p. 108.

"1700. 16*th d.* 4*th mo.* (Lord's day.) I am going to relate one of the most astonishing things that ever befell in all the time of my pilgrimage.

"A particular faith had been unaccountably produced in my father's heart, and in my own, that God will carry him unto England, and there give him a short but great opportunity to glorify the Lord Jesus Christ, before his entrance into the heavenly kingdom. There appears no probability of my father's going thither but in an agency to obtain a charter for the College. This matter having been for several years upon the very point of being carried in the General Assembly, hath strangely miscarried when it hath come to the birth. It is now again before the Assembly, in circumstances wherein if it succeed not, it is never like to be revived and resumed any more. Sundry times, many times, when I have been spreading the case before the Lord, with a faith triumphantly exercised on his power and wisdom and goodness, I have had my assurances, that my father shall yet glorify the Lord Jesus Christ in *England,* renewed unto my amazement.

"But the matter in the Assembly being likely now to come unto nothing, I was in this day in extreme distress of spirit concerning it. My *flesh* indeed would be on all accounts imaginable against my father's removal from me. It will doubtless plunge me into ten thousand inconveniences. But my faith, on the other hand, having been so supernaturally raised for it, the thoughts of that's being wholly disappointed were insupportable. After I had finished all the other duties of this day, I did in my distress cast myself pros-

APPENDIX, No. X.

Extracts from Cotton Mather's Diary.

trate on my study floor before the Lord. Here I acknowledged my own manifold and horrible sinfulness, and my worthiness, by reason of that sinfulness, to be put off with delusions, and have a serpent given to me when I asked and looked for the Holy Spirit. Nevertheless, I, that am dust and ashes, and worthy to be made so by fire from Heaven, craved leave to plead with Heaven concerning the matter of the particular faith which had been wrought in my mind, as I thought by the Lord's own holy operation. I pleaded, that my Lord Jesus Christ had furnished me with his own glorious righteousness, and was now making intercession for me in the Holy of Holies, and because of his interest there I might approach to the most high God, with humble boldness, as to a prayer-hearing Lord. I spread before him the consequences of things, and the present posture and aspect of them, and, having told the Lord, that I had always taken a *particular faith* to be a work of Heaven on the minds of the faithful, but if it should prove a deceit in that remarkable instance which was now the cause of my agony, I should be cast into a most wonderful confusion; I then begged of the Lord, that, if my particular faith about my father's voyage to England were not a delusion, he would be pleased to renew it upon me. All this while my heart had the coldness of a stone upon it, and the straitness that is to be expected from the lone exercise of reason. But now all on the sudden I felt an inexpressible force to fall on my mind, an *afflatus*, which cannot be described in words; *none knows it but he that has it.* If an angel from Heaven had spoken it particularly to me, the communication would not have been more powerful and perceptible. It was told me, that the Lord Jesus Christ loved my father, and loved me, and that he took delight in us, as in two of his faithful servants, and that he had not permitted us to be deceived in our *particular faith*, but that my father should be carried into England, and there glorify the Lord Jesus Christ before his passing into glory; that there shall be illustrious revenues of praise to the Lord Jesus Christ, from our *particular faith* about this concern, and that I shall also live to see it, and that a sentence of death shall be written on the effect and success of our *particular faith*, but the Lord Jesus Christ, who raises the dead, is the resurrection and the life, shall give a new life unto it. *He will do it! He will do it!*

"Having left a flood of tears from me, by these rages from the invisible world, on my study floor, I rose and went into my chair. There I took up my Bible, and the first place that I opened was at

APPENDIX, No. X.

Extracts from Cotton Mather's Diary.

Acts xxvii. 23–25, 'There stood by me an angel of God, whose I am, and whom I serve, saying, Fear not, thou must be brought before Cæsar.' I believe God, that it shall be even as it was told me. A new flood of tears gushed from my flowing eyes, and I broke out into these expressions. 'What! shall my father yet appear before Cæsar! Has an angel from Heaven told me so! And must I believe what has been told me! Well then, it shall be so! it shall be so!'"

"And now what shall I say! When the affair of my father's agency after this came to a turning point in the Court, it strangely miscarried! All came to nothing! Some of the Tories had so wrought upon the Governor, that, though he had first moved this matter, and had given us both directions and promises about it, yet he now (not without base unhandsomeness) deferred it. The Lieutenant-Governor, who had formerly been for it, now (not without great ebullition of unaccountable prejudice and ingratitude) appeared, with all the little tricks imaginable, to confound it. It had for all this been carried, had not some of the Council been inconveniently called off and absent. But now the whole affair of the College was left unto the management of the Earl of Bellamont, so that all expectation of a voyage for my father unto England, on any such occasion, is utterly at an end.

"What shall I make of this wonderful matter? Wait! Wait!"

See p. 134.

"1699. *7th, 10th m.* (*Dec.*) I see another day of temptation begun upon the town and land. A company of headstrong men in the town, the chief of whom are full of malignity to the holy ways of our churches, have built in the town another meetinghouse. To delude many better meaning men in their own company, and the churches in the neighbourhood, they passed a vote in the foundation of the proceedings, that they would not vary from the practice of these churches, except in one little particular. But a young man born and bred here, and hence gone for England, is now returned hither at their invitation, equipped with an ordination to qualify him for all that is intended on his returning and arriving here; these fallacious people desert their vote, and, without the

Extracts from Cotton Mather's Diary.

advice or knowledge of the ministers in the vicinity, they have published, under the title of a *manifesto*, certain articles that utterly subvert our churches, and invite an ill party, through all the country, to throw all into confusion on the first opportunities. This drives the ministers that would be faithful unto the Lord Jesus Christ, and his interests in the churches, unto a necessity of appearing for their defence. No little part of these actions must unavoidably fall to my share. I have already written a large monitory letter to these innovators, which, though most lovingly penned, yet enrages their violent and imperious lusts to carry on the apostasy."

See p. 135.

"1699. *5th d. 11th m.* (Saturday.) I see Satan beginning a terrible shake in the churches of New England, and the *innovators* that had set up a new church in Boston (a new one indeed!) have made a day of temptation among us. The men are ignorant, arrogant, obstinate, and full of malice and slander, and they fill the land with *lies,* in the misrepresentations whereof I am a very singular sufferer. Wherefore I set apart this day again for prayer in my study, to cry mightily unto God."

"*21st d. 11th m.* The people of the new church in Boston, who, by their late manifesto, went on in an ill way, and in a worse frame, and the town was filled with sin, and especially with slanders, wherein especially my father and myself were sufferers. We two, with many prayers and studies, and with humble resignation of our names unto the Lord, prepared a faithful antidote for our churches against the infection of the example, which we feared this company had given them, and we put it into the press. But, when the first sheet was near composed at the press, I stopped it, with a desire to make one attempt more for the bringing of this people to reason. I drew up a proposal, and, with another minister, carried it unto them, who at first rejected it, but afterwards so far embraced it, as to promise that they will the next week publicly recognise their covenant with God and one another, and therewithal declare their adherence to the Heads of Agreement of the United Brethren in England, and request the communion of our churches in that foundation.

"A wonderful joy filled the hearts of our good people far and near, that we had obtained thus much from them. Our strife seemed

APPENDIX, No. X.

Extracts from Cotton Mather's Diary.

now at an end; there was much relenting in some of their spirits, when they saw our condescension, our charity, our compassion. We overlooked all past offences. We kept the public fast with them (on 31st, 11th month, Wednesday), and my father preached with them on following peace with holiness, and I concluded with prayer."

No. XI.—See pp. 82, 86, 87, 89, 95, 126, 136, 138, 150, 156, 193, 201, 203, 207, 223, 256.

EXTRACTS FROM JUDGE SEWALL'S DIARY.

See p. 82.

Extracts from Judge Sewall's Diary.

President Mather's Diary is coincident with the College records. Judge Sewall's states the proceedings thus.

"1696. *October* 12*th*. The Lieutenant-Governor goes to Cambridge,—complimented the President, &c. for all their respect to him, acknowledged his obligations, and promised his interposition for the College, as became such an *alumnus* for such an *alma mater*. Directed the President and Fellows to go on; and enjoined the students to obedience."

See p. 86.

"1696. *December* 18*th*. Mr. Mather, Mr. Allen, Mr. Willard, and Cotton Mather, give in a paper,* subscribed by them, showing

* This paper was in these words.

"Objections made by Increase Mather and others to the above act.

"The act for incorporating the College allows no President, except resident (and so the College rendered incapable of action), before the act be confirmed.

"We observe, that four thousand pounds revenue be reduced to two, and know not what advantage of it. Some Colleges in Oxford have thirty thousand.

"No Corporation meeting is therein to be had, on any occasion, though never so small, without advice given to sixteen, whereof some are far distant; and without the presence of ten, and the consent of nine.

"There can be no execution of any statute, or order, without the incum-

Extracts from Judge Sewall's Diary.

their dislike of our draft of the College charter; and desiring, that their names may not be entered thereon. One chief reason was the appointing the Governor and Council for visitors.

"I do not know that I ever saw the Council run upon with such a height of rage before. The Lord prepare us for the issue. The ministers will go to England for a charter, except we exclude the Council from the visitation. Allege this reason, because the King will not pass it, and so we shall be longer unsettled."

See p. 87.

"1697. *March* 26*th*. This day Mr. Leverett was by the Council denied to be of the Corporation for the College. How the deputies will resent it, I know not."

See p. 89.

"1696. *November* 25*th*. Mr. William Brattle was ordained at Cambridge. He and Mr. Mather (the President) preached. It was, at first, ordered that Mr. Brattle should not preach. But many being troubled at it, 't was afterward altered. Mr. Brattle also procured the church to order elder Clarke should not lay his hand on his head when he was ordained, and he refrained accordingly. So that Deacon Gile, coming home, said, he liked all very well *except the bill of exclusion*."

brance aforesaid; those, that know what it is to govern the College, are of opinion, that these things will render it impossible.

"We see a diminution of respect to the President in the former charter, as to immunity of servants.

"The visitation is such as makes it extremely probable, that the act will not only miss of the Royal approbation, but also give offence by its variation from the directions of the Lords of the Council; which we intimate not from our dislike of the thing, but from our concern to have no part in any thing that may renew or prolong the unsettlement of the College.

"For such causes, we humbly pray to be excused from having our names inserted in the act.

"Signed, Increase Mather.
"James Allen.
"Samuel Willard.
"Cotton Mather."

APPENDIX, No. XI.

Extracts from Judge Sewall's Diary.

See p. 95.

Judge Sewall, in his Diary, thus states the circumstances of the interview between the committee of the General Court and the President, on the subject of his removal to Cambridge, according to their vote passed the 3d of December, 1698.

"1698. *December 8th.* The Speaker, Mr. Eyre, and Mr. Oliver, deputy for Cambridge, were of a committee with Mr. Secretary and me, to acquaint Mr. Mather with the Court's desire of his removal to Cambridge, and to carry him an order for £200 per annum, so long as he should reside there. Mr. President expostulated with Mr. Speaker and Mr. Eyre about the votes being altered from £250, as the Council had set it; and also his name being left out and making him a five years' President.

"Note. By a conference the bill was made as ours, at first, saving fifty pounds less.

"We urged his going all we could. I told him of his birth and education there; that he looked at work rather than wages; that all met in desiring him, and should hardly agree so well in any other. Mr. Speaker, on behalf of the House, earnestly desired him. He objected, — want of a house, — bill for Corporation not passed, his church, — that he must needs preach once every week; which he preferred before the gold and silver of the East Indies. I told him he would preach twice a day to the students; he said that exposition was nothing like preaching." *

See p. 126.

"1701. *October 20th.* Mr. Cotton Mather came to Mr. Wilkins' shop, and there talked very sharply against me, as if I had used his father worse than a negro. He spake so loud, that the people in the street might hear him.

"*Mem.* On the 9th of October I sent Mr. Increase Mather a haunch of very good venison. I hope in that I did not treat him worse than a negro.

"*October 22d.* I, with Major Walley and Captain Samuel Checkley, speak with Mr. Cotton Mather at Mr. Wilkins'. I expostulate with him from 1 Tim. v. 1, 'Rebuke not an elder.' He said he

* For President Mather's account of the same interview, see p. 480.

APPENDIX, No. XI.

Extracts from Judge Sewall's Diary.

had considered that. I told him of his book, of the law of kindness for the tongue. Whether this was correspondent with that, or with Christ's rule. He said, that having spoken to me before, there was no reason for his speaking to me again. And so justified his reviling me behind my back. Charged the Council with lying, nypocrisy, tricks, and I know not what. I asked him, if this were with the meekness as it should be. He answered, Yes. Charged the Council in general, and then showed my share, which was my speech in Council, viz. 'If Mr. Mather should go to Cambridge again, to reside, with a resolution not to read in the Scriptures, and expound in the Hall, I fear the example will do more hurt than his going thither will do good.' This speech I owned. I asked, if I should suppose he had done something amiss in his church, as an officer, whether it would be well for me to exclaim against him in the street for it? (Mr. Wilkins would fain have had him gone into the inner room, but he would not.) I told him, I conceived he had done much unbecoming a minister of the Gospel; and, being called, I went to the Council. 2 Tim. ii. 24, 25."

"*October* 23*d*. Mr. Increase Mather said to Mr. Wilkins, 'If I am a servant of Jesus Christ, some great judgment will fall on Captain Sewall and his family.'"

"*October* 25*th*. This day got my speech copied out, and gave it to Mr. Wilkins, that all might see what was the ground of Mr. Mather's anger. Wilkins carried it to the Mathers. Writ out another, and gave it to Joshua Gee. I perceive Mr. Wilkins carried his to Mr. Mather. They seem to grow calm."

See p. 136.

"1699-1700. *January* 24*th*. Lieutenant-Governor calls me, with him, to Mr. Willard's, where, out of two papers, Mr. William Brattle drew up a third, for an accommodation, to bring on an agreement between the new church and our ministers. Mr. Colman got his brethren to subscribe to it."

"*January* 25*th*. Mr. I. Mather, Mr. C. Mather, Mr. Willard, Mr. Wadsworth, and S. Sewall, wait on the Lieutenant-Governor, at Mr. Cooper's, to confer about the writing drawn up the evening before. There was some heat, but grew calmer, and, after lecture, agreed to be present at the fast, which was to be observed Jan. 31st."

APPENDIX, No. XI.

Extracts from Judge Sewall's Diary.

See p. 138.

"1700. *January* 31*st*. Fast at the new church.

"*A. M.* Mr. Colman reads the writing agreed on. Mr. Allen prays. Mr. Colman preaches, prays, and blesses.

"*P. M.* Mr. Willard prays. Mr. I. Mather preaches. Mr. Cotton Mather prays. Mr. Brattle sets Oxford tune. Mr. Mather blesses.

"His text was, 'Follow peace with all men, and holiness.' His doctrine, — must follow peace, so far as it consists with holiness, Heb. xii. 14. Mr. Colman's text was, Rom. xv. 29, 'And I am sure, that, when I come unto you, I shall come in the fulness of the blessing of the Gospel of Christ.'

"Principal ministers, Lieutenant-Governor, and Council, present.

"Mr. Willard prayed God to pardon all the frailties and follies of ministers and people; and that they might give that respect to the other church due to them, though not just of their constitution.

"Mr. Mather in sermon, and Mr. Cotton in prayer, to the same purpose, and pathetically for Mr. Colman and his flock."

See p. 150.

"1697. *November* 20*th*. Mr. Willard told me of a falling out between the President and him, about choosing fellows, last Monday. Mr. Mather has sent him word, he will never come to his house more till he give him satisfaction."

See p. 156.

"1707. *October* 28*th*. The Fellows of Harvard College met and chose Mr. Leverett President. He had *eight* votes. Dr. Increase Mather *three*. Cotton Mather one. Mr. Brattle one. Mr. White did not vote. And Mr. Gibbs came when voting was over."

See p. 201.

Two contemporaneous accounts remain of the proceedings of the meeting of the Corporation, on this occasion. One in the records of the Corporation, the other in the Diary of Judge Sewall. This last is the most graphic and illustrative of the period.

APPENDIX, No. XI.

Extracts from Judge Sewall's Diary.

"1707-8. *January* 14*th*. Went to Cambridge in Mr. Briggs's coach, with Colonel Townsend, Mr. Bromfield, and Mr. Stoddard. Mr. Eliakim Hutchinson went in his own chariot, taking Mr. Wadsworth with him. Captain Belcher carried Mr. Secretary in his calash. Mr. Pemberton carried Mr. Brown in his sleigh over the ice. Mr. Miles carried Mr. Treasurer Brattle. Mr. Colman there. Major-General Winthrop, Colonel Elisha Hutchinson, Mr. S. Foster, Mr. Sargeant, Dr. Mather, Mr. Cotton Mather, Mr. Bridges. Mr. Allen not there. The day was very pleasant. Colonel Phillips. Mr. Russell, in his black cap. Colonel Lynde met us from Charlestown. Mr. Bradstreet, Mr. Angier, there. Mr. Woodbridge of Medford, Mr. Nehemiah Hobart. In the Library the Governor formed a meeting of the Overseers of the College, according to the charter of 1650, and reduced the number [of the Corporation] to *seven*, viz. Mr. Leverett, President, Mr. Nehemiah Hobart, Mr. William Brattle, Mr. Ebenezer Pemberton, Mr. Henry Flint, Mr. Jonathan Remington, Fellows, Mr. Thomas Brattle, Treasurer. The Governor prepared a Latin speech for the instalment of the President; then took the President by the hand, led him down into the Hall. The books of the College records, charter, seal, and keys, were laid upon the table running parallel with that next the entry. The Governor sat with his back against a noble fire. Mr. Russell on his left, and innermost, I on his right hand. President sat on the other side of the table over against him. Mr. Nehemiah Hobart was called, and made an excellent prayer, then Joseph Sewall made a Latin oration. Then the Governor read his speech, and (as he told me) moved the books in token of delivery. The President made a short Latin speech, importing the difficulties discouraging, and yet that he did accept. Governor spoke further, assuring him of the assistance of the Overseers. Then Mr. Edward Holyoke made a Latin oration, standing where Joseph did, at a desk on the table next the entry, at the inside of it, facing the Governor. Mr. Danforth, of Dorchester, prayed. Mr. Paul Dudley read part of the 132d Psalm, in Tate and Brady version, Windsor tune. Closed with the Hymn to the Trinity. Had a very good dinner upon three or four tables. Mr. Wadsworth craved a blessing. Mr. Angier returned thanks. Got home very well. *Laus Deo*."

See p. 203.

"1707-8. *January* 23*d*. Cotton Mather told me of his letter to the Governor (Dudley) of the 20th inst., and lent me a copy. Dr.

APPENDIX, No. XI.

Extracts from Judge Sewall's Diary.

Mather, it seems, has also sent a letter to the Governor. I wait with concern to see what the issue of this plain, home dealing will be."

"*January* 30*th*. Mr. Pemberton talked very warmly about Cotton Mather's letter to the Governor. Seemed to resent it, and to expect the Governor would animadvert upon him. Said, that, if he were the Governor, he would humble him, though it cost him his head; speaking with great vehemency.

"*February* 5*th*. Mr. Colman preaches the lecture in Mr. Wadsworth's turn, from Gal. v. 25; "If we live in the Spirit, let us also walk in the Spirit." Spoke of envy and revenge as the complexion and condemnation of the Devil. Spoke of other walking. It blotted our sermons; it blotted our prayers; blotted our admonitions and exhortations. It might justly put us upon asking ourselves, whether we did live in the Spirit; whether we were ever truly regenerated or no.

"It is reckoned he lashed Dr. Mather, and Mr. Cotton Mather, and Mr. Bridge, for what they have written, preached, and prayed about the present contest with the Governor. I heard not of it before. But yesterday Colonel Townsend told me of Dr. Mather's prayer, 25th January, wherein he made mention *one* in *twenty-eight* being faithful; which make many look on me with an evil eye, supposing Dr. Mather meant my withdrawing my vote of the 1st of November."

See p. 207.

"1713. *June* 18*th*. As I came from Mr. Stephens' meeting Mr. Pemberton joined himself to me, and told me of the Governor's vehement desire, that Colonel William Dudley might be made Treasurer of the College."

See pp. 193, 223.

"1718. *November* 12*th*. Overseers' meeting, to petition the General Court to make the College one hundred feet long. One calling for the memorial from the end of the table, I stood up and said, what the Honorable Commissioner had in hand was of great moment, but I apprehended there was an affair of greater moment. I have heard exposition of the Scriptures was not carried on in the Hall. I inquired of the President if it were so or no. Was silence

Extracts from Judge Sewall's Diary.

a little while. Then the President seemed to be surprised at my treating him in this manner. I did not use to do so. Neither did he use to treat me so. This complaint was made twice at least. Many spoke earnestly, that what was said was out of season. Mr. Attorney stood up and seconded me very strenuously. When I was fallen so hard upon, I said, I apprehended the not expounding the Scriptures was a faulty omission, and I was glad of that opportunity of showing my dislike of it. President said he had begun to take it up again. I said I was glad of it. At another time said, *that, if he was to expound in the Hall, he must be supported.* It went over. The memorial was voted. Then Mr. Belcher stood up, and moved earnestly, that exposition might be attended. At last Mr. Wadsworth stood up and spoke in favor of it, and drew up a vote, that the President should, *as frequently as he could*, entertain the students with expositions of the Holy Scriptures, and read it. I moved, that '*as he could*' should be left out, and it was so voted. Mr. President seemed to say, softly, it was not till now the business of the President to expound in the Hall. I said, I was glad the Overseers had now the honor of declaring it to be the President's duty."

"*November* 13*th*. Mr. President spake to me again pretty earnestly, and intimated, it was not the President's duty before this order. I said, that it was a shame that a law should be required, meaning, *Ex malis moribus bonæ leges.*"

See p. 256.

"1721–2. *January* 24*th*. Overseers' meeting. Mr. Edward Wigglesworth is presented by the President and Fellows of Harvard College, elected by them the Professor of Divinity, who was approved by the Overseers, by papers, written, *Yes* and *No*. It was voted, it should be done in that manner. Eleven yeas, three noes. Directed he should be called *the Hollis Professor*."

No. XII. — See p. 90.

APPLICATION OF THE CORPORATION TO THE GENERAL COURT.

Application of the Corporation to the General Court.

"1697. *Boston, June 7th*. Upon advice, that an act of incorporating Harvard College is lately passed in the General Assembly;

APPENDIX, No. XII.

Application of the Corporation to the General Court.

we, who are informed that we are named therein, as intrusted with the care of that society, being very sensible that it is of great concernment to these churches, both in present and after times, that the College should no longer labor under the unhappy uncertainties of establishment, have therefore judged it necessary to desire that the Rev Mr. Increase Mather, a person, who may most probably be instrumental in procuring so great a favor for that society, and therein for the whole country, undertake a voyage for England, in order for the obtaining the Royal approbation unto the said act of Assembly, or in case that cannot be, then to endeavour the obtaining such a charter from his Majesty as will be consistent with the constitution of the people and churches in this country.

"And we request the Rev. Mr. Allen, Mr. Torrey, Mr. Willard, and Mr. Thacher, to acquaint the Honorable Lieutenant-Governor and the General Court with this our desire, praying that their great request for so universal a benefit, as that of the College, may still be manifested by their concurrence, countenance, and assistance, to this necessary endeavour for the preservation of that society.

"Signed, with the unanimous consent of the rest,

"CHARLES MORTON."

"*June* 9*th*. Read three several times in the House of Representatives."

"*June* 15*th*. In the House of Representatives put to vote, Whether any assistance shall be allowed out of the public treasury, towards sending Mr. Increase Mather to England, for obtaining a confirmation of the charter, granted to the Corporation of Harvard College by this Court.

"Passed in the negative.

"PENN TOWNSEND, *Speaker*."

No. XIII. — See p. 90.

PETITION OF THE CORPORATION TO THE GENERAL COURT.

Petition of the Corporation to the General Court.

"To the Honorable the Lieutenant-Governor, Council, and Representatives of the Province of Massachusetts Bay, in General Court assembled.

"Having received the grant of a charter for the incorporation of Harvard College, wherein our names are mentioned, as intrusted

Petition of the Corporation to the General Court.

with the government of that society, we judge it our duty to return our hearty thanks unto this great and General Assembly, for the respects therein put upon us.

"And, whereas we have humbly prayed the concurrence and assistance of this Assembly unto our most necessary endeavour to send over one of our members to solicit for the desired settlement, we must now represent our further sense of this matter.

"We utterly despair of attaining our establishment without a personal application to His Majesty. If this Honorable Assembly discountenance our proceedings, it will be so extreme a discouragement to us, that we doubt we shall have little heart to accept the trust now devolved on us. Our care for the effectual support of the College, in the absence of our President, we hope none that know us will think so hardly of us as to question. The time has been, when the College has accommodated this colony with a considerable sum of money, not repaid unto this hour, and we would persuade ourselves, that this Province will, in point of gratitude, not refuse to be helpful unto the good settlement of that society, on which the welfare of the public so much depends.

"Signed, with unanimous consent,

"CHARLES MORTON."

"*Cambridge, June* 14*th*, 1697."

"1697. *June* 15*th*. Read in the House of Representatives.

"*P. M.* Read a second time."

No. XIV. — See p. 93.

MEMORIAL OF THE CORPORATION TO THE GENERAL COURT.

Memorial of the Corporation to the General Court.

"To the Honorable the Lieutenant-Governor, and Council, and Representatives, in General Assembly now sitting in Boston, the address of the Fellows of Harvard College.

"We account it our duty to acquaint this Honorable Assembly, that we have seen a necessity of proposing to our Reverend President the undertaking of a voyage unto England on the behalf of our College, humbly to solicit His Majesty, that the late act for incorporating that society may have the Royal confirmation; or, if that cannot be obtained, then to endeavour for such further settlement as may be judged proper for us, considering the constitution of our churches and of the country. And this for the ensuing

APPENDIX, No. XIV.

Memorial of the Corporation to the General Court.

reasons. 1. It is of great consequence, both to the present and after generations, that the College be settled on a charter foundation, without which it will indeed be no real College, but quickly come to be nothing at all. 2. We cannot but fear, that, if effectual means be not used for expediting this affair, our College may be lost, and those things happen which may frustrate all our hope about it. 3. We have been informed, that the College hath lately been disappointed of considerable donations designed for us, only because we were not by law incorporated, which is no inconsiderable damage to the public. 4. His Excellency, the Earl of Bellamont, our Governor, hath abundantly expressed his apprehension, that His Majesty will not give his Royal approbation to the act for incorporating our College, as it is now worded, but that he believes the President's going to England to solicit that matter will be of use, and, that in such a way, better powers and privileges, for the advantage of the College, may be obtained by a charter from His Majesty than by act of the Assembly; and therewithal declared his worthy desires to have it so qualified by His Majesty's wisdom and goodness, that the statutes and privileges of Harvard College may be secured against invasions that may be vexatious to it. And His Excellency having so graciously and generously signified his apprehension in this matter, we cannot but suppose that all due respect will be paid thereunto. 5. The Right Worshipful agent for this Province, Sir Henry Ashurst, hath also given it as his judgment and advice, that our President be encouraged to undertake a voyage to England, for the service of the College in this matter, and by the late vessels renewed it. 6. We are also desirous that there may be a President residing at the College, and the way to have that accomplished, is to get it speedily settled on a charter foundation. 7. Nor do we know any one amongst us, that better understands the state of the College, or that hath a greater acquaintance and interest in England, or on whose discretion, fidelity, and integrity to the true interest of the College and of our churches, we can have more dependence.

"We therefore pray for such a concurrence and assistance of this Honorable Assembly, as may, by the blessing of God, contribute unto the good success of his undertaking.

"JAMES ALLEN, *Socius Senior*,

"In the name, and with the unanimous concurrence, of the Corporation met in Boston, June 9th, 1698."

"In Council, June 14th, 1698. Read and voted in the negative.

"ISAAC ADDINGTON, *Secretary*."

No. XV. — See p. 95.

LETTER OF PRESIDENT MATHER TO LIEUTENANT-GOVERNOR STOUGHTON.

Letter of President Mather to Lieutenant-Governor Stoughton.

"To the Honorable William Stoughton, Lieutenant-Governor of the Province of Massachusetts Bay.

"Honorable Sir,

"I promised the worthy gentlemen, who acquainted me with the proposal of the General Court concerning the removal of my habitation from Boston to Cambridge, that I would return my answer to your Honor. In the first place, I give my humble thanks as to the General Assembly, so in a special manner to the Honorable Council, and to your Honor in a most peculiar manner, for the respect in this motion manifested. Nevertheless, as to the thing proposed, I do not see my way clear. As to the salary, I make no objection, although it is considerably less than what I have in Boston, through the love and bounty of the people amongst whom God has fixed my present abode. But the objections which are of weight with me are these.

"1st. If I comply with what is desired, I shall be taken off, in a great measure at least, from my public ministry. Should I leave preaching to one thousand five hundred souls (for I suppose that so many use ordinarily to attend in our congregation), only to expound to forty or fifty children, few of them capable of edification by such exercises, I doubt I should not do well. I desire, as long as the Lord shall enable me, to preach publicly every Lord's day; and I think all the gold in the East and West Indies would not tempt me to leave preaching the unsearchable riches of Christ, which several of the Presidents of the College were necessitated to desist from, because of their other work.

"2d. I am now (through the patience of God) grown into years, wanting but half a year of sixty, and of a weak and tender constitution of body, not well able to endure the hardships of the presidentship; a younger and a stronger man would do better.

"*Invalidæ vires ingeniumque mihi.* I have labored much, both in New England, and in England, to obtain a happy settlement of the College. Should I at last go thither myself, the world would say (as I hear some do say), that I sought myself in all those endeavours. Such reproaches will, by a resignation of my relation

APPENDIX, No. XV.

Letter of President Mather to Lieutenant-Governor Stoughton.

to that society, be for ever put to silence. One reason of my retaining my relation to the College thus long has been, because it was thought that would facilitate its charter settlement. Could I see that done, I should with great joy give way to another President.

"4th. I am satisfied, that the church to which I stand related will not set me at liberty. Many say, that God has made me their spiritual father, and how can they consent that I should go from them? Besides, they well know, that I have had a strong bent of spirit, to spend (and to end) the remainder of my few days in England, and that the thing that keeps me here, now the Gospel has a free passage there, is my love to them; for which cause they will not consent to my being discharged of my office-relation, without which I must not remove to the College. For it is not fit I should retain an office without discharging the duties of that office. I neither will nor have I obstructed the settlement of the College in a better hand. I have often (as your Honor well knows) desired to resign my relation to that society; and, if it will not be grievous to you, I shall to-morrow (if you please) deliver a resignation of the presidentship to the Senior Fellow of the Corporation, for him to call a Corporation meeting, in order to the choosing another President. And let the Corporation do as they would do if I were out of the world.

"Thus have I taken the freedom to acquaint you with my present inclinations, and with the reasons thereof, which I cannot answer. Could I see them well answered to my own satisfaction (but of that I despair), I should be capable of changing my mind; until then, and ever, I remain,

"Honorable Sir,

"Yours to serve,

"INCREASE MATHER.

"*December* 16*th*, 1698."

No. XVI. — See p. 103.

LETTER FROM JOHN LEVERETT TO ISAAC ADDINGTON.

Letter from John Leverett to Isaac Addington.

"*Cambridge, August* 10*th*, 1699. I have nothing proper to send to your Honor, unless it be a short account of an election made at College last Monday. As soon as I got home I was informed, that

Letter from John Leverett to Isaac Addington.

Rev. President (I. M.), held a Corporation at the College the 7th inst., and the said Corporation, after the publication of the *new settlement*, made choice of *Mr. Flynt* to be one of the Tutors at College. They have taken off from Mr. Pemberton's salary £ 10 per annum, and have curtailed and docked Mr. Fitch of £ 15, and of a classis, with which they have patched up a pension for a third Fellow. I have not the late act for incorporating the College at hand, nor have I seen the new temporary settlement; but I perceive, that all the members of the late Corporation were not notified to be at the meeting. I can't say how legal these late proceedings are; but it is wonderful, that an establishment for so short a time as till October next, should be made use of so soon to introduce *an unnecessary addition* to that society."

"JOHN LEVERETT."

No. XVII. — See p. 112.

LETTER OF PRESIDENT MATHER TO LIEUTENANT-GOVERNOR STOUGHTON.

Letter of President Mather to Lieutenant-Governor Stoughton

"To the Honorable William Stoughton, Esquire, Lieutenant-Governor.

"To be communicated to the General Assembly.

"Honorable Sir,

"I promised the last General Court to take care of the College until the Commencement. Accordingly I have been residing in Cambridge these three months. I am determined (if the Lord will) to return to Boston the next week, and no more return to reside in Cambridge; for it is not reasonable to desire me to be (as, out of respect to the public interest, I have been six months within this twelve) any longer absent from my family. And it is much more unreasonable to desire one, so circumstanced as I am, to remove my family to Cambridge, when the College is in such an unsettled state. I do therefore earnestly desire, that the General Court would, as soon as may be, think of another President for the College. It would be fatal to the interest of religion, if a person disaffected to the order of the Gospel, professed and practised in these churches, should preside over this society. I know the General Assembly, out of their regard to the interest of Christ, will take care to prevent it. It is, and has been, my prayer to God, that one much more

APPENDIX, No. XVII.

Letter of President Mather to Lieutenant-Governor Stoughton.

learned than I am, and more fit to inspect and govern the College, may be sent hither, and one whom all the churches in New England shall have cause to bless the Lord for.

"So I remain yours to honor and serve,

"INCREASE MATHER.

"*From the College in Cambridge, June 30th*, 1701."

No. XVIII. — See p. 132.

LETTER OF JOHN LEVERETT TO BENJAMIN COLMAN.

Letter of John Leverett to Benjamin Colman.

"*Cambridge, May 25th*, 1699.

"Dear Sir,

"I have wrote several letters to you, but have not been sure of your receiving any more than one of them. However, I hope they have been so happy as to kiss your hands, and to testify to you my regards. This I trust will get safe to you, since it waits upon those that send their invitations to you to come over to do service in your own country. The gentlemen that solicit your return inform me of their doing so, and I hope their hopes of obtaining what they send for, will not be frustrated, nor long deferred. I believe, Sir, you have as advantageous a prospect as any our country can offer. The gentlemen engaged in that affair are able, vigorous, and sincere. They are men of honor, and can't, in an ordinary way, fail a reasonable expectation. The work they have begun had its rise from a zeal that is not common, and the progress of it is orderly and steady. I am heartily pleased with the motion they have made towards yourself, because I shall exceedingly rejoice at your return into your country. We want persons of your character. You will, I doubt not, let the name of your country have a weight in the balance of your consideration. The affair offered to you is great, and of great moment. I pray almighty God to be your director in it. It is he that thrusts laborers into his harvest, and bounds the habitations of the sons of Adam; that yours (if it may be for your advantage) may be where you have this invitation, is heartily desired by all that I have heard speak of it; but it cannot be more agreeable to any body than it is to,

"Sir, your sincere friend and humble servant,

"JOHN LEVERETT."

No. XIX. — See p. 156.

ADDRESS OF THE CORPORATION TO GOVERNOR DUDLEY.

Address of the Corporation to Governor Dudley.

"To his Excellency, Joseph Dudley, Esq., Captain-General and Governor-in-chief in and over her Majesty's Province of Massachusetts Bay, &c. The humble address of the Fellows of Harvard College, in Cambridge, showeth,

"That we have, according to the rules of our House, unanimously declared our desires, that the future Heads of this College may be resident here, and, as resident Presidents were anciently wont to do, may govern the students, and serve them with Divinity expositions, &c. And in pursuance thereof we have chosen the Honorable John Leverett, Esq., our next President, of whom we have good confidence, that he will (when accepted and subsisted) lay aside and decline all interfering offices and employments, and devote himself to said work; and, by the divine help, be a very faithful and able instrument to promote the holy religion here practised and established, by instructing and fitting for our pulpits and churches, and other public and useful services, such as shall in this school of the prophets be committed to his care and charge.

"We recommend the said Honorable person as our President to your Excellency's favorable acceptation, and pray, that you would present him to the Honorable General Assembly, and move for his honorable subsistence, if your Excellency thinks fit.

"So we rest, your Excellency's

"Most humble servants,

"James Allen, Senior Fellow,

"*Harvard College, Cambridge,*
October 28*th*, 1707.

"At a meeting of the Corporation of Harvard College, the 28th of October, 1707. Voted, that the Rev. Mr. Allen, the Senior Fellow, sign the above address, and present the same to His Excellency in the name of the Fellows of Harvard College; and Mr. Treasurer, with the Fellows living in Boston, are desired to accompany the Rev. Mr. Allen, when he waits on the Governor with the said address."

APPENDIX, No. XX.

Address of thirty-nine ministers to Governor Dudley.

No. XX. — See p. 157.

ADDRESS OF THIRTY-NINE MINISTERS TO GOVERNOR DUDLEY.

" May it please your Excellency,

" We have lately, with great joy, understood the great and early care that our brethren, who have the present care and oversight of the College at Cambridge, have taken in supplying the place of the late reverend and learned Mr. Samuel Willard, deceased, by their unanimous choice of Mr. John Leverett, a worthy member of that society, to be the President of that College. And we humbly take the freedom to acquaint and assure your Excellency, that no person whatsoever could be more acceptable to us in that station. Your Excellency personally knows Mr. Leverett so well, that we shall say the less of him. However, we cannot but give this testimony of our great affection to and esteem for him; that we are abundantly satisfied and assured of his religion, learning, and other excellent accomplishments for that eminent service, a long experience of which we had while he was Senior Fellow of that House; for that, under the wise and faithful government of him, and the Rev. Mr. Brattle, of Cambridge, the greatest part of the now rising ministry in New England were happily educated; and we hope and promise ourselves, through the blessing of the God of our fathers, to see religion and learning thrive and flourish in that society, under Mr. Leverett's wise conduct and influence, as much as ever yet it hath done.

" We accept with all thankfulness your Excellency's great, sincere, and constant care and respect to the College, and doubt not you will now readily give an instance of it, not only in approving the choice made, but also in procuring and encouraging, as much as in you lies, an honorable support and maintenance for the President, the granting of which we doubt not but that our great and General Court will cheerfully and readily take effectual care of.

" Your Excellency will easily excuse the freedom we take, when you consider how very near and dear, both to yourself and us, the interest of that society is, and that the support and encouragement of religion and learning in the College is of the last importance to the church and state of New England.

" We shall add no more, but pray for the divine blessing on your

Excellency's person, family, and happy government, and subscribe ourselves,

APPENDIX, No. XX.

Address of thirty-nine ministers to Governor Dudley.

"Your Excellency's sincere and humble servants,

"John Rogers, *Ipswich.*	Samuel Danforth, *Taunton.*
Edward Payson, *Rowley.*	John Sparhawk, *Bristol.*
Benjamin Rolfe, *Haverhill.*	Thomas Greenwood, *Rehoboth.*
Thomas Wells, *Amesbury.*	Samuel Man, *Wrentham.*
Moses Hale, *Newbury Falls.*	Joseph Baxter, *Medfield.*
Samuel Belcher, *Newbury.*	Samuel Cheever, *Marblehead.*
Christopher Tappan, *do.*	Nicholas Noyes, *Salem.*
Joseph Dwight, *Woodstock,*	James Shephard, *Lynn.*
Benjamin Colman, *Boston.*	John Wise, *Ipswich.*
Caleb Cushing, *Salisbury.*	Joseph Capen, *Topsfield.*
Eliphalet Adams, *Boston.*	Thomas Bernard, *Andover.*
Jabez Fitch, *Ipswich.*	Thomas Blowers, *Beverley.*
Joseph Belcher, *Dedham.*	John Swift, *Framingham.*
Moses Fiske, *Braintree.*	Robert Buck, *Marlborough.*
John Norton, *Hingham.*	Israel Loring, *Sudbury.*
Nathaniel Eells, *Scituate.*	Samuel Whiting, *Billerica.*
Nathaniel Pitcher, *Scituate.*	Joseph Estabrook, *Concord.*
James Gardner, *Marshfield.*	John Hancock, *Cambridge.*
John Robinson, *Duxbury.*	John Fox, *Woburn.*"
Ephraim Little, *Plymouth.*	

No. XXI. — See p. 166.

Hon. Leverett Saltonstall, graduated at Harvard College in 1802, elected President of the Senate of Massachusetts in 1831, first Mayor of the city of Salem in 1836, a Representative for Massachusetts in the Congress of the United States in 1838.

No. XXII. — See pp. 182, 269.

JOHN BULKLEY'S DEED TO HARVARD COLLEGE.

John Bulkley's deed to Harvard College.

"1645. *Decembris* 20°. Noverint universi per præsentes, quod egomet Johannes Buckleius, nuper studens Collegii Harvardini, dono Henricum Dunsterum, dicti Collegii Præsidem, utpote eidem ob

APPENDIX, No. XXII.

John Bulkley's deed to Harvard College.

plurima atque ampla accepta beneficia devinctissimus, meâ parte illius jugeris quod ipse cum Domino Downingo, Samuele Winthropo, et Johanne Alcoke, emimus a patre-familias Marritt, viz. Quartâ parte pomarii dudum a nobis plantati, et dimidium reliqui manentis adhuc agrestis, ut, dum hic Præses vixerit, pro suâ vendicet ordinetque. Sin aliquando Præsidium exuerit, aut in eodem vitâ defunctus fuerit, tum velim ut Collegium, tanquam λεπτὸν tenue ab alumno maxime benevolo, sibi in perpetuum appropriaret.

"Hæc ego propriâ manu

"Johannes Buckleius." *

No. XXIII. — See p. 186.

DONATIONS TO THE COLLEGE DURING THE SEVENTEENTH CENTURY.

Donations to the College during the seventeenth century.

These were in money, lands, books, or specific articles.

1. Donations in money. Those received before the year 1654 have been already enumerated, and, with the names of the donors, are contained in Appendix, No. I., except those of Thomas Adams and Christopher Coulson, who paid their donations to Nathaniel Eaton, of which the amount is unknown.

All the subsequent donations in money, during the seventeenth century, including contributions towards the repair of the College edifices, but not including legislative grants for the support of the President, were as follows.

		£.	s.	d.
1654.	Rev. Mr. Allen, of Dedham, gave two cows, valued at	9	0	0
1656.	Richard Dana, (in cotton cloth,)	0	9	0
	John Stedman, of Cambridge, ...	1	0	0
	Edmund Angier, ...	1	0	0
	Edward Jackson, ...	2	12	0
	Nicholas Davison, ...	1	10	0
	Edmund Frost, ruling elder of the church in Cambridge,	0	10	0
	A widow in Roxbury, ...	1	0	0
	Daniel Kempster, ...	0	5	0

* The above was transcribed into the Donation Book of the College, Vol. I. p. 133, with this title; "*Extractum Doni Pomarii Sociorum per Johannem Buckleium.*"

APPENDIX, No. XXIII.

Donations to the College during the seventeenth century.

		£	s.	d.
	Samuel Richardson, of Woburn,	2	10	0
	Richard Russell, of Charlestown,	5	0	0
	Peter Oliver,	5	0	0
	Richard Bellingham,	40	0	0
	John Newgate,	10	0	0
	Increase Newell,	2	10	0
	Robert Keyne,	3	0	0
	Theodore Atkinson,	5	0	0
	Richard Saltonstall,	104	0	0
	Elder Colburn, of Boston,	6	10	0
	Hezekiah Usher, of Boston, merchant,	8	0	0
	Samuel Cole,	0	16	0
	James Oliver,	10	0	0
	Samuel Danforth,	1	4	0
	From Charlestown,	9	9	0
	John Wilson, senior, forty shillings per annum for ten years,	20	0	0
1658.	Edward Hopkins, of Hartford, a legacy, payable in corn and meal, (College Book, No. III. p. 49, pay acknowledged, and cost of transportation of it from Hartford charged,)	100	0	0
	Bridget Wynes, of Charlestown, legacy,	4	0	0
	Thomas Peirce, do. do.	1	0	0
	Mr. Rouse, sadler, do. do.	2	10	0
	Edward Tyng,	9	10	0
	Rev. Mr. Latham, of Bury, in Lancaster county, England,	5	0	0
	Mr. Stranguish, of London,	5	0	0
	William Paine, of Boston,	20	0	0
	John Paine, his son,	10	0	0

These gifts of John and William Paine were laid out in the purchase of land, lying north of the old meetinghouse, on which Dane Hall is now built.

		£	s.	d.
	William Colburne, of Boston,	5	0	0
	The inhabitants of Eleutheria, "out of their poverty,"	124	0	0

This was one of the Bahama Islands, for which collections had been made in New England.*

		£	s.	d.
1659.	Richard Saltonstall, a legacy, in cash,	220	0	0
	and in goods, which cost in England,	100	0	0
	Robert Keyne, of Boston, merchant,	100	0	0
	John Dodderidge, of Bremeridge, in Dover county, gave a yearly legacy of ten pounds for poor scholars.			

* In Flynt's manuscript account of benefactions, there is this statement concerning this gift; "Incolæ et Plantatores Insulæ Segoteæ, sive Eleutheriæ, in testimonium gratitudinis erga Massachusettenses pro necessariis in extremâ illorum indigentiâ transmissis subsidiis, Collegio designarunt."

APPENDIX, No. XXIII.

Donations to the College during the seventeenth century.

		£	s.	d.
	(Nothing was received subsequent to 1684. And, after considerable expense at law, the Corporation abandoned the prosecution in 1737.) paid for 24 years,	240	0	0
1660.	Henry Webb, of Boston, merchant, . .	50	0	0
1669.	Henry Henley, of Lime, in Dorsetshire, England,	27	0	0
		£ 1273	5	0

Contributions for erecting a new College,

		£	s.	d.
1669.	Town of Portsmouth gave sixty pounds per annum for seven years, of which Richard Cutts subscribed £ 20 per annum,	420	0	0
	Boston, of which Sir Thomas Temple subscribed £ 100 and Benjamin Gibbs £ 50,	800	0	0
	Salem, of which the Rev. Mr. Higginson subscribed £ 50, Mr. William Brown £ 40, Mr. Edmund Batter £ 20,	130	2	3
	Dorchester, ...	67	4	11
	Lynn, ...	20	0	0
	Watertown, ...	41	16	3
	Cambridge and the village, . .	199	1	8
	Ipswich, ...	60	3	2
	Newbury, ...	21	4	0
	Charlestown, ...	196	11	1
	Weymouth, ...	39	10	0
	Braintree, ...	87	14	6
	Rowley, ...	40	8	5
	Dedham, of which Ensign Thomas Fuller gave £ 5, ...	61	12	0
	Roxbury, ...	37	16	8
	Concord, ...	33	7	5
	Sudbury, ...	24	0	8
	Marblehead, ...	8	19	6
	Springfield, ...	17	18	9
	Hadley, ...	33	15	3
	Northampton, ...	20	9	4
	Westfield, ...	12	8	1
	Dover, ...	32	15	0
	Kittery, ...	22	0	0
	Salisbury, ...	17	0	0
	Topsfield, ...	6	0	0
	Exeter, ...	10	0	0
	Chelmsford, ...	18	7	0
	Billerica, ...	12	4	0
	Marlborough, ...	11	11	0
	Gloucester, ...	5	0	0
	Andover, ...	12	10	0

APPENDIX, No. XXIII.

Donations to the College during the seventeenth century.

		£	s.	d.	£	s.	d.
	Brought over,				£ 1,273	5	0
	Medfield,	7	16	0			
	Milton,	14	18	0			
	Wenham,	4	11	5			
	Hingham,	19	6	2			
	Hull,	3	18	0			
	Reading,	30	17	6			
	Malden,	10	0	0			
	Haverhill	18	10	6			
	Scarborough,	2	9	6			
	Bradford,	9	3	0			
	Beverly,	13	0	0			
	Hatfield,	14	2	0			
	Woburn,	27	2	0			
	Amount of the contributions,				£ 2,697	5	0
1669.	Sir George Downing,	5	0	0			
	A Gentleman in England, by Peter Serjeant,	27	0	0			
1670.	From England, do.	20	0	0			
1672.	Henry Ashurst,	100	0	0			
1674.	From England, by Peter Serjeant,	24	0	0			
1676.	Judith Finch's legacy,	0	14	6			
	Captain Scarlet gave by legacy an annuity of £ 5 for ever, of which appears to have been received only	10	0	0			
	Richard Russell gave £ 100, payable in provisions, of which appears to have been received only	31	13	4			
1679.	John Smedley, of Concord,	10	0	0			
1680.	David Wilton, by legacy,	10	0	0			
	Henry Clarke, of Hadley, by legacy,	50	0	0			
1681.	Sir Matthew Holworthy, by legacy £ 1000 sterling, in Massachusetts currency	1,234	2	6			
	Capt. John Hull,	100	0	0			
1683.	Nathaniel Hulton, of Newington Green (England), by legacy, £ 100 sterling,	130	0	0			
	Thomas Gunston, of Stock Newington, £ 50 sterling,	65	0	0			
1686.	William Brown, by legacy,	100	0	0			
	William Pennoyer* bequeathed a rent charge upon estates in England, from which was received before 1685,	241	16	6			
1695.	Mrs. Mary Anderson, by legacy,	5	0	0			
					£ 2,164	6	10
	Amount of donations in money during the 17th century,				£ 6,134	16	10

* See above, p. 185.

APPENDIX, No. XXIII.

Donations to the College during the seventeenth century.

Besides the above, the following donations appear on the books of the College, from which it is not known that any thing has been received, viz.

1683.	Henry Ashworth, . . .	£ 128 0 0
	Joseph Brown, . . .	100 0 0
1693.	Rev. Edmund Brown, . .	100 0 0
	Deacon William Trusdale, . .	40 0 0
	Owen Stockton, . . .	20 0 0
		£ 388 0 0

And the following legacies were not obtained until the next century.

1657. Edward Hopkins's legacy of . . £ 500 sterling.
Not received until 1718.

1681. Robert Thorner, of Baddesley, in Southampton (England), ... 500 sterling.
Not received, in the whole, until 1775.

1697. Robert Boyle, for the salary of two ministers to preach to the natives, . . . £ 55 sterling, per annum.

2. Benefactions in lands, or incomes issuing therefrom.

		Acres.
1638.	The town of Cambridge, ...	$2\frac{2}{3}$
	Being part of the land on which the Colleges now stand.	
1640.	The General Court, the Ferry between Boston and Charlestown.	
1645.	John Bulkley and Matthew Day, Fellows' Orchard,*	1 1rd.
1646.	Rev. Nathaniel Ward, ...	600

On Merrimack river, near Andover; said in the books to have been purchased because given in discharge of a debt. President Wadsworth states, that the College

* This gift is thus mentioned in College Book, No. III. p. 32; and Donation Book, Vol. V. p. 12.

"Mr. John Bulkley, first Master of Arts in Harvard College, and Matthew Day, Steward of the College, gave a garden, containing about one acre and one rod of land, situate near and adjoining to the College, and ordered the same to be for the use of the Fellows that should from time to time belong to, and be resident at, the said society, the said garden being now commonly called and known by the name of the Fellows' Orchard."

This is the only record in which Day's name is mentioned. Neither of the books that contain it is an original record. See above, pp. 408, 410, and both refer to Bulkley's deed, which says nothing about Day, and contains no limitation to the use of the Fellows.

Donations to the College during the seventeenth century.

derived no benefit from it, "through the negligence of former times." *College Book*, No. III. p. 104.

Israel Stoughton, by legacy, ... 300

On the northeast side of Neponsit, about Mother Brook, and on the Blue Hill.

Robert Sedgwick, "a shop."

Sometimes called "two shops in Boston, standing by the ordinary called the Ship Tavern." Let by President Dunster for ten shillings annual rent. There is no account of any receipt from it after 1668. *College Book*, No. III. p. 107.

1650. John Newgate, of Boston, gave £ 5 for ever, out of the rents and revenues of his farm at Rumney Marsh.

1652. Town of Cambridge, ... 20

In Lexington.

John Coggan, of Boston, gave seventy acres of Salt Marsh in Rumney Marsh, ... 70

This was leased in Wadsworth's time for £ 20 or £ 25 per annum.

Town of Cambridge, ... 100

On the east side of Shawshin, now Billerica.

Henry Dunster, adjoining and making with the above one parcel, ... 100

1653. John Glover, £ 5 a year, to be raised out of a moiety of his land given to his son, for ever.

1654. Robert Cooke, of Charlestown, 800 acres, confirmed by the General Court.

The College obtained nothing.

1657. General Court, 2000 acres in the Pequod country.

The College obtained nothing by this gift.

1659. Robert Keyne, of Boston, merchant, half of a house in Boston, valued at £ 147, 10*s*. In 1659 it was leased for ten pounds. Situated near the old meetinghouse.

1660. Henry Webb, a house in Boston.

Situated in Washington Street, and extending in the rear to Devonshire Street.

Rev. Ezekiel Rogers, reversion of house and lands in Rowley, upwards of 150

Not received until fifty years afterwards.

1669. Elder Richard Champney, ... 40

In Cambridge.

1670. William Pennoyer, rents out of estates in England, originally £ 34 per annum, sometimes no more than £ 13.

APPENDIX, No. XXIII.

Donations to the College during the seventeenth century.

1671. Theodore Atkinson, 40 rods of land by breadth and length.

The College obtained nothing.

1672. John Hayward, of Charlestown, by legacy, . . 24

Land in Watertown, bounding north on Fresh Pond.

1678. Daniel Russell gave by will 1000 acres at Winter Harbour.

The land was never obtained by the College.

1680. Samuel Ward (Bumpkin's, now) Ward's Island, . 30

Lies between the towns of Hingham and Hull.

1681. Edward Jackson, lands in Billerica.

Never obtained.

1682. General Court, Merriconeag Neck.

Never recovered.

1683. Town of Cambridge, ... 3½

Land in Cambridge.

1696. Samuel Sewall, and Hannah Sewall, his wife, . 500

At Petaquamscott.

Acres, 1,961⅓

3. Benefactions in books.

1638. John Harvard gave, by will, ... 320 vols.

A catalogue of these books is preserved in College Book, No. I.

1642. The magistrates gave from their libraries books to the value of £200 0 0

1658.* Sir Kenelm Digby, 29 books, valued at . . 60 0 0

A catalogue of these is preserved in College Book, No. I.

* Of the scarcity of books at that period, and the value attached to them, the following document, preserved on the College records, is a curious evidence.

"A copy of Mr. Dunster's note, given to Mr. Scottow.

"These presents witness, that whereas Joshua Scottow, of Boston, merchant, hath of his own free accord procured for the library of Harvard College, Henry Stephens his Thesaurus, in four volumes, in folio, and bestowed the same thereon, it is on this condition, and with this promise following; that if ever the said Joshua, during his life, shall have occasion to use the said book, or any parcel thereof, he shall have free liberty thereof, and access thereto. And if God shall bless the said Joshua with any child, or children, that shall be students of the Greek tongue, then the said books above specified shall be unto them delivered, in case that they will not otherwise be satisfied without it.

"In witness whereof this present writing is signed by me, Henry Dunster, President of the College, aforesaid, made at Boston, this twenty-eighth of the eighth month, 1649.

"Henry Dunster."

"Received of Mr. Urian Oakes, President, the above Thesaurus, in four volumes, according to conditions above, upon the demand of my son, Thomas Scottow. I say, received per me, this 30th of August.

"Joshua Scottow."

Donations to the College during the seventeenth century.

Thomas Graves, some Mathematical books.
John Freck gave Biblia Polyglotta.
Ralph Freck, books valued at 10 0 0
John Winthrop, Governor, 40 volumes of choice books, valued at 20 0 0

A catalogue of these is preserved in College Book, No. I.

Sir Richard Daniel, Knight, gave many books.
1660. Rev. Ezekiel Rogers, by legacy, gave part of his library.
1675. John Lightfoot, D. D., his whole library, by legacy.
1678. Theophilus Gale, D. D., bequeathed his library to the College, which made more than half the College library.

See the entry, Donation Book, Vol. I. p. 19.

Joseph Brown, books by legacy, valued at . . 50 0 0
1681. Edward Jackson gave Broughton's Chronology.
1682. Sir John Maynard, Serjeant at Law, gave eight chests of books, valued at 400 0 0

4. Benefactions in miscellaneous articles.

1656. Mr. Thomas Langham, piece of plate, valued at . 3 3 10
Mr. Venn, a fruit-dish, sugar-spoon, and silver-tipt jug.
Richard Harr, one great salt, and one small trencher salt.
1657. Richard Sprague, by will, gave 30 ewe sheep, valued at £ 30
1658. Mr. Wilson, of Boston, merchant, one pewter flagon, valued at 0 10 0
Sir Thomas Temple, Knight, one pair of globes.
John Willet, a bell.
John Ward, of Ipswich, legacy, obtained in horses, 72 0 0
1683. Samuel Paris, a silver tankard, valued at . . 7 10 0
Edward Page, one silver goblet.
Francis Wainwright, one silver goblet.

No. XXIV. — See p. 188.

LAW AUTHORIZING FINES AND CORPORAL PUNISHMENT IN COLLEGE.

Law authorizing fines and corporal punishment in the College.

"It is hereby ordered that the President and Fellows of Harvard College, for the time being, or the major part of them, are hereby empowered, according to their best discretion, to punish all misdemeanors of the youth in their society, either by fine, or whipping in the Hall openly, as the nature of the offence shall require, not exceeding ten shillings or ten stripes for one offence; and this law

APPENDIX, No. XXIV.

Law authorizing fines and corporal punishment in the College.

to continue in force until this Court or the Overseers of the College provide some other order to punish such offences. The magistrates have past this with reference to the consent of their brethren, the deputies, thereunto.

"Voted in the affirmative 21st of October, 1656.

"EDWARD RAWSON, *Secretary*.

"Consented to by the Deputies.

"WILLIAM TORREY."

No. XXV. — See p. 190.

CAMBRIDGE TOWN WATCH AUTHORIZED TO EXERCISE THEIR POWERS WITHIN THE PRECINCTS OF THE COLLEGE.

Cambridge town watch authorized to exercise their powers within the precincts of the College.

"At a meeting of the Corporation, June 10th, 1659.

"Whereas there are great complaints of the exorbitant practices of some students of this College, by their abusive words and actions to the watch of this town, the Corporation, accounting it their duty, by all lawful means, to seek the redress thereof for the future, do hereby declare to all persons whom it may concern, that the watch of this town, from time to time, and at all times, shall have full power of inspection into the manners and orders of all persons related to the College, whether within or without the precincts of the said College houses and lands; as by law they are empowered to act in cases within the limit of their town, any law, usage, or custom, to the contrary notwithstanding. Provided always we judge it not convenient, neither do we allow, that any of the said watchmen should lay violent hands on any of the students, being found within the precincts of the College yards, otherwise than so that they may secure them until they may inform the President or some of the Fellows. Neither shall they in any case break into their chambers or studies without special orders from the President or Fellows, or some other authority; but in all cases, as need may require, shall seasonably inform either the President or some of the Fellows, who will take care to examine the matter for the effectual healing of all such disorders. Also, in case any student of this College shall be found absent from his lodging after nine o'clock at night, he shall be responsible for and to all complaints of disorder in this kind, that, by testimony of the watch or others, shall appear to be done by any student of the College, and shall be adjudged guilty of the said crime, unless he can purge himself by sufficient witness."

No. XXVI. — See p. 190.

COLLEGE DISCIPLINE ENFORCED BY THE CIVIL AUTHORITY.

"At a meeting of the Corporation in Cambridge, March 27th, 1682.

College discipline enforced by the civil authority.

"Whereas great complaints have been made and proved against ——, for his abusive carriage, in requiring some of the Freshmen to go upon his private errands, and in striking the said Freshmen; and for his scandalous negligence as to those duties that by the laws of the College he is bound to attend; and having persisted obstinately in his will, notwithstanding means used to reclaim him, and also refused to attend the Corporation, when this day required; he is therefore sentenced, in the first place, to be deprived of the pension heretofore allowed him, also to be expelled the College, and, in case he shall presume, after twenty-four hours are past, to appear within the College walls, that then the Fellows of the place cause him to be carried before the civil authority."

No. XXVII. — See pp. 15, 190.

"THE LAWS, LIBERTIES, AND ORDERS OF HARVARD COLLEGE, CONFIRMED BY THE OVERSEERS AND PRESIDENT OF THE COLLEGE IN THE YEARS 1642, 1643, 1644, 1645, AND 1646, AND PUBLISHED TO THE SCHOLARS FOR THE PERPETUAL PRESERVATION OF THEIR WELFARE AND GOVERNMENT.

The Laws, Liberties, and Orders of Harvard College, &c.

"1. When any scholar is able to read Tully, or such like classical Latin author *extempore*, and make and speak true Latin in verse and prose *suo* (*ut aiunt*) *Marte*, and decline perfectly the paradigms of nouns and verbs in the Greek tongue, then may he be admitted into the College, nor shall any claim admission before such qualifications.

"2. Every one shall consider the main end of his life and studies, to know God and Jesus Christ, which is eternal life; John xvii. 3.

"3. Seeing the Lord giveth wisdom, every one shall seriously, by prayer in secret, seek wisdom of Him; Proverbs ii. 2, 3, &c.

"4. Every one shall so exercise himself in reading the Scriptures twice a day, that they be ready to give an account of their pro-

APPENDIX, No. XXVII.

The Laws, Liberties, and Orders of Harvard College, &c.

ficiency therein, both in theoretical observations of language and logic, and in practical and spiritual truths, as their Tutor shall require, according to their several abilities respectively, seeing the entrance of the word giveth light, &c.; Psalm cxix. 130.

"5. In the public church assembly, they shall carefully shun all gestures that show any contempt or neglect of God's ordinances, and be ready to give an account to their Tutors of their profiting, and to use the helps of storing themselves with knowledge, as their Tutors shall direct them. And all Sophisters and Bachelors (until themselves make common place) shall publicly repeat sermons in the Hall, whenever they are called forth.

"6. They shall eschew all profanation of God's holy name, attributes, word, ordinances, and times of worship; and study, with reverence and love, carefully to retain God and his truth in their minds.

"7. They shall honor as their parents, magistrates, elders, tutors, and aged persons, by being silent in their presence (except they be called on to answer), not gainsaying; showing all those laudable expressions of honor and reverence in their presence that are in use, as bowing before them, standing uncovered, or the like.

"8. They shall be slow to speak, and eschew not only oaths, lies, and uncertain rumors, but likewise all idle, foolish, bitter scoffing, frothy, wanton words, and offensive gestures.

"9. None shall pragmatically intrude or intermeddle in other men's affairs.

"10. During their residence they shall studiously redeem their time, observe the general hours appointed for all the scholars, and the special hour for their own lecture, and then diligently attend the lectures, without any disturbance by word or gesture; and, if of any thing they doubt, they shall inquire of their fellows, or in case of non-resolution, modestly of their Tutors.

"11. None shall, under any pretence whatsoever, frequent the company and society of such men as lead an ungirt and dissolute life. Neither shall any, without license of the Overseers of the College, be of the artillery or trainband. Nor shall any, without the license of the Overseers of the College, his Tutor's leave, or, in his absence, the call of parents or guardians, go out to another town.

"12. No scholar shall buy, sell, or exchange any thing, to the value of sixpence, without the allowance of his parents, guardians, or Tutors; and whosoever is found to have sold or bought any such things without acquainting their tutors or parents, shall forfeit the value of the commodity, or the restoring of it, according to the discretion of the President.

APPENDIX, No. XXVII.

The Laws, Liberties, and Orders of Harvard College, &c.

"13. The scholars shall never use their mother tongue, except that in public exercises of oratory, or such like, they be called to make them in English.

"14. If any scholar, being in health, shall be absent from prayers or lectures, except in case of urgent necessity, or by the leave of his Tutor, he shall be liable to admonition (or such punishment as the President shall think meet), if he offend above once a week.

"15. Every scholar shall be called by his surname only, till he be invested with his first degree, except he be a fellow commoner, or knight's eldest son, or of superior nobility.

"16. No scholar shall, under any pretence of recreation or other cause whatever (unless foreshowed and allowed by the President or his Tutor), be absent from his studies or appointed exercises, above an hour at morning bever, half an hour at afternoon bever, an hour and a half at dinner, and so long at supper.

"17. If any scholar shall transgress any of the laws of God, or the House, out of perverseness, or apparent negligence, after twice admonition, he shall be liable, if not *adultus*, to correction; if *adultus*, his name shall be given up to the Overseers of the College, that he may be publicly dealt with after the desert of his fault; but in greater offences such gradual proceeding shall not be exercised.

"18. Every scholar, that on proof is found able to read the original of the Old and New Testament into the Latin tongue, and to resolve them logically, withal being of honest life and conversation, and at any public act hath the approbation of the Overseers and Master of the College, may be invested with his first degree.

"19. Every scholar, that giveth up in writing a synopsis or summary of Logic, Natural and Moral Philosophy, Arithmetic, Geometry, and Astronomy, and is ready to defend his theses or positions, withal skilled in the originals as aforesaid, and still continues honest and studious, at any public act after trial he shall be capable of the second degree, of Master of Arts."

No. XXVIII. — See pp. 190, 191.

"ORDERS AGREED UPON BY THE OVERSEERS, AT A MEETING IN HARVARD COLLEGE, MAY 6TH, 1650.

Orders of the Overseers.

"No scholar whatever, without the foreacquaintance and leave of the President and his Tutor, or in the absence of either of them,

APPENDIX, No. XXVIII.

Orders of the Overseers.

two of the Fellows, shall be present at or in any of the public civil meetings, or concourse of people, as courts of justice, elections, fairs, or at military exercise, in the time or hours of the College exercise, public or private. Neither shall any scholar exercise himself in any military band, unless of known gravity, and of approved sober and virtuous conversation, and that with the leave of the President and his Tutor.

"No scholar shall take tobacco, unless permitted by the President, with the consent of their parents or guardians, and on good reason first given by a physician, and then in a sober and private manner.

"To the intent that no scholar may misspend his time to the dishonor of God and the society, or the grief and disappointment of his friends, but that the yearly progress and sufficiency of scholars may be manifest, it is therefore ordered, that henceforth there shall be three weeks of visitation yearly, foresignified publicly by the President of the College, between the 10th of June and the Commencement, wherein from nine o'clock to eleven in the forenoon, and from one to three in the afternoon, of the second and third day of the week, all scholars of two years' standing and upwards, shall sit in the Hall to be examined by all comers, in the Latin, Greek, and Hebrew tongues, and in Rhetoric, Logic, and Physics; and they that expect to proceed Bachelors that year, to be examined of their sufficiency according to the laws of the College; and such that expect to proceed Masters of Arts, to exhibit their synopsis of acts required by the laws of the College. And, in case any of the Sophisters, Questionists, or Inceptors, fail in the premises required at their hands, according to their standings respectively, or be found insufficient for their time and standing in the judgment of any three of the visitors, being Overseers of the College, they shall be deferred to the following year. But they, that are approved sufficient for their degrees, shall proceed, and the Sophisters publicly approved shall have their names publicly set up in the Hall.

"Whereas by experience we have found it prejudicial to the promoting of learning and good manners in the College, to admit such young scholars who have been negligent in their studies, and disobedient to their masters in the schools, and so by an evil custom or habit become utterly unfit to improve, for their own benefit according to their friends' expectation, the liberty of students in the College; it is therefore ordered by the President and Fellows of Harvard College, that no scholar whatsoever, where these be published, shall henceforth be admitted from any such school, unless having the testimony of the master of such school, of his obedience and submission to all godly school discipline, and of his studiousness and diligence, at leastwise for one quarter of a year last before his coming thence; or, in case of discontinuance from school, then it is expected he shall bring the testimony of his sober and studious conversation, under the hand of a magistrate or elder, or two or three competent and pious witnesses."

Orders of the Overseers.

No. XXIX. — See p. 199.

LETTER FROM MESSRS. SEWALL AND ADDINGTON, ACCOMPANYING THEIR DRAFT OF A CHARTER FOR THE COLLEGE AT NEW HAVEN.

"To the Rev. Mr. Thomas Buckingham, at Say Brook, to be communicated to the Rev. Israel Chauncy, Mr. Abraham Pierson, and Mr. James Pierpont.

"Gentlemen,

Letter from Messrs. Sewall and Addington.

"We crave your pardon, that we have made you wait so long for so little. We might frame an excuse from present circumstances, and say, 'Multa nos impedierunt.' But there is another cause which makes us slow and feeble in our progress; — not knowing what to do for fear of overdoing. And that is the reason there is no mention made of any visitation; which is exceedingly proper and beneficial, all human societies standing in need of a check upon them. But we know not how to call and to qualify it, but that, in a little time, it might prove subversive of your design. We on purpose gave the academy as low a name as we could, that it might the better stand in wind and weather; not daring to incorporate, lest it should be served with a writ of *quo warranto*. We pray you to accept of the few inclosed hints for an act; we should have travelled further in it, if your instructions or our invention had dictated to us; not knowing well what scheme to project, because we could not tell how far your government will encourage the design. We should be very glad to hear of flourishing schools and colleges in Connecticut, as it would be some relief to us against the sorrow we have conceived for the decay of them in this Province. And, as the end of all learning is to fit men to search the Scriptures, that thereby they may come to the saving knowledge of God in Christ, we make no

APPENDIX, No. XXIX.

Letter from Messrs. Sewall and Addington.

doubt you will oblige the Rector to expound the Scriptures diligently morning and evening. Praying God to direct and bless you beyond what yourselves do understand or hope for, we take leave, who are your most humble servants,

"SAMUEL SEWALL.
"ISAAC ADDINGTON."

The date of this letter is wanting in the copy, but it must have been written about the end of 1700 or the beginning of 1701.

No. XXX. — See p. 203.

GOVERNOR DUDLEY AND COTTON MATHER.

Governor Dudley and Cotton Mather.

"1712. *May* 16*th*. Upon the President's inquiring of His Excellency concerning the dutiful letters he had been informed had been written to His Excellency by C. M., he was pleased to assure him, that he had never received a letter from him since the undutiful one the said C. M. had sent him *anno Dom.* 1707; which was no small surprise to the President, and a further embarrassing his thoughts with respect to what direction he should think himself obliged to give, as to inserting the new title, he, the said C. M., had lately received from Glasgow, in the new edition of the Catalogue of Graduates to be put out this year; and for what His Excellency was pleased to express upon that matter, the President finds a necessity of concerting the measures to be taken upon that head with the wise and grave. *Det Deus exitum felicem.*"

"1712. *June*. Upon a further discourse with Mr. Pemberton, upon the subject-matter above written, the said Mr. Pemberton had a free conference with His Excellency, from whom he reported to the President, that he would not have the said President to omit inserting the title on his account. Upon the whole of all considerations, the President ordered the Catalogue to be printed with the insertion of the title added to the name of C. M."

Leverett's Manuscript, p. 43.

No. XXXI. — See p. 205.

LETTER OF THE TRUSTEES OF EDWARD HOPKINS'S LEGACY TO THE LORD CHANCELLOR HARCOURT.

"May it please your Worship,

"The agent for Harvard College, who often attended your Lordship in the cause of Mr. Edward Hopkins's charity-legacy to the school and College in New England, has sent us your Lordship's decree thereupon, in which your Lordship has honored us with the name of Trustees, for the improving and applying that charity to the pious intentions of the testator.

Letter of the Trustees of Edward Hopkins's legacy to the Lord Chancellor.

"It is our duty to acquaint your Lordship, that the said decree is come to our hands; but we hold it to be more so, to admire and acknowledge your Lordship's great justice and wisdom, which shine through every intermediate order thereupon, and most illustriously so in the final decree.

"Your Lordship's own great acquirements are a bright evidence of your good affection for learning; and the injunctions and directions your Lordship has given for the application and disposing of the charity, bespeak your great wisdom for the advancement of it. It is by this, as much as by your justice, you have given a more lively countenance than ever it had, to the first, and for a long time, only seminary of good letters in these His Majesty's remote dominions. And it is for this we render to your Lordship our thanks, with the same ardor and sincerity as we acknowledge the justice and equity of your Lordship's decree. We pray your Lordship to believe, that we will exert ourselves to the utmost, that the pious intentions of the testator, and your Lordship's wise and just constitutions and orders, may be pursued with all possible diligence, faithfulness, and integrity, by,

"May it please your Lordship,

"Your Lordship's most obedient,

"Faithful, humble servants.

"*January 25th*, 1713."

Signed by Joseph Dudley and all the trustees.

No. XXXII. — See p. 207.

APPOINTMENT OF MR. WHITE AS TREASURER.

Appointment of Mr. White as Treasurer.

"The President, Mr. Pemberton, and Mr. Flynt, waited on His Excellency, the Governor, to present the election of Mr. White to the Treasurership of the College, and for an Overseers' meeting for the approbation and allowance of the vote of the Corporation. His Excellency was pleased to manifest his dissatisfaction with what the Corporation had done, directed us to consider whether we would insist on a meeting of the Overseers, thought it would be Mr. White's prudence not to accept of the election of the Corporation; but, if we insisted on the Overseers' meeting, to move him by Mr. Secretary."

Leverett's Manuscript, p. 80.

No. XXXIII. — See p. 208.

GOVERNOR SHUTE.

Governor Shute.

"1716. *October 5th.* His Excellency, Colonel Shute, arrived at Boston, and was there received with great acclamations. His commission being read in the Council Chamber, the oaths were administered to him, and after this a proclamation, according to usage, for all officers, civil and military, to continue and act until further order was published."

"*October 15th.* The Governor set out from Boston to visit his government of New Hampshire, passing through Cambridge. He was pleased to visit the College, and was received by the President and Fellows at the gate, and by them conducted into the Hall, where he was saluted by Sir Foxcroft with a Latin oration, to his Excellency's good acceptance, and with the just applause of the learned auditory; he went into the Library, and after a short view and large commendation of the place, and founders, and patrons of it, with assurance of his favors to the House, and blessings upon it, he proceeded on his journey, the President accompanying His Excellency to New Hampshire."

Leverett's Manuscript, p. 117.

No. XXXIV. — See p. 226.

LETTER FROM COTTON MATHER TO GOVERNOR SHUTE.

"*31st d. 8th month,* 1718.

"Sir,

"As in duty for ever bound, I repeat my humble offers of service to your Excellency. That if, at the present session of the General Assembly, there may be any thing within the small sphere of my activity to be done for the public (for I perceive your Excellency knows no other) interests, your commands may be laid upon me.

Letter from Cotton Mather to Governor Shute.

"At the same time I will humbly tender to your Excellency my poor sentiments concerning some affairs of the College, because I am informed a meeting of (those unaccountably called) *the Overseers of the College* is this day expected.

"It appears unto your servant a very strange thing, that, when the life and soul of that society (in its present feeble circumstances) are in your Excellency's favorably looking upon it, and breathing into it, there should be so little acknowledgment of the dependence, as I am informed there was, when Pierpont carried a message from your Excellency.

"It appears a very strange thing, that, when King William and Queen Mary, and my Lord Bellamont, and our General Assembly (many times over), and Governor Dudley, and all the world besides, declared for near twenty years together, that the College had not a sufficient charter to animate it, they should now, by unseasonable challenges and presumptions to act as upon such an one, make their precarious conditions to be inquired into.

"It appears a very strange thing, that, supposing they had all the charter they pretend unto, they should expect that the members of that society should be exempted from the reach of the laws of the Province, and the common law of the nation.

"Which point, if it be this day given to those who know very well, that when the utmost punishments of the College have been inflicted, formerly the civil courts have taken after all a cognizance of the crimes, it will certainly bring the state of the College into the General Assembly, and then — clamor enough, be sure on 't.

"For the abused and oppressed Pierpont, when he has done what your Excellency may order him, to have his degree ordered for him, and so the *βατραχομυομαχία* between him and the pretended Presi-

APPENDIX, No. XXXIV.

Letter from Cotton Mather to Governor Shute.

dent brought to a period, seems to be as compendious a way as any to quiet these academical commotions.

"Though the College be under a very unhappy government, yet for my own part I earnestly desire, that it may go on as easily and as quietly as possible. *And your Excellency's incomparable goodness and wisdom will easily discern and approve the intentions of the freedom used in this letter, and leave it and its writer covered under the darkest concealment.* And the rather, because (for some reasons) I desire to keep at the greatest distance imaginable from all the affairs of Harvard.

"With my supplications to the glorious Lord for his blessing on your Excellency's person and government, and your continuance with an upright heart and skilful hand still to govern us,

"I subscribe, your Excellency's

"Most faithful and obedient servant,

"COTTON MATHER.

"My aged parent, your Excellency's most sincere servant, allows me to write in this manner, with 'his most humble service.'"

No. XXXV. — See p. 226.

LETTER FROM COTTON MATHER TO ELIHU YALE.

Letter from Cotton Mather to Elihu Yale.

"*Boston, New England,* 14*th d.* 11*th month,* 1717–18.

"Sir,

"There are those in these parts of the western *India,* who have had the satisfaction to know something of what you have done and gained in the *eastern,* and they take delight in the story. But that which has made many of them the more sensibly acquainted with it, is, their having felt the testimonies thereof in the overflowing liberalities whereof you find the objects on this side of the wide Atlantic.

"New England values itself upon the honor of being your native country. But you do singularly oblige as well as honor it, in that, although you left it in such an early infancy as to be incapable of remembering any thing in it, yet you have been pleased on all occasions to testify a good will unto it.

"On one of the meetinghouses of another country, the walls have these words engraven on them; 'Not for a faction or a party, but

Letter from Cotton Mather to Elihu Yale.

for promoting faith and repentance in communion with all that love our Lord Jesus Christ.'

" New England is now so far improved as to have the best part of two hundred meetinghouses. On the walls whereof these agreeable words might be very justly engraved. And a people so disposed cannot but be recommended above any in the world unto the charity, the affection, the esteem of all Christians, who understand the catholic and generous principles of Christianity, and have got beyond the narrow span of a party. Your own inclinations to do good, with a view superior to that of a party, have not only enlarged your character with the best of men, but also received already (if we are not misinformed) very conspicuous recompenses from above. The glorious God, who gave power to get wealth, and from whom we have received all that we have, has made us no more than the trustees of his goodness.

" The chief good that we have in our estates lies in the good we do with them. And a serious regard unto the account which we are to give of our stewardship, is most certainly of such importance, that, of them who are strangers to it, it must be said, *What wisdom is there in them?*

" The people for whom we bespeak your favors are such sound, generous Christians and Protestants, that their not observing some disputable right (which no act of Parliament has imposed on these plantations), ought by no means to exclude them from the respects of all that are indeed such, and from the good will which we all owe to the rest of the reformed churches, all of which have their little varieties.

" You have, Sir, been therefore most kindly inquisitive what you may do for such a people. And I will presume upon so much of an answer to your noble inquiries, as to suggest, not what you may do, but whom you have to do for.

" The Colony of Connecticut, having for some years had a College at Saybrook without a collegious way of living for it, have lately begun to erect a large edifice for it in the town of New Haven. The charge of that expensive building is not yet all paid, nor are there yet any funds of revenues for salaries to the Professors and Instructors to the society.

" Sir, though you have your felicities in your family, which I pray God continue and multiply, yet certainly, if what is forming at New Haven might wear the name of YALE COLLEGE, it would be better than *a name of sons and daughters.* And your munificence

APPENDIX, No. XXXV.

Letter from Cotton Mather to Elihu Yale.

might easily obtain for you such a commemoration and perpetuation of your valuable name, which would indeed be much better than an Egyptian pyramid.

" *We have an excellent friend, our agent, Mr. Jeremiah Dummer, who has been a tender, prudent, active, and useful patron of the infant College at Connecticut, as well as many other good interests, and will leave his memory precious with a good people, and among them that survive him, for his having so signally befriended it on all occasions. He will doubtless wait upon you, and propose to you, and concert with you the methods in which your benignity to New Haven may be best expressed.*

" Nor will it be any disadvantage unto your person or family, for a good people to make mention of you in their prayers unto the glorious Lord, as one who has loved their nation, and supported and strengthened *the seminary from whence they expect the supply of all their synagogues.* But having thus far presumed upon your goodness, I shall presume no further, but, with hearty supplications to Heaven, that the blessings thereof may be showered plentifully down upon you and yours,

" I subscribe, Sir,

" Your most sincere friend and servant,

" COTTON MATHER."

No. XXXVI. — See p. 227.

LETTER FROM COTTON MATHER TO GOVERNOR SALTONSTALL.

Letter from Cotton Mather to Governor Saltonstall.

" *25th d. 6th month,* 1718.

" Sir,

" 'T is an unspeakable pleasure unto me, that I have been in any measure capable of serving so precious a thing as your College at New Haven.

" Governor Yale now gives you a sensible proof, that he has begun to take it under his patronage and protection. But I am informed, that what he now does is very little in proportion to what he will do, when once he finds, by the name of it, that it may claim an adoption with him. Yale College cannot fail of Mr. Yale's generous and growing bounty. *I confess, that it was a great and*

Letter from Cotton Mather to Governor Saltonstall.

inexcusable presumption in me, to make myself so far the godfather of the beloved infant as to propose a name for it. But I assured myself, that if a succession of solid and lasting benefits might be entailed upon it your Honor and the Honorable Trustees, would pardon me, and the proposal would be complied withal.

"It is a thousand pities, that the dear infant should be in danger of being strangled in the birth, by a dissension of your good people about the place where it shall be nourished in the wilderness. But probably the Yalean assistance to New Haven will prove a decisive circumstance, which will dispose all to an acquiescence there.

"*When the servants of God meet at your Commencement, I make no doubt, that, under your Honor's influences and encouragements, they will make it an opportunity, in the most serious and mature manner, to deliberate upon projections to serve the great interests of education, and so of religion, both in your College and throughout your Colony, as well as whatever else may advance the kingdom of God, and not suffer an interview of your best men to evaporate such a senseless, useless, noisy impertinency, as it uses to do with us at Cambridge.*

"But I may not presume on the part of a monitor, with such as know much better than myself what that wisdom is, that finds out witty inventions for the doing of good in the world.

"I repeat my humble supplications, that our glorious Lord would multiply his blessings on your honorable person, consort, family, and government; and am,

"Your Honor's most sincere servant,

"COTTON MATHER."

No. XXXVII. — See p. 228.

EXTRACTS FROM LETTERS OF THOMAS HOLLIS TO BENJAMIN COLMAN.

Extracts from letters of Thomas Hollis to Benjamin Colman.

"*London, September* 10*th*, 1720.

"Mr. Dummer, I think your agent, sent for me yesterday to a coffee-house, said he had a letter to show me, mentioning thanks for my bounty to your College, but had mislaid it, and acquainted me about a College, building at New Haven, which he proposed to my bounty. I could only answer, I had not heard of it before."

APPENDIX, No. XXXVII.

Extracts from letters of Thomas Hollis to Benjamin Colman.

"*London, February 9th*, 1721.

"A few days past Mr. Dummer brought me a letter, dated July 4th, but no name to it, which is handsomely worded; recommending to me the collegiate school at New Haven, inclosed in one to him, dated the 3d September, from Mr. G. Saltonstall, Governor of Connecticut, earnestly pressing the same affair. I have answered Mr. Dummer, that, as I am projecting some things in Harvard College, until I have finished, I think not to take his case into consideration. He being a man in a public character, I care not for free conversation with him. He tells me he has £300 sterling for being your agent, £100 for the other, and £50 per annum, well paid, for a third. But what does he do of service for all this money? And what does he do with it? perhaps is a harder question."

See p. 228.

EXTRACTS FROM LETTERS OF THOMAS HOLLIS TO JOHN WHITE, TREASURER OF HARVARD COLLEGE.

Extracts from letters of Thomas Hollis to John White.

"*London, July 12th*, 1721.

"I have now another letter, anonymous, about Yale College. I know not the man, but suppose him to be urged on to it by your agent, Dummer. I inclose it you. I have no inclination to be diverted from my projected design. If you know the author, pray let him know so. I have told Dummer the same."

"*London, August 4th*, 1721.

"I have another letter by this ship from Yale College, by some person, who says he chooses to remain incog., and so I must let him remain. I suppose your agent, Dummer, stirs him up."

No. XXXVIII. — See p. 229.

EXTRACT FROM A LETTER OF THOMAS HOLLIS TO BENJAMIN COLMAN.

Extract from a letter of Thomas Hollis to Benjamin Colman.

"*January 27th*, 1726 – 7.

"I am this day applied unto, at the N. E. coffee-house, by Mr. Oliver, in a letter he showed me from Mr. Prince, of the South Church, in Boston (I think it is called), to help furnish a library for their private use; using this as a motive, we did not know what hands the great library at Harvard College might fall into, but this private one would be secure to posterity. I was disgusted at the suggestion, and refused to read on, and bid him write Mr. Prince word, I disliked his motion, and would not be concerned"

No. XXXIX. — See p. 231.

BENEFACTORS OF THE NAME OF HOLLIS.

Benefactors of the name of Hollis.

Three of these six benefactors bore the name of Thomas; the others, respectively, of John, Nathaniel, and Timothy. The first Thomas, Nathaniel, and John were brothers. The second Thomas was the son of Nathaniel, and heir of his uncle, the first Thomas. The third Thomas was son of the second, and heir of his grandfather, Nathaniel Hollis, and of his father. Timothy was the son of John. Of these, the first-named Thomas Hollis was the earliest and greatest benefactor to Harvard College.

No. XL. — See p. 238.

LETTER FROM THOMAS HOLLIS TO BENJAMIN COLMAN.

Letter from Thomas Hollis to Benjamin Colman.

"*London, September* 10*th*, 1720.

"This gives me occasion to inquire of you, dear Sir, whether this Assembly your letter comes from, will have a vote in the nomination of students to share in my bounty, or if it will remain as I proposed, by your advice, in the President and five Governors of the Corporation and their successors, to nominate the persons that shall have my designed annual gift, after my decease."

No. XLI. — See p. 239.

LETTER FROM THOMAS HOLLIS TO PRESIDENT LEVERETT AND BENJAMIN COLMAN.

"*London, September* 23*d*, 1720.

"Your new proposal, of a suitable stipend for a Divinity Professor to read lectures in the Hall to the students, surprises me. I could

APPENDIX, No. XLI.

not have thought, but, in the standing of your College, you had made such provision long since; however, if not, or if I mistake your meaning, I desire you, at convenient time, to explain more largely that matter to me, and to tell me how much will be called an honorable stipend."

No. XLII. — See p. 239.

HOLLIS'S ORDERS.

"ORDERS MADE BY ME, THOMAS HOLLIS, OF LONDON, MERCHANT, FEBRUARY 14TH, 1720-1,

Hollis's Orders.

"Concerning the disposition of certain sums of money, by me sent over to New England, and already paid or ordered to be paid to Mr. John White, Treasurer to Harvard College, in Cambridge, in New England, subject to such alterations as may be made by me in my lifetime, or by my last will.

"I order such sums of money as are already paid to Mr. John White, Treasurer of Harvard College, or that shall be paid to him by my order in my lifetime, or by my executrix, according to my last will, be placed out at interest, or laid out in good securities, and the produce thereof to be applied in a manner I do here direct.

"*I order and appoint a Professor of Divinity, to read lectures in the Hall of the College unto the students; the said Professor to be nominated and appointed from time to time by the President and Fellows of Harvard College, and that the Treasurer pay to him forty pounds per annum, for his service, and that when choice is made of a fitting person, to be recommended to me for my approbation, if I be yet living.*

"I order and appoint five pounds a year to the Treasurer, for the time being, for his pains in receiving and paying my bounty, and making up an annual account at every annual audit day, for the said College, and the balance to be carried forward to a new account.

"I order and appoint the whole of the remaining annual increase to be disposed of as follows. Ten pounds a year for one exhibition, to assist one pious young man, in the judgment of charity, religiously inclined, in his studies for the ministry of the Gospel of Jesus Christ; one who is poor in this world, and cannot comfortably go forwards without such charitable helps, for three or four years, and he behaving himself well, to be yearly paid to him by the Treasurer; and that so many students be nominated, and exhibitions be granted, and paid, as the annual income will bear, by even, equal sums of ten pounds a year for every one, and this ordinance to be for ever.

Hollis's Orders.

"While I live, I reserve the nomination of the students to myself, intreating the governors of the College to present names of persons and their qualifications to me for approbation. Upon my decease, I do appoint the President and Fellows of Harvard College, of Cambridge, in New England, and their successors for ever, to have the nomination of the students that shall receive the said exhibitions of ten pounds a year apiece, for the time aforesaid, and that as any one dies, or is turned out, or goes off in his course, another be placed in his room, *and that none be refused on account of his belief and practice of adult baptism*, if he be sober and religiously inclined. And I recommend, in a special manner, to avoid nominating any dunces or rakes, as not fit to partake of this bounty.

"I order a register to be kept of such as are taken in upon this foundation, their names, ages, times of entrance, for how long time, and when they go off.

"I order a fair account to be kept of receipts and payments of this my devoted trust, and annually balanced; the whole design hereof being for the glory of God and the good of precious souls.

"May the blessed Lord accept and succeed it. Amen. So prays

"THOMAS HOLLIS."

No. XLIII. — See p. 242.

MINUTES OF A LETTER FROM THE CORPORATION TO THOMAS HOLLIS.

Minutes of a letter from the Corporation to Thomas Hollis.

"At a meeting of the Corporation of Harvard College, in Boston, at Mr. Treasurer White's lodgings, April 25th, 1721.

"The President and Mr. Colman read a letter from Mr. Thomas Hollis, of London, to them; and Mr. Colman a letter from Mr. Neal, of London, written to him by the direction of the said Mr. Hollis, relating to the setting up a Professor of Divinity at the College, and desiring some further advice and information in that affair.

"Voted, That Mr. Wadsworth and Mr. Colman be a committee to prepare and lay before the Corporation a draught of such information at their next meeting, in order to its being forwarded."

Corporation Records, Vol. II. p. 70.

APPENDIX, No. XLIII.

Minutes of a letter from the Corporation to Thomas Hollis.

"At a meeting of the Corporation at Mr. Treasurer White's lodgings, Boston, May 2d, 1721.

"Mr. Wadsworth and Mr. Colman offered to the Corporation a draught of further information respecting the affair of a Professor of Divinity, as they were requested the last meeting, which was read and accepted.

"Voted, To be transmitted to Mr. Hollis and the Rev. Mr. Neal."

"At a meeting of the President and Fellows of Harvard College at the President's House in Cambridge, June 21st, 1721.

"Minutes directory in answer to Mr. Hollis his letters.

"Voted, 1. To acknowledge with thankfulness his last bounty.

"2. To acknowledge his candor and confidence in leaving his institutions open and alterable, and referring them to our consideration and approbation.

"3. As to the Professor, we refer to what has been already written to Mr. Hollis; and further propose to offer it to his consideration, whether the Professor should not be wholly his own, by transferring four of the Exhibitions to the Professorship; yet referring the matter to his determination.

"4. As to what refers to the Treasurer, we thankfully acquiesce.

"5. As to the investing his donation in land at five per cent. That we have no present prospect of doing to the advantage proposed, but shall be ready to embrace an opportunity whenever it shall offer, and advise him accordingly.

"6. As to what he proposes of the General Court's confirming such land as his gift to the uses and designs directed, to refer to a clause in the charter to be transcribed and sent to him.

"7. As to the extending the time of his Exhibitions, we agree to it.

"8. The Professor's lectures are free to the society.

"9. That the students of his foundation will be readily favored, as there is occasion, and one is already.

"10. *As to the Professor's being in communion with a particular church, we judge it highly fitting; and, as to the limitation, we leave it to himself.*

"11. As to the Professor's being chosen anew every third, fifth, or seventh year, we choose the fifth."

Ibid., p. 71.

No. XLIV. — See p. 243.

ELECTION OF PROFESSOR WIGGLESWORTH.

Election of Professor Wigglesworth.

"At a meeting of the President and Fellows of Harvard College at the President's house, in Cambridge, June 28th, 1721.

"Present, the President, Mr. Colman, Mr. Flynt, Mr. Stevens, Mr. Appleton, Mr. Treasurer. The Corporation being informed of ships being ready to sail for London, by which it would be requisite to send answers to Mr. Hollis's letters; and particularly upon his instituting a Professor of Divinity; the question was put, Whether a person should now be elected, in order to be presented to Mr. Hollis for his approbation to be a Professor of Divinity upon his institution? It was agreed and voted in the affirmative. Accordingly the Fellows, met in Corporation, were desired to bring in their votes in writing for the election of a Professor of Divinity, in order to be presented to Mr. Hollis for his approbation. And they did so. Upon numbering the votes, Mr. Edward Wigglesworth was chosen Professor of Divinity, and accordingly so declared. Mr. Wigglesworth's name was sent to Mr. Hollis in the letter signed by the President and Mr. Colman."

Corporation Records, p. 72.

No. XLV. — See pp. 244, 247.

LETTER FROM THOMAS HOLLIS TO BENJAMIN COLMAN.

"*London, August 8th*, 1721.

"Dear Sir,

Letter from Thomas Hollis to Benjamin Colman.

"I have received your letter, dated April 5th, on the 5th of June, and your letter and *scheme* signed by you and Mr. President, dated May 5th, on the 5th of July, the night after I had put mine for Mr. Treasurer into the bag; and now again three letters from you together, by Captain Letherid, August 2d, dated June 6th, 19th, and 26th, the last signed by you and Mr. John Leverett.

* * * * *

"I beseech you to encourage Baptist students equally with Pædobaptists. I am persuaded it will promote true religion, and tend to the peace of the churches of both denominations while I live, and

APPENDIX, No. XLV.

Letter from Thomas Hollis to Benjamin Colman.

them that follow. What I write herein, pray communicate to Mr. President Leverett; and give my humble service to him, and to all the Fellows of the College, who are concerned kindly in this affair. I am mightily pleased with the character you give of the gentleman whom you have proposed to be my first Professor, and have him under my consideration. But I am thinking, whether I am yet ripe for a nomination, my adventures not being yet entered into your Treasurer's cash, and, after that they are, must be placed out to improvement, to produce the designed maintenance for the one and the other purpose; so that, if I proceed presently to nominate, as your letter urges me to do, he must be straitened, or he must break in upon the principal, neither of which is agreeable to me at this writing.

"I also desire to know if this gentleman be in actual communion with some Christian church, as I formerly hinted, and with whom? *In reference to your scheme for the Professor's work, on due consideration, I think it requires some amendments.* I give thanks to Mr. Wadsworth for his paper, and to Mr. President, and to you, for yours; it is a foundation to work upon; and I have consulted several worthy pastors of churches here, who have studied abroad, as at Edinburgh, Utrecht, Leyden, and are acquainted with the Professors of Divinity's work there. And these gentlemen express a great respect and concern for your University, and would willingly lend any advice they can for your advantage. *I have desired them to make some little alterations in your scheme, and some remarks as their reasons for so doing*, which, when finished, I shall send unto you for your more mature consideration; believing you and they have nothing in view herein, but furthering of the glory of God, promoting good literature, and the true knowledge of theology, well understanding of the sacred Scriptures. May the Lord, the Spirit of truth, say, Amen."

No. XLVI. — See p. 248.

"RULES AND ORDERS PROPOSED RELATING TO A DIVINITY PROFESSOR IN HARVARD COLLEGE IN NEW ENGLAND.

"1. That the Professor be a Master of Arts, and in communion with some Christian church, of one of the three denominations, Congregational, Presbyterian, or Baptist.

APPENDIX, No. XLVI.

Rules and orders relating to the Hollis Professor of Divinity.

" N. B. This agrees with the scheme which was sent from New England, approved by the Reverend the President, and the Corporation.

"2. That his province be to instruct the students in the several parts of theology, by reading a system of positive, and a course of controversial divinity, beginning always with a short prayer.

" We apprehend this article to be of the last importance. The want of a Professor, whose *only* work shall be, to make the students *masters* of Divinity, is justly complained of in our Universities, and wisely rectified in the University of Edinburgh, and all the foreign Universities we are acquainted with. It will consequently turn to the great advantage of the students to be thus *regularly* instructed in the several parts of theology without *intermission,* after they have been three or four years in the College. And we are apprehensive it will become very easy to the Professor after he has sat in his chair a year or two.

" 3. That the said Professor read his private lectures of positive and controversial divinity so many times in the week as shall finish both courses within the term of one year.

" The Professors in the Universities of Holland read four times a week on a system, and four times a week on the controversies, each lecture not exceeding three quarters of an hour. The first quarter is spent in examining the students on the heads of the last lecture, then the Professor proceeds; always taking care to finish both his system, and course of controversial divinity, within the compass of a year.

" An hour in the morning is generally employed in the system, on Mondays, Tuesdays, Thursdays, and Fridays, and an hour on the same days in the afternoon in the controversies, by which means the Professors have two days in the week entire to themselves; and by finishing all in one year an opportunity is given for new students to enter every year, and the Seniors may go over the course with the Professor two or three times, which will be of great advantage; nor will this be at all difficult to the Professor, when he has gone over it once or twice.

" 4. That the Professor read publicly twice a week in the Hall, on Church History, Jewish Antiquities, Cases of Conscience, or critical exposition of Scripture, as he shall judge proper, times of vacation always excepted.

" This agrees with the New England scheme.

" We conceive, that though it is impossible these public lectures

APPENDIX, No. XLVI.

Rules and orders relating to the Hollis Professor of Divinity.

should answer the ends of regular instruction, which is the most necessary to make the students masters of theology, and fit them for the pulpit, or the chair, any more than the preaching two sermons weekly in the pulpit can be thought sufficient to fit all the hearers for the pulpit; yet, since they are performed in all our Universities, they are not to be omitted. Give us leave, however, to observe to you, that, notwithstanding the several Universities we have had any knowledge of have laid the strictest injunctions on the Professors to study these lectures, yet in some time they have been generally neglected, and have dwindled into little else than form. We take the liberty to mention critical exposition of Scripture, Church History, Jewish Antiquities, that the Professor may give to the students of Divinity as large and extensive a view as can be of every part of learning, which is proper to enter into the character of a finished divine.

"5. That the Professor set apart two or three hours, one afternoon in the week, to answer such questions of the students who shall apply to him, as refer to the system or controversies of religion, or cases of conscience, or seeming contradictions in Scripture. And this agrees to the New England scheme. And we are informed the Professor of Divinity at Edinburgh allows two or three hours every Thursday in the afternoon to this work; times of vacation excepted.

"6. That the Professor of Divinity, while in that office, shall not be a Tutor in any other science, or obliged to any other attendance in the College than the abovementioned public and private lectures.

"This will make the Professor's work as easy at least, if not more easy than the rest of the Tutors'.

"7. That the Professor read his private lectures to such only as are at least of two years' standing in the College.

"This is intended to remedy an evil too common in most places. When students, upon their first coming to the University, are encouraged to enter on the study of Divinity, they neglect all preparatory studies, and very often enter on the sacred ministry before they are qualified; whereas, by keeping them from the constant and regular study of theology for the first two or three years, you employ them necessarily in other parts of literature, and effectually prevent their going into the pulpit till they are at least of four years' standing. 'T is not intended, by this article, to debar the students of Divinity from attending on any of the lectures of other Tutors, but only that they now begin to make theology their chief study.

"8. That, an honorable salary being provided for the Professor,

Rules and orders relating to the Hollis Professor of Divinity.

it is expected that he require no fee from any of the students for their instruction.

"This agrees with the New England scheme. But, if any gentleman desires his son may run through a course of Divinity, it does not hinder the parent from making the Professor a present, though the Professor is debarred from requiring any thing of such person.

"9. That the said Professor be chosen every five years by the Reverend President and Fellows of the College, for the time being, and be presented by them, when chosen, to the Honorable and Reverend Overseers, to be by them approved and confirmed in his place.

"This agrees with the New England scheme.

"10. That the said Professor be at all times under the inspection of the Reverend the President and Fellows, with the Honorable and Reverend the Overseers for the time being, to be by them displaced for any just and valuable cause.

"This agrees with the New England scheme.

"11. That it be recommended to the electors, that at every choice they prefer a man of solid learning in Divinity, of sound and orthodox principles; one who is well gifted to teach, of a sober and pious life, and of a grave conversation.

"These rules and orders relating to a Divinity Professor in Harvard College, in New England, were drawn up at the request of Mr. Thomas Hollis, and are unanimously recommended by us, as necessary to answer his useful design.

"DANIEL NEAL.
W. HARRIS.
JER. HUNT.
JOSH. OLDFIELD, D. D.
MOSES LOWMAN.
EDW. WALLIN.
ARTHUR SHALLET.

"*London, August* 22*d*, 1721."

No. XLVII. — See p. 249.

FORM FOR THE INAUGURATION OF THE HOLLIS PROFESSOR OF DIVINITY.

Previously to acceding to the eleven preceding articles, recommended by the seven pastors, Mr. Hollis caused the following to be subjoined to them.

APPENDIX, No. XLVII.

"Plan or form for the Professor of Divinity to agree to at his inauguration.

Form for the inauguration of the Hollis Professor of Divinity.

"That he repeat his oaths to the civil government; that he declare it as his belief, that the Bible is the only and most perfect rule of faith and practice; and that he promise to explain and open the Scriptures to his pupils with integrity and faithfulness, according to the best light that God shall give him. That he promise to promote true piety and godliness by his example and instruction; that he consult the good of the College, and the peace of the churches, on all occasions; and that he religiously observe the statutes of his founder."

As the Overseers afterwards inserted, instead of "the Bible," the words "the Old and New Testament," these are given in the text; but the above were the terms used by Hollis in his first draft of this form.

No. XLVIII. — See p. 250.

PROCEEDINGS OF THE OVERSEERS RESPECTING HOLLIS'S RULES AND ORDERS.

Proceedings of the Overseers respecting Hollis's rules and orders.

"At an Overseers' meeting in Boston, January 10th, 1721-2. The President and Fellows of the College having this day laid before the Overseers the pious and generous proposal of Mr. Thomas Hollis, of London, merchant, for the establishing and endowing a resident Professor of Divinity of the said College, as also a draught of rules and orders relating to the said Professor, signed by Mr. Hollis himself;

"It was unanimously voted, that a letter of thanks be sent to the said Mr. Hollis, as for his great bounty in general to the College, so in special for his most kind offer with respect to a Professor of Divinity, and that Mr. Wadsworth and Mr. Colman draw up said letter and send it. Then the Overseers took into their most serious consideration the matter of a Professor of Divinity in general, and, after some debate, unanimously resolved, that the establishing a Professor of Divinity at the said College, under proper regulations, will, by the blessing of God, very much conduce to the advancement

Proceedings of the Overseers respecting Hollis's rules and orders.

of theology among the students there, to promote the interest of the true Christian religion throughout the whole land, and therein very much answer the great and pious end of incorporating the said College. The President continuing his theological expositions and exercises, and the Tutors their instructions in Divinity to their pupils as formerly.

"The next thing, proposed for consideration, was the rules and orders relating to the Professor, signed by Mr. Hollis. The qualifications and regulations of the said Professor being a matter of very great importance to the religion of New England, the founder himself also having been pleased, in his own letter to the Corporation, to desire them duly to consider of the said rules and orders, and send over such needful amendments as should be thought fit;

"The eleven rules and orders being distinctly read over and severally debated on, the Overseers did accept the first, the second, the third, the fourth with this alteration, after the word *publicly*,— '*once a week upon Divinity, either positive, controversial, or casuistical, and as often upon Church History, critical exposition of Scripture, or Jewish Antiquities, as the Corporation, with the approbation of the Overseers, shall judge fit.*' The fifth, the sixth, the seventh, the eighth, the ninth, the tenth, the eleventh, with this alteration, that, instead of the words *that it be recommended to the electors, that at every choice they prefer*, put in '*that the person chosen from time to time to be a Professor, be,*' &c.

"The plan of a form for the Professor of Divinity to agree to at his inauguration was accepted with these alterations, viz. instead of *Bible is* say '*the Scriptures of the Old and New Testament are,*' and after the word *only* blot out *and most.*

"In the last article but one, to the word *churches* add '*of our Lord Jesus Christ.*' In the last article subjoin to the close of it, '*and all such other statutes and orders as shall be made by the College not repugnant thereunto.*'

"The Overseers then adjourned to Wednesday, the 24th current, at 10 o'clock in the forenoon."

Records of the Overseers, Vol. I. p. 21.

No. XLIX. — See p. 261.

EXTRACT FROM A LETTER OF THOMAS HOLLIS TO BENJAMIN COLMAN.

Extract from a letter of Thomas Hollis to Benjamin Colman.

"*London, March 18th*, 1722-3.

"Dear Sir,

"His Excellency, your Governor, with his two brothers, Lord Barrington, and —— Bendish, Esqr., with Mr. Neal and Mr. Hunt, did me the honor to come and dine at my house, March 16th, and after dinner we read over your letter, and debated the President Leverett's answer to the writing obligatory I had demanded under the seal of the Corporation, "that, upon second thoughts, they could not find how to bind themselves faster than they are already, in justice," &c.

"Their unanimous advice was, that I should insist on it, to have such an obligation as strong as may be, according to your promise in former letters I should have; that in all times coming the Corporation will perform my trust in manner appointed by my orders, and not divert the moneys devoted, principal or increase, to any other uses; and, in case of default hereof to my mind, that then by the power I have reserved to myself, I may devise it over to —— for other uses discoursed of ——, which, if you ask your Governor at his return, he will tell you more largely.

"I am of opinion, when you have received the letters sent you as above mentioned, your Corporation will come into it, to send me an obligation as desired, without waiting for a copy of a draft from me. If I do not think it full enough, I may alter it and return it; and it will not be prudent for you to delay it; for, though I think I have sent enough by Osborne, if it arrive safe, to answer all I have as yet appointed, *yet more was designed, as I hinted, in my will. But that is as yet in my own power to alter, if I may not be gratified in this.*"

No. L. — See p. 274.

RESIDENT FELLOWS.

Resident fellows.

"*Anno Dom.* 1666. It is ordered by the Overseers, that such as are fellows of the College, and have salaries paid them out of the

Treasury, shall have their constant residence in the College, and shall lodge therein, and be present with the scholars at meal times in the Hall, have their studies in the College, that so they may be better enabled to inspect the manners of the scholars, and prevent all unnecessary damage to the society."

Resident fellows.

College Book, No. III. p. 25.

No. LI. — See p. 283.

LETTER FROM PRESIDENT LEVERETT TO THE HOUSE OF REPRESENTATIVES.

"To the Honorable Timothy Lyndall, Esquire, Speaker of the Honorable the House of Representatives, Boston.

Letter from President Leverett to the House of Representatives.

"*Cambridge, December 6th*, 1720.

"Mr. Speaker, Sir,

"This is the session you are wont to consider the subsistence and supports of your servants; and, though I have not the least apprehension you will forget that I have the honor to be numbered among them, yet I should neglect my duty both to you and myself, if I should not inform you, and pray you to intimate to the Honorable House,

"1. That the demolition in part, and the removal of the remains, of the President's house, have deprived me of that part of subsistence, which has been always provided by the country for all the Presidents of the College, which even non-resident Presidents for ever have had the benefit of.

"2. That what accrued from the disposal of that house was improved in yon noble additional building.

"3. That above twenty pounds of my own money, disbursed to make the President's house of any significant advantage to me when I could not dwell in it myself, is sunk and carried off in and with it, to so much sensible loss to me, beside that of the yearly revenue which has now ceased for a year and a half.

"I need not tell any body of the extraordinary charges I have been obliged to be at this year, nor mention the melancholy occasion of it; but yet it may be very well thought, that, when such things happen, and are coincident with such diminutions of what was and is necessary for the support of my post and station, difficulties, in-

APPENDIX, No. LI.

Letter from President Leverett to the House of Representatives.

conveniences, and discouragements in public services must unavoidably ensue.

"To be importunate would be impertinent, and may be deemed something worse. I assure you, Mr. Speaker, as I may not, so neither can I, entertain the thought of so much as a possibility, that the Honorable House of Representatives, after the generous care they have taken for the reception of the members of the College, can or will finally neglect the head of it.

"I will do myself the honor, with my humble duty to the Honorable House, and with profound regards to yourself, to subscribe,

"Honorable Sir,

"Your most faithful and humble servant,

"JOHN LEVERETT."

No. LII. — See p. 283.

LETTER FROM PRESIDENT LEVERETT TO JOHN WHITE.

Letter from President Leverett to John White.

"To Mr. John White, Boston.

"*Cambridge, December 14th*, 1720.

"Sir,

"This morning Mr. Boardman tells me, that it was said in the Honorable House of Representatives, that the President had not given the scholars above three expositions in the Hall for a twelvemonth, and that one of the Fellows had said, he would give his oath of it. I pray, Sir, do me the justice, as to declare, in my name, that the assertion is positively false, and demand of the gentleman, that said one of the Fellows would give his oath to the truth thereof, that he should tell which of the Fellows is disposed to be forsworn, and to swear to a falsehood. Such an one is not fit to have any thing to do in the College.

"If it be the mind of the College, that I should be starved out of their service, it is but letting me know their mind; I will not put that House to exercise that cruelty.

"I am, Sir,

"Your humble servant,

"JOHN LEVERETT."

No. LIII. — See p. 284.

LETTER FROM PRESIDENT LEVERETT TO THE HOUSE OF REPRESENTATIVES.

Letter from President Leverett to the House of Representatives.

" *Cambridge, December* 15*th*, 1720.

" Mr. Speaker, Sir,

" It may be justly thought strange, that I should trouble you with a second letter this session, and you will conclude it is something extraordinary that obliges me to do so; for in truth, Mr. Speaker, so it is.

" It is not the denial of what I thought a most reasonable request, and (I think I am sure I designed it) made in an humble and decent manner, that would have induced me to expostulate upon it, or revive it; but the irresistible occasion is what follows, viz. that I was informed, that a gentleman, a member of the Honorable House of Representatives, namely, Colonel Dudley, suggested and averred to the Honorable House, that there had not been in the College Hall above or more than three expositions performed by the President for this twelvemonth; and, repeating it, added, that one of the Fellows would give his oath that it is true. Now I have asked every one of the Fellows, viz. Mr. Flynt, Mr. Sever, Mr. Robie, and Mr. Welsteed, who each and every one of them deny, that ever any suggestion was made by them to any person, and that they neither are ready nor can give their oath to any such representation, for that they none of them suppose it, and some of them know, that it is not true. And I positively declare that it is false.

" The gentleman, I am sure, could not pretend to serve his country by such an averment, and our just country are not willing to be served by such a falsehood. I will not pretend to say what he designed to serve by his representation.

" I have served my country in sundry posts and under various characters, but I never was charged with unfaithfulness in any of them. I acknowledge my imperfections in all of them, but assert my integrity, and can pretend to some good measure of industry too. As for the service I am now in, if it happened the last year through sundry occasions, all relating to the College, some of the necessary duties and services were transposed, that would not by any means expose me to be thought diverting from the service I am devoted to, though some exercises, such as expositions, were not so numerous as sometimes they have been.

APPENDIX, No. LIII.

Letter from President Leverett to the House of Representatives.

"Besides, everybody knows, one great and melancholy diversion from such services as would be duty at other times, would be cruelty to be expected and demanded rigorously at such a time.

"Mr. Speaker, I must protest against the injustice of the representation above mentioned, and that if it has made any impressions upon any of the Honorable members, I pray you to set me right in their thoughts, for I am their and

"Your most faithful (though abused) and most humble servant,

"JOHN LEVERETT.

"To the Honorable Timothy Lyndall, Esquire,
Speaker of the House of Representatives."

No. LIV. — See p. 288.

THE PRESIDENT'S CHAIR.

The antique chair.

The antique chair represented in this vignette has been used in the College for the purpose of conferring degrees on Commencement day, for time beyond the memory of man. Little can be added to the account given by Mr. Peirce in the History of the College, p. 312.

Vague report represents it to have been brought to the College during the presidency of Holyoke, as the gift of the Rev. Ebenezer Turell, of Medford (the author of the Life of Dr. Colman). Turell was connected by marriage with the Mathers, by some of whom it is said to have been brought from England. Mr. Peirce considers it as resembling a class of chairs described by Horace Walpole, and said to be common in the county of Cheshire, being "of wood, the seat triangular, the back, arms, and legs loaded with turnery, and carved and turned in the most uncouth and whimsical forms."

See *Private Correspondence of Horace Walpole, Earl of Orford*, Vol. II. p. 279, and Vol. III. pp. 23, 24.

No. LV. — See p. 307.

MEMORIAL OF THE CORPORATION TO THE GENERAL COURT.

"At a meeting of the President and Fellows of Harvard College, in the Library, December 10th, 1722.

APPENDIX, No. LV.

Memorial of the Corporation to the General Court.

"A Memorial in the words following, viz.

"To his Excellency, Samuel Shute, Esquire, Captain-General, and Governor-in-chief, in and over his Majesty's Province of the Massachusetts Bay, in New England, the Honorable his Majesty's Council, and Representatives, in General Court assembled; the memorial of the President and Fellows of Harvard College, in Cambridge, within the Province aforesaid, most humbly showeth,

"That, the Honorable the House of Representatives having in their Journal of November 22d, past, with a great deal of concern intimated, that it is of the last consequence to that society, that the members of that Corporation take all possible caution that they keep strictly within the rules prescribed in their constitution, in all their acts, that so their ancient and well-established privileges may not in the leastwise be endangered; the members of that Corporation humbly say, that they are not sensible that they have passed any acts at any of their meetings, or that there have been any proceedings of the Corporation in the way and manner they now are, but what are justifiable and maintainable, and warranted by their charter. And the said members further say, that they are very sensible that it is of the last consequence to that society, and they believe it to be so to the whole country and all these churches, that the constitution of the College be entirely preserved, as well as the rules prescribed by the charter strictly pursued. And that their ancient and well-established privileges may not be in the leastwise endangered, the said members of the Corporation humbly think it to be their bounden duty to move to this Honorable Court, that they may be admitted to a hearing upon the premises, the Corporation not having as yet been heard thereupon.

"Wherefore, the said members of the Corporation pray they may be heard, and such a day given them to wait upon the General Assembly, as in their wisdom and justice they shall see meet.

"And your memorialists, as in duty bound, shall ever pray, &c.

"Your Excellencies' and Honors'

"Most humble and obedient servants,

"JOHN LEVERETT, President.

BENJAMIN WADSWORTH,
BENJAMIN COLMAN,
THOMAS ROBIE,
NATHANIEL APPLETON, } Fellows of Harvard College.

EDWARD HUTCHINSON, Treasurer.

"Dated, Cambridge, College Library,

December 10th, 1722."

APPENDIX, No. LV.

Memorial of the Corporation to the General Court.

"Being agreed to, it was voted, that the same should be presented to the General Court now sitting, and put into the House of Representatives by Mr. Treasurer Hutchinson. — *Corporation Records*, Vol. IV. pp. 81, 82.

"December 12th, 1722. In the House of Representatives a memorial of the President and Fellows of Harvard College, praying that they may be heard on the vote of this House, passed the 22d of November, and a day given them to wait on the General Assembly, as in their wisdom they shall see meet, &c. Read and dismissed, for that the prayer of the memorial is altogether groundless and noways to be justified. Ordered, that a message be sent to the honorable board, to inquire whether the vote of the House, passed November 22d, relating to the College, be passed upon by the board." — *Leverett's Manuscript*, p. 246.

No. LVI. — See p. 307.

EXTRACT FROM A LETTER OF THOMAS HOLLIS TO BENJAMIN COLMAN.

Extract from a letter of Thomas Hollis to Benjamin Colman.

"Your Governor (Shute) expresses a great value for your person, and tender regard for your honor. If they do vote you out in May, he will watch it shall not be concurred here. He says he is willing to explain, and enlarge your number of Fellows in the Corporation if advisable it may be done, but seems resolved that your three non-residents shall not be dismissed but on your own application. — *London, March 18th*, 1722-3."

No. LVII. — See pp. 309, 312.

MEMORIAL OF THE CORPORATION TO THE LIEUTENANT-GOVERNOR AND COUNCIL.

Memorial of the Corporation to the Lieutenant-Governor and Council.

"At a Corporation meeting held at the house of the Rev. Mr. Colman, in Boston, August 23d, 1723.

"The representation of the President and Fellows of Harvard College, upon the affairs of said College, now depending in the General Court, occasioned by a late petition of Mr. Nicholas Sever and Mr. William Welsteed, engrossed according to the agreement at the last meeting, being again read over, it was agreed, and

Memorial of the Corporation to the Lieutenant-Governor and Council.

voted, that the President be desired to sign it in the name of the Corporation. The President signed the said representation, accordingly, in the presence of the Corporation.

"The representation of the President and Fellows is as follows.

"To the Honorable William Dummer, Esquire, Lieutenant-Governor and Commander-in-chief in and over his Majesty's Province of the Massachusetts Bay, in New England; and to the Honorable his Majesty's Council, the humble representation of the President and Fellows of Harvard College upon the affairs of said College, now depending in the General Court, occasioned by a late petition of Mr. Nicholas Sever and Mr. William Welsteed.

"It having pleased your Honors so far to regard the memorial lately laid by us before the General Court, as to give us this hearing before you proceed to act upon the late resolves of the honorable House of Representatives, we do thankfully acknowledge your Honors' justice and goodness unto us herein, and make our reply in manner and form following.

"The report of the honorable Committee of the General Court, June 29th, 1722, upon the memorial of the Overseers of Harvard College, on which it has pleased the honorable House of Representatives to come into their resolve, consists of three articles and an introduction. We crave leave to make some short reply to each of them.

"The first article in the report of the honorable Committee is, '*that it was the intent of the College charter, that the Tutors of the said College, or such as have the instruction and government of the students there, should be Fellows and members of the Corporation of said College, provided they exceed not five in number.*'

"To this we reply, that, having had occasion often to peruse and consider the charter of the College, it still appears to us not to be the intent of said charter, that the Tutors of the College, or such as have the instruction and government of the students there, should be Fellows and members of the Corporation of said College, provided that they exceed not five in number. And our reasons are these that follow. First. If this had been the real intention of the General Court, who made and gave the charter, it seems unaccountable to us, that it was not plainly expressed, which might easily have been done, and we humbly think ought to have been. But, instead of that, when the first seven persons are named in the charter, it immediately adds, *all of them being inhabitants in the Bay*. It could as easily have said, *all of them being residents in the College*, or *within the town of Cambridge*, if that had really been the intention

APPENDIX, No. LVII.

Memorial of the Corporation to the Lieutenant-Governor and Council.

of the charter, and there is no doubt with us but it would have said so. But it being only given as a reason or qualification, that they were *inhabitants of the Bay*, it seems plainly to follow, that the charter never intended any such thing, as that the members of the Corporation must be resident Fellows (or Tutors) in the House.

"For we pray your Honors to consider with us, that this description, *all of them being inhabitants of the Bay*, was added for something, or for nothing. To say for nothing, would be such a reflection on that honorable General Court, as we can by no means give in to. If for something, we conceive it must be either for information in matter of fact, or for direction in future conduct. It could not be merely to inform in matter of fact, the thing being notorious to all. Therefore we must necessarily conclude, that it could only be a directory for future conduct; importing this, that, in all times to come, when there shall be occasion to choose a person into the Corporation, he must be an inhabitant in the Bay, as the Massachusetts Colony was then called.

"It seems plain, therefore, that all the record which can be pretended to be found in the College charter, respecting the residence of persons to be elected into the Corporation, is only this; that, as the first seven were inhabitants of the Colony of the Massachusetts Bay, so their successors must be in all times to come.

"If, may it please your Honors, there be any thing else in the charter that seems to require the residence of the Fellows of the Corporation within the House, it seems to be that clause in it, *and, for direction in all emergent occasions, execution of all orders and by-laws, the conclusion shall be made by the major part*, &c. &c. Now from hence some may plead, that the Corporation's residing at the College is necessary for the well-governing the students there, and for the executing the good laws provided for that end.

"To this we answer, that by the charter it is the province of the Corporation, *from time to time, to make such orders and by-laws for the ordering and carrying on the work of the College as they shall think fit, provided these orders be allowed by the Overseers.*

"Now, may it please your Honors, when such laws are made, the *ordinary execution* of them belongs to the President and Tutors residing in the House, who are in the immediate daily government of it, and for this service, among others, they receive their salary. But upon *emergent occasions, and in great and difficult cases*, the direction of the charter is, that the President call the Corporation together to advise and resolve, and, if need be, to *execute*, for the greater honor

APPENDIX, No. LVII.

Memorial of the Corporation to the Lieutenant-Governor and Council.

and service to the College, which accordingly has been the practice, on occasions that have called for severe censures or expulsions.

"May it please your Honors, we humbly conceive, that the College charter, empowering the Corporation to make orders and by-laws, does also authorize and empower them to appoint and require all officers, in their respective places within the College, to execute from day to day the laws made and confirmed for the good order and government of the House. And in a particular manner we judge the Tutors to be such officers, chosen and authorized for this very end, as well as to instruct; and unto the President and them does the execution of the by-laws and orders belong, in the daily ordering of matters within the House. It is not therefore at all necessary (we humbly conceive), that the Tutors be of the Corporation in order to the execution of the laws in the daily government of the House. Nay, what pretence can there be, that persons must needs be lawgivers in order to their having the executive trust and power committed to them?

"We pray your Honors, therefore, to observe, that the execution of all orders and by-laws, wherein the charter directs and expects the convening and acting of the Corporation is only upon *emergent occasions, and in great and difficult cases*, in which cases a non-resident Corporation are easily called together, and have usually been so.

"But, if any should say that this clause, *the execution of all orders and by-laws*, must be taken absolutely and unlimitedly, they must then extend it to all and every particular in the daily administration and ordering the affairs of the House; and then 't would follow, that a student must not have leave to go out of Commons, or out of town, unless there be a major part of the Corporation actually consenting in such a permission to him given. As also that at least four of the Corporation must consent to the punishing a student for being absent from, or tardy at prayers, recitation, or for the least misdemeanor that is punishable by the laws and usage of the House.

"Now this, in our apprehension, is so impracticable, not to say ridiculous, as that none can imagine it to be the meaning of the charter; and that the clause we are now considering refers only to *emergencies* is further confirmed to us from the Appendix to the charter, Anno 1657, which, reciting the paragraph referred to, only says, *all emergent occasions*, silently passing by the other clause, execution of all orders and by-laws. Moreover, also, it is evident in fact, that the orders and by-laws have been executed by the Presi-

APPENDIX, No. LVII.

Memorial of the Corporation to the Lieutenant-Governor and Council.

dent and Tutors upon the spot from time to time, in the daily administration of the House; and they have been always esteemed by the Overseers, and by the Corporation, as well as by themselves also, till of late, sufficiently authorized to execute the same.

"Having thus far argued upon one part and another of the charter, we go on (may it please your Honors) to consider more particularly *the powers granted by the charter to the Corporation*, which we humbly conceive are in their own nature too *great* to be reasonably granted unto the Tutors or resident Fellows to the number of five.

"For will your Honors please again to look over those powers? There is *the electing of the Presidents* from time to time. Will your Honors think the resident Tutors in the House the fittest persons for that great work? Then there is *the choosing, and, upon occasion, removing all officers, and of themselves*, among the rest, which, we think, must make but a very harsh and ungrateful sound in everybody's ear. Then there is *the making of all orders and by-laws*, for which kind of work your Honors (who are in the legislature over us) shall please to say, who are to be ordinarily judged the most capable persons. Then there is the *disposing of all the revenues of the College, and the appointing all salaries and allowances*, for services to be done therein.

"Now (may it please your Honors) when we consider *these powers* granted by the charter to the Corporation, we cannot conceive it to mean, that the resident Tutors, to the number of five, should be so invested. *All these* we think such articles of trust and importance, as call for more years, experience, and judgment, than the Tutors in the House may from time to time be supposed to have; for, generally speaking, they may be younger gentlemen of small experience, and they are often called from College to other work before they can have a proper insight into the weighty affairs and interests of the society.

"We would also add here, that, according to the charter, *no by-laws or orders can be made for the College but by the Corporation*, though the approbation of the Overseers be necessary.

"Therefore, if four or five Tutors be of the Corporation no law can be made directing and requiring said Tutors to do the services of their post, for which they receive salaries, unless those Tutors make it themselves. Now for persons in office, who receive wages or salary for their work, to be under no law referring to their work but what is of their own making, seems contrary to the reason of things, and to the practice of all well-regulated societies.

Memorial of the Corporation to the Lieutenant-Governor and Council.

"To be under no laws in their office work but those of their own making is, in effect, to be under no laws at all; for, if they be evil-minded, they may choose whether they will make any such laws as from time to time may be necessary, none can constrain them, nor make a new law without them.

"And again, if the Tutors should be the major part of the Corporation, and through sloth or otherwise should shamefully neglect the duties of their post, or be abusive or injurious in it, how shall the matter be mended? If new laws are needful, they cannot be made without them; or, if good laws already in being are to be executed, the execution is with them in the case supposed; and shall we think, that they will inflict deserved censure on themselves?

"Or again, let us suppose four resident Tutors, who may be inexperienced, and but lately chosen into the Corporation; then the whole legislature, and the whole executive trust, even upon all emergencies, and in all difficult cases, would be in their hands; which we apprehend would be most dangerous to, if not eversive of, the welfare of the College.

"We pass on, may it please your Honors, to another argument, which is *from custom and usage*, which, with all incorporated bodies, is *a great interpreter* of charters; and we think we may strongly argue thus, that the charter of the College was never interpreted or understood, that we know of, by our worthy predecessors in the state or in the church, to mean, that the Tutors and instructors in the College must necessarily be Fellows of the Corporation.

"None of said General Courts, or Boards of Overseers, have so judged, that we can hear of. The charter of 1672 requires no such thing, nor seems at all to look that way, which act is for the perpetuation of the charter of 1650. And when the government of the Province have in their wisdom gone into the forming of *new charters* for the College (as in the times of Sir William Phips, and in the times of Lieutenant-Governor Stoughton, and the Earl of Bellamont), yet no more than two of the Tutors were allowed to be of the Corporation in any of the draughts or charters by them made, or sent over for the royal approbation, although the Corporation was in those charters enlarged to the number of *ten* and of *seventeen*, and although *the Governor and Council for the time being were named visitors of the College in two of these charters.* This, we think, is a matter worthy of your Honor's special consideration.

"And moreover, when afterwards, under the government of Colonel

APPENDIX, No. LVII.

Memorial of the Corporation to the Lieutenant-Governor and Council.

Dudley, the College was set upon its present foot, there were *three neighbouring ministers* put into the Corporation, and one of the three resident Tutors left out.

"And, since that day, we who are now of the Corporation were approved by the Overseers without any seeking of our own, directly or indirectly.

"So that the way, which we are and have been in, is not in the least of our own devising or projecting, but it is the good old way, which our fathers walked in, and which they have set us in; and, thanks be to God, we have experienced his blessing in it, and the College has increased and prospered therein; and (through mercy) never more than of late years, under the diligent labors of the present Corporation. But the change of late projected and prescribed by some of the Tutors (in favor of themselves, and, as it seems to us, for their own private interest,) is perfectly and entirely novel.

"We ask, therefore, this favor of your Honors, to leave at least this our testimony and witness;—that we apprehend and fear prejudice and detriment to the College in times to come, both as to its estate and also as to the government of it, if this *new and untried* method be gone into. And, if any great inconveniences or damage to the College do ensue thereupon, we are clear of them; nor will they be so easily retrieved, when they may be too late felt and bewailed.

"But there is another thing which we also crave leave to recommend unto your Honors' wise and serious consideration, which is, *that the College Corporation is to have perpetual succession by election as vacancies happen.* So that if those three of the Corporation, whose ejection is thought and endeavoured by some, should be once *quit* of their station in it, or be made to *cease* together from it, the Corporation itself would then cease, and the charter become null and void, inasmuch as there will then remain but one Fellow, with the President and Treasurer, who cannot, by the charter, make an election to fill up the vacancy. For the charter plainly says, that the Corporation is to be continued by elections, and that there must be the *major part of seven* acting in those elections.

"And thus, may it please your Honors, we have made answer to the first article, which is the main and great one, in the report of the honorable Committee; and we submit our reasons, weighty as they seem to us, to your Honors' most impartial and deliberate consideration.

APPENDIX, No. LVII.

Memorial of the Corporation to the Lieutenant-Governor and Council.

"We come now to the second article in the report of the honorable Committee, which is, '*that none of the said Fellows be Overseers.*'

"To this we briefly answer, that, should the Corporation consist of resident Tutors, it is not probable, if possible, that any of them should be of the Board of Overseers, the said Tutors, while such, not being like to be teaching elders in any of the neighbouring churches, nor of his Majesty's Council.

"But then we still add, that some of the Fellows of the Corporation *have been* of the number of Overseers from time to time; and, as we think, to the *great benefit* of the College, so that till *now* it never was judged improper or unfit, or contrary to the intent of the charter, that some of the *Fellows of the Corporation* should be also of the Board of Overseers.

"The last thing in the report of the honorable Committee is, '*that the President and Fellows of the said College, or the major part of them, are not warranted to fix or establish any salary or allowance for their service, without the approbation and consent of the Overseers.*'

"To this we humbly reply; we think, that prior acts of legislature are to be explained, restrained, or enlarged, according to the plain sense of subsequent acts of the same legislature. We readily own, that, from the first constitution of the Overseers, in 1642, the whole management of the affairs of the College was entirely in the hands of the Overseers. But when the same legislature, that had constituted and empowered them, did, in the year 1650, make a charter for the College, and invested a Corporation with the powers therein granted, we humbly conceive, that *thenceforth* there remained no more power to the Overseers than what that charter leaves them.

"We are humbly of opinion, that if the present powers of the Overseers are sought for, they are not so much to be looked for in the act for their original constitution as in the subsequent acts of the General Court, and particularly the charter of 1650.

"That charter plainly supposes the continuance of the Board of Overseers, and reserves sundry powers to them; but we do not find that it leaves them any power in the matter of fixing and establishing any salaries or allowances, or the disposing of the incomes and revenues of the College.

"If this, our opinion, proceeds from our ignorance or weakness, we cannot help it, but should be glad to be enlightened by plain, strong explications of any passage in the charter to the contrary, if any such there be.

APPENDIX, No. LVII.

Memorial of the Corporation to the Lieutenant-Governor and Council.

"And upon all, inasmuch as we think that by the charter it belongs *wholly* to the Corporation to appoint and fix salaries and make allowances to those who do service in the College, therefore we think it the more unreasonable, that even the major part of the Corporation should be of those who receive salaries or allowances from the College. In such cases as these, we think that none ought to carve for themselves.

"In fine, upon this head we judge that the sole power of making allowances is by the charter vested in the Corporation. We know not of such allowances being at any time brought to the Overseers for their fixing them. But if the Tutors are, by charter, of the Corporation, we own it were a most unreasonable thing, that they should have power to fix and establish their own salaries. Neither can we think it decent, that they should have the first naming and appointing any salary for themselves. Wherefore we find here a new argument, if not assurance, that it never was the intent of the charter, that the College Corporation should consist of Tutors, to the number of four or five, receiving salaries.

"And thus we have made some reply to the report of the honorable Committee, in the several articles thereof; only, whereas in the preamble to their report, they are pleased to say, that these *their resolutions, if put in practice, would be more beneficial to the College than the enlarging the number of the Corporation;*

"We must still crave leave humbly to insist on the contrary opinion, and say, that we should be heartily glad, and think it much for the safety of the College, if the honorable Court could in their wisdom think it proper to enlarge the Corporation to twice its present number or more, because of the large powers with which we think it is intrusted; always provided, that the resident Tutors should never be able to make a major part, *because we think it contrary to the light of nature, that any should have an overruling voice in making those laws by which themselves must be governed in their office work, and for which they receive salaries.*

"Having thus answered to the report of the honorable Committee, we come now to offer a few words upon a clause or two in the petition of Mr. Sever and Mr. Welsteed, which they have lately presented to the General Court.

"They recite a proviso, which his Excellency, the Governor, was pleased to make some time the last year, that three of us, ministers, should not be removed from the Corporation.

"On this head we can assure your Honors, that none of us ever

Memorial of the Corporation to the Lieutenant-Governor and Council.

sought after such a proviso in our favor, directly nor indirectly, unless our open arguing and reasoning from time to time before the Board of Overseers may be so interpreted, which we humbly conceive it cannot justly be.

"It has been openly declared before your Honors, again and again, as we do now declare, that we have never meant to argue for our own personal continuance in the Corporation, but only against a majority of the resident Tutors being of it.

"We have no reason at all, for our own parts, to be *unwilling to part with our character* as Fellows of the Corporation, how meanly soever those gentlemen may think and are pleased to say reflectingly of us; and so far are we from desiring to continue in the Corporation, if it has not been, or may not be, for the service of the College, that it would be an ease and a pleasure to us to quit our station in it, and see it better served by others, and more secured by their services.

"Again, their petition has a clause in it to this effect; *the state of the College is now more difficult and perplexed than ever;* and certainly it is so, for which we think the petitioners are to blame themselves, as the first and moving cause of it. They themselves have first perplexed the College, and now they complain of its perplexed estate.

"Again, the petitioners pray the Honorable Court, *that they may be enabled, in their places, to carry on the business of the College to good effect.*

"We reply, that we think if they would, as becomes Christians, study to be quiet and do their own business, they have authority sufficient to do all that work and service in the College for which they were chosen, and they have laws provided for them to go by therein; or, if they need more, the Corporation is ready to provide more, and to lay the same before the Overseers.

"And now, to draw unto a close, we thank God, and we thank your Honors, for this opportunity granted us faithfully to discharge our consciences (how mean soever in themselves or meanly thought of by others), and of humbly and plainly testifying what we really think would be for the good of the College. We truly and seriously declare, that we make not this representation for any by-ends or self-interest. Those of us, whose ejectment is so earnestly sought for, neither seek nor find any reward for all that time we spend, or pains we take, as members of the Corporation. If we have served the College in any kind or degree, we desire to thank God for the

APPENDIX, No. LVII.

Memorial of the Corporation to the Lieutenant-Governor and Council.

time and assistance. We heartily wish and pray for its welfare, and for the flourishing of religion and good literature in it, to the glory of God and the good of all his people, even to the latest posterity, if it may be the divine pleasure so to order it.

"We wish its enemies may not find nor take any occasion against it by its late unhappy discontents and differences, the fault whereof lies at their door who have contrived and fomented them. A house or city divided against itself, what is likely to become of it? God avert the omen!

"We again thank your Honors for the patient hearing which you have given us. We desire to leave the event to the wise disposal of the sovereign God, and to submit ourselves thereunto, whether it be for correction or in mercy. We pray God to be with you in your judgment, and are

"Your Honors' most obedient humble servants,

"JOHN LEVERETT, *President of Harvard College,*

"in the name and at the desire of the Corporation.

"*In Council, August* 23*d*, 1723,

Read, &c."

No. LVIII. — See p. 316.

EXTRACT FROM A LETTER OF THOMAS HOLLIS TO BENJAMIN COLMAN.

Extract from a letter of Thomas Hollis to Benjamin Colman.

"*London, February* 24*th*, 1723-4.

"Mr. Cook, your agent, and his son, did me the honor to visit me at my house last week, and we discoursed of your state and of your College. He tells me your College is in a very bad state and condition; that the Corporation ought to be resident Fellows, and that the gentlemen non-resident are as worthy persons as the country affords, or could be chosen, but by their living at a distance cannot attend the good of the House as were to be desired; and that you cannot alter or increase the number of your Corporation without hazard of the whole; that the wisest men in Boston had thoroughly examined it, and himself also, who seems to understand your constitution very well."

No. LIX. — See p. 326.

MEMORIAL OF THE REV. MR. WADSWORTH AND THE REV. MR. COLMAN TO THE GENERAL COURT.

Memorial of the Rev. Mr. Wadsworth and the Rev. Mr. Colman to the General Court.

"To His Excellency, Samuel Shute, Esquire, Captain-General and Governor-in-chief in and over his Majesty's Province of Massachusetts Bay, and to the Honorable the Council and House of Representatives in General Court assembled, the 31st day of May, 1721.

"The memorial of the Fellows of Harvard College, humbly showeth,

"That, your memorialists having the honor to stand related to the said College for the more immediate inspection and government thereof, and being therefore more peculiarly bound to concern themselves in all respects for the interest and welfare of that society, and having taken into our consideration the necessary annual expense of the President and head of that society in supporting the honor of his station, we crave leave to suggest, that we are humbly of opinion, from the observation that we have made, that what is at present allowed is not sufficient to answer the same; the charge being increased as the Province and the number of those that visit the College and President is increased, and the President wholly taken off from every other way and means of providing for his support.

"Your memorialists therefore humbly supplicate this great and honorable Court, in behalf of the reverend President, as well as on behalf of the society and the interests of learning among us, that some addition (such as in your great wisdom and goodness you shall judge fitting) may be made to his present allowance.

"We should not have presumed to trouble this great and honorable Court with this our request (which has not its rise in any measure from the worthy person it is made for, but from our own mere motion), if our relation to, and many years' concern for, the College had not given us a further knowledge of the reasonableness and necessity of it, than the greatest part of the honorable members of this Court (by reason of their remote dwelling) can be supposed to have.

"We pray, as we are in duty bound, for the presence of God with the General Court in the present session, and for His gracious

APPENDIX, No. LIX.

acceptance of the government in all their cares for the interests of religion and learning, from time to time expressed, and are

"Your Excellency's and Honors'

"Most humble and obedient servants,

"BENJAMIN WADSWORTH.

"BENJAMIN COLMAN."

No. LX. — See p. 342.

COTTON MATHER'S SUGGESTIONS ON POINTS TO BE INQUIRED INTO CONCERNING HARVARD COLLEGE.

Cotton Mather's suggestions, &c.

"Important points relating to the education at Harvard College, needful to be inquired into. Prepared and humbly offered by some who have newly passed through the first four years of their being there.

"The performances of a deceased person, and with what industry and fidelity the churches of New England were served in them, 't is too late to inquire into. But the course of things as they have gone on of late time is a just matter of inquiry among those, who would not see the greatest interest of the country sacrificed, and the churches betrayed.

"It may be inquired,

"I. Whether solid learning be so valued and kept in reputation as it ought to be, and whether there be not rather a sensible and notorious decay of it from what has been in some former years.

"II. Whether the speaking of Latin has not been so discountenanced as to render our scholars very unfit for a conversation with strangers; and whether the undergraduates have not several times petitioned the governors of the College, that the speaking of Latin might be encouraged among them, and their petition been as often denied.

"III. Whether the recitations are such as to instil more solid learning into the pupils. Whether they are not very much of such authors, as are both unprofitable and indeed of little regard in the learned world at this day. Whether the Tutors do not often make their pupils get by heart a deal of insipid stuff and trash, that they bid them at the same time to believe nothing of it. Whether a great part of the exercises be not at best but serious follies.

"IV. Whether the pupils, having learned what is expected of them (which to the more acute sparks requires very little prepara-

Cotton Mather's sugges-tions, &c.

tion), all the rest of the time is not in a manner their own, and little care taken to make them deserve the name of students. Whether it be the custom of the Tutors, with a vigilant inspection, to see that they spend their time well, and assign them such books to read as may be most useful for them, and examine their proficiency, and what improvements they make by reading.

"V. Whether the scholars have not their studies filled with books which may be truly called *Satan's library.* Whether the books mostly read among them are not plays, novels, empty and vicious pieces of poetry, and even Ovid's Epistles, which have a vile tendency to corrupt good manners. Whether the Tutors ever look into this matter as they ought to do.

"VI. Whether the theological recitations, which are made once a week, are not usually carried on after such a cursory manner as to make little impression on the pupils.

"VII. Whether such books of divinity, as have most of the spirit of the Gospel in them, are such as are chiefly recommended into the reading of the students; or not rather such as have many erroneous and dangerous things in them. Whether, when books that have rank poison in them have been recommended to students there has been due care taken to warn them against the poisonous passages, and whether the more faithful writers, that have observed and censured these passages, have not been decried on all occasions.

"VIII. Whether there has been a due concern that the *doctrines of grace,* which are of so much influence on religion, should be understood and espoused by the students. Or whether the highest commendations sometimes given of some that have long been Tutors there have not been, that 'they have not set themselves to instil contrary principles.'

"IX. Whether any thing has ever been done, or one word ever spoken by the Tutors, to acquaint the students with the church state, which is the distinguishing interest and beauty of the churches in this country, and establish them in it.

"X. Whether the Tutors ever confer with their pupils about their interior state, and labor as men in earnest with them for their conversion to God? Whether the souls of the young men are not grievously neglected by those who should remember, that they have the destined ministers of the Gospel under their education.

"XI. Whether many godly persons in the country have not with sad hearts lamented it, that their children, who have left their families with some Gospel symptoms of piety upon them, after they came

APPENDIX, No. LX.

Cotton Mather's suggestions, &c.

to live at College, do quickly lose all, and neither do nor hear any more such things as they had before they went from home.

"XII. Whether the most of these excellent young ministers, who are the gifts of Christ in the service of our churches, will not, upon inquiry, declare, that, before they came to be what they are, they found it necessary to lay aside the sentiments which they brought from the College with them."

No. LXI. — See p. 370.

MEMORIAL OF THE REV. DR. CUTLER AND THE REV. MR. MYLES TO THE GENERAL COURT.

Memorial of the Rev. Dr. Cutler and the Rev. Mr. Myles to the General Court.

"*Province of Massachusetts Bay.*

"To the Honorable William Dummer, Esquire, Lieutenant-Governor and Commander-in-chief in and over his Majesty's Province of the Massachusetts Bay, and to the Honorable the Council and House of Representatives in General Court assembled.

"The memorial of Timothy Cutler, Doctor of Divinity, and Samuel Myles, Master of Arts, and as they are the present incumbents of Christ's Church and his Majesty's Chapel in Boston, within the County of Suffolk and Province aforesaid, most humbly showeth,

"That at a session of the great and General Court the 8th day of the 7th month, 1642, it was ordered in these words; That the Governor and Deputy for the time being, and all the magistrates of this jurisdiction, together with the teaching elders of the six next adjoining towns, that is, Cambridge, Watertown, Charlestown, Boston, Roxbury, and Dorchester, and the President of the College for the time being, shall have from time to time full power and authority to make and establish all such orders, statutes, and constitutions, as they shall see necessary for the instruction, guiding, and furthering said College, and the several members thereof, from time to time, in piety, morality, and learning, &c., provided also, that if any constitution, order, or orders, shall be made, that is found hurtful to said College or the members thereof, or to the weal public, that then, upon the appeal of the party or parties aggrieved to the said

Memorial of the Rev. Dr. Cutler and the Rev. Mr. Myles to the General Court.

Overseers, that they shall repeal the said order or orders at the next meeting, or stand accountable thereof to the next General Court, as by the said act or order, reference thereunto had, more fully will appear. That in observance of your memorialists, Cutler and Myles, likewise the Rev. Mr. Henry Harris, as teaching elders of this town of Boston, have been notified to be present at sundry meetings of said Overseers, and the said Mr. Harris was actually present at several. But so it was, that at an Overseers' meeting at the Council Chamber in Boston, the 18th of May, 1727, his Honor the Lieutenant-Governor informing the board that application had been made to him by your memorialist, Cutler, that he might be notified to be present at the meetings of the Overseers, after a debate had thereon the question was put, whether the said Dr. Cutler be notified accordingly, and it passed in the negative, the board apprehending that he is not entitled thereto. Thereupon your memorialist, Cutler, the 15th of June last, by writing directed to the Overseers, desired to be informed, if he was not entitled to be present at the meetings of the Overseers when notified by their clerk so to be, or at any time since his being an Episcopal minister in the town of Boston, or if he had forfeited that title since, and by what means; and the said Overseers taking the same into consideration, as also their constitution, were of opinion, that the said memorialist has not nor ever had, by the said constitution, a right to sit as an Overseer of Harvard College.

"Also on the said 15th of June your memorialist, Myles, by writing directed to the Overseers, complained that he was not notified by their clerk, as formerly, to sit among the Overseers, and desired this affair might be redressed, and if not, that he might know for what reasons. The board made answer, that he has not nor ever had, by the said constitution, a right to sit as an Overseer of Harvard College.

"Forasmuch, therefore, as the said act of the General Court, that constituted the said Overseers, directs any members grieved with any orders made by said Overseers, to appeal to them, directing at the same time said Overseers to repeal said order or orders, in failure whereof obliging them to be accountable thereof to the next General Court; and that your memorialists think themselves grieved by said order or vote of the said Overseers of the 18th of May last, which induced your memorialist, Cutler, to appeal to said board for the repeal of the same as aforesaid, at their next meeting in June aforesaid, and the said Overseers, at their last meeting, instead of removing the said order, enforced it, and passed another of a like import,

APPENDIX, No. LXI.

Memorial of the Rev. Dr. Cutler and the Rev. Mr. Myles to the General Court.

to exclude your said memorialist, Myles, from the board of Overseers.

"Your memorialists, therefore, pursuant to the said act, Anno 1642, apply to your Honors for redress in the premises; not doubting but that your Honors will be of opinion, that the great and General Court, by their aforesaid act, did, in their great wisdom and justice, design no exclusion of the ministers of the Church of England from the inspection and ordering of Harvard College, since the orthodoxy of the Church of England is questioned by no sound Protestant, and the members of that Church in this government bear an equal proportion in all public charges to the support of said College, and the members of that Church are equally with any others qualified and disposed to promote the interests of religion, good literature, and good manners, the worthy ends propounded in the founding of it; and that your memorialists, by their ordination and canonical induction into their respective churches of the town of Boston are fairly included in the denomination of teaching elders according to its natural and genuine sense and import, and such teaching elders, who, according to said act, have a right to sit as Overseers of Harvard College; and thereupon your memorialists humbly beg an order of this General Court, that, according to the constitution of the body of Overseers, they may be restored the right of Overseers, and may, agreeably to custom, equity, and justice, be again notified and have seats at the meetings of the Overseers of Harvard College, and your memorialists shall ever pray.

"TIMOTHY CUTLER.
"SAMUEL MYLES.

"In the House of Representatives, December 27th, 1727, read again, together with the answer of the Overseers of the College to the said petition, and the House debated thereon; also a reply of the petitioners to the answer aforesaid was read, and the same being duly considered, the question was put, whether it is within the intent and meaning of the charter granted to the said College, that the Reverend memorialists, the said Dr. Timothy Cutler and Mr. Samuel Myles, ought to be deemed as members of the board of Overseers hereof, it passed in the negative. "WM. DUDLEY, *Speaker*.

"Sent up for concurrence.

"In Council, December 28th, 1727, read and concurred.
"S. WILLARD, *Secretary*.

"Consented to. WM. DUMMER.

"In the House of Representatives, January 11th, 1727-8, upon a motion made and seconded, the House entered further into the consideration of the subject-matter of these petitions, and the following question was thereupon put, viz. Whether it is within the intent and meaning of the act of the General Court, Anno, 1642, and referred to in said memorials, constituting the board of Overseers of Harvard College, that the Reverend memorialists, the said Dr. Timothy Cutler and Mr. Samuel Myles, ought to be deemed members of the board of Overseers, it passed in the negative.

Memorial of the Rev. Dr. Cutler and the Rev. Mr. Myles to the General Court.

"WM. DUDLEY, *Speaker.*

"In Council, January 11th, 1727-8, read and concurred.

"S. WILLARD, *Secretary.*

"Consented to. WM. DUMMER."

No. LXII. — See p. 371.

MEMORIAL OF THE REV. DR. CUTLER AND THE REV. MR. MYLES TO THE GENERAL COURT.

"Province of Massachusetts Bay.

Memorial of the Rev. Dr. Cutler and the Rev. Mr. Myles to the Genera Court.

"To the Honorable William Dummer, Esquire, Lieutenant-Governor and Commander-in-chief, and the Honorable the Council and Representatives in General Court assembled.

"The memorial of sundry ministers and others, of the Church of England in New England, humbly showeth, That whereas by the ancient establishment of the General Court, held in Boston, the 8th of September, 1642, the Governor and Deputy for the time being, and all the magistrates of this jurisdiction, together with the teaching elders of six next adjoining towns, that is, Cambridge, Watertown, Charlestown, Boston, Roxbury, and Dorchester, and the President of the College for the time being, are made and appointed Overseers of the College at Cambridge, for the ends and purposes in the same act expressed; and by force and virtue of that act, all those persons, and among the rest the ministers of the Church of England in Boston, lately have been deemed and taken to be Overseers of the said College, and from time to time ever since have assembled and met together, and ordered and disposed the affairs of said College as the Overseers. But so it is, may it please this great and Honorable Court, these three last years the ministers of the Church of England in Boston have been neglected and not

APPENDIX, No. LXII.

Memorial of the Rev. Dr. Cutler and the Rev. Mr. Myles to the General Court.

called to the meetings of the Overseers aforesaid; and, upon application made to them by the Rev. Dr. Timothy Cutler and Mr. Samuel Myles, two of the ministers of the Church of England, on the 15th of June last, the Honorable the Overseers, upon consideration of the constitution aforesaid, voted, declared, and recorded their opinion, that the said Dr. Cutler and Mr. Myles have not, nor ever had, by the said constitution, a right to sit as Overseers of Harvard College. We consider that College as the common nursery of piety and learning to New England in general, as well to them that are of the order of the Church of England as to them that are of the order of the churches of New England; the common interest of both to support it, and a blessing to both when it flourisheth; and therefore apprehend that it is a pity those different orders should be made differing parties, not only in the churches where they are different, but in the College where they are entirely one; and will tend to discourage those of the order of the Church of England from doing those services to the College, or receiving those benefits from it, as otherwise they might.

"We are not so imprudent as to imagine, that the admission of those two gentlemen can make us a party in the ordering of that College, and serve any secret designs or separate interests (which in the nature of the case, is impossible); but only seek that all especial notes of groundless distinction and disesteem towards us may be abated, and an universal good understanding among us all promoted and established. It seems by the vote of the Honorable Overseers above mentioned, as though they did not look upon the ministers of the Church of England to be teaching elders. But we would humbly hope there is no ground sufficient, upon calm thought, to maintain such an opinion; for they have both been ordained teaching elders by the Bishop of London, and have their several credentials for that purpose, and have been both orderly sent to execute that their function in Boston, which they are able to prove; and, as for a minister of the Church of New England, and his being a teaching elder, it has never been questioned and disputed by those of the order of the churches of New England, that we have heard of; indeed, there have been disputes raised and maintained concerning ruling elders, and each several order have claimed to themselves the right of ruling elders, but neither order has ever questioned but the elders of our church were teaching elders before now, if it now be questioned. Wherefore, forasmuch as this great and Honorable Court has the superintending and government of all

APPENDIX, No. LXII.

Memorial of the Rev. Dr. Cutler and the Rev. Mr. Myles to the General Court.

affairs within this Province, for the common good and general quiet and happiness of all his Majesty's good subjects here; and the Rev. Dr. Cutler and Mr. Myles have made this Honorable Court their last resort here, both as the common and impartial patrons of all good men, and the best expositors of your own acts; we therefore, in concurrence with them, humbly pray this Honorable Court, that, according to the original fundamental constitution of the said Overseers, these worthy gentlemen may be deemed, reputed, and declared by this Honorable Court, to be two of the said Overseers of the said College at Cambridge; and your Honors' most humble orators shall ever pray for the prosperity and happiness of this government and that of the College at Cambridge, and every interest of New England, both civil and sacred."

Signed by seventy persons.

"In the House of Representatives, August 25th, 1727, read, and ordered, that these petitions be referred to the next fall session of this Court for further consideration, and that in the mean time Mr. Secretary be directed to serve the clerk of the Overseers of Harvard College with a copy of the said petitions, that the Overseers may make answer thereto at the said session. Sent up for concurrence.

"Wm. Dudley, *Speaker*.

"In Council, August 26th, 1727, read and concurred with the amendments.

"Sent down for concurrence.

"J. Willard, *Secretary*.

"In the House of Representatives, August 26th, 1727, read and concurred.

"Wm. Dudley.

"In Council, August 26th, 1727, consented to.

"Wm. Dummer."

No. LXIII. — See p. 374.

ANSWER OF THE OVERSEERS TO THE MEMORIAL OF THE REV. DR. CUTLER AND THE REV. MR. MYLES.

Answer of the Overseers, &c.

"Province of Massachusetts Bay, in New England.

"To the Honorable William Dummer, Esquire, Lieutenant-Governor and Commander-in-chief in and over his Majesty's Province of the Massachusetts Bay aforesaid, and to the Honorable the Council and Representatives in General Court assembled, at Boston, Nov. 22d, Anno Domini, 1727.

"The answer of the Overseers of Harvard College in Cambridge, to the memorials of the Rev. Dr. Timothy Cutler and Mr. Samuel Myles, with sundry others, in their behalf, presented to the General Court in August last, against the Overseers, and referred to the consideration of this present session, humbly showeth,

"That the said Overseers freely allow, that at a session of the great and General Court, the 8th of September, 1642, the Governor, Deputy, and all the magistrates of this jurisdiction, with the teaching elders of Cambridge, Watertown, Charlestown, Boston, Roxbury, and Dorchester, and the President of the College for the time being, were made and appointed the Overseers of the said College. That, agreeable to this, upon his Honor the Lieutenant-Governor informing the board of Overseers, on the 18th of May last, that application had been made to him by the said Rev. Dr. Cutler, that he might be notified to be present at the Overseers' meetings, the said Overseers did vote, that he be not notified, the board apprehending that he is not entitled thereto; as also about the 15th of June, upon the said Rev. Dr. Cutler and Mr. Myles complaining of not being notified, at a very full board of the Overseers, the said board, taking the same into serious consideration, and examining the said memorialists' pretended right by the act or constitution aforesaid, did by a very great majority vote, that they had not, nor ever had, by the said constitution, a right to sit as Overseers of Harvard College; and they found their judgment on the following reasons.

"1. It is a most clear, undeniable, and universal rule, that the signification of terms must be decided in every country according to the known and general acceptation of them, in the several countries where they are used, and laws must needs be explained according to the general use of the terms in the places where they are made, in times when they are enacted, and agreeable to the known principles of the legislators.

"Thus, a deacon, in England, both in general use and in all their public acts, signifies a person ordained to preach the gospel; but a deacon, in this country, always signified a person chosen to take care only of the churches' temporal matters. And thus, the signification of magistrate in England, and even now in New England, extends to every one of his Majesty's Justices of the Peace; but in the time when the act abovesaid was made, wherein the said term is used, the known signification extended only to those who were Assistants to the Governor in Council, and therefore must be still so explained.

"2. Agreeable to this undeniable rule, the phrase expressed in the abovesaid act of a 'teaching elder,' must for the same reason be construed.

"Now the known construction of these terms in this country, from the very beginning, is this, namely, the pastors and teachers of a complete and Congregational church, the very same which the Scriptures call by the name of bishops, who have the full power both of teaching and administering the sacraments, and of ruling in the said church, and are called teaching elders, to distinguish them from another sort of elders, which have the power of ruling only, which latter are therefore called, for distinction's sake, ruling elders. This is the known signification of the term 'teaching elders' among us; in this sense it has been used from the beginning. It indeed lay in the foundation of this ancient colony; is agreeable to all the public writings in defence of these churches, to their judgment declared in the synods, approved by their General Courts, and the laws of the said jurisdiction; and this is the known and general meaning of these terms to this very day. For the proof of this, we would observe,

"1st. There was not one assembly, nor so much as one minister, magistrate, or representative in the General Court, professedly of the Church of England, for above fifty years after the settlement of the said colony, and for above forty years after the act abovesaid, there being no others but teaching elders of Congregational churches then in being in this country, and it is such elders only that it can refer to.

"2d. To make this evident we shall cite some of the laws of the

APPENDIX, No. LXIII.

Answer of the Overseers, &c.

said jurisdiction in those times wherein the united body both of magistrates and people declared, that by the 'churches' they meant Congregational churches, and by 'elders' the elders of those churches. Among the laws of the said jurisdiction of the Massachusetts, title *ecclesiastical*, are the following passages.

"'*Sec.* 1. All the people of God within this jurisdiction, who are not in a church way and be orthodox in judgment, and not scandalous in life, shall have full liberty to gather themselves into a church state, provided they do it in a Christian way, with the observation of the rules of Christ revealed in his word.'

"'*Sec.* 4. Every church hath free liberty of election and ordination of all her officers from time to time, provided they be able, pious, and orthodox.'

"'*Sec.* 5. Every church hath free liberty of admission, recommendation, dismission, and expulsion, or disposal of their officers and members, upon due cause, with free exercise of the discipline and censures of Christ according to the rules of the word.'

"'*Sec.* 13. Considering the rich blessing of God flowing from the good agreement of the civil and church state, it is therefore ordered, that henceforth no person shall be ordained to the office of a teaching elder, where any two organic churches, Council of State, or General Court, shall declare their dissatisfaction thereat; and, in case of ordination of any teaching elders, timely notice thereof shall be given to three or four of the neighbouring organic churches for their approbation.'

"See also Sec. 3, 6, 12, 14, and last.

"But, to put the matter beyond all possibility of evasion, we shall here produce the most approved and public declaration of the judgment both of magistrates and ministers, churches, courts, and people, in those days, and this is in their well-known Platform of church discipline. As previous to which we shall (1st) observe, that the General Court, on the 15th of May, 1646, made an order for the calling of a synod from all the churches of this country, in the following words; 'To agree on a form of government and discipline for the main and substantial parts thereof as that which they judge agreeable to the holy Scriptures, that it may receive from the said General Court such approbation as is meet; and our posterity may not so easily decline from the good way when they shall receive the same thus publicly and solemnly commended to them.'

"2d. The said synod accordingly met, agreed on the said Platform, and presented it to the General Court, who sent it to all the

APPENDIX, No. LXIII.

Answer of the Overseers, &c.

churches in the government, desiring them to signify how far it was suitable to their judgment and approbation. Upon return of the same by the Representatives of the several towns, the General Court took further care to remove all objections, as appears from their records, and then in their session of October 14th, 1651, declare their approbation, concluding with the following words; 'Accounting themselves called of God, especially at this time, when the truth of Christ is so much opposed in the world, to give their testimony to the said Book of Discipline, that, for substance thereof, it is what we have practised and do believe.' Agreeable to this most public declaration of their preceding practice and continued belief, we shall now show to your Honors what their said practice and belief were in said book.

"In Chap. II. Sec. 5, they declare their judgment, that the state of the members of the visible church walking in order since the coming of Christ is only Congregational (the term Independent we approve not), therefore neither national, provincial, nor classical.

"Chap. IV. Sec. 3. That the form of a church is a visible covenant.

In Chap. VI. Sec. 3. That the officers of a church were either extraordinary, such as apostles, prophets, evangelists; ordinary, as elders and deacons.

"Sec. 4. That the elders are also in Scripture called bishops, and of these some attend chiefly to the ministry of the word, as the pastors and teachers; others attend especially to rule, who are therefore called ruling elders.

"Chap. VII. Sec. 1. That ruling elders are not so called to exclude the pastors and teachers from ruling, because rule and government is common to these with the others.

"Chap. X. Sec. 5. They assert the power of the church and brotherhood (1st) to choose their own officers, whether elders or deacons; (2d) to admit their own members, and both to excommunicate and otherwise censure them for offences, and to restore the penitent.

"Sec. 8. That the power that Christ has committed to the elders is to feed and rule the church; and Sec. 11. That the ordaining power of government belongs only to the elders, the power of judge remains with the brotherhood; and that, in an organic church and right administration, no church act can be perfected without the consent of both. This is the substance of said Platform, whereby it essentially differs from most other schemes of church order and

APPENDIX, No. LXIII.

Answer of the Overseers, &c.

discipline, and which the said General Court has borne their testimony to, have been their practice, and what they believed. And by these things it appears as clear as the light, that by churches were meant, by the framers of those ancient laws, no other than the Congregational churches; by elders, no other than elders of these particular churches, which elders they also accounted to be such as are chosen by the said churches, and have full power both to teach, to feed, and to rule them, and therefore no others but such elders as these were by them intended and appointed to be the Overseers of the College by the act abovesaid.

"And hence the said Overseers draw the undeniable conclusion, that the said Reverend memorialists neither have, nor ever had, by the said act, a right to sit among us as Overseers of Harvard College; that all insinuations of the said memorialists about their being teaching elders, and of groundless notes of distinction, &c., are entirely vain, not only because the said denomination can never be found attributed to them in any public acts whatever, either abroad or here, but is only now assumed to serve their present turn and break in upon our ancient constitution; and even they themselves in the title of their memorial carefully avoid the style where one would especially on such an occasion expect it, and, instead of calling themselves teaching elders of Christ Church and his Majesty's Chapel in Boston, they chose to entitle themselves the incumbents of the said church and chapel, a style that is unknown among us, and can't be found in any of our public instruments. But especially all the memorialists say on this head is wholly beside the question, inasmuch as the said Reverend memorialists never pretended, nor may they pretend, to be such sort of elders as the framers of the act aforesaid have so fully declared to be their intention, which would be for the Reverend memorialists to assert themselves to be the same with bishops in Scripture, and have the full and unsubordinate power both to teach, feed, and govern their particular churches. Nor is their discourse about their notification any more to their purpose; for it is well known, that, for many years after there were ministers of the order of the Church of England in the town of Boston, they were never deemed to be Overseers, never notified, never complained of their not being notified, and, when they were notified some few years since, it was done without the direction of the Overseers; and, though the error was not so well considered in the time of it, it has since been noticed and corrected, and for some years past has ceased accordingly. And it cannot be supposed, that a notification gives

APPENDIX, No. LXIII.

Answer of the Overseers, &c.

right to any to be Overseers, who have no previous right by the plain intention of the act aforesaid. For then the Overseers or their clerk may convey a right to whom they please, in defiance of the said act, and so alter the constitution at their pleasure.

" And, as for the Reverend memorialists, they neither of them ever met, or acted, or ordered, or disposed of the affairs of the College, as is wrongly insinuated in some of the memorials. And, as for their arguments from the College being a nursery of piety and learning to New England in general, not only to those of the order of the churches of New England, as the memorialists term it, but also to them of the Church of England, the common interest and charge of both to support it; it is easily answered, that we account it distinguishing honor to our College, that the education there is free, without oaths or subscriptions to any particular sort of church order or discipline; and that, though the governors of the College be of the Congregational order, yet, agreeably to their known principles of liberty, the sons of the Church of England are as welcome to the learning and academical honors there as any of our own children; and this is as much as the memorialists can, in honor or justice, desire of those who are intrusted with a constitution settled for above fourscore years before the said Reverend memorialists, or any of their order, pretended to a right to come among us, and even above forty years before there were any of the said reverend order settled in this country; but the Overseers account the said act and constitution as a sacred deposit put into their hands to keep inviolate, by the excellent and ancient fathers of this country in General Court assembled, which they cannot, either in law or conscience, in the least vary from; and for the same reason that the memorialists have made this Honorable Court their last resort, as the best expositors of their own acts, the said Overseers cannot doubt but your Honors will adhere to the said ancient constitution, and not adjudge the Reverend memorialists to be such teaching elders as the abovesaid act intends, nor ever declare them to be of the number of the Overseers of Harvard College. All which is humbly submitted to the great wisdom and justice of this Honorable Court by the Overseers of the said College. In the name and by the order of the Overseers of Harvard College.

" HENRY FLYNT, *Clerk Curator.*

" In Council, December 18th, 1727, read and ordered to be sent down.

" SAMUEL TYLEY, *Clerk.*"

No. LXIV. — See p. 375.

REPLY OF THE REV. DR. CUTLER AND THE REV. MR. MYLES TO THE ANSWER OF THE OVERSEERS.

"Province of the Massachusetts Bay.

Reply of the Rev. Dr. Cutler, &c.

"In the great and General Court, November 22d, 1727. The reply of Dr. Cutler and others to the Overseers of Harvard College, their answer.

"May it please your Honors, the said Dr. Cutler and Mr. Samuel Myles, present incumbents of Christ Church and the King's Chapel in Boston, are (as we humbly conceive) by the act of the General Court of the 8th of September, 1642, made two of the Overseers of Harvard College, for,

"(1st.) They have been duly ordained, instituted, and inducted into their respective churches, and are in fact proper teaching elders of these churches, as we have alleged, and are ready to prove, and this has not been denied by the answer aforesaid; and therefore they are by the act made Overseers, and have a right to sit as such.

"(2d.) The Presbyters or ministers of the Church of England were meant and intended by the terms of teaching elders in the act aforesaid, for the plain force of the terms includes them to every man's understanding; and therefore we can't imagine the legislature intended by those terms to exclude them. The gentlemen, that made that law, honored these ministers as the Lord's ministers, and that church as their dear mother, as by their letter but twelve years before this act, dated April 7th, 1630, subscribed John Winthrop, Governor, George Phillips, Richard Saltonstall, Charles Fines, Isaac Johnson, Thomas Dudley, William Coddington. When this act was made, the gentlemen that made it had no more power to hinder any of the Church of England from coming into this place, nor any assurance they would not be here the next year; and, if they had, it is not possible these gentlemen should say to them, Your ministers are not teaching elders, nor have any right to sit as Overseers. These things laid in the foundation.

"(3d.) We are humbly of opinion, that the memorialists have as good a right to sit now, as they would have had if they had come forty years ago, for in that they are but in the common case of all the rest in reality, and therefore 't is no argument against them, that they came here but lately.

Reply of the Rev. Dr. Cutler, &c.

"(4th.) Though the ecclesiastical laws gave good men a liberty to gather into a church, and that church liberty to elect and ordain their officers, to admit, expel, and dispose of their officers and others, but, when they did ordain any, they should have the approbation of the neighbouring churches, yet they never say, that, if any number of those good men be of the Church of England, they may not give up these liberties we here give them; if they do, and send to the Bishops for a teaching elder, he shall not exercise his function here. But 't is plain those laws, according to the opinion of those worthy men in these disputed points, gave liberty for the people to erect such a church among them, and at the same time never thought the Church of England no church, the ministers no teaching elders, nor had a thought of depriving them of liberty of conscience here.

"(5th.) The Platform indeed doth seem to give us a pretty clear description of teaching elders, that they are such as are also called Bishops, and have power both to teach and rule the churches; and yet we are humbly of opinion, that don't prove the memorialists have no right to sit as Overseers of Harvard College; for those reverend and worthy gentlemen that compiled the Platform, though they herein gave their opinion in a disputed point, yet they never meant this opinion was such a fundamental article of the Christian faith, that he that being ordained a teaching elder could not think himself therefore a bishop, and to have all the power of ruling the church committed to him, was therefore in fact degraded, was no minister at all, and that the inferior clergy of the Church of England were not to be acknowledged as ministers and teaching elders; such austere sentences are no consequence from private opinions differing in point of modo and form. Besides, if there be any thing in these declarations of the Platform compared with the ecclesiastic laws aforesaid, it seems to be entirely in the memorialists' favor; for the said laws seem to give all the power and rule to the fraternity, to ordain, expel, and dispose of the pastors and others, and leave nothing but the faculty of teaching and feeding to the teaching elders. These laws are made in 1641, and then in 1642 the act is made to make teaching elders Overseers of the College. Wherefore it seems plain, that the memorialists, who claim but to be teaching elders, not to be bishops, nor to have the full and unsubordinate power both to teach and govern their particular churches, thereby keep themselves duly within the primary sense of the legislature in those terms of 'teaching elders'; while the gentlemen that follow the Platform plainly depart from the law, deny the entire

APPENDIX, No. LXIV.

Reply of the Rev. Dr. Cutler, &c.

power of the fraternity, and claim a full unsubordinate power to rule their particular churches, and to be the same with bishops, and that by the Platform made some years after the said laws and the act appointing the Overseers, by this departure from the laws to the Platform, seem to put themselves out of the intention of these terms of 'teaching elders' in the act aforesaid. So that, upon the whole, we account the College a common interest, and beg leave, with the answerers, to call it *our College*, and the said act our depositum. They will have nevertheless benefit of it, and we shall all have the more charity, and the better title to a blessing on it, which is and shall be the constant prayer of your Honors' most humble orators, &c.

"We flatter ourselves that your Honors will candidly attribute all the imperfections of this replication to the contractedness of the time we had to put in the same. We were only from eight last night till this morning.

"JOHN READ, *Pro Quer.*"

No. LXV. — See p. 388.

OVERSEERS' COMMITTEE OF INQUIRY.

Overseers' committee of inquiry.

On this committee there were, of the Council, the Honorable Thomas Hutchinson, Spencer Phips, and Jonathan Remington; and of the clergy, the Rev. John Webb, William Cooper, Thomas Foxcroft, and Joshua Gee.

No. LXVI. — See p. 394.

CASE OF MR. LONGLOISSORIE, FRENCH INSTRUCTOR

Case of Mr. Longloissorie, French instructor.

An account of the errors of this individual is given by Dr. Wigglesworth, Hollis Professor of Divinity, in his "Letter to the Rev. Mr. George Whitefield, by Way of Reply to his Answer to the College Testimony against him and his Conduct," * written for the purpose of illustrating the tendency of that enthusiasm, for which he condemned Whitefield, to mistake "dreams and suggestions, and any thing which bears strongly upon the mind, as from

* Printed at Boston, 1745, 4to.

APPENDIX, No. LXVI.

the Spirit of God," and which proved destructive to faith, as in other instances to good conscience.

Case of Mr. Longloissorie, French instructor.

"We very sensibly felt its ill effects in the society under our care not more than ten years ago, when a gentleman, who had been permitted to teach the French tongue in the College, where he had behaved himself to all appearance unblamably, at length began to give too much heed to certain dreams, which he supposed to be of divine original. And, when once he had gotten his imagination thoroughly heated with these, he soon began to fancy himself favored frequently with visions too, and these sometimes attended with articulate voices to instruct him in the divine meaning and design of them. Upon this he very industriously, though with as little observation as he could, endeavoured to propagate among his intimate friends several strange and pernicious doctrines; such as the unlawfulness of magistracy among Christians, and consequently of any temporal punishments for evil doers from men; that punishment from God in the future state would be sure not be eternal, nor any other, nor perhaps more, even for a time, than what wicked men now suffer in this world, by being abandoned to the outrage of their own and others' passions, &c. That a standing ministry, ordinances, the Christian Sabbath, and social worship, were all without warrant from the New Testament; that, beside our blessed Lord of the tribe of Judah, who was in his account but a mere creature (if not a mere man), there was quickly to be expected a second Messiah of the tribe of Ephraim, who is the Shepherd, the Stone of Israel, spoken of Gen. xlix. 24. And the person 'like the Son of Man, whom Daniel saw in the night visions, to whom there was given dominion, and glory, and a kingdom, &c.' Dan. ix. 13, 14., that this person was then in being; that he had been often presented to him in vision, and was one whom he knew very well. And though he declined telling who he was, under pretence of wanting a permission for it, yet, by many circumstances it appeared highly probable that he himself was the man, in his own conceit. Nor was his being by birth a Frenchman an objection of force enough to be set in opposition to his heavenly visions; for multitudes in the world (as he said) are undoubtedly of Israelitish extract, who are not known to be so, either by themselves or others. And since the posterity of Jacob have utterly lost their genealogies, it was impossible that Ben Ephraim should know his own descent, otherwise than by revelation, or be able to make it out to others but by the gifts of prophecy and miracles.

"And these gifts, he once and again, before very credible witness,

APPENDIX, No. LXVI.

Case of Mr. Longloissorie, French instructor.

declared that he knew by revelation he should shortly be endued with from on high, in as great a degree as ever the Apostles were, to say nothing more.

"These extraordinary things *Monsieur* did not broach all at once, but by little and little; the most plausible of them, or rather some plausible deductions from them, first, and only to such as (to use his own expression) he found of a teachable spirit; till at length the secrets were imparted to too many to remain such any longer.

"The propagator of them, now waxed bold,* professed the strongest assurance imaginable of the divine original of his dreams and visions, and of the sacred truths of those doctrines and interpretations of Scripture which he had by these means been led into; and sometimes went so far as to declare, that, if the event should prove these things to be delusions, he should doubt for his part whether God had ever made any revelations at all to men.

"We soon perceived, that too great a respect was paid by several in our society, and elsewhere, to his pretences to visions and revelations; that one of his greatest confidents began to be favored with visions too, in his own conceit; and that others were in suspense, whether he might not be a teacher sent from God, and waited with some impatience to see him begin to prove his mission, and were likely to take up with evidences slight enough.

"As the gentleman's notions were now no longer privacies, it soon appeared that they had been industriously spread by some among their friends, in places far and near; that many people's minds were greatly moved with them; and strange apprehensions and expectations raised, of what these things would come to.

"It would be beside our present business to relate by what means, through the good providence of God, it was at length made manifest that these high pretences to extraordinary divine communications were all mere delusions; and so the minds of people again quieted.

"It would be of more importance to remark, what was the end of these things with respect to the enthusiastic gentleman himself; namely, that, when he began to be exalted above measure with the abundance of his imaginary revelations, he withdrew himself entirely from the public worship of God, which he before diligently and (so far as appeared) devoutly used to attend; and he has since returned to the idolatries of the church of Rome, from which he had professed himself a sincere convert."

"* Longed to suffer persecution."

No. LXVII. — See p. 15.

LAWS, RULES AND SCHOLASTIC FORMS, ESTABLISHED BY PRESIDENT DUNSTER.

Laws, rules, and scholastic forms, established by President Dunster.

"Statuta, Leges, Privilegia, et Ordinationes, per Inspectores et Præsidem Collegii Harvardini constitutæ An. Chr. 1642, 1643, 1644, 1645, 1646, et promulgatæ ad scholarium salutem et disciplinam perpetuò conservandam.

"1. Cuicunque fuerit peritia legendi Ciceronem aut quemvis alium ejusmodi classicum authorem ex tempore, et congruè loquendi ac scribendi Latinè facultas oratione tam solutâ quam ligatâ, suo, ut aiunt, Marte, et ad unguem inflectendi Græcorum nominum verborumque paradigmata; hic admissionem in Collegium jure potest expectare. Quicunque verò destitutus fuerit hac peritiâ, admissionem sibi neutiquam vendicet.

"2. Considerato unusquisque ultimum finem vitæ ac studiorum, cognitionem nimirum Dei et Jesu Christi, quæ est vita æterna. Joh. xvii. 3.

"3. Cum Deus sapientiæ sit largitor, privatis precibus sapientiam ab eo singuli ardenter petunto. Prov. ii. 2, 3, &c.

"4. In Sacris Scripturis legendis bis quotidie unusquisque se exerceto; quo paratus ac peritus sit rationem reddendi suorum profectuum, tam in theoreticis philologicis observationibus, quam in spiritualibus practicis documentis, quemadmodum tutores requirent pro suo cujusque captu, quum 'aditus verbi illuminat.' Psal. cxix. 130.

"5. In publico sanctorum cœtu omnes gestus, qui contemptum aut neglectum præ se ferunt sacrarum institutionum, studiosè cavento, atque ad rationem tutoribus reddendam quid profecerint parati sunto; omnibusque legitimis sibi scientiam reponendi mediis utuntor, prout à suo quisque tutore institutus fuerit.

"6. Omnem profanationem Sacrosancti Dei nominis, attributorum, verbi, institutionum ac temporum cultûs, evitanto; Deum autem et ejus veritatem in notitiâ retinere, summâ cum reverentiâ et timore, studento.

"7. Honore prosequuntor, ut parentes, ita magistratus, presbyteros, tutores, suosque omnes seniores, prout ratio postulat; coram illis tacentes nisi interrogati, nec quicquam contradicentes, eis exhibentes honoris et reverentiæ indicia quæcunque laudabili usu recepta sunt, incurvato nimirum corpore salutantes, aperto capite adstantes, &c.

APPENDIX, No. LXVII.

Laws, rules, and scholastic forms, established by President Dunster.

"8. Ad loquendum tardi sunto; evitent non solum juramenta, mendacia, et incertos rumores, sed et stultiloquium, scurrilitatem, futilitatem, lasciviam, omnesque gestus molestos.

"9. Nequis se intrudat vel rebus alienis immisceat.

"10. Dum hîc egerint, tempus studiosè redimunto, tam communes omnium scholarium horas, quam suis prælectionibus destinatas, observando; prælectionibus autem diligenter attendunto, nec voce nec gestu molesti. Siquid dubitent, sodales suos, aut (nondum exempto scrupulo) tutores modestè consulunto.

"11. Nequis sub quovis prætextu hominum, quorum perditi sunt ac discincti mores, consuetudine seu familiaritate utitor. Neque licebit ulli, nisi potestate ab Inspectoribus Collegii factâ, bellicis lustrationibus interesse. Nemo in pupillari statu degens, nisi concessâ priùs à tutore veniâ, ex oppido exeat; nec quisquam, cujuscunque gradûs aut ordinis fuerit, forum frequentet, vel diutius in aliquâ oppidi plateâ moretur, aut tabernas, cauponas, vel diversoria ad comessandum aut bibendum accedat, nisi ad parentes, curatores, nutricios, vel hujusmodi, accersitus fuerit.

"12. Nullus scholaris quicquam, quod sex denarios valeat, nullo parentum, curatorum, aut tutorum approbante, emito, vendito, aut commutato. Quum autem secus fecerit, à Præside pro delicti ratione multabitur.

"13. Scholares vernaculâ linguâ intra Collegii limites nullo prætextu utuntor, nisi ad orationem aut aliud aliquod exercitium publicum Anglicè habendum evocati fuerint.

"14. Siquis scholarium à precibus aut prælectionibus abfuerit, nisi necessitate coactus aut tutoris nactus veniam, admonitioni aut aliusmodi pro Præsidis prudentiâ pœnæ, si plus quam semel in hebdomade peccaverit, erit obnoxius.

"15. Scholarium quisque donec primo gradu ornetur, ni sit commensalis, aut nobilis alicujus filius, aut militis primogenitus, suo tantum cognomine vocator.

"16. Nullus scholaris quâvis de causâ (nisi præmonstratâ et approbatâ Præsidi vel tutori suo) à suis studiis statisve exercitiis abesto, exceptâ horâ jentaculo, semihorâ merendæ, prandio verò sesquihorâ, pariter et cœnæ concessâ.

"17. Siquis scholarium ullam Dei et hujus Collegii legem, sive animo perverso, seu ex supinâ negligentiâ, violârit, postquam fuerit bis admonitus, si non adultus, virgis coërceatur, sin adultus, ad Inspectores Collegii deferendus erit, ut publicè in eum pro meritis animadversio fiat; in atrocioribus autem delictis, ut adeò gradatim

Laws, rules, and scholastic forms, established by President Dunster.

procedatur, nemo expectet, nec ut admonitio iterata super eâdem lege necessario fiat.

" 18. Quicunque scholaris, probatione habitâ, poterit sacras utriusque instrumenti Scripturas de textu originali Latinè interpretari et logicè resolvere, fueritque naturalis et moralis philosophiæ principiis imbutus, vitâque ac moribus inculpatus, et publicis quibusvis comitiis ab Inspectoribus et Præside Collegii approbatus, primo suo gradu possit ornari.

" 19. Quicunque scholaris scriptam synopsin vel compendium logicæ, naturalis ac moralis philosophiæ, arithmeticæ, geometriæ, et astronomiæ exhibuerit, fueritque ad theses suas defendendas paratus, nec non originalium ut supra dictum est linguarum peritus, quem etiamnum morum integritas ac studiorum diligentia cohonestaverint, publicis quibusvis comitiis probatione factâ, secundi gradûs, magisterii nimirum, capax erit."

"IN SCHOLARIBUS ADMITTENDIS.

" 1. Præbebis omnimodam debitam reverentiam honorandis magistratibus ac reverendis Presbyteris et Præsidi Collegii unà cum Sociis singulis.

" 2. Debitam diligentiam studiis incumbendo adhibebis, studiis inquam linguarum et artium liberalium, obsequendo tutori tuo et salutaribus ejus præceptis, quamdiu in statu pupillari versatus fueris in hoc Collegio.

" 3. Religiosè in te suscipies curam, dum hîc commoraberis, observandi singulas salutares leges, statuta, et privilegia hujus societatis quantum in te situm est; atque etiam, ut observentur ab omnibus hujus Collegii membris in singulo uniuscujusque munere, fideliter curabis.

" 4. Sedulò prospicies nequid detrimenti Collegium capiat, quantum in te situm est, sive in ejus sumptibus, sive in ædificio et structurâ, fundis, proventibus, cæterisque omnibus, quæ nunc ad Collegium pertinent, aut, dum hîc egeris, pertinere possunt.

" Quod ad nos, Præsidem et Socios scilicet, spectat, pollicemur nos tibi non defuturos quibuscunque nostrâ intererit; imo verò in studiis tuis et pietate progressum, quantum in nobis fuerit, promovebimus."

" SOCIIS ADMITTENDIS.

" 1. Præbebis omnimodam debitam reverentiam honorandis magistratibus ac reverendis Presbyteris et Præsidi, Collegii Inspectoribus.

APPENDIX, No. LXVII.

Laws, rules, and scholastic forms, established by President Dunster.

"2. Religiosè in te suscipies curam, dum hîc commoraberis, observandi singulas salutares leges, statuta, et privilegia hujus societatis, quantum in te situm est, atque etiam, ut observentur ab omnibus hujus Collegii membris in singulo uniuscujusque munere.

"3. Omnes et singulos studentes, qui tutelæ tuæ committuntur aut in posterum committendi sunt, ut promoveas in omni tam divinâ quam humanâ literaturâ, pro suo cujusque captu, atque, ut moribus honestè et inculpatè se gerant, summopere curabis.

"4. Sedulo prospicies, nequid detrimenti Collegium capiat, quantum in te situm est, sive in ejus sumptibus, sive in ædificio et structurâ, fundis, proventibus, cæterisque omnibus, quæ nunc ad Collegium pertinent, aut, dum hic egeris, pertinere possint.

"Quod etiam ad nos (Collegii Inspectores) spectat, pollicemur nos non tibi defuturos esse, quibuscunque tuâ intererit; imo verò te confirmabimus authoritate ac potestate nostrâ in omnibus tuis legitimis administrationibus, contra quoscunque contumaces. Et pro Collegii facultatibus erogabimus tibi idonea stipendia (i. e. pro modulo nostro), quæ sufficiant ad victum et amictum et literaturam tuam promovendam."

"PRÆSENTATIO BACCALAUREORUM.

"Honorandi viri, vosque, reverendi Presbyteri, præsento vobis hosce juvenes, quos scio tam doctrinâ quam moribus idoneos esse ad primum in artibus gradum suscipiendum pro more Academiarum in Angliâ."

"ADMISSIO.

"Admitto te ad primum gradum in artibus, scil. ad respondendum quæstioni pro more Academiarum in Angliâ, tibique trado hunc librum unà cum potestate publicè prælegendi (in aliquâ artium, quam profiteris) quotiescunque ad hoc munus evocatus fueris."

"PRÆSENTATIO MAGISTRORUM.

"Honorandi viri, vosque, reverendi Presbyteri, præsento vobis hosce viros, quos scio tam doctrinâ quam moribus esse idoneos ad incipiendum in artibus pro more Academiarum in Angliâ."

"ADMISSIO INCEPTORUM.

"Admitto te ad secundum gradum in artibus pro more Acade-

APPENDIX, No. LXVII.

Laws, rules, and scholastic forms, established by President Dunster.

miarum in Angliâ; tibique trado hunc librum unà cum potestate publicè profitendi, ubicunque ad hoc munus publicè evocatus fueris."

"FORMULA PUBLICÆ CONFESSIONIS.

"Ego, S. W., qui à cultu divino in aulâ Collegii tam matutino quam vespertino toties per aliquot menses abfui (in quâ absentiâ monitis et aliis in me animadversionum gradibus non obstantibus hactenus perstiti), nunc culpam meam agnosco, et publicæ agnitionis hoc testimonio me reum profiteor, et majorem in his exercitiis pietatis diligentiam in posterum (Deo volente), dum hîc egero, polliceor."

CERTIFICATE FOR AN UNDERGRADUATE.

"Per integrum biennium quo apud nos pupillari statu commoratus est A. B., Collegii Harvardini Cantabrigiæ in Nov-Angliâ alumnus, publicas lectiones tam philologicas quam philosophicas audivit, necnon declamationibus, disputationibus, cæterisque exercitiis, pro sui temporis ratione adeò incubuit, ut nobis certam spem fecerit illum suis coætaneis etiam in aliis collegiis (si admissus fuerit) non disparem fore. Quapropter hoc de illo testimonium omnibus, quorum interesse possit, perhibemus nos, quorum nomina subscripta sunt.

"Datum."

CERTIFICATE FOR A BACHELOR OF ARTS.

"Per integrum illud tempus quo apud nos commoratus est C. D., Collegii Harvardini Cantabrigiæ in Nov-Angliâ alumnus, et in artibus liberalibus Baccalaureus, bonarum literarum studiis vitæ probitatem adjunxit; adeò ut nobis spem amplam fecerit se in Ecclesiæ et Reipublicæ commodum victurum. Quapropter hoc de illo testimonium omnibus, quorum interesse possit, perhibemus nos, quorum nomina subscripta sunt.

"Datum."

CERTIFICATE FOR A MASTER OF ARTS.

"Per integrum illud tempus quo apud nos commoratus est E. F., Collegii Harvardini Cantabrigiæ in Nov-Angliâ alumnus, et in artibus liberalibus Magister, bonarum literarum studiis sedulò incubuit, sinceram veræ fidei professionem inculpatis suæ vitæ mori-

APPENDIX, No. LXVII.

Laws, rules, and scholastic forms, established by President Dunster.

bus exornavit, adeò ut nobis certam et amplam spem fecerit se in Ecclesiæ et Reipublicæ commodum victurum. Quapropter hoc de illo testimonium omnibus, quorum interesse possit, perhibemus nos, quorum nomina subscripta sunt.

"Datum."

"BACCALAUREORUM PRÆSENTATIO.

"Supplicat Reverentiis vestris A. B., ut quadriennium ab admissione completum, quo ordinarias lectiones audiverit unà cum disputationibus, declamationibus, cæterisque exercitiis per statuta Col. requisitis (licet non omnino secundum formam statuti), sufficiat ei ad primum gradum in artibus suscipiendum."

"MAG. PRÆSENTATIO IN ANGL.

"Supplicat Reverentiis vestris N. N., ut novem termini completi post finalem ejus determinationem, in quibus ordinarias lectiones audiverit (licet non omnino secundum formam statuti) unà cum omnibus oppositionibus, responsionibus, declamationibus, cæterisque exercitiis per statuta regia requisitis, sufficiant ei ad incipiendum in artibus."

"CERTAIN ORDERS BY THE SCHOLARS AND OFFICERS OF THE COLLEGE TO BE OBSERVED, WRITTEN 28TH MARCH, 1650.

"The Steward, receiving a just and clear account of the visible store or treasury of the College, as it is a society, either in visible provisions, or in debts acknowledged or proved, due by the members of the society, shall be bound with sufficient security, quarterly to give an account thereof within ten days to the President, when he shall require it, together with the just and necessary disbursements, which by the President's allowance have been issued out (for necessary provisions) to the steward himself, butler, cook, or any other officer of the House, as also to and for the necessary provisions of fuel, reparations of outworn utensils, &c., towards all which charges the steward is to see (besides the stock maintained) that one third part be reserved of all payments to him by the members of the House quarterly made, and the other two parts in suitable provisions to the scholars to be returned as the season and state of the year doth require, and answerably thereto shall deliver in such provisions to

Laws, rules, and scholastic forms, established by President Dunster.

the cook and butler, or brewer and baker, and of them require weekly or quarterly accounts.

"Forasmuch as the students, whose friends are most careful to discharge their due expenses, have sundry times sorely and unjustly suffered by such as neglect to pay their debts; therefore the steward shall not permit, but upon his own peril, any students to be above two pounds indebted, but, acquainting the President, with his leave send them to their friends, if not above a day's journey distant; if otherwise, then shall the steward, at the admission of such scholars, inform himself from whom he shall be supplied, or to whom they shall have recourse in the aforesaid case of debt; neither is the steward at any time to take any pay that is useless, hazardful, or importing detriment to the College, as lean cattle to feed, turning over of bills to shops, &c., but at his own discretion and peril.

"Whereas young scholars, to the dishonor of God, hinderance of their studies, and damage of their friends' estate, inconsiderately and intemperately are ready to abuse their liberty of sizing besides their commons; therefore the steward shall in no case permit any students whatever, under the degree of Masters of Art, or Fellows, to expend or be provided for themselves or any townsmen any extraordinary commons, unless by the allowance of the President or two of the Fellows, whereof their Tutor always to be one, or in case of manifest sickness, presignified also unto the President, or in case of a license, of course granted by the President to some persons whose condition he seeth justly requiring it.

"The butler and cook are to look unto, and, in case detriment befall, fully to be accountable for, all the College's vessels and utensils, great and small, delivered by inventory unto them, and once every quarter to deliver in unto the President in writing an inventory thereof, particularly showing what detriment is befallen the College, in what particular, and by what means, whether by wearth in their just usage (which the steward is to repair by the College charges), or by any abuse of any person or persons whatever, from whom the President shall see that the butler and cook shall have just and full recompense, if they be members of the society; but, if detriment come by any out of the society, then those officers themselves shall be responsible to the House; because they may not but at their peril communicate any thing that is the College's to any without.

"*Item.* They are to see, that the said utensils, to their several offices belonging, from day to day be kept clean and sweet and fit for use, and they shall at meal-times deliver them out as the public

APPENDIX, No. LXVII.

Laws, rules, and scholastic forms, established by President Dunster.

service of the Hall requireth to the servitor or servitors, who shall be responsible for them until that they return them after meals to the butteries or kitchen; but they are not bound to keep or cleanse any particular scholar's spoons, cups, or such like, but at their own discretion.

"And if any scholar or scholars at any time take away or detain any vessel of the College's, great or small, from the Hall out of the doors from the sight of the buttery hatch without the butler's or servitor's knowledge, or against their will, he or they shall be punished three pence, but more at the President's discretion, if perverseness appear. But, if he or they shall presume to detain any vessel, great or small, that it be wanting the next meal, he shall be punished the full value thereof; and, in case any shall lose, mar, or spoil any such vessels, then shall they pay double thereof; and, if they conceal it until by examination it be found out fourfold the value thereof.

"The butler and cook shall see that all the rooms peculiar to their offices, together with their appurtenances be daily set and kept in order, clean and sweet from all manner of noisomeness and nastiness or sensible offensiveness. To the butler belongs the cellar and butteries, and all from thenceforth to the farthest end of the Hall, with the south porch; to the cook the kitchen, larder, and the way leading to his hatch, the turret, and the north alley unto the walk; neither shall the butler or cook suffer any scholar or scholars whatever, except the Fellows, Masters of Art, fellow commoners, or officers of the House, to come into the butteries or kitchen, save with their parents or guardians, or with some grave and sober strangers; and, if any shall presume to thrust in, they shall have three pence on their heads; but, if presumptuous and continually they shall so dare to offend, they shall be liable to an admonition and to other proceedings of the College discipline, at the discretion of the President.

"The butler upon every sixth day of the week at noon is to give an account to every scholar demanding his week's sizings in the buttery, and is not bound to stay above half an hour at bevers in the buttery after the tolling of the bell, nor above a quarter of an hour after thanksgiving in the Hall at meals. The cook on the sixth day at noon shall give in the week's expenses of the whole society, which the butler shall enter into his book, according to custom, and shall keep the bills from quarter to quarter, and show them to the steward at his demand for his satisfaction.

"The butler and cook may not deliver at meal-times, save in case

APPENDIX, No. LXVII.

Laws, rules, and scholastic forms, established by President Dunster.

of sickness, or just cause, to the President (if it may be) presignified, and by him allowed, any commons to any scholars, save unto the servitor, nor see to any save their dues to the scholars sitting orderly in their places, in the Hall; neither may any scholar rise from his place or go out of the Hall at meal-times before thanksgiving be ended, unless liberty be given by the President, if present, or the senior Fellow, or such as for that time possess their place.

"If any officer of the College whatsoever shall make any secret contract with any scholar or scholars, either to conceal their disorderly walking or to draw from them any valuable things, as books, wearing apparel, bedding, or such like, by any direct or indirect course, not before allowed by the President or their Tutor, the said officer or officers shall be liable to be punished at the discretion of the President.

"Whereas much inconvenience falleth out by the scholars bringing candles in course into the Hall, therefore the butler henceforth shall receive at the President's or steward's hands twenty shillings in money, ten at the thirteenth of September, and ten at the thirteenth of December, toward candles for the Hall for prayer time and supper, which, that it may not be burdensome, it shall be put proportionably upon every scholar who retaineth his seat in the buttery."

THE FORM OF EXEMPTION FOR COLLEGE SERVANTS.

"Whereas our much honored magistrates and deputies in General Court assembled, in the third month of the year one thousand six hundred and fifty, have, for the furtherance of good literature, by charter privileged the officers and servants of Harvard College to the number of ten from all personal offices, civil and military exercises and services, watching and wardings, and their estates, not exceeding a hundred pounds a man, from all country rates and taxes whatever;

"We therefore, A. B. C., having chosen our well-approved neighbour D. E. to serve us for the space of one whole year from the date hereof, in his calling of F., to attend the College work upon a week or ten days' warning, so often as thereunto he shall be called, do by virtue of the privileges given unto us, exempt the aforesaid D. E. from all the aforementioned incumbrances and charges, in witness whereof we have given, and he hath accepted, these presents signed with our hands."

No. LXVIII.* — See pp. 15, 33, 38, 68, 84, 90, 100, 108, 159.

ACTS RELATING TO THE CONSTITUTION AND GOVERNMENT OF THE COLLEGE FROM 1636 TO 1780.

GRANTS OF THE GENERAL COURT.

["At a Court holden September 8th, 1636, and continued by adjournment to the 28th of the 8th month (October, 1636).

"The Court agreed to give £ 400 towards a School or College, whereof £ 200 to be paid next year, and £ 200 when the work is finished, and the next Court to appoint where and what building." — *Records of the General Court*, Vol. I. p. 183.

"At a General Court, holden at Newtown on the 2d of the 9th month (November 2d) 1637.

"The College ordered to be at Newtown." — *Ibid.* p. 204.

"For the College, the Governor, Mr. Winthrop, the Deputy, Mr. Dudley, the Treasurer, Mr. Bellingham, Mr. Humphrey, Mr. Herlakenden, Mr. Stoughton, Mr. Cotton, Mr. Wilson, Mr. Davenport, Mr. Welde, Mr. Shepard, and Mr. Peters, these, or the greater part of them, whereof Mr. Winthrop, Mr. Dudley, or Mr. Bellingham, to be always one, to take order for a College at Newtown." —*Ibid.* p. 213.

"At a Court, holden the 13th of the first month (March) 1638-9.

"It is ordered, that the College agreed upon formerly to be built at Cambridge, shall be called Harvard College." — *Ibid.* p. 241.

"At a Court, holden the 7th day of the 8th month (October), 1640.

"The ferry between Boston and Charlestown is granted to the College." — *Ibid.* p. 288.]

* This Number presents, in chronological order, all acts passed, and bills proposed, in relation to the constitution and government of Harvard College, from its foundation in 1636 to the adoption of the Constitution of Massachusetts in 1780. Those acts or parts of acts, which were never in force, or, if so, only temporarily, or which were not general in their character, are printed in smaller type, and included in brackets. Those in larger type, include all acts or parts of acts, which were regarded during the Colonial period of Massachusetts as the Constitution of the College, and comprehend the "general Charters," referred to in the Constitution of Massachusetts, Chap. V. Sect. I. Art. II. All these acts and bills have been carefully compared with the originals, in the records or on file in the office of the Secretary of State.

THE ACT ESTABLISHING THE OVERSEERS OF HARVARD COLLEGE.*

The act establishing the Overseers of Harvard College. 1642.

"At a General Court held at Boston in the year 1642.

"Whereas, through the good hand of God upon us, there is a College founded in Cambridge, in the county of Middlesex, called HARVARD COLLEGE, for the encouragement whereof this Court has given the sum of four hundred pounds, and also the revenue of the ferry betwixt Charlestown and Boston, and that the well ordering and managing of the said College is of great concernment;

"It is therefore ordered by this Court, and the authority thereof, that the Governor and Deputy Governor for the time being, and all the magistrates of this jurisdiction, together with the teaching elders of the six next adjoining towns, viz. Cambridge, Watertown, Charlestown, Boston, Roxbury, and Dorchester, and the President of the said College for the time being, shall, from time to time, have full power and authority to make and establish all such orders, statutes, and constitutions, as they shall see necessary for the instituting, guiding, and furthering of the said College, and the

* The above act has been carefully copied from the act printed in "The General Laws of the Massachusetts Colony, revised and published by order of the General Court, in October, 1658."

This was "the second impression" of the laws of the Colony, and a copy of it is now preserved in the Law Library of Harvard College. Having been revised and published by the authority of the General Court, at that early period, the above may well be regarded as the exact and authentic College charter of 1642.

It is, however, deemed proper to subjoin the act as it was originally passed by the General Court, not only as a matter of curiosity and of history, but because, in the controversy between Dr. Cutler (see above, p. 560) and the Overseers (see above, p. 566) both parties obviously made use of that original draft as it stands in the Records of the General Court (Vol. II. p. 24), in the words following.

"At a General Court at Boston, the 8th of the 7th month, 1642.

"Whereas, by order of the Court in the 7th month, 1636, there was appointed and named six magistrates and six elders, to order the College at Cambridge, of which twelve some are removed out of this jurisdiction.

"It is therefore ordered, that the Governor and Deputy for the time being, and all the magistrates of this jurisdiction, together with the teaching elders of the six next adjoining towns, that is, Cambridge, Watertown, Charlestown, Boston, Roxbury, and Dorchester, and the President of the College for the time being, shall have, from time to time, full power and authority to make and

APPENDIX, No. LXVIII.

The act establishing the Overseers of Harvard College. 1642.

several members thereof, from time to time, in piety, morality, and learning; as also to dispose, order, and manage, to the use and behoof of the said College, and the members thereof, all gifts, legacies, bequeaths, revenues, lands, and donations, as either have been, are, or shall be, conferred, bestowed, or any ways shall fall, or come, to the said College.

"And whereas it may come to pass, that many of the said magistrates and said elders may be absent, or otherwise employed about other weighty affairs, when the said College may need their present help and counsel, — It is therefore ordered, that the greater number of said magistrates and elders, which shall be present, with the President, shall have the power of the whole. Provided, that if any constitution, order, or orders, by them made, shall be found hurtful to the said College, or the members thereof, or to the weal-public, then, upon appeal of the party or parties grieved, unto the company of Overseers, first mentioned, they shall repeal the said order, or orders, if they shall see cause, at their next meeting, or stand accountable thereof to the next General Court."

establish all such orders, statutes, and constitutions, as they shall see necessary for the instituting, guiding, and furthering of the said College, and the several members thereof, from time to time, in piety, morality, and learning; as also that they shall have full power to dispose, order, and manage, to the use and behoof of the said College and members thereof, all gifts, legacies, bequeathalls, revenues, lands, and donations, as either have been, are, or shall be, conferred, bestowed, or any ways shall fall to the said College.

"And whereas it may come to pass, that many of the said magistrates and elders may be absent, or otherwise employed in weighty affairs, when the said College needs their present help, counsel, and authority; — Therefore it is ordered, that the greater number of the said magistrates, elders, and President, shall have the power of the whole. Provided also, that if any constitution, order, or orders, shall be made, that is found hurtful to the said College, or the members thereof, or to the weal-public, that then, upon the appeal of the party or parties aggrieved to the said Overseers, they shall repeal the said order, or orders, at their next meeting, or stand accountable thereof to the next General Court."

APPENDIX, No. LXVIII.

THE CHARTER OF THE PRESIDENT AND FELLOWS OF HARVARD COLLEGE, UNDER THE SEAL OF THE COLONY OF MASSACHUSETTS BAY, AND BEARING DATE, MAY 30TH, A. D. 1650.*

The charter of 1650.

"Whereas, through the good hand of God, many well-devoted persons have been, and daily are, moved, and stirred up, to give and bestow, sundry gifts, legacies, lands, and revenues, for the advancement of all good literature, arts, and sciences, in Harvard College, in Cambridge in the County of Middlesex, and to the maintenance of the President and Fellows, and for all accommodations of buildings, and all other necessary provisions, that may conduce to the education of the English and Indian youth of this country, in knowledge and godliness.

"It is therefore ordered and enacted by this Court, and the authority thereof, that for the furthering of so good a work, and for the purposes aforesaid, from henceforth that the said College, in Cambridge in Middlesex, in New England, shall be a Corporation, consisting of seven persons, to wit, a President, five Fellows, and a Treasurer or Bursar; and that Henry Dunster shall be the first President; Samuel Mather, Samuel Danforth, Masters of Art, Jonathan Mitchell, Comfort Starr, and Samuel Eaton, Bachelors of Art, shall be the five Fellows; and Thomas Danforth to be present Treasurer, all of them being inhabitants in the Bay, and shall be the first seven persons of which the said Corporation shall consist; and that the said seven persons, or the greater number of them, procuring the presence of the Overseers of the College, and by their counsel and consent, shall have power, and are hereby authorized, at any time, or times, to elect a new President, Fellows, or Treasurer, so oft, and from time to time, as any of the said persons shall die, or be removed; which said President and Fellows, for the time being, shall for ever hereafter, in name and fact, be one body politic and corporate in law, to all intents and purposes; and shall have perpetual succession; and shall be called by the name of President and Fellows of Harvard College, and

* This charter is thus introduced on the Records of the General Court, Vol. IV. p. 10. "At a General Court of elections, held at Boston, 22d May, 1650. In answer to the petition of Henry Dunster, President of Harvard College, ... and to his desires for a Corporation, the Court doth grant his request in these terms. Whereas," &c.

APPENDIX, No. LXVIII.

The charter of 1650.

shall, from time to time, be eligible as aforesaid, and by that name they, and their successors, shall and may purchase and acquire to themselves, or take and receive upon free gift and donation, any lands, tenements, or hereditaments, within this jurisdiction of the Massachusetts, not exceeding five hundred pounds per annum, and any goods and sums of money whatsoever, to the use and behoof of the said President, Fellows, and scholars of the said College; and also may sue and plead, or be sued and impleaded by the name aforesaid, in all Courts and places of judicature, within the jurisdiction aforesaid.

"And that the said President, with any three of the Fellows, shall have power, and are hereby authorized, when they shall think fit, to make and appoint a common seal for the use of the said Corporation. And the President and Fellows, or major part of them, from time to time, may meet and choose such officers and servants for the College, and make such allowance to them, and them also to remove, and after death, or removal, to choose such others, and to make, from time to time, such orders and by-laws, for the better ordering, and carrying on the work of the College, as they shall think fit; provided, the said orders be allowed by the Overseers. And also, that the President and Fellows, or major part of them with the Treasurer, shall have power to make conclusive bargains for lands and tenements, to be purchased by the said Corporation, for valuable consideration.

"And for the better ordering of the government of the said College and Corporation, Be it enacted by the authority aforesaid, that the President, and three more of the Fellows, shall and may, from time to time, upon due warning or notice given by the President to the rest, hold a meeting, for the debating and concluding of affairs concerning the profits and revenues of any lands, and disposing of their goods (provided that all the said disposings be according to the will of the donors); and for direction in all emergent occasions; execution of all orders and by-laws; and for the procuring of a general meeting of all the Overseers and Society, in great and difficult cases; and in case of non-agreement; in all which cases aforesaid, the conclusion shall be made by the major part, the said President having a casting voice, the Overseers consenting thereunto; and that all the aforesaid transactions shall tend to and for the use and behoof of the President, Fellows, scholars, and officers of the said College, and for all accommodations of buildings, books, and all other necessary provisions and

The charter of 1650.

furnitures, as may be for the advancement and education of youth, in all manner of good literature, arts, and sciences. And further, be it ordered by this Court, and the authority thereof, that all the lands, tenements, and hereditaments, houses, or revenues, within this jurisdiction, to the aforesaid President or College appertaining, not exceeding the value of five hundred pounds per annum, shall, from henceforth, be freed from all civil impositions, taxes, and rates; all goods to the said Corporation, or to any scholars thereof appertaining, shall be exempted from all manner of toll, customs, and excise whatsoever. And that the said President, Fellows, and scholars, together with the servants, and other necessary officers to the said President, or College appertaining, not exceeding ten, viz. three to the President, and seven to the College belonging, shall be exempted from all personal civil offices, military exercises, or services, watchings, and wardings; and such of their estates, not exceeding one hundred pounds a man, shall be free from all country taxes or rates whatsoever, and no other.

"In witness whereof, the Court hath caused the seal of the colony to be hereunto affixed. Dated the one and thirtieth day of the third month, called May, anno 1650.

THOMAS DUDLEY, *Governor.*"

[A copy of the original, engrossed on parchment, under the signature of Governor Dudley, with the colony seal appendant, is in the custody of the President and Fellows of Harvard College.]

AN APPENDIX TO THE COLLEGE CHARTER, GRANTED BY AN ACT OF THE GENERAL COURT OF THE COLONY, PASSED ANNO 1657.

An Appendix to the College Charter. 165-

"At a General Court held at Boston the 14th of Oct. 1657.

"In answer to certain proposals, presented to this Court by the Overseers of Harvard College, as an Appendix to the College Charter it is ordered, The Corporation shall have power, from time to time, to make such orders and by-laws, for the better ordering and carrying on of the work of the College, as they shall see cause, without dependence upon the consent of the Overseers foregoing. Provided always, that the Corporation shall be responsible unto, and those orders and by-laws shall be alterable by, the Overseers, according to their discretion.

APPENDIX, No. LXVIII.

An Appendix to the College Charter. 1657.

"And when the Corporation shall hold a meeting for agreeing with College servants; for making of orders and by-laws; for debating and concluding of affairs, concerning the profits and revenues of any lands, or gifts, and the disposing thereof (provided that all the said disposals be according to the will of the donors); for managing of all emergent occasions, for the procuring of a general meeting of the Overseers and Society in great and difficult cases, and in cases of non-agreement; and for all other College affairs to them pertaining, — in all these cases the conclusion shall be valid, being made by the major part of the Corporation, the President having a casting vote. Provided always, that in these things also, they be responsible to the Overseers, as aforesaid.

"And in case the Corporation shall see cause to call a meeting of the Overseers, or the Overseers shall think good to meet of themselves, it shall be sufficient unto the validity of College acts, that notice be given to the Overseers, in the six towns mentioned in the printed law, anno 1642, when the rest of the Overseers, by reason of the remoteness of their habitations, cannot conveniently be acquainted therewith."—*Records of the General Court*, Vol. IV. p. 265.

INTENDED CHARTER OF 1672.

Intended charter of 1672.

["At the second session of the General Court for elections, held at Boston, 8th of October, 1672, on their adjournment.*

"Whereas, by the good hand of God there hath been erected and continued a College in Cambridge, in the county of Middlesex, called by the name of 'Harvard College,' and that by an instrument or charter, dated the

* The connexion between this act and the appointment of Dr. Hoar, as suggested in the text (p. 33), is established by the fact, that the following vote immediately precedes that act on the records of the General Court.

"The Court having duly considered of the motion in reference to allowance to be given to the maintenance of a President at the College, and the settlement of what may give due encouragement to that work, do judge meet, and order that there be allowed one hundred and fifty pounds per annum, to be paid in money by the country Treasurer, out of such revenues as are paid in money into the Treasury, *provided that Dr. Hoar be the man for a supply of that place now vacant*, and that he accept thereof. And that when this order of one hundred and fifty pounds per annum takes place, the former order of one hundred a year, settled upon the President in the printed law, be made void, and that this allowance be continued until the General Court or Overseers shall find some other way for the making it good, and that the annual allowance be paid quarterly."

APPENDIX, No. LXVIII.

Intended charter of 1672.

31st of May, in the year 1650, the President and Fellows thereof were established to be one body corporate by the authority of this Court. And whereas several gifts and donations have been made, and are still making, by many well-devoted persons, inhabitants of this country, as also strangers, for the maintenance of the governors and the government thereof, and for all the accommodations of the scholars thereof, in books, buildings, lectures, scholarships, and all other necessary and fitting provisions, that may conduce to the education of English and Indian youth, there residing in all good literature and godliness. Now, for the perpetuation and further advancement of so good a work, and for the better encouragement of all persons therein concerned, or to be concerned, it is ordered and enacted by this Court and the authority thereof, that Leonard Hoar, Doctor in Physic, be the present President of said Harvard College, Mr. Samuel Danforth, Fellow of the said College, Mr. Urian Oakes, Pastor of the church of Cambridge, Mr. Thomas Shephard, teacher of the church of Charlestown, Mr. Joseph Browne and Mr. John Richardson, Masters of Art, be the Fellows, and Mr. John Richards the Treasurer, of the said College and Corporation, for the time being; and that the President, Fellows, and Treasurer of the said College, or the Fellows alone, when there is no President established, and their successors from time to time, be the immediate governors thereof, and shall in name and fact for ever hereafter be one body politic and corporate in law, to all intents and purposes, and shall have perpetual succession, having power and authority by these presents (procuring a meeting of the Overseers, and by their counsel and consent), to elect successors into the place of any one or more of them which shall be by death or removal made vacant. Be it also hereby authorized and enacted, that the said Corporation and their successors shall have the power of constituting, and again at their pleasure removing, all inferior officers to the said society appertaining, — and all the next and immediate government of every member of the said society according to such orders and laws as are or shall be established by the said Corporation; the Overseers of the said College allowing or not contradicting the said laws, upon notice of them given to them at their next meeting. And also the said Corporation and their successors may purchase and acquire to themselves, or take and receive upon free gift any lands, tenements, hereditaments, annuities, services, goods, moneys, or other emoluments whatsoever, or from whomsoever, and (observing straitly the will of the donors) dispose of the same to the use and behoof of the said College or any members thereof; and that the President may warn a general meeting of the said Corporation for debating any of the affairs aforesaid. In all which cases the conclusion shall be made by the major part present, the President having a casting voice. And that the said Corporation, with their distinct Treasurer (if any such be chosen) by the name of the President, Fellows, and Treasurer of Harvard College, may sue and plead, or be sued or impleaded in all Courts and places of judicature within this jurisdiction of the Massachusetts Colony, to all intents and purposes in law and with effect,

APPENDIX, No. LXVIII.

Intended charter of 1672.

as may any private person or body incorporate; only the estate to the Corporation belonging, and not that which belongs proper to any member of the said Corporation, being liable to such impleadments; also that the said Corporation, or any three of them, the President being one, in all crimes by the laws of this country punishable by one magistrate, shall have the full power of sconsing, fining, or otherwise correcting, all inferior officers or members to the said society belonging, as the laws of the country provide in such cases, or the laws of the College not repugnant unto them; and for that end any of the said Corporation shall, and hereby have power personally with such aid of the society as they shall think meet, taking the constable along with them, to enter into any houses licensed for public entertainment, where they shall be informed, or may be suspicious, of any enormities to be plotting or acting by any members of their society; and all constables and all other inferior civil officers in that place are hereby authorized and commanded to be readily aiding and assisting to them, or any of them in the premises. Neither shall any person or persons legally expelled the College, abide above ten days in the township of Cambridge, unless their parents live in the said township. And be it also ordered and enacted by this Court and the authority thereof, that all the lands, tenements, hereditaments, or annuities within this jurisdiction, to the said Corporation appertaining, not exceeding the value of five hundred pounds per annum, shall be henceforth freed from all ordinary civil impositions, taxes, and rates, and all goods to the said Corporation or to any scholars thereof appertaining, shall be exempted from all manner of toll, customs, and excise whatsoever, except in cases of war, or extraordinary exigencies of the country. And moreover, that the said President, Fellows, and scholars, together with their menial servants, and other necessary officers (not exceeding the number of ten), shall be utterly exempted from all personal and civil offices, military exercises, watchings, and wardings, or the like public services. And the personal estates of the said Corporation and their officers (not exceeding one hundred pounds a man) shall be also freed from the like country taxes for ever. All and every of which premises we do ordain and enact to be fully established for law, any law, grant, or usage to the contrary in any wise notwithstanding."] — *Records of the General Court*, Vol. IV. p. 707.

CHARTER PROPOSED IN 1692.

Charter proposed in 1692.

["Province of the Massachusetts Bay.

An act for incorporating of Harvard College, at Cambridge, New England.

"Whereas there hath been for many years, in the town of Cambridge, in the county of Middlesex, in New England, a society commonly known by the name of Harvard College, where many persons of known worth have, by the blessing of Almighty God, been the better fitted for public employments, both in the church and in the civil state. And whereas the due encouragement of all good literature, arts, and sciences, will tend to the

APPENDIX, No. LXVIII.

Charter proposed in 1692.

honor of God, the advantage of the Christian Protestant religion, and the great benefit of their Majesties' subjects inhabiting this Province, both in the present and succeeding generations. And considering that many persons have bestowed legacies, gifts, hereditaments, and revenues on the said College. Be it therefore enacted and ordained by his Excellency the Governor, Council, and Representatives, of their Majesties' Province of the Massachusetts Bay, in New England, convened in General Assembly; and by the authority thereof it is enacted and ordained, that the said College, in Cambridge, in the county of Middlesex, in their Majesties' Province of the Massachusetts Bay in New England, shall be a Corporation consisting of ten persons, that is to say, a President, eight Fellows, and a Treasurer, and that the Rev. Mr. Increase Mather shall be the first President, James Allen, Samuel Willard, Nehemiah Hobart, Nathaniel Gookin, Cotton Mather, John Leverett, William Brattle, Nehemiah Walter, Masters of Art, shall be the eight Fellows, and John Richards, Esq., the Treasurer, all of them inhabitants in said Province, and the first ten persons whereof the said Corporation shall consist, which said Increase Mather, James Allen, Samuel Willard, Nehemiah Hobart, Nathaniel Gookin, Cotton Mather, John Leverett, William Brattle, Nehemiah Walter, and John Richards, and their successors, shall for ever hereafter, in name and fact, be one body politic and corporate in law, to all intents and purposes; and shall have perpetual succession, and shall be called by the name of the President and Fellows of Harvard College; which persons, or the greater number of them, shall have power and are hereby authorized at any time or times to elect a new President, Fellows, and Treasurer, so often, and from time to time, as any of the said persons shall die or be removed, provided no such election be made without notice given in writing under the hand of the President or senior Fellow unto the persons concerned, seven days at least before such election be made. And the said President, Fellows, and Treasurer, and their successors elective, as aforesaid, shall and may purchase and acquire to themselves, or take and receive upon free gift or donation any lands, tenements, or hereditaments within the Province aforesaid, not exceeding the value of four thousand pounds per annum, and any goods or sum of money whatever to the use and behoof of the said President and Fellows of Harvard College, and also for the encouragement of learning, and may sue and plead or be sued and impleaded by the name aforesaid, in all courts and places of judicature; and that the said President and Fellows, and their successors may have for ever one common seal to be used in all causes and occasions of the said Corporation, and the same seal may alter, change, break, and new make, from time to time, at their pleasure. And the said President and Fellows, or the major part of them, from time to time may meet and choose officers, and menial servants for the College, and them also to remove, and, after death or removal, to choose such others, and to make from time to time such statutes, orders, and by-laws, for the better ordering the affairs of the College, as they shall think fit. And also, that the President and Fellows, or major part of them, with the Treasurer,

APPENDIX, No. LXVIII. Charter proposed in 1692.

shall have power to make conclusive bargains for lands and tenements to be purchased by the said Corporation for valuable consideration. And for the better ordering the government of the said College or academy, Be it enacted by the authority aforesaid, that the President and Fellows, or any six of them, shall and may from time to time, upon due notice or warning given by the President to the rest, hold a meeting for the debating and concluding of affairs concerning the profits and revenues of any lands, and disposing of their goods, provided, that all the said disposals be according to the will of the donors, and for direction in all emergent occasions, and the execution of all statutes, orders, and by-laws; in all which cases aforesaid, the conclusion shall be made by the President and major part of the Fellows. And all the transactions aforesaid shall tend to, and for the use and behoof of the President, Fellows, scholars, and officers of the said College; and for all accommodations of buildings, books, and all other necessary provisions and furniture, as may be for the advancement and education of youth in all manner of good literature, arts, and sciences. And further be it enacted by the authority aforesaid, that all the lands, tenements, and hereditaments, houses, or revenues, within said Province, to the aforesaid President, Fellows, or College appertaining, shall from henceforth be freed from all public ordinary rates and taxes appertaining to the Province in general. And that the said President, Fellows, and scholars, with the said servants, and other necessary officers to the said President or College appertaining, which servants and officers are not to exceed fifteen, viz. three to the President and twelve to the College belonging, shall be exempted from all personal, civil offices, military exercises, watchings, and wardings. And the estate of the said President and Fellows, under their own management, to be free from all rates and taxes, provided they reside and dwell in the College. And whereas it is a laudable custom in Universities, whereby learning has been encouraged and advanced, to confer academical degrees or titles on those who by their proficiency as to knowledge in theology, law, physic, mathematics, or philosophy, have been judged worthy thereof, it is hereby enacted and ordained, that the President and Fellows of the said College shall have power from time to time to grant and admit to academical degrees, as in the Universities in England, such as, in respect of learning and good manners, they shall find worthy to be promoted thereunto. And whereas there have been at sundry times and by divers persons, gifts, grants, devises of houses, lands, tenements, goods, chattels, legacies, conveyances, heretofore made to the said Harvard College in Cambridge, in New England, or to the President and Fellows thereof successively, the said gifts, grants, devises, and legacies, are hereby for ever confirmed according to the true intent and meaning of the donor or donors, grantor or grantors, devisor or devisors.

"WILLIAM PHIPS.

"WILLIAM BOND, *Speaker*.

"Boston, passed June 27th, 1692, Anno Regis et Reginæ Gulielmi et Mariæ quarto.

"ISA. ADDINGTON, *Secretary*."]

CHARTER PROPOSED IN 1696.

Charter proposed in 1696.

[" Province of Massachusetts Bay.

An act for incorporating of Harvard College, at Cambridge, in New England.

" Whereas there hath been for many years, in the town of Cambridge, in the county of Middlesex, within this his Majesty's Province, a society commonly known by the name of Harvard College, where many persons of known worth have, by the blessing of Almighty God, been educated and the better fitted for public employments, both in the church and in the civil state. And, whereas the due encouragement of good literature, arts, and sciences, will tend to the honor of God, the advantage of the Christian Protestant religion, and the great benefit of his Majesty's subjects inhabiting this Province, both in the present and succeeding generations. And considering that many persons have bestowed legacies, gifts, hereditaments, and revenues on this said College;

" Be it enacted and ordained by the Lieutenant-Governor, Council, and Representatives, in General Court assembled, and by the authority of the same, That the said College, in Cambridge, in the county of Middlesex, in his Majesty's Province of the Massachusetts Bay, in New England aforesaid, shall henceforth be a Corporation consisting of sixteen persons, that is to say, a President, fourteen Fellows, and a Treasurer, and that ——— ——— shall be the first President, Charles Morton, I ——— ——————— ——————— shall be the fourteen Fellows, and ——— ——— the Treasurer, all of them inhabitants in said Province, and the first sixteen persons whereof the said Corporation shall consist; which said ————————— and their successors, shall for ever hereafter in name and fact be one body politic and corporate in law, to all intents and purposes, and shall have perpetual succession, and shall be called by the name of the President and Fellows of Harvard College, in New England; which persons shall have power, and are hereby authorized, to elect a new President, Fellows, and Treasurer, when and so often, from time to time, as any of the said persons shall die or be removed, the President, Fellows, and Treasurer, or any of them, being removable for disability or misdemeanor, and may be displaced by the Corporation, saving to the party grieved his appeal to the Visitors; provided no such displacing or new election be made without notice first given in writing to each member of the Corporation, or left at the place of his usual abode, eight days at least before the meeting for such purpose; and nine at least of the Corporation shall be consenting in every removal and new election of any member; — *all elections to be made by votes in writing.*

" And the President and all Fellows receiving salary shall dwell and reside at the College; and no one shall enjoy a Fellowship with salary for more than ten years, except continued by a new election. And upon any vacancy happening by the death, removal, or deprivation of any of the Corporation, the same shall be filled up by a new election, within the space of twelve months next after.

" And the President, Fellows, and Treasurer, and their successors elec-

APPENDIX, No. LXVIII.

Charter proposed in 1696.

tive as aforesaid, shall and may purchase and acquire unto themselves, or take and receive upon free gift or donation any lands, tenements, or hereditaments, within the Province aforesaid, not exceeding the value of two thousand pounds per annum, or any goods or sum of money whatsoever, to the use and behoof of the President and Fellows of said Harvard College, and also for the encouragement of learning ; and may sue and plead, or be sued and impleaded by the name aforesaid in all courts and places of judicature. And that the said President and Fellows, and their successors may for ever have one common seal of the said Corporation, and the same seal may alter, change, break, and new make, from time to time, at their pleasure. And the said President and Fellows, and their successors, or the major part of them, from time to time may meet and choose officers and menial servants for the said College, and them also remove, and upon death or removal choose such others, and from time to time make such statutes, orders, and by-laws, for the better ordering of the affairs and government of the said College, as they shall think fit; so as such statutes, orders, or by-laws, be not repugnant to the laws of the Province, and notice first given as aforesaid, for a general meeting for that purpose. And also, that the President and Fellows, or major part of them, shall have power to make conclusive bargains for lands and tenements to be purchased by the Corporation, for valuable consideration. And for the better ordering of the government of the said College or academy, Be it enacted by the authority aforesaid, that the President and Fellows, or any ten of them, upon due notice or warning as aforesaid given to the rest, shall and may, from time to time, hold a meeting for the debating and concluding of affairs concerning the profits and revenues of any lands, letting and selling of the same; and disposal of their goods; provided that all the said disposals be according to the will of the donors; and for direction in all emergent occasions, and the execution of all statutes, orders, and by-laws. In all which cases aforesaid, the conclusion shall be made by the major part of the Corporation. And all the transactions aforesaid shall tend to and for the use and behoof of the President, Fellows, scholars, and officers of the said College, and for all accommodations of buildings, books, and all other necessary provisions and furniture, as may be for the advancement and education of youth in all manner of good literature, arts, and sciences. And further, be it enacted by the authority aforesaid, that the President, Fellows, and scholars, as also the steward and cook for the time being, and one servant for the President, shall be exempted from all personal civil offices, military exercises, watchings, and wardings.

" And, whereas it is a laudable custom in Universities, whereby learning has been encouraged and advanced, to confer academical degrees or titles on those who, by their good manners and proficiency as to knowledge in theology, law, physic, mathematics, or philosophy, have been judged worthy thereof; Be it further enacted by the authority aforesaid, that the President and Fellows of the said College shall have power, from time to time, to grant and admit to academical degrees, as in the Universities in

England, such as in respect of learning and good manners they shall find worthy to be promoted thereunto. And, whereas there have been at sundry times, and by divers persons, gifts, grants, devises of houses, lands, tenements, goods, chattels, legacies, and conveyances, heretofore made unto the said College, or to the President and Fellows thereof successively, the said gifts, grants, devises, legacies, and conveyances, are hereby for ever ratified and confirmed according to the true intent and meaning of the donor or donors, grantor or grantors, devisor or devisors.

Charter proposed in 1696.

"And for the more assurance of the well governing of the said College, it is enacted and declared, by the authority aforesaid, that his Majesty's Governor and Council of this Province for the time being, shall be the Visitors, and have, use, and exercise the power of visitation.

"December 15th, 1696, read.

"December 16th, read a second time and debated.

"Read a third time.

"Mr. Increase Mather, *President.*	Mr. John Danforth.
Chas. Morton, *Vice-President.*	Cotton Mather.
Michael Wigglesworth.	John Leverett.
James Allen.	William Brattle.
Samuel Torrey.	Nehemiah Walter.
Samuel Willard.	Paul Dudley.
Nehemiah Hobart.	Benjamin Wadsworth.
Peter Thacher,	Thomas Brattle, *Treasurer.*

"Voted and approved of, December 17th."]

CHARTER PROPOSED IN 1697.

["Province of Massachusetts Bay.

An act for incorporating Harvard College, at Cambridge, in New England.

Charter proposed in 1697.

"Whereas there hath been for many years, in the town of Cambridge, in the county of Middlesex, within his Majesty's Province of the Massachusetts Bay, in New England, a society commonly known by the name of Harvard College, where many persons of known worth have, by the blessing of Almighty God, been educated and the better fitted for public employment, both in the church and in the civil state; and, whereas due encouragement of good literature, arts, and sciences, will tend to the honor of God, the advantage of the Christian Protestant religion, and the great benefit of his Majesty's subjects inhabiting this Province, both in the present and succeeding generations; and considering that many persons have bestowed legacies, gifts, hereditaments, and revenues, on the said College;

"Be it enacted and ordained by the Lieutenant-Governor, Council, and Representatives, in General Court assembled, and by the authority of the same, that the said College at Cambridge, in the county of Middlesex, aforesaid, shall henceforth be a corporation, consisting of seventeen persons; that is to say, a President, Vice-President, fourteen Fellows, and a Treas-

APPENDIX, No. LXVIII.

Charter proposed in 1697.

urer. And that Increase Mather shall be the first President, Charles Morton, Vice-President, and James Allen, Michael Wigglesworth, Samuel Torrey, Samuel Willard, Nehemiah Hobart, Peter Thacher, John Danforth, Cotton Mather, John Leverett, William Brattle, Nehemiah Walter, John White, Paul Dudley, and Benjamin Wadsworth, Masters of Art, shall be the fourteen Fellows, and Thomas Brattle, Master of Art, the Treasurer; all of them inhabitants within the said Province, and the first seventeen persons whereof the said Corporation shall consist; which said Increase Mather, Charles Morton, James Allen, Michael Wigglesworth, Samuel Torrey, Samuel Willard, Nehemiah Hobart, Peter Thacher, John Danforth, Cotton Mather, John Leverett, William Brattle, Nehemiah Walter, John White, Paul Dudley, Benjamin Wadsworth, and Thomas Brattle, and their successors, shall for ever hereafter be one body politic and corporate in fact and name, to all intents and purposes in law, by the name of the President and Fellows of Harvard College in New England, and that by that name they shall have perpetual succession, and by the same name they and their successors shall and may be capable and enabled as well to implead as to be impleaded, and to prosecute, demand, and answer, and be answered unto, in all and singular suits, causes, quarrels, and actions, of what nature and kind soever; and also to have, take, acquire, and purchase, or receive upon free gift or donation, any lands, tenements, or hereditaments, within the Province aforesaid, not exceeding the value of three thousand pounds per annum, and any goods, chattels, sum or sums of money, whatsoever, to the use and behoof of the said Corporation; and the same to lease, grant, demise, employ and dispose, and the revenues, issues, and profits thereof, for the encouragement of learning, and of the President, Fellows, scholars, and officers, of the said College, as also for accommodation of buildings, books, and all other necessary provisions and furniture, as may be for the advancement and education of youth in all manner of good literature, arts, and sciences; provided, that all the said disposals be according to the will of the donors.

"And the said President and Fellows, and their successors, may have for ever one common seal, to be used in all causes and occasions of the Corporation; and the same seal may alter, change, break, and new-make from time to time, at their pleasure.

"And be it further enacted and declared by the authority aforesaid, that the said Corporation shall be and hereby are authorized and impowered to elect a new President, Vice-President, Fellows, and Treasurer, when and so often, from time to time, as any of the said persons shall die or be removed. The President, Vice-President, Fellows, and Treasurer, or any of them being removable for disability or misdemeanor, and may be displaced by the Corporation; saving to the party grieved his appeal to the Visitors. A Vice-President to be annually elected, although not occasioned by death or removal, as aforesaid. And when any of the members of the said Corporation shall settle himself without the bounds of this Province, he shall be *ipso facto* dismissed, and no longer continue to be of the Corporation, and his place be supplied by the election of a new member.

APPENDIX, No. LXVIII.

Charter proposed in 1697.

"And the President for the time being, or in case of his death or absence the Vice-President, shall and may, from time to time, appoint and order the assembling and meeting together of the said Corporation to consult, advise of, debate, and direct the affairs and businesses of the said Corporation, to choose officers and menial servants for said College, and them also to remove, and upon death or removal to choose such others, and to make statutes, orders, and by-laws for the better ordering the affairs and government of the said College or academy, so as such orders, statutes, and by-laws, be not repugnant to the laws of this Province. And any nine or more of the members of the said Corporation, together with the President or Vice-President being so assembled, shall be taken, held, and reputed to be a full, sufficient, and lawful assembly, for the handling, ordering, and directing of the affairs, businesses, and occurrences of the said Corporation. And, in case of the death, removal, or absence, of the President and Vice-President, the senior Fellow for the time being may call and hold a Corporation meeting, until the return or new election of a President or Vice-President. Provided, nevertheless, that no meeting shall be held for the displacing or new election of any member or members of the Corporation, Fellows of the House, or the making of statutes, orders, or by-laws, for ordering of the affairs and government of the said College, without summoning a general meeting as aforesaid, for such purpose, each member of the Corporation to be notified, either verbally or in writing, eight days at least beforehand, of the time and occasion of calling such meeting. And in the passing of all votes and acts of the said Corporation in any of their meetings, the determination shall be made by the major part, the President to have a casting voice in case of an equivote.

"And it is further declared by the authority aforesaid, that, after this act shall be confirmed, the President, as well as all the Fellows receiving salary, shall reside at the College, and that no one shall enjoy a fellowship with salary for more than seven years, except continued by a new election. And that the housing and lands in Cambridge aforesaid, belonging to the said Corporation, and being in the personal occupation of the President and Fellows residing at the College, shall be free from all province or country rates and taxes. And that the President, Fellows, and scholars, with the servants and necessary officers to the President and scholars appertaining, who shall reside at or be constantly employed in services for the College (which servants and officers are not to exceed ten; viz. three to the President, and seven to the College belonging), shall be exempted from all personal civil offices, military exercises, watchings, and wardings.

"And, whereas it is a laudable custom in Universities, whereby learning has been encouraged and advanced, to confer academical degrees or titles on those who, by their good manners, and proficiency as to knowledge in theology, law, physic, mathematics, or philosophy, have been judged worthy thereof;

"Be it further enacted by the authority aforesaid, that the President and Fellows of the College shall have power, from time to time, to grant and admit to academical degrees, as in the Universities in England, such as in

APPENDIX, No. LXVIII.

Charter proposed in 1697.

respect of learning and good manners they shall find worthy to be promoted thereunto.

"And, whereas there have been at sundry times and by divers persons gifts, grants, devises, of houses, lands, tenements, goods, chattels, legacies, and conveyances, heretofore made unto the said College, or to the President or Fellows thereof successively, the said gifts, grants, devises, legacies, and conveyances are hereby for ever ratified and confirmed according to the true intent of the donor or donors, grantor or grantors, devisor or devisors.

"And, in order to the preventing of irregularities, and for the more assurance of the well government of said College, we pray his Majesty, that it may be enacted, and it is hereby enacted and declared, that his Majesty's Governor and Commander-in-chief of this Province, and the Council for the time being, shall be the Visitors of the said College or academy, and shall have, use, and exercise a power of visitation as there shall be occasion for it.

"Read in Council, 26th March, 1697. Voted and passed in the affirmative, and sent down for concurrence.

"ISA. ADDINGTON, *Secretary.*

"In the House of Representatives, March 27th, 1697, read a first time.

"March 30th, read a second time.

"Read in Council, 29th March, 1697.

"Read again, March, and voted in the affirmative, and sent down for concurrence.

"ISA. ADDINGTON, *Secretary.*

"Read in Council, May, 1697.

"Read again, May, 1697. Voted in the affirmative.

"ISA. ADDINGTON, *Secretary.*

"May 31st, read in the House of Representatives.

"1697, June 1st, read a second time and debated.

"1697, June 2d, read a third time. Voted with the emendations. Sent up for concurrence.

"PENN TOWNSEND, *Speaker.*

"June 2d, 1697, voted a concurrence in Council.

"ISA. ADDINGTON, *Secretary.*"]*

CHARTER PROPOSED IN 1699.

["*An Act for incorporating Harvard College, at Cambridge, in New England.*

Charter proposed in 1699.

"Whereas there hath been for many years in the town of Cambridge, in the County of Middlesex, within his Majesty's Province of the Massachusetts Bay in New England, a society commonly known by the name of Harvard College, where many persons of known worth have, by the bless-

* It appears by the engrossed act, that on the 4th of June, 1697, it received the consent of William Stoughton, Lieutenant-Governor.

APPENDIX, No. LXVIII.

Charter proposed in 1699.

ing of Almighty God, been educated and the better fitted for public employments both in the church and in the civil state; and whereas due encouragement of good literature, arts, and sciences, will tend to the honor of God, the advantage of the Christian Protestant religion, and the great benefit of his Majesty's subjects inhabiting this Province, both in the present and succeeding generations; and, considering that many persons have bestowed legacies, gifts, hereditaments, and revenues, on said College;

"Be it enacted and ordained by his Excellency the Governor, Council, and Representatives, in General Court assembled, and by the authority of the same, that the said College, in Cambridge, in the County of Middlesex, aforesaid, shall henceforth be a Corporation consisting of seventeen persons, that is to say, a President, Vice-President, and fourteen Fellows, *and a Treasurer*. And that Increase Mather shall be the first President, Samuel Willard, Vice-President, *James Allen*, *Michael Wigglesworth*, *Samuel Young*, *Nehemiah Hobart*, *Nicholas Noyes*, *Peter Thacher*, *John Angier*, *John Danforth*, *Cotton Mather*, *John Leverett*, *William Brattle*, *Nehemiah Walter*, *John White*, *and Benjamin Wadsworth*, *Masters of Arts*, *shall be the fourteen Fellows*, and Thomas Brattle, Master of Arts, the Treasurer, all of them inhabitants within the said Province, and the first seventeen persons, whereof the said Corporation shall consist; which said Increase Mather, Samuel Willard, —————— and their successors, shall for ever hereafter be one body politic and corporate, in fact and name, to all intents and purposes in law, by the name of the President and Fellows of Harvard College, in New England, and that by that name they shall have perpetual succession, and by the same name they and their successors shall and may be capable and enabled as well to implead as to be impleaded, and to prosecute, demand, and answer, and be answered unto, in all and singular suits, causes, quarrels, and actions, of what nature and kind soever, and also to have, take, acquire, and purchase, or receive upon free gift or donation, any lands, tenements, or hereditaments, within the Province aforesaid, not exceeding the value of three thousand pounds per annum, and any goods, chattels, sum or sums of money whatsoever, to the use and behoof of the said Corporation, and the same to lease, grant, demise, employ, and dispose, and the revenues, issues, and profits thereof, for the encouragement of learning, and of the President, Fellows, scholars, and officers of the said College, as also for accommodation of buildings, books, and all other necessary provisions and furniture, as may be for the advancement and education of youth in all manner of good literature, arts, and sciences; provided, that all the said disposals be according to the will of the donors. And the said President and Fellows, and their successors, may have for ever one common seal to be used in all causes and occasions of the Corporation, and the same seal may alter, change, break, and new-make, from time to time, at their pleasure.

"And be it further enacted and declared, by the authority aforesaid, that the said Corporation be and hereby are impowered and authorized to elect a new President, Vice-President, Fellows, and Treasurer, when and so often,

APPENDIX, No. LXVIII.

Charter proposed in 1699.

from time to time, as any of the said persons shall die or be removed; the President, Vice-President, Fellows, and Treasurer, or any of them, being removable for disability or misdemeanor, and may be displaced by the Corporation, saving to the party grieved his appeal to the Visitors. A Vice-President to be annually elected, although not occasioned by death or removal, as aforesaid.

Dele. (*Provided, that no person shall be chosen, and continued President, Vice-President, or Fellow, of said Corporation, but such as shall declare and continue their adherence unto the principles of Reformation, which were espoused and intended by those who first settled this country, and founded the College, and have hitherto been the profession and practice of the generality of the churches of Christ in New England.*)

"And when any of the members of the said Corporation shall *settle* himself without the bounds of this Province, he shall be *ipso facto* dismissed, and no longer continue to be of the Corporation, and his place be supplied with the election of a new member. And the President for the time being, or, in case of his death or absence, the Vice-President, shall and may, from time to time, appoint and order the assembling and meeting together of the said Corporation, to consult, advise, debate, and direct the affairs and businesses of the said Corporation, to choose officers and menial servants for the said College, and them also to remove, and upon death or removal to choose such others, and to make statutes, orders, and by-laws, for the better ordering the affairs and government of the said College or academy, so as such orders, statutes, and by-laws be not repugnant to the laws of this Province; and any *seven* or more members of the said Corporation, together with the President or Vice-President, being so assembled, shall be taken, held, and reputed to be a full, sufficient, and lawful assembly, for the handling, ordering, and directing of the affairs, businesses, and occurrences of said Corporation; and, in case of the death, removal, or absence of the President and Vice-President, the senior Fellow for the time being may call and hold a Corporation meeting until the return or new election of a President or Vice-President. Provided, nevertheless, that no meeting shall be held for the displacing or new election of any member or members of the Corporation, Fellows of the House, or the making of statutes, orders, or by-laws, for ordering of the affairs and government of the College, without summoning a general meeting as aforesaid for such purpose, each member of the Corporation, to be notified, *either verbally or* in writing, eight days at least beforehand, of the time and occasion of calling such meeting; and in the passing of all votes and acts of the said Corporation in any of their meetings, the determination shall be made by the major part, the President to have a casting vote in case of an equivote.

"And it is further declared, by the authority aforesaid, that, *after this act shall be confirmed*, the President, as well as all the Fellows receiving salary, shall reside at the College, and that no one shall enjoy a fellowship with salary for more than seven years, except continued by a new election, and that the housing and lands in Cambridge aforesaid, belonging to the said

APPENDIX, No. LXVIII.

Charter proposed in 1699.

Corporation, and being in the personal occupation of the President and Fellows residing at the College, shall be free from all Province or country rates and taxes, and the President, Fellows, and scholars, with the servants *and necessary officers to the President and scholars appertaining, who shall reside, or be constantly employed in services for the College,* (*which servants and officers are not to exceed ten, viz. three to the President and seven to the College belonging,*) shall be exempted from all personal civil offices, military exercises, watchings, and wardings.

"And, whereas it is a laudable custom in Universities, whereby learning hath been encouraged and advanced, to confer academical degrees or titles on those, who, by their good manners and proficiency as to knowledge in Theology, Law, Physic, Mathematics, or Philosophy, have been judged worthy thereof; Be it further enacted by the authority aforesaid, that the President and Fellows of the said College shall have power from time to time to grant and admit to academical degrees, as in the Universities in England, such as in respect of learning and good manners they shall find worthy to be promoted thereunto.

"And, whereas there have been *at sundry times and by divers persons,* gifts, grants, devises of houses, land, tenements, goods, chattels, legacies, and conveyances heretofore made unto the said College, or to the President and Fellows thereof successively, the said gifts, grants, devises, legacies, and conveyances are hereby ratified and confirmed according to the true intent of the donor or donors, grantor or grantors, devisor or devisors.

"And, in order to the preventing of irregularities, and for the more assurance of the well government of said College, a power of visitation is hereby reserved to his Majesty, and his Governor or Commander-in-chief for the time being of this Province.

"July 8th, 1699. Read a first time and a second time. Read a third time and passed, &c.

"Sent up for concurrence.

"JAMES CONVERSE, *Speaker.**

"July 11th, 1699. In Council read a first time.

"July 12th. Read a second time, and committed to a Committee of the whole board.

"July 13th. This bill was passed as amended below.

"July 18th, 1699. The Governor (Bellamont) objected to the bill on account of the clause marked *Dele,* and, the Council adhering, the bill was lost." — See *General Court Records.*

"July 13th, 1699.

"Amendments to the College Bill proposed and agreed to by a Committee of the whole Board.

"The words, *and a Treasurer,* to be left out in the Constitution.

"The members of the Corporation to continue seventeen.

* The words printed in Italics were contained in the original draft, and were either erased, or proposed to be expunged prior to the final passage of the bill.

APPENDIX, No. LXVIII.

Charter proposed in 1699.

"The two senior Tutors resident at the College from time to time to be Fellows of the Corporation.

"A Vice-President to be annually elected on the day of Commencement, from time to time.

"Instead of the word *settle* the word *remove* to be inserted, so as to be absent out of the Province by the space of one whole year.

"Upon the death or dismission of the President, Vice-President, or any of the Fellows, such vacancy to be filled up within three months next after.

"The word *verbally*, in the notification of Corporation meetings, to be left out.

"The word *domestic* to be added to servants, and the words *and necessary officers to the President and scholars appertaining, who shall reside at or be constantly employed in services for the College*, to be expunged, and the number of servants to be left out.

"In the paragraph about gifts, grants, &c., the words *at sundry times and by divers persons* to be expunged, and the words *heretofore* and *divers* to be inserted next foregoing the word *gifts*.

"The words *after this act shall be confirmed* to be expunged.

"Members of the Corporation.

"Mr. Increase Mather, *President*.
Samuel Willard, *Vice-President*.

William Stoughton,
Wait Winthrop,
Elisha Cooke, Esq.
Samuel Sewall,
Isaac Addington,
Mr. James Allen,
Michael Wigglesworth,
Samuel Torrey,
Nehemiah Hobart,
John Danforth,
Cotton Mather,
William Brattle,
Nehemiah Walter,
} *Fellows*,

with the two senior Tutors resident at the College for the time being.

"That there be a quarterly meeting of the Corporation at the College on the first Wednesday in September, the first Monday in December, March, and June, from time to time in every year successively.

"And, whereas five of the members of the Council are nominated and appointed by the present Constitution to be Fellows of the Corporation, when it happens that any of them die or be otherwise removed or dismissed, such vacancy to be filled up out of the Council from time to time.

"That there be eight or more members of the Corporation, together with the President or Vice-President, to constitute a Corporation meeting.

"Agreed, and voted that a bill be drawn accordingly.

"James Converse, *Speaker*.

"And, whereas the first planters of this country, and founders of this College, were, as to their persuasion in matters of religion, such as are known by the name of Congregational or Presbyterian, and the general profession and practice of the churches throughout this land hath been and is according thereunto, and the College being intended as a nursery to these churches, It is enacted, that no one shall be the President, Vice-President, or a Fellow of said Corporation, but such as shall declare themselves, and continue to be, of the said persuasion in matter of religion.

"Agreed to be inserted.

"Agreed.

"JAMES CONVERSE, *Speaker.*"]

CHARTER PROPOSED IN 1700.

Charter proposed in 1700.

["July 12th, 1700.

"*Draught of a Charter of Incorporation for Harvard College, at Cambridge, in New England, agreed to by the Council and House of Representatives of his Majesty's Province of the Massachusetts Bay, to be humbly solicited for to his Majesty.*

"William the Third, by the grace of God, of England, Scotland, France, and Ireland King, Defender of the Faith, &c., to all unto whom these presents shall come, greeting. Whereas there hath been for many years in the town of Cambridge, in the County of Middlesex, within our Province of the Massachusetts Bay, in New England, in America, a Society commonly known by the name of Harvard College, where many persons of known worth have, by the blessing of Almighty God, been educated, and the better fitted for public employments both in the church and in the civil state, and whereas due encouragement of good literature, arts, and sciences, will tend to the honor of God, the advantage of the Christian Protestant religion, and the great benefit of our subjects inhabiting within our Province aforesaid, both in the present and succeeding generations; and whereas the Governor, Council, and Assembly, of our said Province of the Massachusetts Bay, in New England, by their humble address have supplicated our royal grace and favor in the settlement of the aforesaid College, that it may be done in such manner as may effectually secure the same to be a nursery for the supplying the churches in our said Province with able, learned ministers, agreeable to the chief end and intent of the first founders of said College;

"We therefore, being graciously pleased to gratify our said subjects, of our special grace, certain knowledge, and mere motion, have willed and ordained, and we do by these presents, for us, our heirs, and successors, will and ordain, that the said College in Cambridge, in the County of Middlesex, within our Province of the Massachusetts Bay, in New England aforesaid, shall henceforth be a Corporation consisting of seventeen persons, that is to say, a President, Vice-President, and fifteen Fellows, and that Increase Mather shall be the first President, Samuel Willard, Vice-President, James Allen, Michael Wigglesworth, Samuel Torrey, Nehemiah Hobart, Peter Thacher, Samuel Angier, John Danforth, Cotton Mather, Nehemiah Walter, Henry Gibbs, John White, Jonathan Pierpont, and Benjamin Wadsworth, Masters of Art, and all of them inhabitants of our Province of the

APPENDIX, No. LXVIII.

Charter proposed in 1700.

Massachusetts Bay aforesaid, together with the two senior Tutors resident at the said College for the time being, shall be the fifteen Fellows, and the first seventeen persons whereof the said Corporation shall consist. Which said Increase Mather, Samuel Willard, James Allen, Michael Wigglesworth, Samuel Torrey, Nehemiah Hobart, Peter Thacher, Samuel Angier, John Danforth, Cotton Mather, Nehemiah Walter, Henry Gibbs, John White, Jonathan Pierpont, Benjamin Wadsworth, and the two senior Tutors residing at the College for the time being, and their successors, shall for ever hereafter be one body politic and corporate, in fact and name, to all intents and purposes in law, by the name of the President and Fellows of Harvard College, at Cambridge, in New England, and that by that name they shall have perpetual succession, and by the same name they and their successors shall and may be capable and enabled as well to implead as to be impleaded, and to prosecute, demand, and answer, and be answered unto in all and singular suits, causes, quarrels, and actions, of what nature and kind soever; and also to have, take, acquire, and purchase, or receive upon free gift or donation, any lands, tenements, or hereditaments, not exceeding the value of three thousand pounds per annum, and any goods, chattels, sum or sums of money, whatsoever, to the use and behoof of the said Corporation; and the same to lease, grant, devise, employ, and dispose, with the revenues, issues, and profits, thereof, for the encouragement of learning, and of the President, Fellows, scholars, and officers of the said College; as also for accommodation of buildings, books, and all other necessary provisions and furniture, as may be for the advancement and education of youth in all manner of good literature, arts, and sciences. Provided, always, that all the said disposals be according to the will of the donors. And we do further grant and ordain, that the said President and Fellows, and their successors, may have for ever one common seal, to be used in all causes and occasions of the said Corporation; and the same seal may alter, change, break, and new-make from time to time at their pleasure.

"And further, we do for us, our heirs, and successors, grant, establish, and ordain, that the President, Vice-President, and the Fellows of the said Corporation, or any of them, shall be removable, and may be displaced, by the said Corporation for disability, or misdemeanor, saving to the party grieved his appeal to the Visitors. And that when and so often from time to time as any of the said Corporation shall die or be removed, the said Corporation shall be and is hereby impowered and authorized to elect a new President, Vice-President, or Fellows, in the room and stead of such member or members of the Corporation so dying or removed. And that a Vice-President of the said Corporation be annually elected upon the Commencement day from time to time, although not occasioned by death or removal as aforesaid. And we do further, for us, our heirs, and successors, will and establish, that, when and so often as any Fellow of the said Corporation shall remove himself so as to be absent out of our Province of the Massachusetts Bay aforesaid by the space of one whole year without leave of the Corporation, he shall *ipso facto* be dismissed, and no longer continue to be of the Corporation, and his place shall be supplied with the election of a new mem-

APPENDIX, No. LXVIII.

Charter proposed in 1700.

ber. And that upon the death, or removal and dismission, of the President, Vice-President, or any of the Fellows, such vacancy shall be filled up within the space of three months next after. And further, we do, by these presents, for us, our heirs, and successors, grant, establish, and ordain, that the President for the time being, of the said Corporation, and in case of his death or absence, the Vice-President for the time being, of the same, shall and may from time to time appoint and order the assembling and meeting together of the said Corporation to consult, advise of, debate, and direct the affairs and businesses of the said Corporation, to choose officers and menial servants for the said College, and them also to remove, and upon death or removal to choose such others, and to make statutes, orders, and by-laws, for the better ordering the affairs and government of the College or Academy, so as such orders, statutes, and by-laws be not repugnant to the laws of our said Province of the Massachusetts Bay. And that any ten or more of the members of the said Corporation, whereof the President or Vice-President to be one, being so assembled, shall be taken, held, and reputed to be a full, sufficient, and lawful assembly, for the handling, ordering, and directing of the affairs, businesses, and occurrences of the said Corporation. And that, in case of the death, removal, or absence of the President and Vice-President, the senior Fellow, for the time being, of the said Corporation, may call and hold a Corporation meeting until the return or new election of a President or Vice-President. Provided, nevertheless, and our will and pleasure is, that no meeting shall be held for the displacing or new election of any member or members of the said Corporation, for the appointing of Tutors, for the making of statutes, orders, and by-laws for ordering of the affairs and government of the said College, or for the purchasing, selling, or letting of lands and tenements, or disposal of the stock or revenues belonging to the said College, without summoning and notifying each member of the said Corporation, in writing, of the time and occasion of calling such meeting eight days at least beforehand. And our further will and pleasure is, that in the passing of all votes and acts of the said Corporation in any of the meetings thereof, the determination shall be made by the major part of those assembled, and that the said President have a casting vote in case of an equivote. And also, that there shall be held and kept a quarterly meeting of the said Corporation at the College aforesaid on the first Wednesday in March, June, September, and December, from time to time in every year successively. And we do by these presents, for us, our heirs, and successors, further grant, establish, and ordain, that the President of the said Corporation, as also the Fellows and Tutors thereof receiving salary, shall reside at the College aforesaid, and that no one shall enjoy a fellowship, or a tutorship, with a salary, for more than seven years, unless continued by a new election. And that the housing and lands in Cambridge aforesaid, belonging to the said Corporation, and being in the personal occupation of the President and Fellows residing at the said College, shall be exempt and free from all rates and taxes. And likewise that the President, and resident Fellows, with their domestic servants, shall be

APPENDIX, No. LXVIII.

Charter proposed in 1700.

exempted from all personal civil offices, military exercises, watchings, and wardings.

" And, whereas it is a laudable custom in Universities, whereby learning hath been encouraged and advanced, to confer academical degrees or titles on those, who, by their good manners or proficiency as to knowledge in Theology, Law, Physic, Mathematics, or Philosophy, have been judged worthy thereof; We do therefore further, by these presents, grant and ordain, that the President and Fellows of the aforesaid Corporation shall have power, from time to time, to grant and admit to academical degrees, as in the Universities in our kingdom of England, such as in respect of learning and good manners they shall find worthy to be promoted thereunto.

" And, whereas there have been heretofore divers gifts, grants, devises of houses, lands, tenements, goods, chattels, legacies, and conveyances made unto the aforesaid College, or to the President and Fellows thereof, successively, we do hereby, for us, our heirs and successors, ratify and confirm the said gifts, grants, devises, legacies, conveyances, each and every of them, according to the true intent of the donor or donors, grantor or grantors, devisor or devisors.

" And, for preventing of irregularity in the government of the said College, we do hereby reserve a power of visitation thereof in ourself, our heirs and successors, by our Governor and Commander-in-chief, together with our Council, for the time being, of our Province of the Massachusetts Bay aforesaid, to be exercised by our Governor or Commander-in-chief, and Council, when and so often as they shall see cause.

"July 10th, 1700.

" In Council, read a first and second time, and, the question being put, was agreed to.

" Sent down for concurrence. ISAAC ADDINGTON, *Secretary.*

" July 10th, 1700. Read a first time in the House of Representatives.

" July 11th, Read a second time. And a third time July 12th.

" Voted a concurrence.

"JOHN LEVERETT, *Speaker.*"] *

* The following documents, in addition to those before published in this Appendix, pp. 503, 504, contain all the proceedings antecedent to the passing of the final Resolve.

[" In Council, 11th November, 1707.

" Upon reading an humble address of the Fellows of Harvard College, in Cambridge, respecting their choice of Mr. John Leverett to be the present President of said College, and recommending him to his Excellency's favorable acceptation, withal praying that he would please to present him to the General Assembly and move for his honorable subsistence; the aforesaid address being also accompanied with addresses from thirty-nine ministers;

"*Voted,* That the said election be accepted, and that Mr. Leverett be desired

APPENDIX, No. LXVIII.

FINAL RESOLVE OF THE PROVINCIAL LEGISLATURE, DECLARING THE COLLEGE CHARTER OF 1650 NOT REPEALED, AND DIRECTING THE PRESIDENT AND FELLOWS OF THE COLLEGE TO EXERCISE THE POWERS GRANTED BY IT.

Resolve of 1707.

Anno Regni Annæ Reginæ Sexto.

"At a Great and General Court or Assembly for her Majesty's Province of the Massachusetts Bay in New England, begun and held at Boston, upon Wednesday the twenty-eighth of May, 1707; and continued by several prorogations unto Wednesday the twenty-ninth of October following, being the third session.

"In Council, Thursday, December 4th, 1707.

"The Governor and Council, having accepted and approved the choice made by the Fellows of Harvard College in Cambridge, of Mr. John Leverett, to be present President of the said College, to fill up that vacancy,

"Propose, that the House of Representatives consider of and grant a suitable salary to be paid to the said President annually, out of the public Treasury, for his encouragement and support, during his continuance in said office, residing at Cambridge, and discharging the proper duties to a President belonging, and entirely devoting himself to that service.

"And inasmuch as the first foundation and establishment of that

and empowered to take the care and government of the College, as President accordingly.

"Sent down for concurrence. ISA. ADDINGTON, *Secretary.*

"November 28th, 1707. Read and concurred.

"In the House of Representatives, November 29th, 1707.

"*Voted,* That a message be sent up to the Board, moving them to join with this House in choosing a suitable person to take care of the College until the session of this Court in May next. JOHN BURRILL, *Speaker.*

"Die predict. Read in Council. December 3. Again read and not concurred.
"ISA. ADDINGTON, *Secretary.*

"In the House of Representatives, December 2d, 1707.

"*Resolved,* That the vote of this Court passed in July, 1700, in the words following, viz. Resolved, that the sum of two hundred and twenty pounds per annum be allowed and paid out of the public Treasury to the President already chosen, or that shall be chosen by this Court, he residing at the College, had respect only to the choice then made or making, and has had its full effect, and is now of no further power or efficacy, but for ever void.

"Sent up for concurrence. JOHN BURRILL, *Speaker.*

"In Council, December 4th, 1707. ISA. ADDINGTON, *Secretary.*"]

APPENDIX, No. LXVIII. Resolve of 1707.

House and the government thereof hath its original from an act of the General Court, made and passed in the year one thousand six hundred and fifty, which has not been repealed or nulled;

"The President and Fellows of the said College are directed from time to time to regulate themselves according to the rules of the Constitution by the said act prescribed; and to exercise the powers and authority thereby granted for the government of that House and support thereof.

"Voted.

"Sent down for concurrence. ISA. ADDINGTON, *Secretary.*

"In the House of Representatives, December 5th, 1707. Read and concurred, and voted, that the sum for salary be one hundred and fifty pounds. JOHN BURRILL, *Speaker.*

"Agreed to in Council, 6th December, 1707.

"ISA. ADDINGTON, *Secretary.*

"Consented to, J. DUDLEY."

END OF VOLUME I.